PRAISE FOR *MAKING A NEW VOW*

"This book might well be the difference between shipwreck and success in remarriage. Warren Kniskern helps you navigate the treacherous waters of dating, finances, children, and blending families. With *Making a New Vow* as your guide, you can anticipate success and God's blessing as you remarry."

—Steve Grissom
Founder, DivorceCare

"What a blessing is Warren Kniskern's book, *Making a New Vow*! This is a tremendous resource for people who find themselves considering, approaching, or knee-deep in a remarriage. The author approaches the difficult and practical problems of remarriage thoroughly, thoughtfully, and biblically. This is a must-read for those who desire biblical insight and wisdom when facing the overwhelming hurdles associated with remarriage and blended families. It is also an indispensable resource for pastors and counselors who are called to provide direction for the growing population of non-traditional families."

—Julianna Slattery, Psy.D.
Author, *Finding the Hero in Your Husband*

"I have been a pastor for over thirty-five years, and divorce and remarriage may be the most difficult issue families face. Blending children, uniting relatives, handling embarrassment, and dealing with loneliness often constitute a small portion of the difficulties accompanying divorce. Easy answers are few, and complications numerous. Remarriage then becomes a monster of a decision. *Making a New Vow* will be a major contributor in dealing with all these issues. Warren also has produced a masterpiece on the major question, 'Am I Scripturally Free to Remarry?' This book is a must-read and will be a key volume on this subject."

—Dr. Dino J. Pedrone, Senior Pastor and
President, Florida Association of Christian Colleges and Schools

"Making and keeping our initial wedding vows is hard enough; doing it a second time is even more challenging. By God's grace, Warren and Cheryl have walked this complex road with success. I am delighted that they are sharing their experiences and insights with others."

—Ken Sande, President of Peacemaker Ministries and
Author, *The Peacemaker* and *The Peacemaking*
for Families

"It's always difficult to be confident about issues of divorce and remarriage. People come with problems, and they need answers. *Making a New Vow* challenged me to reexamine what I believe. It is an honest look at Scripture and the situations we face without trying to insist on a particular point of view. Warren Kniskern gives new light to difficult situations with historical perspective and spiritual insight. The answers aren't always easy, but there are answers!"

—Terry Singleton, Minister

"Warren Kniskern's keen insights and clearly communicated information in *Making a New Vow* covers what couples need to succeed after saying, 'I do.' It contains a wealth of well-organized material, practical tips, and suggestions that will help blend families in the love of Christ, while inspiring each family member to strive toward deeper intimacy and joy."

—Karen H. Whiting
Author, *Family Devotional Builder* and
God's Girls series

"*Making a New Vow* is written from the perspective of a faithful Christian man who has experienced the devastation of an unwanted divorce, lived the difficult "single again" life, and successfully navigated the minefield of courtship and remarriage. Warren Kniskern is a thoughtful student of the Bible, an able teacher, and a father committed to leading his family in the paths of righteousness. His earlier book, *When the Vow Breaks,* has been helpful to us in counseling Christians considering, or forced into, divorce. I am sure *Making a New Vow* will prove helpful to many as well. The author has dug deeply and prayerfully into the Word in dealing with many challenging divorce and remarriage issues in a forthright, but compassionate manner. This book will make you think . . . and it will make you study!"

—J. R. Perkins, Jr., Church Elder

"How I wish *Making a New Vow* had been in print thirty-three years ago! My husband and I have struggled blindly through many of the issues Warren addresses in his comprehensive guidelines for Christians considering remarriage. Emotional baggage! Finances! Blended family! Estate planning! The "Ex"! Only the Lord has given us grace to tackle the problems. Christians are not exempt from divorce or widowhood . . . or God's promises for blessings in this life. *Making a New Vow* should be on every Christian's bookshelf—for themselves or someone they know."

—Lynne Cooper Sitton

"I have found Warren Kniskern's writings to be a treasured resource in my library and a valuable tool in my ministry. The author's insight into the realities of divorce and issues concerning remarriage is dead center on the truth. I believe every professor of Christian counseling, pastor, and marriage counselor should require their clients to read it. Anyone considering remarriage should read this book for enlightenment on issues they will face and guidance about how to ultimately strengthen their marriage and blended family."

—Tim Meadows
Development Director, Florida Baptist Children's Home

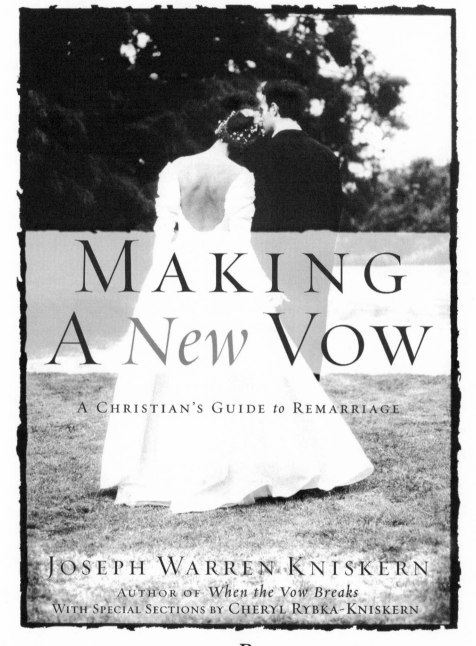

MAKING
A *New* VOW

A CHRISTIAN'S GUIDE *to* REMARRIAGE

JOSEPH WARREN KNISKERN

AUTHOR OF *When the Vow Breaks*

WITH SPECIAL SECTIONS BY CHERYL RYBKA-KNISKERN

BROADMAN
&HOLMAN
PUBLISHERS

NASHVILLE, TENNESSEE

0-8054-2616-7

Published by Broadman & Holman Publishers
Nashville, Tennessee

Dewey Decimal Classification: 306.84
Subject Heading: REMARRIAGE \ DIVORCE THERAPY

Unless otherwise noted, Scripture quotations are from the Holy Bible, New International Version, copyright © 1973, 1978, 1984, by International Bible Society.

1 2 3 4 5 6 7 8 9 10   08 07 06 05 04 03

This book is lovingly dedicated to

The Bride of My Life

This book would not have been possible without the unselfish service and encouragement of these good people who are among my dearest family and friends:

Ms. Danielle Aguire
Ms. Pamela Harty
William Jacobs, Esquire
Douglas B. Kniskern, Esquire
Mr. and Mrs. Kenneth F. Kniskern
Mr. Wayne F. Kniskern
Pastor Tim Meadows
Antonio Martinez Jr., Esquire
Mr. Juan D. Milian
Dr. Kieth A. Mitchell
Dr. Dino Pedrone
Elder Robert Perkins
Dr. Michael Rybka
Minister Terry Singleton
Dr. Juliana Slattery
Dr. Stephan Tchividjian
Mrs. Karen Whiting
Ms. Peggy Wilson
Evangelist Rusty Wright
All of the members of the Miami-Dade and Broward County, Florida, chapters of the Association of Christian Writers

With special recognition and gratitude to

Steve and Cheryl Grissom
Ms. Kim Overcash
Mrs. Lynne Sitton
Ms. Janis Whipple

Table of Contents

Foreword

I slipped the wedding band off my finger and gently placed it in a box in my dresser. I had worn the ring faithfully through two years of separation, financial negotiations, weekend visitation with my daughter, shame, anger, embarrassment, and depression.

This was the day my divorce became final. I had worked hard and prayed long for a reconciliation that did not come. This was the day to release my marriage and move on with my life.

I tried. A sense of release briefly subdued my grieving. I hung on to the hope that a new relationship with the right woman would take away the ache and emptiness.

The months passed but the pain did not. I wanted to date but did not have the courage to ask a woman to join me for a simple dinner. My life was not improving, despite the closure that should have accompanied the divorce decree. In fact, I realized closure had eluded me. I needed more than an unwanted legal pronouncement. I needed closure in my soul.

My thoughts often returned to my gold wedding band. At times trying to figure out what to do with it obsessed me. Do I keep it? Sell it? It became a festering irritant—a symbol of my inability to accept my new status as a single man. I reasoned that I needed a ceremonial, spiritual closure. My solution was to plan a "funeral" for my wedding band. At 11:00 P.M. one night, I took it to a bridge over a stream near my home. After pausing to watch the water swirl fifteen feet below me, I let go of the ring. With a faint plunk, it hit the water and sank to the bottom of the stream. I paused for a moment in prayer, asking the Lord to finish healing me. I felt great. I felt release! Until the next day, that is. Once again, closure and healing had eluded me.

It took nearly two more years for me to reach measurable emotional and spiritual health. Much of what I learned during that time appears in part 1 of this book. I wish that *Making a New Vow* had been available then! It offers profound truth and essential reading for anyone who has lost a spouse through divorce or death.

It *is* possible to heal from the soul-level hurt that accompanies the loss of a mate. I experienced many awkward, unsuccessful attempts to "get on with my life" in those dark months following my divorce, but I can now look back with the perspective of fifteen years and promise you that God can heal you and bless your future!

He has united me with Cheryl—my wife, soulmate, friend, and lover. He allowed me to form a new family as I embraced her daughters, then ages four and six. Even more, He gently restored me to wholeness, helping me find the closure that was impossible to find on my own.

CHERYL'S STORY

Like Steve, I traveled a lengthy and often rough road to healing after my husband left me.

I was a stay-at-home mom, caring for our daughters, when my first husband left. The oldest was four; the youngest was just 11 months. To exist, I returned to work quickly. I trained as a pharmacist, which meant the work I could find typically involved unusual hours. Often I received twelve-hour-shift assignments.

Unlike Steve, I have few specific memories of those times. My life felt like an endless loop alternating between work and caring for my daughters. I searched constantly for people and childcare facilities to keep the girls while I worked.

I was too tired (and probably too depressed) to do much else. Often, when my daughters were away for the weekend visiting their father, I would not leave my apartment. Instead, I would remain in bed . . . for two days. I simply did not have the energy or will to do anything or be around other people.

I clung to God's promise to be "a father to the fatherless, a defender of widows" (Ps. 68:5). The next verse of that psalm promises that "God sets the lonely in families."

He set me in two "families" within my church—a Bible study for hurting women, and a home fellowship group. I was around people who cared genuinely about me, prayed for me, and helped me face some real-world problems as a single-again mother.

It was the Lord's tender care and the nurture of others that helped me gain strength and hope. I now believe what others too quickly dismiss as a cliché—that he really is sufficient to meet all my needs and be the source of my joy!

We've shared our story to help illustrate two crucial points:

• Healing from divorce or the death of a spouse is possible, but it is a difficult process that will take longer than you might expect. If you don't heal sufficiently, you will sabotage future relationships. Because you are reading this book, we assume you have an interest in the potential for remarriage. It is our fervent desire that you succeed and thrive!

• Healthy remarriage *is* possible, even predictable, when you follow the Lord's plan, direction, and timing. You can defy the odds and succeed where so many who remarried fail. This book is an invaluable roadmap to the process!

By our own measure, Cheryl and I have a wonderful marriage. I think it's fair to say that most outside observers would agree. Through the painful lessons of our prior marriages and a constantly growing appreciation of the importance of keeping Christ at the center of our family, we face married life with confidence and purpose.

After Cheryl and I married and had some time to merge our families and lifestyles, we sensed God's direction to begin reaching out to others who were experiencing the hurt of separation and divorce (2 Cor. 1:3–4). Ultimately, he led us to establish the DivorceCare ministry, which equips local churches to provide weekly divorce recovery support groups. Later, he guided us to create the GriefShare support group program for people who have lost a friend or loved one through death. We now have the privilege of working with thousands of churches worldwide.

Through DivorceCare and GriefShare, we've met many wonderful people who are making the same journey as you. We have seen them at their rawest, witnessed the healing process, and then shared their joy and hope as they moved beyond their loss toward restoration.

We especially cherish our long-standing friendship with Warren and Cheryl Kniskern. We first met Warren when he was single. He had just written *When the Vow Breaks* in the early 1990s. We had the privilege of interviewing him about his own experience with divorce and his extraordinary insight into the healing process.

Soon after that first meeting, Warren met Cheryl and began the process of getting to know her, courting her, and ultimately "merging" together as a family with Cheryl and her son, Chase. Warren and Cheryl have lived firsthand the lessons they share in this book. They are honest and transparent about what they write, passionate in their desire to help you succeed, and are outstanding examples of the Lord's ability to heal and redeem lives. We love them, and you will too!

—Steve and Cheryl Grissom
Founders, DivorceCare/GriefShare Church Initiative Ministries

HOW THIS LABOR
OF LOVE CAME INTO BEING

As a Christian lawyer, once divorced and now happily remarried to a wonderful Christian wife, I am writing this book for you as a friend would write to a friend. Sharing my own experience with those facing the aftermath of divorce or death of a spouse and now considering remarriage is a personal ministry—one I believe the Lord committed to me in August 1991.

In early July 1984, when I was thirty-three years old, I married a beautiful young Christian woman. We weathered the ups and downs experienced by any married couple, but my partnership in a Miami law firm required too much of my time. This often left my young wife alone at home.

Highly capable and eager to be sociable, my wife chose to rejuvenate a successful career in the theater. She avoided loneliness at home, and blossomed in the adulation of her excellent performances before a live audience. At the same time, her affections for me waned. In the early morning hours one day in late July 1989, she returned home to announce, "Warren, I love someone else more than you. I want an immediate divorce. You draw up the papers, and I'll sign."

This announcement shocked me! Although we agreed to seek counseling, my wife declined meeting with a Christian counselor. Our secular counselor's advice to my wife? "Follow your heart." (Of course, Scripture clearly warns that the heart is deceitful above all things and beyond anyone's understanding [Jer. 17:9].) But my wife would not be dissuaded from divorcing me. The divorce finalized in July 1991. (My ex-wife and I had honeymooned by cruising through the Greek Islands on the ship *Oceanos*. In a fitting event of utmost irony, this great ship capsized and sank off the South African coast days after completion of our divorce.)

Life-changing lessons inundated me during that extremely difficult and challenging time following our divorce. At each step, the Lord touched my heart. He knew I wanted to help others work through their divorce crises. Early one morning in August 1991, the outline for a book from a Christian perspective on how to survive and recover from divorce came to me. Although I had never written a book before, the ideas flowed together faster than I could write them down.

This personal awakening led to publication of *When the Vow Breaks: A Survival and Recovery Guide for Christians Facing Divorce.* I dedicated that book of love and reconciliation to my first wife, trusting the Lord would guide it into the hands of hurting individuals who needed it most. It sent a message of grace and forgiveness to many unknown readers. How amazing to watch God prosper that work and move it across North America with little help from me! I can rejoice and step back from that first book to give him the glory.

But there's more to this wonderful story! If my first wife had not divorced me, I suppose we would have had a child or two together by now. The greatest tragedy for me was losing that opportunity for parenthood. I resigned myself to contentment as a divorced Christian man in the aftermath of publication of *When the Vow Breaks.* But I had no idea that a divorced Christian woman in Akron, Ohio, had begun searching her church library for help in recovering from divorce. She was single-parenting the most beautiful, sweet little three-year-old blond boy you've ever seen! Did she select *When the Vow Breaks* from the shelf by chance? Only the Lord knows for sure. But reading that book prompted her to call me in South Florida and invite me to lunch on her next business trip to my area.

I thought meeting this nice woman from Ohio would be just another ministerial visit. But Cheryl and I had a wonderful first lunch together. We laughed and shared our life experiences for hours while discovering many common interests.

Over a two-year courtship with Cheryl, I relinquished my initial prejudice against a remarriage to a divorced spouse with children. But Cheryl raised her young son well in the nurture and admonition of the Lord. This sweet little boy endeared himself to me by reciting Psalm 23 from memory. The Lord's lesson for me? Don't close doors on remarriage options that are acceptable and pleasing to him!

After seeking counsel from many advisors, Cheryl and I married in a small wedding ceremony in 1998. In fact, our decision to marry included all three of us—Chase participated and received his own special gold "family ring," reminding him that he is a vital part of our relationship with each other. What a blessing from the Lord! I have received a small taste of what Job experienced when God restored his lost fortunes. Now I have a loving Christian wife and a son who is about the same age as the child I had desired almost ten years ago!

Because Cheryl and I gained so much practical experience from dating after divorce and facing the many issues involving remarriage, we want to share our knowledge with you. We hope your journey will be safer and sweeter than ours! We invite you to share in our victories and learn from our mistakes.

As you read this love letter, occasionally Cheryl will add notes and personal insights from the perspective of a Christian mother entering remarriage. Be sure to look for these thought-provoking sections!

Cheryl and I hope and pray that as you journey into your future you will consider the many issues and practical Christian advice within the following pages. May our efforts bring you closer to God and your loved ones and enrich and encourage you in every way that God intends!

Introduction

ISSUES TO CONSIDER BEFORE YOU REMARRY

Samuel Johnson once described a second marriage as "the triumph of hope over experience." Indeed, for those contemplating remarriage, hope springs eternal when a new suitor appears. Yet, though love may be better the second time around, frequent complications make remarriage more challenging as well!

If you are remarried, and especially if you're part of a blended family with children from a prior marriage, you may feel stressed out, frustrated, and disillusioned by all the responsibilities, hard work, and surprises filling your life. You may be investigating some answers and solutions to help ease your load. If so, take heart! This book will help and encourage you!

Perhaps you harbor some skepticism about remarriage. "Remarriage? Dating's too frustrating to even think about it!" "I've been burned once—that's enough! I'd rather die than make another mistake in marriage!" If you're young, single, widowed, or divorced, these comments are understandable. Yet, with years of life ahead, you trust that God will heal your frustrated or wounded spirit. Chances are that a special someone will emerge to dazzle and amaze you. So it's wise to prepare for remarriage while you have a clear head and a guarded outlook.

In these hectic and troublesome times of the twenty-first century, quite often a remarriage goes far beyond joining two individuals. It's really a marriage of two *families* of strangers with unique habits and quirks, and vastly different ways of resolving differences and setting up family traditions.

Monetary minefields exist as well. Consider each partner's ingrained spending habits, child support payments, debts, retirement plans, and college funds. How will you pay for the additional costs for food, day care, entertainment, and other day-to-day expenses? Remarriage with kids means bigger families, bigger cars, and bigger budgets to manage. Are *you* ready to tackle these issues?

Consider several key questions influencing your decision to remarry:

Can I be content as a single person? Who could deny that inner craving to share one's life with someone else, and have an aching back rubbed in the middle of the night? A soul mate helps stave off the common terrible fear of ending up alone in life, isolated from society. What if something happens to you that no one knows about? Who would care for you if you needed help? What would life be like without a mate around, with whom to share all the daily details of life?

Of course, we're really never alone with Christ abiding in our lives. But we still yearn for the touch of another person—someone close who shares our days. Even so, we need to use caution that we don't allow our need for companionship to rush us into a new relationship with someone who may not be *suitable.* We always need to seek God's best partner for us.

Seeking remarriage out of fear of independence or loneliness is a recipe for disaster. It can sow seeds of destruction in the new relationship. However, if you are content with the many positive benefits in remaining single, but desire to marry *after* putting your heart at rest and surrendering to God's will, then considering remarriage is appropriate. Marry with the sincere desire to share with someone else the abundance of what you have in your own life, not out of deficit neediness for another person to fulfill you.

Am I scripturally free to remarry? There are some serious scriptural issues about remarriage, which no formerly married Christian should ignore. Jesus tells us in Matthew 19:9: "I tell you that anyone who divorces his wife, except for marital unfaithfulness, and marries another woman commits adultery." Luke 16:18b goes further: ". . . and the man who marries a divorced woman commits adultery."

"Marital unfaithfulness" in Greek is *porneia,* meaning "fornication and all forms of illicit or unlawful sexual intercourse in general." Does this term require some sexual involvement on the part of a marriage partner? Can it simply mean breaking faith with one's partner by forsaking the marriage relationship without any sexual involvement with others? As we shall see in chapter 3, according to Greek authorities, the word has a very broad *sexual* connotation. It appears to require more than mere "covenant-breaking," marital incompatibility, or disloyalty. Thus, if there is no marital unfaithfulness *(porneia),* divorce and remarriage to another person while both spouses to the first marriage remain alive may cause the parties to that remarriage to commit adultery. These warnings from the Lord are controversial but warrant careful, prayerful consideration before seriously considering any remarriage. This book will give you enough information to review your situation and prayerfully seek the counsel of God before you proceed.

Why wait to remarry? "Don't remarry right away." That's the advice most formerly married folks will hear. Why? Because losing a mate through death or divorce shakes anyone up enough that one's identity is a little uncertain for awhile. You need time to adjust from being "Michelle's husband" or "Jack's wife" to being just yourself. After the loss of a spouse, changing these labels is uncomfortable and difficult, so some people rush back into a marriage as quickly as possible to keep their familiar labels.

Who can escape from the harsh statistics of divorce? Almost half of first marriages end in divorce, as do a majority of remarriages. Remarriages with children are even more likely to fail. A *Bizarro* comic strip some years ago cynically illustrates a remarriage cycle by showing a mother reading a bedtime story to her young daughter from "Grim Reality Fairy Tales": ". . . and the prince kissed her and they fell in love,

dated for awhile . . . broke up, got back together, got married, had a baby, got separated, got back together, broke up again, divorced, spent time alone rediscovering
themselves, met someone new, fell in love, and repeated the pattern habitually ever
after."[1] It's a sobering scenario!

We also hear horror stories of a forty-five-pound bundle of joy who steadfastly
resists any stranger coming into Mommy or Daddy's life—a kid who almost instinctively
knows just how to wreck a romance and torpedo a new relationship. And that's before the
little angel learns the "You're not my mommy!" thrust to the heart after a remarriage
occurs. Remarriages—especially with children—require extreme patience and wisdom.

Have I met the right person? Before considering remarriage, any courting couple
would do well to consider the usual questions: Do I enjoy talking to this person? Can
we communicate openly and honestly? Do I genuinely like this person? Can I care for
her needs? When the car breaks down on the highway, how does he react? Where is this
person spiritually? Can we discuss matters calmly and work out a mutually acceptable
solution whenever we disagree? Does this person have the character I want to see reproduced in my children? Unless a potential mate is spiritually, intellectually, emotionally,
and physically compatible *over a reasonable time period of dating and openly sharing
each other's lives,* you should question whether that person is right for you.

What about parenting the children? Single parents have additional concerns.
Potential mates in remarriage may be personally compatible, but will they be good
parents? Experience discounts the naïve notion that a new stepparent will become an
"instant parent," with the newly remarried couple immediately functioning smoothly
as coparents. No matter what a stepparent does, and no matter how interactive he/she
may be with stepchildren, that person will never really replace the biological parent. A
stepparent, merely by assuming the role, threatens children in a number of ways—
especially if the stepparent comes into the remarriage with his/her own children in
tow: "Does loving my stepdad mean that I can't love my daddy anymore?" "Why do
I have to call her Mom, when she's *not* my mom?" "I didn't ask for these stepsiblings.
Why do I have to share my room?"

Adults in love with each other frequently rush into remarriage and overlook the
suspicious and sometimes hostile reactions of the children involved. Even *grown* children aren't immune to problems. What priority do our natural and stepchildren have
in this situation? Children who come *with* a remarriage can come *between* the married couple too! No one can force togetherness. Remarriage today quite often is a
family decision involving children from both spouses, ex-spouses who are biological
parents of one or more of the children, as well as grandparents and even other
extended family members.

What about finances? Family research experts and marriage counselors uniformly
confirm that four primary issues break up marriages—money, sex, kids, and in-laws
(present and former). The money issue is more complicated in a remarriage. Do you
both know how to budget properly? Will financial settlements from a prior relationship cause problems? What about unpaid debts? Do you agree on spending priorities?
Missing or late child support payments can strain a blended family budget to the limit.

Remarriage after widowhood has its own financial hazards as well. There may be concerns about honoring a deceased spouse's wishes in distributing insurance funds and personal possessions among natural children, for example.

Remarriage can be an exhilarating experience, but it's a major life commitment. If you are scripturally free to marry and wish to do so, explore different options. But be cautious. Take your time and ask many questions!

Given the many life-changing issues and decisions any marriage requires, it's *vital* to receive counseling—not only marital but family-related as well. Seek the counsel of many advisors (Prov. 11:14). Don't rush! Remarriages are extremely complex unions—much more so than first marriages.

These are but a few of the many issues facing those considering remarriage after death or divorce of a spouse. But take heart! They are part of what makes remarriage and blended families intriguing and absolutely life-fulfilling! So let's begin at the end of your prior marriage and review the matters that make for a good foundation in any remarriage.

A Message from Cheryl

Even bad first marriages have a natural advantage over potentially good remarriages. Why? We were young, childless, without long-term financial commitments, and wonderfully naïve. Plan the honeymoon, open a checking account, and you were on your way!

Remarriages are more difficult and much more likely to end in divorce. It's no wonder! There's so much to argue over. Who has the time? Even before finalizing the honeymoon plans, children can sabotage the relationship. There may be two homes to rework or sell. Two sets of debts to merge. Ex-spouses pop in periodically—often unannounced—to wreak havoc. This onslaught hits you when you may be reeling with issues, fears, and doubts.

Where do we go for advice? The Bible doesn't specifically tell us how to brace children for a stepparent. Mom never went through this trial, and Oprah may not be the best source!

Counselors warn that remarriage is more difficult than a first marriage. It *will* take longer to merge and blend, sometimes as long as five years. Be prepared and patient! It is not for the faint of heart—particularly with children at stake. Are you ready to love unconditionally during five years of turmoil? There's no turning back. If you're not ready to meet the challenges of remarriage, don't risk it. Some couples wait ten years for their children to be fully grown before considering remarriage. They find it's easier on themselves and their children.

But if you're ready, able, and willing to enter remarriage, Warren will provide you with many issues to consider, and excellent suggestions in this book. As one who has been through divorce and remarriage, however, I would offer the following biblically based suggestions:

- Another divorce will *never* be an option without scriptural reason (God hates divorce).
- We need to be at peace with everyone (including ex-spouses!) as much as it depends upon us (Rom. 12:18).
- Children are to honor and obey their parents (Eph. 6:1) which, I believe, includes stepparents.
- Seek a competent and experienced Christian counselor. You *will* need this input! Begin sessions with your husband or wife-to-be *before* you remarry.
- Although the rewards are worth the journey, fasten your seatbelt—it will be a bumpy ride!

How to Use
This Book Wisely

As you read this book, you need to understand where you've come from, where you are right now, and where you want to go in remarriage. As your servants, Cheryl and I are asking the Lord to help us come alongside you in a very personal way to *encourage* you. In doing so, we'll share some insights and suggestions from personal experience and from other remarriage veterans.

Although we won't ignore them (see appendix A), we also won't overwhelm you with statistics as to death, divorce, and remarriages. Why? Because there are just too many unique twists and turns in life to make general statistics truly relevant to what you may experience. It really doesn't matter how many marriages in the United States end in divorce over a period of years if we've lived through it ourselves. And what benefit comes from knowing that remarriages are more likely to end in divorce than first marriages? Others' failures may result from any number of reasons, most of which probably won't apply to us. But we do want to *learn* from the mistakes of others without becoming fixated on the sad results reaped from those errors.

Are you recently divorced or widowed? If you haven't yet remarried, you may want to begin reading part 1 of this book. These chapters deal with reentering single life after death or divorce of a spouse. We explore grief and recovery issues to help you examine your heart and mind in an effort to understand where you have come from in your prior relationships and where you are right now. This section also has a comprehensive review of the vital biblical considerations to help you determine whether you are scripturally free to remarry.

Are you remarried, or about to remarry? Part 1 of this book will help you examine your life to make sure you've released your prior marriage so you can devote yourself fully to your new partner and family. Part 2 will guide you through many perplexing problems and circumstances of remarriage and blended families—from dating and engagement to a suitable mate for you (and your children) through managing the issues of remarried life.

You don't need to read this book in chronological order. Each chapter is written independently. Skip around and read chapters dealing with the subjects that interest or apply to you the most. Above all, keep an open heart and mind. Let the Lord whisper his message to you as you read.

PART ONE

Dawn of Recovery

Healing the Wounds of Divorce or Death of a Spouse

I would love to reassure you that your remarriage will be a guaranteed joy without having to work hard at it. Itching ears long to hear this message! But it isn't true. The truth is, remarriage takes a *lot* of hard work.

Many remarriages fail because people enter the relationship as broken and hurting individuals. Like it or not, we must acknowledge that hurt people . . . hurt people. If you break your leg, you can anesthetize yourself enough to believe that you have conquered the pain and are ready to put the episode behind you, but this won't work because you have to reset your broken leg and give it time to heal. Remarriage candidates are no different. Ignoring broken spirits and crushed dreams, or being captive to deep-seated anger and resentment, they think they can walk on broken legs into a remarriage without reaping the consequences of a hasty decision. Result? Another sad divorce statistic.

To build a truly successful remarriage fully grounded in commitment, intimacy, and joy, we must know who we are in Christ. We also need to understand how our prior marriages affected us, where we are in our personal recovery process, and how well prepared we are for remarriage. This means undergoing an honest self-appraisal and realistically looking at our lives the way God views us—both good and bad. It also means using the living and active Word of God to explore the thoughts and attitudes of our hearts (Heb. 4:12).

Shouldn't we let our life experience as formerly married individuals mature us? Shouldn't we use this time to take a direct, in-depth look inside ourselves with a greater desire for personal growth and expanding awareness? When we're ready to sift through the fantasies and fairy-tale promises of a mythical romance and a trouble-free remarriage and face the realities of married life in a blended family, we can feast on the meat of what *really* works!

To the uninitiated, there's a tempting quick answer to the common question, "How can I avoid the mistakes made in my former marriage?" What is it? "I'll marry a better person this time!" Wrong! You first must *be* a better person for someone else.

We are the major cause of breakdown in remarriages, often because we haven't allowed the Lord to prepare us adequately for the relationship.

If we want to avoid repeating mistakes from our former marriage, we can and *must* first yield ourselves to God. We must be healed sufficiently from the grief and loss of our former marriages without blaming the past or our former spouses for where our marriages fell short. Unfinished business from our prior relationships needs completion and closure to allow room for a new partner.

In my own recovery I realized I couldn't be a responsible and loving husband again until I honestly looked at how I failed my first wife. This was so difficult! I could point the finger at her in some ways, but God's resounding answer was for me to give up my pride and self-reliance so I could fully yield to him. I needed to open my heart wide for extensive surgery on my own selfishness, anger, and bitterness. I needed the pain of his discipline and correction before I could heal enough to move on in my life.

But healing from a prior relationship isn't the full story. Something equally important needs to occur. The absolute best preparation for remarriage is . . . *be content as a single person.* Sound odd in a book on remarriage? Yet it's true. You must realistically assess yourself and get to know who you are *without* a partner. Only after you are content and secure as a single person—in your relationship with God and with other people—will you have the best chance of making your remarriage a success. This means fully experiencing your hunger and need for companionship but resisting the impatient urge to fulfill it with the first suitor who comes along. It means not envying the marrieds. Dare I say it? It means being content to remain single . . . for the rest of your life if necessary.

The goal for a successful remarriage is simply this: A single whole person entering into an interdependent relationship with another single whole person—not half a person pairing up with another half person.

In part 1 of this book, you'll find help for taking a good look inside your heart. How far along are you in your recovery from the grief and pain arising from your former marriage? Have you released the bitterness and resentment of your loss? How well have you dealt with the inevitable issues of being comfortable as a single person once again? Are you willing to accept God's will for your life—even if his Word makes it clear that you may not be scripturally free to remarry?

The chapters in part 1 will test your resolve and inspect your foundation for remarriage. The hard work begins now.

Chapter 1

EMBRACING SINGLENESS
Where Do I Go from Here?

After death or divorce of a loved one, the first priority is to embrace singleness and restore your identity as a person. Being content and fulfilled as a single person is absolutely necessary before considering remarriage.

"I am . . . single . . . once again." Saying those words can grip your soul in frightening despair. What will happen to me? How can I move on in life without my mate? How will my children grow up without their missing parent? What will happen to my extended family members and friends? It's been so long since I was single, how can I survive returning to the dating world? Loneliness. Isolation. Even hearing about a "singles event" sends chills up and down one's spine.

"I am single . . . once again." I have been a single person most of my adult life. In many ways I was comfortable being single. Still, I must tell you that after crossing over the bridge to married life in 1984, I fully expected to leave singleness behind forever. So in coming to grips with my wife divorcing me out of love for another person, I felt as shocked and unprepared to deal with becoming a single, formerly married man as you may have experienced. I wasn't ready. I really wasn't *willing* to be single *again.*

When the full weight of coming out the back end of a marriage hits you, perhaps you feel the temptation to say to yourself, "I need to remarry." I did. You may think it strange that a book on the virtues of remarriage would counsel you in this fashion, but before going any further in this book, every "single-again" person needs to ask one crucial question: "Have I *embraced singleness?*" If the answer is no, then I encourage you to read through all of part 1 of this book carefully. *Then put this book away* for a while as you think and pray about the message of these vitally important chapters.

PEACEFUL, RATIONAL SELF-EVALUATION

The most important aspect of embracing singleness is discovering who you are as an individual—right now and also in the context of your past. Are you fully aware of your feelings about leaving a marriage behind and becoming single? Don't rush into remarriage until you learn who you are, where you have come from, who and what you like—and especially *why*.

Consider where you are right now in your life. Do you frequently tell your "divorce story" to others? Are you more interested in reminiscing about your deceased spouse than finding out what's going on in the lives of others? Do you go to an event only because you might meet another eligible person instead of to learn more about yourself and others? Do you need someone in your life to define who you are? Do you feel guilty and think you're a second-class citizen because you don't have a mate? Do you blindly follow the personal assessments and advice of friends instead of being in touch with who *you* are and what *you* need? If so, you've got it all wrong! Rediscover yourself *first*. See whether you are fully surrendered to the Lord. The rest most likely will fall into place in good time.

Why is time for personal reflection and embracing singleness so important? It resists the inevitable desperation some of us feel in wanting to plunge into another marriage right away. We tend to repeat the errors and negative patterns of the past if we don't have time to learn from our mistakes. This is why, as essayist Oliver Wendell Holmes once astutely noted, "A moment's insight is sometimes worth a life's experience." Proverbs 26:11 warns us: "As a dog returns to its vomit, so a fool repeats folly." Desperate people lack objectivity. They become *reactive* and "fall into a new relationship" rather than being *proactive* in choosing a suitable mate after careful reflection and receiving wise counsel. Reflection is the most noble way to *learn* from our mistakes and gain wisdom.

Shortly after my first wife divorced me, I spent too much time working during the week and staying indoors to read and write on weekends. I really was in my own world, just doing what I enjoy, but life was passing me by. So I decided to become a power walker. Several times each week, I strapped on weights and found different routes to walk through my neighborhood. I discovered my neighbors, ran into fellow walkers, and became friends with local pets. I enjoyed glorious sunsets, flowers blooming, and how people tended their yards. But it also gave me time to pray, seek the Lord . . . and just listen for him. I found that many of the pieces of my life began to settle into place and make sense once again just by having this recreation and reflection time without distraction. It connected me with the world around me that I was ignored for too long. Life was fulfilling, and even thrilling, me once again as a single man.

So much of life is the little things that we too quickly ignore. Don't skip all these little episodes coming between major events—*learn* from them! As you think ahead to remarriage and all the other wonderful goals you want to accomplish in life, it's tempting to see life as a series of page-one headlines. The truth is, life is actually all the little stories between the front and back pages.

So how do you embrace singleness? How do you *learn* from the past and prepare for remarriage by being content and at peace?

FEELING THE SHOCK AND WEIGHT OF LONELINESS

As a single person, you are spending more time alone than you ever did as a married individual. How does it feel? Are you comfortable with it?

How did you feel in the first few months after losing your spouse? Many of us felt impact. Shock. Denial. Numbness. Amnesia. Disorientation. Isolation. You are left alone and feel very alone—one single solitary life, even with kids around to keep you busy. You know this may mean the end of many family traditions, such as holiday dinners or reunions. A cold wind blows through your life. Each day brings another layer of snow to cover the glacier that entombs your life. You go through the motions of daily life, but with no real destination.

I was struck by the feeling of loneliness so vividly pictured in Tom Hanks's movie *Cast Away.* Hanks plays Chuck Noland, a man who rules his life by the clock and a pager. His life as a FedEx troubleshooter is breathlessly frenetic. He rushes through Christmas with his girlfriend, Kelly Frears (played by Helen Hunt), to the point that they exchange gifts in the car. "I'll be right back," Noland tells her, delaying his marriage proposal to rush off on yet another emergency in a cargo jet bound for Tahiti.

But Noland goes down with a FedEx plane in the South Pacific, miraculously survives, and washes up marooned on a deserted island where he stays for four years—alone. He now is cut loose from all human contact, struggling to survive, and overwhelmed by forces beyond his control or comprehension.

Ironic relics of his life wash ashore in the form of FedEx packages—videotapes, ice skates, and a volleyball. He must learn the basics of existence—how to make fire, crack a coconut, spear fish, weave rope, build a raft—to keep life going. But throughout the movie you feel his utter, soul-destroying loneliness and despair. In desperation for companionship, Noland develops a friendship with the volleyball, which he names "Wilson" and upon which he's drawn a face with his own blood. The hardships Noland faces and the primal emotions he experiences undermine his will to live. It is deeply moving.

When Noland finally escapes from the island, he returns to the world he left behind but realizes that he's no longer part of it. His girlfriend is no longer available—she has married someone else. He is emotionally adrift in civilization, forever changed by his island experience. Eventually he rediscovers himself and accepts that his situation has changed. He is now a single man with a different life ahead of him.

While going through the divorce process with my first wife, her lawyer instructed her not to talk with me. When her divorce lawsuit against me bogged down in court, she and her attorney finally agreed to participate in mediation. Ultimately this mediation provided the catalyst necessary to complete the divorce more amicably. It also gave my wife and me our first real chance in too many months to simply talk with each other. She was committed to seeing the divorce through to the end, but as we talked about really mundane things, I remember admiring how beautiful and sweet she was, and I grieved in my heart at how we had come so far in our marriage only to reach this point of really saying good-bye and becoming strangers. It was very sad . . . and lonely.

Throughout our separation and the divorce process, I steadfastly wore my wedding ring. It reminded me of the vows we had made to each other—to be faithful to God and to each other until death parted us. Divorce never was an option for me. On the day the judge signed the divorce decree, I took it off and spent a few minutes looking at it. It was a melancholy moment. Like my wife and our marriage, the ring looked so beautiful and sparkled as it turned in the light. It was so difficult dropping it into an envelope and burying it in the safe deposit box. At that moment, the heavy burden of singleness fell on my soul.

Some people coming out of an unhappy marriage feel an almost instant relief and release by escaping from a hurtful or controlling spouse. They're glad to free themselves from the grip of their mates. This isn't a loss, but a triumph of freedom. But for many of us experiencing death or divorce of a spouse—even in unhappy marriages—there is an almost unbearable sadness for awhile.

When you wake up alone the first couple of mornings, you immediately realize your mate is gone. The absence is all around you. He or she is no longer there to greet you with a smile or a caress. Sometimes there's nothing better to do than to weep and rail at the emptiness.

Many times we think, *My life is over.* Our histories will overshadow whatever future we have—forever. We feel like postponing living and letting time—days, months, and even years—pass us by, *precious time that is lost forever.* We feel . . . invisible.

We also know the memories of one's mate linger on for months and years, tucked away in our subconscious, resting quietly until some life trigger brings them freshly to mind as if they never left. Grief specialists call these little ambushes of grief "secondary losses." Family counselor Irving Kermish knows this feeling well. He spotted a woman wearing a hairstyle similar to that of his deceased wife. "I said to myself, 'There's Nola,'" he remembers. "Then I laughed out loud and told myself, 'How silly of me. Nola is dead.' Then my next thought was, 'I must go home and tell Nola how silly I just was.' It all happened in a fraction of a second."[1] These memories aren't simply pressed between the pages of our minds—they can emotionally overwhelm us.

Even so, to cope with our loss we keep something personal from our departed loved one—an old shirt or pair of pajamas—anything to keep the scent near. We sit in his/her favorite chair that has been empty for too long. We sleep diagonally across the bed at night.

Single parents see their former mates in their children. A child's appearance highlights the genetic link to a departed spouse. Sometimes it's just a certain look or a favorite phrase that brings the loss to mind. Or it may be nothing more than a question about how Daddy used to do things, or what dress Mommy liked to wear. These matters connect with our consciousness in many different ways.

Our memories will always be there, reminding us of our life history, our identity, and serving as a guidepost for our future. They are part of us—who and what we are.

God allows them for a reason. Treasure them. Live with them. *Learn* from them. Then build new memories where you are right now.

How loss of a spouse and loneliness affect many men. Older widowed and divorced persons, particularly men, face an even more daunting challenge—a penetrating loneliness spurred by declining health and resources. You may have seen photographs of Israel's former prime minister, Menachem Begin, in the period after his wife passed away in November 1982. Begin began looking terribly depressed and physically wasted after she departed.

Many men have a very tough time with loss of a spouse. Most of us are heavily dependent upon a nurturing spouse for physical, emotional, and other kinds of support. When this support is ripped away, the reality of being single again affects us deeply.

Men generally don't cope well with grief. We are less likely to cry or talk about our feelings. Rarely do men choose to join grief support groups or seek counseling. We might not want to ask for help because we may believe it's not manly to do so. In addition to this natural reluctance to talk matters out, it's not uncommon for male friends to encourage us to "keep a stiff upper lip" and bear up under this crushing loss. Female friends may withhold much-needed emotional support in fear of having their efforts misinterpreted sexually. Result? Missing out on a special hug from a caring friend when their wounded and hurting souls so desperately need it.

This lonely situation drives many men to an early grave. A Johns Hopkins study of more than four thousand widowed persons revealed a mortality rate for widowers that was 26 percent higher than for married men, and *61 percent* higher in men 55 to 64 years of age.[2] "If an early death doesn't get me," men often think, "my life expectancy today is 76, compared to 47 in 1900. I'm going to be alone for a *long* time yet!"

So how do many men cope with their loss? They begin dating and remarrying sooner. It's easy for them to do so because at almost any age, single women outnumber available men.[3]

How loss of a spouse and loneliness affect many women. Most women accept the loss of their husbands quite well. Why? Because they are more open to sharing their grief with others. But adapting to the circumstances surrounding their loss remains a significant challenge. In a heartbeat, a wife becomes a widow facing life alone.

After her husband, Leo, died of a massive heart attack at 37, *Miami Herald* columnist Ana Veciana-Suarez provided some insight into a widow's life:

> I used to get mad at him for the stupidest things . . . like leaving
> dirty socks on the bathroom floor. Like eating the last of the Heavenly
> Hash ice cream. Like reading the paper while I was swamped with
> morning chores. . . . [But now] I cry at anything, at the smell of his
> Paco Rabanne cologne, at the sight of his favorite University of Miami
> Hurricanes T-shirt, at the taste of Triscuits and cheese. Even when
> I think I'm all cried out, when surely no more tears are left, I weep
> again, and again, and again. And in this fog of agony, I hear our

children plead, 'Mom, please don't cry. Please don't cry, Mom.
Please!' . . . Then I think, Who will finish my sentences when I don't?
Who will love me when I'm down, encourage me in rejection? Who
will answer when I call, calm me when I rant? Who has lived a parallel
life? Who shares a history? Who will tell me the truth when I don't
want to hear it? Who will do something silly because I think it's funny?
Who will tell me—and believe it—that I look best without makeup?
Who will look at my children and know, without a doubt and with a
considerable amount of pride, that there is a bit of us in their shapely
arms, their long legs, their upturned faces.[4]

It's a very lonely feeling.

Sometimes loneliness is laced with anger. A widow may be angry that her
deceased spouse didn't take better care of himself. If he had, she wouldn't have to face
life alone now. Perhaps a husband didn't leave enough money for a comfortable
retirement—an often frightening situation in these financially troublesome times.

Some years ago, I urged one of my clients to secure more life insurance and obtain
estate planning for himself and his young wife, then pregnant with their first child. He
put it off, only to be mortally wounded by a runaway car in downtown Miami.
Although he was on life support for only twenty-four hours before he died, the
cost of that treatment wiped out the small life insurance policy they had. This compelled his stunned widow to sell their home and return to live with her parents.
Circumstances like these understandably make widows angry in their loneliness. Then
guilt comes from feeling anger toward the departed spouse.

Eventually, loss of a spouse leads many women to long for another meaningful
relationship with a male suitor. This urge quite often brings frustration and disappointment. A woman's need to have another man in her life sometimes tears at her
soul. As my wife, Cheryl, confesses, life without a husband was particularly challenging for her as a single mother. "A young single parent can experience a deep yearning
for the opposite sex that is—almost primal—something inside that you haven't felt for
years, almost driving you to do things you never imagined. I used to be so desperate
for the scent of a man that I would douse my little three-year-old, Chase, with
cologne. And guess what? His middle-aged single female teachers actually requested
the cologne . . . apparently we shared the same sense of desperation!"

Sure, not all women need male companionship. But if you feel this need in your
own heart, you know that each passing day without it is a fresh source of loneliness.

The perils of single parenting. Single parents have the toughest challenge of all.
God created team parenting of children—and it does take two to do it right! But single parents persevere in this heroically lonely venture, often lived out in eighteen-hour
days or more. Working full-time—sometimes with more than one job—while fixing
meals, helping with homework, paying bills, cleaning house, banking, grocery shopping, and on and on with little or no support is a very lonely pursuit.

But single parents do have an advantage here. Cheryl remembers one particular
Mother's Day when all of her friends and family were busy or out of town: "There

I was alone with a three-year-old little boy, too young to know about the significance of that day. Depressed after attending church, I crawled into bed for a nap as he napped downstairs. But after awhile I heard Chase wake up and begin climbing the stairs to my room. He crawled into my bed, hugged me, and said, 'I love you, Mommy.' It was as if the Lord knew my need for just such a moment of appreciation!"

The heartbreak of being left behind. When you first learn that your former spouse has remarried, fresh loneliness rides on a flatbed of guilt and regret after a divorce. This news can hit you like a ton of bricks—especially if your ex-spouse made noble efforts to avoid divorce and desperately wanted reconciliation but you resisted it. You may second-guess your decision to divorce while dealing with jealousy. You may recall your honeymoon and some great times with your ex-mate. All the while, your memory blocks out the bad times or how he/she cheated on you.

You may ask yourself the painful, self-defeating question "How can he love her when he couldn't love me?" Guilt grows quickly with this mind-set. You think, "There's something wrong with me." It won't be long before more withdrawal from society seems to be the soothing choice, which only feeds the loneliness you already may feel.

The dating scene. Reality strikes many women who find themselves single again. Women in their twenties find decent men everywhere. For women in their thirties and beyond, however, the situation is quite different. It seems that the men worth marrying have curiously disappeared. One widow echoes a common complaint: "I'm not as young as I once was, and there aren't as many men around. And women are desperate. They're barracudas when it comes to a free man."

Pat Sullivan, a widow with five children, expressed the shock of adjusting to the singles environment this way: "I felt I had nowhere to go. It's a couples-oriented world, and you don't think about it until you have to see it." In trying to date others, she faced a harsh reality. "Once [men] found out that I have five children, they wouldn't dance with me for the rest of the evening." Then another stigma surfaced. "Your friends will do anything for you at first, but then they seem to get jealous. One friend I finally confronted said she was afraid I could just go and do anything I wanted with her husband."[5]

Many young formerly married women find themselves the target of much older men—old enough to be their fathers or grandfathers. One elderly gentleman approached a young divorcee in her twenties with the age-old come-on, "Where have you been all my life?" Shocked at his advance, she blurted out, "Teething."

Many men don't fare much better. William, a divorcee, notes, "Women seem to warm up to me quite well . . . that is until they find out that I'm divorced. Then it's like I have the plague. They don't want to waste valuable time to see if I would be worth the risk of developing a relationship."

For men and women, between events like these is the waiting . . . and waiting . . . and waiting, hoping to find someone, *anyone,* who might be suitable for a relationship. All of these scenarios can be very discouraging and lonely indeed!

Churches may compound the loneliness. Upon death or divorce of a spouse, you may experience the pain of losing your "place" as part of the married couples group in church. Not only do you lose your family, but you may feel like an outcast in your home congregation.

Church leaders, many of whom are ill-equipped to deal with formerly married folks—especially divorced Christians—quite often consider single-again people as some kind of strange species. They really don't have a clue about what to do with them. Result? Many single Christians feel like second-class citizens in church fellowship. One insensitive pastor even announced a "Sweetheart's Banquet" for Valentine's Day, open only to couples, adding that he and his wife would have an open house later for "all the rejects."

Unfortunately, avoidance of singles prevails in too many churches. The leadership focuses on the intact family. They bring in family experts and hold marriage encounter weekends, while secretly hoping single Christians will get remarried and resume a "normal" family life to ease their discomfort of ministering to those who "always seem to be in need." This isn't true in all churches, of course. For example, some enlightened congregations set up special ministries to help those valiant single parents who cannot balance everything by themselves. But this seems to be more the exception than the rule.

By ignoring singles, church leaders may unwittingly, and prematurely, push people into marriage with the wrong person. The wise church will focus on helping singles become spiritually and emotionally healthy—and be lovingly honest when it sees potential problems in relationships—*before* singles choose to remarry.

But, in fairness, let's also remember that, for all its failings in ministering to divorced souls, the church remains the Lord's primary ministry agent on earth. DivorceCare/GriefShare Founder, Steve Grissom (who wrote the foreword to this book) remarks, "The church does many things poorly (especially in divorce matters). I have personally had to work through a number of hurts and issues related to the church and divorce, yet I have come away from that experience passionate that the church (local body of believers) is central to divorce and grief ministry." He's right! Many upsides to church ministry can counteract loneliness—biblical teaching, consistent safe fellowship, opportunities to participate in small group "families," access to church-based benevolence, opportunities to minister to others (which is so effective in the healing process), mechanisms for accountability and confrontation of sin (Matt. 18), ministry to children, and when the time is right—an excellent place to meet potential mates.

Some consequences of loneliness. Loneliness, which ages poorly over time, can lead to alternative gratifications to ease the pain—such as filling up with alcohol, becoming shopaholics, flirting with sexual temptations, or overeating. When we feel terrible inside, we can become listless and begin eating all the wrong foods instead of dieting and limiting ourselves to only healthy fare. It won't be long until we hole up in our rooms watching risque movies while balancing a buffet of finger foods and junk meals on an unmade bed as we cry into our Häagen-Daz pints. When loneliness covers you like a blanket, it's the rare person indeed who doesn't feel the need to go to the fridge to try and fill up the emptiness inside.

Ironically, some of us may really *want* to experience this lonely sadness and regret fully. Moving ahead with life can come later. Right now, for awhile, we may want to experience the pain of loss and sadness. Why? Because feeling too good about moving on too quickly often means you're leaving your mate behind. And it hurts. We may want to feel bad for awhile just to keep in touch a little longer. But too often this is only another form of self-punishment when one's self-esteem is in the gutter.

Learning to Cope with Loneliness

So where does this loneliness lead us? We wish we could meet the person of our dreams—someone to share life with us, to hold hands, to hug and kiss, laugh with and so much more. We have a gnawing hunger to belong to someone else, to be understood and loved. We may think that remarriage and finding another lifelong companion is the antidote to loneliness. Not so! Christ is. Here are a few proven steps to deal with loneliness in a spiritually healthy way:

Admit you are lonely. Sounds simple enough, but too often it's so hard to do! It does no good to deny that you feel emotionally disconnected. Too many people run away from loneliness, guilt, and pain. They fear others view them as inferior if they admit having these problems. But God wants us to be truthful and realistic about our situations and how we feel about them. (He knows what's going on anyway, so who do we think we are fooling?) Want some honesty? How about praying, "Lord, I'm lonely and depressed. I need someone to be my friend. Please help me." God loves you and wants you to be a joyful Christian. Communicating this in prayer *will* bring results!

Admitting loneliness like this will wake you up to the realization that quick cures, like playing more golf or working longer hours, just won't solve the problem. Don't worry, you aren't alone in feeling lonely. Elijah was lonely when he thought he was the only one left as a prophet of God (1 Kings 19:10). The apostle Paul experienced loneliness when "everyone deserted me" (2 Tim. 4:16). Christ certainly experienced loneliness on the cross (Mark 15:34). Evangelist Billy Graham says that, in his experience, more people suffer from loneliness than any other problem. Once you admit that you are lonely, you'll be ready to seek out the next positive step to change your life for the better.

Talk about the sources of loneliness. During holidays, for example, many widowed persons don't feel comfortable enough to even mention a deceased mate's name or reminisce about him/her. But even the sound of that person's name can be just like medicine! While the first mention of it may bring tears, soon will follow the joy of sharing stories filled with "Do you remember when he . . . ?" Even divorced spouses can find some funny or tender experiences to share about their ex-mates. Finding someone with whom you can *honestly* share how you really feel during the holidays, or any other time of the year for that matter, keeps emotions from getting bottled up and catching you off guard.

Understand the causes of loneliness. First, loneliness can be the result of major life transitions. Going to school for the first time is lonely. Interviewing for a new job is lonely. Beginning the job is lonely. Moving away from family and friends is lonely. Growing older is lonely. And yes, being single again certainly is very lonely.

Second, we feel loneliness because of separation. We are isolated from others—in this case our ex-spouses and mutual friends perhaps. We ask ourselves many times over, "Why did he leave me?" Mostly we just miss our mates and the happy times we once shared. The good news is that new opportunities await. God promises us: "In *all* things God works for the good of those who love him, who have been called according to his purpose" (Rom. 8:28). He uses our life events for our ultimate good, with the goal that each of us will become more like Jesus.

Third, we need to understand that our natural defense against loneliness is self-protection, to avoid pain and fear. When we feel lonely, we may withdraw and become introspective. We build walls to keep the world out. Or perhaps we try to become extroverts, losing and sacrificing ourselves to be in the company of others. These coping mechanisms for dealing with our pain only prolong recovery. Result either way? Even more loneliness. It's easy to withdraw and miss out on life. One common way is to lose oneself in the "bondage of busyness"—filling one's life with countless trivial or meaningless tasks to avoid the pain.

As a native Floridian, it continually perplexes me why so many folks encase their ears with headphones hooked up to metal detectors and wander aimlessly along the most beautiful beaches in the world while hoping to find a treasure. What do they usually find? Only a dime or soda can poptop. What drives them to spend their lives this way? They must experience frequent frustration and disappointment after so many days of this drudgery without success. All the while, God faithfully paints his skies each afternoon with glowing sunset colors that trumpet, "Look up to the heavens and see the majesty around you!" "Not interested," seems to be the reply of these beachcombers as they trudge along with their heads down, listening for a hopeful "ping" in the sand. How sad. And yet lonely people pursuing lonely pursuits like this will surely reap what they sow—even more loneliness.

Lastly, loneliness is the ultimate curse of abandonment, rejection, or betrayal by a former spouse whom you loved more than life itself. We need acceptance. We need recognition from others. When we don't receive this from others or, even worse, when we *do* receive it but then lose it, loneliness is the result.

But admitting you are lonely and understanding *why* you're feeling this way is the beginning of self-awareness, which will steer you in the right direction.

Inventory your life. What needs to change? Identify what contributes to your loneliness. Ask yourself some hard questions. Am I intentionally keeping myself marooned on my own lonely island, or do I come back to civilization and move on with my life like Chuck Noland? Do I feel better sitting alone on my couch each night having a pity party rather than reaching out in a healthy way to give and to serve others? Do I *like* being lonely? If you answer yes, *stop!* Be willing to *learn* from the lonely times and use them to examine your life to reveal holes needing to be filled with the good things of God. Look deep into your life long enough to do this vital work!

Part of inventorying your life is committing yourself to pursue priorities. Beyond merely organizing our lives into the "must dos," "should dos," and "could dos," we need to ask, "What's truly important in my life?" What would you leave undone if you had only weeks to live? Are you living for Jesus or a house mortgage payment? Are you seeking to make a name for yourself or glorifying his name? What was more important to the Good Samaritan—to continue his trip or change his plans to help the injured man (Luke 10:25–37)?

You won't find the real cure for loneliness in your life on paper. Examine yourself and let God point the way: Check your heart. Where are you headed in life? Check your schedule. Who controls your time? Check your possessions. How much is enough? Check your Savior. Who *really* sits on the throne in your life? Then redeem the time (Eph. 5:15–16).

Being *other*-centered chases away loneliness. Jesus always put people ahead of his schedule and personal convenience. He was accessible, and took interruptions in stride. Though weary, he ministered to an entire city (Mark 1:32–34). Though thirsty and tired, he changed the life of the woman at the well (John 4). Despite the pressing crowd, he reached out to the hemorrhaging woman (Luke 8:43–48). As hurried as he was, he didn't overlook blind Bartimaeus (Mark 10:46–52).

The most valuable time is neither taken nor given—it is shared with love and leisure. Lack of significant moments coming from serving others can lead to a lifetime of regret. Investing *quality* time in individuals is a priority, even if it means spending more time with fewer people.

Appreciate the blessings of loneliness. Loneliness isn't something to avoid. It can be a very healthy feeling to experience. Why? Because enduring it confirms that you can stand alone with God if necessary. Author Bruce Larsen believes loneliness is best understood as a gift that motivates a relationship with God and others. The intense, painful loneliness Christ experienced in the Garden of Gethsemane was overwhelming for him (Mark 14:35–36), but it also strengthened him to walk alone down that final road to the cross.

Loneliness cuts deep into our hearts and souls. But as it does so, it opens up new pathways for God's love to penetrate all of the hidden places in our lives where we desperately need him the most. Had it not been for our painful experiences, would we feel God's presence as deeply? Listen once again to Paul, this time in his letter to the brethren in Rome: "We rejoice in our sufferings, because we know that suffering produces perseverance; perseverance, character; and character, hope. And hope does not disappoint us, because God poured out his love into our hearts by the Holy Spirit, whom he has given us" (Rom. 5:3–5). What does loneliness produce in us? Perseverance. Character. Hope. Everything we need the most to carry with us into remarriage!

Yield yourself to God. We can learn something from those who suffered ultimate loneliness and isolation. During the Vietnam War, captors separated American prisoners and placed them in solitary confinement to break them down. The long days and nights of total silence and darkness devastated many of these men psychologically. But not all of them. The ones who survived best were those who yielded themselves to God. They constantly remembered Scripture. They prayed continually. In doing so, God's presence in that still, cold, dark little cell became all too real.

How many lonely hours do you spend worrying about crises that never happen? Listen with your heart to the words of Jesus: "Do not worry, saying, 'What shall we eat?' or 'What shall we wear?' For the *pagans run* after all these things, and your heavenly Father knows that you need them. But seek *first* his kingdom and his righteousness, and all these things will be given to you as well" (Matt. 6:31–33, emphasis added). Then increase your faith in God's providence (Ps. 127:2).

Where is our comfort? The psalmist David realized he would never be truly alone: "Where can I go from your Spirit? Where can I flee from your presence? If I go up to the heavens, you are there; if I make my bed in the depths, you are there. If I rise on the wings of the dawn, if I settle on the far side of the sea, even there your hand will guide me, your right hand will hold me fast" (Ps. 139:7–10).

Do you believe the promise in Scripture? Jesus said, "I will not leave you as orphans; I will come to you" (John 14:18). God said, "Never will I leave you; never will I forsake you" (Heb. 13:5). The Lord is an inseparable companion, always and everywhere. We can be lonely, but not alone—he is always with us, as the Father was with Jesus when he faced trial and crucifixion (John 16:32). We must let Christ *breathe* in every dimension of our lives. That daily intimacy begins with using Bible study, prayer, and Christian fellowship to *focus* on him.

Be content with your life. Day after day, in a damp cell with eyesight failing, the apostle Paul awaited execution. Yet in the midst of this painful circumstance, the Lord prompted him to pen one of the most beautiful and encouraging letters in history: "For I have learned to be content whatever the circumstances. I know what it is to be in need, and I know what it is to have plenty. I have learned the secret of being content in any and every situation, whether well fed or hungry, whether living in plenty or in want. I can do everything through him who gives me strength" (Phil. 4:11–13). We cannot always control our circumstances, but we can control our *attitude* as we adapt to what is going on around us.

Having a positive attitude during dark days is important. It all depends on whether you can appreciate the opportunities in perceived adversity. During the 1985 season, Miami Dolphins receiver Joe Rose shared a hotel room with famed quarterback Dan Marino while on a dreary road game in Green Bay. Being a California native, Rose complained about having to play the Packers in severe cold weather. Marino walked over to the window, briefly assessed the dark skies and cold rain, and remarked confidently, "Looks like a four-touchdown day to me!" (Marino threw five.)[6] Now that's the type of optimism needed to turn loneliness around!

You also cannot combat loneliness by plunging into the bondage of busyness. Harness the chaos. Decelerate. Don't rush. Roy Clark's 1973 hit "Yesterday When I Was Young" laments the years that went by so fast he never really appreciated life. Is the urgent really urgent? Slow down. Don't let the tyranny of urgent things crowd out the important, the essence of life.

Time is God's way of keeping everything from happening all at once between two eternities. Solomon said it well: "There is a time for everything, and a season for every activity under heaven" (Eccl. 3:1). Step back and see life in phases once again. Day. Night. Eat. Sleep. Work. Quiet time with God. Family time. The need for speed and enjoying the quality of life are quite often irreconcilable. We need time to dream and nurture vision for the future. God uses this time to grant us *peace* in the midst of life's storms.

Follow your godly passions. As you become more aware of who you are, where you've come from in life, and where you are right now, having a dream to hope for and pursue gives you purpose and direction in life. It's difficult to dwell in loneliness when passionately pursuing a dream to improve your life!

Think about it. Was there some goal in life you always wanted to achieve but put off for some reason? Is there a ministry you wanted to undertake? Is there some job you wanted to do? While I love practicing commercial real estate law, my life's passion is to write articles and books to encourage and challenge others. Having this wonderful opportunity to reach readers like you is so fulfilling! Do you have a similar desire? Find it and pursue it!

Never remarry out of loneliness. Columnist Ann Landers received many queries over the decades from lonely single-again men and women. "Too many women marry because they are afraid to be alone," she frequently pointed out in her columns. "I've received hundreds of letters through the years from women who wish they had settled for 'being alone.' Their poor choices brought nothing but grief. I've said it before and I'll say it again: Being alone is not the worst thing that can happen. If you marry an alcoholic, a drug abuser or a man with an incurable roving eye, you'll know what I'm talking about."[7]

Loretta, a thirty-eight-year-old widow with two small children, has the right attitude: "I personally believe that if you can cope with the sadness and grief life has brought you, you become a much better person. You learn to treasure the joys and pleasures in life, not overlook so much that is taken for granted. As they say, 'You stop and take the time to smell the roses.' Whether or not you ever re-enter the 'sea of matrimony' is left to the future. But I know I shall never enter it again just because of loneliness, but only out of great love and respect for someone who will be so special to me that I would want to incorporate and merge my hopes and dreams with that person. I would rather, after being single for three years, try to find what happiness and joy there is within me. No one can make another happy; we have to be happy with ourselves." Remarrying out of loneliness is a recipe for disaster.

Use loneliness as an asset rather than a liability. Don't let loneliness trap you into doing nothing. Make the best of your situation. God can use loneliness for good. Accomplish something worthwhile. Take on a personal ministry to others. While dealing with loneliness in prison, John Bunyan wrote *Pilgrim's Progress.* Beethoven and Mozart composed some of history's greatest classical music as they battled loneliness. You can excel also. Use your loneliness to open up new avenues of personal creativity and ministry as a single-again person!

Just say no to everything that reverses your forward progress toward a full and happy single life. *No* is the greatest time-saving word in the English language when used appropriately in proper circumstances. Just say *no* to walking the beach with a metal detector strapped on while missing the beauty around you. Just say *no* when your ex-spouse, family, or friends try to make you feel guilty about the past. Just say *no* to letting loneliness consume and paralyze you.

Overcoming loneliness as a single person without jumping into a remarriage is one vital part of properly preparing for a remarriage. But there is more . . .

LETTING GO OF THE PAST

We mark marriages with formal, public ceremonies full of joy and celebration. But when it ends in divorce, too often spouses leave each other with a slammed door and a muffled curse. If a spouse suddenly dies, there's an abrupt end with no chance to say "I love you" or good-bye. There's no closure of feelings and emotions. One important step in bringing closure to a relationship and embracing singleness is striving for peace by letting go of our former spouses.

Letting go is very biblical. Remember how the father loved the son in the parable of the prodigal son, but still let him go to a far-off land (Luke 15:11–32)? Do you recall how Jesus didn't stop the rich young ruler (Mark 10:17–23), or even his own disciples (John 6:60–69), when they wanted to leave him? It was *their choice* to turn their backs on a personal relationship with him. This didn't make their decision right, but Jesus let them go. Even in the context of divorce (1 Cor. 7:15) there's a time when a believing spouse is to let an unbeliever go if he/she abandons the marriage.

Letting go doesn't mean we stop loving our ex-spouses. Of course it's easy to love our mates claimed by death. For those with an unlovable divorced spouse, however, it's the essence of unconditional love to still wish them the best in life. Letting go leads us to a crossroads. We accept the truth that it's time to stop investing further emotional energy into a relationship that is over. We must move on with our lives.

In some ways, letting go is one area where it's more difficult for widowed individuals than for divorcees. Those widowed do receive some closure through having a funeral with caring friends and family available. Still, many keep their spouses' clothes in the closet, pictures on the walls, and other mementos around for days and years on end. Most divorcees are quicker to put memories of the departed spouse away and avoid painful reminders of the failed marriage. In either case, there comes a time when all those losing a spouse must let go.

Accept reality. We feel the sting of embarrassment and failure as we helplessly watch our marriages die. We married with the expectation that the relationship would last "till death do us part." But we thought that day would be a long time off in the future. We would live with our spouses, work and laugh together, raise our children to be loving and responsible citizens, and die in each other's arms. Now we know that won't happen as we planned.

To arrive at peaceful acceptance of our situations, we need to accept reality and come to an awareness of where we are in our own grieving process (discussed in chap. 2). We must deal firmly with whatever hinders our effort to let go—denial, guilt, anger, fear of rejection, and low self-esteem. Each of us must make a very personal psychological inventory of where we are in our lives. Our goal is to move through the grieving process to a point of full acceptance of our situations. Where that point of personal acceptance is, of course, depends upon you.

Acceptance of divorce or death of a spouse begins with taking a good hard look at your life and finding out what's best for you.[8] We can fool others. Perhaps we can even fool ourselves for awhile. But ultimately we must confront ourselves honestly. And certainly, we'll *never* fool the Lord. Therefore, as we let go of everything from our prior marriage that weighs us down in life, we need to hold onto some things—consistency with our values, honesty in dealing with others, acknowledging our true feelings, and the integrity and courage to stand up for what's right.

Admit powerlessness. Florida raccoon hunters know that they don't have to find and shoot their prey. Why? Because a good way to catch a raccoon is to put a treat at the bottom of a heavy jar with a narrow bottleneck opening. With the treat in hand, the raccoon's paw is too large to fit through the narrow opening. But the raccoon is so intent on getting the prize in the jar, that it grabs hold of the treat and will *not* let go—even when the hunter returns! Sometimes we trap ourselves by holding onto various aspects of our prior marriages too.

We may desperately want to chain ourselves emotionally to former spouses who are no longer in our lives. But we cannot control this loss. This is why using "tough love" is such an important part of letting go. Limiting communication with ex-spouses who wanted out of marriage helps restrain our temptation to jump in and control their lives against their will. If they wanted to get out of a marriage, forcing them to deal with our feelings of regret and loneliness only makes them more determined to avoid us, or even exploit us. We increase our pain by not releasing people and events that must be set free.

Gradually let go. Bend so you won't break. As a modern beatitude encourages us, "Blessed are the flexible, for they shall not be bent out of shape."

Get rid of blame. We may want to blame our former spouses for leaving us alone. We want to view ourselves as nurturing and responsible mates. Our divorced spouses are the unreasonable and angry ones making unjust attacks. Grieving widowers may blame their deceased mates for abandoning them. But deep down we know this isn't right or fair. No one can truly ruin our lives without our permission.

How do you honestly feel about your ex-spouse and former in-laws? What is their attitude toward you? Get rid of blame that has no purpose except to distort how you view yourself. Then, consider how you can become a better person.

Acceptance of our circumstances and making the most of ourselves mandates that we acknowledge our own mistakes. As some have said, "Bless those who curse you—they may be right!" In fact, Jesus commands us to love our enemies and pray for those who have harmed us so we can become children of God (Matt. 5:44–45). Our focus obviously shifts more toward how *we* will live, with less focus on our former mates.

Use "tough love." In using tough love, we allow others to make mistakes. Others must have this freedom to affect their own destinies without unwelcomed interference from us. Don't soften the blow of consequences flowing from any bad decisions.

It is often sad to see others make wrong choices in life that ultimately hurt them. If others stubbornly decide to self-destruct, we cannot protect them from themselves. That's tough love—so necessary in cutting the cord to our former spouses. (We'll discuss "tough love" issues further in chap. 6.)

But there's another side to consider. Edmund Burke once remarked, "There is a limit at which forbearance ceases to be a virtue." How true! We must not become sappy wimps who look the other way while our ex-spouses make poor decisions. By *irresponsibly* "turning the other cheek" through accepting emotional or physical harm without complaint or accountability, we leave ourselves vulnerable to the manipulation and control of unscrupulous people who may attack and control us. Unconditional love does *not* mean unconditional acceptance of whatever wrongs others commit. There is a way to *responsibly* "turn the other cheek," to overcome evil with good (Rom. 12:21). It comes through having the integrity and love to disrupt sinful practices of others by encouraging them to do what's right, rather than to ignore them meekly. Let them make their own decisions, but urge them to do what's right.

Forgive without forgetting biblical perspectives on past wrongs. To "forgive and forget" is impossible. A playwright once said that God gave us memory that we might have roses in December. If we truly could willingly forget events in our lives, think of how we could lose precious memories of good times we want to remember—our grandparents, special holiday events, or restful vacations. Can we ever really forget our past? In 1992 a zealous youth cleanup crew ventured into the prehistoric Bruniquel caves in Southwest France to remove some modern graffiti. They proudly displayed the spic-and-span walls until curators discovered that the kids had also scrubbed away Cro-Magnon paintings thousands of years old! Fortunately, God created us so no one scrubs our personal memories into oblivion as easily as those paintings!

The truth about what has happened to us in the past is this: we cannot change it and we will never fully forget it. When we try to forget wrongs others have done to us, we may be trying to rewrite our personal history to make it less disappointing and distressing, but this causes us to lose perspective. We fail to learn from our own mistakes.

Let's not go too far though. We *should* quickly put behind us bad memories that stir up bitterness, resentment, or despair. Holding grudges is like the army that carried heavy cannonballs wherever it went out of fear of meeting up with the enemy and having nothing to shoot with. Aren't grudges just as heavy? There comes a time when we need to let go of our grudges after closing our divorce cases and stack cannonballs up on the courthouse lawn.

The principles of letting go and keeping a proper perspective on the past intimately tie into a correct understanding of biblical forgiveness. Contrary to popular thought, forgiveness isn't overlooking wrongs of others while pretending everything's fine. It's a continuing desire to see justice done by restoring and rebuilding, to the glory of God, what has broken down.

Overcome self-pity. Some years ago Marla Hanson was a beautiful, talented actress and model with a skyrocketing career. All this changed in an instant when she was brutally attacked and stabbed. After receiving more than one hundred stitches in her head, no amount of makeup could ever hide the hideous scars that cut across her face from her nose to her left ear, and from the right corner of her mouth. After many months in recovery and rehabilitation, someone asked Marla whether she felt self-conscious about her disfigurement. "Everyone has scars," she replied. "Mine show. Most others carry theirs on the inside."

How true that is! It's foolish to think we'll ever again be the persons we were before the death or divorce of a spouse. This tragedy left its mark upon us. We will carry it with us for the rest of lives. But as healed survivors, our inner scars should not enslave us in self-pity. Instead, they should propel us forward with experience and hope. "We also rejoice in our sufferings, because we know that suffering produces perseverance; perseverance, character; and character, hope. And hope does not disappoint us, because God has poured out his love into our hearts by the Holy Spirit, whom he has given us" (Rom. 3:3–5). The scars of our painful past remind us of how much we have to live for.

Release relationships tied to former marriages. This is a sad part of losing our spouses and marriages. The time comes when it's best to say good-bye to some who cannot really accept us as single persons.

This is particularly true of our in-laws. You may find that you can maintain relationships with your in-laws after divorce. If so, and you can still fully accept your divorce situation as a newly single person, you are most fortunate. If you have children, you won't have much choice—you cannot cut their ties with relatives. But if children aren't involved, don't deceive yourself and rationalize the thoughts and attitudes of your heart. Check your feelings to see if preserving relationships with in-laws interferes with your own recovery. It may be best for everyone concerned to cut the ties lovingly with in-laws and those friends keeping a strong bond with our ex-mates. Bring a closure to these relationships as well.

After my divorce, I wrote a letter to my former in-laws expressing sincere regret over the divorce and thanking them for sharing my private pain in trying to save the marriage, even as they quietly bore their own sorrow over the situation. I also acknowledged what we all knew was true—it was time to recognize, sadly, that a broken marriage needed closure of family ties as well. We would have to say good-bye to each other. It wasn't what any of us wanted, but it was reality. I expressed to them how much this hurt me, since I wasn't only losing my wife, but her family as well. But seeing or hearing from each other would only be a reminder of the painful divorce process all of us endured.

A related problem arises when our ex-spouses ask us, "Can we still be friends?" Answering yes or no depends upon individual situations. Again, you may be able to handle a friendship, but I suspect that most people will have trouble with it. Why? Because ending a marriage is serious business. This isn't a matter easily ignored or brushed away with time. From a practical viewpoint, it could be awkward to continue a friendship. (Of course, with children involved it's important to have friendly relations with ex-spouses for the sole purpose of working out custody and visitation issues, as we discuss in chaps. 9 and 11.)

These are only suggestions. Ultimately, the decision about how to manage post-divorce relationships with ex-spouses and in-laws requires much prayer, advice from competent counselors who are familiar with the situation, and sensitivity to everyone concerned. Do what is best for you. Just be sure to let go fully, and complete your personal grieving process and recovery as you embrace single life.

Trust in ourselves less, and rely upon God more. Are we ready to take counsel that we may not like from the Lord? Are we truly committed to putting our faith into action—no matter what? An old story tells of the man who fell off a cliff only to stop his fall by desperately grabbing a small bush growing from an outcropping. After screaming for help, the man noticed an angel sitting leisurely on the cliff's edge. "Will you trust me to save you?" the angel asked. "Yes!" the man pleaded, "I'll do anything you ask—just help me!" "*Anything?*" the angel said thoughtfully. Growing more impatient with each moment, the man agreed, "Yes, anything!" "Okay," came the reply, "if you want to be saved, let go of that bush!" After a short pause, the man yelled, "Is there anyone else up there?"

Most of us can empathize with this man. We want help, but we want it to come *our* way—when and where *we* want it. It isn't always comfortable to lay ourselves aside at times and trust God enough to do what he says. Yet it's the only sure way out of the valley of the shadow of death we often find ourselves in after death or the divorce of a spouse. Right now, is your divorce or death of your spouse drawing you *toward* God or pushing you *away* from him?

God is the author of new beginnings. It's time to let go of our former spouses and let God work in our lives—and in theirs.

The Truth and Beauty of Embracing Singleness

Singleness is normal. Singleness prevails in America. This wasn't always the case. Single adults made up less than 4 percent of our population from the earliest days of America and into the 1800s. Married couples were the norm.

After World War II and during the Baby Boom of the following decade, people married at an unprecedented rate. As a result, the single population dropped. But during the second half of the twentieth century and now into the twenty-first century, singles now comprise almost half of our population. The 1995 U.S. Census confirmed more than 75 million single adults. The 2000 U.S. Census reports that almost half of all householders in America are unmarried. Only 23.5 percent of U.S. households are traditional families (married couples with children).

Unlike any time in America's history, our culture is gearing up to the single life. Men and women are opting for careers rather than families, and postponing marriage because of educational and economic demands. While the breakdown of the family is tragic indeed, it does mean that being single definitely doesn't place you into a small minority of society.

Unparalleled fellowship with God. Singleness allows one to fully experience God's love in ways married folks aren't able to share. This isn't to say that singleness is God's preferred way of life. He graciously ordained marriage for men and women as part of populating the earth and taking care of children. But God did not command that *all* men and women marry. In fact, we know from Jesus' words in Matthew 19:12 that some may renounce marriage because of the kingdom of God.

How would Jesus have been able to fulfill his mission on earth if he had married? In living an exemplary life as a single adult, he was totally focused on his ministry. As the apostle Paul counseled:

> For this world in its present form is passing away. I would like you to be free from concern. An unmarried man is concerned about the Lord's affairs—how he can please the Lord. But a married man is concerned about the affairs of this world—how he can please his wife— and his interests are divided. An unmarried woman or virgin is concerned about the Lord's affairs: Her aim is to be devoted to the Lord in both body and spirit. But a married woman is concerned about the affairs of this world—how she can please her husband. I am saying this for your own good, not to restrict you, but that you may live in a right way in undivided devotion to the Lord. (1 Cor. 7:31b–35)

Why would Paul recommend staying single? Perhaps because he believed that singles had the potential to be the most productive members of the church. They were in the unique position of having an "undivided devotion" to the Lord—a single-minded commitment to Christ.

It's no surprise that Paul's own single adult Christian life reflects rejoicing in the Lord *always,* and accomplishing his goals through God's strength (Phil. 4:4, 12). Neither Paul nor Jesus ever pushed marriage. Marriage is our *choice*—not a command or necessity. They both made it clear that God's best blessing in life is to have a relationship with him.

Being single brings great freedom. God assures us of certain freedoms as single-again individuals. Even more, we are free to have faith in God in unique ways. Like all believers, our faith sustains us when the storms of life wipe us out. It is having the assurance of what we hope for and being certain of what we do not see (Heb. 11:1). Faith gives meaning to our lives and circumstances. Believing in God's promise to provide for us frees us from the prison of dwelling in former marriages.

But God gives us freedom to make our own decisions as single individuals. We can respond positively or negatively to people and events as we choose, and we are free to count the cost of the inevitable results of our choices.

We also have the freedom to change our lives as single-again persons as the Lord leads us. We can learn to accept suffering without resentment or bitterness as formerly married persons. How? Through faith we understand and appreciate how God stretches and strengthens us in our trials. Knowing that *all* things work together for good in the lives of those who love God helps make troublesome times more bearable (Rom. 8:28). We adapt and adjust with his help.

Finally, we are free to love in new ways. After the sharp edges of death or divorce have cut us to the bone, the experience changes our perspective on life. As we tap into God's resources for survival during a crisis, we appreciate life more. Suddenly we become more aware and empathetic of the suffering of other wounded souls. We are brothers and sisters who know real pain. The sacrifice Jesus made on the cross for us has far greater power than it ever did before.

Being single means great opportunities. The old motto is, "There are no problems, only opportunities." Singles who see their singleness as a problem miss opportunities. True, if you're a single parent, you may not have some of the flexibility that many singles enjoy. But even single parents have unique opportunities beyond those of married couples. Take full advantage of the opportunities available to you. Take a mission trip, choose your friends, go to church socials, and build your own schedule.

Christian singles receive a great opportunity to be a beacon of light to non-Christians. Christian singles can empathize with unbelievers living in shallow relationships without God—those resigned to restaurant tables for one, having few alternatives to immoral dating relationships, and facing personal crisis and tragedy without the tears of a friend. God can sensitize you before sending you out into the world to meet the needs of lost friends.

Most single adults in the Western world have been blessed with more time, money, and talent than any other group in God's kingdom. But with such riches comes great responsibility to be good stewards and not to allow laziness and irresponsibility to reign. Single adult Christians need to be counted among the two good and faithful servants who did well with what they had been given in the parable of the talents (Matt. 25:14–30).

WE'LL KNOW WE'VE EMBRACED SINGLENESS WHEN . . .

We come to the end of our rope before we come to the end of our lives. We realize that we cannot make it in life without God's help. Our failures and weaknesses wake us up to this truth. Only then can we depend upon God and take hold of that which is truly life (1 Tim. 6:19)!

Tough times like surviving death and divorce relieve us of complacency in life. Tragedies and crises in life do scare us. But when they pass, the relief we feel brings a new perspective. Knowing what happened to us and learning from the experience makes us wise and free.

Anne Alexander once said, "The circumstances of life, the events of life, and the people around me in life do not make me what I am, but reveal what I am." That's what trials are for—to show us what we're made of. And God makes tough people! He gives us more character and strength to survive than we realize. When we embrace this truth, and can thank God for it all through our intense pain, we can experience a miraculous release and freedom filled with hope and optimism. Believe it—surviving death or divorce reveals the *real you.* Receive the revelation with gratitude.

We're not shackled by the opinions of others. I love the old fable about an elderly man traveling with a boy and a donkey. The man led the donkey through one village, with the boy walking close behind. The villagers called the old man a fool for walking instead of riding. To please them, he climbed on the animal's back. But the people in the next town criticized him severely for making the child walk while he enjoyed the ride. So to please them, the man got off, set the boy on the animal's back, and continued on his way. In the next town, the people accused the child of laziness for making the old man walk. They suggested that both ride the donkey. The old man climbed on and they set off again. In the last village, the people were incensed and indignant at the cruelty to the donkey because he had to carry two people. The frustrated man was last seen carrying the donkey down the road.

We obviously cannot please everyone. If we try to do so, we could end up with a greater burden. It is always a challenge to risk displeasing our critics. Yet trying to please people to win their respect can be fruitless. It restricts our freedom in Christ. Pleasing God is where it's at (2 Cor. 5:9; Gal. 1:10)!

Too often others will not have our best interest in mind anyway. Former Los Angeles Dodgers manager Tommy LaSorda once said, "I found out that it's not good to talk about my troubles to everyone. Eighty percent of the people who hear them don't care, and the other twenty percent are glad you're having trouble!"

Advice and encouragement of others is helpful to a point, but we must remain on guard not to become enslaved by baseless opinions of others. In this book, we stress the critical importance of receiving advice from *competent* and godly advisors. As Christians, we must be shrewd as snakes, but as innocent as doves (Matt. 10:16). We must seek the counsel of those who will tell us what we *need* to hear. "Wounds from a friend can be trusted, but an enemy multiplies kisses" (Prov. 27:6). But when we feel overloaded to the point of frustration and confusion, we also must feel secure and free to decide what is best for us by relying upon wisdom from God's Word.

We no longer fear independence. For awhile after a death or divorce, it is only natural that we automatically think of our ex-spouses whenever something goes wrong, illness comes, or a crisis arises. But slowly, over time, dependence upon our missing mates will change into a natural, comfortable independence that helps us care for ourselves.

In exercising independence, we must *learn* to cope and adjust. We will survive and find new ways to take care of ourselves. In doing so, we experience more confidence in ourselves, helping us mature as individuals and better equip us to deal with life and enjoy *inter*-dependent, healthy relationships.

Independence does *not* mean isolation. Isolationists become detached and out of touch. We do not seek independence only to become dependent on television or content to live in our home or apartment cocoons. Shutting ourselves off from the world forfeits our freedom to experience new relationships. Instead, we must launch out into the world, mindful of who we are and what we want to accomplish in life.

Intimacy returns to our relationships. Understandably, we are on guard against others for a while after a death or divorce of a spouse. Losing intimacy—one of the first and greatest casualties in a failing marriage—can leave us shell-shocked for a time. But as emotional beings, we still deeply desire intimacy. We can restore it, beginning with our personal relationship with God. New, close relationships with others grow from that spiritual bond we feel with the Lord.

Intimacy doesn't come without some personal risks however. It begins with self-disclosure. If we will not open ourselves up to others, healthy bonding in new relationships is rare. But treasuring our freedom and slowly feeling more secure about ourselves gives us the confidence to be open and vulnerable to others. Of course, there will be disappointments as we take these risks. First encounters with potential friends can raise our hopes. Sometimes we see that nothing clicks. But then a match will come, and it will feel so good and refreshing to have someone special take an interest in us. And if God sustains us, we can risk laying aside our defenses to allow others to know us as we are.

We are willing to be vulnerable in our love and risk feeling pain. Being willing to risk again opens the way to a greater freedom. Sometimes we are overcautious. Too guarded. What happens when we fear taking risks or become tentative when times are good? The temptation often is to ignore God and rely upon ourselves. As a result, we miss out on some joys in life and opportunities to grow and enjoy our freedom.

The essence of the Christian way of life is to "live by faith, not by sight" (2 Cor. 5:7). This simply means that when God says anything, we trustingly rely on him, whether or not we can fully understand the reasons. It is the willingness to take risks by putting our faith into action during times of uncertainty. Our *faith,* not what we see, gives us our footing for action. When we are willing to step out in faith, as Peter did on the Sea of Galilee (Matt. 14:28–29), we experience freedom as God intends.

What can increase our faith? Relying on God in a crisis. What kills our faith? Not putting what faith we have *into action.* As James tells us, "faith by itself . . . is dead" (James 2:17).

We respect God's boundaries. Being personally responsible for ourselves means respecting where God has drawn the lines. For awhile after death or divorce, seeking company of the opposite sex can be a stumbling block with emotional and sexual temptation. Many will tell you that sex outside of marriage is okay. But you know it's not. Though we live in a society—and a "formerly married" subculture—that is increasingly tolerant of extramarital sex, it makes no difference. Paul tells us plainly:

It is God's will that you should be sanctified; that you should avoid
sexual immorality; that each of you should learn to control his own
body in a way that is holy and honorable, not in passionate lust like the
heathen, who do not know God; and that in this matter no one should
wrong his brother or take advantage of him. The Lord will punish men

for all such sins, as we have already told you and warned you. For God did not call us to be impure, but to live a holy life. (1 Thess. 4:3–7)

We can be equally happy and complete as single or remarried. Question: What would you receive out of marriage that you wouldn't receive by being single? Psalm 23:1 tells us, "The LORD is my Shepherd, I shall not be in want." Paul tells that, in Christ, "I have learned to be content whatever the circumstances" (Phil. 4:11). The danger, of course, is in feeling incomplete as a single person and falsely believing that you will only be happy and free if you remarry.

As we have said, seeking remarriage out of fear of independence or loneliness is a recipe for disaster. If we remarry because of a negative self-image or a need to have sexual relations, we are sowing seeds of destruction in the new relationship before we begin. If we see positive benefits in remaining single but desire to remarry *after* putting our hearts at rest and surrendering to God's will, then considering remarriage is appropriate. We remarry with the sincere desire to share with someone else the abundance of what we have in our own lives, not out of deficit neediness for another person to fulfill us.

Remarriage becomes an option if we desire intimate companionship with another person out of a sacrificial love for them. It is good if a couple begins with a goal of working together to fulfill each other's needs in a godly way.

We don't take ourselves too seriously. Do you have a sense of humor to help keep matters in perspective? Evangelist Billy Graham believes a keen sense of humor helps us to overlook the unbecoming, understand the unconventional, tolerate the unpleasant, overcome the unexpected, and outlast the unbearable.

Can you step back and laugh a little bit at your situation? Comedienne Joan Rivers, whose husband, Edgar, committed suicide in 1987, dealt with her grief by getting back to work. Five weeks after her husband's death, she joked that she'd scattered his ashes in her favorite department store so he'd be sure to see her every day. "I knew what people were saying: 'If I'd been married to her, I'd kill myself,'" Rivers said in an interview. "So my attitude was, We all know what's happened, let's get it out of the way. It's very comforting to talk about it. It's like therapy."[9]

We certainly don't mean to minimize the serious nature of marriage and divorce, but laughter is good for the soul—especially after a devastating life crisis. Look for harmless ways to find some humor in your situation if you can—ways that don't hurt your ex-spouse or others around you. People are drawn to those who are cheerful and optimistic. A person enjoying freedom is someone who laughs frequently and can take good-natured kidding from others. Proverbs 17:22 tells us, "A cheerful heart is good medicine, but a crushed spirit dries up the bones." Allow God and others in your life to help you have a cheerful heart. It's an excellent painkiller!

We are experiencing God's love more deeply day by day and year by year. We know God feeds and watches over the sparrow, but after death or divorce, we may feel like the one who fell to earth. God watches over us *all*—twenty-four hours a day for the rest of our lives. Do we truly believe this? It's much easier to focus on our tasks in life if we know that God is backing us up. He's our safety valve in times of trouble.

David certainly knew sorrow and pain in his life, but see where he seeks his strength:

> When my heart was grieved
>   and my spirit embittered,
> I was senseless and ignorant;
>   I was a brute beast before you.
> Yet I am always with you;
>   you hold me by my right hand.
> You guide me with your counsel,
>   and afterward you will take me into glory.
> Whom have I in heaven but you?
>   And earth has nothing I desire beside you.
> My flesh and my heart may fail,
>   but God is the strength of my heart
>   and my portion forever.
> (Ps. 73:21–26)

If we struggle with experiencing God's love and assurance, it's hard not to worry about the many pitfalls in this life. This is why we need to return continually to reading the Bible. We need reminders of those great and precious promises God gives us to participate in the divine nature and escape the corruption in the world caused by evil desires (2 Pet. 1:4).

We need to communicate with God more through prayer. Prayer is the language of this most intimate, spiritual relationship. It is having daily communion with someone who genuinely cares about us. When we talk with God, we *heal* where we are hurting the most. We begin to understand ourselves better. It's a peaceful time for release, relief, joy, and renewal.

Our prayer life is a barometer of our faith. As we consider Nehemiah's enormous task in rebuilding the destroyed walls of Jerusalem, repeatedly we see how much he was a man of faith and prayer. He begins with a worshipful and humble prayer for success in the face of distress (Neh. 1:4–11). Throughout the rebuilding effort, Nehemiah goes back to God in prayer—time after time. He prays for God to strengthen his resolve. He asks God to remove all hindrances to his work. What an example of faith and prayer he is for us! We need to have the faith and daily commitment to prayer that Nehemiah had as we rely upon God's power day to day.

Do you see some common themes in recovery from death or divorce and freedom to live a fulfilling single life in Christ? There is an optimism in being glad to be alive. There is a commitment to, and daily involvement with, God and other people. Life calls us to be active and engaged in new challenges. When we lose a relationship, we cultivate an ability to adapt by making new relationships. Our faith in God increases as we face our pain and depend upon him more. We keep our sense of humor and avoid easy anger. We ease into a peace that surpasses all understanding. These measures make our lives as single individuals, a springboard toward a joyful existence!

STAGE OF LIFE OR LIFELONG STATE?

Being single is a very special time in your life. This isn't an inconsequential side road or detour. It is part of your life journey and a richly worthwhile opportunity. It's a good place to be for someone coming out of a former marriage. The common assumption is that being single gets worse, when in fact it frequently gets better! Being single isn't a social disease, although too many act as if it is one. Take it slow. Enjoy singleness. Don't rush to escape into remarriage.

If you are considering remarriage, are you ready to sacrifice the many freedoms that singleness offers? If not, maybe singleness is where you need to stay for a while longer so you'll be a better candidate for remarriage in the future. Accept and embrace singleness with a balanced and objective long-range view.

At the same time, check your motives if you *want* to remain single. After all, it is one thing to be a whole person comfortably living the single life with peace and contentment because God has not opened up any doors to another relationship yet. It is another matter, however, to *remain* single due to pride or selfishness. God certainly approves the former case but never intended the latter. Selfishness is a debilitating sin and a major temptation for the person who has no real responsibility for anyone but himself. This is why a *realistic* self-appraisal is necessary before considering remarriage.

But there is more work to do in personal preparation for remarriage. A major part of this preparation is to understand the grieving and recovery process we all experience following death or divorce of a spouse. Have you fully recovered from your loss? If not, or you are not sure, then the next chapter is for you!

A Message from Cheryl

When you are married, you take many things for granted—things that haunt you in singleness. I loved going out to a great restaurant. No one needs a night out as much as a single parent. One night, just wanting a wonderful meal, I gathered up my courage to dine alone at a formal restaurant. The couple next to me felt moved by my obvious solitude. They sent over a message: "Don't give up . . . you will find the right man." I couldn't escape my own loss and loneliness, not even for one night! After that experience, I began taking my little man, Chase, with me for "dates." We formed a special, perhaps impenetrable, bond during those special times together.

But loneliness affected both Chase and me. The most crushing loss to me was seeing how our solitude highlighted a wound in Chase that I could not heal. He once visited a dear friend with a wonderful intact family. When I came by to take my little one home, I was met with great trepidation. He cried for a solid hour. "Please don't make me go home," he pleaded. Chase and I enjoyed a close bond that perhaps only a single parent might understand. His pleas cut me to the core. I asked him, "Dear, tell me, why are you so downcast?" He sobbed uncontrollably. Between heaves he cried out, "Daniel has a daddy at home, but I will *never* have a daddy!" A wound I could not kiss and make better . . . a promise I could not make . . . a broken vow I could not mend for myself, much less so for my son! I could only rest upon God to be a Father to my fatherless son, and desperately seek out godly men, grandfathers, uncles, and friends to help me bandage over the deep hole of need in my son's heart. And by God's grace, he covered our lives.

QUESTIONS FOR PERSONAL REFLECTION

1. What effect has loneliness had on my life? What are some lonely times I have experienced? How have I reacted to these lonely times?
2. Do I find myself thinking a lot about my former spouse? Are there aspects of this relationship that I am not willing to let go of yet? Is there anything from my prior marriage that is holding me back from moving on in life?
3. What specific aspects of being single again are preparing me for remarriage? Is there anything occurring in my life that might keep me from wanting to remarry?
4. How much have I embraced singleness as a formerly married person? Do I feel comfortable being single again and enjoying life, or do I feel the need to rush into another relationship?

Chapter 2

THE RECOVERY BRIDGE
Learning from the Past While Preparing for the Future

How long does it take to recover from losing a spouse? What happens in your life as you deal with the aftermath? A necessary life transition—a recovery bridge—will help you leave behind the anger, heartbreak, and sorrow of your loss so you can move forward confidently in becoming a whole person once again, truly ready for remarriage.

If you believe you are ready to remarry, take a few moments to ask yourself some questions:

- Are you wanting to remarry within a year after the death or divorce of your spouse?
- Do you have any doubt that your ex-spouse is not going to return to you?
- Do you keep mementos or personal effects of your former spouse indefinitely in the place where he/she left them?
- Does your ex-spouse's absence make you dread holidays, birthdays, and anniversaries?
- Do you wish you could somehow undo the loss of your spouse?
- Are you preoccupied with thoughts and dreams of your ex-spouse?
- Do you view your ex-spouse as a perfect "saint," or as an evil person, while thinking of yourself in opposite terms?
- If your ex-spouse offended or wounded you in any way, do you find it difficult or impossible to have a forgiving heart and release the bitterness and resentment you feel?
- Do you brood about the past while being pessimistic, if not hopeless, about the future?
- Do you believe something is missing in your life without your former mate around and that you need to "replace" him/her?

- Do you feel the need to remarry to "prove" you have recovered from the death or divorce of your spouse?
- Do you feel a profound sense of guilt and betrayal of your ex-spouse or your children as you consider remarriage and having marital relations with a new mate?
- Do you fear making a commitment to a remarriage partner because of anxiety that he or she also may die or divorce you?

If you find yourself answering "yes" to some or all of these questions, then this chapter is for you. You need to take the time necessary to complete your grieving process fully. You may not be ready for remarriage at this point in your life. Some vitally important work needs completion before you can realistically and confidently move forward into a new marriage with another partner.

THE RECOVERY BRIDGE

Think of a countryside scene with a brook running through it, filled with fresh clear water rushing over and around stones, tree branches, and leaves. On one side of this brook is land burned by a fire. The once-green trees are black, charred skeletons now. The grass is a smoldering dark carpet of charcoaled earth. It is a desolate place— almost like a moonscape. Smoke fills the air and blocks out the sun. It chokes your lungs as you breathe in.

On the other side of this brook is lush green grass covering gently rolling hills. Beautiful green trees with wide canopies dot the landscape. A light breeze brushes your face, carrying with it the sweet aroma of sunflowers in bloom. Under one large tree there is a wooden bench where a couple of your best friends sit, one with an arm around the other as they are smiling, laughing, and talking with one another. More friends encircle them, sitting on blankets having a picnic. Underneath another large green tree in the pasture is a group of folks singing and reading the Bible together.

Spanning the brook between the burned-up landscape and the beautiful pasture is an arched wooden bridge. A few more friends lean on the bridge railing, looking at you with warm smiles. They wave and beckon you to come over the bridge with them. You see them clearly as you tearfully survey the whole scene. You can make out a sign, in colorful letters, running along the arch of the railing. It says, "This is *your* recovery bridge." You know it means moving from an ugly landscape to a place of peace and beauty, from a harsh existence to new beginnings. The recovery bridge is your pathway from death to life.

A lost marriage strikes at the core of our self-esteem. It can lead to the most personal form of despair. It breeds self-doubt and feelings of inadequacy. We think *I'm alone. How will I survive? Can I bear this terrible pain? When will I ever feel normal again? Who will want me now?* Of course the best way to survive this crisis is to let go of emotional ties to the relationship. When a spouse departs, it is time to free ourselves from them so we can move on with our lives. But how is this done? It's done by experiencing a grieving process—something that God graciously gives us as a recovery bridge.

This chapter will encourage you. It will help show you the way over your own recovery bridge to a new life in Christ. This is so important! Why? Because you should only consider remarriage *after* completing your grieving process and achieving a reasonably complete recovery from any pain and loss of your former marriage.

WHAT YOU CAN EXPECT FROM EXPERIENCING GRIEF

The first step in understanding your own grieving process is to know what to expect from it:

- Grief is much more than just sadness and depression—it involves the entire range of emotions from fear and anxiety to anger and guilt, with intermittent times of confusion and relief amid feelings of differing levels of insecurity and loss of control over your life.
- No one will grieve exactly like you do. Grief is individualized, depending upon the physical, social, psychological, and spiritual factors influencing your life.
- Men and women don't have separate grieving processes, but they do experience the same process differently.
- The intensity of your grief will fluctuate over time.
- Completing your grieving process takes longer than you, or most other people, think, and it requires more work than you ever imagined.
- Your grieving process depends on how you perceive the loss of your ex-spouse.
- You not only grieve over the loss of your ex-spouse but also your unfulfilled hopes and dreams with that person.
- Losing a spouse often brings up unresolved conflicts, needs, and desires of the past—not only from your marriage but also from your life experiences going back to childhood.
- You may question God, or your religion, in a search for meaning of your loss.

Having unrealistic expectations about how your grieving process affects you, as well as your children and others, keeps you from completing the process.

WHAT IS THE PURPOSE OF GRIEF?

God created us to experience grief so we can learn to adapt and adjust to losses in life. It keeps us from living in a world that no longer exists by helping us to face reality. The goal of grief is to move us beyond the losses so we can live normal lives once again.

In order to allow grief to work in our lives fully, we must

- let our ex-spouses go, realizing that they, whether deceased or divorced, aren't returning.
- change our identity and relationship with our former mates.

- build a new, healthy life in Christ as single-again individuals.
- develop new ways to serve and love ourselves and others as God loves us.

The goal is to recover from loss of a spouse; therefore, it's important to realize what "recovery" really means. It doesn't mean you are always happy, without any more pain. It doesn't mean a once-and-for-all closure. It doesn't mean you will ever stop grieving your loss.

Recovery involves adapting to your new life by successfully resolving the issues stemming from your former marriage and your departed spouse while integrating this history into your life as you move on. In some ways you really never recover from losing a spouse because you'll never be exactly the same as before. But you *can* recover your God-given talents and abilities, and the essence of who you are, despite the changes in your life. You can integrate your prior marriage's good, healthy, and useful qualities into your future. You can use adversity to become a much stronger person! While you may not have had any choice or control over losing your mate, you *do* have a choice over how your loss affects you.

HOW LONG DOES IT TAKE TO RECOVER?

There are no easy answers. How long does it take to fall in love? For some, it can happen almost overnight. For others, romance takes years. The same is true with falling out of a relationship.

Don't fool yourself. Too many people assume it will take only a fraction of the time it actually takes to recover. And forget experts who say that recovery from loss of a spouse takes one month for every year, or one year for every five years, of marriage. Recovery takes as long as *you* need. It depends upon how much the loss of your spouse means to you and the circumstances of his/her death or divorce that you experienced, in addition to the physical, social, psychological, and spiritual forces at work in your life. But it definitely does take time—even in the *best* cases, at least a year or two from the date one loses a mate.

Sometimes it's difficult to see the end of the tunnel in going through the grieving process. You may think it has no end, but it will come when you are most ready for it. A stonecutter hammers away at his rock a hundred times without as much as a crack showing in it. It is long and frustrating work! Yet the 101st blow will split it in two. Still, it wasn't the final blow that did it but all those that had gone before. Recovery in the grieving process is no different.

This healing time is helpful to you *if* (and only if) you deal with your loss without delaying or inhibiting the grieving process. You do need time to put your life in proper perspective, process feelings, and adapt to the many changes in your life alone. If you ignore the wound in your heart and don't seek proper treatment and care, the painful infection of getting trapped in the past and being unable to move on could paralyze you. Even if the wound heals, you may carry some scars for the rest of your life. In some ways, your grieving process never really ends. But take heart—you *will* recover. Remind yourself that the tough times will pass. Life will be happy once again—*before* you remarry!

Recovery begins with the right attitude. We view changes in our lives as challenges and opportunities rather than threats. Then, when we're ready, we rebuild our lives with the Lord's help to gain a new sense of normalcy. We commit ourselves in a different way to our remaining family and friends, our work, and our church. We cling to the spiritual values rooted in our personal relationship with God. In doing so, we let go of what we cannot change. We heal at our own pace.

GRIEVING OVER OUR LOVED ONES: THE HEALING PROCESS

If one must suffer loss, who wouldn't prefer to bear it without feeling the pain? But facing reality is part of life. Pain is unavoidable. Even so, we are afraid of it. Why? Because our anticipation of pain can be much worse than the pain itself. Our fear paralyzes us into dysfunctional and self-destructive circumstances rather than encouraging us to follow through with a mourning process. As Franklin Roosevelt said years ago, "The only thing we have to fear is fear itself."[1] It is best, and healthiest, for us to complete our grieving process *fully.* The quicker we accept reality, the easier it is to move on.

How do people grieve? By going through various stages of mourning, we find healing.[2] The sting and intensity of our pain dissipate. Research describes these phases as: (1) *Denial,* the immediate psychological defense of not accepting the obvious by saying to ourselves, "He didn't really leave me. He'll come back. This isn't happening to me." (2) *Anger* at the source of our pain, often expressed in demanding, "How could you leave me all alone after all I've done for you." (3) *Guilt* in turning our anger inward and running ourselves down by thinking, "It's all my fault—I wasn't good enough to keep this from happening." (4) *Bargaining* through often unrealistic beliefs that circumstances will change if we change or make concessions, such as "If only this loss could be reversed somehow, I would do anything." (5) *Depression* as we face the reality that matters are beyond our control and acknowledge: "It's really true. Our marriage is over." (6) *Acceptance* of the finality involved and freedom to leave the past behind for a new life.

There's no right or wrong way to go through this grieving process. Experts now believe that anyone can experience any stage at different times and in a different order while coping with a loss. We may go through the entire cycle several times before we really come to a peaceful acceptance of our circumstances. Regardless of how the process occurs, it's critical that we allow God to instill his peace within us. The end of the crisis and turmoil is in accepting the reality of where we are in life, and then deciding how to move forward from there.

DENIAL: A MEANS OF *SLOW* HEALING

What is denial? It is use of an unconscious mental defense mechanism by which we refuse to see and understand the obvious. We protect ourselves against painful or unacceptable realities of life. If our ego feels threatened by a perception or memory, it is automatically taken away from our conscious thought as if it didn't exist. We think, *There must be some mistake.*

One of my favorite cartoons shows General Custer riding with his troops through the valley as, along the rims of the hills in all directions, Indians on horses peer down at him. Custer is saying, "Oh, they'll *never* find us!" That's denial.

Even well-meaning friends and supporters can reinforce denial. They can be like the trainer encouraging his boxer undergoing a fearful whopping: "Keep it up, champ! He ain't laid a glove on you!" The battered fellow spits blood in his bucket, saying, "Well, you better keep an eye on the referee then, because somebody in this ring sure is beating the heck out of me!" When we hurt deeply inside, we know *something* is happening, although we may not know why. That too is denial.

One famous example of denial was Queen Victoria. She continued to lay out the clothes of her deceased husband, Prince Albert, as if he was only away for the day. She did this for many years after his death. But dead husbands will not be coming home. Somewhere deep inside, a widow knows it's true, but still . . .

Denial does help reduce our anxiety by keeping unwanted thoughts and feelings out of our conscious mind. We can deny or "stuff" our feelings about a matter (repression) or refuse to admit the truth of what happens to us, but the result is the same— we escape reality. In a predivorce situation, how is it that family and friends may be acutely aware of how our marriages are falling apart, or how one spouse is cheating on the other, while we are blissfully ignorant? Quite simply, we look back now and realize that we may not have wanted to face the truth.

Denial can serve a necessary function. The stress of divorce, or death of our mates, wears down our bodily immune systems. This can lead to dependency and addictions to alcohol or drug abuse (or both), cause physical and mental illness, and even premature death. We need protection from emotional overloads like this. It is then that denial provides us with a gracious anesthetic. It shields us from overwhelmingly stressful events in our lives. What a blessing this is for those with spouses struck down by sudden death. Without denial, it would be difficult to live normal lives in a hectic and dangerous world. After all, if we didn't believe we were reasonably safe from muggings and death on the highways, we might never leave home.

But denial and repression that is too frequent, too intense, or too continuous becomes unhealthy. It keeps us from correcting the real problems that are making our lives unbearable. The key is to gradually sensitize ourselves throughout our grieving process. We need to alert ourselves to denial that unreasonably disrupts our relationships and our ability to work.

Using denial for constructive healing. There is no universal prescription for how to grieve. The timing for healthy denial varies from person to person. Don't let others tell you when your time is up. If you aren't ready to receive the full measure of pain from your situation, let it come naturally. But don't delay the process. Here are some suggestions to help you move through the denial stage at your own pace with a minimum of difficulty:

- *Don't be afraid to cry.* Crying is a natural emotional and spiritual cleansing that releases some of those pent-up feelings inside, making it easier to deal with the emotions of the situation in a truthful way. Crying is a release given to us by God for our comfort and healing. When you are alone, shout or scream if you feel like it. The Bible tells us that Jesus often offered up prayers and petitions with loud cries and tears to the Father (Heb. 5:7). Certainly, if the Son of God felt the need to do this, we can too!

- *Use the power of prayer.* What does the Bible say about dealing with anxiety and stress? "Cast your cares on the LORD and he will sustain you; he will never let the righteous fall" (Ps. 55:22). "Do not be anxious about anything, but in everything, by prayer and petition, with thanksgiving, present your requests to God. And the peace of God, which transcends all understanding, will guard your hearts and your minds in Christ Jesus" (Phil. 4:6–7). The first verse in the old hymn "What a Friend We Have in Jesus" says it so well: "What a friend we have in Jesus, all our sins and griefs to bear! What a privilege to carry everything to God in prayer! Oh, what peace we often forfeit; Oh, what needless pain we bear, all because we do not carry everything to God in prayer."[3] That lonely pain of going to an empty bed, or eating dinner alone, packs less of a punch as we feel the presence of the one who always stands with us. *Prayer is vital at every stage throughout the grieving process.*

- *Sorrow and sadness are okay.* If you feel distress and sorrow, let it come out when you're ready rather than bottle it up inside. New events may bring back memories of when your spouse was at your side. You may hear your mate's favorite song. Seeing your spouse in your child may be a reminder of that frantic trip to the hospital before sharing a joyous birth together. And perhaps saddest of all, you try to hug your missing companion in bed during the night. Over time, the pain slips away. But for now, it's natural and good to feel some sadness. If possible, talk it out.

- *Seek trustworthy friends.* In dealing with denial, we must find others who will help us accept the truth. If we can confess to our closest friends that we aren't coping well in specific ways, then we are moving well through the denial stage of grieving. Having concerned friends who are willing to *listen* to you, rather than give advice you haven't asked for, are a blessing. No one, except the Lord, can truly know how we feel. True friends express caring concern by simply asking, "Would you like to talk?" or "It must be hard to live without Wally. How are you adjusting?" Having someone there to talk to and hug means so much.

- *Be open to face reality.* The best antidote for denial is facing reality as soon as we are ready. Previously you may have thought death or divorce of a spouse only happens to other people. Now you know better. Get a grip on the difference between fantasy and reality. We may "see" our spouses in crowds or hear their voices only to turn around and see a stranger. A car coming into the driveway may cause us to think our mates are returning home. After each of these fantasies, it's healthy to say, "I must accept that my mate is gone forever." Recognize these secondary losses and grieve them as they come up one at a time. For widowers, this is why it's so important to view the dead body of one's mate as the ultimate proof that he or she is dead. It is a very human quality to require some evidence that one's spouse is gone for good before grieving really begins.

• *Try to adjust your lifestyle gradually.* As soon as possible, adjust daily routines to meet your own needs and those of your children and loved ones. If your world is upside down and the silence in the house deafening, start a new life with little details. Bring order and joy to your home once again. Put flowers in the kitchen. Straighten up the bedroom. Get new sheets and bedspreads. Watch a favorite TV show or go to a movie with a friend. Invite church members to lunch after services. Do the things that can make your life happy once again.

ANGER: A CONTROLLED, FOCUSED RESPONSE

Feeling anger is a step in the right direction. Why? Because it's the beginning of acceptance of a loss. We now recognize that a problem exists, but we refuse to accept it. We're angry at our mates, angry at ourselves, and even angry at God for letting death or divorce happen.

What is anger? Anger is an emotion of control and manipulation to undo actions we perceive to be unjust, unfair, foolish, or negligent. We have experienced an unwanted and, as we may perceive it, undeserved and unfair loss. When we cannot control others (or events) to do our bidding, we may become frustrated and hostile. We want life to meet *our* expectations, which can often be unrealistic or unreasonable.

Do you feel significant only if you are in control? Are you easily hurt by what others say or do? Do you somehow feel you have the right to hurt them as well? Do you want your ex-spouse to suffer somehow for leaving you behind? If your answer is yes, anger could be controlling you.

What causes anger? Anger is a natural result of losing something valuable. Some believe anger instinctively arises within an individual, rather than from circumstances in life. Emotions build until our restraints rupture. Others contend that the heart of anger comes from frustration in not achieving one's goals. As achievements fall short of expectations, our self-esteem takes a nose dive and frustration builds into an eruption of anger. Still others believe anger is an emotion we learn through experience and seeing how others achieve success through aggressive behavior.

We fuel anger's fire by holding grudges spawned from the pain of losing face in front of others, assuming the worst motives in others who have hurt us, overreacting against harsh criticism, and even basic personality conflicts. Stoked-up anger then erupts in different ways. There is the explosive, loud outburst. We lash out whenever the world shortchanges us. Then there are those who become cool—icy cool—by turning hostility into a cold, suppressed silence. Anger turns inward for fear that others will punish or abandon them. "Cool anger" is a slow burn leading to depression, cynicism, or sarcasm.

In separation or divorce, anger comes quickly through unfulfilled expectations in resolving property distribution and child custody or visitation rights. The most trivial of incidents can spark a firestorm of protests. After a divorce, parents may use children as informers against each other. But power, control, and hurting others in revenge for personal gain are self-defeating reactions.

Using anger constructively. After death or divorce, how can we deal with anger in a healthy and constructive way? Here are some suggestions:

• *Realize that not all anger is sin.* God is described as being angry in Psalm 2:5–9. Jesus also showed anger in Matthew 23:1–36, Mark 3:4–5, and John 2:13–17. The apostle Paul makes a distinction between anger and sin in Ephesians 4:26–27: "'In your anger do not sin': Do not let the sun go down while you are still angry, and do not give the devil a foothold."

The account of Jesus clearing the temple of the moneychangers in Mark 11:15–19 and John 2:15–17 is an excellent contrast between sinful anger and being angry without sinning. Notice that: (1) Jesus had *altruistic anger* for the benefit of those wronged (exploitation of worshipers and desecration of God's temple), rather than for some personal offense; (2) he *focused his anger on the behavior deserving of rebuke* rather than venting anger at innocent people; (3) he *controlled his expression of anger* and used it in a socially constructive way (by letting everyone know of God's moral position on the matter); and (4) he *did not nurse a grudge* in bitterness that eats away at the soul with a seething vengeance. Sinful anger cultivates a retaliatory spirit. It is intolerant of the failings of others, as Jonah exemplified in not wanting to preach to Nineveh (Jonah 1:1–3; 4:1–3). It makes no distinction between the sinner and the sin involved.

How can we use anger constructively? James 1:19–20 tells us: "My dear brothers, take note of this: Everyone should be quick to listen, slow to speak and slow to become angry, for man's anger does not bring about the righteous life that God desires." Proverbs 29:11 also says, "A fool gives full vent to his anger, but a wise man keeps himself under control." Self-control is a fruit of the Holy Spirit (Gal. 5:22–24). We can use our anger positively by having a vigilant love for others, regardless of what they may have done to us.

• *Cool off—stop and think, rather than stop thinking.* Losing control of ourselves as we are unsuccessfully trying to control others is a humiliating experience. We lose credibility, loyalty, and respect while earning a reputation for intimidation—especially in front of our children! We gain nothing if others respond to us out of fear. Instead, we need *patience.* "A patient man has great understanding, but a quick-tempered man displays folly" (Prov. 14:29). We need to get a grip on ourselves. This may mean breaking off a confrontation with an ex-spouse to take a long walk, talk to a friend, or pray for a peaceful spirit. Keeping a journal of events prompting anger helps us understand what triggers it and allows us to prepare against future overreactions.

• *Honestly express feelings to others.* This means calmly describing what we see, how we feel about it, and what we believe needs to be done. In doing so, it is good to address the issues and problems while not attacking the *person* angering us. How is this done? Why not follow the steps in Matthew 18:15–17? Meet *face-to-face* with whoever is offending us to discuss the problem. Use a neutral competent third-party adult mediator (*not* your child) for unresolved matters. It's a good idea to write a letter to the person first, describing your irritation in detail, and then throw it away. This helps purge bitterness and revenge *before* meeting the person, and encourages us to focus on the most important issues—forgiveness and peaceful reconciliation! (We will discuss specific biblical conflict resolution measures in chap. 6.)

• *Negotiate rather than self-detonate.* Avoiding a conflict doesn't make it go away—that's a "lose-lose" proposition. Dominating and intimidating others into submission makes victims resentful and desire to seek revenge. Acquiescing to the expectations of others makes us doormats for further abuse. But don't confuse compromise with being compromised. The best way to negotiate peacefully with a warring spouse in a postdivorce situation is through collaboration on creative "win-win" solutions, if possible. (See chap. 11.) Through negotiation and give-and-take, everyone feels fulfilled to some degree.

• *Admit some expectations may be unreasonable.* We must recognize when our need for love, freedom, and control is out of balance. Even if others unfairly offend us, it's best to let some matters go without confrontation—especially if we have no control over the situation or it involves a trivial matter. "A man's wisdom gives him patience; it is to his glory to overlook an offense" (Prov. 19:11). *Forgiveness* is critical.

• *Allow others to experience logical results of their own conduct.* This is the concept of using "tough love." (See chap. 6.)

GUILT: ACCOUNTABILITY FOR ERRORS

Frequently in a divorce situation, the initiator feels guilt for ending a relationship with a spouse. Perhaps he or she thought about divorce for some time while trying to work up the courage to challenge the noninitiator. In contrast, the noninitiator often feels rejection and guilt for being an inadequate marriage partner. Widowed persons blame themselves for not telling their mates that they loved them enough, or that if they had done more they think they might have made a difference in whether the person lived or died. Whatever the reasons, feeling guilty about our circumstances and our roles in bringing everything about is natural. But there is a positive and healthy way to experience guilt. A negative and destructive guilt can affect us adversely for years to come. *Guilt is where many people get stuck in the grieving process.*

What is guilt? Feeling guilt comes from the imbalance we perceive between ideals and realities. The key is in understanding the difference. Unhealthy or illegitimate guilt crops up from unrealistic expectations. It condemns us with responsibility for matters truly beyond our control. Mistakes flash through our minds. We feel like failures as spouses. We condemn and torture ourselves with the "I should haves," "maybe ifs," and "if onlys" as we withdraw into our own private world of suffering. We dwell on all that went wrong, while overlooking all that went right.

Even well-meaning family members and friends may innocently make matters worse through uninformed judgments or implied blame. Whether we are recovering from death or divorce, insensitive comments spear us with guilt and increased pain at a very vulnerable time. But we are human. We make mistakes. We need to correct any irrational beliefs and change any unrealistic expectations. We need to forgive ourselves and move on.

There is a cycle to feeling guilt. We search our souls and find faults, mistakes, and inadequacies. This creates guilt. We make an effort to change. This brings mixed results, but we fear that we can never completely change, and we doubt we have the power to overcome our weaknesses. This leads to more self-searching and fault-finding. More reasons to feel guilty. We spiral downward into self-pity.

But is all guilt self-destructive? Certainly guilt can be a punitive measure—we punish ourselves, or allow others to punish us with it. Healthy guilt feelings are not neurotic and destructive, however.

Objective vs. subjective guilt. Guilt can be *objective* (arising from violation of an objective standard, such as when we disobey God's Word or a civil law) or *subjective* (arising from violation of personal, internal standards of conduct). Certain standards, whether God's law or civil law, exist as reasonable codes of conduct to benefit the greatest number of people. When we violate these external standards of conduct, quite often the guilt we feel in doing so motivates us to change in healthy ways. That's *objective* guilt. It helps us to see our relationship to others and the world around us better. *Subjective* guilt, however, cuts from a flawed perspective. It relies upon subjective internal standards coming from often inconsistent rules and expectations given to us by our parents, peers, and life, as we alone perceive it. We don't always test or challenge the truth of our internal standards. So if inconsistencies and distortions riddle our internal subjective standards of conduct, we reap a harvest of self-punishment, self-rejection, and low self-esteem.

The apostle Paul distinguishes between these two types of guilt in 2 Corinthians 7:10–11:

> Godly sorrow [objective guilt] brings repentance that leads to sal-
> vation and leaves no regret, but worldly sorrow [subjective guilt]
> brings death. See what this godly sorrow has produced in you: what
> earnestness, what eagerness to clear yourselves, what indignation, what
> alarm, what longing, what concern, what readiness to see justice done.
> At every point you have proved yourselves to be innocent in this
> matter.

Self-centered subjective guilt roots itself in selfish anger. It focuses on past failures and condemnation rather than on the problems at hand. But objective guilt is forward looking. It leads us to consider damage done to others and fosters a desire to see justice done. We confess our wrongs, seek forgiveness, and change with hope for a better future.[4] Relief from objective guilt comes through penance and restitution (civil law) or repentance and forgiveness through Christ (God's law). Subjective guilt, however, can punish without end. Subjective guilt turns inward with introspective, excessive self-examination to discover what fault within us causes others, and (we think) even God, to reject us. In contrast, objective guilt helps us see ourselves more clearly and discover healthy ways to change in how we relate to others.

Using guilt constructively for accountability and change. In the grieving process, objective guilt used in a healthy way keeps us from rebellion. It's the shortest route toward a positive, more fulfilling life in harmony with God and others. Here are some ways to use guilt in a positive way:

• *Readjust thinking processes.* How do we deal with guilt? We can isolate the causes of the guilt we feel. We can think of some matters we didn't handle very well in our marriages. But we cannot go back and change things. Instead, we rely on the Lord to help us understand our errors and change course for the future. This means ridding ourselves of self-destructive mental images and replacing them with positive and true statements about ourselves. How does God see us? How does Jesus love us? Make a list of positive and negative qualities, sifted through the eyes of the Lord. As we can become more aware of each, we then rely upon God's forgiveness to forgive ourselves. We also can then focus on constructive solutions to the problems causing us to feel guilty.

• *Get rid of perfectionism.* We do some tasks well and others not as well. Within our abilities and limitations we can still live, love, and laugh with others. Aim for balance in all areas of life. Learn from the past and let it go.

• *Form realistic expectations.* There's great truth in the famous Serenity Prayer: "God grant me the *serenity* to accept the things I cannot change; *courage* to change the things I can; and the *wisdom* to know the difference." We *cannot:* change anybody but ourselves, change the past or rewrite history, always get our own way about matters, or always make people do what we want them to do. We *can:* change ourselves, change our present and future, change how we *feel* when we don't get our own way, and change how we *act* when people will not do what we want them to do. This also means that we must accept and acknowledge the sovereignty of God. Many folks who have suffered great losses, after praying earnestly for God's intervention, respond to his "NO" with guilt and anger. We must let God be God, trusting that he knows what's best for us and our loved ones.

• *Seek freedom through forgiveness and letting go.* The best relief from guilt is *forgiveness.* Confessing our wrongs and seeking forgiveness from God and those we have sinned against, and forgiving ourselves in the process, frees us to move on in life with wisdom of experience. We also may need to ask our ex-spouses to forgive us for our sinful mistakes. First John 1:9 reassures us: "If we confess our sins, he is faithful and just and will forgive us our sins and purify us from all unrighteousness." With confession and forgiveness, it's time to release the past and let go.

BARGAINING: EXPLORING OPTIONS

In this stage of grieving, we want to try and recover what we have lost with our former spouses. For the widowed person, bargaining sometimes goes hand-in-hand with denial about the finality of death. "I want just a few more hours with him, a last chance to mend fences, to take back harsh words—to say good-bye the right way." "If only I hadn't worked overtime." "If I had just kissed her good-bye one last time." But there are no second chances with the death of a spouse. Divorcees also try to bargain with God for a second chance at marriage: "Lord if I change this in my life, will you bring my ex-spouse back?" But efforts like these are only mind games that sap energy and time, postponing acceptance of a loss.

Why is bargaining often such a futile process? Because we also bargain away our feelings and perhaps even sacrifice our identity in the hope that matters will change. It is only when we see that bargaining is useless that we can move on with our grieving process toward acceptance of our circumstances.

Using bargaining constructively. Bargaining can interfere with letting our spouses go and moving on with our lives. Here are some suggestions to make this stage of the grieving process work in your favor:

• *Stop bargaining.* Stop wasting mental and emotional energy thinking of the infinite number of "what ifs," and "if onlys."

• *Rely on the sovereignty of God.* Accept the fact that life brings people and events our way over which we have no control. Every time you're tempted to hash over the "if onlys," remind yourself of God's sovereignty and leave matters in his capable hands. Realize that you are powerless, but God will cause all things to work for his glory.

• *Face reality.* For widowed persons, accept the ultimate reality of death. It's important to realize that nothing will change the fact that your spouse is dead. You cannot work any harder, behave any better, pray any longer, or bargain with God any more intensely. Trust in God, and look forward to meeting your loved one again in heaven.

For divorcees, let your ex-spouse go if he/she clearly has no intention of reconciliation. You cannot change anyone against their will. Avoid compromising your life, and the lives of your children, by falling into appeasement postures with your former mate. Accept the divorce decision and move forward with the Lord without looking back.

Freedom from the past, and a healthy acceptance of the reality and finality of death or divorce of a spouse, begins when the "if onlys" of bargaining end!

SADNESS AND DEPRESSION:
FACING REALITY BEFORE EXPERIENCING FREEDOM

What is depression? If uncontrolled anger marries excessive guilt, often the sad child born of that union is depression. Many psychologists believe depression is anger turned inward. It occurs when we avoid expressing any anger toward our ex-spouses or others for fear of reprisals or further abandonment. As we do, we become easy targets for our own anger. Inward anger springs forth in self-criticism. Eventually this feeling of worthlessness lowers our self-esteem. Depression leads to disappointment as we cope with death or divorce of a spouse—even spiritual dryness. We experience an overwhelming sense of despair and hopelessness.

The difference between sadness and depression. Sadness and "feeling blue," a relatively temporary unhappiness, is different from depression, a chronic and more painful deep sorrow that can cripple daily life. Who wouldn't feel sad over the loss of a spouse? Sadness can lead to a temporary period of withdrawal from family and friends.

A brief period of isolation and tears is healthy and appropriate to cope with a loss. But then adjustment and recovery helps us to move on and overcome the grief of loss.

Feelings of sadness may make us think we're getting worse when in fact we are getting better. Sadness, crying, and releasing one's feelings are God-given, healthy events. They free us to face reality and accept our circumstances. If we don't release our bottled up feelings, however, we can fall into depression. Depression lasts much longer than shortlived sadness. It can destroy us emotionally.[5]

The confusion of depression can lead to a cyclical, downward spiral. Depression brings indecision, which leads to self-blame. This destroys self-esteem, which leads to further despair, and so the hopeless cycle goes. Some describe this feeling as being like a pitcher so full of pain that *any* added hurt or stress makes it overflow. Unless one deals aggressively with depression, it can put anyone into a psychological cage of isolation and despair until he/she just gives up on life.

Recent studies confirm that the number of Americans treated for depression soared 271 percent to 6.3 million during 1987–97.[6] Many researchers believe that those between the ages of twenty-five and forty-four have the greatest vulnerability for depression. Women are more prone to depression than men by a factor of two to one. Those in higher socioeconomic groups experience it three times more often than other groups.

Few of us are immune to depression. Winston Churchill was beset by what he called the "black dog" of depression. Abraham Lincoln had frequent depressive moods. King David experienced some depression through self-punishment over his adultery with Bathsheba. He describes himself as experiencing physical weakness, mourning, feeling spent and crushed, having tumult in his heart, longing, sighing, alienation from others, and apathy (Pss. 6, 32, 51). Moses, Job, Elijah, Jeremiah, Jonah, and many others in the Bible went through periods of deep depression as well—even to the point of wanting to die (see 1 Kings 19:4; Jonah 4:9). Judas, the betrayer of Jesus, became so distressed that he sought relief through self-destruction instead of forgiveness from the Lord (Matt. 27:3–5).

Using sadness or depression constructively. How can we deal with sadness and depression in a positive and healthy way?

• *Realize that we are not alone in our suffering.* One of Satan's best weapons against us is despair and thinking that we're alone in our suffering. But this is a lie. "No temptation has seized you except what is common to man. And God is faithful; he will not let you be tempted beyond what you can bear. But when you are tempted, he will also provide a way out so that you can stand up under it" (1 Cor. 10:13). Everyone goes through tough times and circumstances in life. Knowing that others experience what we do gives us hope that we can survive whatever comes our way. Many times in working through my own sadness I reassured myself by saying aloud, "You and me forever, Lord." I found Romans 8:35–39 to be of particular personal comfort:

Who shall separate us from the love of Christ? Shall trouble or
hardship or persecution or famine or nakedness or danger or sword?

As it is written: "For your sake we face death all day long; we are considered as sheep to be slaughtered." No, in all these things we are more than conquerors through him who loved us. For I am convinced that neither death nor life, neither angels nor demons, neither the present nor the future, nor any powers, neither height nor depth, nor anything else in all creation, will be able to separate us from the love of God that is in Christ Jesus our Lord.

Like a child feeling the security of snuggling up in a parent's arms during a stormy night, it's comforting to know God is near. Even if family and friends fail us and we walk through the valley of the shadow of death, God is always with us (Ps. 23).

• *Live as victors rather than victims.* Sadness and depression thrive on hopelessness, powerlessness, and inactivity. The more inert we are, the less we *want* to do. You may think you *can't* do anything because of depression. Even so, it's time to be accountable for ourselves and take some action! By scheduling small, doable tasks from day to day, we can rejoice in making progress. Learn to be flexible and adjust fully to changing circumstances. If severe depression makes you unable to do this for any length of time, however, seek medical help.

• *Focus on positive thoughts and optimism.* Let's face it. Pessimism is "in" as routine comment on the state of the world today with the breakdown of families. We can laugh with our children at the morose donkey Eeyore in the *Winnie the Pooh* stories, but his outlook on life can mirror our own pessimism. In an environment of pessimism, sad or depressed individuals can become preoccupied with the pain of past or present experiences, while ignoring positive or neutral events.

But there's reason to have hope! We can reverse the process through training ourselves to focus on the positive qualities of ourselves, others, and life in general. "Finally, brothers, whatever is true, whatever is noble, whatever is right, whatever is pure, whatever is lovely, whatever is admirable—if anything is excellent or praiseworthy—think about such things . . . And the God of peace will be with you" (Phil. 4:8, 9b). Pleasant words and thoughts are "sweet to the soul and healing to the bones" (Prov. 16:24). We can concentrate on all that we do well, rather than upon whatever is beyond our abilities. Read Psalms and other uplifting material. Find ways to laugh—do silly or relaxing things to help relieve the stress. Whenever questions arise, assume the best of others rather than the worst.

Optimists are happier, healthier, and better problem solvers. They consider options and new possibilities. Pessimists see failure as personal, permanent, and pervasive. Optimists see reversals of fortune as impersonal, short-term, and specific setbacks overcome with time. As Proverbs 23:7 tells us, it's so true that as a man thinks within his heart, so is he (cf. Mark 7:21–23). Keep these matters in perspective, knowing that "weeping may remain for a night, but rejoicing comes in the morning" (Ps. 30:5). The Lord heals all wounds—*if* we submit to him and complete the grieving process.

• *Develop a servant's heart.* Serving others can reinforce our value and self-worth while countering our feelings of neediness. Community service, volunteer work, and church activities counteract the temptation to withdraw from the world. Touching other people and their hearts is a healing process all the way around. We also need to let others give to us. This combats the powerlessness we may feel and elevates the spirit!

• *Rely upon a support network of family and friends.* The best defense against sadness and depression is: Don't face it alone. In fact, you *cannot* do all of the work discussed in this chapter by yourself. A strong, personal relationship with God makes a difference. Family and friends can offer advice and encouragement when you need it most. We all need these "reality checks" from others to make sure we're not missing something important in our recovery.

• *Act responsibly in seeking help.* It isn't advisable to use medication too soon in order to avoid the pain of a loss. However, it's also not wise to *ignore* situations when medical treatment is necessary. Have doctors, friends, and family help you with a "reality check." Do you need specialized interpersonal therapy and medication? Sometimes depression can be so severe that medication is necessary to live a normal life. Making a decision to receive medication, with the wise counsel of doctors and supporters, isn't escape or a lack of faith. Lynn, a fellow Christian writer who struggles with depression, shares the dilemma this way: "Christians have a fear of antidepressants. I was even warned by a pastor's wife that they 'block' the Holy Spirit! I felt *very* guilty in taking drugs to cope emotionally. But whenever I stopped taking the medication, the symptoms returned immediately. My doctor finally said, 'Your endorphin levels aren't right. Taking this medication is for you what insulin is for a diabetic.' *Many* Christians throw a guilt trip about this matter. It's a spiritual stigma: 'You aren't able to handle life with the Lord—you need drugs!'" But sometimes taking medication is unavoidable in order to restore normal physical health.

Acceptance: The Truth Will Set Us Free

These suggestions for working through each stage of grief focus on facing existing circumstances. This can be tricky at times! Why? Because what we may *perceive* as real life sometimes isn't reality—especially in emotionally volatile situations. That's why help from others and "reality checks" are so important. Throughout the grieving process, we need faithful input from the Lord through his Word, and from trusted Christians, to help us discern the truth.

But the critical point of acceptance comes from realizing that our happiness doesn't depend upon needing people to please us or experiencing a change of circumstances. It comes from seeing our situations honestly as the Lord sees them, witout exaggeration or understatement, and dealing with issues responsibly. We tell ourselves, "This is how matters are. I'll accept the situation." This frees us to have vision for ourselves and to make and act upon our own choices in life.

Isaiah prophesied that Jesus would be a man of sorrows, familiar with suffering and grief (Isa. 53:3). The Lord knew the depth of grief over loss of a loved one as he wept over the death of his friend Lazarus (John 11:35). After hearing of the beheading of his cousin, John the Baptist, he withdrew to a lonely place to deal with his sorrow and grief (Matt. 14:13). Not being able to gather Jerusalem to himself before his crucifixion grieved him (Matt. 23:37). In the Garden of Gethsemane, his anguished prayers brought sweat like drops of blood falling to the ground (Luke 22:44). The agony of the cross, in comparison, is almost beyond comprehension. Yet Jesus always faced reality unselfishly. He relied upon the Father for strength and perseverance. In every way, he epitomized the freedom that comes through acceptance of his mission in life and never giving up.

Acceptance of our circumstances isn't easy! If it brought extreme anguish to Jesus as he accepted the cross, we shouldn't be surprised that this may be the most difficult part of our grieving as well. But acceptance is a time for stabilization and reconstruction, moving beyond feeling resentful and bitter. We find renewed trust in the Lord, ourselves, and others. Although we feel deep loss over our former spouses, we *choose* to invest no more time and energy than reasonably necessary to lay our relationships down gently and move on with our lives.

The winter of grief passes. In our valleys of defeat, hope blooms again. We can still praise God, whether our ex-spouse was unfaithful or our children are rebellious. Life isn't as we expected, but we begin to see new possibilities for ourselves. Laughter comes into our lives once again. We can embrace church fellowship, not to numb our pain but to rejoice with God's people and praise him—the source of life and hope! Once again, we receive the joy of living.

Shakespeare once wrote, "Everyone can master a grief but he that has it."[7] But, with God's help, *anyone* can master grief. More than that, we can become "wounded healers," encouraging others through their own grief. In my own sorrow of divorce, I have become a brother to others who suffer. Now as one who has successfully remarried a wonderful Christian wife with a beautiful young son, I also can set an example of hope and vision for the future. Turn your own loss into victory, helping others to bear their burdens. Set your course for bigger and better things that the Lord has in store for you!

As we accept our situation after death or divorce, however, some inevitable consequences of our circumstances will test that acceptance from time to time. We may experience these "secondary losses" for the remainder of our lives. But being able to work our way through these aftershocks in a healthy way is vital to achieving renewal in life.

But let's dig a little deeper to prepare ourselves for the journey over our recovery bridge. Now that we understand how important it is to move through the cycle of grieving over the loss of our loved one, and that acceptance means facing our shortcomings, we need to put on some good walking shoes of forgiveness to get over that bridge.

THE HEALING POWER OF FORGIVENESS

Why is forgiveness so difficult? One major reason is that we live in a world founded on the principle of rewards and punishments. If we perform well, we are rewarded. If we fail, we are punished. But God doesn't always require the scales of legal justice to balance. As Dr. James Dobson so succinctly states many times on his national radio program, "Forgiveness is giving up my right to hurt you for hurting me." That isn't natural for us, but it is the gracious way of God. After all, doesn't God have the authority to make everything right? *He* is in charge of justice—not us (Rom. 12:17–21).

What does it really mean to forgive someone? It means to "remember no more." It does *not* mean to "forgive and forget." If we really could forget life events, then we wouldn't learn from our mistakes. We would lose some precious memories as well. Yet forgiving doesn't prohibit *learning* from the offense and reasonably guarding yourself against it happening again.

The essence of responsible biblical forgiveness is to: (1) *release bitterness and resentment* that is self-destructive; (2) *focus our anger* toward motivating repentance in those who have wronged us for *their* benefit; and (3) *offer to restore and reconcile* broken relationships whenever possible, even if others will not repent and accept it. If the person we forgive repents and desires reconciliation, *then* we should restore the relationship promptly if (and to the extent) *reasonably* possible (Luke 17:3b–4).[8] Biblical forgiveness encourages repentance from sin by offering the best incentives to heal and recover from the pain of fractured relationships. And we should desire to forgive our former spouses. Why? Because God has forgiven us. That's what the parable of the unmerciful servant is all about (Matt. 18:21–35). Forgiveness accepts a score that may never come out even.

Forgiveness also blesses others through our personal pain. It amazes me to consider Jesus hanging in agony on the cross and saying, "Father, forgive them for they do not know what they are doing!" (Luke 23:34). He concerned himself with those spitting and cursing accusers at the foot of the cross, even in the midst of his own pain and anguish.

Since forgiveness isn't natural for us, we may need some time to let it well up within us. Divorce can be *very* hurtful. You may not feel entirely good about forgiving your ex-spouse, but feelings aren't the benchmark of biblical forgiveness. Jesus didn't "feel good" about us on the cross; he did it while he was in agony! We forgive because God forgave us. We forgive because it's the *right* thing to do. So let it come from your heart when you are ready, but let it come without delay. Don't use time as an excuse not to forgive.

Forgiveness accepts repentance without judging the reasons. Sometimes we expect our ex-spouses to come to repentance about our divorce for rational reasons. We demand that they fully realize their part in killing our marriages. We want to hear our ex-spouses admit that we are saints and they are skunks. But genuine forgiveness doesn't work that way. Jesus tells us, "If your brother sins, rebuke him, and if he repents, forgive him. If he sins against you seven times in a day, and seven times comes back to you and says, 'I repent,' forgive him" (Luke 17:3b–4). Now that's *tough* to do! Even the apostles thought so as they said to Jesus, "Increase our faith!" (v. 5).

As we let our spouses go, we also must leave room for their repentance about what happened. God's way is *active* forgiveness toward those who have wronged us. If those who have done us wrong truly come to their senses and apologize, we should be glad and accept it. After all, it's not easy to say, "I'm sorry for my part in our divorce." Let their hearts speak to us and their actions show us the fruit of their repentance. Unconditional love accepts this response. It doesn't insist upon its own way. We must be ready to love them when they repent, even if it was too late to save the marriage.

But we also should note that forgiveness is *not* conditional on our ex-spouses meeting our expectations for repentance. They may never acknowledge their wrongs. If we harbor bitterness and resentment, we actually restrict our own yieldedness to God's forgiveness of us! As Christians, *we* are to take the initiative. Why? Because Jesus forgives *us*. This is the essence of what Jesus tells us to do in the Lord's Prayer in Matthew 6:9–15.

Forgiveness of our former spouses is for our benefit. Why is unconditional love and forgiveness so important? Because *we* need it! Having a forgiving heart frees us from the spiritual bondage of hatred, resentment, and a desire for revenge. *We need this release to move on with our lives.*

We may think forgiveness is our gracious act toward those who hurt us. We may think it is for *their* benefit. Not so! Forgiveness is primarily for *our* good! It allows us to lay down a marriage relationship gently and move on. Experiencing release of our resentments through forgiveness allows us to pick up the pieces of our lives and start over without requiring that others suffer for our satisfaction. Christ already paid that price!

Our former spouses also need forgiveness. The prodigal son needed forgiveness as much as the father needed to give it (Luke 15:18–20). Both needed to experience release in order to live joyfully. The wrongdoer and the person wronged needed forgiving attitudes to let mercy reign in the heart, free of resentment.

Even if our former mates reject our forgiveness, our hearts and attitudes can affect them in life-changing ways. When Germany was divided some years ago, some East German residents threw their garbage over the border into West Germany. The West Germans retaliated—but not as you might expect. They delivered a stockpile of canned goods and other food—with a note, "Each gives of what one has." As the apostle Paul urged, "If your enemy is hungry, feed him; if he is thirsty, give him something to drink. In doing this, you will heap burning coals on his head" (Rom. 12:20).

Compassion and mercy smooth the pathway over the recovery bridge leading home. What is compassion? It is your ex-spouse's pain in your heart. What is mercy? It is the unmerited favor of not letting problems and offenses become more important than loving your former mate unconditionally. Is this difficult to do when your ex-spouse continues to offend you and your children? You bet! But a successful person is one who can lay a firm foundation with the bricks that others throw at him. And forgiveness is what makes this happen.

FAILURE IS NOT FATAL UNLESS WE FAIL TO FORGIVE

What can we say about forgiveness? It isn't easy to do. It is on God's terms, not ours. It releases bitterness and resentment in the heart. Feelings aren't the barometer of forgiveness—it is our willingness to allow God to change our hearts. Reconciliation (peace) becomes a reality in our lives when we take the initiative to ask for forgiveness from our ex-spouses for causing them pain, while letting go of our own unforgiving attitudes. It creates a willingness in our hearts to let go of the offenses of our former mates, entrusting God to take care of the judging, so we are truly *free* before him to start over fresh in a new relationship.

What happens if we cannot (or will not) forgive others? "For if you forgive men when they sin against you, your heavenly Father will also forgive you. But if you do not forgive men their sins, your Father will not forgive your sins" (Matt. 6:14–15). In the parable of the prodigal son (Luke 15), the older brother lost what his younger brother gained simply by having an unforgiving attitude. As Christian apologist Josh McDowell cogently remarked, "The failure to forgive burns the bridge over which you must someday travel." How true that really is!

Forgiveness is an invitation, not a threat. It is a sweet aroma beckoning those coming out of a fractured relationship to receive peaceful restoration as single, whole persons prepared and responsibly willing to enter into new relationships.

Another important aspect of walking over our recovery bridge is enduring pain. We are experiencing a whole range of emotions as we move from a dead marriage to a new life on our own. It is painful at times. But how we face pain will make all the difference in whether we depend upon ourselves and reject God in the process, or turn to him and depend upon his strength, mercy, and grace to complete our recovery.

WALKING THROUGH THE PAIN

Why don't we turn to God when our world is in turmoil? The simple answer is that we want to relieve our inward pain and restore order to our lives immediately. Is that necessarily wrong? No, but if our desperate search for fast relief pushes us toward everything in life competing for our attention, while turning us *away* from God, then it's a major problem. In our race to numb the pain, we grab for the nearest anesthetic or rush for an easy escape rather than depend upon God for the cure. We don't have the patience to wait upon God. This is a major reason why too many people rush into remarriage before being properly prepared to do so.

When a crisis occurs, we can become obsessed with relieving our pain. We want quick fixes with minimum effort. The world is always there to give us lots of "handles" to grab when we are desperate—escape hatches, emergency brakes, ripcords, pills to take—all types of "saviors" to pull in a hurry when trauma hits us. Reaching out for God in a spiritual sense can be unsettling and uncertain. God doesn't give us that feeling of flesh or metal that tells us we're connected with help. It can feel like walking in the dark around obstacles while listening to instructions from someone we cannot see.

Even if we go to church with that inner ache for something more in life, well-meaning church members can pacify us with inferior substitutes for God. Why? Because too many believe that the church's primary mission is to relieve or ignore pain in a sinful world, instead of seeing it as a natural reminder of our own helplessness and need for God. We are too quick to avoid pain instead of understanding *why* we hurt, *who* can really help us, and *how* to get that help!

Think about it. Pain is universal. Everyone struggles with it; no one escapes. No one. Much of our inner spiritual pain comes from a void within us. We know those personal, inward thoughts, fantasies, secrets, and private sins that no one else knows about us. In shame, we go into deep denial about where we are in life. We avoid probing questions and intimate contact with others. We hide in our secret gardens just like Adam and Eve did from the Lord. Outwardly to others, we know how to offer up evidence to make ourselves look good and exhibit a fake sense of well-being. But inwardly we know it's there—the pain of powerlessness, emptiness, and hypocrisy that won't go away. We may deceive others or ourselves with outward charades. But God isn't fooled. He knows how we *really* are on the inside (Pss. 14:2; 94:11; 1 Cor. 4:5; Heb. 4:13). Pain is God-given to protect us from hurting ourselves more. It leads us into depending primarily upon him.

So what do we do about this? Instead of going to God, we constantly rearrange our lives and seek maximum comfort through escapism or a quick new relationship instead of learning contentment in spite of our circumstances. Or we *demand* that others love us and meet our needs. This is particularly tough in recovering from death or divorce of a spouse. Self-obsession with our own pain breeds selfishness. We expect others to ignore their own pain and prostrate themselves in service to us first.

Avoiding pain brings out the worst in us. It pushes God out of our lives. It doesn't satisfy us. It simply doesn't work in making our lives more fulfilling. What's the answer? Instead of avoiding our inner pain, why not use a major life crisis, such as a divorce or death of a mate, as a catharsis for change?

Life's trials build character and maturity. Norman Rockwell, the late artist whose pictures appeared for years on the cover of the *Saturday Evening Post,* was famous for capturing the essence of America in his paintings. When asked how he so vividly portrayed scenes from real life, even in his drawings of animals, he replied, "Whenever I need a dog model, I always get it from the pound. Dogs that have taken a beating from life have character." There's a lot of truth in that statement. It's so true that those who take a beating in life develop more character than those who don't. Romans 5:2b–5 tells us: "And we rejoice in the hope of the glory of God. Not only so, but we also rejoice in our sufferings, because we know that suffering produces perseverance; perseverance, character; and character, hope. And hope does not disappoint us, because God has poured out his love into our hearts by the Holy Spirit, whom he has given us."

Facing the pain requires a decision. And it's best to do it quickly. As General Norman Swartzkopf once noted, "If you have to swallow a frog, do it as quickly as possible. If you don't, the longer you look at it, the bigger that thing will be!"

Life experiences toughen or soften us up as necessary, helping us to mature and allow God into our circumstances. In his excellent book *Inside Out,* Dr. Larry Crabb eloquently states the goal of Christian maturity this way: "Christ wants us to face reality as it is, including all the fears, hurts, resentments, and self-protective motives we work hard to keep out of sight, and to emerge as changed people. Not pretenders. Not perfect. But more able to deeply love because we're more aware of his love."[9] As we resist the urge to fix matters ourselves, and yield ourselves to his loving discipline, this produces perseverance, character, and hope.

But how can we face our pain? By depending upon God—*totally!* What cures can mankind offer to any distressed person compared to what God delivers to us? Can we come close to harnessing the power God has in his very nature? No problem we face is an obstacle for God. People may compliment us directly, and rip us up behind our backs on the same day. Hidden agendas control. But our God is a steadfast rock.

> This is what the LORD says: "Cursed is the one who trusts in man,
> who depends on flesh for his strength and whose heart turns away
> from the LORD. He will be like a bush in the wastelands; he will not see
> prosperity when it comes. He will dwell in the parched places of the
> desert, in a salt land where no one lives. But blessed is the man who
> trusts in the LORD, whose confidence is in him. He will be like a tree
> planted by the water that sends out its roots by the stream. It does not
> fear when heat comes; its leaves are always green. It has no worries in a
> year of drought and never fails to bear fruit." (Jer. 17:5–8)

How do we depend upon God? How can we have the inexpressible joy that Peter speaks of in 1 Peter 1:8 after death or divorce of a spouse? To understand and experience the power of God in our situation fully, we must get out of our lifeboats, as Peter did on the Sea of Galilee, and keep our eyes on Jesus (Matt. 14:22–33). We must resist the inner temptation toward self-protection and self-reliance and launch out in faith, focused fully on him.

The apostle Paul expresses the answer well:

> We do not want you to be uninformed, brothers, about the hardships
> we suffered in the province of Asia. We were under great pressure, far
> beyond our ability to endure, so that we despaired even of life. Indeed, in
> our hearts we felt the sentence of death. But this happened that we
> might not rely on ourselves but on God, who raises the dead.
> (2 Cor. 1:8–9)

> But we have this treasure in jars of clay to show that this all-sur-
> passing power is from God and not from us. We are hard pressed on
> every side, but not crushed; perplexed, but not in despair; persecuted,
> but not abandoned; struck down, but not destroyed. We always carry
> around in our body the death of Jesus, so that the life of Jesus may also
> be revealed in our body. . . . Therefore we do not lose heart. Though
> outwardly we are wasting away, yet inwardly we are being renewed day
> by day. For our light and momentary troubles are achieving for us an
> eternal glory that far outweighs them all. So we fix our eyes not on
> what is seen, but on what is unseen. For what is seen is temporary, but
> what is unseen is eternal. . . . We live by faith, not by sight.
> (2 Cor. 4:7–10, 16–18; 5:7)

Do you see any common denominators in Paul's devotion and dependence upon God? Outwardly, he groaned and felt burdened by life—perplexed, persecuted, and struck down. But *inwardly,* he renewed himself by fixing his eyes on Jesus. In doing so, he did not lose heart. Why? Because he walked by *faith* in God's promises—not by *sight* in a disapproving world.

What about us? Our marriages came to an end. Our mates are gone. Confusion and fear gripped our children. Friends backed away. Relatives took sides. But who rides upon the storm? God tells us to look beyond our daily trials of faith and be confident! He calls us to look beyond our difficulties with concentrated faith in his deliverance—*no matter what!* This is the essence of biblical faith according to Hebrews 11:1: Being *sure* of what we hope for and *certain* of what we do not see. God gives us this faith as we learn from his Word (Rom. 10:17). In our trials and hardships, we can know that if God is all we've got, he is surely all we need!

This isn't an impossible ideal—it just seems that way. That's the irony of having faith in God. The question is whether we are willing to let go of our lives to walk on troubled waters. Will we reach out for God, or for a quick fix from the world around us? God provides the recovery bridge for us—will we walk over it?[10]

MOVING FROM DEATH TO LIFE OVER YOUR RECOVERY BRIDGE: HOW DO YOU KNOW WHEN YOUR GRIEF IS RESOLVED?

Remember, God's plan and purpose for grief in our lives is to help us accept the loss of our spouse, adapt to the reality of that loss, and move on into a new world, depending upon him as never before. This is the recovery bridge he provides for us.

How do we know if we have adequately completed our grieving process to move on with our lives and into a remarriage? Here are some encouraging signs:

We've accepted our loss and understand how it happened. Intellectually, emotionally, psychologically, and spiritually, we accept that our ex-spouses left us and will not return—at least not in this life. We are comfortable with the explanations for how and why our marriages are over. We have done our best to make sure we have *accurate* information about everything we've experienced.

We have realistic expectations about our grieving process and what the future holds. We accept responsibility for defining the problems we face, determining the priority of our concerns, and deciding how best to deal with them in ways that help us heal. We don't let anyone interfere with our completion of this vital work. While we may hurt or feel overwhelmed at times, we don't feel that God has abandoned us or that we're going crazy. We know that the grieving process goes back and forth in ebbs and flows. We accept that it takes a lot of time to complete—even for the rest of our lives. We are willing to be patient before changing our surroundings, remarrying, or making other important life changes.

We've sorted out our feelings over our loss and its consequences. We experience and feel comfortable with *all* of the positive *and* negative feelings about our ex-spouses, our former marriages, and how our loss affects us now and in the future. We don't feel helpless or out of control any longer. We have a peace about letting go of our former mates.

We've faced the pain of our loss without minimizing its effect. We know there's no way around it—healing in the grieving process comes *through* facing the pain of our loss. We no longer wish that our world could go back to the way it was with our spouses. We also trust God and don't give up hope that our pain decreases over time. We lead the pain—it doesn't lead us any longer.

We accept help from others. We realize that we may be so close to our own situations that we may lose sight of the big picture. We welcome faithful counselors and encouragers who gently guide us to the way, the truth, and the life of how Christ impacts our daily existence. We accept their love, security, and feedback in motivating us toward a life without resistance and isolation in a selfish lifestyle.

We've embraced singleness. We have crossed over into a new existence with attractive possibilities and opportunities and have hope for the future without yearning for the past. We enjoy the pleasures of each day. We are comfortable being alone. We commit ourselves to make the most of every opportunity to live, to love, and to glorify God.

We can remember our ex-spouses without pain. We can think about our ex-mates, or tell stories about them, without ripping apart inside. Hatred and anger about what happened in our lives doesn't consume us. Our hurt is now limited, manageable, and understood. We can appreciate the good and bad aspects of our former marriages. We can appreciate life more because of having known, and loved, our departed mates. The composite memory we have of our ex-spouses now more accurately reflects *all* that we experienced with them. We treasure the valuable qualities of our former mates and the lessons learned from them, while relinquishing what is no longer needed.

We rejoice in a new identity in Christ as single, formerly married persons. After entering a "one flesh" marriage with our ex-spouses, we know that a piece of us goes with them. We will not be the same person after losing our mates. But we adjust and adapt to the world without them. We accept and affirm our new identities in Christ as formerly married individuals without complaint or regret.

CROSSING THE BRIDGE

Do you have a "life verse" from the Bible that inspires you in your walk with the Lord? My favorite is Hebrews 12:1–3, which sums up so well all that we've reviewed in this chapter:

> Therefore, since we are surrounded by such a great cloud of witnesses, let us throw off everything that hinders and the sin that so easily entangles, and let us run with perseverance the race marked out for us. Let us fix our eyes on Jesus, the author and perfecter of our faith, who for the joy set before him endured the cross, scorning its shame, and sat down at the right hand of the throne of God. Consider him

who endured such opposition from sinful men, so that you will not
grow weary and lose heart.

We are not alone. We are part of a long line of people who have struggled with pain and self-doubt. These predecessors held onto their faith despite overwhelming circumstances. They are watching us cross our recovery bridge now, cheering us on. With God's help, our challenge is to throw off anything that hinders us, deal with sins of our hearts that drag us down, and cross our recovery bridge while looking to Jesus. We also look forward to the joy of his personal welcome into heaven with the words, "Well done, good and faithful servant!" What greater motivation is there to keep going when everything within us wants to give up?

This is the path over your recovery bridge—understanding the grieving process and reaching acceptance of your new life as a single person. It means having a humble attitude and forgiving heart, crucifying bitterness and resentment. It involves nurturing unconditional love for others, letting go of the past, facing the pain of post-marital circumstances, and exercising perseverance in depending upon God.

The key to personal dependence upon God is making a *commitment* to him. Jesus asks each one of us, "Will you do this?" This vital foundation, your personal recovery bridge to a new life—be it as a single person or a remarried individual—is necessary for everything else in this book. This is especially true in chapter 3, an in-depth biblical study to determine whether it is God's will that you remarry.

A Message from Cheryl

Have you ever met someone bitter and crippled by divorce, and then you discover it took place twenty years ago? The divorce ruined that person's whole life! The anger is as fresh as the day it happened.

As you recover from divorce, if there was one thing you could do to improve the rest of your life, would you do it? If you held the power to protect your children from much of the pain, would you? If God called you to do one thing above all else, would you? Will you forgive? Release your entitlement for revenge? Unforgiveness and revenge poison your life and the lives of your family. Want to squash your children? Each critical word about a parent may as well be spoken about each child personally—nothing can hurt them more. Is there any question God requires us to forgive?

Those of us rejected by spouses tend to regress, thinking it's all about us. We are self-absorbed enough to think that an ex-spouse meant only to hurt us. The reality often is that any Christian who walks away from a marriage voluntarily, or by continued adultery, is a sinner running from God. Our spouses rebel against *God* more than they reject us. We are likely the bystanders (as are our children), nevertheless vulnerable to the consequences of our spouses' disobedience of God.

If we are able to forgive and move closer to the Lord, his promises to us and our children remain. He *will* give us peace. He *will* work all things together for good. Years later the divorce becomes a distant memory, a chapter of change in our lives. One that leads us in a different, but still good, direction in our walk with God.

The choice is yours to make. The alternative is to spend your life seeking revenge, moving away from God's rich promises every day for the rest of your life. No one can ruin your life without your cooperation.

QUESTIONS FOR PERSONAL REFLECTION

1. Looking over the list of questions at the beginning of this chapter, which ones ring true in my life?
2. Considering the grieving process of denial, anger, guilt, bargaining, sadness, depression, and acceptance, which phase has been the most difficult for me in resolving the loss of my former spouse?
3. Am I willing to be patient with God and myself and not make any major decisions or commitments to remarry, unless and until I am fully convinced that my own grieving process over my former marriage is reasonably complete?
4. Can I honestly say that I've forgiven my ex-spouse for what happened in my former marriage?
5. Of all the painful experiences I've had with my ex-spouse, which one has been the most difficult to face? Forgive?

Chapter 3

AM I SCRIPTURALLY
<u>FREE TO REMARRY?</u>
The Divorce Dilemma
from a Biblical Perspective

"Am I scripturally free to remarry after death or divorce from a former spouse?"
For Christians considering remarriage, this is one of the most
critical, primary questions of our living faith.

If you're a Christian considering remarriage, you certainly want to know—in fact, you *need* to know—whether you have the freedom and blessing of God to remarry. It doesn't matter what a civil court of law tells you about completing your divorce from an ex-spouse. God's Word is the standard upon which we will be judged for eternity.

Why is God's view of a Christian marriage, and any remarriage, so vitally important? To answer this question, we must first understand his plan, his unique concept of the marriage relationship. Then we need to review the most critical Scriptures addressing remarriage issues after death or divorce of a mate. (To help your understanding, we added a question-and-answer section applying Scripture to many situations of interest to most readers.)

Author's note: The endnotes contain useful information and in-depth analysis. Be sure you check out this supplemental material as you read!

THE BIBLE ON MARRIAGE, DIVORCE,
WIDOWHOOD, AND REMARRIAGE

Here's what we know from the teachings of Moses, Jesus, and Paul:

• God joins a male and female, who leave their parents and cleave together in marriage, into a strong, sexually exclusive bond of fidelity and trust.

• Once a marriage has occurred, no human being should separate a married couple.

• Anyone who has never married may, without sin, marry anyone of the opposite sex as long as that other person is eligible to marry in God's view.

• If a spouse is sexually unfaithful to his/her mate *(porneia)*, God *permits* (not commands) the faithful spouse to divorce and remarry another person. (Unfortunately, neither Jesus nor Paul tells us whether, or when, the unfaithful spouse may remarry another person while the faithful spouse is still alive.)

• Spouses divorced for reasons other than porneia (sexual unfaithfulness) *may not remarry* anyone else without committing adultery while both spouses remain alive. *However,* Paul tells us that, in the limited case where an unbeliever leaves or divorces a Christian, the Christian is "not bound" to the unbeliever. This may free the Christian to remarry, but this isn't conclusive. (The safe course is remarriage only after an ex-spouse commits porneia or remarries.)

• Anyone who marries an unscripturally divorced person commits adultery if that person's ex-spouse is alive and hasn't remarried or committed porneia.

• For Christian spouses, Paul states that they are "not bound" to their unbelieving spouses if the unbeliever decides to abandon the marriage. This implies that Christian mates may be released from the marriage (and therefore free to remarry another scripturally free individual), but this isn't conclusive.

• If a marriage involving a Christian is incestuous or adulterous, the church should exercise discipline to disfellowship the unrepentant person(s) (see 1 Cor. 5:1–5). It is probable, but not conclusive, that repentance requires ending a sinful relationship as a condition to restoration into the fellowship once again. (Certainly one's heart must be repentant!)

• Death of a spouse releases a Christian widowed person from the marriage. He or she may remarry another person who also is scripturally free to marry. However, Paul indicates that the remarriage partner should also be a Christian (see 1 Cor. 7:39).

• God may not permit remarriage to one's former spouse after a divorce if either party to the prior marriage married and divorced a third person in the intervening period (see Deut. 24:1–4).

Before you jump to any personal conclusions about your situation, take time to study the Scriptures carefully and understand more about your experience. For purposes of this chapter, however, let's begin with God's original plan for marriage and see how humankind altered this plan over time.

WHAT IS MARRIAGE?

Perhaps when you divorced from a former spouse, you asked yourself, "Where did I go wrong?" But this leads us to a larger question: Did we ever really understand God's view of marriage at the outset? Keeping God's marriage plan in perspective is crucial to understanding the Scriptures. "Never lose sight of the big picture," a dean told my law school class. That's good advice. We easily can get bogged down with minutia, and we forget our primary goals.

What's the true foundation of any marriage relationship? Dictionaries blandly define marriage as the social institution under which a man and a woman show their decision to live as husband and wife by legal commitments and religious ceremonies. But God's definition roots itself in the creation of man and the original union of Adam and Eve. If we don't understand the foundational aspects of marriage, we distort our view of divorce and remarriage and make it unrealistic. So let's look at God's original blueprints for the relationship:

Then God said, "Let us make man in our image, in our likeness, and let them rule over the fish of the sea and the birds of the air, over the livestock, over all the earth, and over all the creatures that move along the ground." So God created man in his own image, in the image of God he created him; male and female he created them. (Gen. 1:26–27)

The LORD God took the man and put him in the Garden of Eden to work it and take care of it. And the LORD God commanded the man, "You are free to eat from any tree in the garden; but you must not eat from the tree of the knowledge of good and evil, for when you eat of it you will surely die."

The LORD God said, "It is not good for the man to be alone. I will make a helper suitable for him."

So the LORD God caused the man to fall into a deep sleep; and while he was sleeping, he took one of the man's ribs and closed up the place with flesh. Then the LORD God made a woman from the rib he had taken out of the man, and he brought her to the man.

The man said, "This is now bone of my bones and flesh of my flesh; she shall be called 'woman,' for she was taken out of man."

For this reason a man will leave his father and mother and be united to his wife, and they will become one flesh. (Gen. 2:15–18, 21–24)

Jesus Christ commented on these verses this way: "Haven't you read," he replied, "that at the beginning the Creator 'made them male and female,' and said, 'For this reason a man will leave his father and mother and be united to his wife, and the two will become one flesh'? So they are no longer two, but one. Therefore what God has joined together, let man not separate" (Matt. 19:4–6).

God created man and woman as complementary and necessary beings for each other—equally yoked partners.[1] In the beginning, Adam and Eve were God's total creation of humankind. One husband for one wife. Jesus reminds us that God's plan from the beginning was that the "two become one." How can that be split apart? Splitting a single unit of anything destroys the whole. This union is God's creation plan for marriage.

What does it mean to "become one"? From God's perspective, a marriage means "leaving" parents and family, and "cleaving" to a spouse in starting a new home. They become "one flesh," not only physically through consummation of the marriage, but with a *total commitment* to God and each other. God isn't only a witness but a *participant* in joining the two together into one. It is the ultimate interdependent relationship.

"To leave" *(azab)* (Gen. 2:24) means to forsake, leave behind, and depart from, in the sense of letting go or setting loose. It describes a change in one's devotion and loyalty from one person to another. It doesn't mean abandonment of parents—sons and daughters are to always honor them (Exod. 20:12). It simply means that one's role as a child in the parent's home changes to that of a husband or wife in his/her own home.

"To cleave" *(dabaq)* means to cling onto, keep close by, or to stick to someone as if glued together. Husband and wife join in the closest union possible between two human beings. It is more than a physical sexual relationship. It is more than love among close friends. Wholehearted *commitment* and sacrificial submission to each other transcends changes in emotions and feelings. It's a covenant for the lifetime of the man and woman so joined.

After leaving and cleaving, God didn't say that the two become "one team" or "one mind" or "one goal," but "one flesh." It's the most intimate of relationships on earth, far greater than with one's father, mother, or closest relationships. The Hebrew word for "one flesh" almost is inadequate to express God's meaning fully. Man and woman bond to each other in a way that rivals the blood relationship between parent and child.[2]

God made marriage to *serve*, not enslave, marriage partners. God looks on the *hearts* of husbands and wives. The covenant-love vows of fidelity, unity, and trust they make to each other mean much more than the outward ceremony in most weddings.

THE FALL OF HUMANKIND

In Genesis 3, problems arise in paradise. Everything right started to go wrong with Adam and Eve. The serpent deceived Eve into violating God's command against eating the forbidden fruit of the Tree of Knowledge of Good and Evil. Adam also ignored God's command and took the fruit from Eve. Believing the serpent's lies, husband and wife fell for the oldest, and most difficult, temptation known to man—wanting equality with God. This sinful rebellion began a sad journey of tears and heartbreak for all humankind, who likewise sinned against God. This spiritual death reigned from generation to generation until Christ paid the penalty for sin in full with his own death on the cross in our place (Rom. 5:12–21).

After this fall of man in the Garden, pride, selfishness, and even hate gripped people's hearts. Men and women quickly rebelled against God by marrying and divorcing indiscriminately. Sexual immorality increased. God's beautiful plan for husbands and wives in marriage quickly became distorted. Seeing how the hardheartedness of humankind was destroying them, in grace God permitted (not commanded) divorce to occur for a time. But how God's heart must have ached to see his creation malfunction in this way!

DEUTERONOMY 24:1–4: LIMITED PERMISSION TO DIVORCE

Given the breakdown of marriage and the increase of divorce throughout history from the Garden of Eden, let's review how God graciously teaches and guides us through the maze of sin and broken relationships. The first major instruction on marriage, divorce, and remarriage comes from Moses.

> If a man marries a woman who becomes displeasing to him because he finds something indecent about her, and he writes her a certificate of divorce, gives it to her and sends her from his house, and if after she leaves his house she becomes the wife of another man, and her second husband dislikes her and writes her a certificate of divorce, gives it to her and sends her from his house, or if he dies, then her first husband, who divorced her, is not allowed to marry her again after she has been defiled. That would be detestable in the eyes of the LORD. Do not bring sin upon the land the LORD your God is giving you as an inheritance. (Deut. 24:1–4)

Not many years after the fall of man in the Garden, "quickie divorces" became common. A husband simply told his wife, "You are no longer my wife," and gave her a certificate of divorce.[3] The divorced wife had to leave home without entitlement to her husband's property.

Moses acted to regulate the aftermath of divorce among the Israelites by including Deuteronomy 24:1–4 in the law. Some believe this Scripture shows God's implicit approval of divorce. In context, however, it appears to address only remarriage *after* a divorce *and* an *intervening marriage* have occurred. If so, the only command from God is in verse 4. In that verse only, God prohibits any remarriage of a man to his former wife after the wife remarries someone else.

Many disagree about the meaning of "something indecent" in verse 1. The Hebrew words *erwat dabar* literally mean "nakedness of a thing" or a "naked matter." Some believe it means infertility or other physical deficiency. Others argue that it refers to a shameful or repulsive act (like that referred to in Deut. 23:13). Whatever the meaning, it probably does *not* refer to adultery, because the law commanded *death*, not divorce, for an adulterer (see Lev. 20:10; Deut. 22:22–24).

Why does God prohibit remarriage to the former spouse? Verse 4 tells us that the second marriage makes the wife "defiled."[4] Any such remarriage was "detestable in the eyes of the Lord." Why? Some believe it was the result of a sexual sin (e.g., incest) in violation of Leviticus 18.[5] Another possibility is that the first husband might take material advantage of his former wife.[6] Still others believe it refers to a prohibition against wife-swapping. We can only guess at the reasons. The Law of Moses doesn't tell us why. We only know that any remarriage by a wife to her former husband *after an intervening marriage* is detestable to God. The larger question is whether this circumstance *continues* to be detestable to God under the new covenant that Christ proclaimed.

Jesus and the Pharisees indirectly address this Scripture in Matthew 19:1–12. Jesus acknowledged that God *permitted* divorce to occur under Mosaic law because men's hearts were hard. It was futile to ask for obedience from those whose hearts were cold, hateful, stubborn, rebellious, and without spiritual perception. But he quickly added that God never abandoned his original plan for marriage of one husband for one wife in a one-flesh relationship for life.

Now let's review Jesus' teachings about marriage, divorce, and remarriage in more detail. In Matthew 19, one of the most controversial passages in the Bible, we find that Jesus brings us full circle back to God's original intent and plan for marriage.

Matthew 19:1–12: Jesus on Marriage and Divorce

Jesus . . . left Galilee and went into the region of Judea to the other side of the Jordan. Large crowds followed him, and he healed them there.

Some Pharisees came to him to test him. They asked, "Is it lawful for a man to divorce his wife for any and every reason?"

"Haven't you read," he replied, "that at the beginning the Creator 'made them male and female,' and said, 'For this reason a man will leave his father and mother and be united to his wife, and the two will become one flesh'? So they are no longer two, but one. Therefore what God has joined together, let man not separate."

"Why then," they asked, "did Moses command that a man give his wife a certificate of divorce and send her away?"

Jesus replied, "Moses permitted you to divorce your wives because your hearts were hard. But it was not this way from the beginning. I tell you that anyone who divorces his wife, except for marital unfaithfulness, and marries another woman commits adultery."

The disciples said to him, "If this is the situation between a husband and wife, it is better not to marry."

Jesus replied, "Not everyone can accept this teaching, but only those to whom it has been given. For some are eunuchs because they were born that way; others were made that way by men; and others have renounced marriage because of the kingdom of heaven. The one who can accept this should accept it."

At the time of this incident, divorce was commonplace. Men and women had ignored God's ideal plan for marriage for a long time. Even so, some realized that divorce wasn't morally right. Consequently, there was continuous debate within religious circles on when divorce was acceptable. The controversy centered on "something indecent" in Deuteronomy 24:1.

Two distinct rabbinic schools of thought on divorce received the most credibility. Rabbi Shammai held to the conservative view that "something indecent" referred to unchaste behavior. A wife could be mean and extremely difficult to live with, but no divorce could occur unless she committed some sort of adulterous act. Rabbi Hillel, however, held the liberal view that a man could divorce his wife for *anything* not pleasing to him. This Hillel-Shammai divorce controversy intrigued the Pharisees. They decided to put Jesus to a test by challenging him in public debate on this issue.[7]

Is it lawful to divorce for any reason? The Pharisees lead off with a question to Jesus that follows the Hillel position: "Is it lawful for a man to divorce his wife for *any and every reason*?" It's a loaded question. It guarantees that almost any answer will offend someone and stir up controversy. Jesus responds to this question throughout the entire passage.

By asking "Is it lawful . . ." in context with verse 7, the Pharisees refer to the Law of Moses. They believed that greater obedience to the law would raise one up another rung in the spiritual hierarchy. But was this the right question? Instead, purer hearts might have asked, "Is it lawful for a man to remain married to his wife when there are *good reasons* to divorce?" My hunch is the Pharisees really wanted some reasons to *break up* a marriage. Jesus responds by emphasizing what *keeps a marriage together*—God's way.

Haven't you read the Scripture? In verse 4 Jesus reminds the Pharisees of God's original purpose and design for marriage from creation. He begins by challenging their pride. "Haven't you read," he asks, knowing they knew well the creation account in Scripture, "that at the beginning the Creator made them male and female?" God created one man (Adam) for one woman (Eve). God designed and created men and women for each other from the creation of humankind.

From the beginning, marriage means leaving and cleaving. In verse 5 Jesus confirms that the creation ideal is the reason *anyone* leaves parents and cleaves to his or her mate in a one-flesh relationship. Anything that destroys the new family structure is contrary to God's will.

Husband and wife must not separate. Jesus concludes by adding, "Therefore what God has joined together, let man not separate" (v. 6). God joins husband and wife together—not civil contracts or a sexual relationship. They become like one person. No human being is to separate them. This is a creation law of God given *before* the Law of Moses.

How are two persons "joined together"?[8] Marriage is a binding, and bonding, *commitment* between husband and wife. They make lifelong vows of fidelity. God is a witness to these vows. He yokes them together. Those in a single yoke cannot separate themselves without removing the collar.

In context, the last part of verse 6 literally says, "and keep on not letting man separate."[9] This is a *continuous* command throughout a marriage. Is it possible for a husband and wife separate? Yes. *Should* they separate? No.[10] Why? God's will is that husband and wife remain yoked together as "one flesh."

The Pharisees' question was: "Is it lawful for a man to divorce his wife for *any and every reason*?" They understood that Jesus had answered no to their first question. Man and woman leave parents and cleave to each other in a one-flesh relationship. God joins them together. Some may seek separation. They may want to end a marriage, but that wasn't God's plan.

Why did Moses permit divorce? The Pharisees consider Jesus' response and believe they see an apparent contradiction with Deuteronomy 24:1–4. They immediately ask Jesus about this in verse 7. "Why then did Moses command that a man give his wife a certificate of divorce and send her away?"[11]

Because of the hard hearts of men. In verse 8, Jesus answers the Pharisees by giving them the reasoning behind Deuteronomy 24:1–4.[12] First, Moses *permitted*[13] the Israelites to divorce their wives. It was *not* a *command* as the Pharisees suggested. Nor did Moses create divorce—it was already a common practice among the Israelites. The Law of Moses was really damage control as divorces occurred.

Why was divorce permitted under Moses? "Because your hearts were hard."[14] Nevertheless, Jesus points out, "It wasn't this way from the beginning." God never wanted divorce. It was not part of his plan for marriage. Jesus says this creation law still governs *all* humankind.[15]

Anyone who divorces. Now we come to the most controversial statement of all. Jesus says in verse 9, "I tell you that anyone who divorces his wife, except for marital unfaithfulness, and marries another woman commits adultery." He restores God's creation law, rather than merely commenting on the Law of Moses. But what is Jesus really saying here?

Jesus consistently looks beyond mere outward compliance with the law to a deeper obedience from the heart. He frequently refers to the limited Law of Moses,[16] and then contrasts it to the eternal principles of God.[17] Christ refers to the law, and then probes deeper into the thoughts and attitudes of the heart. That is part of how Jesus fulfilled the law. Jesus is saying that coming into the kingdom of God requires a righteousness that exceeds that of merely seeking justification under the law (Matt. 5:20). The law only pointed man toward righteousness. Christ *is* our righteousness (2 Cor. 5:21).

The second controversy about verse 9 concerns *who* Jesus is addressing. Some say he spoke only to Jews (that is, the Pharisees). Therefore, they believe the verse doesn't apply to Christians today. But the word *anyone* can apply to all humankind.[18]

Others argue that Jesus spoke verse 9 while the Law of Moses was still in effect. This is true. Therefore, they reason, it might have passed away with the law after Christ's death on the cross. That is a disputable conclusion.[19] To the contrary, in Luke 16:16 Jesus says that the Law of Moses was proclaimed *until* the time of John the Baptist. Since then, he spoke of the coming new covenant.[20]

The remainder of verse 9 is very difficult to receive. Jesus speaks of two classes of persons who commit adultery: (1) explicitly, husbands who divorce their wives, except for "marital unfaithfulness" (NIV), and marry other women; and (2) implicitly, women who marry husbands who have divorced their wives for reasons other than "marital unfaithfulness." Let's review the meaning of the operative words.

The word *divorces* is the same term that the Pharisees used in verses 3 and 7.[21] It means "letting go." Also, *marries*[22] refers to the marriage bond between a husband and wife. These words grammatically link together, and equally relate to the word *anyone*.

What does the exception for "marital unfaithfulness" mean? Divorce that does *not* lead to adultery on any remarriage arises from "marital unfaithfulness" (NIV). Its meaning is critical to understanding verse 9.

The word *except* usually *excludes* what follows it from the main thought. There are differing views on whether this word modifies the word "divorces" preceding it, or "marries" following it.[23] But clearly Jesus is telling the world that divorce for marital unfaithfulness is the only divorce *with God's permission* that applies to all people from that time forward.[24]

"Marital unfaithfulness" in Greek is *porneia,* meaning "fornication and all forms of illicit or unlawful sexual intercourse in general." *The proper application of this single term is the most important key to understanding verse 9.* Does this term require some sexual involvement on the part of a marriage partner? Can it simply mean breaking faith with one's partner by forsaking the marriage relationship without any sexual involvement with others?[25] According to Greek authorities,[26] the word has a very broad *sexual* connotation—including unlawful heterosexual relationships, homosexuality (also sodomy and lesbianism), incest, and bestiality. Many of the offenses in Leviticus 20:11–21 could apply. It appears to require more than mere "covenant breaking," marital incompatibility, or disloyalty.

Does the exception used by Jesus for marital unfaithfulness refer only to *adultery?* No. Jesus did not use the specific word for "adultery"—the Greek root word *moicheia* (discussed below). Is this important? In emphasizing the purity of the marriage bond, Jesus speaks broadly against *any* sexual involvement with others *(porneia)* that breaks the sexually exclusive bond between husband and wife. He did not restrict this sin to adultery only, but rejects it and *all* other forms of sexual infidelity.[27] Jesus *permits* divorce whenever a spouse commits *porneia,* not just *moicheia.*

How much *porneia* must a spouse commit before the divorce exception applies?[28] Is it a one-time act, or must it be a continual, unrepentant state of marital unfaithfulness? How does one know for sure if, and when, *porneia* occurs, especially since it is usually a secretive act? The word and context don't tell us. The exception could apply *immediately* upon any sexual infidelity. The first act could break the exclusive sexual bond between husband and wife. It also may require a continuous and unrepentant *lifestyle* of sexual infidelity with a hard heart before divorce occurs scripturally.[29] There's no clear consensus on this issue. But God permits divorce if *porneia* is present and active.

How does one prove marital unfaithfulness? Under Mosaic law, witnesses must verify adulterous behavior (cf. Lev. 20:10; Num. 35:30; Deut. 17:2–7; 19:15–21). No such biblical requirement exists today.[30] Some civil courts struggling with legal proof of adultery in divorce cases resolve the problem this way:

> Because adultery usually takes place in secret or seclusion, proof
> thereof in most instances is by circumstantial evidence, through show-
> ing *desire,* by evidence of mutual affection or otherwise, coupled
> with *opportunity* under conditions or circumstances from which a

reasonable judge of human nature would be led to conclude that adultery was committed. (emphasis added)[31]

We must act wisely to arrive at an honest conclusion on this important matter. If reasonable Christians, aware of the relevant facts, believe that the circumstances (through desire and opportunity) support sexual infidelity *(porneia)*, perhaps that is enough to fulfill the intent of verse 9.[32]

Divorce, except for porneia, and remarriage is adultery. If there's no marital unfaithfulness *(porneia)*, divorce and remarriage to another person while both spouses to the first marriage remain alive causes the parties to that remarriage to "commit adultery." This holds true unless another provision in God's Word applies (such as 1 Cor. 7, reviewed below). (The Greek root word is *moikaomai,* meaning "to have unlawful sexual intercourse with another's wife, to commit adultery with.") But does this term refer to a *one-time act* of adultery or a *continuing adulterous act?*

For example, an unscriptural divorce occurs (without *porneia*). One spouse remarries another person. Both parties to that remarriage commit adultery. Does this adultery continue? Some believe it doesn't. They argue that once an adulterous marriage occurs, there's no way to undo it.[33] At that instant, the remarriage becomes legitimate.[34]

Alternatively, does *moikaomai* mean such a remarriage is a *continuing state of adultery?* As opposed to a one-time adulterous act, is it adultery that continues while the *relationship* exists? This means Jesus is saying that when one *divorces* (past tense, one-time event) one's spouse and *marries* (past tense, one-time event) another person, he or she *commits adultery* (present tense, *continuous* action—as in "keeps on committing adultery").[35] This may mean that anyone remarrying after an unscriptural divorce from a living spouse enters into a *lifestyle* of adultery.

The debate on this critical point continues. However, if a *continuous state of adultery* truly exists in the remarriage, who would argue against ending this relationship? Repentance would clearly require breaking off the adulterous relationship.[36]

Many questions arise. Does the exception Jesus makes in verse 9 for marital unfaithfulness permit a *divorce* to occur, but not remarriage? This is a very strict construction. Jesus clearly addresses a situation where divorce *and* remarriage have occurred, not each action as an isolated incident.

• May a spouse *divorced* by a mate ("divorcee") for reasons other than porneia remarry? Verse 9 doesn't tell us, but a parallel passage in Matthew 5:32 (discussed below) addresses this issue. (Jesus appears to say that a divorcee, under these circumstances, may commit adultery upon any remarriage.)

• What about the divorcee who's guilty of *porneia?* Does he/she give up any chance to marry again? Jesus doesn't say anything about this person. The one engaging in *porneia* commits a grievous sin in breaking up the marriage bond. What are the consequences? Jesus doesn't mention any penalty in verse 9. Many would say, however, that the adulterer dies spiritually (being the parallel spiritual consequence of what literally and physically occurred to adulterers under the Mosaic law). The only redemption is through repentance and forgiveness from God. But this may not allow remarriage. Others argue, however, that if the marriage ends in God's judgment, why would both parties not be free to remarry another as if the marriage had never occurred?[37]

• What rights does the *divorcing* spouse ("divorcer") have when *porneia* has occurred? When the exception *does* apply, Jesus doesn't say whether the divorcer may remarry. However, by implication, if a divorce is permissible for porneia, then the marriage is broken. It is as if a death of the unfaithful spouse has occurred.

• What happens to the divorcer who remarries after an *unscriptural* divorce? Jesus says in verse 9 that the divorcer commits adultery.[38] If the remarriage is a *continuing* state of adultery, are the parties now required to end their new marriage as part of repentance? If they do divorce, can the spouses ever marry again? Must they return to their former mates from their first marriages?[39]

As you can see, many remarriage issues remain unanswered by Jesus. The Scriptures don't tell us much about how a *scriptural remarriage* may occur after a scriptural, or unscriptural, divorce. It appears that we are to answer these questions for ourselves, using the Scriptures as God leads us.

The teaching that an unscriptural divorce followed by remarriage is adultery is a *very* hard principle to receive! It shows how important the purity and longevity of a marriage is to God.

Is it better not to marry at all? Verse 10 tells us that Jesus' statements shocked his disciples. If this was the way God viewed divorce and remarriage, why marry at all? In saying this, did the disciples prefer easy divorces over being obedient to God's plan for marriage? Were they so concerned about sin in marriage that they would turn their back on marriage altogether? (Fortunately, the disciples must have resolved their doubts about this since at least some of them married [1 Cor. 9:5].)

The disciples show how far we all fall short of God's ideal. They missed the point. Jesus didn't tell anyone to avoid marriage. His focus was always on loving God with all of one's heart, mind, soul, and strength. If a decision to marry, earn money, or seek anything else keeps one out of the kingdom of God, then it's better to say no to that decision.

How did Jesus respond to the disciples' attitude on marriage? He only added, "Not everyone can accept this word, but only those to whom it has been given. For some are eunuchs because they were born that way; others were made that way by men; and others have renounced marriage because of the kingdom of heaven." He relies upon God helping them through *any* situation. This goes beyond the question of marriage and divorce. It's a faith problem. Will the disciples trust in God or themselves?

Who can accept this teaching? In verses 11 and 12, Jesus adds: "The one who can accept this [teaching] should accept it." Marriage is a matter of free choice. God doesn't coerce anyone into it. If anyone wants to marry, then he/she should accept the responsibilities of marriage. The couple should glorify God through their union as he intended from creation and honor its permanence and fidelity. Likewise, if anyone remains single, he/she should glorify God as an unmarried individual.

Mark 10:10–12: Further Teachings of Jesus on Divorce and Remarriage

When they were in the house again, the disciples asked Jesus about
this. He answered, "Anyone who divorces his wife and marries another
woman commits adultery against her. And if she divorces her husband
and marries another man, she commits adultery."

The *circumstances* of Jesus' teaching to the Pharisees in Mark 10:1–12 are very
similar to Matthew 19:1–12. It is very likely they are different accounts of the same
meeting. There are some differences, however. In Mark 10:2–5, for example, the
Pharisees ask whether it is lawful for a man to divorce his wife.[40] Jesus replies, "What
did Moses command you?" The *Pharisees* respond, "Moses *permitted* a man to write a
certificate of divorce and send her away." Jesus then says that hard hearts were the reason for this permission. However, the content and meaning in Mark 10:1–9 mirror
Matthew 19:1–8. Important differences from Matthew 19 are: (1) Mark entirely omits
the exception for "marital unfaithfulness" *(porneia)* in Matthew 19:9; and (2) Jesus'
teachings apply to *both* husbands and wives if they are the divorcers.

Since Jesus didn't restate the "marital unfaithfulness" exception in Mark's Gospel,
some argue that Jesus: (a) didn't really mean for the exception to apply at all; or
(b) made a public statement to the Pharisees using the exception, and then made
another to his disciples privately without any exception; so, different rules apply to
nonbelievers and believers. But the missing exception in Mark doesn't nullify Jesus'
statement in Matthew's version. Also, since Jesus roots all his teachings in God's
creation plan for marriage, these general principles as to marriage, divorce, and
remarriage apply to all people for all time without limitation to any particular
group.

Matthew 5:27–32: The Sermon on the Mount

"You have heard that it was said, 'Do not commit adultery.' But
I tell you that anyone who looks at a woman lustfully has already
committed adultery with her in his heart. If your right eye causes you
to sin, gouge it out and throw it away. It is better for you to lose one
part of your body than for your whole body to be thrown into hell.
And if your right hand causes you to sin, cut it off and throw it away. It
is better for you to lose one part of your body than for your whole
body to go into hell.

"It has been said, 'Anyone who divorces his wife must give her a
certificate of divorce.' But I tell you that anyone who divorces his wife,
except for marital unfaithfulness, causes her to become an adulteress,
and anyone who marries the divorced woman commits adultery."

In verses 29–30 Jesus figuratively points up the serious nature of sin. Don't miss
the point he is making here—to rid ourselves of evil motivations and desires, our
hearts must change. People violate God's law not only by *outward* acts but also by
inward motivations of the heart leading to those actions. Murder begins with anger

(Matt. 5:21–22). Adultery begins with lust in the heart (Matt. 5:27–28). Jesus seems to say that the *desire* is as wrong as the actual act.

Verses 31–32 tell us that a husband's unscriptural divorce (without *porneia*) of his wife causes her to become an adulteress. Also, anyone who marries a divorcee *not* divorced for marital unfaithfulness (*porneia*) commits adultery *(moikaomai)*. Does a divorce literally *cause*[41] a divorcee to become an adulterer, even *before* any remarriage? No, the divorcee may be an innocent and faithful spouse subjected to an unscriptural divorce by the divorcer. But Jesus warns that this divorcee is in a position of *being vulnerable to becoming* an adulterer upon any remarriage while the divorcer is still alive. Jesus warns that if the divorcee, unscripturally divorced, remarries an eligible third person, *both* become adulterers. This is difficult because both persons could be innocent parties.

Why does Jesus take this harsh stand against "innocent" persons? Perhaps it's because the first marriage still exists in God's sight until it is scripturally broken through *porneia* while both spouses are alive. God wants the first husband and wife to either remain unmarried or reconcile with each other to fulfill his plan for marriage.[42] By warning married persons of adultery, Jesus reinforces the relationship.

Jesus' Teachings on Divorce and Remarriage Are Tough!

The unanswered questions about divorce and remarriage don't make matters any easier for us. In reviewing our own situations, some of us may find ourselves on the short end of one of these principles. What then? What if we disobey what Jesus told us about divorce and remarriage? Welcome to the realities of life. Everyone has sinned and fallen short of the glory of God. By acknowledging this truth, however, we certainly don't mean to be callous in excusing the sin involved here! But when we find ourselves trapped in sin, the good news is that God justifies us freely by his grace through the redemption given us in Christ Jesus (Rom. 3:23–24). If adultery occurs, repentance brings forgiveness from our merciful God. If, in obedient faith, we return to God and seek his forgiveness and guidance to correct our situation, he will shower us with his loving grace and mercy!

Even so, some would ask of Jesus, "Why is it so tough to get out of a failing (or failed) marriage?" But if we really understand how God feels about divorce, the answer to this question becomes clear. God was there when each man and woman loved each other and made the vow, "For better or for worse; for richer or for poorer; in sickness and in health, for as long as we both shall live." Broken vows are serious concerns to him. God doesn't just feel "disappointed" by our sin in this situation—he detests it! The Lord is very protective of the helpless children Jesus loves so much, caught in the crossfire of mommies and daddies tearing each other apart. He hates divorce when wives and husbands deal treacherously with each other. He hurts for all of them.

Now we come to the apostle Paul's inspired New Testament interpretation of Jesus' teachings about marriage, divorce, and remarriage—also built upon God's creation plan for marriage. While Jesus emphasized the commitments of marriage, Paul deals with those sticky situations when marriages go wrong for Christians and the later consequences.

WHY LISTEN TO PAUL AS MUCH AS JESUS?

Paul's concern was unity among Christians (1 Cor. 1:10). He was jealous of anything that disrupted this unity. He confronted wrong. He forged solidarity among all Christians. This could be why God commissioned him to deal with Christians whose marriages were in shambles.

Paul was unmarried, at least during his ministry to the church in Corinth.[43] If so, why should we listen to him? Because he speaks with the authority of God as an apostle of Jesus Christ. Although Paul was not among the first apostles chosen by Jesus, the risen Christ confronted him and commissioned him to preach the good news (Acts 9:1–19). Paul credited Jesus with his teachings (Gal. 1:12). The apostles and disciples closest to Christ during his ministry accepted Paul as an apostle of Christ (Acts 9:26–30). His competence came not as one qualified under the old covenant Law of Moses, but as a minister of reconciliation under the new covenant of grace. The same Holy Spirit Jesus promised to send to believers (John 17) also inspired Paul.

Did Paul address marriage issues that Jesus did not? Yes. We find many examples of this in Paul's letters to the Christians in Corinth. Is this important? Yes. Knowing the background and context of Paul's writings is critical to our understanding how his teaching coincides with that of Jesus.

THE CORINTHIAN LETTERS: ADDRESSED TO CHRISTIANS IN A WORLDLY CITY

Corinth was a seaport city, fourth largest of the Roman Empire, of about six hundred thousand people (mostly slaves). It was a multinational city, much like New York City or Miami today. Corinth had a reputation for being very immoral. Even so, Corinth also had many teachers speaking about Christ (1 Cor. 4:15).

In this environment, many Christians struggled to live in Corinth without compromising their faith (1 Cor. 7:31). There were easy divorces at law, mixed faith marriages between believers and nonbelievers, adultery, and incest. No wonder Paul agonized over all the churches (2 Cor. 11:28)!

Who was Paul writing to in the Corinthian letters? In 1 Corinthians 1:2, he addresses his letter to the "church of God in Corinth, to those sanctified in Christ Jesus and called to be holy, together with all those everywhere who call on the name of our Lord Jesus Christ—their Lord and ours." Unlike Jesus addressing the world at large in Matthew 19, Paul speaks primarily to *Christians*—directly in the Corinthian church and indirectly throughout the world. This is a *very* important consideration to keep in mind! He deals with problems foreign to unbelievers—divisions in the church, Christian marriages, celebration of the Lord's Supper, propriety in Christian worship, and church contributions. Paul clearly distinguishes between problems of those *outside* the church and issues of those *inside* the church (1 Cor. 5:12–13). This distinction becomes more apparent as we review the biblical passages that follow below.

First Corinthians 7: Prelude to Paul's Teaching on Marriage

With 1 Corinthians 5 and 6 in mind (reading these chapters now will give you context for the discussion to follow), Paul then gives the only major New Testament discourse on marriage in general beyond Christ's teachings.

Before we review 1 Corinthians 7, however, let's briefly note some factors that will help our understanding of this Scripture. First, *Paul is answering specific questions of Christians—not unbelievers.* His letters to the Corinthian church responded to their specific questions (1 Cor. 1:11; 5:1; 7:1; 8:1; 12:1; 16:1). Unbelievers would have little interest in much of what Paul writes to the Corinthians. Second, *Paul addresses Christians under unusual circumstances.* His teachings on marriage consider the severe distress (the "present crisis" in 1 Cor. 7:26) affecting the Corinthians at that time. Therefore, some instructions may apply to that specific time and abnormal circumstance. Third, *some of Paul's answers address specific groups of Christians.* In 1 Corinthians 7, note the specific instructions Paul gives to different groups of men and women within the Corinthian church. Finally, *Paul carefully distinguishes between the Lord's commands and his own spiritual judgment.* In a manner rarely found in the New Testament, Paul writes on issues that Christ gave no specific command (1 Cor. 7:6, 10, 12, 25, 40). Therefore, some may question divine inspiration of these verses. Were they merely Paul's opinion? In context, Paul didn't disclaim inspiration from the Holy Spirit.[44] He merely acknowledged that Jesus didn't specifically address these matters.

Paul offered three kinds of responses to questions of the Corinthians: (1) answers that follow Jesus' teachings (1 Cor. 7:10); (2) answers *not* specifically addressed by Jesus, but which the Holy Spirit inspired Paul to give as a divine commandment (1 Cor. 7:12); and (3) answers not addressed by Jesus, but where Paul used spiritual judgment as one having the Spirit of God (see, for example, 1 Cor. 7:6–9). In the last instance, the Spirit inspired Paul to *advise* rather than to *command.* But Paul's advice was more than just personal preference—it was the advice of a highly qualified apostle of God. It still merits our serious consideration today.

In Matthew 19:1–12, Jesus addressed the Pharisee's questions about the *grounds* for divorce. He added warnings about adultery in any remarriage after an unscriptural divorce occurs. Paul applied these teachings to *different* questions from concerned Christians about marriage for virgins, the unmarried, widows, and Christians married to unbelievers ("mixed faith marriages").

Now let's review the specific words of Paul in 1 Corinthians 7.

First Corinthians 7:1–7: The Need for Marriage

Now for the matters you wrote about: It is good for a man not to marry. But since there is so much immorality, each man should have

his own wife, and each woman her own husband. The husband should
fulfill his marital duty to his wife, and likewise the wife to her husband.
The wife's body does not belong to her alone but also to her husband.
In the same way, the husband's body does not belong to him alone but
also to his wife. Do not deprive each other except by mutual consent
and for a time, so that you may devote yourselves to prayer. Then come
together again so that Satan will not tempt you because of your lack of
self-control. I say this as a concession, not as a command. I wish that
all men were as I am. But each man has his own gift from God; one has
this gift, another has that.

Paul responds to the implied questions: (1) *Is marriage acceptable to God?*
(2) *Should married persons have sexual intercourse?* He answers yes to both questions.
After speaking against sexual immorality *outside* of marriage in 1 Corinthians
6:13–20, Paul begins 1 Corinthians 7 saying that sexual abstinence *inside* marriage is
going too far. Marriage avoids sinful temptations for those without the gift of celibacy
(cf. Matt. 19:12). Verse 5 shows that any abstention from sexual relations within a
marriage should (not *must*) be mutually agreed upon, temporary, and have a spiritual
goal.[45] Mandatory celibacy for those not able to handle it may lead them into the sexual immorality that Paul spoke against in 1 Corinthians 6.

First Corinthians 7:8–9: Instructions to the Unmarried and Widows

Now to the unmarried and the widows I say: It is good for them to
stay unmarried, as I am. But if they cannot control themselves, they
should marry, for it is better to marry than to burn with passion.

Question: *Should the unmarried (formerly married) or widowed remarry?* Answer:
It is good to be single, but if they cannot live a pure life, it is better to marry again.[46]

Paul believes that the best option for the unmarried and the widowed is to remain
single. Why? Two reasons: because of the "present crisis" (v. 26), and so they can give
themselves fully to the service of the Lord without distractions (v. 35).

First Corinthians 7:10–11: Instructions to the Married

To the married I give this command (not I, but the Lord): A wife
must not separate from her husband. But if she does, she must remain
unmarried or else be reconciled to her husband. And a husband must
not divorce his wife.

Question: *Are Christians who divorce, without scriptural authority to do so, allowed
to remarry others?* Answer: No. If a divorce is unscriptural, husband and wife must reconcile with each other or live separate lives without remarriage to others as long as
they both live.

This instruction is the *Lord's* command. Spouses must not separate.[47] The term
separate isn't merely a temporary physical separation—it is ripping a marriage apart
as in a divorce.[48] Though Paul mentions, "but if she does (separate)" in verse 11, he

doesn't condone a couple leaving their marriage. This only introduces God's will that unscripturally divorced spouses "be reconciled"[49] or remain unmarried. No spouse referred to in verses 10–11 should remarry another person as long as his/her mate remains alive.[50] There are no other alternatives pleasing to God.

First Corinthians 7:12–16:
Instructions to Christians Married to Unbelievers

> To the rest I say this (I, not the Lord): If any brother has a wife who is not a believer and she is willing to live with him, he must not divorce her. And if a woman has a husband who is not a believer and he is willing to live with her, she must not divorce him. For the unbelieving husband has been sanctified through his wife, and the unbelieving wife has been sanctified through her believing husband. Otherwise your children would be unclean, but as it is, they are holy.
>
> But if the unbeliever leaves, let him do so. A believing man or woman is not bound in such circumstances; God has called us to live in peace. How do you know, wife, whether you will save your husband? Or, how do you know, husband, whether you will save your wife?

Verses 12–16 answer such questions as: (1) Should Christians divorce unbelieving spouses? (2) Are Christians made unclean before God through marriage with unbelievers? (3) Are children born into such marriages unclean? (4) Do Christians sin if unbelievers leave a marriage? Paul's answers (in order) are: (1) No, if an unbeliever wishes to stay in a marriage, it should continue. But if the *unbeliever* wants a divorce, let the unbeliever go. (2) No, the Lord sanctifies the unbeliever "through" the Christian. (3) No, the children also are acceptable to God through Christ. (4) No.

Who is an "unbeliever"? "Unbelievers"[51] are those who have not received, or who have rejected, Christ as Savior and Lord.

The problems of a mixed-faith marriage. A mixed-faith marriage between a Christian and an unbeliever probably arose through conversion of one, but not both, spouses in an existing marriage. Some Christians also may have married unbelievers. Regardless of how it arises, what can happen in a marriage between a believer and an unbeliever? Some fundamental differences exist between them.

A believer examines and reevaluates every aspect of life. Through self-denial, a Christian's motivation focuses more on a love for God and a desire to please him. Believers see beyond mere daily circumstances toward eternity and one's ultimate purpose in life. The Christian cannot share the deepest longings in life arising out of a personal relationship with God. Loneliness and lack of fulfillment settle in. Inevitably, "spiritual" competition often increases between the Christian and his/her unbelieving mate. If the spouses in a mixed-faith marriage have children, these young ones may see no family unity. There may be no sense of togetherness where each family member desires to see the others reach their fullest potential. The parents are more likely to disagree on how to raise the children and on matters of discipline.

Paul's primary concern in verses 12–16 is this: Christians in mixed-faith marriages cannot share their love for Jesus with their spouses, while unbelievers frequently yearn for mates who love the world. Who will give in? *Does the believer compromise his or her faith to save the marriage, or continue the Christian life and risk divorce from the unbeliever?*

Mixed-faith marriages do not please God. God strongly discourages any marriage (or other close relationship) that unequally yokes his people to unbelievers. He urged the Israelites not to intermarry with Gentiles, as described in Malachi 2:10–16 and Ezra 9 and 10. Does the same warning apply to Christians married to unbelievers? How does God, through Paul, deal with this matter?

Consider this strong warning from Paul in 2 Corinthians 6:14–16a, 17a:

Do not be yoked together with unbelievers. For what do righteousness and wickedness have in common? Or what fellowship can light have with darkness? What harmony is there between Christ and Belial? What does a believer have in common with an unbeliever? What agreement is there between the temple of God and idols? For we are the temple of the living God.

"Therefore come out from them and be separate," says the Lord.

How does God view a binding marriage relationship between a Christian and an unbeliever? Any relationship or circumstance that could destroy a Christian's faith is not pleasing to him. Would God ask a Christian to break up a marriage to an unbeliever (as Ezra and Shecaniah did of the Israelites in Ezra 9 and 10)? Paul does *not* recommend this action to preserve the peace of an existing marriage. Verses 12–13 affirm that, despite the many disadvantages of a mixed-faith marriage, the Christian is *not* to divorce[52] an unbeliever who wishes to remain in the marriage. *But* if the unbeliever wants to leave the marriage, the Christian is to let the unbeliever go. The Lord is not quick to salvage a failing mixed-faith marriage because his greater concern is for the faith of his people.

Don't resist an unbeliever who wants a divorce. Verse 15 makes it clear that if the *unbeliever* chooses to separate (divorce), the Christian is not to resist it. Compare this instruction to that given to Christian spouses in verse 10. Paul doesn't command unbelievers to stay in the marriage. He doesn't address the unbeliever in the same manner as a Christian divorced from another believer.[53]

In leaving the marriage, an unbeliever clearly violates God's plan for marriage.[54] But more importantly, through unbelief he/she has already rejected the Lord altogether. This is even more grievous.

If an unbeliever leaves a marriage, a Christian is "not bound." In verse 15 Paul says a Christian is "not bound"[55] if an unbeliever leaves a marriage. This is a controversial statement. What does Paul mean by "not bound"? Is Paul only releasing a Christian from *resisting* the divorce, or does he mean that the marriage bond *dissolves* with God's permission? Is the Christian then allowed to remarry? If so, does Paul contradict Jesus in Matthew 19:9?

Paul's primary objective is to preserve the peace. A Christian spouse cannot force salvation upon an unbelieving mate who stubbornly refuses to accept it. If the unbeliever decides to divorce and leave, the Christian clearly has no further responsibility to that person. But does being "not bound" change a Christian's *marital status* before God? Is the Christian free to remarry "in such circumstances"? Notice that Paul doesn't tell the *Christian* in verse 15, as he did in verse 11, to remain unmarried or reconcile to his/her spouse (the unbeliever). *Why?* If a Christian remarries after a divorce by the unbeliever for reasons other than *porneia,* is this consistent with Matthew 19:9? Opinions are split.

One viewpoint holds that verse 15 means only that Christians are "not bound" to chase after unbelieving mates who leave marriages, since this could lead to compromising one's faith. The Christian and unbeliever remain bound to the marriage, however, unless and until the unbeliever commits "marital unfaithfulness" or dies. Any remarriage by the Christian under these circumstances contradicts Jesus' statement that any divorce, except for marital unfaithfulness *(porneia)*, followed by remarriage is adultery. Jesus never made an additional exception anywhere in the Gospels for instances where an unbeliever divorces a believer. Others argue that "not bound" means what it says—the Christian isn't bound to the marriage any longer, nor is the unbeliever. In a legal contract, both parties remain bound to an agreement or neither is bound. Paul thus fulfills God's will for marriage *and* his desire that his people not yoke themselves with unbelievers. This doesn't conflict with Jesus' words in Matthew 19:9, speaking to the world at large about marriage in general—not special marriage problems between *Christians* and unbelievers.

The key question is whether a Christian remains married, or is scripturally released from a marriage, when an unbeliever voluntarily leaves the relationship.[56] Since there are no clear answers from Scripture on this point, we must make our own decision. In keeping with his grace, we ask God to give us individual insight into Matthew 19:9 and 1 Corinthians 7:15.

Does a Christian who divorces his/her faithful Christian spouse qualify as an "unbeliever" in 1 Corinthians 7:15? Does verse 15 apply to a Christian marriage if one believer divorces the other for unscriptural reasons—especially after the divorced spouse follows the biblical conflict resolution procedures in Matthew 18:15–18? In other words, does this make a divorce by an unrepentant Christian divorcer— although not technically an "unbeliever"—enough like an unbeliever that verse 15 applies, thereby possibly opening the way for his or her divorced Christian mate to remarry? If so, does this interpretation conflict with the Lord's command to married Christians in verse 11? Once again, it isn't easy to resolve these controversial issues.[57]

Now let's shift ahead to see what advice Paul has for widowed persons.

First Corinthians 7:39–40 and Romans 7:2–3: Advice for Widows

A woman is bound to her husband as long as he lives. But if her husband dies, she is free to marry anyone she wishes, but he must belong to the Lord. In my judgment, she is happier if she stays as she is—and I think that I too have the Spirit of God. (1 Cor. 7:39–40)

For example, by law a married woman is bound to her husband as long as he is alive, but if her husband dies, she is released from the law of marriage. So then, if she marries another man while her husband is still alive, she is called an adulteress. But if her husband dies, she is released from that law and is not an adulteress, even though she marries another man. (Rom. 7:2–3)

Question: *May a widow remarry?* Answer: Yes, but only in the Lord. A marriage ends when one spouse dies or the couple scripturally divorces. The widowed may then remarry if they wish.

These passages also highlight a point made earlier. The word "bound"[58] in verse 39 and in Romans 7:2 is the same root word in Greek as used in 1 Corinthians 7:27. It is *not* the same word used in 1 Corinthians 7:15, speaking of a Christian being "not bound" to an unbeliever, although the meanings are similar. Others contend, however, that the *meanings* in verses 15 and 39 are the same. Use of different words with such similar meanings is a technical distinction without any real difference. For example, in 1 Corinthians 7:39, a wife is bound until her husband "dies."[59] Paul uses a *different* Greek word for "dies"[60] in Romans 7:2. But both terms describe the same event— physical death of a husband.

It is clear that if one's spouse dies, the surviving spouse is *completely* free in the sight of God to remarry another scripturally eligible mate. Paul describes the survivor as being "free"[61] and "released."[62] The only other consideration is Paul's command in 1 Corinthians 7:39 that the widowed who choose to remarry do so only "in the Lord." What does this limitation mean?[63] There are two views. The widowed person must remarry: (1) a *Christian* (meaning one is *not* free to marry an unbeliever)[64] or (2) *any* person (Christian or unbeliever) who is *scripturally free* to marry as God has ordained. To test the difference between these views, consider this example: Ephesians 6:1 commands children to "obey your parents in the Lord." Under the first view, are children only to obey *Christian* parents? What if the children are Christians and the parents are not, or only one parent is a believer? Even so, the admonitions against being unequally yoked with unbelievers in 2 Corinthians 6:14–18, when coupled with Paul's charge in 1 Corinthians 7:39, is more compelling. Therefore, the first view may be more reasonable.[65]

As we look at some specific questions applying the Scriptures reviewed above in this chapter, let's be sure to keep the big picture in mind as to how God views matters.

SOME TOUGH QUESTIONS TO FOCUS THE ISSUES

Now let's review some troublesome questions about divorce and remarriage. By doing so, hopefully you'll have a better understanding of how each question may affect your life and marital situation. But always be sure to scripturally test *everything* before drawing your own conclusions (Acts 17:11; 2 Thess. 5:21–22).

My spouse is deceased. Am I free to remarry? We have a clear answer on this question—*yes!* Of course, the remarriage partner also must be previously unmarried, widowed, or scripturally divorced. The only question is whether the command in 1 Corinthians 7:39 to remarry "only in the Lord" means you also must marry another Christian. Some argue that the answer to this isn't as clear, but the wisest course of action is to marry a believer since we know this pleases God.

I divorced my spouse for porneia *committed during our marriage. My ex-spouse has made it clear that reconciliation will not occur. Am I free to remarry?* If a marriage is *scripturally* broken, or if a death of a ex-spouse occurs, God *permits* (not requires) remarriage to others who also are scripturally free to marry. This is a concession—not a command. It flows from God's gracious nature. He calls all people to lives of peace—not discord and strife. Those faithful to him have a chance for a new life.

My ex-spouse divorced me and has remarried. Does God permit me to remarry? The answer depends upon whether *porneia* occurred during your former marriage. If *your* sexual misconduct was the reason your spouse divorced you, biblical scholars don't agree on whether you may remarry. If your spouse committed sexual misconduct, followed by your divorce, then you may be free to remarry. Finally, if your spouse divorced you for nonscriptural reasons, you may still be free to remarry since your spouse may have committed *porneia* by entering into remarriage with a third party first.

Who is eligible to remarry? It depends upon one's *marital status* before God—whether a person, at the time of remarriage, is *married* or *unmarried*.[66] A spouse can *scripturally* divorce his or her mate for *porneia* and probably remarry another person without committing adultery. But may an *unscripturally* divorced person remarry without committing adultery? Not if his/her spouse still lives and neither spouse commits *porneia* before the remarriage, according to Jesus. We know that *porneia* (which also can occur upon a remarriage by either spouse) or death can break the first marriage. And by definition, when no marriage exists, there can be no adultery (although the sin of fornication occurs). So the key factor to remember in studying the Scripture is to determine what your marital status is *in God's view* before you consider remarriage.

God doesn't specifically tell us whether those divorced for committing *porneia* may remarry. It'sarguable that if God views a marriage as dissolved for one spouse, it ends for *both* marriage partners. *Both* spouses may be free to remarry regardless of who committed *porneia*.[67] But this challenges our sense of justice.[68] One would hope, however, that God's graciousness would minister to those with a repentant heart and unchain them from their past mistakes.

My spouse, an unbeliever, divorced me. Am I free to remarry? Many biblical scholars would say yes, on the basis of 1 Corinthians 7:12–16. But other scholars disagree, since Paul's words appear to conflict with those of Jesus in Matthew 19:9. This may be a matter for you to consider prayerfully before God. Of course the most secure course of action would be to postpone remarriage until after your unbelieving ex-spouse has committed *porneia* or dies. As unpleasant as this scenario may seem, unfortunately it really becomes a waiting game.

In Matthew 19:9, Jesus says that an unscriptural divorce followed by a remarriage to another person is adultery. My ex-spouse and I divorced for unscriptural reasons, and I have already remarried. Is there any penalty for continuing in my remarriage? If adultery occurred upon remarriage, when did it begin? Is there ever a time when it will end? How can anyone repent of this sin once it has occurred? Should I now divorce my current spouse?

Unfortunately, Matthew 19:9 (and parallel passages in the Gospels) don't address *all* aspects of marriage, divorce, and remarriage. Unanswered questions remain. Why? Was it Jesus' intent to be ambiguous?

It is reasonable that Jesus would address divorce and remarriage issues from different perspectives, depending upon the needs of the people he taught. For example, consider his teachings about salvation. In some instances he speaks only of repentance (Luke 13:3). On other occasions, he speaks only of faith (Luke 7:50; 8:12). Sometimes he speaks of some, but not specifically all, requisites of Christian salvation (Matt. 28:19–20; Mark 16:16). To see the complete picture, we simply bring together *all* the Scripture. In the same way, we review all Scripture addressing marriage, divorce, and remarriage issues. Jesus and Paul warn us of what to honor and what to avoid. Unfortunately, we don't find *all* our questions answered—including how one repents of an adulterous remarriage. But can we make a reasonable inference about this matter?

What's the penalty for adultery in Matthew 19:9? This verse doesn't specifically tell us. Do other verses help? Romans 13:9 says the commandments of God sum up in this: Love your neighbor as yourself. It states no penalty for disobeying this command. But 1 John 3:4 says sin is lawlessness (breaking the commands of God). Romans 6:23 tells us that the penalty for sin is (spiritual) death. That's the penalty for *all* sin when a person doesn't repent. Adultery therefore has the same penalty as hate and murder—loss of eternal life *if* one's heart is unrepentant and separated from God. The Bible clearly says that unrepentant adulterers cannot inherit the kingdom of God (1 Cor. 6:9–10; Rev. 21:8). The wages of sin are eternal death, but the gift of God is eternal life in Christ (Eph. 2:8–10). Divorce isn't the unpardonable sin. Neither is adultery. All sinners with repentant and believing hearts receive redemption by God's grace through Christ's sacrifice on the cross.

How can one repent of entering into an adulterous (at least initially) relationship?[69] "Go and sin no more" is what Jesus said in John 8 to the woman caught in adultery. First Corinthians 6:11 says that some of those Christians *were* adulterers. What changed them? Scripture tells us they were washed, sanctified, and justified by the blood of Christ. But the Bible says nothing about the details of their repentance. How was this done? Was one required to divorce a mate if an unscriptural marriage existed? Were vows of the remarriage to be broken? Must remarried spouses abandon homes and families created by the remarriage? Unfortunately, God doesn't specifically tell us in Scripture. Would God really condone *more* divorce by requiring remarriage partners to split up in a questionable effort to restore their former marriages? For the sake of peace and order, and to spare further heartbreak to innocents (children), isn't it better for the couple to stay as they are and to seek repentance and forgiveness in the existing remarriage?

There are no conclusive solutions to this problem. We know that without repentance adulterers are out of favor with God. However, no Scripture commands divorce for any Christian couple in a nonincestuous relationship that may have involved adultery at one time between the parties.[70] Although adultery preceded murder in their case, God permitted David and Bathsheba to continue in their marriage. Their example shows that the key to forgiveness for adultery is whether our *hearts* are truly repentant and devoted to God.

Adultery is a serious sin—but it isn't unforgivable. God always beckons all sinners to come to a heart-piercing repentance to receive the benefits of his forgiveness continually offered to everyone in Jesus Christ (1 John 1:8–10). God also can exercise his grace to withhold any penalty as our righteous Judge. The faithful sincerity of our hearts expressed in submissive repentance to God is a key to receiving his grace and forgiveness. He'll guide us into making the necessary decisions in expressing our repentance. Quite often this means reconciliation with a spouse, if that's still possible. Or it may mean accepting divorce and its consequences. But *commanding* termination of a remarriage may compound sin's destruction rather than alleviate it. It requires careful thought and prayer.

I was unscripturally divorced before becoming a Christian. If I remarry after becoming a Christian, is the remarriage acceptable to God? Many believe that an unscriptural divorce, or an unscriptural divorce followed by a remarriage that is adulterous, is forgiven upon one becoming a Christian. *All* sins are forgiven in Christ. An unscriptural divorce or later remarriage is not an unpardonable sin. Christians are *new* creations in Christ. Second Corinthians 5:17 tells us: "Therefore, if anyone is in Christ, he is a new creation; the old has gone, the new has come!" Everything about a Christian is "new," "fresh," and "cleansed of sin"—completely forgiven. That's why Christianity is such good news! God doesn't hold our sins against us. He removes our sins from us as far as the east is from the west (Ps. 103:10–12).

Christians are forgiven, set apart as belonging to God, and *justified*—"just as if I'd" never sinned. If so, why would an unscriptural divorce and remarriage (that isn't inherently sinful due to incest, etc.) be the only sin *not* covered by the blood of Christ? Stated another way, unbelievers don't live godly lives. Why? Because their sinful natures control them (Rom. 8:5–8). They commit many acts contrary to Scripture before coming to Christ. Given this fact, why shouldn't new converts receive a "fresh start" with Christ as new creations without breaking up families who want to stay together?

But let's also consider the alternate view. Are unbelievers *exempt* from obeying Scripture? If this is true, no unbeliever could become a Christian. Why? Because God's Word must *apply* to one's life before anyone can *obey* it. If the Bible doesn't apply to them, unbelievers cannot claim the promises of salvation in God's Word.[71] But forgiveness offered by Christ is complete to *anyone* who will receive it, and becoming a Christian does indeed make one a new creation. But receiving forgiveness requires repentance.[72] What were those referred to in 1 Corinthians 6:9–11 implicitly required to do? Thieves must no longer steal. Drunkards must stop their drinking. Idolaters must no longer worship idols but instead worship the true, living God. Homosexuals must stop their perversion. Likewise, adulterers must no longer commit adultery. In all cases, the Corinthians *were* engaging in these sinful practices. But repentance occurred as part of their conversion. Repentance is always necessary to receive forgiveness (Acts 2:38; 3:19; 17:30; 26:20).

This brings us back once again to the critical issues of one's *marital status* before God and the *nature* of a remarriage relationship after an unscriptural divorce. Is a remarriage a *continuing state of adultery?* Is it so because one also remains married to a former spouse in God's sight? Or is the remarriage the result of a single, adulterous act that immediately *breaks* the former marriage such that the adultery doesn't continue? If it is the latter, and the persons involved sincerely repent from the heart against repeating this act, then few would deny that God forgives them upon coming to Christ. If, however, the relationship *continues as an adulterous relationship* in God's eyes, then few dispute that the remarriage must end as part of repentance. In all events, the sin of adultery cannot continue if one truly desires forgiveness.

Does the risk of entering into an adulterous remarriage after an unscriptural divorce in effect force a divorced couple to reconcile? What if domestic violence or sexual abuse threatens a spouse or children? Does Scripture require an abused spouse to return to the abuser?

After an unscriptural divorce, a Christian couple has the option to remain separate (and therefore celibate) or to reconcile with each other, according to 1 Corinthians 7:11. God seems to encourage reconciliation in every way by removing tempting distractions of third parties. But if this is impossible, a separated or divorced Christian must remain unremarried. This is a tough choice for spouses who really desire a marriage relationship. It can tempt a spouse to return to a dangerous marriage.

Mutual submission is important in a marriage. Paul addresses this point in Ephesians 5. He relates it to the relationship between Christ and the church. He tells wives, "Submit to your husbands as to the Lord . . . as the church submits to Christ, so also wives should submit to their husbands in everything" (Eph. 5:22, 24). To husbands he says, "Love your wives, just as Christ loved the church and gave himself up for her. . . . In this same way, husbands ought to love their wives as their own bodies" (Eph. 5:25, 28). But what happens to the many women who don't have husbands like this? Must a spouse submit to a mate who threatens him/her physically or emotionally?

Domestic violence and sexual abuse are very serious problems. Too often insensitive outsiders blame victims for somehow bringing this abuse upon themselves. They feel those abused need to work harder in the marriage to please their mates. Many well-meaning people will counsel the abused spouse to suffer silently and endure the abuse, perhaps thereby winning the abuser over by continuing submissiveness (1 Pet. 3:1–2). But this is bad advice under these circumstances, as well as a misapplication of Scripture! No Scripture approves of a spouse being violent, nor of family members enduring it.

What is a spouse to do in these circumstances? First, don't think that God over-looks abuse like this. He definitely moves *against* those who use violence. He abhors violence against any person. "Don't you know that you yourselves are God's temple and that God's Spirit lives in you? If anyone destroys God's temple, God will destroy him; for God's temple is sacred, and you are that temple" (1 Cor. 3:16–17). Many familiar with God's sentiment expressed so strongly in Malachi 2:16: "I hate divorce," neglect the rest of that same verse—"and I hate a man's covering himself with violence as well as with his garment."

What should one do about domestic violence? When faced with personal vio-lence, David quickly turned to the Lord: "Rescue me, O LORD, from evil men; protect me from men of violence, who devise evil plans in their hearts and stir up war every day. They make their tongues as sharp as a serpent's; the poison of vipers is on their lips. Keep me, O LORD, from the hands of the wicked; protect me from men of vio-lence who plan to trip my feet" (Ps. 140:1–4).

God doesn't turn away from such pleas. Notice how Jesus warns against harming the most precious of God's creations—his children: "But if anyone causes one of these little ones who believe in me to sin, it is better for him to have a large millstone hung around his neck and to be drowned in the depths of the sea. Woe to the world because of the things that cause people to sin! Such things must come, but woe to the man through whom they come!" (Matt. 18:6–7).

But how can an abused spouse cope with a marriage marred by domestic violence or sexual abuse and still be faithful to Scripture like 1 Corinthians 7:11, which gener-ally commands spouses not to separate?

1. *Separate from the abuser.* Scripture acknowledges that there may be situations when a Christian couple separates (1 Cor. 7:11a). God knows that an unreasonably abusive relationship is not really a marriage as much as it is a murderous relationship fueled by hate and violence (see 1 John 3:15). God always provides a way of escape if our circumstances are more than we can reasonably bear so we can stand up under the pressure (see 1 Cor. 10:13). If counseling and reasoning have failed, then it is proper, and sometimes even absolutely necessary, for victims of abuse to separate themselves from their abusers for physical safety reasons. It's *time to move* to a safe environment among church friends or a safehouse for victims of abuse. There's nothing wrong with avoiding further injury to oneself or other innocent family members. Separation allows time for sorting out options. It is reasonable *after* exhausting all other reason-able measures of protection.

2. *Report the abuse to those competent to help.* Abused spouses need help! This means notifying those who can be a positive force for change. The abuser needs proper confrontation. Governmental studies prove that women who report their abu-sive husbands to the proper authorities were less susceptible to another attack within the following six months. More importantly, if one parent abuses children, the other parent has a moral and legal responsibility to protect these young ones.

3. *Seek comfort and counsel from faithful Christians.* It's critical to find family members and friends who believe your reports of abuse and truly *understand* your situation. They must empathize with the trap a victim spouse faces by enduring continuing abuse. You need help in moving to a safe and secure environment without delay *and* without skepticism about your complaints.

4. *Don't place undue reliance on the legal system.* The Public Broadcasting System production *My Husband Is Going to Kill Me* powerfully details the last month in a thirty-year-old woman's life. She sought help from friends, social workers, police, and the courts without success. Her husband forced his way into her home and held her hostage at gunpoint while trying to rape her. Eight days later, he shot and killed her in front of her two children in a Denver restaurant parking lot. Obviously the legal system was too slow or ineffective in dealing with criminal abuse in this particular case. You must fully utilize the protection of civil law to shield yourself from your abuser(s). But also be realistic. All the court injunctions and protective orders the legal system has to offer won't shield anyone against bullets, knives, or fists when in extreme jeopardy like this. Take reasonable measures to protect yourself as well.

5. *Churches should use scriptural discipline against abusive spouses.* Domestic violence and abuse cries out for the discipline procedures Jesus outlined in Matthew 18:15–17. This isn't a problem of the abused spouse only. Everyone in the Christian community has a responsibility to help bring an abusive spouse to repentance (see 1 Cor. 5:2, 12–13; 12:24b–26).

Certainly God wants reconciliation of marriages. But if there's a matter that God hates more than divorce, it's one whose hands shed innocent blood! (Prov. 6:16–17). You have options with which to deal with domestic violence itself, but Scripture doesn't provide those who are unscripturally divorced with the option of remarriage as long as the abuser remains alive and is open to reconciliation (after repentance, of course). First Corinthians 7:11 still applies to abusers who are Christians. First Corinthians 7:12–16 applies to nonbeliever husbands who didn't agree to the divorce. God wants you to remain as you are or, if the abuser truly repents,[73] reconcile with your spouse.

How can one cope with a life alone if reconciliation with one's spouse cannot occur and yet remarriage isn't a scriptural option? Some acknowledge that the only option open to a couple in an unscriptural divorce situation is reconciliation or mandatory celibacy. But they cite 1 Timothy 4:1–3 (which says that false teachers will oppose marriage) to make an interesting argument: Forbidding people to marry breeds lust, fornication, and other sensual sins. Denying marriage to anyone condemns that person to celibacy. This thrusts formerly married spouses into a state of extreme temptation for sensual sin. God created men and women with sexual desires. First Corinthians 7:8–9 says that those unable to control themselves in a sensual way should marry rather than burn with passion. Therefore, can 1 Corinthians 7:11 really mean what it says in requiring unscripturally divorced persons to remain unmarried if reconciliation with their mates doesn't occur? Some argue this is a recipe for disaster in the real world. It's too much to ask of many distressed individuals. Requiring celibacy without consideration of whether individuals can control themselves sensually is too harsh. It seems counter to Paul's admonition in 1 Corinthians 7:9 that it is "better to marry than to burn with passion."[74]

The alternative view is that God can make such judgments about who must remain celibate—especially if it violates the marriage relationship. The fact is that God denies sexual intimacy to many people. These include single persons who cannot find suitable mates or who find it expedient or impractical to marry. There are also *married* persons who cannot, or will not, fulfill their marital responsibilities. Celibacy isn't an unnatural or extreme condition foreign to most human beings. In any event, sexual tension cannot justify an unscriptural, or improvident, marriage. If it were otherwise, many parents would have their children marry at puberty to avoid fornication. Individuals who cannot control themselves sensually, such as rapists, also could justify their sin. God's command is clear that no one may take another person's spouse and live with him/her in adultery simply because one's passionate desires need satisfaction.

God surely knew of these difficulties in giving us the principles in 1 Corinthians 7:11, but his will is plain. Any spouse who separates from, or divorces, a mate without scriptural reason must remain unmarried or reconcile to his/her mate. Remarriage to another person isn't an option. These persons are not being denied marriage. They have a choice—live separately or return to their marriage. This is biblical instruction. To ignore it or act contrary to it violates our relationship with God. But remember, as Jesus tells us, "All things are possible with God." This isn't a trite or simplistic promise to us in coping with our difficult feelings and circumstances. God promises to provide us with the grace sufficient to meet our needs (2 Cor. 12:9). He also promises to keep us from being tempted above what we can bear. He provides a way of escape so we can bear up under the pressures we feel within us without committing adultery (1 Cor. 10:13). Jesus wouldn't ask those in an unscriptural divorce situation to remain unmarried without his help.

We could review many other issues and controversies. Sometimes there are clear statements in Scripture. When there isn't, biblical principles exist that apply to issues not directly addressed. The best advice is to obey the truth as far as it is clear to us, regardless of our personal feelings. God always calls each of us to use spiritual judgment in *prayerfully* working out our problems. In doing so, we need to wrestle with some of these Scriptures rather than to compromise or ignore them. It's our task to move forward with confidence and trust him—not to deceive ourselves into denial of his truth.

THE BOTTOM LINE: WHERE IS YOUR HEART?

Helen Kooiman Hosier tells the story of how a young woman once asked Saint Francis whether or not it was a sin to use rouge. "Well, some theologians claim it's all right," he replied, "but others disagree." "But what should *I* do—use rouge or not?" the woman persisted. "Why not follow the middle course?" counseled the saint. "Rouge only one cheek." I can sure relate to that!

Scholarly theologians camp on all sides of many of these controversial marriage, divorce, and remarriage issues. It's hard to find any consensus. As a divorcee, I struggled with these questions. To me they weren't just interesting theological points of debate—they directly affected my life with the Lord! What can you do to sort through all the viewpoints to find God's truth? You may not agree with the biblical analysis in this chapter.[75] That's okay. But you must decide what's best for you as God grants you wisdom. If your conclusions are heartfelt and, most importantly, *consistent with Scripture,* no one should chastise you for your convictions.

Paul expresses well the ultimate accountability each Christian has about the issues we've been discussing. Listen to what he shares about his own life:

So then, men ought to regard us as servants of Christ and as those entrusted with the secret things of God. Now it is required that those who have been given a trust must prove faithful. I care very little if I am judged by you or by any human court; indeed, I do not even judge myself. My conscience is clear, but that does not make me innocent. It is the Lord who judges me. Therefore judge nothing before the appointed time; wait till the Lord comes. He will bring to light what is hidden in darkness and will expose the motives of men's hearts. At that time each will receive his praise from God. (1 Cor. 4:1–5)

We are to make judgments about right and wrong within the church as Scripture guides us (1 Cor. 5:12). There are some matters that *outwardly* appear wrong or right, but God looks *inward* to our hearts (1 Sam. 16:7; 1 Chron. 28:9). No human can really know the thoughts and motivations of another's heart (1 Cor. 2:11). Therefore, when people who profess an obedient faith in Jesus make personal decisions in legitimately disputable matters of Scripture, who among us can condemn them? They cannot be condemned by matters of our own consciences (1 Cor. 10:29). If their hearts are *not* right in making *any* decisions about marriage, divorce and remarriage, God is the judge—not us.

Accept him whose faith is weak, without passing judgment on disputable matters. . . . Who are you to judge someone else's servant? To his own master he stands or falls. And he will stand, for the Lord is able to make him stand.

For none of us lives to himself alone. If we live, we live to the Lord; and if we die, we die to the Lord. So, whether we live or die, we belong to the Lord.

For this very reason, Christ died and returned to life so that he might be the Lord of both the dead and the living. You, then, why do you judge your brother? Or why do you look down on your brother? For we will all stand before God's judgment seat. It is written: "As surely as I live," says the Lord, "Every knee will bow before me; every tongue will confess to God." So then each of us will give an account of himself to God.

> Therefore let us stop passing judgment on one another. Instead, make up your mind not to put any stumbling block or obstacle in your brother's way. . . . Do not allow what you consider good to be spoken of as evil. For the kingdom of God is not a matter of eating and drinking, but of righteousness, peace and joy in the Holy Spirit, because anyone who serves Christ in this way is pleasing to God and approved by men. (Rom. 14:1–4, 7–13, 16–18)

By all means possible, we must interpret Scripture honestly. We do this by: reading verses in context, testing our understanding against examples and patterns seen throughout the Bible, and verifying our conclusions with the grace of God as a foundation for everything we learn. We must let God tell us, through his Word, how he sees our situation and what he asks of us. We cannot stress rules and laws if it nullifies God's grace. On the other hand, we must not emphasize God's compassion and mercy to such an extent that "anything goes" with conclusions that contradict Scripture.

Also, as God has consistently rejected legalism in responding to his commands, we must avoid legalism as well. What is legalism? It is coldly and heartlessly going through the motions of faith through outward obedience to God's commands. It is having a form of godliness, but denying its power (2 Tim. 3:5). Since the Law of Moses consists of rules and regulations, it invites legalistic compliance. But God clearly disapproves of legalism under the old and new covenants. Neither covenant was an end in itself. The eternal purpose of both was continually to *lead us to Christ* (Gal. 3:24; Heb. 8–10). God earnestly searches for those who devote their *hearts* to him (2 Chron. 16:9; Matt. 22:34–40).

In making decisions about disputable matters, we must exercise our best judgment in devotion to him. But *whatever* we do should not serve our own selfish ends. Instead, we should unselfishly give of ourselves and always seek to glorify God (1 Cor. 10:31). "And God is able to make all grace abound to you, so that in all things at all times, having all that you need, you will abound in every good work" (2 Cor. 9:8).

A Message from Cheryl

There are no New Testament biblical guidelines on how to divorce a spouse when it becomes necessary. And yet, through each phase of divorce, dating, and remarriage, God's Word gives us many principles we can practically apply to ex-spouses, ex-inlaws, and other relatives; single-parenting of our children; and the blending of families. God calls us to peace. Is that applicable to our relationships with our ex-spouses? You bet!

God calls us to forgive. That too? Yes. As parents we have a responsibility to meet the needs of our children, even if that leaves us wanting or alone. Is it hard? Yes. But *if* we are obedient, we also have the promise of God's blessings—peace that surpasses all understanding and a spiritual Father for our often fatherless children.

A divorce need not draw you out of God's plan and his will, but sin, resentment, and bitterness will. Don't let the end of your marriage undermine your walk with the Lord.

Can you "save your marriage alone"? No. Is an abandoned spouse resigned to a life of pining away after an unfaithful mate? At first glance, it may seem that his/her hardness of heart and disobedience may destroy the hope of a whole family. But God, in his mercy, offers plan B to those of us left behind.

I'm spending the rest of my life on plan B—and what God has allowed me to enjoy is beyond anything I may have asked or thought.

QUESTIONS FOR PERSONAL REFLECTION

1. Do I really understand and accept God's original plan for marriage?
2. What conclusions have I reached about marriage, divorce, and remarriage? (Write them down and think and pray about these conclusions.) Are they consistent with what I learn from Scripture?
3. What is my marital status in God's sight? Am I willing to remain unmarried if God hasn't granted permission for me to remarry?
4. In what areas of my life do I most need the Lord's grace and mercy right now?
5. Do I really believe that God understands both my personal pain in going through a divorce as well as my desire to find another mate and remarry?

PART TWO

To Love Again

Building a Healthy and Joyful Remarriage—God's Way!

In Matthew 7:24–27, Jesus shared a parable about wise and foolish builders. The wise man built his house on the rock. When the rain came down, the streams rose, and the winds blew and beat against that house; yet it did not fall. Why? Because its foundation was on the rock. However, the foolish man built his house on sand. When the rain came down and the elements blew and beat against that house, it fell with a mighty crash.

In preparing for remarriage, we need to act like wise builders. This is why we devoted so much time in part 1 to dealing with loneliness, letting go of prior marriages, embracing singleness, completing the grieving process, having a forgiving and loving heart, facing the pain in our lives, praying, and depending upon God like never before. It is also why we carefully examined Scripture in chapter 3 to see whether God permits us to remarry. These are *foundational* principles that will prepare you to build your remarriage on the rock of Jesus Christ. Fortify your remarriage to stand up through the inevitable storms of life. Dig *deep* into the solid ground of faith and then, using great patience and careful instruction, build your remarriage on that foundation! Without that foundation, the worries of this life and the pressures of remarriage and blended families will shake your relationship to pieces like an earthquake.

Another equally important principle is needed to build a healthy remarriage—*flexibility.* In his book *The Enormous Exception,* Earl Palmer wrote that the San Francisco Golden Gate Bridge, constructed right on the San Andreas fault, was built to sway about twenty feet at the center of its one-mile suspension span. This flexible sway was a key feature to the bridge lasting so many years. But that's not all! By design, every part of the bridge's concrete roadway, steel railings, and cross beams hinged from one welded joint to another up through the vast cable system. Each part ties to another on up to the top of two great towers standing tall from two enormous land-anchor piers. Because these towers bear most of the weight, they sit deeply embedded into the rock foundation in San Francisco Bay. What's the secret to the longevity of the bridge? Flexibility *and* foundation!

How does flexibility affect remarriage and building a blended family? It means acting in faith to study the Scriptures, and restructuring our lives as God desires rather than trying to call all our own shots. It means seeing ourselves as God sees us—nothing less, and nothing more—and acting accordingly. It means *learning* from our past relationships. An oft-recited phrase applies here as well: "Those who fail to learn from history are condemned to repeat it."

Flexibility also means being willing to *change* our hearts, minds, and lives as necessary to reach our full potential as loving and committed remarriage partners. (No one else can make this change for us!) It means having reasonable and realistic expectations of our remarriage partner, as well as each member of our blended families. We need to learn how to cope successfully with disappointments, frustration, and anger, and to manage conflict well by using good communication skills. We need to honor and respect healthy boundaries in our blended families. We need to be generous in giving quality time in making blended family *relationships* a priority. And we need to seek competent and spiritual help when we need it!

As we prepare for remarriage and building our blended families, we naturally will want to be very careful to find a person with whom we want to spend the rest of our lives. We might be tempted to think that our choice of a mate makes all the difference. Should we experience trouble and hardship with our chosen one, we might think we made the wrong decision. Not so! Every relationship has trouble and hardship. The key to success is building on the foundation of Jesus Christ and yielding to God in flexibility. We must allow him to bend and shape us into wise and experienced remarriage mates and parents for our children.

Part 2 of this book will help guide you through building a healthy remarriage on the rock of Jesus Christ. Look to him as you work through the maze of issues and challenges unique to remarriages and blended families.

Chapter 4

PREPARING FOR REMARRIAGE
Finding a Mate Suitable for
You and Your Children

Remarriage is weaving your life (and the lives of your children) into the life of another person (and his or her children). It will change everything about your existence for the rest of your life! This is why it is so crucial that your remarriage partner be suitable for you.

How will you beat the odds against a successful remarriage? How will you go the distance as others fall by the wayside? Are there ways to reduce the risk of failure and improve marital happiness in remarriage? How do you avoid unwelcome and unsettling surprises after it's too late to reconsider a relationship? The answers are simple (although living it out isn't so easy): You must allow God to lead and guide you to find a *suitable* mate, as he provided for Adam (Gen. 2:18).

Getting acquainted with prospective remarriage partners through dating and courtship is a major key in determining the bond you'll have in remarriage. This is why it's so important not to rush this critical phase of the relationship. Preparing for remarriage takes *time* for careful evaluation and prayer. If we seek God, he will answer. As Jesus promised, "Ask and it will be given to you; seek and you will find; knock and the door will be opened to you. For everyone who asks receives; he who seeks finds; and to him who knocks, the door will be opened" (Luke 11:9–10).

Crises and stress test every marriage through personality differences, child-parenting problems, in-law problems, job changes, relocations, serious illnesses, financial problems—you name it! But if the partners share the same vision and dream and truly *want* to make it work with God's help, the relationship *will work*. This chapter separates wheat from chaff in helping you make a responsible and wise choice before God about whom you remarry—someone with whom to share your vision and commitment to make the relationship *work*.

The Vital Difference between Biblical Love and Romantic Infatuation

The bedrock of marriage, and particularly remarriage, is building a very special union based on *biblical love,* strongly rooted in the nature and essence of Jesus Christ. The *primary* goal of marriage isn't to please one's partner romantically (although that certainly should occur as the relationship grows), but to bring each spouse closer to God.

What is romantic infatuation? As *Webster's New World Dictionary* defines it, romantic infatuation is "a fictitious tale of wonderful and extraordinary events, characterized by much imagination and idealization; without basis in fact; an exaggeration or falsehood." Infatuation is an emotional joyride without the selfless commitment inherent in biblical love.

Infatuation deals with fantasies and "settings" that move the emotions—moods, weather, soothing words, music, gifts—not reality. It's a fickle "love at first sight," identified by changeable and unstable affections. It's insecure, plagued by nagging doubts and unanswered questions. Infatuation leaves lives unexamined since resolving problems might spoil the dream. Finally, infatuation leaves us as orphans when those emotions fade after a few rounds of "Romantic Roulette." It's no substitute for love. It ignores the most important element necessary for a lasting relationship—*commitment.* Truly, infatuation builds on sand instead of the rock of Jesus Christ.

In contrast, true biblical love depends on *commitment*—to God and to a marriage partner. *Vine's Expository Dictionary of New Testament Words* defines love this way: "Love, whether exercised toward the brethren or toward men generally, is not an impulse from the feelings, it does not always run with the natural inclinations, nor does it spend itself only upon those for whom some affinity (or closeness) is discovered. Love seeks the welfare of all (Rom. 15:2), and works no ill to any (Rom. 13:8–10), love seeks opportunity to do good to 'all men' (Gal. 6:10). (Also see 1 Cor. 13 and Col. 3:12–14)." Love is calm, secure, and unthreatened *trust* that makes your partner feel trustworthy and appreciated.

Biblical love strengthens you, uplifts you, and fills the empty spaces in your heart. Unlike infatuation that pushes and pulls in jerky motions, love steadily and patiently says, "I will not panic. I will plan my future with confidence as the Lord guides me." Time does not bother love, for it will wait. Distance cannot separate lovers. Love grows from quiet understanding and mature friendship that accepts another person without feeling the compulsion to change them.

Consider the track record of actress Elizabeth Taylor, a famous remarriage veteran: Upon marrying hotel heir Nicky Hilton (May 6, 1950): "I'm so very happy." In just over a year they divorced and Taylor married actor Michael Wilding (February 21, 1952): "I hope you will all be as happy someday as I am right this moment. This is to me the beginning of a happy end." But five years later, she began her third marriage to producer Mike Todd (February 2, 1957): "I have given him my eternal love. . . . This marriage will last forever. For me it will be third time lucky." Thirteen months later, Todd died in a plane crash, but Taylor quickly moved on to marry singer Eddie Fisher

(May 12, 1959): "I have never been happier in my life. . . . We will be on our honeymoon thirty or forty years!" By March 15, 1964, however, the honeymoon ended. Taylor shelved Fisher and entered her first marriage to actor Richard Burton, exclaiming: "Oh God, I'm so happy you can't believe it. . . . This marriage will last forever!" They divorced, but later married again on October 10, 1975, when Taylor pledged: "There will be bloody no more marriages or divorces. We are stuck like chicken feathers to tar—for lovely always." When the second Burton marriage fell apart for good, Taylor wed Virginia senator John Warner on December 4, 1976: "I have never been so happy. I'm really so very much in love with John. I don't think I have ever felt this good and lucky about being in love before!" They later divorced, followed by Taylor's eighth marriage to construction worker Larry Fortensky, whom she met in a rehabilitation program. That marriage also ended in divorce shortly thereafter.

On January 15, 2001, sixty-nine-year-old Taylor, then single after eight marriages, appeared on *Larry King Live* to say "eight is enough." "That's it?" host Larry King (another remarriage veteran with an equally interesting history) asked incredulously. "Yes!" she gasped. "You're done?" he quizzed. "Yes," she insisted, adding, "[But] I'd live with someone if he were cute, intelligent, compassionate, adorable, and had a good sense of humor!"[1]

About 60 to 65 percent of remarriages end in divorce. Too many spouses watch their marriages crumble into quiet desperation and utter despair. Why? Because we marry with shallow and superficial "love" that is merely lust or infatuation in disguise. We are drawn by physical attraction, wealth, and temporal *external* qualities rather than what's in a *heart* truly devoted to God. Plus, we don't expect marriage to be *so* difficult—but it almost always is!

The apostle Paul defines biblical love in 1 Corinthians 13:4–7: It is patient and long-suffering, but doesn't condone evil. Love is kind, but speaks the truth in righteousness with gentleness and respect. Love doesn't envy others, but guides one to deny oneself unselfishly in seeking God's will for the benefit of others. Love doesn't boast or seek the attention of others, but appreciates and encourages others. Love isn't proud, doesn't shift the blame, or assess others with a cool, patronizing haughtiness. With humility, grace, and thanksgiving, it receives the blessings God bestows. Love isn't rude, coarse, vulgar, or indecent, but gives due respect to everyone. Love isn't selfish. It doesn't seek its own way at others' expense, but encourages and esteems others in ways that glorify God.

Love isn't easily angered in emotional outbursts with a desire to punish or seek revenge. Instead, it is self-controlled, sensitive, alert, and willing to listen. It is slow to speak and slow to become angry (James 1:19–20). And yet love defends truth and righteousness to the death. By forgiving without letting offenses pass, love keeps no record of wrongs. It rejoices in reconciliation of wounded people from broken relationships, in the spirit of the father and the prodigal son (Luke 15:18–24). Love doesn't delight in evil or gossip, or receive pleasure in the harm it causes others. Instead, love tries to restore sinners to God in humility and empathy. It rejoices in the truth with consistent honesty, integrity, loyalty, and trustworthiness, and weeps when others reject the truth.

Love always *protects* and assumes the best—rather than the worst—of others. It guards those incapable of defending themselves from injury or attack. Love always *trusts* in God with faith and has confidence in the character of others free from deceit of false rumors. Love always *hopes* with expectation of fulfillment as God wills and provides, while not letting this hope slip away. Love always *perseveres* and endures without quitting easily, even when the going gets tough.

Love never fails. It isn't weak. It isn't compromised by circumstances. Why? Because God *is* love (1 John 4:16), and he never fails! As Jesus loved us, love is willing to lay down one's life for one's family and friends even when they're unloving towards us (John 15:9–17)! "Jesus Christ laid down his life for us. And we ought to lay down our lives for our brothers" (1 John 3:16).

How does this apply to finding a prospective remarriage partner? Joshua Harris, author of *I Kissed Dating Goodbye,* describes the difference between what he calls "smart love" (which desires God's will after knowing and obeying his rules) with "dumb love": "I was primarily interested in what I could get, such as the popularity a girlfriend could give me or the comfort and pleasure I could gain physically or emotionally from a relationship. . . . I lived 'dumb love'—choosing what *felt* good for me instead of what was good for others and what pleased God."[2] What type of love prompts a man to sleep with his girlfriend when it scars her emotionally and damages her relationship with God? What type of love motivates a woman to lead a man along only to break up with him when she finds someone better? "Smart love" (biblical love) is a sincere, God-focused love concerned for others. "Dumb love" (romantic infatuation), by contrast, is self-centered and flirtatious.[3]

As you determine if a remarriage partner is suitable for you, resolve yourself to do so with biblical love. Keep romantic infatuation in check. Naturally, this commitment to biblical love carries into remarriage as a foundation for everything else. Yet there is another vital prerequisite for Christians to embrace *before* finding a suitable remarriage partner—the importance of *contentment.*

CONTENTMENT AND WAITING ON THE LORD

The apostle Paul captures the essence of how to deal with *every* type of life experience this way: "I have learned the secret of being content in any and every situation, whether well fed or hungry, whether living in plenty or in want. I can do everything through him who gives me strength" (Phil. 4:12b–13). How does this relate to finding a potential mate? Simply put, it means letting go, being patient, and letting *God* open doors to a new relationship.

Without contentment, *desperation* to find a remarriage partner creeps in. Cheryl and I live by a lake where a large great blue heron calls out day and night in a loud voice during mating season, "EEEEE-ya, EEEEE-ya, EEEEE-ya!" Translation: "I need a mate *now!*" As I lie awake during the early morning hours listening to this racket, I wonder if the old bird will ever find satisfaction. (Cheryl and I sure hope he does . . . and soon!) The point is, without contentment, those searching for a suitable mate can give off the same "EEEEE-ya!" signals, pushing too hard for a relationship. There is a better way than this annoying turnoff!

With an external focus, we find only temporary pleasure—it will fade or disappear. With each failure or disappointment, the natural urge is to pick up the pace, *push* our own agenda, *pursue* more romance and adventure, and *grab* for an easily available relationship. But true contentment comes from being *patient*—watching quietly, praying silently, and waiting upon the Lord to open doors rather than trying to force our way in. This is why we emphasized the importance of *embracing singleness* from the beginning of this book. If we don't have complete confidence and trust in God, we may begin demanding that others meet our needs, manipulating and controlling them to please us at their expense.

Scripture reminds us that godliness with contentment is great gain (1 Tim. 6:6). Seneca, the Roman stoic philosopher who lived during the time of Christ, said, "If you would make a man happy, do not add to his possessions, but subtract from his desires." Scottish novelist and dramatist James M. Barrie once observed, "Not in doing what you like, but in liking what you do, is the secret of happiness." The word *contentment* literally means *sufficiency* and *containment,* and refers to a person who is "self-contained." A content person derives satisfaction from *inner* resources and blessings received from the Lord, rather than from *external* sources.

Paul also tells us that contentment is "learned." One of the most critical lessons to learn is to know *who* you are, to know *why* you are the way you are, and then to be satisfied in both categories. Learning also means making some tough choices—like pressing on when the going gets tough; forgetting what is behind while striving toward a goal; standing firm when it's easy to compromise; and rejoicing greatly in challenging circumstances. Contentment is the fruit of obedience in *seeking the Lord first* rather than trying to meet our own needs (our natural tendency). This is God's way.

How do we gain "godliness with contentment"? Here are a few ways:

Desire and pray for contentment. Who receives contentment when he/she doesn't really *want* it? We need to *desire* it and *pray* for it! God cares for his own. He hears us when we ask him to take away our anxieties: "Humble yourselves, therefore, under God's mighty hand, that he may lift you up in due time. Cast all your anxiety on him because he cares for you" (1 Pet. 5:6–7). We must be *yielded* and *willing* to allow the Lord to help us with our needs. Then he will lift us up "in due time." Praying for contentment also may mean asking the Lord to take away feelings for someone you love if you know God isn't pleased with the relationship.

Surrender to God. Do we want God's will or what *we* want in a remarriage partner? With Christ, Paul says we can do "all things" (including finding a suitable partner, if it is the Lord's will). This means acknowledging, "Your timing, your way, and your outcome, Lord." Psalm 37:4 urges us, "Delight yourself in the Lord, and he will give you the desires of your heart." This doesn't mean that God wants to fulfill all *our* desires. David tells us that if our focus is on the Lord, then he will transform our desires so they will actually reflect *his* desires. He will then satisfy those wants. The

Lord has no intention of fulfilling our selfish desires. But if we're experiencing Christian contentment, we really won't care!

What is your overriding passion in life right now—to find a remarriage partner or to serve and glorify God? Seeking *first* the kingdom of God and his righteousness is the key (Matt. 6:25–34). God's promise is that he will then "meet all your needs according to his glorious riches in Christ Jesus" (Phil. 4:19).

Have an appreciative and grateful heart. Gratitude means appreciating what you have rather than yearning for whatever you don't possess. It is saying, from the heart, "Dear God, what a wonderful life I lead. I feel blessed to be alive and to have so many conveniences that make my daily chores lighter. But most of all, I'm grateful and satisfied with my relationship with you." Are you grateful to God for your present circumstances? For a moment, think about the last time you prayed. How much of your prayer time did you spend thanking the Lord for his many blessings rather than asking him for something more?

Focus on today—not the past. It is *so* important to let go of the past—the ways we have failed, as well as the ways others have failed us. Receiving God's forgiveness freely and then graciously extending it to others depends entirely on *our* willingness to forgive and move ahead. When we live each day one day at a time, trusting God for the future and allowing him to handle the pain and injustices of the past, we pave a road to contentment. We commit ourselves to this attitude: Joy and contentment will *not* depend upon the circumstances of our day but on the dedication of our hearts to God.

Accept powerlessness. We have no control over many of life's circumstances. Finding a suitable remarriage partner may be one of them. But God opens new doors we cannot see. Certainly I didn't expect a sweet, spiritual young single mother in Ohio to call and invite me to lunch after she read *When the Vow Breaks.* In my entire life I never would have crossed her path if the Lord hadn't opened this door for us, but it happened when I least expected it *and* when I wasn't looking for it! Paul affirms, "Therefore I will boast all the more gladly about my weaknesses, so that Christ's power may rest on me. That is why, for Christ's sake, I delight in weaknesses, in insults, in hardships, in persecutions, in difficulties. For when I am weak, then I am strong" (2 Cor. 12:9b–10).

What is contentment? It's more than a feeling—it's an *attitude, mindset, discipline, dependence on God,* a *miracle!* Christian contentment is God-given *satisfaction* and *self-containment* with his loving provision in every situation. The contented Christian is peaceful, hopeful, thankful, generous, energetic, and has a *giving spirit.* But being content doesn't mean you lay back and take life easy either! We still have the responsibility to be part of the solutions to life's problems (such as finding a suitable remarriage partner). Ask God for direction. Expand your circle of friends, increasing your opportunities to meet potential partners. But check your motives. Are you involving yourself to get what you want or to represent and serve the Lord? To paraphrase Francis Schaeffer, love God enough to be contented while loving others enough not to envy and covet what they have that you don't.

"But I Haven't Dated in Years!"

A "Cathy" cartoon by cartoonist Cathy Guisewite shows a girlfriend quizzing Cathy on her readiness for marriage: "Are you available?" asks the friend. "Yes!" Cathy responds excitedly. "Open-minded?" "Yes!" "Confident?" "Yes!" "Interesting?" "Yes!" "Willing to give? Willing to share? Willing to try? Willing to learn? Willing to risk?" continues the friend. "Yes!" to all, Cathy replies. "Do you ever leave your home except to drive to the office?" "No," confesses a surprised Cathy. "You're hopeless," says the friend with a disgusted look as she marches off throwing away her list of questions.[4]

In another "Cathy" adventure, we find her marching up to her friend, boldly proclaiming: "I'm beautiful, bright, charming, talented and ready to share my life with someone, Charlene! I want to dream with someone . . . plan with someone. . . . I want to be there for someone, and I want someone to be there for me!" Charlene then perks up to say, "My husband has a really cute friend who . . ." but an exasperated Cathy interrupts: "AACK!! A *fix-up??* Are you out of your mind?? *No Fix-ups!!*" As Cathy walks away, she remarks, "I'm ready to be married. I'm not ready to date."[5]

Deciding to date and, hopefully, remarry is a good decision if you're ready for this relationship, but moving beyond this decision to building a relationship with a suitable partner requires *action*. It means meeting Christian people and spending quality time with them. Does this make you nervous or afraid? Perhaps you're saying, "I just don't know if I can do it after being married. I haven't dated in years!" Maybe if it is asking too much, you aren't ready for remarriage. But if you're experiencing the usual anxiety we all feel in being vulnerable as we reach out to others, then take heart! Some suggestions follow to keep you on track in finding a person suitable for you.

Work with the Lord. Unfortunately, Scripture doesn't give us specific guidance for dating. This is even more true for those dating after death or divorce of a spouse. Even so, we do see God's hand in leading people to each other. For example, God was active in opening the door for the servant of Abraham when he sought a wife for Isaac (Gen. 24). God was part of the process that brought Ruth (a widow) and Boaz together (Ruth 1–4). God was certainly involved when Esther married the king and, through that relationship, helped God's people (Esther 1:10). A careful reading of these accounts confirms that these people used personal responsibility in finding their mates. Abraham's servant traveled, prayed, spoke to Laban and Bethuel, and made decisions that positioned him where God could introduce him to Rebekah. Similarly, Ruth and Boaz took actions that eventually brought them together. Esther's obedient choices also resulted in marriage.

What can we learn from these examples? They tell us that God does act in our lives to provide us with opportunities to find suitable mates. He opens doors and offers choices. But we still have personal responsibility to pursue the opportunities God gives us and to be willing to do whatever is necessary to receive it. Above all, God expects us to listen for his guidance in Scripture and to use common sense. This means avoiding circumstances leading into sin or corruption of God's standards and values. To steer clear of trouble, associate only with other single individuals who share your faith and values.

Deal with guilt and fear. As you launch into new relationships, you may face one especially thorny matter: "survivor guilt" about dating. Some widowed individuals may feel dating is an unfaithful act against their deceased mates. Former Beatle Paul McCartney, whose first wife (Linda) died some years ago, talked about the struggles a widower feels in considering a new relationship. "I had all these questions," he explains, "like, 'Oh, my gosh, I've had a wife for thirty years. Is this allowed?' But I soon felt, yeah, it is. Actually what I felt was that if Linda was alive, I'd be dead meat. She'd kill me! No way would I be getting away with this. But I felt that if she was around, this wouldn't even be happening. But, as she wasn't, she would want me to be happy."[6]

If you experience survivor guilt about dating, review chapter 2 and the section on guilt. It's part of completing the grieving process. If you are widowed, or divorced with no hope of reconciliation and are scripturally free to remarry (see chap. 3), then trust in God. Forge ahead without guilt or shame when you're ready to remarry.

What about dating fears? "I'm too old—nobody will want me." "Can I make a new commitment?" After a divorce, finding a new partner also may rekindle memories of pain, rejection, and loss of personal identity. Put these fears to rest and trust God! Too old? There are more people over age fifty today than at any other time in history! Remembering the hurt, anger, and mistrust of a prior marriage partner before divorce? Learn to let go and look forward to a brighter future. Feeling defeated? Learn from your mistakes and move on with your life in God's wisdom and grace. As dramatist and poet William Moulton Marston observed, "Defeat strips away false values and makes you realize what you really want. It stops you from chasing butterflies and puts you to work digging gold."[7] Don't let yourself become a victim—take a chance again whenever you're ready.

What about the children? By January 2000, there were 12 million single-parent households in the U.S., according to the U.S. Census Bureau. Millions of those parents are dating. One common element among many of those dating millions is having fifty pounds and three feet of determined resistance—a child who wants you to stay home! NBC *Today Show* host Katie Couric, widowed for several years, recalls how her young daughter once told Couric's date that Couric was a "compulsive gambler" and that she "had gambled away all my college funds."[8] Dealing with children poses one of the most difficult scenarios faced by single-again parents. That resistance can sabotage a promising new relationship!

Children of single-again parents are naturally suspicious and jealous. Bridging the gap of resistance requires *both* the single parent and the dating partner reaching out to each child to affirm his/her worth and significance. How is this accomplished? Let's consider one good example.

Kurtis, the supermarket stock boy, decided to ask Brenda, the new checkout girl, for a date. "May I see you sometime when we're not working?" he asked politely. "That's really not possible," she declared. "I have two children at home and really can't afford a baby-sitter." Not to be outdone, he quickly countered, "How about if I pay for the baby-sitter?" Reluctantly, she accepted his offer for a date the following weekend.

When Saturday night came, he arrived at her door right on time and knocked. She greeted him at the door with a look of concern. "The baby-sitter called and canceled. I just can't go with you tonight." "Well," Kurtis added simply, "let's just take the kids with us!" "But you don't understand," she protested. After thinking for a moment, however, she decided to open her life up a little more. "Maybe you should meet my children. Maybe then you will see the reason."

Brenda had a cute older daughter. But then she brought out her son in . . . a wheelchair. He was born a paraplegic with Down's Syndrome. Kurtis was undeterred. "I still don't understand why the kids can't come with us." Brenda was amazed. Most men would run away from a woman with two kids—especially if one was disabled. (Her prior husband, the father of the kids, had done that.) But Kurtis and Brenda loaded up the kids for a wonderful evening of dinner and the movies. Whenever Brenda's son needed anything, Kurtis was right there to take care of him. When the boy needed to use the restroom, Kurtis gently lifted him out of his chair and carried him to the facilities. By the end of the evening, Brenda knew this man was someone she wanted to know better.

The relationship blossomed. Eventually they married and Kurtis adopted both children. Then they were blessed with two more children of their own. So what happened to the stock boy and the checkout girl? They became Mr. and Mrs. Kurt Warner of St. Louis. Kurt became the starting quarterback for the St. Louis Rams, leading them to multiple Super Bowls while being named the NFL's Most Valuable Player.[9]

Another way to bridge the gap of juvenile resistance is to help the *children* develop biblical love for others—including dating partners. Certainly single parents should delay introducing a potential suitor to the children prematurely. Exercising caution avoids potential rejection if the relationship doesn't work out. However, a dating partner doesn't need to be a stranger either! Gently including children helps them develop empathy for others, even as you calm their natural fears and anxieties.

Cheryl recalls one particular telephone call with me relatively early in our courting relationship. As she remembers it: "I was visibly grimacing as Warren described his bachelor meals of canned tuna and applesauce. As I hung up the phone, I lamented to Chase, 'Poor Mr. Warren.' Chase asked, 'What's wrong?' I looked at him with a sad expression. 'He has nothing good to eat at his house.' Chase felt empathy. He immediately went to our pantry and gathered a handful of each of his favorite treats—five marshmallows, a fruit roll, a sucker, a piece of chocolate, a graham cracker, and an oreo cookie—and put them in a plastic baggie. He asked me to mail everything to Mr. Warren so he could share with him." Cheryl began helping Chase work through any resistance he might have had against our budding relationship. She introduced him slowly to my lifestyle while also teaching him about the importance of sharing with others.

Should you engage in casual dating? Cartoonist Cathy Guisewite portrays Cathy's friend running down another dating checklist with her: "Blind date? Ick. Personal ad?

Ick. Dating service? Ick. Online chat room? Ick. Coffee shop? Ick. Gym? Ick. Singles group? Ick. Chance encounter while wandering around aimlessly? *Yes!* That has possibilities! *Yes!!"*[10] But how does this sound to *you?*

Casual dating has a flaw—it is temporary and doesn't emphasize *commitment.* Purely recreational and casual dating breeds disillusionment, inevitable breakups, and broken hearts. It often mistakes a physical relationship and emotional excitement for biblical love. It isolates a couple from other relationships. It tempts a couple—particularly those who are single again—into dissatisfaction with embracing singleness the way God intended. Casual dating is an artificial setting for testing another person's character and values. Too often it involves playing emotional games with others' feelings. The inevitable result of many instances of casual dating? Another broken relationship.

What about friendship, dating, and courtship? Because of the possible flaws of casual dating, many Christians are moving toward using friendship dating and old-fashioned *courtship.* Why? Because this process encourages men and women to develop (emotionally and spiritually) significant brother-sister friendships *first.*

• *What is friendship dating?* "Friendship dating" is going out socially with someone you already know fairly well from church or Christian family contacts—not a relative stranger. Dating a friend from church, for example, is an existing wholesome, God-honoring relationship. There is minimal pressure while considering personal readiness for remarriage. Many churches encourage reflection, prayer, and seeking the counsel of many competent spiritual advisors in guiding the couple to determine whether they are suitable for each other from a godly perspective. Brothers and sisters in Christ also help keep the couple focused on the truly important aspects of a dating relationship—*commitment* and *accountability* to God, each other, and the church.

In friendship dating, each partner asks lots of questions to evaluate his/her heart and motives: "Why do I want to be with this person more than others? Are there any issues I need to deal with personally first? Am I using this person to meet needs that only God can meet?" The goal is to evaluate and clarify the true direction of the relationship.

One very important question to ask is: "How do I   God about this person and a possible future together?" Seeking the Lord's leadership and guidance prompts each person to submit his/her heart, and decisions about each other, to him. The Lord provides a sense of proper timing if both persons' hearts yield to him.

If a couple mutually agrees that they have the Lord's blessing to continue the relationship after an adequate time of "friendship dating," they may prayerfully decide to begin courting each other.

• *What is courtship?* Courtship involves a time of deeper fellowship. When courting, the couple makes joint decisions and sets boundaries and limits. Before entering into a more committed relationship, they agree in advance to use self-control and live within scriptural limitations (although boundaries really should be in place before dating even begins). Courtship isn't a game of conquest or manipulation, but of request and mutual submission in seeking each other's greater good before the Lord.

Courtship fosters an opportunity for deeper communication and learning more about each other. It helps build a good and wholesome friendship grounded in confidence and trust. Courtship maintains sexual purity and establishes godly control of normal sexual attraction. Knowing that raw sexual attraction only masquerades as "love," limiting sexual temptation may mean avoiding too much time alone.

Courtship also promotes trustworthy behavior, sincere interest in the other's welfare, and good listening skills. Each partner learns to encourage and serve the other without smothering each other. It is interceding for one another in prayer together. As a courting relationship deepens, there is purposeful intimacy with integrity, leading a couple to engage themselves for marriage.

During courtship, the couple earnestly seeks the feedback and advice of family, friends, and Christian counselors. Asking others lots of questions usually reaps helpful insight: "What do you think about our relationship? Do you see any potential problems? Is there anything you would recommend that we could work on together? Do you have any reservations about us getting married someday? How can we parent our children during our courting period?" In every way, you seek what's best for you and your beloved—not just serving your own interests.

Above all, make sure that you give the relationship enough *time* to breathe and grow. We recommend *at least two years* from the time you begin "friendship dating" until the date of any remarriage, depending on your circumstances. Why two years? That period seems optimal to discover how you and your beloved bond. You need to experience a wide variety of situations and circumstances as you grow and adjust to each other. Dr. Neil Warren, author of *Finding the Love of Your Life*, counsels, "[I]t's crucial that you spend time with your spouse-to-be early in the morning and late at night; in heavy traffic and on country roads; in times of stress and easygoing moments. Observe him or her playing with children, doing household chores and balancing the checkbook." In addition, Dr. Warren cites researchers at Kansas State University, who completed an empirical study of the subject and found "a strong correlation between the length of time spent dating their current spouses and current marital satisfaction." They further found that "couples who had dated more than two years scored consistently high on marital satisfaction, while couples who had dated for shorter periods scored in a wide range from very high to very low."[11] The most important point here is that if a relationship doesn't stand the *test of time*, it may not be a good foundation for a remarriage lasting for the rest of your life. Don't rush!

Other ways to meet potential mates. Other options are available to meet prospective remarriage partners, although they may not be as reliable and rooted in biblical love and commitment as "friendship dating" and courting. Here are just a few:

• *Dating services.* Dating service agencies (some of them Christian) interview potential clients and conduct screenings (usually taking social security, driver's license, and work numbers to verify employment). They prepare client profiles by either videotaping clients or using staff members to interview candidates. These profiles form a database that matches clients according to their interests and expectations. The Bible doesn't say dating services are wrong. In fact, in Genesis 24 the servant of

Abraham essentially performed the same function. The servant received clear instructions (as would an agency), leading him to find a woman for Isaac (as a dating service would do for you). Isaac then decided to marry her (just as you would make the decision to date or deepen the relationship with someone you meet). It's not the dating service that matters most, but how you associate with them.

• *Internet contacts.* Many people, including Christians, are finding other interesting people on the Internet. The movie *You've Got Mail,* starring Tom Hanks and Meg Ryan, is a good example. Unfortunately, the Internet breeds similar hazards of romantic infatuation and casual dating. Relationships can evolve in a cyberworld of imagination safe from preconceptions. But imagination may take off in unhealthy ways. Only a few keystrokes separate truth from deceit. Still, the Internet does have its advantages—participants aren't swayed by looks, so they take the time to get to know each other, falling in love from the inside out. It also provides a quick and inexpensive way to communicate with an out-of-town prospective partner that expensive telephone calls and snail mail cannot match. Even so, many well-known safety risks exist in using the Internet— including deceitful introductions and chat rooms for cheating spouses. Be careful!

• *Personal ads.* Many Christians believe these aren't appropriate measures to find a suitable marriage partner. For one reason, the scope is much too broad. Ads invite too many different people from unknown backgrounds to come into your world without proper screening or social context. Responding to ads of others carries the same red flag. Remember, these messages are only ads—not affidavits. But the most important question is whether using such ads suggests desperation rather than contentment in God's providence. It is much better, and certainly less risky, to stay with the familiar—those you already know through church, family, and friends.

Let the Lord lead. In discussing dating options, we certainly don't mean to imply that you should have the mind-set, "Lord, I'm out here beating the bushes for a mate. When I find one suitable for me, please bless us." Obviously, this is backwards! Keep in step with the Holy Spirit as you meet others. There's a big difference between waiting with expectancy for the Lord to open some doors, and focusing on our own expectations. Seek the Lord's guidance through prayer and advice from competent counselors. Ask, "Lord, is this person someone with whom you want me to spend my life? What should I be doing? Show me your will for my life, and help me live it out today, trusting you for tomorrow. Help me be content and seek your wisdom and discernment." Let him lead in your dating life.

If you are in a serious courtship, within six months from the time you and your beloved first consider marriage you should receive some confirmation from the Lord as to whether the relationship is pleasing to him. If after six months you don't receive this confirmation, then perhaps it's best to move on—gently and with biblical love.

The Best Way to Find a Suitable Mate—Just Let Go!

Time after time you hear it: "I found the person who is right for me in marriage . . . when I stopped looking!" Kelly summed up her experience this way: "I had trouble finding a decent relationship. I spent a lot of time looking, dating the wrong men, and feeling sad, lonely, and left out. One day I realized I might *never* get married. I took a good, long look at my life and decided it wasn't so bad. I stopped yearning for what I didn't have and focused on what I did have, and concluded that I had more than most people. I filled my life with friends and fun activities. At one of those fun activities, I met the most wonderful man in the world. We were married two years later."

Certainly no one will tell you that you'll meet a remarriage partner suitable for you if you stop looking. You may not. But do you trust God to lead you into green pastures of a fulfilling and rewarding life no matter what happens? Stop worrying about all the "what ifs" and just *relax*. That instantly makes you more attractive to others! The Lord knows what you need, even before you ask him (Matt. 6:8)! If no prospective partner comes into your life, perhaps God believes the time isn't right or a relationship isn't suitable for you in your current circumstances. Be content enough to go with the flow of your life and just let the Lord lead. You may be surprised to find the person of your dreams revealed at the most unexpected time!

DATING CONCERNS FOR FORMERLY MARRIED CHRISTIANS

Dating again with a view toward remarriage is a mixed blessing of excitement, inconvenience, and discomfort. Here are a few suggestions:

Prepare yourself. More than anything else, this means wrapping you and your children in prayer and sensitizing your family to the Lord's direction. You're ready to date when your attention and focus are on the Lord and his will for yourself and your children. If you feel trapped in any way by the past and earlier relationships, you need to complete your recovery work, as outlined in part 1.

Prepare your children. Depending upon the age and maturity of each child, let each one know you will be spending time with certain people so they will not be overly concerned. Assure them no one will take their place. Accept the fact that there will be at least some jealousy and resistance and that your children may not be happy with your choices. Be honest with them, but you need not go into specifics—just say that you're "going out with friends." Also, use caution when expressing your feelings for a dating partner. Limit the time you spend with a dating partner while making sure not to ignore your children. Introduce change *gradually*. Always maintain a healthy sense of *balance* between your interests and those of your children, making sure the needs of your children always remain a high priority. Above all, it's wise to avoid introducing dating partners for any *extended* interaction with your children until after the relationship enters a serious courting stage. Try to arrange initial meetings on neutral ground—rather than the home—until everyone feels comfortable with each other.

Be warm, relaxed, and confident. If you enjoy your date's attention, let him/her know you are having a good time by being expressive and sincere in your conversation. Use humor, and laugh with your date. Be other-centered, focusing on your date's needs and interests. Be positive and encouraging. Remember that everything good will occur in God's timing, so you don't need to push or rush. Show your date that you are comfortable with yourself.

Act in a godly manner. Live and act in a pure way. Don't lie about yourself. Don't compromise your beliefs or allow yourself to be pressured into doing anything that would violate those beliefs. Reveal yourself slowly, guarding your heart. Be courteous and understanding. Take communication at your own pace. Above all, *pray* about how you will act with this person before you meet!

Make dates a meaningful experience. Encourage fluid conversation. Listen and pay attention to your date without being distracted. Be alert and responsive. Avoid dominating the conversation. Dating experts tell us there are three primary "conversation stoppers" on dates: (1) What do you do for a living? (2) Where do you live? and (3) Just how old are you anyway? Why? Because people often use these questions as excuses not to dig a little deeper and get to know someone better. Try more interesting questions, such as: "What is your idea of a great date?" "Where do you see yourself in three to four years from now?" "If your house was on fire, what would you take out and why?" A key is to get to know a potential partner on a deeper level, allowing both you and that person to be yourselves, before any automatic defenses kick in. You have to feel safe so you can be who you truly are. You also need reliable information about the other person.

Matters to avoid on dates:

• *Don't date to look for instant parents for your children.* Use friendship dating and courting to find someone suitable for *you,* as God guides you. Once you find that person, *then* you can move on to see how well that person will be able to coparent with you. Remember that the Lord faithfully serves as "a father to the fatherless . . . (and) sets the lonely in families" (Ps. 68:5–6). One of the primary goals of friendship dating and courting is to better discern God's will for a godly marriage partner, as well as a spiritual, sensitive, and compassionate stepparent to your children.

• *Avoid talking about problems.* Remember Paul's admonition in Philippians 4:8: "Finally, brothers, whatever is true, whatever is noble, whatever is right, whatever is pure, whatever is lovely, whatever is admirable—if anything is excellent or praiseworthy—think about such things." *Share* the blessings of life so you don't sound like a complainer.

• *Don't push the relationship.* Don't be too desperate to please. Don't interrogate your date. After all, a date shouldn't be a job interview. Most importantly, avoid making commitments you don't intend to keep throughout the relationship. The old adage, "What you do to get him, you will have to do to keep him" is true.

• *Don't wear your wedding ring.* If you're a widowed person, you may be wearing your wedding ring for sentimental reasons. If you're ready to date, take the ring off. It will be an uncomfortable distraction to those spending time with you. If this is too difficult an adjustment to make, then it would be wise to postpone dating until it's no longer a problem for you.

• *Limit discussion about former mates.* Don't tell your date that your deceased husband was a saint. Avoid talking about how your divorced ex-spouse created problems for you and your children. If the subject of past relationships comes up, be careful to tread lightly and avoid any negatives. The Lord wants us to love those who mistreat us and to speak well of others! Especially avoid gossip. As James warns us, "Consider what a great forest is set on fire by a small spark" (James 3:5). Instead, focus on your current life—what you are doing now and where you hope the Lord will lead you in the future. No one wants to listen to betrayal, misery, or anger on a date.

• *Avoid getting overly physical before remarriage.* It goes without saying that a Christian dating relationship should remain pure and holy for the entire term. As the relationship and intimacy grows, it's appropriate and good to express physical affection with restraint. But God expressly forbids engaging in sex before marriage (1 Cor. 6:12–20; Gal. 5:19–21; Rev. 21:8; 22:15). This is a *very* serious matter that should be avoided at all costs!

Don't let the "don'ts" of dating unduly upset you. The most important thing to do on a date is to *relax* and have good, wholesome fun in a spiritual context!

Now let's look at some ways we can miss the Lord's leading in dating relationships.

UNREALISTIC EXPECTATIONS AND ASSUMPTIONS— THE LIES THAT BIND

Many World War II marriages survived because the partners, even those who really didn't know each other well, had more realistic expectations of marriage. Today we demand that our spouses be our soulmates, best friends, and psychiatrists, and hold down a full-time job while looking like Heather Locklear or Tom Cruise. What an impossibly heavy burden! No wonder so many remarriages hit the rocks within months of the wedding, as pressures and disappointments escalate daily.

Personal expectations arise from our own perspective of what is good or bad— *not* God's. They run counter to "waiting expectantly" for the Lord's direction and provision. They breed a sense of entitlement—that we are "owed" fulfillment of our needs or desires by God or other people. Naturally, this sense of entitlement too often gives way to ingratitude. When we feel we aren't receiving our due, we get angry or resentful. Why? Because we aren't looking at what God *has* given us, and we ignore his blessings. Personal expectations not only are unrealistic, they're selfish!

What unrealistic expectations should we avoid before finding a suitable remarriage partner?

Thinking of ourselves more highly (or lowly) than we are. We shoot ourselves in the foot if we think, "I'm hot stuff! Someone would be crazy not to want me!" It is equally self-defeating to say, "I'm damaged goods from a failed marriage. I have nothing to offer." Both lies could bind you into isolation.

Having realistic expectations first comes from knowing who you are, appreciating the gifts and talents God gives you while being realistic about what you have to offer others. Newspaper columnist Diane White saw this vital task as being particularly difficult, in different ways, for men and women: "Women look in the mirror and see flaws; men look in the mirror and see why women find them so fascinating!"[12] I'm also reminded of the fable telling of how, in the Garden of Eden, Adam asked God, "Why did you make Eve so beautiful?" "To attract your attention," was his reply. "Why did you give her so sweet a personality?" "So you would love her." Adam thought about this for a while. "Why, then, did you make her so *dumb?*" "So she would love *you!*"

The apostle Paul said it succinctly: "For by the grace given me I say to every one of you: Do not think of yourself more highly than you ought, but rather think of yourself with sober judgment, in accordance with the measure of faith God has given you" (Rom. 12:3). Evaluate your own character, strengths, and weaknesses. Ask the Lord to help you humbly and realistically assess what you have to offer to prospective partners.

Expecting replacements for departed spouses. A "Bizarro" cartoon shows a young, blonde woman chatting with another woman at a party, with a green, Frankenstein-looking man standing by. "This is Frank, my fifth husband," she explains to her fellow guest. "He's a combination of all the best qualities of the first four."[13]

One who has lost a beloved spouse by death may think, "I only want to remarry if I know that he'll be as good and kind as Jack." Widows want a man to step into the sizeable shoes (which may still sit in the widow's closet!) of their loving husbands—mates perhaps idealized larger than life. For divorcees, the sentiment may be the opposite: "I only want to remarry if she *won't* be like Nancy!" Divorcees want major improvements over ex-spouses—perhaps an impossibly high standard for anyone to meet. In either instance, the former mate is the standard by which to measure and compare everything else.

It's vital that you let go of the past and consider new relationships with a clean slate. How can you see and evaluate prospective remarriage partners with God's eyes if you view someone through the dark glasses of preconceived expectations? Ask the Lord to give you renewed vision for *new* opportunities!

Wanting an ideal mate. Our favorite cartoon character, Cathy, earnestly types a personal ad on her computer as follows: "Fabulous woman seeks fabulous man. You must love women, but not be with one. . . . Love children, but not have any. . . . Love dogs, but not live with one. You must be a dynamic self-starter who waits for no one, yet simultaneously have your whole life on hold while waiting to meet me! Also, you should have impeccable taste, but no furniture, towels, or dishes yet." A friend looking over Cathy's shoulder can only shrug and say, "Very realistic!"[14]

Robert Schuman once remarked, "When I was a young man, I vowed never to marry until I found the ideal woman. Well, I found her—but alas, she was waiting for the ideal man!"

Scouting for an *ideal* mate presents more trouble than waiting for someone to replace your ex-spouse. The bar keeps rising to impossible heights. Scrap the notion of the idealized mate. Be open and receptive to whatever the Lord brings your way. Be aware that there are certain expectations on which you should *never* compromise. Look at suitable remarriage partners as God would—search for those enduring qualities of biblical love, maturity, good character, and integrity. Too many people "settle" for less because they are lonely or desperate.

Are you dismissing potential partners too quickly because of a tiny flaw? There may be a weird mannerism, a strange laugh, a wry sense of humor, or a minor personality flaw. Is that all it takes to think, "This person is weird!" Perhaps that little quirk will make that person special and lovable over time. Give God time to show you *his* view of this person. Be patient and dig deeper! Charles Dickens summed up this principle this way: "Estimate [a woman] by the qualities she has, and not by the qualities she may not have. This is marriage."[15] Find out about the person's *heart* and what he/she treasures in life before making judgments.

Changing our beloveds. One key quality to look for in a prospective mate is the ability to grow and change. Does he or she seek wisdom? Make adjustments based upon new information and changing circumstances? Receive feedback well? Although it's true that you really cannot change a relationship partner against their will and make it stick, you do want someone who is mature and flexible in all the right ways. The problem is that too often *we* want to *force* change on others. This simply won't work!

The only person you can really change with the Lord's help is *you.* The Lord may call you to love someone in *spite* of personal flaws. Can you accept your prospective partner the way he/she is now? If not, why not? This could be a signal that this person may be unsuitable for you.

Ignoring unequal yokes. Unequally yoked relationships are uneven mismatches between opposite personalities. Perhaps you find an interesting person who needs Christ and appoint yourself as conversion coach to pursue a "Christian relationship." Or one person wants to rescue and help a victim in a relationship between two very needy people. Or a fifty-year-old wants to remarry a twenty-year-old bride. What do these relationships spell? P-R-O-B-L-E-M-S!

The words are sadly familiar: "I married a nonbeliever because he promised me he would go to church with me after we married." But that didn't happen. Now this couple is unequally yoked spiritually. Why didn't this wife heed the warning? If he wasn't interested in getting right with God *before* the marriage, is it reasonable to assume he would do so after the wedding?

Just how critical is it that your beloved share your Christian faith? It is *essential* to avoid marriage problems later on. As the apostle Paul cautions, "Do not be yoked together with unbelievers. For what do righteousness and wickedness have in common? Or what fellowship can light have with darkness? . . . What does a believer have in common with an unbeliever? . . . As God has said: . . . 'Come out from them and be separate'" (2 Cor. 6:14–18).

Finding a genuine Christian remarriage partner should be one of your *highest* priorities. If not, you are binding yourself to a lie—chained to someone who doesn't love God and doesn't share your Christian values.

Overreliance on appearance. An interviewer asked former Beatle Paul McCartney about the floor-to-ceiling gold and platinum records on the wall in his London office. He wondered whether one could actually play the metallic discs. "Not anymore," McCartney laughed. "When the Beatles got their very first gold album, 'Please Please

Me,' they excitedly took it home and gave it a spin. It played all right," McCartney remembers, "but, much to our dismay, what we heard was the Rolling Stones!"[16] Sometimes we may accept others because they claim to be Christians, but what plays out in their lives is a worldly tune!

Another Paul—the apostle—warns us that Satan himself can masquerade as an angel of light (2 Cor. 11:13–14). How will we know the truth? Jesus tells us, "By their fruit" (Luke 6:43–45). *Listen* to how your partner speaks. Jesus tells us, "The evil man brings evil things out of the evil stored up in his heart. For out of the overflow of his heart his mouth speaks" (v. 45). Be sure you know who you're dealing with!

Jesus warns, "Stop judging by mere appearances, and make a right judgment" (John 7:24). Don't let physical appearances fool you. Looks fade. Be sure you know the whole person! And find someone close to your own age, since shared history and life experiences far outweigh surface features. As comedienne Phyllis Diller once observed, "Whatever you may look like, marry a man your own age—as your beauty fades, so will his eyesight!"[17]

Making unwarranted assumptions. Humorist Will Rogers hit the nail on the head: "It isn't what we don't know that gives us trouble; it's what we know that ain't so." It's *so* important to ask many questions and take a lot of *time* in building up a relationship before remarriage. Is your partner ready for remarriage? Has he/she really come to a point of healthy closure on a prior marriage? What is this person like while away from you? We can easily make incorrect assumptions based upon a person's best behavior while spending time with us. Find out the facts—and don't move forward in the relationship until you do!

Unwarranted assumptions about others can work the opposite way too. Just because someone appears to take an interest in you doesn't justify pursuing remarriage. Be sure to check out *why* people are warming up to you, and give them plenty of time to reveal the thoughts and attitudes of their hearts.

Overlooking family-of-origin influences. Another "Bizarro" cartoon shows a respectably suited man sitting next to his friend in a restaurant. "I'm bringing Liz home to meet my mother tonight," the man tells his friend. "You getting serious about her?" the friend asks. "No. I'm trying to run her off!"[18]

It's easy to underestimate the powerful impact that one's parents and extended family could have on your new blended family. If you're compatible with your partner, do you have the same level of comfort with his/her parents and siblings? After all, your partner's parents will become instant step-grandparents to your children. Do you see any problems or concerns there?

Cheryl's family and mine are very different. My family has close ties with each other . . . but not too close. When we were living in the same house, we were a lot like a group of porcupines huddled together to keep from freezing on a cold winter's day. If we got *too* close to each other, we would feel the prick of our quills and move apart. But if we moved too far away, our need for family warmth nudged us back together. Back and forth we'd go until finding the optimal separation to provide maximum warmth with a minimal amount of quill stab pain.

In contrast, Cheryl's family (the Rybkas) is a large Polish/Italian clan. They absolutely *love* being together! Mom and Dad Rybka welcome all six children, with scores of grandchildren in tow, for extended visits in their home. They even take them on fabulous vacations. Family members sleep everywhere in the Rybka home. They eat together, play games, and stay up late talking and laughing together. I kid Cheryl that her family is like a herd of gerbils, flopped over each other in a cage corner for the night after chasing each other around the wheel and water bottle all day!

We often choose partners who somewhat remind us of significant family members, or even ex-spouses. And we often carry into a remarriage all the baggage associated with those people. Result? We can find ourselves caught up in the same problems plaguing those earlier relationships! Pray for the Lord to reveal choice or behavior patterns that spell trouble.

Origin influences don't end at home either. Most of us grow up with people of similar social circumstances. We hang around with folks from the same town. We have friends with the same educational backgrounds and career goals. And, of course, relationships and fellowship in a local church can rival family ties many times. Since we're most comfortable with these familiar folks, we may want relationships with those whose families are much like our own. All these influences shape our beliefs and behaviors more than we know, deeply affecting the expectations we have for each other.

As you date others, part of being content and waiting on the Lord is not having false hopes or unrealistic expectations. Prepare yourself. Expect disappointments and letdowns—even *plan* for them if you can.

Now let's get even more specific about what to watch out for in order not to remarry the wrong person.

YOUR RELATIONSHIP EARLY WARNING SYSTEM— SEVEN CRITICAL "STOP SIGNS"

Real estate executive Donald Trump may have his faults, but he does know how to evaluate offers and propositions. "Experience taught me a few things. One is to listen to your gut, no matter how good something sounds on paper. The second is that you're generally better off sticking with what you know. And the third is that sometimes your best investments are the ones you don't make."[19] Before you invest your future, and that of your children, into a remarriage partnership with your beloved, *watch* and *listen* very carefully. Be sure you know who and what you're dealing with. If you have any reasonable doubts about your beloved, or nagging uncertainties about your relationship, perhaps, like Trump, the best investment of your life would be to pass on the relationship and wait for God's best.

There truly is nothing worse than marrying the wrong person for the wrong reasons. Here are a few relationship "stop signs" the Lord may use to say, "This relationship isn't suitable for you":

1. *Rushed or blind "love."* You know from experience that recovering from death or divorce of a spouse takes a *lot* of time and healing. So what does that tell you about

someone who is only months out of a prior marriage and now wants to remarry you? Love on a quick rebound is a stop sign—don't ignore it! Like a teenager, you also may experience a blind, romantic "puppy love" for someone that clouds your judgment. Test yourself and the relationship. See if the signs point more toward romantic infatuation than biblical love.

2. *Excessive loneliness, immaturity, self-pity, or defensiveness.* If your love interest retreated from society and lived a sheltered life after a prior marriage ended, will he/she be ready, willing, and able to actively interact with you and your children? Is your partner mature enough to be a spouse and a parent? If he/she is impatient and doesn't consider the consequences of impetuous decisions, these tendencies will carry over into any remarriage. Remarriage and blended family situations are much too complex for the immature to handle.

If you find yourself feeling sorry for your partner, or vice-versa, this also isn't a healthy basis for a relationship. While it's nice to feel needed, if your partner is too emotionally dependent upon you, trying to fill his/her needs will wear you down over time. A problem also exists if your partner never takes responsibility for whatever goes wrong and blames everything on others. Like lies, accusations and self-justification indicate bigger spiritual problems. If your partner spends an entire evening out detailing how he/she was wronged by an ex-spouse, a boss, a parent, or others, pick up the check and check out of the relationship quickly.

3. *Possessive control and abusive behavior.* Does your partner "advise" you on ways to change yourself so you'll be "more acceptable" to her and her family and friends? Does he frequently criticize, correct, or try to "fix" you?

Sara gives us this revealing look at control and possessiveness: "I first met my husband at a party. He told me his name, and made me spell it to make sure I would remember it. He asked if I wanted a drink. When I said, 'I'd like a milkshake,' he told me I would have to stop eating high-calorie foods if I wanted to hold his interest. He then asked how late he could call me. I said, '10 P.M.' He called at 1 A.M. After we started to date, he insisted we cut back on visiting my parents and friends. They were 'boring.' Before I met his parents for the first time, he gave me orders: 'Don't wear your best outfit. I don't want them to think you are extravagant or vain about your appearance, or clothes-crazy.' When things turned serious and he asked me to marry him, I said I would love to have an engagement ring. He said, 'Engagement rings don't mean anything. They are just pieces of jewelry that women like to show off.'" Here's a picture of an emotional abuser. When an abuser successfully flatters someone, the abuser rides on that flattery to become overbearing. If the flattery catches one's heart, the victim hangs on to the abuser for fear of rejection and being alone. *Run!* This definitely is *trouble!*

Does your partner pressure you to do things against your will? Is there a persistent interest in sexual matters prior to marriage? These pressures could increase and create multiple problems for you and your children! How does your partner communicate with waiters and service people? Do you witness judgmental, critical, demanding, unforgiving, insensitive behavior? While driving, does he call other people "jerks, morons, and idiots"? *You* could be on the receiving end in the future! If your partner doesn't get along with parents, siblings, neighbors, or people at work—watch out!

After decades of dealing with relationship problems and misunderstandings, columnist Abigail Van Buren is convinced that the best indications of a person's character are: how he treats people who can't do him any good and how he treats people who can't fight back. If you find your partner using a double standard in how he treats you and how he treats others, beware!

Above all, *never* continue a relationship with a person who threatens, hits, or humiliates you or your children, no matter how many other good qualities the person may have.

4. *Unhealthy personality types.* If you experience trouble with your partner's personality, such as jealousy, temper, stubbornness, lying, moodiness, regular unhappiness, or lack of dependability, ask yourself whether you want to spend the rest of your life coping with these problems. Some people are so absorbed in themselves and their lifestyles that their entire personality becomes a red flag:

• *The Religious Fanatic.* Winston Churchill once remarked, "A fanatic is one who can't change his mind and won't change the subject." We're not talking about serious, evangelical believers or those having legitimate religious differences. These are the fanatics—those excessively legalistic and dogmatic religionists who really don't care as much about pleasing God as they do about making their own rules and distorting Scripture. They feed their own selfish needs by manipulating others in the name of religion.

Abusers of Christianity will tell unsuspecting partners in a relationship, "God wants you to marry me—he meant it to be!" But this is only a cover for their own manipulation and control. Don't take their word for it or let them take God's place! Check out the Scriptures, pray, and seek the counsel of many advisors before going further.

• *The Dominant Dictator.* A dictator personality is a classic perfectionist or control freak. They are dominant people who love making decisions for themselves—and others! Initially they may seek to control the friends you can see and how you spend your money. This control becomes pervasive as the relationship grows.

Dominant dictators love being around passive people who admire and follow their "leadership." They secretly fear weakness, so they are know-it-alls who must always be right about everything. They must be in control of their own destiny since they don't trust God or any spouse to look out for them. Be forewarned: dictators are preset to behave in ways that will eventually degrade and humiliate their partners emotionally, socially, and sexually while robbing them of dignity and worth.

• *The Dependent Doormat.* This passive person may be the single-again woman who comfortably let her deceased husband take care of the finances and all important marital decisions, but who now experiences a deep void with the loss of her spouse. There is "no one to take care of her." This person quickly becomes infatuated with anyone powerful who will "tell her what to do." She wants a man to rescue her and take control of her life. (Of course, this happens to men too! Weak men often look for "mamas.") A "yes, dear" dependent doormat lacks confidence, direction, and strength and avoids conflict at all cost. Doormats crave a dominating personality because they fear making decisions for themselves.

• *The Selfish Saint.* Selfishness is fairly obvious early in most relationships. Those who are thoroughly acclimated to thinking only of themselves tend to tip their hands early. But the selfish saint is more subtle due to masking his/her motives and hiding behind seemingly charitable acts of kindness. This might be the divorced single father so busy working at church or "doing God's work" that he neglects his children. But selfishness is selfishness, obvious or not. There's no room for sensitivity or caring for others. Every decision first hinges on one question, "How will this affect *me?*"

• *The Responsible Rescuer.* Rescuers live to supply the needs and meet the demands of others while making their own needs invisible. Their relationships wrap themselves around the weaknesses of others in a codependent manner. They assume responsibility for others in need for two primary reasons—to protect them from themselves and to take control of others' lives. In some ways they are like benevolent dictators as they overtly and covertly make decisions for their wards. But because of the significant control issues, they really don't help those they deal with.

Outwardly, these servants have a Christlike quality of seeking out others and wanting to meet their needs, but the motivation is fear and weakness rather than love and conviction. They fear rejection, thus working hard to meet the needs of others struggling with problems. Unfortunately, they lose touch with their true identities. The rescuer is so intent on helping and "fixing" others that the person's *own* needs get lost in the process—ignoring the vitally important first phrase in Philippians 2:4.

• *The People Pleaser.* Remember the comedy *Mrs. Doubtfire* with Robin Williams and Sally Fields? When the movie begins, their characters are married with three children. Williams, however, is the man-child who indulges his kids with a barrage of junk food, crazy antics, loud music, and twenty-four-hour entertainment. The kids love it! But the movie reveals how this act quickly wears thin on his responsible and sensible wife, played by Fields. She hates parenting *four* children—husband included! Eventually she gets fed up and divorces him. The rest of the movie details the extreme lengths Williams's ostracized character invents to be one of the kids again. A people pleaser might be the fun-loving father with a gang of kids from a deceased wife. He wants to find a mate to join the gang. In reality, he's looking for a mother to take care of everyone. These folks may care more about how they appear to others than how they please God!

5. *Poor communication.* Does your partner carefully listen to you and show genuine concern for your feelings, or just brush you off? Does your partner really seem to understand how you feel, or just go through the motions to appease you? Is your partner judgmental and accusatory so you cannot tell him/her what you're really feeling? Does your partner shut down the conversation or leave you whenever negative feelings or conflicts arise? This type of conduct obviously isn't the way to begin any remarriage.

6. *Inadequate conflict-resolution skills.* Researchers confirm there are two primary "marriage killers": unrealistic expectations and inadequate conflict-resolution skills.

The ability to talk about problems and to resolve them in a biblical manner is as important as how much the couple loves each other. If you and your partner disagree about too many issues, and especially if you even disagree about how to *resolve* your disagreements, then the relationship is failing early. This isn't a good sign. Do you and your partner avoid conflict? Blow up at each other? Manipulate with guilt? A controlling person eventually will control you. Conflicts like these may be beyond resolution! Fervently pray for God's guidance.

7. *Serious problems with children and extended family.* Is your partner ready, willing, and able to interact with and love your children? These relationships are as important to the success of any remarriage as your partner's relationship with you. "I really don't have any interest in being a father to your children. I've already raised my children, and am not looking to do it again." If your partner is honest enough to say it, how will you handle these remarks? If your partner has children, do you want to "marry" them too? They'll be part of the package. And, of course, these children always will be a direct link to your partner's ex-spouse. If you and your partner cannot accept and love each other's children, do your kids (and yourselves) a favor—*stop!*

Have you met your partner's family, friends, and coworkers? If your partner has kept them hidden, this is a red flag. Perhaps your partner doesn't want you to get involved with people who know him/her best. Does your partner disrespect his/her family members or yours? Is there excessive devotion to one's family that might interfere with your relationship with your partner? If your partner is devoted to a parent and that parent isn't very fond of you, problems may be unavoidable. Is there a "fantasy bond" where your partner holds the illusion that you resemble a former mate or parent? Do you see any relationship problems in the extended family that might adversely impact you and your children? Use caution!

Red flags like these are *stop* signs! They should stop you in your relationship well before you consider remarriage. This isn't always easy to determine or do. As David Russell once observed, "The hardest thing in life to learn is which bridge to cross and which to burn." This is why testing the relationship over time and seeking the counsel of many advisors are so crucial to your prayerful decision.

Some relationships may have no outward "red flags." Even so, our partners may not be good remarriage candidates for us—not because they are unlovable but because they aren't suitable to our personalities or don't meet our needs (or those of our children).

It's also important that we add a note about judgment here as well. A divorcee may fear abandonment in a remarriage, which leads to a controlling and jealous nature. This may only be a temporary condition due to that person's wounded and unhealed heart. Still, remarriage calls for two *whole and healed hearts.* Lovingly move on to those with healed hearts without judging the wounds in those left behind. Our point in addressing "stop signs" isn't to judge others, but merely to recognize wounded hearts that need the Lord's healing *outside* of any remarriage affecting you and your children.

Give yourself adequate time to review, assess, and pray about your relationships. This is the most vital prerequisite to making a right decision. Your judgment cannot be better than the information on which you base it. Get the facts, be compassionate and loving, but don't ignore the stop signs! Listen for God's still, small voice in your heart. Also, don't compromise your values and beliefs for the privilege of keeping a questionable relationship. To paraphrase former President Dwight D. Eisenhower, someone who values the *privileges* of a relationship above its *principles* soon loses both!

Above all, don't feel bad about ending a relationship (or having it end for you). Humorist Robert Henry remarks, "Don't ever be afraid to admit you were wrong. It's like saying you're wiser today than you were yesterday."[20] Use your experience with prior relationships to your advantage. Rejection sometimes is God's way of keeping two people apart who shouldn't be together.

HOW DO YOU RECOGNIZE A SUITABLE REMARRIAGE PARTNER?

Many Christians believe that God's will for their lives is very specific—including one right marriage partner selected for them by the Lord. Of course this belief becomes more problematic for those considering remarriage. Was the prior spouse the "right one" or the "wrong one"? Will your remarriage partner now be the "right one"?

We need to weigh this belief carefully against Scripture in the context of marriage. What happens when the couple faces inevitable difficulty in marriage? Will they begin to question whether they made the right decision in remarriage? This leads to serious problems that compound as time goes on. Doubts may lead a spouse to rationalize divorce because he/she married the "wrong person."

Other Christians believe God provides general biblical guidelines for our decisions, with the expectation that we make wise decisions of our own using these biblical principles. And so our sovereign God graciously provides us with many options and choices in life—including multiple persons who might be suitable remarriage partners for us. I believe this is the most scripturally consistent position, which is why we've gone into such detail in this chapter with checklists of qualities to look for (and avoid) in a suitable remarriage partner.

So how can you know when you find one of those suitable remarriage partners? Godly remarriage candidates share many of the following characteristics:

They are wholeheartedly devoted to God. You can tell because of the focus of their conversation and action in their lives. They are consistently, intelligently, and without reservation serving the Lord with all of their hearts, minds, souls, and strength. God tops every priority list in their lives. And they desire spiritual priorities in life (Matt. 6:33; 2 Cor. 7:1; Eph. 5:15–20). Not only are they spiritual people but they are spiritually related to you through Christ by being Christians.

They thrive on biblical love. They know it, show it, and grow it in their lives.

They embrace commitment. Director George Lucas spoke about his famous *Star Wars* series when he said it, but the same principles apply to those who understand the nature of commitment: "You have to find something that you love enough to be able to take risks, jump over the hurdles, and break through the brick walls that are always going to be placed in front of you. If you don't have that kind of feeling for what it is you're doing, you'll stop at the first giant hurdle."[21] This is just a small picture of the commitment Christians are willing to make to God and to their spouses and family in remarriage. Commitment like this continues even when disease or old age comes. Truly committed spouses desire to stand by their mates in sickness and in health.

They model consistent integrity, character, maturity, and experience. They consistently act lovingly with grace and poise—when they're competing in groups, have a flat tire, lose their money, or suffer stress from work or family obligations. They are responsible, mature, and self-disciplined persons (Prov. 23:20–21, 29–35; Gal. 5:22–26; 2 Pet. 1:5–9). Adlai Stevenson astutely noted, "A sign of maturity is accepting deferred gratification." These individuals know how to exercise self-control and restraint in dealing with the sins of the flesh. They believe Christian character is essential for godly families, and they consistently live out that belief *daily* (Prov. 16:3; 1 Cor. 15:58; 1 Thess. 5:16–28).

They value friendship. Great remarriage candidates don't sacrifice the real "glue" of any relationship—friendship between partners—for the sake of romance or privileges with another person. They value the worth and significance of the person first before seeing their partners as love interests.

They can communicate. They know that listening, talking, and being responsive to the wishes of others is extremely important in remarriage and a blended family (Prov. 15:1; 16:18; 20:5). You can talk to them about almost anything without fear of judgment or a put-down.

They appreciate others. One of the greatest acts of love is attentiveness. This leads to empathy, understanding, and appreciation. Even the iconoclast Voltaire acknowledged, "Appreciation is a wonderful thing; it makes what is excellent in others belong to us as well."

They desire emotional intimacy. Intimacy dwells in almost every quality marriage, but it is almost always absent from terminal marriages. Intimacy is sharing our lives and allowing the Lord to weave us together at the deepest levels of our existence. Great remarriage candidates yearn for a deeper spiritual and emotional intimacy with their partners.

They are peacemakers. Great remarriage candidates put into practice the principles of conflict resolution that Jesus set out for us in Matthew 5:23–26 and 18:15–17. They know how to manage anger with the Lord's help (Prov. 14:17, 29; 15:18; Eph. 4:26; James 1:19–20). They are slow to anger and quick to rid themselves of it before it wounds anyone.

They quickly forgive. They know marriages fail where there is no forgiving attitude (Prov. 24:17; Matt. 5:7; 6:14–15; Eph. 4:32).

They love children. They are compassionate and loving while being good role models for children—even if children may not be a part of the remarriage.

They are graciously flexible. My parents' former housekeeper, Olis, is a bright and joyful soul, and a pleasure to be with. But the family chuckled whenever lunchtime came because she was very particular about her meals. Many times we would ask her,

"Olis, what would you like to have for lunch?" She would reply with a smile, "Oh, just anything will do!" We then offered a number of menu items for her approval, always ending with her telling us, "Oh, I can't eat *that!*" After a time we discovered that what Olis really wanted was fried chicken without skin and a Twix bar!

Great remarriage candidates have no hidden agendas. They are willing and dedicated to thinking about the needs of others first, above their own needs. They are not rigid and inflexible. Instead, they want to do whatever is reasonably necessary to make the relationship *work*. Actress Carrie Fisher, a divorcee, once observed: "If you want to work out a relationship, everything is negotiable. If you don't, everything is a door."[22]

They know how to laugh. Research confirms that appreciating good clean humor, and being able to laugh about the ups and downs of daily life with a partner is one of the top five qualities most everyone wants in a mate. Without it, life in any marriage— and particularly a remarriage with a blended family—can become burdensome and dreary.

They learn the song in the hearts of their beloveds. Arne Garborg observed, "To love a person is to learn the song that is in their heart, and to sing it to them when they have forgotten." Great remarriage candidates are *encouragers* and *healers*. They keep hope alive. They capture the fire of their beloveds' vision and dreams and heat them up more! They truly want their partners to succeed, and they rejoice greatly when they do!

They are soulmates. The bottom line is that you really don't have to select someone to marry. When you meet the "right one," your lives just fall into step with each other because you are fit and suitable for one another. Each of you has a life to *share* with each other, not *tame*. You are willing to make genuine personal sacrifices—one of the best litmus tests of any relationship. If your partner has a 6:30 A.M. flight, you gladly offer a ride to the airport. You are willing to bend for the sake of the relationship.

You and your beloved can talk, listen, read each other's body language, encourage, nurture, and fight fairly. You respect, cherish, and trust each other. You feel romantic about each other much of the time, but also experience a comfort and contentedness with one another. It is paradoxically feeling both vulnerable and powerful at the same time. You know all the tiny details of your beloved's life—the ones that would be insignificant to anyone else. Each interesting insight brings deeper fascination. You can't stop talking to each other, and never go two or three days without touching base with each other. There's a special intimacy between you that's uniquely personal and private. Your souls are being knit together in harmony and peace at the deepest levels of your existence.

Above all, you and your beloved *agree* on the kind of remarriage you want, and you *accept* one another as Christ accepts both of you. Both of you know that remarriage is, and always will be, a work in progress that requires constant attention to keep it from going dry.

Godly people want mates who will challenge them to depend upon God rather than trying to control them or other people. They seek those who truly feel compassion for others in ways that the seekers haven't fully experienced in their walk with the

Lord. They desire mates who will challenge their thinking and stretch their perceptions and life experiences in ways that will deeply *unite* them with God and their mates.

Strong, godly relationships are built on communication, appropriate boundaries, biblical conflict resolution, and with remarriage, a lifetime commitment. But more work is still necessary to test whether a relationship is ready for remarriage. It comes from getting valuable feedback and insight from objective third-party sources.

SEEKING OBJECTIVE OPINIONS: PREMARITAL EDUCATION AND EVALUATION

There are some excellent resources available to help you double-check your evaluation of your relationship with your beloved. Consider some of the following options:

Premarital inventory evaluation. Hundreds of thousands of couples each year take a premarital inventory evaluation test called PREPARE.[23] With astonishing accuracy—most years more than 70 percent—these tests predict which couples are most at risk of divorce. They perform an "X ray" of the couple's strengths and weaknesses, isolating how each person gives—positively and negatively—to the relationship.

Cheryl and I participated in the PREPARE-MC evaluation (for unmarried couples with children) at a local church a year before we married. Our evaluation showed we had great strength in children and parenting, religious orientation, conflict resolution, financial management, sexual relationship issues, and family adaptability and cohesion. We were about even in personality issues, leisure activities, and egalitarian roles. Our report alerted us to the need for better communication and being more realistic about the demands and difficulties facing us in remarriage and blended family life. (Perhaps that's why throughout this book we stress the need to have realistic expectations and good communication!)

Our report also revealed that we shared leadership in stable roles, using "somewhat democratic" discipline while changing and adapting when necessary. Cheryl had a strong "we" focus on the relationship, very high closeness and loyalty scores, with above-average dependency. I had a more "I–we" view with moderate-to-high closeness, high loyalty, and a more interdependent outlook. As a couple, we shared very similar strengths and weaknesses, with above-average cohesion and more structured relationship roles. While not determining our decision to marry, this encouraging evaluation helped identify areas where we needed to grow before we remarried.

Mentor couples. Whenever you go scuba or skin diving, the cardinal rule is that you always use a buddy to help you in times of trouble. Couples facing remarriage benefit from "buddy couples" or mentors.

What is a mentor? Some describe this person as "a brain to pick, an ear to listen, and a push in the right direction." The Uncommon Individual Foundation, a mentor research and training organization, reports that mentoring is the third most powerful relationship for influencing human behavior after marriage itself and the extended family.

A young pianist once approached the master Leonard Bernstein, asking to be mentored by him. Bernstein told the young man, "Tell me what you want to do, and I will tell you whether or not you're doing it." Bernstein's message? You're responsible for playing and practice, but you may not be able to hear yourself play as a great pianist would. I can do that for you. Then mentor and apprentice compare notes. That's the essence of a mentor relationship.

Compare notes and tap into the wisdom and experience of a mature Christian couple in a successful marriage. They can help you steer through the maze of challenges and opportunities in remarriage and a blended family. Trial-and-error is one way to gain experience, but learning successful skills through a mentoring couple and adapting their ideas to one's own situation is a lot smarter. Consulting like this quickly highlights what works, and what doesn't, in critical areas.

A pattern for mentoring comes from Jesus Christ, but mentoring differs from discipling. Those who disciple others seek to convince the discipled to adopt the discipler's viewpoint and manner. A mentor seeks to encourage more than persuade, without monitoring or controlling the apprentice or seeking to clone the apprentice. Mentoring couples serve apprentice couples as: (1) spiritual guides, providing direction to bring God into the relationship more; (2) teacher/counselor/consultants, giving specific suggestions on how to work out their own relationship; 3) coach/cheerleaders, to listen and encourage; and (4) role models, showing how good things come together in marriage. Mentor couples always seek to bring out the best in apprentice couples rather than training them in specifics.

When Cheryl and I began courting each other, we spent a lot of time with Kieth and Diane Mitchell—Christian counselors married for several decades while raising four children (including an adopted son). Whenever Cheryl visited me in Miami, she'd stay with the Mitchells (who have known me for more than twenty years). I encouraged Kieth and Diane to be very candid and detailed in sharing their evaluation of my good and bad qualities so Cheryl could then develop an informed opinion about whether we were suitable. (I must admit that after having her first lengthy discussion with the Mitchells, she came out with a rather stunned expression on her face! But fortunately she worked through whatever information she received to marry me anyway!)

Cheryl and I received wise counsel from the Mitchells as we came closer to remarriage. What tremendously helpful mentors they were for us—and continue to be! Kieth, also a minister and church elder, even officiated at our wedding!

What couple facing remarriage couldn't use a "brain to pick, an ear to listen, and a push in the right direction"? Find a strong Christian couple with a good track record of success to serve as mentors to you and your beloved. You'll emerge well prepared for remarriage.

Marriage seminars and conferences. Many excellent marriage—and premarriage—Christian seminars, workshops, and other resources are available to those considering remarriage. Among these is Marriage Savers, cofounded by Michael J. McManus of Potomac, Maryland, and author of *Marriage Savers: Helping Your Friends and Family Avoid Divorce.*[24] Dr. Willard F. Harley Jr.'s organization, Marriage Builders, offers an excellent "Marriage Builders Weekend" seminar around the country.[25] Family Life of Little Rock, Arkansas, overseen by noted author and counselor Dennis Rainey, began its ministry to families throughout America in 1976. This organization provides FamilyLife Marriage Conferences and a special "Weekend to Remember" seminar in major cities all over the country each year—excellent seminars helping couples plan for and work through marriage issues.[26] (Before we remarried, Cheryl and I committed to attending at least one Christian marriage conference each year. Our first was the "Weekend to Remember," which we highly recommend to you!)

Focus on the Family ministries, begun by Dr. James Dobson, also offers many excellent resources for couples considering marriage. Cheryl and I are so grateful this powerful ministry helps so many couples prepare for solid, biblical marriages while thoroughly equipping them for a lifetime together!

Of course many local churches across the country have good premarital courses. For example, First Baptist Church of Fort Lauderdale has counselors teaching personal finance, parenting skills, and conflict resolution in an eight-week course for individuals considering marriage. Catholic couples also must undergo a rigorous premarital education course and testing in their local parishes.[27]

There's no shortage of excellent Christ-centered and good secular materials available for couples serious about preparing for remarriage with a suitable partner. But of all these options and resources, nothing is so valuable and revealing as receiving premarital counseling from a competent Christian counselor. Counselors can minister to you and your beloved on the deepest levels based upon your particular circumstances.

THE BEST PREMARRIAGE PREPARATION: COMPETENT CHRISTIAN COUNSELING

It's easy to fool yourself as you fall in love with someone who seems like the "perfect partner." You and your beloved spend countless hours getting acquainted over many months, or perhaps even years, of quality personal time. Why bother with the time and expense of premarital counseling? Quite simply, as Dr. James Dobson affirms, "Premarital counseling is a must and can literally be a marriage-saver."

As Dr. Dobson correctly points out:

The typical couple spends much time talking. . . . Still, they don't know each other as well as they think they do. That is because a dating relationship is designed to conceal information, not reveal it. Each partner puts his or her best foot forward, hiding embarrassing facts, habits, flaws, and temperaments. Consequently, the bride and groom often enter into marriage with an array of private assumptions about life after the wedding. Then major conflict occurs a few weeks later when they discover they have radically different views on nonnegotiable issues. The stage is then set for arguments and hurt feelings that were never anticipated during courtship. That's why I strongly believe in the value of solid, Bible-based premarital counseling. *Each engaged*

couple, even those who seem perfectly suited for one another, should par-
ticipate in at least six to ten meetings with someone who is trained to help
them prepare for marriage. The primary purpose of these encounters is
to identify the assumptions each partner holds, and to work through
the areas of potential conflict.[28] (emphasis added)

Who is the best counselor? Of course nothing can ever replace the confidence of
relying upon God's wisdom in the Bible. The psalmist wrote, "Your statutes are my
delight; they are my counselors. . . . I have more insight than all of my teachers, for
I meditate on your statutes" (Ps. 119:24, 99). In Isaiah, the prophesy of the coming of
Jesus Christ describes him as "Wonderful Counselor." In promising the Holy Spirit,
Jesus said: "And I will ask the Father, and he will give you another Counselor to be
with you forever—the Spirit of truth" (John 14:16–17). Second Peter 1:20–21 tells us
that Scripture doesn't have its origin in the will of man, but men spoke from God as
the Holy Spirit moved them. "All Scripture is God breathed and is useful for teaching,
rebuking, correcting and training in righteousness, so that the man of God may be
thoroughly equipped for every good work" (2 Tim. 3:16). As a Christian, these verses
tell me that wise counsel first comes from the Lord in the Bible.

From the very beginning God's intent has been that *he* be your primary counselor. He will be your first source of problem diagnosis. Insight into options and alternatives, and guidance in making the right decisions, will be most reliable coming from
the one who loves you the most. Through Scripture and prayer, God can give you
guidance about a prospective remarriage partner, as well as a competent marriage
counselor to help you in your remarriage decision.

Qualities to look for in a marriage counselor. Marriage counselors aren't miracle
workers or prophets who foretell which relationships last. Even those sensitive to biblical concepts in counseling make mistakes. But be wary of those who promise more
than they can deliver. Here are some qualities any counselor should have:

• *Faithful Christian, knowledgeable about God's Word.* You may be able to find
many admirable qualities in a qualified secular counselor, but he/she won't be able to
counsel you on vital spiritual aspects of your relationship. Therefore, seek a competent, spiritual Christian counselor. Settle for an experienced secular counselor who
takes marriage seriously only if you find no Christian counselors.

• *Good communicator.* Careful listening is critical to the success of the counseling
process. The counselor hears everyone out, not giving decisions like a judge, but clar-
ifying issues so the couple can arrive at their own conclusions.

• *Married.* You wouldn't go to your pastor for guidance on filing your income tax
or to a financial consultant for advice about your marriage, so why go to an unmarried counselor for advice on building a good marriage? Ideally, the counselor will be
familiar with the many issues and challenges of remarriage and blended families as
well.

• *Strongly empathetic.* There is a significant difference between *empathy* and *sympathy.* Empathy focuses on understanding the hurts and problems of the people
involved. The counselor's participation in feelings of clients allows him/her to see

matters as they do, without losing objectivity or the goal of healthy problem solving. Sympathy, however, focuses too much on feeling the pain without understanding its origin. Sympathy isn't objective, but subjective. The best counselors are like harpists. A harpist's fingers become callused so they don't bleed in stroking the strings, yet they remain sensitive enough to feel the special qualities of each string. So the counselor strikes a balance: caring for others, but without falling apart in difficult circumstances.

• *Neutral and impartial.* Few counselors are completely immune from favoring one partner over the other. The counselor can, and should, help the couple clarify issues and correct destructive or inappropriate behaviors. But the fate of the relationship rests with the couple alone. Sometimes counselors temporarily align with one partner to help the counseling process, but the best counselor resists manipulation while consistently facilitating the couple's understanding of issues and goals in the relationship. The couple then determines what's best. A good counselor patiently respects every ambivalence, point of indecision, and procrastination, waiting until clients reach personal catharsis and resolve to take action.

• *Applies proper balance and tension between affirmation and confrontation.* Many counselors use two approaches: (1) *affirmation,* with encouragement to love each other; and (2) *confrontation,* stressing personal accountability and responsibility for voluntary choices. Affirmation uses the biblical principle of loving your neighbor as yourself (Matt. 19:19). Many interpret this as a command to love ourselves as a prerequisite for the selfless love that the Bible consistently commands. But self-love can become destructive and sinful if it ignores repentance (2 Tim. 3:2). Some need affirmation and acceptance to grow. However, troublesome personal problems, such as perfectionism and control, may require direct confrontation with a clear ultimatum and a healthy response. What's the proper balance between affirmation and confrontation? Wise counselors know *what* is needed, *when* it is needed. Above all, competent counselors are comforters. In the New Testament this means "to come alongside." Counseling best serves people by coming alongside them without manipulation. Our task, as those receiving counsel, is to remain alert. We must discern a counselor's personal failings and protect a good potential remarriage relationship.

• *Keeps all discussions confidential.* It takes extraordinary restraint and discretion to preserve the client's trust and confidence in these circumstances. Few feel comfortable sharing personal problems with another if there is fear of gossip. Sadly, this is why many Christian pastors are subject to doubt. Even if a pastor is trustworthy, too often church members feel great discomfort in knowing that a relative stranger in close contact has personal information about them, so they end up leaving the congregation. It's simply too great a risk that the minister will bring up their problems, directly or indirectly, in the Sunday sermon. Select a counselor with no ties to either partner. This retards gossip and avoids bias.

How do you prepare yourself for premarital counseling? Notice what God tells us to do:

• *Prepare with prayer.* Prayer, before and after a counseling session, is essential. Counseling involves delving into the heart. Why not keep in close communication with the only one who truly understands each person's heart? Pray separately and together before each session, asking for openness to see whatever needs to change. David expressed this attitude well in Psalm 139:23–24: "Search me, O God, and know my heart; test me and know my anxious thoughts. See if there is any offensive way in me, and lead me in the way everlasting." Attending counseling sessions with this godly attitude surely brings change for the better!

• *Realize that you can be your own worst enemy.* We think we know what's best. Some marriage counselors urge, "Follow your heart." God knows better. Through the prophet Jeremiah, he tells us, "The heart is deceitful above all things and beyond cure. Who can understand it?" (Jer. 17:9). Proverbs 14:12 reaffirms this point: "There is a way that seems right to a man, but in the end it leads to death." Can you fully trust your heart right now with the emotions you experience for your beloved? Can you really be objective about your situation? Proverbs 12:15 clearly says, "The way of a fool seems right to him, but a wise man listens to advice." Follow God's advice—be very skeptical of your own judgments. Rely upon the advice of competent and trustworthy people who can be objective and see the "big picture" in your relationship.

• *Develop a deep friendship with someone who tells the truth.* We need a close friend sticking with us during a crucial remarriage decision. God will always be with us. Treasure also a confidant who will tell you what you *should* hear, rather than what you *want* to hear. Seek advice from someone who has no personal interest except your friendship and the satisfaction of serving you. "Perfume and incense bring joy to the heart, and the pleasantness of one's friend springs from his earnest counsel" (Prov. 27:9). Accept godly discipline faithfully administered by this caring friend. Make it *easy* for others to tell you the truth.

• *Seek the wisdom of several counselors.* By seeking advice from different people we respect and trust, we greatly reduce the risk of questionable counsel. If several competent counselors advise the same action, that may be a wise plan to follow. If an action plan receives mixed blessings, it's best to rethink matters. Universally good advice is: "When in doubt, don't do it!" Using several competent advisors with different perspectives protects you from the few well-intentioned folks who may not have godly views on a particular issue.

• *Follow wise counsel against your own interest.* We must train ourselves to be humble and accept godly advice. For example, if we receive wise counsel about letting a relationship go that we really want to keep, will we accept that advice? Pleasing God is more important than holding on to any premarital relationship, isn't it? If we reject godly advice meant for our good, we may reap what we sow and taste the bitter fruit of having our own way (Gal. 6:7–8; Prov. 1:29–33).

• *Eagerly desire to learn from your circumstances.* We must allow our advisors to highlight our weaknesses and errors in judgment, so we can learn from our mistakes. "Listen to advice and accept instruction, and in the end you will be wise" (Prov. 19:20). "No discipline seems pleasant at the time, but painful. Later on, however, it produces a harvest of righteousness and peace for those who have been trained by it" (Heb. 12:11). Use premarital counseling as an opportunity for self-evaluation and deeper dependence upon God. Staying alert with an eagerness to learn transforms routine sessions into triumphant ones!

• *Strive to communicate like never before.* Any relationship without good communication, negotiation, and conflict resolution will die. Counseling determines whether a couple can reach compromises and solve problems or whether they are better off terminating the relationship entirely. To give counseling its best chance of success, focus on a few important communication skills. Keep harmful emotions in check, not by suppressing feelings but by controlling destructive emotions. Keep the counseling setting open for calm, rational discussion. Try to see matters from other perspectives, learning what affects your partner's choices and desires. Paraphrasing what he/she shares *before* making any response reassures your partner that you listened and focused on the issues of concern. Avoid attempts at power or control tactics in communication, such as: (1) attacking the person rather than addressing the problem, (2) trying to win an argument rather than solving the problem, (3) presenting final solutions before receiving input, (4) focusing on one answer to the exclusion of other options, (5) trying to break your partner's will rather than appealing to what's fair, or (6) threatening action unless your partner agrees with your analysis. Whenever possible, communicate acceptance of your partner and agreement with legitimate complaints without belittling or stereotyping your partner. (See chap. 6 regarding vital communication skills.)

• *Be gracious and loving in giving constructive criticism.* There are helpful, and destructive, ways to give criticism. Some say *all* criticism is inappropriate because it is meant to *change* the other person. But *feedback* about irritations and causes of frustration with the other person is appropriate. For criticism to be constructive, serve it up with generous helpings of sincere appreciation. Show genuine interest in your partner's welfare. Ask yourself what you want to accomplish. Why do you feel the need to criticize? Do you have all the facts? Can you give examples to help your partner understand? If you don't have the answers, wait until you do. Above all, if we criticize only to vent personal anger, hurt or demoralize our partners, or give advice that we pridefully believe will impress them, it's probably best to keep silent. Consider your partner. Helpful criticism requires planning to guard against assaults on self-esteem, sarcasm, or undue blame and accusations. Is your criticism positive, or will it undermine your partner's confidence? *Timing* and *delivery* are so important. After giving criticism, be open for any responses. Communicate a cooperative spirit and flexibility in considering options and solutions to a problem. Above all, emphasize your partner's positive qualities.

• *Be gracious and loving in receiving criticism.* Before reacting to positive or negative criticism, be sure you understand and thoughtfully consider the complaint. Give calm, sensitive, and gracious responses—your attitude will mean more than your response! Is the criticism justified? Request help and suggested changes. If the criticism is invalid, honestly say so with due regard for your partner's feelings. Be on guard for personal defense mechanisms. There are essentially three: (1) *identity defenses* rooted in low self-esteem, which affect our self-image; (2) *emotional defenses* to mask pain, such as crying, anger, or depression that cover feelings of insecurity or inadequacy; and (3) *mental defense mechanisms* to avoid taking action, such as denial, rationalization and excuses, avoidance, distancing oneself from painful situations (leaving the room), or projecting our own faults onto others. These mental gymnastics keep us from looking at ourselves honestly or dealing with underlying feelings. Maintain an openness and accountability for your own shortcomings.

• *Keep a personal diary or journal.* We learn more about ourselves while with our partners and counselors than ever before. Don't miss this excellent opportunity to examine the thoughts and attitudes of your heart and submit them to the Lord. It's an excellent time for prayer, repentance, and learning to receive God's comfort and help. Journal writing helps us get even more in touch with our feelings in a soothing and relaxing way. It's a rewarding time of solitude for personal reflection, providing a record of our difficulties and how we worked through them. We gain perspective in reviewing our thoughts later.

How do you handle resistance to premarital counseling? It definitely takes *both* partners participating in premarital counseling for this valuable resource to have full effect. You and your partner may want to bypass counseling due to its expense. Don't do it! While expensive, the cost of counseling is far less than dealing with a failing remarriage.

What if your partner asks, "Why should I take personal advice from a stranger who doesn't know as much about us as we do ourselves?" Perhaps he/she simply doesn't feel comfortable talking about feelings with a counselor. (Men sometimes perceive therapy as a "woman's thing," to which they can't relate.) Reason with your partner. For example, you might point out that your partner receives medical advice from doctors (also strangers) who know less about the symptoms than your partner does. Why? Doctors have the training and experience to diagnose the cause of problems and prescribe remedies. Your partner doesn't. Why would a marriage counselor be any different? Stress the value of having a neutral observer provide feedback. Areas not obvious to you and your partner may be readily apparent to third parties looking in on the relationship. If your partner still balks at receiving counseling, propose a compromise. Ask for his/her participation in one consultation in a safe, confidential setting. Explain that the session will deal with how each person values the relationship and how to explore options for improving it. Often, after trying counseling, the reluctant partner is quite surprised to find therapy much less threatening, and more helpful, than expected.

Ultimately, receiving premarital counseling for yourself alone is much better than receiving none at all. You cannot force your partner to attend, but if your beloved refuses counseling, this might reveal a dangerous precedent for the remarriage. When this occurs after exhausting all other efforts to encourage cooperation, you might consider if your relationship really has a future.

Preparing for remarriage is serious, hard work! But if you take these suggestions to heart and apply them in your life, with the Lord's help, you will have the best opportunity to find a suitable remarriage partner and give your remarriage the best chance of success. Prove the critics and statisticians wrong!

A Message from Cheryl

Remarriage will be the greatest risk of your life. We don't just put our wounded selves at risk, but our already traumatized little ones as well. Many of us realize our previous mistake of ignoring the warning signs before a first marriage, and yet we often are inclined to make the same mistake before a remarriage. If you're unhappy as a single person, work on your life. No other person can make you happy.

The greatest lesson I brought with me in dating again was to avoid emotional attachment with anyone until I knew they were a "safe candidate" for remarriage. History proved I could be vulnerable to the wrong man and avoid the warnings of others!

Be as objective as possible: Was he dedicated to serving God *before* you met? Was he faithful to his first wife? Did he forgive her? Is he still kind to her? Does he care for his children? Does he spend time with them? Does he support them financially without resentment? Don't be foolish. Don't think you're so special that the entire pattern of his life will change. Until you know his faults (and he, yours) as well as his strengths, you aren't ready for remarriage.

If you think he's "perfect," you don't know him well enough. If he had faults but is changing, just wait . . . they will return. If you find him rather impatient or dull, perhaps you're realistic. *Then* ask yourself if you're equipped to spend your life with such a person. And make sure he knows you're bad at handling money and can't cook! Now *this* may be the person for you!

QUESTIONS FOR PERSONAL REFLECTION

1. Do I really know and appreciate the difference between romantic infatuation and biblical love?
2. Am I content with my life and relationship with God no matter what happens to me and my children?
3. What unrealistic expectations do I have about finding a suitable remarriage partner?
4. What relationship "stop signs" and "red flags" are most important for me to watch out for?
5. Specifically how can I make counseling sessions with my partner more effective and meaningful?

Chapter 5

MYTHS, EXPECTATIONS, AND REALITIES OF REMARRIAGE
Sorting out Feelings, Needs, and Goals

What will we face in remarriage? How should we prepare ourselves
for this wonderful new relationship—this second
chance—with children and many other related
family members?

Sometimes you get a second chance in life . . . and in marriage. You know all too well how it feels to see a loved one slip away. For you, it may have been your beloved spouse who was unable to resist death. For me, it was watching my first wife drive away from our home for the last time—on the road to divorce without any intention of returning. But we may have felt some of the same emotions—the sadness of loss, the bondage of guilt, the uncertainties and self-doubt of life alone, and the inevitable question: "Where do I go from here in my life?"

But then, perhaps when we aren't even looking for it, someone comes along—a new hope for a life partner. Someone who brings light into the darkness of our aloneness. Life becomes sweet with anticipation and plans for the future. This time we'll treasure the moments more. We'll be wiser and make the most of our opportunities. We *won't* repeat the mistakes of the past. With experienced eyes open, we invite remarriage into the reality of our lives through God's guidance. This time we'll make it *better* than our prior marriage. We're committed to making it *work!*

Throughout this book our focus is on these three phases of our lives: where we've come from, where we are right now, and where we want to go in remarriage. So let's begin with what we desire most right now in life—remarriage to a devoted and loving spouse. What can we expect from it? How do we prepare for it in terms of where we've come from in life and where we are right now? And what about the others coming into the family with remarriage?

BLENDED FAMILY LIFE IS DIFFERENT!

Like it or not, we must acknowledge that biological families with one husband/father and one wife/mother having children of their own and living out their lives together (which we will refer to as the *"traditional family"*) no longer is the prevailing family form. The stepfamily is rapidly becoming the most common form of family in America.

In remarriage we define a new family reality. It may not be the intact, traditional husband-and-wife-for-life *first* marriage that God intended. Nevertheless, it is a *family* unit more in conformity with God's will than single parenthood. We all want the best for our children. Ideally we want them to grow up in an intact traditional family, but that's not where we are right now in life. Even so, is growing up in a stepfamily so bad? I think not.

Sure, stepfamilies are more complex than traditional biological families. Even single-parent families are easier to deal with at times. A stepfamily, or what we will refer to as a *blended family,* arises from the marriage of a husband and wife, either or both of whom have been previously married, with or without children from prior relationships. Blended families offer the unique opportunity of bringing adults and children into an instant collage of multidimensional relationships and personal differences that make life so very special!

Blended families, unlike traditional families, are marked more by differences than similarities. People who don't look alike, think alike, or act alike, with the Lord's help, *unify* themselves in a mutual commitment to struggle together in meeting the challenges of blended family life. They become an underdog *team* that is willing to work against extraordinary odds—with the Lord's help—to make their family work successfully. These differences do create stress, but they also can bring rich personal satisfaction and sweet success! Blended families bring together people from different family backgrounds, traditions, and special histories. Think about how these life events can meld together into a beautiful new tapestry!

First-time traditional families frequently take each other for granted. Those entering remarriage and blended family life know the pain of earlier marriages shortened by death or divorce. Most have learned a valuable lesson: *Carpe Diem!* (Seize the day!) Make the most of every opportunity *each day,* rather than wait for a tomorrow that may never come (Eph. 5:15–16).

It's shortsighted to think of blended families as "secondhand" or "recycled." Yes, some of life's wonderful list of "firsts"—first steps, first teeth, first dates—may not be part of a blended family experience. But plenty of other "firsts" can fill special days for blended families to enjoy together.

So how do you prepare for this wonderfully new, but challengingly different, experience? What can you expect? Begin by asking yourself some fundamentally important questions.

AM I READY FOR THE CHALLENGE OF CHANGE?

If one word can describe the reality of remarriage and blended family life, it is *change*. And if two words could describe my initial attitude toward this new experience, they would be: *No change!* I wasn't prepared for this first reality. My attitude about change created a lot of conflict for Cheryl and me.

I'm a creature of habit—logical, methodical, predictable, and comfortable with routines that work. (Cheryl may tell you that I'm "rigid and inflexible" at times, although perhaps "defensively pigheaded" might be more accurate!) When I must go from point A to point Z, I research my move from point A, to point B, to point C, etc., before taking any action. I also like structure, order, and few surprises. Cheryl, by contrast, is the opposite—fluid, flexible, pragmatic, easily adaptable, and ready to go with the flow. (I might say she's somewhat "impulsive.") She'll fly to point Z by the quickest and shortest route, with her goal firmly in mind and without worrying about the hurdles in between. She loves to solve problems "on the fly" if unexpected difficulties arise. Structure and order aren't high priorities for her. Great change is no problem for Cheryl, but it's a *big* problem for me.

Cheryl saw an opportunity to open my eyes when she read the bestselling book, *Who Moved My Cheese?* by Dr. Spencer Johnson. The book is an allegory on how people react to and resist change. "Cheese," of course, is a metaphor for what you want in life—a good job, a loving relationship (such as a remarriage), health, or spiritual peace of mind. The book chronicles how two simple mice, Sniff and Scurry, and two more sophisticated little rodents, Hem and Haw, work their way through a maze (translation: life) to hunt for cheese "to nourish them and make them happy." When the cheese runs out in one location (station C), Sniff and Scurry simply move on through the maze, bouncing around until they find more. Not Hem and Haw, who are immobilized by change. Initially they succumb to the "paralysis of analysis" while refusing to find cheese elsewhere in the maze. Hem steadfastly resolves not to look elsewhere, and suffers from starvation. Haw, however, undergoes a character change— moving from denial to acceptance. He changes by abandoning the cheeseless fortress of station C, manned by Hem, and launches out into the maze.

Anyway, Cheryl, with a sneaky grin, shoved this book under my nose, saying, "Honey, here's a great book that you may find *very* interesting!" My reaction? "Uh-oh!" But as I read through the book, the message was clear: The cheese keeps moving. Move with the cheese. *If you don't change and adapt, you may become extinct!* Even so, I overreact to change agents who triumphantly declare, "Change is *good!* Change is *fun! Enjoy* change! Change will make you a better person! Change quickly— again and again!" In my Hemlike nature, too much change occurring too suddenly for a habitual, predictable person of comfortable routines is threatening, confusing, and unsettling. Thinking of those (like Cheryl) who thrive on change, I joked, "You know, sweetheart, instead of naming this book *Who Moved My Cheese?* maybe it should be *Where Is My Cheese Today?!?*"

Change. It's a *powerful* word. To some, it's a wonderful word; for others, an *impossible* word! Change is one force you can expect in life. Change brings with it anxiety of ambiguity, an uncomfortable feeling of losing touch with ourselves and reality as we perceive it. Because we don't know where change will lead us, it can frighten us! And let there be no doubt—remarriage into a blended family requires *change,* and *lots* of it!

Here I was, a relatively young (to me, anyway!) lawyer and Christian author, living the single life alone in my comfortable home in South Miami. When I went to work, I left things out of place. They'd be waiting right where I put them when I returned home. I worked, ate, slept, and watched television whenever I wanted to— even at odd hours. But when sweet Cheryl came into my life with young Chase in tow, I knew I wanted to go after that "cheese." Even so, I struggled with all of the usual questions: Do I really want to remarry? Can I still do many of the things I enjoy in life? Can I handle the responsibility of a new wife *and* a young son and instant family? What if the relationship doesn't work out again? It was all a jumble, pushing and pulling at my heart and mind!

Although I knew it before she said it, Cheryl also made it clear: "Chase and I are a package deal. Make sure you have no problems loving my son as you love me." Of course this wasn't much of a challenge since Chase was a wonderful, well-behaved little golden-haired boy. But in counting the cost of remarriage to Cheryl, there was more: "Warren," she said somewhat regretfully, "I also want to be honest with you. People who have seen your home in Miami tell me that it is the only five-room den they've ever seen in their lives! Also, I'm not comfortable living in the house you shared with your first wife. I would feel a lot better living somewhere else. Oh, and by the way, I've heard enough about life in Miami-Dade County schools that I really don't want Chase to go to school in Miami either. Maybe we can find a nice home in another county." I felt like my cheese was not only moving, but on a rocket to Mars!

Although I wanted Cheryl and Chase in my life, I had to make a decision . . . a decision to *change!* I fought it. Resisted it. Even *grieved* over it. But I *needed* that cheese in my life. To find and embrace it, I knew I had to change. As Jesus noted in Mark 2:22, "No one pours new wine into old wineskins. If he does, the wine will burst the skins, and both the wine and the wineskins will be ruined. No, he pours new wine into new wineskins." My life needed to become a new wineskin to receive Cheryl and Chase. So I prayed, "Penetrate my prideful heart, Lord. Break down my resistance to change that's locking me out of one of the most precious joys of living—having a family to love and to return my love. Give me the strength to yield to you and to my new family."

I feared the unavoidable changes remarriage would bring, but I also remembered the Scripture "There is no fear in love. But perfect love drives out fear" (1 John 4:18). Would God give me the perfect love for Cheryl and Chase to chase away my doubts and fears? When love is the dominating force, there are no fears of change, tough questions, or even doubts. Biblical love seeks what is most pleasing to God and those we want to love.

The many blessings of remarried family life motivated me to review, rethink, and renew my life's goals. As Cheryl and I talked about our future together before we remarried, it really excited me! I found myself saying, "Yes! I can make these major life changes with the Lord's help. More than that, I *want* to do it." I saw something better in the Lord's blessing of remarriage to Cheryl. I felt God's call that this was what he wanted for my life. I was ready, willing, and able to absorb the losses of my single life.

Think about the many unique differences—*changes*—in life that remarriage and blended families bring into our lives:

- Unlike first marriages, one or both partners in a remarriage have experienced marriage, and perhaps also parenthood.
- Often one or both remarriage partners carry unfinished business and other emotional baggage into the relationship from former marriages.
- In blended families, remarriage partners have no time alone in the relationship—children are present from day 1.
- In blended families, remarriage partners, children, *and* other family members (including ex-spouses, ex-inlaws, and others) strive to interact with each other—all at once!
- Children from prior marriages go in and out of the home to spend time with biological parents.
- Names of blended family members won't always match, which can create identity confusion and a sense of not belonging.
- Remarriage may mean relocation of home, work, schools, and relationships—affecting not only the remarriage partners but potentially multiple sets of children as well.
- Since a blended family includes more than just husband and wife, family expenses can be a major drain on finances.
- Stepparents must become "instant parents," assuming parenting roles with their partners' children with whom they have no prior history or relationship.
- Unlike biological parents, stepparents have no legally recognized relationship with their partners' children.
- Pecking orders for children in each remarriage partner's family can change dramatically when the "two become one."

The list goes on and on. All these factors require major change and adjustment!

What process of change can we expect in typical blended families? In her excellent book *Stepfamily Realities,* Dr. Margaret Newman highlights several phases of change in blended family life (similar to the phases of the personal grieving process we discussed in chap. 2) as follows:

• *The fantasy phase.* This is the "honeymoon stage" of remarriage, full of idealism and possibly delusion. Children of single parents now have a "father" and "mother" once again living in the same home. Family members tend to disregard existing "microfamily" relationship boundaries temporarily in the emotional joy of being in a totally new environment.

• *The confusion phase.* The novelty of the new family structure slips away. Reality creeps in, bringing tension and waning romance between remarriage partners. Differences in daily living and future goals become much more apparent. Issues begin to crop up, perhaps too many to handle. Everyone tries to deny or ignore problems in the vain hope that everything will work itself out over time. Different family members withdraw into the more comfortable "microfamily" groups they knew prior to the remarriage. Communication breaks down.

• *The conflict phase.* Conflicts increase as needs and interests collide on a daily basis. Power struggles surface. The family may divide into camps and shift alliances. Family skirmishes and wars flare up. Anger, guilt, and manipulation breed cold shoulders and the "silent treatment" toward different family members. *This very normal but extremely critical turning point in the life of everyone in the home can make or break the blended family.* Family life and individual relationships break down and spiral downward from this point on *unless* the family *earnestly* practices conflict-resolution skills. (We review vital blended family communication, boundaries, and biblical conflict-resolution measures in chap. 6.)

• *The coming-together phase.* Although battle-weary partners may feel depressed and defeated, more family members are learning to resolve conflicts, be solution-oriented, and build bridges rather than walls. A growing awareness of personal and corporate identity is forged, individually and collectively. Family members begin to *understand* each other better and to *accept and love* each other more. Upsets and conflicts aren't as long or bitter as members confess and forgive each other more quickly. They learn to overlook minor offenses. Hope dawns as each family member discovers healing and recovery. They feel more like a *family* and less an association of individual members. But be prepared—this phase may take *years* to complete!

• *The resolution phase.* Individual family members, for the first time perhaps, feel they can be themselves and get comfortable in blended family life. Family life demonstrates genuine loving relationships, laughter, and relief more than conflict. Ideally, all family members fully invest in collective decision making and brainstorming on creative options and solutions. Family life improves.

Similar to the grieving process, the whole family, or individuals, can experience one or more of these phases of blended family life simultaneously. There's no guarantee that families ever reach the last two phases, although that's the goal. But understanding the *process* of blended family change and growth helps everyone get on the same page in identifying behaviors and attitudes along the way. In doing so, each family member develops personal skills to help keep family life on an even keel with the Lord's help.

But change isn't the only effect of remarriage and blended family life. Each marriage partner also needs another reality check . . .

AM I READY TO MAKE A NEW COMMITMENT?

Ask yourself some questions:

Have I resolved and learned from mistakes made during my prior marriage? If the answer is no, then you may want to read through part 1 again.

Am I truly ready, willing, and able to commit myself to another partner? If the answer is yes, how consistent have you been in your walk with the Lord and your commitment to him? *Commitment* is absolute in your relationship with God and with your remarriage partner—not "while our love shall last."

Am I ready for the responsibilities of blended family life? Test yourself. Given the choice, would you do what you *want* to do or what you *need* to do? If you find yourself doing only what you want to do, it would be better to remain single. How sad it is to see people jump hurdles to remarry and care for someone else when they've proven they're barely able to care for themselves!

Am I willing to be honest and transparent to a new spouse? Any marriage built on the quicksand of secrets and deception risks destruction. Do you find it difficult to be open and transparent? Remarriage isn't the best place to begin learning.

Am I willing to be submissive? If you're more concerned about being in control of the marriage and being the boss, not a *partner,* it's best to stay single. Marriage is built on *mutual* submission out of reverence for Christ (Eph. 5:21). Can you accept your place in God's plan, whatever it may be? How have you overreacted when you've been under authority of parents, employers, teachers, and others having power over you?

Am I ready, willing, and able to love? This type of love is Godlike—a decisive will and desire to do good for someone even when you don't feel like it (grace) and when they don't deserve it (mercy). It is loving someone else without getting any love back—a genuine unselfish, sacrificial, servant-hearted biblical kind of love. Or is the love you feel contingent upon how your beloved looks, makes you feel, or treats you?

I guess you could group me with the "typical males who won't commit to a relationship." Cheryl and I dated for about two years. We developed a good friendship, worked through a *lot* of issues, and began the process of blending our lives together. As we dated, Cheryl was very loving and quite expressive in her feelings for me, which felt great! Of course, I loved her too. We were definitely gearing up for remarriage. But it was difficult for me to tell her that I had some reservations about committing myself fully to her.

Deep down, I was *afraid* of committing my life to her because I didn't want to be disappointed or abandoned again in marriage. I feared manipulation and exploitation in a relationship. Cheryl said and did all the right things. But like a typical male, I wanted to keep my dating options open. I wanted to make sure there wasn't someone even better coming down the road (which really was difficult to believe since Cheryl was so special!). The problem was mine—I didn't want to face my fear and work through my feelings.

As a lawyer, I always want options too! This relationship was no different. I wanted an exit strategy if the premarital relationship didn't go the way I wanted. Noncommitment gave me a way out, but I had to resolve these problems if our remarriage was to become a reality. *How unfair to Cheryl!* I put her in a "wait on me" position while exercising control over our relationship. She met my needs in our dating relationship, but I wasn't giving her what she needed most from me—a committed heart!

Eventually I knew I had to make a "commit or quit" decision, to either move forward into a remarriage with Cheryl (including Chase) and continue to invest in the growth of our relationship or to cut everyone loose. I asked myself, "Am I truly willing and able to *commit* to Cheryl and Chase?" After searching my heart for a long time and praying hard about this major life change, I knew I was ready.

But what about Cheryl? Once she knew me, would she bail out of our relationship? I had to face the other side of my own commitment dilemma—"Is Cheryl really committed to me?" Only by dating for an extended time, and seeing me in a *lot* of different situations (where I was at my best *and* my worst), did Cheryl make it clear that she wanted me—no one else.

Cheryl loves to tell the story about how after her divorce she moved from Florida to her home state of Ohio. She never intended on coming back to the Sunshine State. "In fact," she would swear to her family, "even if Dr. James Dobson himself were to ask me to marry him and come to live in Florida, I wouldn't do it!" Well, here she is—living in Florida . . . with me! Imagine how important and special that makes me feel!

What is commitment? It's the glue that binds mates together. It means barring the exits and burning the bridge out of remarriage. You and your mate are in the relationship together, no matter *what* happens. It means pledging yourself totally and exclusively to your beloved—as you are now *and* as you will become in the future. Commitment puts all the world outside the garden where your relationship will grow. It is the confined space of a remarriage—a place of refuge without self-defense, nourishment without fantasies or manipulation, vulnerability without power games or opportunism, and *acceptance*. Remarriage is ideal for those who have servants' hearts—those who *choose* to love despite unpleasant circumstances and feelings at times.

Commitment to a marriage is difficult enough, but a remarriage takes it up several notches! With a first marriage, romance and excitement bind a couple's hearts together as they work on a clean canvas. In remarriage, you don't have a clean canvas, but one with a lot of shapes and colors already drawn on it—and you are asked to blend it together into a fabulous new painting! Remarried spouses desperately want to avoid making mistakes, and have less time to discover whether a relationship is right for the future. Decisions of this magnitude obviously must be covered in prayer! But *commitment* is what keeps their work in progress going when they feel like putting their paintbrushes away.

Commitment in remarriage also carries accountability. Bill McCartney, founder of Promise Keepers, stated it best for husbands: "What America desperately needs today is men who take responsibility for their actions, who are faithful to their families, who keep their word, even when it's difficult or costly."[1]

Doug and Naomi Moseley, marital counselors and authors of the very thought-provoking book *Making Your Second Marriage a First-Class Success,* had this to say about the pain and cost of commitment in remarriage:

The cost of committing is high. It means loss of freedom, major
increases in responsibility, and a big shift away from the comforts of

egocentricity . . . a shift into the need to take account of another person moment to moment for a very long time. *Forever.* It means comforting, dealing with, and possibly defusing the secret specialness he feels—that we all feel—along with uncovering his usually unseen sense of powerlessness. It means a lifetime of struggling through all manner of impossibly complicated issues with a less-than-perfect person, with much less-than-perfect tools. Worse than all that, their relationship might fail in the end, which will lead to even greater possibilities for pain than can be imagined right now. In short, it means dealing with reality.[2]

Commitment absolutely does mean cutting through the romance, the unrealistic expectations, and the dashed hopes and dreams of former relationships to deal with reality. Commitment permits us to say, from the heart, to our beloved on our wedding day, "I am choosing you to be my husband, my friend, my love, the father of our children. I will be yours in plenty and in want, in sickness and in health, in failure and in triumph. I will cherish you, and respect you, comfort and encourage you, and together we shall live, freed and bound by our mutual love for the Lord and each other."

None of us will fulfill our commitments perfectly . . . in fact, we will fail many times! Why? Because we're sinners. But as Ecclesiastes 4:12 reminds us, "Though one may be overpowered, two can defend themselves. A cord of three strands is not quickly broken." Our marriage partner—the Lord—helps pick up the slack when we fall short. Commitment and trust come in knowing that ultimately we *want* to be there for our partners. Our heart's desire is to fulfill our new vows before God and our mates. We express our desire to commit fully—in words and actions. Then when we or our spouses fail to live up to these commitments, it is much easier to forgive one another when our common denominator is Jesus Christ.

Change. Commitment. These are challenging issues! But there's more to consider.

WILL I HAVE COMPASSION FOR EVERYONE IN MY BLENDED FAMILY?

Some blandly define compassion as a sympathetic awareness of the distress of others and a desire to relieve it. But the word originates from two Latin words that literally mean "to suffer with." The Greek word translated "compassion" in Scripture means "to feel something deep within the heart" or "to have one's inner being stirred." I like this simple phrase: "Compassion is *your* pain in *my* heart." It involves not only feeling but action! It is love that moves us to do something positive and beneficial for wounded and hurting individuals. Compassion also motivates us to "carry each other's burdens and . . . fulfill the law of Christ" (Gal. 6:2).

I recall a poignant story about Mother Teresa, a sincere woman known throughout the world for her compassion. Shortly before her death, she met a man eaten up with terminal cancer. The stench was so bad that one of the workers aiding the man vomited. Mother Teresa gently led the worker aside and kindly took over. This pitiful patient looked up at her and cried, "How can you stand the smell?" She replied, "It's nothing compared to the pain you must feel." That's compassion.

As we have said, commitment is vitally important in remarriage. But if we sacrifice compassion for the sake of commitment, we become legalistic tyrants. Conversely, if we sacrifice commitment for compassion, we may become weak, ineffective, and spiritually soft. Commitment *and* compassion are both from the Lord and work together to overcome difficult situations.

The New Testament uses the term for compassion nine times to describe Jesus' disposition toward a person or group. When Jesus saw a large crowd of people searching for help, understanding, and relief, "he had compassion on them, because they were like sheep without a shepherd" (Mark 6:34). The very nature of Jesus is *compassion.*

How compassionate are you toward other people—especially those who will become members of your blended family? Are you willing to empty yourself of pride and self-centeredness to *see* not only the needs of your family members but also to *feel* those needs? Hebrews 4:15 says that Jesus, our high priest, *feels* for us. He knows us *as we are.* He *understands* us. If we truly love the Lord and want to be like him, we must love others as Jesus loves us. Compassion is more than mere words—it's a *way of life!*

How can we open our hearts to make compassion a reality in our lives? By approaching people where they are and on their own turf. Obviously we don't accept or approve of sin in their lives, but we just love them as persons and try to come alongside them to feel their pain. Whatever they need—even if it's only a touch, a smile, or a hug—we try to deliver. Then we establish a *relationship,* communicating and empathizing with them in a clear and compassionate manner. We become involved in their lives. Compassion *seeks* and *serves.*

For people wounded by loss of a spouse or parent through death or divorce, the most effective therapy is compassion from those sharing similar experiences. Why? Because hurting people desperately need to be *understood.* As Gilbert Beers once noted, "To become healers, we have to be wounded. And because our wound was deep, ugly, and painful, our balm of healing was more therapeutic than it would have been had life superficially scratched us." This is one very special reason why remarried couples and blended families are so good for each other! Second Corinthians 1:3–4 reassures us: "Praise be to the God and Father of our Lord Jesus Christ, the Father of compassion and the God of *all* comfort, who comforts us in all our troubles, so that we can comfort those in any trouble with the comfort we ourselves have received from God" (emphasis added).

And who needs our compassion most? Our kids and stepkids. As the powerful changes and emotions caused by death or divorce of parents whirl in their lives, children twist and turn in a world of bewilderment, confusion, and fear. What will they do now that Daddy is gone? Why is Mommy crying all the time? Why can't we be a happy family like other children at school? If divorce is like death to us, we can only begin to imagine the devastating impact it has on our children. They may bravely bear up under the pressure and turmoil, but they pay a price. They lose a loved one—an irreplaceable parent. Some children have suffered even more—emotional, physical, and even sexual abuse from a parent, which can absolutely suffocate them. In desperation, they must break free to survive.

Our children are our heritage, blessed by God himself. They are the innocents. The humble. The trusting. Examples of how we should approach God. In Matthew 18:1–4, the disciples came to Jesus with the question "Who is the greatest in the kingdom of heaven?" How did Jesus respond?

> He called a little child and had him stand among them. And he said: "I tell you the truth, unless you change and become like little children, you will never enter the kingdom of heaven. Therefore, whoever humbles himself like this child is the greatest in the kingdom of heaven.
>
> "And whoever welcomes a little child like this in my name welcomes me. But if anyone causes one of these little ones who believe in me to sin, it would be better for him to have a large millstone hung around his neck and to be drowned in the depths of the sea."

Too often we lose children in the shuffle of business among busy adults, but Jesus knew the worth of children. Even after Jesus praised the childlike attitudes of humility and trust, his disciples still missed the high regard God has for children. We need to step into the shoes of these youngsters. How would you feel if you were a child whose parent died or divorced? How would you react if compelled to share a room with a stranger in a new blended family? If we don't have sufficient compassion for our children, we aren't ready to remarry.

Stay open to *change.* Make a *commitment* to your spouse and *all* the children in the new blended family. Have *compassion* for everyone concerned—especially the children. You cannot do this in your own strength. Ask God for his help! These vital elements are only a few of the many realities facing those who want to remarry.

DO I HAVE REASONABLE EXPECTATIONS?

We know that the statistics for the survival of remarriages are worse than for first marriages. What are the most common "sticky issues" leading to marital distress? Marriage counselors and psychologists cite the four most commonly stated reasons for divorce among first-time marriage partners as: (1) lack of clear communication between spouses, (2) unrealistic expectations of the marriage or spouse, (3) personal power struggles, and (4) role conflict. Remarriages fall prey to these same problems more frequently.

If you've been tracking divorce statistics in recent years, you know that in the late twentieth and early twenty-first century, born-again Christian couples have been divorcing at a *higher* rate than non-Christian couples! *Why?* (Statistics might be skewed by many non-Christian couples, incompatible over the long haul, living together rather than marrying, so their broken relationships aren't included in divorce statistics. But the question remains relevant: *Why* are born-again couples, who profess total commitment to Christ, leading the way in divorces?) After studying the subject for some years, and through personal experience, I believe one major factor is having *unreasonable expectations.*

We marry for any number of reasons, many of which may be absolutely wrong. We were young, idealistic, and immature, or maybe we thought marriage would be the cure-all for loneliness. Maybe we bought into the "romance myth" and looked to our marriage partners to give us the "happily ever after" life we craved. Perhaps we married because all our friends were marrying, and it seemed the "right thing to do." We wanted to get away from home and leave authoritarian parents, or we wanted a "substitute parent" in a mate. Perhaps we looked forward to sharing a proper sexual relationship with a spouse. Maybe, as we made a living, we didn't want to have an unfulfilled existence and miss out on life without sharing it with someone special. And, through it all, we may have overlooked asking God to guide our lives and decisions.

Before experiencing it, how many of us *thought* we had reasonable expectations of what a marriage was all about? I remember a "Cathy" cartoon some time ago that featured a single secretary asking two married coworkers, "Tell me what it's like to be married." One wife responds, "It's exactly like dating, except you see each other at your absolute worst and he never comes home!" The other married colleague observes, "It's a 24-hour-a-day, 365-day-a-year job of compromise, compromise, compromise!" Then the same question is posed to single Cathy, who gushes with heart aflutter, "It's a blissful union of two souls, intertwined in unending passion and joy!!!" The last frame shows the inquisitor wondering to herself, "Funny how you only get the truth when you ask someone who hasn't been there."[3] Unreasonable expectations and denial—a recipe for delusions that only a disastrous marriage can cure!

What will it take for us to wake up to having *realistic* expectations in marriage? While Christians and non-Christians alike certainly allow our human qualities and frailties to influence marriage decisions unduly, Christians also expect one additional distinctive quality in their mates—*spiritual maturity.* Though a desirable characteristic, that expectation can skyrocket to a level that requires one's mate to have Christlike sinless perfection or the marriage is a failure. Even more, many Christians aren't aware of the most basic principles of marriage and what God requires of marriage partners. So when we discover our mates are sinners (just as we are), our expectations shatter. Then we may want to distance ourselves from them so we don't stumble! Result? Another marriage breakdown.

It was a very good attorney friend—an unbeliever, no less—who gave me the very best premarital advice I've ever received: "Warren, don't ignore any little annoyances you see in a prospective mate while you are dating. Each annoyance, which you probably won't be able to change, becomes predominant and will aggravate you more after you marry. If you can accept these annoyances, then marry. If you can't, *don't!*" How true that is! Annoyances are symptoms of bigger issues—those behaviors, fears, mindsets, and other barriers that come back to haunt us if we aren't alert and wise.

But other wrinkles surface as well. People change for better (or worse) during marriage. My first wife impressed me to the core of my being when we met in the early

1980s. On the postdivorce side of my marriage, I've learned I really idealized her. I underestimated her significant need for guidance and support, while overestimating her maturity, strength, and wisdom, as well as her resolve to stand up against the worldly pressures and temptations. I also foolishly thought that we would remain the same people we were when we married, simply growing closer to each other with time. The final revelation dawned, shortly before our divorce, when my first wife told me, "Warren, I am no longer the woman you knew when we married." Her confession cut my heart and shattered my hopes for our life together, but I knew it was true. Growth and change are part of life.

Compare the unrealistic expectations we carried into our first marriages with our thoughts and desires as we consider remarrying now. Are we using more *wisdom* in evaluating our prospective remarriage partners? (I define true "wisdom" as *true and accurate knowledge,* tempered by *experience*—vital life resources those who remarry should have that many first-time married persons don't!) Are we more able to acknowledge and face our shortcomings and truly submit them to God? Are we seeking his guidance in decision making?

In many ways we're wiser for experiencing marriage before remarriage. We know more about what to expect from our partners than the first time around. But we also have to contend with the flip side of this equation. Perhaps we also experience more anxiety and tension over minor disturbances in remarriage than previously. We may be more self-protective and less vulnerable or open-minded. When conflict arises, we may think, *Uh-oh. Here it comes again! Is this the beginning of the end?*

Do unreasonable expectations plague us because we're remarrying too soon? We think we can handle the new relationship, but we haven't really dealt with prior marriage issues. In our heart we may still carry the torch for an ex-spouse. Or we may remarry "on the rebound" to show our former mates their mistake in throwing us away. We're still first-rate marriage material, thank you very much!

It's also important to avoid the *other* extreme in entering remarriage. We shouldn't unreasonably *lower* our expectations instead of desiring the best in a remarriage partner. Not everyone is as cavalier as singer-songwriter Joni Mitchell, who once told how she met her husband of many years: "I was kind of lonely at the time. And I actually prayed . . . an embarrassed prayer. I said: 'Look, God, I know I don't write, I don't call. However, I don't need that much. All I need is a real good kisser who likes to play pinball.' So two days later, [bass player Larry] Klein said to me, 'How would you like to go to the Santa Monica pier and play video games?' And I looked up at the sky, and I said, 'Close enough!'"[4] You and I know the temptation to reach out for anyone and try to make the relationship work.

Even in the best remarriages, two partners won't connect perfectly. Our spouses won't fully understand some of who we are as persons, despite our deepest desire to be soulmates. I don't think Cheryl will ever be a fan of my beloved Miami Dolphins and Florida Gators football teams. It's not a long shot to assume that I won't share her love for Cleveland, Ohio, either. The *reasonable* expectation in our remarriage anticipates moments—vital and critically important moments—when Cheryl turns to me in desperate search of a reassuring, "I know what you mean," only to have me respond with "Huh?" and a look of total incomprehension! That's the reality of *any* marriage.

Here are a few other myths and unreasonable expectations many people share about remarriage:

Blended families are similar to traditional families. Nothing could be further from the truth! Blended families rise from the ashes of broken dreams and shattered memories caused by loss of a spouse or parent. And that's only the beginning.

Our love will last forever. In fact, more remarriages fail than first marriages. Be positive, but also be realistic. The adage is, "Know what you're getting into *before* you say, 'I do.'"

Stepparents are from another planet. Fairy tales like "Cinderella," "Hansel and Gretel," and "Snow White" all portray stepparents as harsh and wicked persons. Often children wonder which planet their stepparents came from, and view them as silly or out of touch with life. But stepparents aren't much different from biological parents.

Stepparents are "snap-on" moms and dads. The other side of the "stepparents are from outer space" myth is that families can pop stepparents in like replacement parts. But they don't immediately handle problems with ease and elegance like the parents in *The Brady Bunch*!

Loving me means immediately loving my child. Not necessarily! Love takes time— especially when it involves kids wounded by death or divorce of a parent. Sometimes it's very hard not to take personally a child's reservations about you as a parent.

We'll shut out all the exs. Wrong! Numerous studies and research confirm that children need regular contact with their biological parents in order to become healthy and well-adjusted adults. If anyone interferes with these relationships, expect the affected child to rebel, considering those who interfere as the bad guys!

Don't worry; be happy. God gives us many great, useful principles for working through problems and interpersonal relationship issues in remarriages. But blended families come with no instruction manual. Each family needs to change and adapt to their own particular interests, desires, and needs. What works for one blended family could be disaster for another family. Remarriage partners definitely need to "read more about it" in Scripture and at the local library or bookstore! You also can't realistically expect to do it alone. That's why family counseling, stepparenting support groups, and seeking input from competent and experienced spiritual advisors are so vital!

We've arrived. Each developmental stage in remarriage has its own new problems. There's really never any time when the remarriage partners can sit back and say, "The worst is over; we can coast from here on out and take life easy." If anyone thinks otherwise, prepare for some nasty surprises! Successful remarriages, like first marriages, take a *lot* of work with one major difference—*remarriages* take a lot *more* work!

Unreasonable expectations leading into remarriage—sticky issues indeed! You and your loved one must sit down before you remarry and work through at least five major problem areas that may arise in your remarriage. With the help of competent spiritual marriage counselors, each partner absolutely must come to terms with the reasons and conditions each person's prior marriage(s) failed. Then together focus on the specific measures each of you will take to keep the problems from reoccurring in remarriage. This requires honest definition of the problems that could arise. After all, a problem well defined is a problem half solved. It's much better to *prevent* a problem than try to *solve* a problem after it happens in remarriage!

No matter how uncomfortable it makes you and your beloved, thoroughly air your personal expectations of remarriage and your differences of opinion well in advance of any wedding. If both of you cannot, or will not, irrevocably commit to preventing the problems you discuss, have the courage to back off. Let the relationship die a graceful death before significant entanglements of remarriage bring misery your way.

Can I Trust My Partner?

If you're considering remarriage to your beloved, one or both of you likely may have some regrettable experiences facing some serious issues from former marriages, such as adultery, alcoholism, homosexuality—not to mention the horror of the divorce process itself. Coming out of experiences like these, it's very natural to guard against "making another mistake" and to be *very* slow in trusting someone again. When we find someone who might be our next soul mate, we hear the whispers, *"Be careful!"* and feel some anxiety in our soul. Can I *really* trust this person? This fear blocks trust as partners teeter between relief of finding a new mate and anxious uncertainty about each partner's true character.

Let me share one personal anxiety with you. When I first married in 1984, I resolved that divorce would never be an option for me. I burned the bridge out of the marriage and clearly was in the relationship for the long haul. Unfortunately, my first wife didn't share those views. She initiated the divorce against my wishes and saw it through to the end without wavering. In contrast, Cheryl filed for divorce from her first husband for scriptural reasons. She secured support from her church fellowship that it was the right thing to do before God under those circumstances. But it made me pause—did Cheryl share my conviction about avoiding divorce? Would she bail out on me when times were tough? At the same time, Cheryl's concern was our age difference. (I'm twelve years older.) She also felt somewhat vulnerable to my legal background and exacting nature. Would she be comfortable trusting me?

During my first marriage, I delighted in telling family and friends that I trusted my Christian wife 100 percent. But after she left me because of loving another man and wanting an immediate divorce, I wondered whether I could completely trust another woman. Suffering a breach of trust is bad enough, but being blindsided is much worse! Yet, how can you have intimacy in any relationship without wholeheartedly trusting your partner?

What if your beloved (or you) is a repentant adulterer? How can you really trust someone who's been duplicitous and has broken faith with a spouse, without fear of recurrence? Betrayals are extremely hard to forget! In this circumstance, it's the duty of the erring spouse to do whatever is necessary in establishing trust: being accountable, keeping the remarriage partner informed, and ensuring actions remain consistent and transparent. Even then, it's extremely difficult to build up trust—especially under pressure of one's mate having a skeptical mind-set of "guilty until proven innocent." The pattern of our lives quite often is more predictable than words. Ultimately, we must trust in the Lord's faithfulness and his work in each remarriage partner's life.

What's the fruit of mistrust? Insecurity leading to power plays, backstabbing, betrayal, and undermining of the relationship. Mistrust isolates marriage partners and fuels suspicions and deep anxiety about the relationship. You don't feel safe relaxing or thinking aloud with your spouse. You wonder what *else* might be hidden from you!

Some years ago, one of my legal colleagues carried a heavy workload, requiring long hours at the office and a wife left home alone. To help with the office work, a divorced female paralegal gladly helped him long into the night. You can guess what happened. It wasn't long before the attorney divorced his wife and married the paralegal. But the most curious thing about this remarriage was seeing how this paralegal, now working in another office, felt the need to call continually and check up on her new husband. I guess she knew that if he could cheat on his wife once, it might happen again! Result? Suspicion. Anxious moments. Mistrust—perhaps well-founded.

Trust. We desire it. More than that, we *need* it desperately. If you cannot trust your remarriage fiancé, whom can you trust? In fact, the word *fiancé* traces back to the Latin word *fidare*, which means, you guessed it, "to *trust.*"

Building trust requires lots of time. Dating for a long period and sharing a variety of experiences before considering remarriage is essential. How does your beloved handle conflict? How about keeping personal confidences? Does he self-destruct when the pressure is on? Does she let her emotions override reason? When there's no time to build a common history, we become impatient and jump too quickly. Then remarriage can be like walking over a narrow rickety wooden bridge hanging precariously over a deep gorge of doom—blindfolded and alone!

So how can you build trust, loyalty, honesty, integrity, and security—words that have fallen out of favor in today's world—as you enter remarriage? How do you avoid further "relationship roulette"? Can you rely on your gut feelings to know whether to trust your beloved? Is the romantic chemistry of dating enough to justify making a remarriage commitment to someone who, in many ways, remains a stranger?

Trust thrives with building a common history. You and your partner need to share a common frame of reference—faith in God and a proper perspective on families, friends, and the world. This is why it is *so important* to have sufficient time to build up your relationship with your beloved before any remarriage. Different counselors and experts may give you different answers, but here's my suggestion: (1) allow no less than two years buffer between the end of your prior marriage and when you begin a serious dating relationship with someone else; (2) date in moderation until you find someone you want to date exclusively; and (3) build up a common history by dating your special honey in all kinds of circumstances and scenarios for one to two years *more* before proceeding into a remarriage. Simply put, this will give you a reasonable amount of *time* to recover from your prior marriage. It allows you to use *caution* to keep from jumping at the first relationship that comes along. And it also allows you to build a *shared history* by having the time needed to really know one another.

Cherish your partner and family with biblical love. This roots itself in a solid and undeniable commitment to your beloved and to your new family. Husbands are to love their wives as Christ loved the church (Eph. 5:25). And wives are to respect their husbands. Love and trust like this absolutely cannot be conditional or situational. How do we express love for each other and build trust? Love notes (those special, specific, and solid expressions of love tucked into lunchboxes, taped to the bathroom mirror, E-mailed, or placed under the pillow) work wonders to let your sweetheart know he/she is appreciated, respected, treasured, and loved. How can we develop a "love mind-set"? Focus on the biblical love characteristics in 1 Corinthians 13:4–8a, and put them into daily practice! Love and trust truly are *choices* made and *decisions* implemented. *Choose* to love. *Choose* to trust, and let your actions show it!

Make your beloved (and your children) a priority. It seems almost too obvious to suggest, but so many of us forget this primary commitment. Relationships require *daily* monitoring and maintenance. Complacency isn't trust. Your beloved needs to know that your joint remarriage investment will always be an *active* account that is *secure.* It comes with a *guaranteed return* of unconditional love despite any adverse circumstances, a *mutual fund* relationship between the Lord, husband, and wife. How does this happen? Simply turn off the television and lay aside the mail to go walking. Watch a sunset together, meet for an impromptu lunch, or go out for a romantic dinner. Keep this priority time by regularly scheduling "date nights" to do a wide variety of new and different fun things together. Also, love your children and give them your full attention during the time set aside for them. But be careful not to let children encroach the vital time necessary for you and your spouse.

Communicate and ventilate. Each remarriage partner needs enough time to explore feelings fully. Sharing our hearts in honesty and humility while patiently encouraging our partners develops intimacy. Intimacy springs from reciprocally sharing sensitive personal information with each other, and being forthcoming and cooperative in dealing with mistakes and shortcomings. It means avoiding any opportunities to capitalize on each other's goodwill or taking advantage of embarrassing secrets.

Promote empathy. Identifying the sources and symptoms of each other's fears and anxieties is a critical prerequisite to empathizing with each other's pain. Share personal doubts and weaknesses and help put those fears to rest. Patient and positive support is the best healing agent.

Focus on the positive. Get time alone and reflect on the positive benefits of your remarriage. Take care that you don't just "problem solve." Although it is certainly necessary to identify problems, fears, options, and solutions, it's also important to learn to relax, laugh, play, and "escape" together. Focusing on the positive aspects of life, without also ignoring the problems, does take a *lot* of patience and practice.

Pump up the passion. After your wedding, sexual intimacy is God's remarriage gift to you and your partner—resolve yourself to take advantage of it! Commit now to not letting your bedroom devolve into a large laundry hamper rimmed with books, magazines, and tossed-aside items after you remarry. Make it an *inviting* and beautiful place—clean, orderly, and restful. Let it be your sanctuary away from the world—a spot that is your own intimate refuge.

What is the very best environment for building trust in a remarriage? It grows where two whole, complete, and joyful individuals have an abundance of life to share with each other. They freely and voluntarily come together in a marriage partnership out of a loving *choice* to love each other, rather than any neediness to fulfill unmet emotional needs. There is parity and equality. There is an *interdependent* closeness that endures, yet doesn't trap or smother the partners. There is a realistic perspective on each one's strengths and weaknesses, rather than an idealized or romanticized image of each other.

Trust allows remarriage partners to merge and blend their lives completely while allowing room for personal growth. But how much personal space do remarriage partners (and their children) need? This brings us to . . .

CAN I ACCEPT SOME SEPARATENESS?

God's intent is that one man and one woman leave their parents, marry, and cleave to each other in a "one-flesh" relationship for life. Couples then give birth to and raise their own children in an intact traditional family. When you have these natural bonds and blessings, it's much easier to share things in common. It's a relatively easy fit without a lot of competing interests. But that's not our situation. What do we face? A network (some might say, *cobweb*) of *microfamilies* and competing interests. Consider the circumstance in which Cheryl and I found ourselves.

After my first wife divorced me, she left to pursue her own life (and has since remarried). She has her own microfamily. As a single, formerly married man, I became a microfamily living in my own house. Although I still had some contact with my former in-laws (also microfamilies in this puzzle), because there were no children from my first marriage, these relationships eventually faded away over time.

Cheryl and her first husband, Michael, conceived and bore Chase during their marriage—an intact traditional family. Unfortunately, they divorced and became two microfamilies—Cheryl and Chase in one, and Michael in the other. Since Cheryl and Michael had a child, this meant that Cheryl's parents and extended family (all independent microfamilies) *and* Michael's parents and extended family members (also independent microfamilies) would have some continuing interaction with Chase and Cheryl. Then Michael remarried, combining his microfamily with his new wife's microfamily unit. Finally, Cheryl and I remarried, assuming joint parenting responsibilities for Chase—a combination of two microfamilies.

Now what happens when all these microfamilies interact? I can tell you it's a lot like living together in a condominium. Blended families really are like *remarriage condominiums*. And what do you find in some real condominiums today? Frequent squabbles and conflicts as each unit owner tries to live as though he/she owned the whole building! Communities today require even more give-and-take than neighborhoods of

Americans before us. As a result, many condominium associations have mediation measures in place to resolve all types of neighbor complaints. Like condominium living, all our microfamilies also must learn to adjust and cooperate as we live in such close quarters with each other.

But there's another inescapable reality of remarriage—an inherent *separateness,* or natural buffer, between each microfamily. What do I mean? To Cheryl, Chase is her life. The natural bond of mother and child is God-given, and uniquely theirs to enjoy forever. Everyone can understand this very special relationship. But because of this wonderful bond, everything in Cheryl's world is influenced by how it affects Chase. Many mothers in Cheryl's position will have strong unspoken and perhaps even subconscious feelings: "I will stick by my children no matter what happens; I will always be closest to my own children; I will love others more if they are kind to my children; I will have less respect for those who are unkind to my children." These very natural and God-given maternal protection feelings form at least a minimal buffer against anything or anyone potentially endangering one's child.

Now I come into the picture. To her credit, in every way Cheryl stated her intent and desire to entrust her son to me as a father. But deep down she knew: "I want Warren to be the at-home father that Chase is missing. But Warren is a single man. He has never had children of his own. Can I really trust his judgment without more parenting experience?" Result? A little bit of separation until time and experience reinforces her trust.

What about Chase and Michael, his biological father? From the beginning of our marriage, Chase has felt comfortable calling me Dad without confusion about Michael, whom he also calls Dad. It's understandable that Michael would feel at least a little jealousy hearing his son call a newcomer "Dad." So Michael will naturally want to put some separation between us to make sure Chase knows who his "real dad" is. After several years of calling me Dad, however, Chase (and every stepfather in the world knows this is coming) told me at our family dinner recently, "You know, you aren't my real dad—you're just my stepdad." Cheryl and I asked him, "Did you think of this yourself, or did someone tell you this?" Chase remarked, "Well my real dad explained the difference to me." So Chase was putting a little separation between us as he sorts out his place in these microfamilies (which is very natural and expected).

Separation isn't always a bad situation—it can be a *good* thing. In football, a receiver makes moves and runs precise routes with primarily one goal in mind—to get some separation from the defender so the quarterback can complete the pass to his teammate without getting intercepted. This is true in relationships and life as well! Cheryl and I both earnestly yearn for Chase to grow up and become a devoted and loving Christian man. But it is natural to keep a little separateness from any parenting inexperience I may have so both of us can complete our joint parenting passes to Chase. It is understandable that Michael and Chase keep a little separateness from my daily stepparenting role so they have room to live and breathe in their relationship as well.

Separateness. It's a reality of remarriage and blended family life. We cannot reasonably expect our microfamilies, with our own unique histories of family life, to fit together seamlessly at the outset, any more than we can force it with a large number of *individuals* having different identities, backgrounds, and experiences. Each microfamily, and each person in that family, has different issues and unfinished business to deal with from the past. Single parents need time to adjust to married life once again and become accustomed to sharing decisions about their children and themselves. Children naturally will want to resist a new stepparent, whom they may see as an intruder. Stepsiblings will need time to sort out pecking orders and learn to coexist. To many remarriage partners who feel swamped with issues, some separateness is a blessing! In fact, it is actually healthy. These little buffers act like oil, greasing all the potential points of friction between all the different microfamilies. So don't think it strange when you encounter some separateness—especially in the early years of blended family life. Above all, don't *force* unity and togetherness on those who don't feel fully comfortable with it yet. It's a normal part of "getting to know you" better! Over time, these little buffers of separation will fall away as their usefulness becomes unnecessary and trust builds between individuals in each microfamily.

Here are a few suggestions to keep these temporary separateness buffers from becoming permanent, impenetrable walls between blended family members:

Keep looking for common interests. Think of the many areas in your blended family life where there's *no* need for separation. First, you and your partner love the Lord and each other. That's a vital common interest! Most parents—biological *and* stepparents—love their children and enjoy providing them with the best life they can provide. Finding the right house to live in, church and schools to attend, vacations to enjoy, and similar interests are good places to build family consensus. Notwithstanding the separateness found in most blended families, each member in the immediate family needs to feel more "we-ness" than "I-ness." Any communication or event toward that noble goal is a good idea.

Keep separateness in perspective. Don't assume separateness means "I don't love you." It only means, "I'm not comfortable just yet in receiving more closeness in this area of my life." That's okay. Don't force issues or try to control other's feelings.

Keep communication lines open. Sometimes separateness may mean a stepchild loving a stepsibling from a distance for a while because they must share living quarters. Perhaps ex-spouses are too intrusive and create stress in the blended family. Maybe the remarriage partners are weary in putting out all the fires and need some time alone. Regardless of the circumstances, *just keep listening and communicating.* The idea is to build love and trust bridges over time, spanning all those little gaps of separateness.

Keep the family focused. As each blended family member draws nearer to God, it isn't surprising that they draw nearer to each other as well. The Christian role models provided by remarriage partners also need to be the strongest daily life force for the children. With all the necessary shifting and adjusting of lives, hopes, and dreams, parents need to assume responsibility for promoting flexibility and merging the interests of the microfamilies enough to allow everyone to live cooperatively and lovingly with each other as much as possible. Mutual *acceptance* and looking to the interests of others is the key (Phil. 2:4).

Keep intimacy alive. Remarriage partners need the freedom to let their guard down with each other. Once again, actions speak louder than words. Setting aside private time for prayer and couple devotionals, undivided attention to each other, and sharing confidences builds intimacy and helps dissipate separateness over time. Being quick to understand and "come alongside" each other to the fullest extent possible keeps the home fires burning in each other's hearts.

Commitment. Compassion. Trust. Intimacy. These are wonderful "glue words" enhancing the "one flesh" remarriage relationship. But nothing really solidifies the remarriage relationship more than simply honoring God's roles for husbands and wives in *any* marriage.

AM I WILLING TO ACCEPT BIBLICAL ROLES AND SUBMISSION?

We serve a very complex God, whose mind and heart truly are beyond our understanding. So complex, in fact, that he created males and females with uniquely different talents and skills to express his nature fully. The usual tendency is for men to take charge of a marriage—and especially a remarriage with so much at stake. Certainly there is biblical support for male headship, but we must not miss God's mandate for a shared *servant* leadership and *mutual* submission in many aspects of married life.

"For God is not a God of disorder but of peace" (1 Cor. 14:33a). Order is the purpose of submission. God ordained (through the apostle Paul, as referenced in 1 Cor. 11:3 and Eph. 5) order for marriage and family this way: (1) he is the ultimate authority; (2) Christ, his Son, is the only mediator between God and humankind and is the head of the Church, his body; (3) husbands are the head of their wives, as Christ is the head of the church, and are to sacrifice themselves for their mates; (4) wives are to respect and submit to their husbands out of reverence for God; (5) children are to obey their parents, as the Lord. You cannot have submission if there is no order in the home or there is confusion about roles. Neither can you have order without submission, as each member in the family does his/her part to make God's plan a reality.

True submission is threefold: husband submits to God, wife submits to God, and because of their individual and personal love for the Lord, they willingly submit to each other as God desires (Eph. 5:21–33). In God's eyes, *mutual* submission is the liberating force, husband and wife imitating Christ's supreme example in submitting to the Father's will. God wants us to frame our perspectives on marriage with a focus on respecting each other and appreciating and honoring each other's gifts, rather than grabbing for power, authority, and dominance.

Mutual submission means *communicating* about marital decisions with honest and loving sharing of feelings and ideas, jointly working toward a goal of *unity.* The husband isn't a superior being by having headship in the family, but rather is a *leader* with equal value and worth as the wife before God. The wife may not agree with everything the husband does in asserting that leadership. She may need to give him some room to make some poor decisions as well. But her primary task is to strive for *unity* with him as he exercises that leadership, to the full extent it conforms to biblical principles.

Biblical submission becomes an issue when you reach a deadlock in your remarriage. After reviewing relevant facts and considering options, who decides when there's an impasse between husband and wife? That's the critical time when submission requires strength of character.

The idea of submission is very difficult for many people to accept—even if God's Word asks for it. In a Gallup poll several years ago, nearly 70 percent of people polled said they *disagreed* with the following statement: "A wife should graciously submit to the servant leadership of her husband." But when the question included the phrase, "statement taken from the Bible" (asked of a different group), the number disagreeing fell to 60 percent.[5]

Because so many have misused and abused God's Word on the issue of husband and wife roles, many women have become extremely sensitive to the subject. This reminds me of the couple who attended a marriage seminar by a well-known author. The speaker pounded away at the biblical issue of the husband being the head of the wife. (In reality, the speaker violated the spirit of the Scripture and essentially abused the scriptural text.) There was an eerie silence between the couple in the car on the way home from the seminar. Before stepping across the threshold of the front door, the husband paused and said, "What that guy said tonight—that's exactly how it's going to be around here from now on!" He didn't see his wife for several days. And then one eye began to open . . .

But God means what *he* says (not what we *think* he says), and his Word stands forever. Christians need to accept the Father's will in this matter, rather than seek to explain it away or bend it to make the Bible "politically correct" and fit in with our culture.

In the New Testament, the Lord's message for husbands is in 1 Peter 3:7 and Ephesians 5:1–2, 21, 25–33. Husbands are to love their wives as Christ loves the church. How does Christ love the church? He came to *serve* and to give his life as a ransom for many (Mark 10:45). He literally sacrificed himself for her (the church). This is the example for a Christian husband's leadership in Ephesians 5:25–30.

In his role as head of his bride, the church, Christ dedicates himself to do what is best for her always. He is the source of life for the church (Eph. 4:15–16). He nurtures, sustains, and protects her as a shepherd watches over the sheep. He encourages and enriches her. He willingly assumes responsibility for her growth and maturity. He is fully accountable for her. He also corrects her (Rev. 2:4–5; 3:15). In every way, Christ *leads* the church as her servant to enable her to reach her full potential. That also is how a husband is to love his wife. No manipulation, coercion, or control issues. No intimidating power plays. No abuse and fear. No grandstanding. You lay down your life for the one you love!

Husbands are to treat their wives with great respect, being encouraging, support-ive, and considerate of their needs and interests. Husbands do *not* have the right to dominate their wives. Men are to resist the natural temptation to use their position as head of the wife and their physical superiority to become dictatorial or self-absorbed. For "alpha male" husbands who think this way, it's time to have a heart-to-heart talk with the Alpha and Omega!

Fulfilling the vital role of loving one's wife as Christ loves the church is an awe-some task for any husband! How could any man possibly do it—even with God's ever-present power working in his life? Wives yearn to be loved and cherished in ways that seem beyond most husbands' grasp. So many women are looking for that Prince Charming to protect and serve them, and to slay the dragons in their lives. What wife wouldn't want a highly intelligent and sensitive husband who is confident in his life and work yet tender and loving at all the right times and places? But what husband can fully and consistently meet her expectations?

And that's where a godly wife comes in. She helps and encourages her man to be the best husband he can be—first for the Lord and then for her. As he changes from one degree of spirituality and fulfillment of his responsibilities to the next, struggling each step of the way to give her the best he can offer, his wife is always with him, urg-ing him on to still higher planes. Result? Husbands give even more to their wives. This cycle of giving and receiving between husbands and wives is part of God's plan for any marriage—a consistently uplifting experience!

God's message to wives is in 1 Peter 3:1–6; Ephesians 5:1–2, 21–24, 33; and Colossians 3:18: Husbands are to be the loving leaders of the home and family in God's arrangement (1 Cor. 11:3). Wives are to submit to their husbands' leadership because of God's command—not because of the husband's personal worthiness or capabilities as a leader. Her submission flows from a quiet and gentle spirit (1 Pet. 3:4), of great value in God's sight, in being respectful of her husband. This submission is a sign of strength—not weakness. It definitely *doesn't* mean inferiority or lack of ability. It also doesn't mean loss of equality of status with men before God (Gal. 3:26–28)—it simply means the Lord assigned different roles and functions to husbands and wives to maintain order in the remarriage. As her husband's helpmate, he needs her *active* involvement in his life, adding her special voice of encouragement and advice, and contributing constructive influence on him and the family in the same spirit as the noble woman described in Proverbs 31.

Our primary submission is to God as we willingly turn away from sinful pride and self-will (James 4:7). We willingly put ourselves under governmental authorities (Rom. 13:1–7; 1 Pet. 2:13). Children are to submit to their parents (Eph. 6:1–4; Col. 3:20). The younger are to submit to the older (1 Pet. 5:5). All of this is in accord with God's divine will in structuring society and maintaining order. In this same way, wives are to submit to their husbands (Eph. 5:22; Col. 3:18; 1 Pet. 3:1). Literally, wives are to "arrange under" their husbands in the same way all of us should arrange our lives under the Lord.[6] But be careful not to take this too far! Obviously the Lord doesn't expect any wife to submit herself or her family to domestic violence or abuse, since this is *disorder* of the worst kind!

Having a submissive, quiet, and gentle spirit means being a faithful encouraging helpmeet to one's husband in a nonargumentative spirit, without continual nagging and ostentation. Wives are to resist the temptation of using their words and emotions to usurp the husband's God-given leadership role or undermine his influence so she can control the family. They are not to be pushy, selfishly assertive, or insist on having their own way.

Wives can, and should, proactively share their thoughts, ideas, and confidence without usurping their husbands' leadership. There is a stable balance between being a strong and self-assertive wife while also being able to trust and give to the strength of her husband with dignity, wisdom, and courage. I really like the way Dr. Juliana Slattery expresses this balance in her excellent book *Finding the Hero in Your Husband*:

> The submissive wife uses all of her God-given influence to build her husband's ability to lead. . . . Her goal is not to take his leadership away, but to empower him daily to grow into this difficult role. She does not use his mistakes to prove his inadequacies, but she succeeds and fails with him. She convinces him that she believes in him and will be by his side. She is able to wait for his leadership, even if she believes that she could do a better job. She tells him daily, through her trust, that she needs him to be a strong and capable leader. Her goal is to convince him that he can trust her with everything he is. The message that her submission communicates is: "I know you are not perfect, but I trust in your love. I believe you are capable of being the great leader for our family that God has called you to be. I will help you with all that I am to achieve this goal, even if at times my love hurts you. I will not expect you to be more than you are or allow you to be less than you are."[7]

In Ephesians 5:21–33, submission carries the sense of "attachment to," or "identified with." This means husbands and wives are to divest themselves of obligations to the world, as much as reasonably possible, and to attach and identify themselves *with each other* in mutual respect without intimidation or domination. Husbands and wives are to pour themselves out in complementing and completing each other. They willingly sacrifice themselves to make their mates, and the remarriage, whole.

There's great strength in biblical submission. It isn't strength as the world values it. It's rooted in our willingness to subjugate our will to God first and then to one another. Obedience to God and love for our mates are the tandem forces that makes biblical submission a true blessing. God planned marriage this way—our lives at home are a training ground for learning what biblical submission to him truly is all about. Remarriages are no different.

Remarriage partners would do well in making a mutual commitment to serve each other, challenge each other, encourage each other, and create a mutually submissive partnership where both spouses bloom and grow together.

BLENDED FAMILY UNITY WITH DIVERSITY

Nothing wrecks a remarriage more quickly than *disunity* between husband and wife. It's better by far to weather the results of a poor decision or two than to experience the many negative consequences of not being unified. Being *unified* in remarriage is more important!

As Philippians 2:1–8 reminds us, we are to strive for the same love, being of one accord and like-minded, looking out for the interests of our spouses as well as our own. "If it is possible, *as far as it depends on you*, live at peace with everyone" (Rom. 12:18, emphasis added). You *can* have unity without being in total agreement on every decision. But you *cannot* have unity when pride and selfishness rule the home.

More so than first marriages, remarriages thrive best in acknowledging that you can still have unity, notwithstanding the great amount of diversity in so many blended families. *Unity in diversity*—a strong partnership with a workable balancing of interests bringing peace and harmony to remarried family life. We explore practical ramifications of this principle in blended family life in the chapters to follow.

A Message from Cheryl

Merging of two middle-aged adults can be *very* complicated. He has a condominium. She has a home. Her kids are laid back. His children are overly active. He is a charismatic Christian. She likes more traditional denominations. Merging these and many more differences takes lots of time.

When children are involved in a blended family, adjustments obviously need to be gradual. Children need consistency (don't we all?). Often their needs must be considered before our own.

When we first fall in love, it seems we can make any sacrifice for this new spouse-to-be. But if we bend too far, it will come back in resentment later on—in months or even years down the line. Be wise enough to know your needs, and the needs of your children so you can make the best remarriage decision.

Many family experts warn that a remarried couple, and their blended family, must not require too much adaptation from the life either spouse knew prior to the remarriage. But it may be impossible for "his" home to become "our" home without some significant change. Physically, and symbolically, we need to seek a new home that is "ours."

Make sure your remarriage is indeed a merger—not a hostile takeover!

QUESTIONS FOR PERSONAL REFLECTION

1. How much change can I accept in remarriage? Do I have any reservations against making a total commitment to my remarriage partner and all other members of my blended family? Is there any area in my life that hinders me from having compassion for *every* member of my family?

2. What are some unreasonable expectations about remarriage with which I have struggled?

3. Do I trust my remarriage partner? Are there any areas where trust is difficult for me? What fears do I have about making a commitment to everyone in my blended family?

4. How do I feel about having some separateness in remarriage—especially in areas where it wasn't as apparent in my prior marriage? In what specific areas is separateness most apparent in my relationship with my remarriage partner and the children?

5. Do I accept God's plan for order and authority in marriage? Is there any specific area of my life that might hinder me from having a servant's heart for everyone in my family?

Chapter 6

FOUR ESSENTIAL KEYS TO LAUNCHING A SUCCESSFUL REMARRIAGE

You've now found a suitable mate and are preparing to remarry. What are the four most important keys to making your remarriage relationship and blended family a success with the Lord's help?

Once upon a time, not so very long ago, it seemed that television's Cleaver family—Ward, June, and the boys of *Leave It to Beaver* fame—seemed to epitomize most American families in the late fifties and early sixties. They always appeared to resolve their problems with little effort. They never raised their voices or appeared overly angry or upset. Children could play in the neighbor's house, and mothers wouldn't have to worry. Each episode had a happy ending. But the reality in American families, even then, was much different. This is even more true today.

At the breakfast table, over the holidays, and on the way to the bathroom at night, you may find yourself running into relative strangers in your own home during the first few years of blended family life. During holidays, it may be hard to know exactly which extended family members will show up. There may be constantly shifting boundaries, strange alliances, and rather awkward intimacies, punctuated by a few jealous anxieties. Each family member may have to struggle with the "name game"—what does everyone call themselves?

Children have "instant parents" and perhaps new brothers and sisters overnight. These adjustments may lead to competition for parental attention, personal space at home, and other material comforts that strain family finances. If the blended family welcomes newborn children, these half-siblings bring still another dimension of difficulties and adjustments.

Stepparents have even more adjustments to make. They aren't biological parents, nor are they adoptive or even foster parents. Although a stepparent may be, in every way, a true "psychological parent," many courts view him/her as a "nonparent" without any legal rights because there's no blood relationship to the stepchild. This is true even though the stepparent assumes daily responsibility for spiritual, emotional, and physical care of a stepchild. With all the uncertainties about stepparenting roles in disciplining children in the blended family, a stepparent also may go to extremes. Either the stepparent overdisciplines the children or withdraws from a parenting role—perhaps entirely! Result? Children in many blended families receive less attention and supervision than those in traditional families.

Then, on top of all the internal blended family challenges are external stresses and pressure. How does one properly deal with the divorced biological parent or ex-spouse, grandparents, and extended family members? Many times this leads to expensive legal battles over custody, visitation, and support. Ex-spouses experience their own frustration by being caught in the middle between their children, former mates, and unfamiliar new spouses and stepparents "baby-sitting" their children.

Romanticized notions of blended family life fade away in the realities of daily problems and struggles. Each family member may feel he/she is giving up more than what is received. With all these family and personal stresses and pressures, it's common for family members to feel confused, isolated, lonely, anxious, insecure, angry, resentful, overwhelmed, and even despairing at times!

This book is designed to guide you in recognizing potential remarriage and blended family issues while suggesting how to build up your remarriage and blended family with the Lord's help. You know that you *will* run into challenges and difficulties. However, if you've built your family on the rock of Jesus Christ using biblical principles, you needn't panic when challenges come; you'll know where to look to fix the problems. When the going gets rough, simply ask yourself, "Is my family still together? Are we still moving in the right direction?" If yes, then *relax* and start dealing with the problems one by one as you move along.

FOUR VITAL KEYS

"Teacher," a lawyer once asked Jesus, "Which is the greatest commandment in the Law?" Jesus' response?
"'Love the Lord your God with all your heart and with all your soul
and with all your mind and with all your strength.' This is the first and
greatest commandment. And the second is like it: 'Love your neighbor
as yourself.' All the Law and the Prophets hang on these two commandments. There is no commandment greater than these."
(Matt. 22:34–40)

Jesus' statement summarizes how we're to live in relationship with the Lord and everyone else—including a blended family. Loving God is our first priority. Loving each other as we love ourselves is the second.

But how do these commandments apply in remarriages and blended families? I believe obedience requires four essential elements: (1) Put God first in your home, and keep your family devoted to him. (2) Encourage loving and effective communication among all family members. (3) Maintain healthy boundaries among those within the family, as well as with ex-spouses and extended family members. (4) Promptly resolve conflicts in a loving, biblical, and responsible manner. These vital relationship builders should be in place among all family members even *before* the wedding.

Key No. 1—Put God First in Your Home

Build on a foundation of Christ and biblical love. Remember, unless the Lord builds the house, its builders labor in vain (Ps. 127:1). Christ is the bedrock for blended family homes that truly grow and succeed, and the cement holding those building materials together is biblical love (discussed in chap. 4).

Reflect the Lord's glory, grace, and unconditional love. Psalm 136:1 assures us that the Lord's steadfast "love endures forever." Romans 8:38–39 teaches us of the depths of God's love: "For I am convinced that neither death nor life, neither angels nor demons, neither the present nor the future, nor any powers, neither height nor depth, nor anything else in all creation, will be able to separate us from the love of God that is in Christ Jesus our Lord." If this is how God loves each member of the family, how can we do anything less?

How do we put God's love first in our family? We need to *empathize* with them in the same spirit as the father in the parable of the prodigal son (Luke 15:11–32). Just as God treats us, we need to reflect his mercy and grace in deciding that there's *nothing* our partners or our children could ever do that will keep us from loving them. How? By *choosing* to love them unconditionally without making them *earn* it. We love and accept our family members for who they are—not because of what they do. This love needs *daily* reaffirmation![1] Unconditional love like this requires that moments of disappointment or anger with family members don't give the false impression that we love them any less. *As a safeguard, never withhold or withdraw your love as means of discipline or punishment.*

Think like God thinks. As Christians, "we have the mind of Christ" (1 Cor. 2:16), which means we have the knowledge and power to live, love, and serve as Christ did during his time on earth. That's *amazing!* The only conditional element is our *desire* to think and act like him. We must *choose* to see matters God's way.

The disciples missed this vital point when they tried to keep children from bothering Jesus in Matthew 19:13–15. Jesus *wanted* them to come to him for a blessing. Similarly, when a stepparent has difficulty accepting a stepchild, he/she may be forgetting how God lovingly accepts us. As his adopted sons and daughters, he *lavishes* us with his love, wisdom, and understanding (Eph. 1:3–8). How can we say we love God and yet not love the children in our own home?

How can we think like God? Scripture is full of ways to help us see matters from God's perspective, but the apostle Peter gives us one critical element: "Therefore, prepare your minds for action; be self-controlled; set your hope fully on the grace to be given you when Jesus Christ is revealed" (1 Pet. 1:13). Preparing one's mind for action begins with having the right attitudes—those attitudes that God has: holiness, peace, patience, compassion, forgiveness, empathy, commitment, faithfulness, and love.

Recognize these qualities? They're fruits of the Spirit (Gal. 5:22)! By keeping in step with the Spirit, we "grow" these fruits into our lives as we set our hope fully on God's grace, practice obedience, and yield to him. Changing our attitudes about our mates and blended families to mirror God helps us rely upon him for self-control as we prepare ourselves for action.

Open wide your heart. In 2 Corinthians 6:11–13, the apostle Paul captures the essence of how we're to treat each other as God treats us: "We have spoken freely to you, Corinthians, and opened wide our hearts to you. We are not withholding our affection from you. . . . As a fair exchange—I speak as to my children—open wide your hearts also."

God poured out his love into our hearts by the Holy Spirit, whom he has given us (Rom. 5:5). He poured out his grace, with faith and love found in Christ Jesus (1 Tim. 1:14). The very nature of "leaving" the single life and "cleaving" to one's remarriage partner in a "one flesh" relationship (discussed in chap. 3) means pouring out our very selves for our mates. We do so in a gracious and loving manner that makes us vulnerable, and encourages them to trust in their love for us. This involves assertive and effective communication by revealing our true selves and letting our mates know what we think, feel, and desire (or not desire) with honesty, integrity, and sensitivity.

How worthless to fill our heads with endless blended family relationship skills if our *hearts* aren't in it too! Family members won't *hear* each other's words, no matter how eloquently and sensitively expressed, if they don't *feel* sincere empathy and warm acceptance. Use your head *and* your heart to open the door to the Lord and intimate bonding with your family. You must *want* to come alongside a family member with the consistent message, "I really want to understand why you feel the way you do."

We also need to open our hearts wide to the children in our blended family. They do need this special place in our lives so desperately—especially after experiencing the trauma and confusion of divorce or death of a parent. This need may lead a stepparent to tell his stepchild, "I'll never replace your father, but I'll love you, and protect you, and provide for you as my own child."

Reaffirm personal commitment to the family. Commitment is a voluntary choice to fulfill the responsibilities of being a husband or wife and a coparent to all the children in the blended family as the Lord expects and commands. This means spending one-on-one quality time with each family member as much as reasonably possible, giving each person emotional support while nurturing spiritual growth. It also means providing personal and financial security to protect everyone so each member feels safe, secure, and significant with a growing sense of *belonging* to the family.

Each family member needs to encourage and nurture a unified "we-ness." Include other family members in events and activities as much as possible, and defend them from others putting them down or diminishing them. Above all, admire the accomplishments of each family member and don't take anyone for granted. This fosters an emotional partnership among everyone concerned.

Promote a spiritual focus for the family. There are few better statements of Christian relationship dynamics that will make any remarriage and blended family situation work better than what the apostle Paul expresses in Romans 12:9–21:

> Love must be sincere. Hate what is evil; cling to what is good. Be devoted to one another in brotherly love. Honor one another above yourselves. Never be lacking in zeal, but keep your spiritual fervor, serving the Lord. Be joyful in hope, patient in affliction, faithful in prayer. Share with God's people who are in need. Practice hospitality.
>
> Bless those who persecute you; bless and do not curse. Rejoice with those who rejoice; mourn with those who mourn. Live in harmony with one another. Do not be proud, but be willing to associate with people of low position. Do not be conceited.
>
> Do not repay anyone evil for evil. Be careful to do what is right in the eyes of everybody. If it is possible, as far as it depends on you, live at peace with everyone. Do not take revenge, my friends, but leave room for God's wrath, for it is written: "It is mine to avenge; I will repay," says the Lord. On the contrary: "If your enemy is hungry, feed him; if he is thirsty, give him something to drink. In doing this, you will heap burning coals on his head." Do not be overcome by evil, but overcome evil with good.

How can a blended family go wrong if these qualities reign in relationships?

Paul then adds another important ingredient to this family recipe in Philippians 2:1–4:

> If you have any encouragement from being united with Christ, if any comfort from his love, if any fellowship with the Spirit, if any tenderness and compassion, then make my joy complete by being like-minded, having the same love, being one in spirit and purpose. Do nothing out of selfish ambition or vain conceit, but in humility consider others better than yourselves. Each of you should look not only to your own interests, but also to the interests of others.

Looking out for each other. Serving one another in love. Striving to be "like-minded," having the same love, and being united in spirit and purpose. How does this happen?

• *Worship together.* Look for every opportunity to attend the same church and worship together as a family. Get involved in church family activities. Carry the sermon messages through the week by discussing practical applications.

• *Make family events and meals special.* After the wedding, blended family members may head off in a thousand different directions with busy work schedules, after-school activities, church activities, and everything else. At the beginning, set the right tone for building up the family and encouraging intimacy and regular fellowship with each other. Do things together as a family *now—before* the wedding. Share meals with each other, and spend as much time together as reasonably possible. Discuss spiritual victories and personal defeats. Making family times a priority now *and* after the wedding builds relationships and bolsters a sense of bonding. You're making one of the best investments in your children and your family's future. Take time to *listen* carefully about cares and passions while giving each other undivided attention. And have some fun—don't just eat and run! Dream and plan your future together.

• *Devotionals.* Even before the wedding, remarriage partners need to work together diligently in keeping everyone in the blended family focused on spiritual goals. Ideally, the couple is having private devotionals and praying together regularly. But get *all* family members studying Scripture and praying together *before* the wedding as well. Christian bookstores carry a wide variety of guides to family devotions to make the time enjoyable and worthwhile. (See chap. 7.)

• *Build family intimacy.* Intimacy comes from sincere warmth, honesty, openness, genuine affection, sincere appreciation, empathy, shared experiences, and bonding of family members. It grows when family members learn to be emotionally present for one another with a caring concern and commitment to each other. To achieve intimacy we must *actively* discover the unique abilities, and strive to meet the individual needs, of each family member. Building intimacy involves giving regular, consistent, positive affirmations; sharing in each person's goals and dreams; and encouraging him or her to achieve those goals and dreams.

Intimacy also grows from a "mutual fund" of accountability, respect, acceptance, and love:

• *Mutual accountability.* Each member knows and relies upon the premise that each person is accountable to everyone else. Everyone lives by the same house rules, while lovingly respecting and honoring each other's boundaries. No one plays God, pursuing selfish wants and expecting others to comply. No one hypocritically demands that other family members do anything he/she fails to do. The blended family is a team, with each member sharing the workload to help the family grow (see 1 Cor. 12). Humility and forgiveness reign.

• *Mutual respect.* Creating a family environment that encourages all family members to share their thoughts and feelings openly builds intimacy. Each member can have meaningful input in major family decisions and disagree with each other respectfully without penalty or punishment. Mutual respect involves giving others appreciation and admiration, rejecting opportunities to manipulate or control each other. It seeks every opportunity to honor needs, values, and rights of all family members as much as reasonably possible. It speaks the truth in love without controlling others, and helps them face the logical results of their decisions. Mutual respect also honors individual privacy—personal time and space—to the fullest extent reasonably possible. It gives others space to grow and enjoy life in personal ways vital to each person's age and maturity. (Obviously, parents do need to act responsibly in monitoring the needs of minor children as part of their coparenting.)

Part of this process is learning to "walk in another's shoes," honoring each person's freedom to be different. Being respectful and loving may mean giving up personal desires at times for the greater good of all. Sometimes it's difficult (if not impossible) to understand another's mind-set. But when we accept someone else's *perspective* on an issue, even if we heartily disagree, we can still come alongside them, help them bear their burdens, and empathize!

• *Mutual acceptance and love.* Romans 15:7 urges us: "Accept one another, then, just as Christ accepted you, in order to bring praise to God." Everyone in the blended family needs acceptance. Yet too often we fall short on this vital spiritual affirmation. Christ accepts us. And so we should eagerly accept one another. How do we do it? By having a patient, gentle, kind, and forgiving heart full of compassion, as Jesus models for us in loving the little children in Luke 18:15–17. Acceptance roots itself in biblical love. By trusting in God and accepting each other we open our hearts wide to receive the full measure of joy that Christ promises in John 15:10–11.

When blended family members reside together for the first time—unpacking totally different experiences, values, and beliefs from their life suitcases—acceptance can be elusive. A wife may insist on having everyone sit down for dinner at 6 P.M. sharp, while the husband and his children enjoy more flexible dinnertimes. Some children love to play video games all weekend, while new stepsiblings feel comfortable with rules limiting video gametime. Accepting each other means discussing, compromising, and adjusting to one another to help the family gel. Without mutual acceptance and love, competition and battles for control dominate life where no one wins.

• *Achieve unity and oneness between remarriage partners.* Jesus tells us the truth: "Every kingdom divided against itself will be ruined, and every city or household divided against itself will not stand" (Matt. 12:25). As you prepare for remarriage, are your relationships with your partner and your children marked more by unity or division? Is there a basic agreement among all family members to live together?

The spiritual focus of the blended family—indeed its best chance for success with God's help—hinges on the *unity and oneness* of husband and wife after they leave the single life and cleave to each other as God intends. Your relationship with your mate thrives on it. Your children depend upon it (although they may unwittingly try to sabotage it at times). The preservation of your family from unreasonable outside pressures and intrusions from ex-spouses and extended family hinges on it. In fact, the only calm and rational force for order and growth in the chaos of blended family life may be your relationship with God and your spouse.

Sure, there'll be times when you won't feel united with your mate. As imperfect people, we all make mistakes. But focus your energy and appreciation on the many positive qualities you share in your relationship. *Together,* commit to putting God first in your lives and homelife, always seeking to live his way. As Edward and Sharon Douglas (themselves remarried after divorce) so eloquently expressed in their book, *The Blended Family: Achieving Peace and Harmony in the Christian Home*:

> As flawed women married to flawed men, couples will have the desires of their hearts if they work towards oneness in their marriage. Couples must work toward eliminating selfishness and focus more on developing a Christlike character. Couples should spend more time on learning what their individual godly roles are as husband, wife, and parent rather than spending energy on what is deficient in their mate.

If couples do this, they will appreciate more the person God has given to them.[2]

Key No. 2—Loving and Effective Family Communication

What do most couples say is the greatest problem in marriages? Poor communication. (You may have experienced this truth firsthand if your prior marriage ended in divorce.) When's the best time to begin developing marital communication skills? According to researchers, it's *before* you marry, since that's when a couple feels extraordinarily good about each other. Matters are running smoothly, and the blended family responsibilities haven't kicked in yet.

If Christ is the lifeblood of any Christian marriage, then communication surely is its heartbeat. Learning how to listen so your mate can *talk* is as important as learning how to talk so your partner will *listen*. But communication is a much greater challenge for couples who remarry. Added to all the other complexities in a blended family, each family member uses different communication styles that may (or may not) be compatible with everyone else. These styles spring from prior relationships and can set the scene for potential misunderstandings and conflicts.

Learn what builds up family members. To communicate within the family in the loving way God intends, we must take Ephesians 4:29 to heart: "Do not let any unwholesome talk come out of your mouths, but only what is helpful for building others up according to their needs, that it may benefit those who listen." Is your communication encouraging to others? Does it build up your mate and family members or tear them down? Do your loved ones benefit by listening to what you have to share? Nothing else matters if you ignore this divine command!

Learn the blended family language. Family communication styles can be complex codes. How do we translate all the messages, body language, feelings, and emotions involved? After we married, Cheryl noticed Chase getting up some mornings with a big frown on his face. She'd greet him with a big hug and kiss while asking him, "Hey, little guy! Why the 'foonja face' [phonetically written]?" I thought this was some reference to ninja movies! But it was an expression from Cheryl's Italian great-grandfather that means "sad face." How was I to know? Then, of course, Cheryl and Chase had their "secret handshake" together—three quick squeezes of each other's hands meaning "I . . . love . . . you!" They enjoyed a whole different language together while I felt like a foreigner! Some families are quite vocal and demonstrative in their communication. Others rely more on nonverbal actions and reactions. Some use humor and mild sarcasm to make points and resolve differences. Others are more unemotional, introspective, and serious. We gain a common language by talking out our differences.

Besides learning each other's family languages, it's important to develop a new blended family language, perhaps with one family member acting as "translator" for each microfamily involved. "Blending" means compromising and *melding* these communication styles so everyone will be on the same page. If family members learn to relate and communicate in a loving and comfortable way—even before the wedding—the family will have a great start in the crucial first years of living together.

How can each family member learn good communication skills? Here are some suggestions:

Timing. Nothing is more critical to good communication than finding the proper time to talk. Proverbs 15:23: "A man finds joy in giving an apt reply—and how good is a timely word!" Proverbs 25:11: "A word aptly spoken is like apples of gold in settings of silver." The tricky and delicate aspect of timing, knowing when to speak up, is as important as knowing when it's better to remain quiet and wait for a better time. Careless, untimely words wound others—sometimes permanently. Robert Fulghum said it best: "Sticks and stones may break my bones, but words will break our hearts." That's why we need to *think* and *pray* about what to say, how to say it, and especially *when* to say it. Then, before taking any action, we'll have appropriate sensitivity and concern about the other family members' feelings. This requires a cool head and a warm heart, assuming the best of others, and not jumping to conclusions until having all the facts.

Give family members needed space rather than forcing communication. Perhaps a family member really needs some time alone to meditate, pray, forgive, or cool off anger. Sometimes kids (particularly adolescents) don't feel talkative at all to adults (although they spend hours on the telephone with friends). Good timing involves patience, waiting for them to feel ready to talk. Forcing the issue inevitably collides with a concrete wall of silence or conflict. Young people especially protect their privacy, and normally establish some individuality and independence by controlling communication.

The best time to talk is during uninterrupted "one-on-one" time with other family members. This time is absolutely critical between husband and wife, but it is extremely important with the children as well. All blended family members can benefit from spending time together fixing dinner or washing dishes, going to a sports event, running errands, playing a game together, or just taking a walk with one other family member.

To encourage family communication in general, consider a regular time for holding a Family Conference (see chap. 8), where each can discuss personal concerns. Family Conferences really help clear the air and promote bonding and intimacy. Given these special times for discussing family problems, have everyone agree *not* to discuss problems during times of rest and relaxation. Reserve family meals or recreational times for fun activities, nourishment, and refreshment without controversy.

Stimulate conversation. Children in the blended family need to know the stepparent's family history. Familiarity helps lessen natural fears and suspicions about this new parental figure coming into their lives. To meet this need, the stepparent may want to share personal childhood memories and photographs or tell humorous stories giving each child room to relate and laugh. Sharing memories helps the stepparent bond with children.

Biological parents, especially, need to keep in touch with their children and "take their emotional temperature." How well are they adjusting to the new family situation? "Honey, how did you feel about not going with us on the picnic because you visited your dad and his new family?" "In what ways are you and your new stepsister getting to know each other better?" More than stepparents, biological parents need to assume primary responsibility for monitoring problems with their children.

Encourage *all* family members to begin reaching out to each other by asking timely, specific, open-ended, nonleading questions designed to promote healthy and insightful communication. Once again, timing is extremely important. Make sure the family member is ready, able, and willing to respond. Pray beforehand!

Specific questions ("What did you most enjoy doing at work today?") are better than vague questions ("How was your day?"). Vague questions usually reap only equally vague responses—"Fine." Open-ended questions ("What was on the science test?" rather than "Was the science test hard?") can't be answered with one word, such as yes or no. Nonleading questions ("What topic do you think we should cover in our family devotion tonight?") invite sincere, creative responses, while leading questions ("Do you think we should study Jesus walking on the lake tonight?") may compel other family members to agree and rubberstamp *our* conclusions and desires.

Specific, nonleading, and open-ended questions like these, asked at the proper time, engage the personality, mind, and opinions of other family members in ways that open the soul, inspire visions and dreams, and promote family bonding. Creative discussion is an excellent way to begin a shared family history, which is vital in building trust and keeping family members actively investing in their relationships for the future.

Communicate with clear, accurate, and consistent messages. Poet Robert Frost once remarked, "Families break up when people take hints you don't intend and miss hints you do intend."[3] Why does this happen? Probably because we fail to communicate clearly with each other. Merely talking isn't necessarily *communicating.* Some folks talk a great deal without really saying anything meaningful. Others can share profound messages and engage in very effective communication by saying very little. Clear, accurate communication occurs when all parties to a conversation clearly say what they want to say while carefully listening to, and hearing, what others say.

Communicating *consistent* messages is as important as stating a matter clearly and concisely. A classic example is the husband who asks his obviously upset wife, "Honey, I can tell something's bothering you. What's wrong?" only to be given a curt and stiff, "*Nothing's wrong!*" Or it can be the husband restlessly waiting for his wife to get ready for an evening out, saying through gritted teeth, "Take your time dear, I don't mind waiting." Rest assured, he *doesn't* want you to take your time, and he *does* mind waiting!

Be specific about feelings. It's much better to say, "I need some quality personal time with you, but I feel shut out when you spend your free time opening mail and reading the newspaper," as opposed to only sharing, "I don't get enough time with you."

Sometimes it's hard to discuss difficult or emotionally charged issues with others. If you can't talk about a matter, why not write it out? In fact, it may even work better to write down an important message at times. Writing out your feelings gives you an excellent opportunity to sort everything out. This helps minimize the risk of mis-understanding. It also provides the recipient with a record of your thoughts that he or she can reread and pray about. Many times written apologies or encouragement mean much more than expressing the same thoughts verbally!

Be quick to listen. "We don't talk anymore" usually means"We don't *listen* to one another anymore." James 1:19 urges us, "My dear brothers, take note of this: Everyone should be quick to listen." Listening involves making a prompt, personal engagement to hear others out.

There's a difference between truly listening and holding a hearing. Hearings are for those with quick agendas to discover facts and rush to judgment. Listening involves putting the other person first and responding to his/her needs while sensitively considering that person's feelings.

How can we listen to family members? First, devote positive attention to them by listening without distraction. Don't try to multitask by shuffling through the mail, reading the newspaper, or watching television. *Look* at the speaker and give your full attention. Don't answer the telephone. Above all, don't walk away in the middle of a conversation without proper closure.

Set the scene for active listening. Choose a private place to talk. Eliminate any barriers between you and the speaker. Some of my fellow lawyers love to hide behind their desks to look "professional" in their conferences—even to the point of having their chairs slightly elevated above clients' chairs! But I have a couple of comfortable chairs in front of my desk where I ask clients to join me. We can be closer to one another for meetings without any barrier, which helps put people at ease. Isn't this especially necessary with family members at home?

Be aware of your body language as you listen. Since listening is a very *visual* practice, look attentive and engaging. Show openness and approachability as you listen. Make it a point to listen and talk with your whole body. Have everyone take a seat to talk—this reduces the risk of intimidating body language. Turn your body in the speaker's direction and lean forward. Don't cross your arms or shift your body from side to side if you are standing. Look pleasant. Nod your head periodically to show you are tuned in and understanding the comments shared. These are encouraging ways to show your speaker that you want more information.

Be slow to speak. James 1:19 goes further, "My dear brothers, take note of this: Everyone should be quick to listen, slow to speak." Try not to interrupt a family member sharing feelings. Don't think you have to fill in a brief period of silence as the speaker gathers some thoughts. Pauses allow all parties in the conversation to process information and focus on understanding each other. This time prepares the way for more honest communication.

Proverbs 18:13 says it well: "He who answers before listening—that is his folly and his shame." When a family member asks you to listen, try to avoid giving advice. Telling the person why he/she shouldn't feel that way doesn't help either. Just *hear* and *understand* what's behind those feelings. Don't think you have to say or do something to solve the problem. If you do, and it's a problem your family member really needs to resolve without your help, you may worsen matters by contributing to that person's fears or feelings of inadequacy. Simply ask, "What kind of help would you like me to give you right now?"

What if your family member is *quick* to speak and *slow* to listen to whatever you feel you need to say? Try the "ten minute rule" of communication. Your family member has ten minutes to speak without interruption. Then you have ten minutes to respond. Can't figure out which one should start a conversation? Simple, just flip a coin!

But allow everyone to express themselves in ways that feel natural for them. Consider the words a gift. Take time to unwrap them. Act as though the only important thing in the world to you at that particular moment is listening to what your family member is sharing. Communicate, "If you ever need to talk about something, I care."

Be slow to become angry. The passage in James 1 concludes, "My dear brothers, take note of this: Everyone should be quick to listen, slow to speak, and slow to become angry, for man's anger does not bring about the righteous life that God desires" (James 1:19–20). This divine "communication formula" in a nutshell really works in blended families!

Give constructive feedback while validating feelings and emotions. Communication isn't effective unless there's a complete exchange of information. The speaker gave a message. How did the listener receive it? If the message carried certain feelings and emotions, was it understood in the same context? Don't be satisfied in your listening role if you receive statements from family members but miss the accompanying feelings and emotions. Ask for clarification. Look beneath the surface of emotions. Whenever reasonably possible, accept a family member's feelings, acknowledging each person's perceptions as his/her assessment of a situation. Also respect the person's freedom to hold views different from your own.

In his article "Ineffective Communication—The Fine Art of Disagreeing," communications researcher Kenneth Heiting notes that many spouses fear losing control of feelings and experiencing personal invalidation. Expecting the worst, some couples "draw up a pact" (an unwritten one) *not* to share their feelings openly with each other. This is put into effect in five ways: (1) one partner gives in; (2) one assumes the blame; (3) one places responsibility on the other for any problem; (4) one consistently interrupts during a conversation; or (5) one consistently treats the other's feelings lightly. Heiting concludes his assessment with this observation:

> Effective communication is characterized by a willingness to really listen to what your partner is saying, thinking and feeling. Respect for your partner's self-disclosure—his or her feelings of excitement, frustration, sadness, or shame, etc.—is another important ingredient. If you want your partner to be open with you, you must be accepting of what he or she says. This doesn't mean that you must agree on all matters, but at least you must allow them to express their own outlook.[4]

Above all, be empathetic. Show that you really do understand what others share. Whenever possible, give *positive* feedback. Proverbs 16:24: "Pleasant words are a honeycomb, sweet to the soul and healing to the bones." Confirm your understand-ing—and agreement if possible—by telling the speaker, "Now I understand what you're saying. I think you're right about that particular point. I agree with you." Or, if you understand but don't agree, you might say, "I really appreciate your insight on this matter because you have brought up some things that I haven't thought of. After I think and pray this matter through a little bit, may we talk again?"

Accept/agree/apologize/forgive. We've already emphasized how important it is for family members to always feel accepted, no matter what the topic of conversation. This *doesn't* mean always accepting their opinions as practical or truthful—they may not be! However, accepting the *person* expressing the thoughts and feelings allows him/her to be the unique person God created.

Agree with the truth whenever possible. One common marriage complaint is, "My spouse never admits being wrong about anything!" This prideful mind-set brings division. I recall a court clerk once asking a groom-to-be applying for a marriage license, "Would you like an exercise guaranteeing a successful marriage?" "Sure," the man replied. The clerk elaborated, "Repeat after me, and lower your head a little more after each sentence: First, 'You're absolutely right!'; Second, 'I'm so sorry, honey!'; and third, 'I'll never do it again!'" Amusing advice, but not a bad idea when our partners have a valid criticism! Agreement with the truth requires a humble heart.

As we mentioned in key no. 1, mutual accountability is crucial to the success of a blended family. Part of that accountability involves making prompt, sincere, simple apologies. A sincere apology loses its effectiveness with each hour that passes between an offensive event and the time of actually voicing the apology. The apology should be *personal and direct* by facing the offended family member, communicating concern for the offended, and expressing sincere regret for hurtful words or actions. It should be short and to the point, without qualifications that try to excuse or shift blame. *Receiving* an apology graciously ranks as important as giving one. Make it an experi-ence that reinforces family bonding and understanding.

In every way possible, communicate to the family that forgiveness brings healing and restoration of relationships when members have been hurt by others. An even better and more gracious practice is desiring a forgiving heart, even when other family members won't acknowledge their errors or seek forgiveness. This takes lots of prayer, preparation, and persistence!

The essential need for touch. One of the most beautiful and moving experiences of courting before marriage is the close, good feeling of embracing your beloved fre-quently. It doesn't matter whether it is hugging, holding hands, or sitting close together—you desire that constant touch literally and figuratively. This desire to be touched and to touch others is a God-given need from infancy. It provides a tangible connection between human beings that displaces insecurities, and calms fears and anxieties.

Children need to see affection between their parents as well. Many times I'll approach Cheryl in the kitchen and give her a warm hug and kiss. When he was younger, Chase felt threatened by someone else hugging his mommy, so he'd jump up and try to squeeze himself between us. But now he knows we love him, so he just looks up and smiles at us. And many times we also include him in a "group hug"!

Touching family members communicates, many times without words, "I love you. You're important to me. I won't abandon you. I'm glad we're together." Spontaneous, sincere, nonsexual, meaningful affection sustains emotional closeness in the family. And, of course, touching is even more special if it is accompanied by verbal expressions of praise and acceptance.

Of course, there's a "good touch" and a "bad touch" as well. Some become affectionate in manipulative ways—only selectively touching others when they selfishly want something. This does nothing more than breed resentment and distrust. In addition, some stepparents engage in inappropriate touching or sexual misconduct because there's no natural biological tie between adult and child. Obviously, conduct like this is biblically and morally wrong and reprehensible to Christ (Matt. 18:6–7).

Affectionate and pure bonding of blended family members needs to be the first line of defense against the world. Affirmation and touching within the family builds trust and self-acceptance to face the dragons outside the front door!

How ineffective communication causes family breakdowns. When family members don't communicate effectively, they miss the golden opportunity to get to know each other as they really are in the blended family. But, unfortunately, it doesn't always end there.

Family members find themselves saying yes to matters and agreeing to requests when they really feel like saying no. Anger or frustration follow because they fail, neglect, or refuse to let the family know how they really feel. Eventually frustrated family members may become more assertive in selfish and destructive ways. Then when communication breaks down, family members no longer feel safe, secure, and significant. Result? Withdrawal and distancing occurs—gradually at first, and then more rapidly. Initially, a distancing family member ignores offenses and insensitive comments from others by walking away, staying busy, or even staying away from home. But intimacy breaks down as disappointment and bitterness increase. Emotional separation follows close behind.

As distancing continues to separate family members, conflicts escalate, with more criticism, contempt, defensiveness, and stonewalling. As conflicts increase, the available means of resolving those conflicts become overloaded and ineffective. There's simply too much conflict to deal with at one time! A void in the family relationships develops. Since families, like nature, abhor a vacuum, family members seek to fill the void by having their personal needs met outside the family. The primary purpose of blended family existence fails.

As distancing and withdrawal increase, the family becomes more polarized. The entire family experiences severe distress as each family member now more openly shows discontent and pain in manipulative, demeaning, and devaluing ways. They assume the worst of each other. The meltdown is complete as family life breaks down completely into unstructured chaos and negativism. At this point, remarriages collapse into divorce. Satan has won.

Don't let this happen to you and your family! Encourage effective personal communication *before the wedding*. Carefully nourish and maintain family communication as the blended family launches into the first critical two to four years of living together.

Graceful communication requires gentle, compassionate hearts devoted to God and to other blended family members. Psalm 19:14 sums up the godly spirit of it all this way: "May the words of my mouth and the meditation of my heart be pleasing in your sight, O LORD, my Rock and my Redeemer."

Putting God first in your home. Encouraging effective communication among family members using biblical love. These are excellent tools for successful blended family life. But they won't have full impact without respecting healthy family boundaries and using biblical conflict resolution measures to maintain order and peace in the home.

Key No. 3—Maintaining Healthy Boundaries

Much has been said in recent years about the importance of maintaining healthy boundaries among those in close relationships. Rightly so!

A boundary is like a property line in real estate—a line marking one person's land from that owned by someone else. Boundaries are vitally necessary in life. Where would a football halfback run if there was no goal line? What if you went to your car only to find someone drove off with it? What would you think if a waitress joined you at your table in a restaurant and began eating your meal? Boundaries bring order and predictability to our lives. Without them, there would be chaos and confusion. Who wants to add even more complexity and uncertainty to what is already a challenging blended family situation?

A boundary marks what is special, unique, and personal to you, in contrast to everything and everyone else in the world. It reinforces each person's basic need to assert some individuality and separateness from other humans. Everyone needs reaffirmation of personal identity to answer life's ultimate questions: "Who am I?" and "How am I different from everyone else?" In a blended family, of course, a new larger boundary encircles the two microfamily boundaries of the individual husband and wife that says, "This is now *our* family." It identifies them as a couple, and keeps out strangers and intruders.

Physical boundaries. A blended family soon learns daily physical boundaries by observing each other's habits and preferences. Many of these boundaries are obvious—such as not entering a closed bathroom or bedroom door when someone is dressing.

Early in our marriage, Cheryl and I had a classic boundary conflict (an argument) when she removed some of my favorite old shirts and other items from my drawers and closet. She placed the items in a box and mailed them to missionaries in Mexico, without any prior discussion. As a single mother, she was so used to doing this with Chase's baby clothes and toys that she overlooked the fact that now there was another adult in the mix. That incident was an eye-opener for all of us! (Even so, Chase and I have our suspicions at times. Whenever something's missing, we wonder if it too is "on its way to Mexico"!)

Psychological boundaries. Boundaries can be *psychological,* such as saying to yourself, "I just need to get away from everything and everyone for a while to have some peaceful time alone." We know the need for a psychological boundary of personal time—especially when a peaceful soak in a bubble bath, quietly listening to soothing music, is drowned out by loud music blasting from the teen's room!

Psychological boundaries also may be "competence based." Call it a quirk, but I use uncommon Germanic precision in carefully logging all entries in the checkbook when paying household bills. I enter each transaction to the penny, with an accurate running total. Cheryl, on the other hand, is . . . well . . . different. Writing checks with no descriptions, rounding check entries (many times randomly located in the debit or credit columns), and keeping an occasional running balance pose no problem for her. She knows exactly what she did and what it all means—but I don't have a clue! Because I take some pride in being so precise, Cheryl's style bumps up against my psychological boundary of technical competence. Sometimes it drives me nuts! But we worked through these boundary issues by reaching a marvelous compromise—we now have two checkbooks!

Common psychological boundary encroachments arising in blended families occur when parents, understandably eager to speed up the blending process, unwittingly pressure their children to call stepparents Mom or Dad. Unfortunately, this puts children into a classic "loyalty bind." "If I recognize my stepdad as my father, what happens with my 'real' dad?" "Have I betrayed my mom if I treat my step-mother like I would my own mother?" A child psychologically may wall off a noncustodial biological parent who remarries. The pain of seeing the child's original family disintegrate—coupled with the anger of perceived personal betrayal by the child's parent—may be too much to bear. So the child makes an emotional break with the non-custodial parent, marked by distancing and withdrawal, to cope with the pain.[5]

Relational boundaries. Relational boundaries arise as part of our instinctual need to feel protected and secure and, yes, even territorial at times. For example, when people feel shy and want to avoid too much closeness, they may sit alone at social gatherings. They protect themselves by being isolated and noncommunicative. Another example is wanting privacy without interruption from others when talking on the telephone.

In blended families, relational boundaries arise when a child living with a custodial ex-spouse visits the blended family home and feels like an outsider. "I don't want to watch your television shows." "We're playing this game by ourselves. Go away!" Resident children may feel an uneasy edginess at having this intruder-child around, but the visiting child feels the full force of a relational boundary that says, "You don't really belong here." That really hurts! Or a mother may think, "My children and I are my only family while I've been single. I don't want to lose what we have together after

I remarry." This acknowledges her relational microfamily boundary prior to entering into a blended family.

Stepparents regularly bump against relational boundaries in blended families. When a biological parent cuddles up to his/her child or they spend a lot of personal time together, it's common for a stepparent to feel like an outsider, resulting in many powerful negative feelings of inadequacy, jealousy, resentment, and loneliness. In fact, many stepparents struggle with having stepchildren in their home. A stepparent's inner voice may say, "I really want you to stay in your own space in the house until I can feel more at ease with you being around." But positive relational boundaries exist between stepparents and stepchildren as well: "Timmy and I are taking a short walk after dinner so we can spend some time together. We won't be long."

Dealing with relational boundaries of teenagers can be particularly difficult in blended families. Teens naturally pull away from parental authority as part of asserting their own individuality. But experiencing loss of a parent, coupled with adjusting to a new blended family, can be especially challenging. The teen may have matured in a single-parent family situation—especially if the parent relied on the teen to complete some adult tasks. Now, with remarriage of the parent, the teen may fear reverting to a "child" position in the new blended family; therefore he/she resists family bonding. Teens also want more input into family decisions. If they feel taken for granted or excluded, they may withdraw and forego family activities.

Also be aware that relational boundaries that *force* conformity ironically can work *against* blended family unity. How? The greater the pressure any family member feels to conform to the thoughts, desires, and behavior of other family members, the more personal boundaries tend to prompt him/her to pull away. Family members naturally resist conformity to keep some individuality and separateness.

Spiritual boundaries. Boundaries also can be spiritual, as when one says, "I just can't worship at the family's congregation anymore. I need to find spiritual nourishment elsewhere," or "The Lord seems to be leading me away from my job and into the full-time ministry." A couple may love the Lord, but if there are doctrinal differences between them or they don't enjoy the same worship experience, this boundary affects all relationships in the blended family.

As if all these types of boundaries weren't enough to deal with, boundaries also can be *visible* and *invisible, rigid* or *fluid, double-sided* or *one way,* and *automatic* or *nonautomatic.* They can expand and contract—even from moment to moment in any given day—to draw others close or keep them at a distance, depending upon one's need for privacy or fellowship. Now imagine the complexity as all these boundary dynamics reel into motion while you and your partner are trying to launch a blended family!

Why do we need boundaries? In their excellent book *Boundaries in Marriage,* Drs. Henry Cloud and John Townsend shared this personal observation:

> In our work with couples over the years, we have observed that, while many dynamics go into producing and maintaining love, over and over again one issue is at the top of the list: boundaries. When

boundaries are not established at the beginning of a marriage, or when they break down, marriages break down as well. Or such marriages don't grow past the initial attraction and transform into real intimacy. They never reach the true "knowing" of each other and the ongoing ability to abide in love and to grow as individuals and as a couple—the long-term fulfillment that was God's design. For this intimacy to develop and grow, there must be boundaries.[6]

This is even more true in blended family situations!

Creating boundaries is normal and natural human behavior. We simply need personal time and space as a basic element of our existence and happiness. In relationships, boundaries are a way to define who we are, what we desire, and where we're going in life. They help us sort out feelings, attitudes, and behaviors and find out to whom they belong. This is the essence of being able to define and distinguish ourselves from others.

In blended families, *all* members lived in other families beforehand. They have different experiences and differing levels of unfinished business coping with grief and loss. Now diverse microfamilies merge into a larger blended family, where strangers rub shoulders with other strangers. No one can make microfamily decisions anymore—everything now becomes a blended family decision. Single-parent autonomy disappears. The new coparent must consider the interests, needs, and desires of the family at large. No wonder many or all blended family members feel like foreigners in their own home, becoming anxious, angry, and despairing since they aren't able to live life in the normal way! Without boundaries to help define family members' choices and actions, as well as to trace motives or sources of conflict, blended families would be a chaotic mish-mash of emotions and unresolved frustrations—a hopeless mess! Boundaries help set loving, godly standards to foster healing and respect in relationships.

How do Boundaries help blended families? Boundaries provide five essential functions critical to blended family harmony. They: (1) ensure protection and security of individual family members and the family at large, (2) preserve each person's God-given freedom of choice, (3) reinforce personal awareness and identity, (4) promote personal responsibility and self-control, and (5) provide the best environment for love and acceptance among all blended family members. Without any one of those elements, the result will be poor communication and increasing conflict.

• *Boundaries protect the blended family.* Boundaries shield us from sin. They raise our consciousness about how sin can encroach into blended family life while alerting us about where to wall off sin and protect ourselves from evil. For example, sexuality is more noticeable in a blended family situation, where children live with other children with whom they haven't grown up. Protective boundaries allow the family to set clear, age-appropriate limits on acceptable dress, nudity, and privacy in the home—especially among teenagers. Godly standards help children know what is acceptable behavior, and keep the family properly focused on the Lord rather than the world. Also, since it's as difficult for your new family to move into your existing home and adjust to your way of home management as it would be for your microfamily to relocate into theirs, it's a loving and protective measure to have the new blended family move into an entirely new home environment. This helps reduce territorial feelings and conflicts (see chap. 7).

Proactive (rather than reactive) boundaries lovingly protect and preserve the freedom of each family member. For example, to reassure a child visiting from the home of a custodial ex-spouse, establish some affirmative physical boundaries. Set aside a special, private area in the home that will be that child's own space *always*. It may be a bed, or a closet, or a drawer, but it will be his/her own without interference from other family members. These boundaries communicate to the child, "Indeed, you *do* belong here when you visit. You are an equal partner in our family, and we all love you!"

• *Boundaries preserve freedom of choice.* One of God's greatest gifts to each individual is the freedom to *choose* how he/she will live. God's law also limits the ways others adversely affect this freedom. We're free agents whom God created to love each other freely. We aren't held hostage or enslaved to become victims of others—unless we *choose* to be so by turning away from God, giving ourselves over to others who control or manipulate us, or by surrendering to sin or self-centeredness. Boundaries therefore help define the *limits* of our freedom with God and others.

Without boundaries, if one family member interferes with, or controls, the choices of another member, the controlled person loses his/her God-given freedom. The loss is complete if the controlled family member isn't willing or able to say "Stop!" and stand firm. When a blended family truly celebrates freedom, everyone seeks to unite and appreciate each other's minds, values, and feelings rather than insisting that other family members "see things my way." Each blended family member has enough time to grow and develop caring relationships, without any expectations of "instant love." Forced interaction, especially between stepparents and stepchildren, only results in disappointments and problems.

Boundaries also help preserve the freedom of mature, responsible adults to say no and make it stick. But don't become selfish and irresponsible in exercising this freedom. Galatians 5:13 reminds us, "You, my brothers, were called to be free. But do not use your freedom to indulge the sinful nature; rather, serve one another in love." Is our freedom harming other family members and hindering their growth? Are we using our freedom to punish or hurt other family members or to seek revenge? If so, our freedom *crushes* love in the family. Healthy boundaries that ensure freedom of choice also promote responsibility and mutual respect. Then everyone benefits from well-defined, loving, enforced boundaries that respect and preserve personal freedoms.

• *Boundaries reinforce personal awareness and identity.* Boundaries allow each family member to experience his/her own feelings and emotions independently without unreasonable pressure or interference. Each individual is a separate person from other family members with different beliefs and opinions. Some separateness is a good thing for a blended family. It encourages family members to be whole and complete individuals, free to enjoy their own thoughts, feelings, and actions. Separateness also provides time and space for each person to ask, "How do I really feel about this family?

How do I feel about what's happening around me? Do I have any prideful or selfish attitudes that would disrupt family unity?" Only by having this separate sense of self-awareness is each person able to examine the thoughts and attitudes of his/her own heart.

It's vital that husbands and wives acknowledge and honor each other as separate individuals going into remarriage. This process is necessary to form the "one flesh" nature and "we-ness" of the new relationship. As one of the most interesting paradoxes and ironies of life, we first respect each other's *separateness* before unifying in *oneness*. A mature couple entering remarriage understands the biblical concept of *two* becoming *one* within the context of "you are not me, and I am not you, but *together we* will live, work, and love as the Lord allows and guides us." Each mate feels free to express opinions with an appropriate sense of power and assertiveness without being unduly controlled by external pressure or internal stress. Each knows how to connect emotionally, be vulnerable, and share feelings without retreating into self-protection. Then remarriage becomes a voluntary and cooperative partnership of two mature and responsible adults—a *cooperative oneness*. The goal is for husband and wife to "be mature and complete, not lacking anything" (James 1:4).

• *Boundaries promote mutual responsibility and self-control.* What are two of the greatest temptations we face in accepting responsibility? We really want others to become responsible for us, and we want others to pay the price for our own mistakes so we can avoid personal pain (see chap. 2). But boundaries highlight areas where *we* need to assume responsibility for personal change and growth. If we know we've crossed our own line, it's a wake-up call to repent and change. That's a good thing, because it encourages us to agree with truth and reality. It also discourages our tendency to deny, rationalize, and excuse our weaknesses, pride, or selfishness. Boundaries are *not* manipulative mechanisms to expand our freedom selfishly at the expense of another family member. We make no power plays or force choices we selfishly want others to make using boundaries. To the contrary, boundaries graciously and loving *protect* what God has given *us*. The primary purpose of a boundary is *self-control*—not controlling someone else.

But boundary encroachments also create consequences. How much will we permit another's sinful conduct to encroach into our lives, or the lives of other blended family members? Those encroachments reveal boundaries . . . and consequences for violating them. When others ignore reasonable requests or warnings, we place a boundary on the offensive conduct. If the offender persists, we take action to protect that boundary. Consequences for that boundary encroachment, which cause pain or loss, engage the attention and repentance of offenders.

But how does this happen? Allowing consequences to bring others to repentance is the essence of using "tough love." Paul's disciplinary measure against the sexually immoral church member in 1 Corinthians 5 is a classic example of using tough love— a very biblical concept. What's "tough love?" It's a *firm and measured response* to the sinful decisions and ungodly actions of those we love. It helps them feel the full weight of responsibility and inevitable consequences caused by their decisions and actions. Using tough love allows an unruly and selfish blended family member to reap the full effect of selfishness and irresponsibility. It says to the offender, "We love you, but we're not going to enable you to continue destroying yourself and others. We won't rescue you from the consequences of your rebellion." This keeps the trouble with the troublemaker.

Tough love sets up limits (boundaries) on what *God* tells us is acceptable conduct. With courage to speak the truth in love (Eph. 4:15), tough love also helps create options for repentance and forgiveness in the offender's favor, rather than seeking personal revenge. Sometimes it requires releasing someone who doesn't want to continue in a relationship, such as a disobedient child who wants to live with an ex-spouse (see chap. 9). Though tough love takes firm action in dealing with imbalanced and sinful situations, you never lose sight of the *person* and his/her worth. It still means loving the person despite the sin or the predicament.[7]

• *Boundaries create the best environment for love and acceptance.* We should gratefully thank God for boundaries in marriage! By its very nature, marriage reveals our pride and selfishness in living color. Simply by being in this ultimate antiselfish relationship, it exposes our weaknesses and failings like nothing else in the world! It forces us to change for the better. Boundaries consistent with God's Word primarily promote self-control, personal responsibility, and an awareness for personal change. But these boundaries also remind us that godly change and repentance come from loving and wanting to please God and our family, as well as ourselves. Loving God and loving each other is the highest calling of our faith (Matt. 22:37–40). Boundaries are good, healthy, and constructive measures to build up family harmony and unity when they spring from loving, sensitive, other-centered, servant hearts reflecting the nature of Jesus Christ.

Boundaries educate and guide us, revealing our part in helping (or hindering) blended family growth. We learn how our feelings affect others. We see how our attitudes generate those feelings. When we act on improper attitudes and feelings, we also see how our behaviors and reactions are part of the problem—not the solution.

How do all these boundary functions work? When you consider putting God first in your home and seek effective communication, the concept of boundaries may seem contradictory or excessively territorial. The first two keys almost suggest that "anyone in the blended family is welcome, anywhere, anytime," while boundaries seem to pull back and say, "Not so fast!" How do all these keys integrate and work together?

God designed a wonderful *balance* in healthy relationships that flows in a full circle. God created us to be uniquely ourselves and to have free choice. He also created us with a need for companionship. We decide if and when we want others in our lives to meet that need for companionship. The result is a family—a mate, and perhaps some children, too, in a remarriage. If the couple is a union of two complete and whole individuals, they complement each other but also acknowledge and respect each other as separate individuals. This separateness leads each mate, with the Spirit's guidance, to exercise personal freedom by venturing into different pursuits in work, ministry, and hobbies. But enjoying one's separateness for a time soon becomes less fulfilling, or even less desirable, due to a longing for the company of one's mate. Each partner then draws near to each other once again to enjoy the full "we-ness" of togetherness. And so, on this loving "life-tension" cycle goes—until the couple, and the blended family at large, achieve the proper balance of separateness and a comfortable "we-ness," or cooperative oneness.

God uses each of the three keys mentioned—godliness in the home, effective communication, and boundaries—to create *balance* through giving and receiving among all blended family members. But there's a critical fourth key that keeps that balance from self-destruction.

Key No. 4—Timely and Conciliatory Family Conflict Resolution[8]

Novelist F. Scott Fitzgerald, who certainly had his share of family conflict, rather bitterly summarized his experience this way: "Family quarrels are bitter things. They don't go according to rules. They're not like aches or wounds; they're more like splits in the skin that won't heal because there's not enough material."[9] Noted marriage therapists Les and Leslie Parrott have a different perspective:

The goal of marriage is not to avoid conflict. Not by far. Conflict—if handled correctly—can help build a stronger marriage. We have said it at least a hundred times: *Conflict is the price smart couples pay for a deepening sense of intimacy.* Without conflict it is difficult to peel away the superficial layers of a relationship and discover who we really are.[10]

What can cause a remarriage and blended family to self-destruct? The cumulative effect of hundreds of small unilateral decisions, unwarranted remarks, insensitive responses, unresolved differences, and instances of emotional neglect. What helps promote close and fulfilling blended family relationships? Timely and conciliatory conflict resolution.

Some family conflicts are as unavoidable as they are complex! Consider this true example: In a few months, Hector will be marrying Jill, who has a fifteen-year-old son, Mike. Mike is very friendly with Hector's son, Juan, who's the same age as Mike. Mike and Hector get along reasonably well, but they haven't had time to develop the close relationship Hector would like. Recently, Juan told his father, in the strictest of confidence, that he's seen Mike buying and using drugs. Jill has no idea this is going on. Hector is in a quandary. If he tells Jill, he'll violate his confidentiality promise to Juan. Juan's trust in his father is very important to Hector. He doesn't want to betray his son. Also, Mike will know Juan talked to Hector, which will wound their relationship. This could cause real problems when everyone is living together under one roof. On the other hand, if Hector withholds this information from Jill, is he being unfair to her and preventing her from helping her son? If Jill discovers Hector knew about Mike's drug problem but said nothing to her, will this revelation damage their relationship? Hector believes he cannot violate Juan's confidence without destroying the trust built between them. But if Hector remains silent, Mike won't be getting the help he needs, and Jill may never forgive Hector. *What would you tell Hector to do?* Certainly there are no easy answers!

What is conflict? Conflict is "a difference in opinion or purpose." It may range from good-natured differences and minor friction to aggressive (even physical) confrontation among blended family members. It also is "a struggle for influence or power." Conflicts range from minor disagreements to active battles for control (in total disregard of the God-given roles and responsibilities). Conflict is an inevitable part of *any* relationship—not just marriage. Why? Because no two people have exactly the same interests, ideas, expectations, or timetables. More to the point, conflict exists whenever there's *free choice!* In itself, conflict isn't always sin—but how we handle it often can be! When it's repetitive, disruptive in the blended family, or divides family fellowship, conflict is a *major* problem.

What causes conflict in blended families? Here are some common causes:

• *Misunderstandings.* Inaccurate or insufficient information, or when family communication is absent, erratic, incomplete, confusing, or only one-way, conflict is sure to arise!

• *Competition for limited resources.* Genesis 13:1–12: Abram and Lot split because "the land could not support them while they stayed together, for their possessions were so great that they were not able to stay together. And quarreling arose." In a blended family, quarreling is more likely to arise because of shortages—in finances, housing space, family activities and trips, and personal time with biological parents, to name a few!

• *Dysfunctional blended family organization.* When roles of husband and wife are fuzzy or out of balance, or where there is no clear "chain of command" in making fair and consistent family decisions, there will be confusion, misunderstandings, and conflict about family responsibilities.

• *Differences in needs, goals, expectations, style of relating, or opinions.* These are inevitable differences that create conflict in any blended family.

• *Competition over status/power.* Who's in charge? Will there be power plays in your family? Who craves the attention of others the most? Is a family member dabbling in someone else's area of responsibility or expertise? Just as the disciples quarreled over "Who's the greatest disciple?" (Matt. 20:20–28), grabbing for status and power in the blended family causes many conflicts.

• *Sinful attitudes and desires that lead to sinful words and actions.* James 4:1–3: "What causes fights and quarrels among you? Don't they come from your desires that battle within you? You want something but don't get it. You kill and covet, but you cannot have what you want. You quarrel and fight. You do not have, because you do not ask God. When you ask, you do not receive, because you ask with wrong motives, that you may spend what you get on your pleasures."

God's Word tells us that the fundamental reason behind conflict with others within (and outside) the blended family is sin in our hearts.

Although causes may be actual or perceived, conflict exists if even *one* family member *thinks* it exists. And it exists as the type of conflict *that* family member *thinks* it is, even if others don't view it that way!

Negative consequences of blended family conflict. Conflict compounds distorted, absent, or ineffective communication and overly emotional reactions. It creates an atmosphere of tension and increasing discomfort. It shatters trust, leading family members to check on matters previously taken on faith. Conflicts begin the destructive process of family members distancing and withdrawing from each other, resulting in the downward spiral discussed at the end of the section on key no. 2 (communication). The family begins sliding down a slippery slope, with matters going from bad to worse.

Positive results of blended family conflict. On the other hand, blended family conflict can stimulate family problem-solving. It can cause family members to unite around an issue and bring underlying problems to the surface. Conflict can encourage cooperation among family members, create new learning opportunities, and spark a search for new ideas and solutions. It encourages the family to prioritize relationships, identify issues, and implement creative options for resolution. Promptly dealing with conflicts prevents more serious problems while fostering a healthy pattern of giving and receiving forgiveness and biblical love. Conflicts help stimulate mutual understanding and growth, that leads to greater intimacy. When others challenge our beliefs and compel us to defend these beliefs through conflict, we grow intellectually. When we learn how to resolve disputes, we become peacemakers while gaining a godly self-confidence and maturity. And with every conflict resolved that results in forgiveness, acceptance, and love among family members, everyone grows spiritually.

Responses to conflict. What are we to do when conflicts arise with our spouse or another blended family member? We can: seek to even the score; walk away and forget about it; throw up our hands in exasperation and tell him/her, "Okay, do whatever you want. I give up!"; capitulate and compromise what we know to be true; or sensitively and humbly meet with the person, speaking the truth in love. The first four options *avoid* conflict. Only the fifth option promotes conflict *resolution.* The last option springs from a peacemaker's solution-seeking mind-set. Biblical resolution comes through confrontation—not avoidance—but with *gentleness* and respect for our spouse or family member. There's no room for hostility, cruelty, revenge, or retaliation. How the messenger speaks, acts, and loves is as important as the message given to those confronted.

How do we respond to family conflicts? Peacemaker Ministries summarizes possible reactions this way:

"Work-it-out responses" (a/k/a "reconciliation responses"). Some battles need to be fought, while others can be finessed! Here are the *personal peacemaking responses that involve only the family members actually involved in the conflict:*

1. *Overlook an offense:* "A man's wisdom gives him patience; it is to his glory to overlook an offense" (Prov. 19:11). One family member may deliberately and unilaterally decide to forgive a wrong and refuse to perpetuate the conflict.
2. *Face-to-face discussion:* "If your brother has something against you . . . go and be reconciled" (Matt. 5:23–24). "If your brother sins against you, go and show him his fault, *just between the two of you*" (Matt. 18:15, emphasis added). Resolve personal offenses too serious to overlook through loving confrontation and/or confession, leading to forgiveness and reconciliation.

3. *Negotiation:* "Each of you should look not only to your own interests, but also to the interests of others" (Phil. 2:4). Resolve *substantive* issues about money, property, and other rights (rather than personal and relationship issues) through a bargaining process. Seek a consensus and a mutually agreeable settlement of differences by negotiating options and solutions while meeting the interests of all family members involved. Summarize the negotiated agreement with an exchange of promises.

If these personal peacemaking responses don't achieve conflict resolution and reconciliation of the parties, some *assisted responses* may be necessary. This involves bringing in other family members to help resolve the conflict or, if that isn't available or appropriate, asking competent and wise Christian counselors or trusted friends for help. Assisted responses are:

1. *Mediation:* "If he will not listen [to you], take one or two others along" (Matt. 18:16). Ask one or two others (counselor or family friends) to meet with you and your blended family member(s) to help improve effective communication, explore possible solutions, and facilitate a resolution. (Mediators give advice and suggest solutions, but have no power to impose settlements.)
2. *Arbitration:* "Therefore, if you have disputes about such matters, appoint as judges even men of little account in the church!" (1 Cor. 6:4). When the parties cannot come to a voluntary solution, they explain the matter to a trusted arbitrator (such as a church elder or family counselor) who listens to arguments on all sides and thereafter gives a binding decision on the matter.
3. *Corrective discipline:* "If he refuses to listen to [others], tell it to the church" (Matt. 18:17). If a person who professes to be a Christian refuses to do what's right and just to resolve conflict, the blended family, other family members, Christian counselors, or church elders may intervene with the goal of promoting justice, repentance, forgiveness, and reconciliation.

"Escape responses." These usually ineffective responses that avoid conflict are:

1. *Denial:* Pretend that a conflict doesn't exist, or refuse to do what you can and should do to resolve it properly. These responses bring only temporary relief, and usually allow matters to grow worse (see 1 Sam. 2:22–25).
2. *Flight:* Withdraw from the family member with whom you are in conflict. This may involve working late at the office, staying alone in the garage or den, or even changing churches. Withdrawal may be a legitimate response only when it is presently impossible to resolve the conflict in a constructive manner (see 1 Sam. 19:9–10; Rom. 16:17). In most cases, however, it only prevents a proper solution to a problem.
3. *Separation/suicide:* When people lose all hope of resolving a conflict, they may seek to escape the situation or make a desperate cry for help by running away from the family (abandonment or separation) or even going to the extreme of taking their own lives (see 1 Sam. 31:4). Obviously, these *escape* responses don't resolve conflict.

"*Attack responses.*" These responses bring as much pressure on family members as seems necessary to defeat their complaints and end their opposition. People use attack responses when they only want to *win a conflict,* not *preserve a relationship.* Attack responses are:

1. *Verbal or physical assault:* Use of aggression to compel a family member to give in to your demands. Some people mistakenly believe it's better to overcome an opponent by force or intimidation, such as verbal attacks (including gossip and slander), physical violence, or damaging a person financially or professionally (see Acts 6:8–15). Conduct like this is ungodly and unnecessarily inflammatory.

2. *Litigation:* This involves taking a family conflict before civil authorities for a decision (e.g., divorce). At times, court action may be a legitimate response (such as in domestic violence or child-abuse situations), but use it only after exhausting the "work-it-out" responses (with rare exceptions). Some conflicts legitimately may be taken before a civil judge for a decision (see Rom. 13:1–5); however, lawsuits usually damage relationships and often fail to achieve complete justice. More importantly, it's not faithful for Christians to litigate against other Christians (1 Cor. 6:1–8). It's better to make every effort to settle matters out of court whenever reasonably possible (see Matt. 5:25–26).

3. *Murder:* Some people may be so desperate to win a dispute that they'll murder those who oppose them (see Acts 7:54–58). Murder is evil and wrong. Even if we don't attack a family member physically, *we're guilty of murder in God's eyes when we harbor anger or contempt in our hearts toward others* (see Matt. 5:21–22; 1 John 3:15).

Here's a summary chart comparing each form of response to conflict:

	Focus On:	May Be Called:	Frequent Result:
Escape Responses •Denial •Flight •Separation/ suicide	Me	Peace-faking	KYRG (<u>K</u>iss <u>Y</u>our <u>R</u>elationship <u>G</u>ood-bye)
Attack Responses •Assault •Litigation •Murder	You	Peace-breaking	KYRG
Reconciliation Responses •Overlook offense •Face-to-face talk •Negotiation of options •Mediation •Arbitration •Corrective discipline	Us	Peace-making	Reconciliation

Obviously, for blended families to succeed, they must focus together on using the "work it out" peacemaking reconciliation responses noted above. By applying these to family conflicts, they'll enjoy the sweet benefits of resolving problems—forgiving and reconciling with each other in a biblical manner.

The biblical conflict resolution process. Specifically, how do we resolve conflicts among blended family members in a biblical, responsible, and loving way? Jesus teaches us, "[I]f you are offering your gift at the altar and there remember that your brother has something against you, leave your gift there in front of the altar. First go and be reconciled to your brother; then come and offer your gift" (Matt. 5:23–24).

Worship is a time of searching one's heart and life (Ps. 139:23–24). What will God find? Conflict? Division? Bitterness? Unresolved conflict and broken fellowship with others adversely affect our fellowship with God. How can we say we love God, whom we have not seen, when we haven't dealt lovingly with our family members, whom we have seen (1 John 4:19–21)? This passage isn't telling us to put off worship. It's a command to go the distance *with urgency,* reconcile with an offended family member, and then to *return* to worship.

Repentance and reconciliation with those we've offended isn't a "tomorrow" agenda item—the Lord means for it to happen *now.* Why? Because we'll be too busy with "tomorrow" matters and won't get to the items held over from today. By tomorrow, matters may boil over and become worse. Tomorrow also may never come (see 1 Thess. 5:3). *Today* is all we have for sure. Take it from a remarried divorcee lawyer: If you don't neutralize problems when they first arise, these difficulties take on a life of their own and steamroll over the people involved!

What if our family member is being unreasonable in feeling offended? Must the alleged "offender" (us) still take the initiative in seeking peace and reconciliation? Yes! Jesus addresses situations where we notice someone who has "something" against us—not necessarily a valid complaint but anything that could break fellowship or become a breeding ground for sinful thoughts. It may be an unfounded complaint, or even a misunderstanding on the part of the other person, but we still have a responsibility to act and personally go to that person. If the complaint is valid, confession and repentance are appropriate. If it isn't, we're to help the offended person understand the error and reaffirm the relationship so peace prevails (Rom. 12:18).

But Jesus goes further:

> "If your brother sins against you, go and show him his fault, just
> between the two of you. If he listens to you, you have won your
> brother over. But if he will not listen, take one or two others along, so
> that 'every matter may be established by the testimony of two or three
> witnesses.' If he refuses to listen to them, tell it to the church; and if he
> refuses to listen even to the church, treat him as you would a pagan or
> a tax collector." (Matt. 18:15–17)

In Matthew 5:21–26, Jesus sends the *offender* immediately to the offended to seek forgiveness and reconciliation in any conflict—even before the offender makes an offering in church. Here, in Matthew 18:15–17, he sends the *offended* to the offender in the same spirit. This passage is for those who may say, "Wait a minute. I'm not the offender here. He sinned against me. Let him come to me!" Jesus dismisses this rationalization. The offended person must take the initiative in pursuing peace too! Taken to heart, all sides to a conflict will meet on their way to see each other.

We'll discuss the specific steps of biblical conflict resolution in Matthew 18:15–17 more specifically in a moment, but first let's make sure *our* hearts are right before God by properly preparing *ourselves* for action.

Perform an attitude check. Making sure our *attitude* is right before seeking to resolve conflict with a family member is a necessary part of taking the log out of our own eyes so we can see clearly to remove the speck from our family member's eye (Matt. 7:1–5). Family disputes are secondary. The real motivation behind Jesus' command in Matthew 5:21–26 is to *guard our hearts* against roots of resentment, bitterness, and division. These evils cause us to brood over conflict, harbor malice, and think of revenge. They fester and eventually become uncontrollable. Root it out. Don't give anger a foothold in your heart. If reasonably possible, don't let the day pass by without seeking some just and peaceful resolution (Eph. 4:26–27). Do this as you are on your way to seek forgiveness from, and *reconciliation*[11] with, your family member. Then you replace the chaos of sinful division with peace, order, and harmony in ways that honor God, keep the family intact, and reclaim offenders. What should our attitude be? (read Phil. 4:2–9): (1) *rejoice* in the Lord *always,* (2) let your gentleness be evident to all, (3) replace anxiety with prayer, (4) see things as they really are, and (5) *practice* what you have learned. Peacemaker Ministries expounds on these biblical principles this way:

• *Have a humble attitude of confession* (Prov. 28:13; Luke 19:1–9). "The Seven A's of Confession" are: (1) *address* everyone involved; (2) *avoid* "if," "but," and "maybe"; (3) *admit* specifically—get to the *root* of the conflict (James 4:1–3); (4) *apologize*; (5) *accept* the consequences; (6) *alter* your behavior; and (7) *ask* for forgiveness. That says it all!

• *Have a forgiving heart.* True forgiveness is motivated by God's forgiveness for us (Matt. 18:21–35). Since Christians are the most *forgiven* people in the world, we also should be the most *forgiving* people in the world. "Bear with each other and forgive whatever grievances you may have against one another, Forgive as the Lord forgave you" (Col. 3:13). Some common attempts at forgiveness really aren't forgiveness at all: "I'll never forgive you for what you've done to me," "I'll forgive you as soon as my feelings change," "I'll forgive you as soon as I'm able to forget what you did," and "I forgive you; I just don't want anything more to do with you." The "Four Promises of Forgiveness" (Ps. 103:12; Isa. 43:25; 1 Cor. 13:5) are: (1) I won't think about this incident. (2) I won't bring this incident up or use it against you. (3) I won't talk to others about this incident. (4) I won't allow this incident to stand between us or hinder our relationship. Remember, the power of forgiveness doesn't fail even though the scales remain unbalanced. Forgiveness accepts scores that may never come out even for the greater victory of winning our family members over.

Use the family conflict resolution "toolbox." Before beginning any project, you need the right tools. What tools do we need before confronting others? Peacemaker

Ministries uses the acronym PAUSE to describe the "tools" necessary for effective biblical conflict resolution: (1) Prepare/Plan. (2) Affirm relationships. (3) Understand needs, interests, positions. (4) Search for creative solutions. (5) Evaluate options objectively and reasonably. These principles work very well in blended family conflict situations.

• *Prepare/plan.* Prepare yourself for *responsible* discussion with the family member in conflict. Begin with prayer for God's guidance in solving the problem and softening your heart in the process. Pray about your attitude, the family member involved, and what needs to be said. Get the facts underlying the conflict. Plan your words in advance. Decide what words and topics to avoid. Develop a *neutral*, specific description of the problem and relevant behavior. Develop a *neutral* description of the effect the situation has had on everyone involved in the conflict. Anticipate reactions, and plan responses. Seek godly counsel of others as to any uncertain aspects of your action plan (to the extent you don't engage in gossip before meeting directly with the family member involved). Select an appropriate time and place to talk, and remove all distractions—ringing phones, interrupting waiters, etc.

• *Affirm relationships.* This means showing genuine respect for another family member, concern for his/her needs and interests, and a desire to protect and preserve your relationship. Ways to affirm relationships include: separating personal issues from substantive issues, expressing sincere appreciation and concern for your relationship, showing respect for authority, and communicating in a loving and courteous manner. Exercise authority with wisdom and restraint. Commit to earnestly understanding your family member's viewpoint. When you're wrong, be ready to admit it. Be sure to allow room for the family member to save face and avoid embarrassment whenever reasonably possible. Be lavish in praise and thanksgiving for good things the family member has done.

• *Understand issues, needs, interests, and negotiating positions.* *Issues* are identifiable, concrete questions about matters in conflict. Issues may be *personal* ("This remark hurt me deeply") or *material/substantive* ("We can't afford this purchase"). One blended family conflict issue might be, "If the family moves after the wedding, I'm going to live with my father!" *Needs* are vital concerns or limitations affecting one's livelihood. A child may say, "I need time in the restroom, but Sarah's always in there!" Legitimate needs like these must be addressed to reach a satisfactory agreement. *Interests* are what really motivates people—something a family member values or desires. A teenager may say, "I don't mind family devotionals, but I feel like a little kid if I can't lead our family worship sometimes." This isn't a need, but instead is the teen's important interest in wanting to assume a greater role in serving the family. Praise God for that! *Positions* are desired outcomes or definable perspectives on an issue. Mom may say, "Since you kids are old enough to care for yourselves, I expect each of you to put your laundry in the hamper without leaving it for me to pick up."

Needs and interests are the *reasons* behind the positions. Positions usually are mutually exclusive and incompatible, which is where conflicts surface most. (Everyone *needs* a family vacation break, but some want to go to the beach while others want to hike in the mountains—mutually exclusive *positions.*) Why not help others *under-stand* the reasons underlying positions as a means of reaching agreement? Interests dovetail more easily than positions. (Stepfather wants to spend more time with his stepdaughter; stepdaughter wants to see a Disney movie. They satisfy both interests by going to the movie together.) The better you *understand* others' needs and interests (as well as your own), the more likely you are to develop acceptable solutions (see 1 Sam. 25:1–44).

• *Search for creative solutions.* Invent options for resolving conflict through brainstorming. Pray for wisdom, insight, and creativity. List all possible options in writing. Mix and combine options creatively (one idea may trigger another). Separate option *creation* from evaluation (criticism). Initially, simply explore options without commitment. Strive to satisfy interests whenever possible, seeking solutions where everyone "wins," if possible. (See chap. 11 for an example of how to work with ex-spouses in using child support payments for a child's education.)

• *Evaluate options objectively and reasonably. Objectively* means not based on per-sonal feelings or prejudice, but on facts and unbiased assessments. *Reasonably* means "in accord with sound judgment," not irrational or groundless. Keep the focus on facts and issues. As much as possible, use Scripture as a guide (*not* a weapon) and seek ver-ifiable or measurable facts rather than personal opinions. If an option worked before, use it again!

After making sure we have a godly attitude and after gathering our peacemaking tools together, we're now ready to follow Christ in resolving conflict responsibly and lovingly.

Follow Jesus' command for conflict resolution. In Matthew 18:15–17, Jesus outlines an important step-by-step process for conflict resolution. This isn't optional—it's a command of Christ! There's divine thought behind each step of this process and the specific order of it. The key link for each step is whether the offending person will "listen" to the reason of others. This obviously requires time, patience, and multiple attempts in completing each step.

1. Meet personally with the offending family member. Contain the problem in an informal and private manner. Keep the meeting as narrow as the offense. Remember, it's a loving gift to overlook a minor offense (Prov. 19:11b). But one cannot ignore a problem if it creates lingering resentment or family division. It's also not responsible to "look the other way" if another is in sin. Also address an offense quickly; otherwise the offender could make matters worse—especially if he/she is unaware of the prob-lem.[12] Notice that Jesus *doesn't* say we're to gossip about the specific problem to other family members—or, even worse, talk to others *outside* the family—before discussing the matter first directly with the person involved.

God gives us an early example of going to meet with offenders. When Adam and Eve sinned against God, he searched for them and called out to them even while they hid from him (Gen. 3:8–9). After finding them, he was careful to allow Adam and Eve to explain their situation (though, being God, he obviously knew the truth already) (Gen. 3:10–13). Only then did he begin to deal with the problem.

Approach the offender sensitively and lovingly. Assume the best instead of the worst (1 Cor. 13:7). Can anyone really have all the facts *before* talking to the offender and considering that person's perspective? Perhaps a misunderstanding occurred. Matters aren't always as we perceive them (see Mark 4:12). This isn't the time for suppositions, preconceived judgments, or reckless accusations. Instead, it's a time for constructive fact-gathering and enlightened, gentle confrontation. This private meeting isn't an opportunity to "hit and run" by venting anger and quickly dodging further conversation. It's a time for understanding, reasonable compromise, and reconciliation rather than berating a family member for rude or thoughtless conduct.

The point of Jesus' words in Matthew 18:15–17 is to unite, not divide, us. There should be no lingering problems. If an offender won't "listen," however, it's imperative to go to step 2. Don't leave the matter unresolved.

2. If no reconciliation comes from this private meeting, bring one or two other *mature and spiritual* individuals along. For what purpose? To aid communication and show there's a deep concern. These mature, wise, and (hopefully) unbiased persons should have a loving concern for all parties involved, with no personal stake in the dispute. They should resist any effort by either party to lobby for particular positions in advance of a meeting. Their role is to help conflicting parties bear their individual burdens and faithfully restore them to full fellowship in spirit and in truth (Gal. 6:1–2). These other individuals should remain *neutral observers,* not "yes-men."

Who should these "two or three others" be? They could be other adult extended family members, a Christian family or marriage counselor, a mediator qualified to act in this type of family conflict), and/or trusted church family members, provided they can be neutral and objective.

3. If an erring family member fails, neglects, or refuses to "listen" and repent after steps 1 and 2, it's time for the blended family to use a Family Conference to apply appropriate discipline (see chap. 8).

What if family conflicts defy resolution? Even in the best blended families, there may be some unresolvable conflicts. Without compromising biblical principles, you've done all you can. What then? It's time to give the conflict *fully* over to the Lord. Receive some satisfaction in knowing you tried to be a peacemaker in the spirit of Matthew 5:9 and "[made] every effort to live at peace with all men and to be holy" (Heb. 12:14). For personal peace, there eventually comes a time to say, "I've done all I can do about this. Now it's up to you, Lord. Grant me serenity to accept these things I cannot change."

Glorifying God in family conflicts. Glorifying God and following the example of Christ should be our *primary* objective in resolving family conflicts. Conflict isn't always an accident, but it's almost always an *assignment* to put Christian love into practice. In conflict, we demonstrate our faith in God and draw attention to his holiness, wisdom, power, goodness, and love. We become Christlike (Rom. 8:28–29) and learn to love each other as Christ loves us (John 15:12–13). Loving God and loving others as ourselves lead us to make *every effort* to resolve conflict and reconcile with others as Jesus commands.

USE THESE KEYS TO UNLOCK THE HEARTS OF YOUR BLENDED FAMILY

In the chapters to follow we'll review some specific examples of how each of these four keys work together toward the greater good of each blended family member. These keys *will* work if we truly love and cherish each other enough to use them regularly. Loving God and appreciating the way he created our partners and children is what really motivates us to practice these measures. One remarried man interviewed by Author Helen Kooiman Hosier for her book *To Love Again: Remarriage for the Christian* beautifully captures the essence of *why* we want these keys to work:

> I wake up every morning wondering what new miracle is going to take place today. The big difference in this marriage is that we read the Bible together, we have fun—no longer do I go around looking like I've been baptized in vinegar—when we do have things that bug us, we get it out in the open and talk about it intelligently rather than fussing, fuming, and fighting. We are real with each other. We are authentic. Above all, we are open to God's will. I am deeply in love with my wife; she is an incredible gift from God.[13]

God help us all to have that same attitude as we live, and move, and have our being in our remarriages and blended families!

A Message from Cheryl

Remember the idea of plan B? As you come together in remarriage, it may become apparent why this isn't God's original plan! After years alone, many of us have become very set in our ways. Our habits and selfishness are easily hidden when there's only one decision-maker in the home.

As a single-again person, hundreds of little decisions come flooding at you daily. You take them as they come, and make them. Then you marry someone doing the same thing and . . . *whoa!*

I vividly remember my first grocery store trip with Warren. As I waltzed down the pancake mix aisle, I reached for syrup. Warren said, "Uh, sweetheart? Why would you buy that syrup when this fine one (translation: the one I usually buy) is half the price?" "Well," I replied, "the expensive one (I usually buy) is *maple* syrup. Yours is sugar water with artificial maple flavoring. See on the label there?" Since neither Warren nor I had any intention of him doing the grocery shopping or cooking in our home, we soon agreed to a boundary. I shop, select, and cook. These decisions are mine. He eats!

So, we return to the purpose of remarriage. Is it only to meet our needs? I believe our relationship with God highlights the primary purpose as ministry—perhaps the most difficult ministry you may ever have! As Christ did, we'll need to sacrifice our own needs (habits and selfishness) for the benefit of others—others we may feel estranged from at times. As in many applications of our faith, if we allow feelings to dictate our actions, we will fail our Lord and our new families.

QUESTIONS FOR PERSONAL REFLECTION

1. Specifically, how have my partner and I reflected the grace and love of Christ to each other and to our children?
2. What communication barriers have I faced with my mate and others in my blended family? How have I tried to overcome them?
3. What boundaries do I have in my life? What boundaries have I encountered with my mate and our children?
4. What are the five most difficult conflicts I've experienced with my partner and/or our children over the past year? What did we do to resolve them? Are they resolved now? In what ways do I avoid or promote conflict?
5. Do I have a pattern of forgiveness in my life? Can I forgive unconditionally?

Chapter 7

PREPARING FOR BLENDED FAMILY LIFE:
Matters to Consider before and after the Wedding

Blended family life is an entirely new experience. Along with many unique joys, there are more than enough challenges.

Jesus knew the value of timing and how to help people distinguish between old and new concepts. He was masterful in sharing this parable with a large crowd of lawyers and Pharisees during a great banquet at Matthew's house:

> "No one tears a patch from a new garment and sews it on an old one. If he does, he will have torn the new garment, and the patch from the new will not match the old. And no one pours new wine into old wineskins. If he does, the new wine will burst the skins, the wine will run out and the wineskins will be ruined. No, new wine must be poured into new wineskins. And no one after drinking old wine wants the new, for he says, 'The old is better.'" (Luke 5:36–39)

In this passage, Jesus makes a comparison between the incompatibility of the old Law of Moses and the new covenant of Christian grace and mercy. The Pharisees saw no need to change the "old ways" of the Law. Jesus, the Son of God, offered them a taste of new wine, but they couldn't receive it. They wanted no part of Jesus' ministry of new faith, new life, and spiritual renewal (John 3:3–5; 2 Cor. 5:17; Eph. 4:22–23; Col. 3:10; Titus 3:5). They trapped themselves into old legalism and rigidity. This kept them from moving where God wanted to lead them.

So what does all this have to do with remarriage and blended families? For many, the family left behind is old wine. To them, the former family ways taste better. They don't want to give up the old ways of doing things. But they forget that their former marriages are old wineskins that have burst. Remarriage with children is new wine, and new wine needs the new wineskin of a blended family structure. Those adequately prepared and willing to receive this new wine in "blended family wineskins" enjoy satisfying and successful family relationships.

Remarriage is another chance in life—for yourself and your children. It's a time of *redemption*. Remarriage is a time of bringing the broken gold wedding ring of your life to the Lord and allowing him to melt the pieces, refine them in his fire, and fashion a new ring for you to wear. It's your new opportunity to enter into a stable, emotionally satisfying, and spiritually fulfilling relationship with a suitable mate.

CHARTING OUT A BLENDED FAMILY PLAN

You and your remarriage partner have now successfully completed all the important foundational work for your remarriage. You believe you truly are suitable for each other, hopefully with confirmation from family, friends, and counselors. Your children have met and begun preparations to live together (see chap. 9). You've jointly worked out a preliminary family budget and have agreed on many financial issues (see chap. 10).

Now, before going any further, you and your mate-to-be need to discuss your individual and collective ideas and expectations about your remarriage and blended family. Make a written list of "his" and "hers" (*and* each child's) goals and expectations so you can see your family's world of ideas at a glance. Remarriage is a time of great change and transition, where nothing feels quite right. Careful planning and preparation minimizes the initial chaos many blending families experience.

Chart your course through the months leading up to your wedding and the first two years afterward. Pray about this together with your children. Will both spouses work? Have you considered relocation possibilities? Who will be the primary caregiver for the children? How will you assign household chores? What responsibilities will children have? Who will handle the finances? What checking, savings, and investment accounts will you need? Will you have a night for family fun? Will you have a date night just for you and your mate? What about scheduling child visitation with ex-spouses, grandparents, and other extended family members? Run through a typical week on a day-to-day basis—even hour-by-hour—anticipating your family's needs.

Wise and effective blended family management begins with this premarital planning, and carries over through at least the first two years of family life. You and your partner have a lot of discretion about laying this foundation, but the most important principle to keep in mind is this: "Unless the LORD builds the house, its builders labor in vain" (Ps. 127:1).

Always begin from a point of unity. In working out a plan, both partners need to focus on the goal of promoting *stability* in the family with security and mutual respect. There should be no scorekeeping of rights and wrongs, but a mutual caring commitment to the entire family more than individuals in it.

Confront head-on the myth that you and your mate can change each other. Each partner must accept personal responsibility to change, regardless of what the other does in remarriage. This begins by exchanging the question "What's wrong with *her?*"

with the more appropriate inquiry "What's wrong with *me?*" You will change your remarriage by changing *yourself.*

I like the way Edward and Sharon Douglas expressed this point in their book *The Blended Family:*

> If you apply the Word of God to your marriage, your *marriage* will change. Scripture doesn't reveal that we must make sure our life partner loves, respects, and gives us all the affection or financial and physical satisfaction we long for. The Bible never promises that God will make our mates into the kind of people *we* pray they should be. It does tell us, however, what kind of heart God can enable us to have *if we do our part in bringing out the best in our mate.* Marriage demands spiritual growth. To live with and love someone else requires us to put our spouse's interests ahead of our own.[1] (emphasis added)

Each spouse should commit to taking the steps necessary to become more Christlike. Each mate needs to encourage and love the other in a biblical manner with the goal of *enhancing* the remarriage. This means exercising mutual affirmation, empathy, and patience with each other on a *daily* basis. When the couple does these things, then God can really use the remarriage for his glory!

Reject any future temptation to resign yourselves to certain incompatibilities. Deal with inevitable conflicts as they arise. Make a joint plan to: (1) immediately acknowledge personal anger when it flares up, (2) commit not to attack each other, (3) uncover the sources of each other's anger, (4) determine what's at stake in the conflict, (5) turn to each other for help in brainstorming on available options and alternatives for resolving the situation, (6) carry out the most workable solution, and (7) practice forgiveness for each other just as Christ has forgiven you.

Accept that each partner will make *lots* of mistakes in remarriage. Working together as a team means taking those setbacks in stride without blaming or demeaning each other. Many times mistakes are unavoidable oversights or reasonable misunderstandings. The only responsibility each partner needs to accept personally is how he/she *reacts* to those mistakes. All fallout from mistakes is manageable *if* each partner's *reactions* are appropriate and don't make problems worse.

Embrace the *permanence* of the upcoming remarriage. Capture the vision of growing old with your partner for the rest of your life. Have the mind-set that you'll allow yourself no other option but to do your part to make the remarriage *work*. This may be difficult to do, especially if your ex-spouse failed you in your prior marriage. If you enter remarriage with any strong doubts about it lasting, take this last opportunity to stop it before it begins.

Most importantly, develop a "we-ness" by preparing to meet each other's needs for spiritual, emotional, and sexual intimacy from day one in the remarriage. Passion can fizzle, and commitment can become dry, routine, and obligatory over time. But if there's no meeting of the souls in *intimacy,* the remarriage cannot be sustained on any deep level (see chap. 8).

Nurture empathy for each other. Remarried partners make all the sacrifices former spouses do—and more! Like it or not, you're marrying a person with a history you can't ignore. Both of you may have to raise children you didn't bring into the world—kids who may forget your sacrifices in later years when you need their help. It's extremely challenging to send that support check to an ex-spouse when times strain your finances to the limit. The challenges and difficulties unique to remarriage are endless. Empathize with each other's situation, and pray for each other. Empathy builds up and restores relationships. It comes through being kind, not disrespectful. Empathy means forgiving your beloved instead of being quick to take offense, holding grudges, or throwing your mate's past mistakes up in his or her face.

Cherish and praise each other. One key element is identified by most marriage experts as keeping a marriage alive and growing. What is it? *Cherishing* each other! What does it mean to truly cherish your mate? The essence of it is to say two things: "You are of great value to me, a worth far beyond measure," and "I am devoting the rest of my life to honor and respect you because of your great worth to me and our family." Worth and commitment. Your mate needs to *feel* that as well as intellectually know it. Your children hunger for it as well. Cherishing your partner becomes especially necessary when tempers flare. It's letting him/her know that you're always in your mate's corner, even if conflicts arise or you feel hurt or ignored. Be sure to nourish this in your marriage and blended family life on a daily basis.

Now, before the wedding, practice those warm and wonderful "cherishing words" with your beloved: "I love you." "You look absolutely fabulous!" "Can I help you in some way?" "Why don't we all go out to eat tonight!" And don't forget the all-time ultimate cherishing words: "Here's the remote, honey. Let's watch what *you* want tonight!"

Seek the Lord's guidance. It's as fundamental as eating healthy food and getting a good night's sleep—that's what prayer and Bible study provide to a couple searching for God's wisdom and guidance. Praying together brings transparency to a couple as you and your partner learn to speak honestly of joys and disappointments, victories and defeats, hopes and fears. Searching God's Word together for answers and encouragement keeps you and your partner spiritually alive. It keeps you properly focused on your priorities in life and in your upcoming remarriage.

Prepare for colliding worlds! In the old *Seinfeld* television comedy series, the short and balding George Costanza character would go to extreme lengths in separating his relationships so he could act differently with each group. If, by chance, members of one of Costanza's groups happened to intermingle with those of another group, Costanza would fret, "Oh *no!* Worlds are colliding!" This meant that Costanza could no longer act the same with the interminglers—"colliding worlds" revealed his inconsistencies with each group.

Remarriage and blended families are the ultimate in colliding worlds. Very seldom will everyone feel comfortable that he/she is coming into a blended family on equal terms with everyone else. During the first years of the remarriage, it's natural that either or both spouses will experience some intimidation and self-doubt about how to make their relationship work. But don't despair! With time, patience, and a lot of empathy and understanding, your different worlds can blend into one. Here are a few suggestions:

• *Be your spouse's advocate.* Christians have the comforting assurance of knowing that Jesus always intercedes for us with the Father (Rom. 8:34; Heb. 7:24–25). Your spouse needs you to be his/her advocate at this challenging time in life—especially when ex-spouses, children, superiors at work, and others may make your mate feel as if the entire world is full of adversaries. Support the new love of your life when he/she needs it most! This also means being supportive if your mate has legal battles with an ex-spouse over child support or custody issues. Try to find ways to help your partner disengage from the struggle through mediation and settlement, if possible. Above all, look for ways to help carry your mate's burden in the spirit of Christ (Gal. 6:2).

• *Understand your spouse's mind-set and feelings.* Use *empathy*—not sympathy. Come alongside your beloved. Try to understand the real source of your mate's frustrations. See the world through his/her eyes. Be there to talk out problems and offer constructive, positive solutions without being defensive if your partner's problems spill over on you. Work toward having the same mind-set on as many issues as possible to promote unity and guard against division (see 1 Cor. 1:10).

• *Be a positive and encouraging resource in all areas.* Avoid issues of sensitivity for your mate until he/she is better able to deal with them. Use compassion and tact—with a good eye on proper timing—to best meet the needs of your beloved. If an ex-spouse criticizes your mate's shortcomings, habits, or idiosyncrasies, avoid reinforcing your beloved's guilt in this regard–particularly if you see efforts to change. If a former wife criticized your husband for being underemployed, come alongside and encourage him where he is right now, while looking together for better options in the future. Curb any jealousies and encourage your mate to spend quality time with all the children. Encourage your partner to fulfill support obligations of each child without reinforcing his/her guilt in doing so—even if this support requires you to make personal sacrifices as well. Keep your mate focused on being a person of integrity who cares for his/her family, no matter how difficult or expensive it becomes (Prov. 20:7; 28:6)!

• *Take a reality check on your mate's expectations.* The worst thing to do with a remarriage partner is to make unreasonable demands or have unrealistic expectations. Let Christ, and your mate, breathe in your relationship. *Test* your expectations, perhaps with a Christian counselor or close Christian friend, before making them known to your mate. Are they realistic? Are they reasonable? What's in the best interest of your mate and other family members? Each remarriage partner also needs to lovingly allow the other both time and space to be *human* and to make mistakes.

• *Avoid comparisons and competition with ex-spouses.* Each spouse to a remarriage needs to establish and build upon his/her own roles and identity in the new relationship without falling into the trap of comparisons with an ex-spouse, or becoming engaged in a futile game of "one-upmanship."

Anticipate blended family dynamics. In a traditional family, family members essentially "grow up together." They tend to respond to economic and social difficulties as a unit, rather than individually. But remarriage often forms a blended family with members having a wide variety of different backgrounds, experiences, and aspirations. What happens when challenges come? Probably individuals will have unique responses, or react as others do in their microfamily unit. For the first year or so, expect these individualized reactions.

Children in the blended family may align with their microfamily relationships, since these will be most natural and comfortable. Therefore, at least initially, children in each microfamily may tend to exploit one another or play one parent against the other. Ideally, a truly *unified* couple will work together to break down microfamily boundaries at a reasonable pace, with the goal of unifying the blended family. But even for the best prepared couples, the usual blended family dynamic is fluid, since roles can switch daily. To further confuse matters, stepparents tend to serve their stepchildren in ways they wouldn't do so for their own children in order to win their favor. Alternatively, each parent may favor his/her biological children and align with microfamily groups. The reality is that competition and rivalry are quite common in blended families, pitting one family member (or microfamily) against the other.

But blended family dynamics don't end there. In many families there's a lot of *transference* occurring—often without anyone being aware it's happening. (Transference occurs when someone shifts displeasure or dislike for another person to a third person.) For example, Marta's ex-husband, Ron, is an unrepentant adulterer, chronic alcoholic, and violent abuser. It's very difficult for Marta to even look at him. But Marta and Ron's son, John, looks just like Ron. It also doesn't help that John has picked up some of Ron's slang and mannerisms. Marta has to struggle with her feelings for John at times because of this physical similarity.

But why not take this blended family dynamics bull by the horns? *Be proactive* by sitting down with your partner and doing the following:

1. *Prepare.* Talk to your remarriage partner about how, when, and why these blended family dynamics arise. *Plan* for them so when they do come up, each spouse will calmly say, "Okay, we talked about this one. I remember what we agreed to do about it." The alternative is to emotionally overreact after thinking, "Uh-oh! This was an unexpected surprise. What do I do now?" Especially prepare for disciplining children in a timely, consistent, and loving manner so that neither spouse inherits the role of being the "heavy" all the time. Agree in advance to discuss all discipline matters *privately*—not in front of any children. Also prepare for some rejection by stepchildren, who may naturally align with biological parents. Commit yourself to be loving, giving, and forgiving by reaching out to each stepchild—even if you receive nothing in return.

2. *Plan for personal space and privacy.* If children must fight each other for toys, time spent alone, or personal clothing or beds, there will be conflict. In many instances it may not be possible to provide a separate bedroom for each child in the blended family home. Children sharing bedrooms then becomes unavoidable. Most likely result? More dissension and conflict! As much as possible prior to the wedding, make sure each person has enough space and privacy in the blended family home. Personal space need not be large in cramped housing, but it must be secure (probably a

lockable area such as a toy chest or file cabinet) and assigned for one family member's exclusive use. Teach all children to respect each other's privacy and possessions.

AGREE ON BLENDED FAMILY GOALS

Some basic foundational goals help assure success in almost every remarriage and blended family situation. Here's a summary:

As husbands and wives, accept the roles of being the family guardians. We serve a God of peace and order—*not* confusion, disorder, and chaos (1 Cor. 14:33). He holds our world together—otherwise there would be total chaos. In similar fashion, as we follow him, it's the remarriage couple's responsibility to bring the Lord's order and peace to the new family. How? By following the Lord's direction and honoring his ordained marital roles and responsibilities (see chap. 5). *Above all, the couple must be the strongest relationship in the blended family, with husband and wife caring for each other first, and supporting one another as each mate works to support the family.* Everyone in the blended family must acknowledge and respect that the adults are in charge. Without this "couple bond" of family strength, a growing void will creep into the family, resulting in imbalanced marital roles, children usurping parental authority, family disintegration, and chaos.

Encourage family unity. The primary prescription to remedy disunity among siblings is to encourage mutual cooperation and appreciation rather than rivalry and competition. How? By making every effort to tell and show each child that he/she is loved and accepted individually. Each child must know and feel that each parent fully considers his/her needs, interests, and desires. No child will have to compete for either parent's attention in the home.

Honor existing relationships between biological parents and children. Each child needs significant and regular contact with *both* biological parents, as long as there's no abuse or other misconduct. Children have natural feelings for their biological parents. Look for ways to be cooperative with a child's absent parent and grandparents. Don't criticize a child's biological parent in front of the child or ask a child to reject a parent for whom he/she may feel strong loyalty. Rather, encourage children to maintain relationships with *both* biological parents, as long as it's safe and reasonable to do so.

Encourage honest and candid family communication. Problems are inevitable—*significantly* more so than in a traditional family. The best defense against these challenges is keeping the lines of family communication open. Honest dialogue allows family members to use biblical measures to resolve conflicts *promptly* and achieve reconciliation, rather than withdraw into opposing splinter groups with blaming, complaining, and disunity. Any reasonable measure designed to *encourage* family communication (such as a regular Family Conference, discussed in chap. 8) protects family unity and preserves order and peace. Candid communication extends to significant relationships outside the family as well, such as ex-spouses, grandparents, and other extended family members. Without cooperation and at least minimal polite discussion, blended family life will be *much* tougher to handle.

Encourage and enforce healthy boundaries. Boundaries are necessary for any family to work, particularly blended families. Remarriage partners must make sure that the family environment provides for reasonable boundaries to work in a positive manner, since everyone benefits from their proper use. The couple must make sure proper boundaries keep ex-spouses and extended family members from taking actions harmful to any family member. The couple also must monitor and enforce boundaries and limits on conduct of all children in the home. The adults must enforce limits by appropriate discipline in a timely and loving, but firm and consistent, manner. While preserving healthy family boundaries, it's equally important to tear down walls of isolation and resentment that disrupt family harmony.

Operate under consistent rules and realistic godly expectations. Promote consistency. Override human nature's tendency to let forgetfulness and stress result in inconsistent discipline. Discuss and agree on rules of conduct, being sure to *write them down.* This encourages family unity and harmony. (Consider using the Blended Family Covenant, discussed in chapter 8 and appendix B, as a starting point for your own "family covenant" so everyone knows what to expect and how to address problems *before* they arise.) Agree on a consistent disciplinary plan as to biological children and stepchildren. Who will be the primary disciplinarian? What age-appropriate corrections are necessary? How can each parent support the other in disciplinary matters? As the couple plans out these goals and objectives, it's important that no child receive unwarranted favor above others as to family responsibilities and discipline.

Model biblical conflict resolution. Expect a lot of conflict in the blended family during the first few years of living together. Different beliefs, experiences, and values that each family member brings into the home guarantees it. It's absolutely essential that husband and wife take the lead in using biblical conflict resolution measures in a prompt, loving, flexible, and open manner whenever conflict arises. The children need parental mentors in this vital area. They need to know what Jesus would do in any situation arising in their lives. Keep everyone focused on the real problems hindering family growth, without wasting time and energy in power struggles over minor issues. If a conflict resists resolution, but the situation also is intolerable, the couple must be willing to seek mediation from a professional Christian counselor, mature and spiritual Christian family friends, or local church elders (see chap. 6).

Don't overlook any blended family member. Too often, family members foolishly believe relationships somehow will nurture and maintain themselves. There are so many fires to put out at the beginning of blended family life, it's easy to put relationships on hold. One remarried couple focused so much on each other's happiness, they went away together on their first Christmas, leaving their teenage kids to fend for themselves. Their justification? "We'll only have our kids for a few years, but we'll have us forever." Result? Feelings of resentment and abandonment by the youngsters during an all-too-crucial stage of beginning blended family life. And those feelings won't be forgotten! Family members too often get taken for granted and lost in the shuffle—that is, until a family crisis arises (many times after the damage is done). Instead, have all family members check in with each other *daily.* Encourage awareness of each other's needs. The first step is having all family members share this commitment. You might consider making every family dinnertime an opportunity for each family member to share about his/her day, a particularly meaningful Scripture, an answered prayer, or other personal thoughts. There's more than enough love to share—make sure it works its way around to everyone each day!

Encourage positive family attitudes and mutual respect. Nothing upsets family unity and peace more than negative and critical words or actions toward others! Turn negativism around by writing down a list of all the blessings God gives to each family member, and to the family in general. Avoid fantasy wishes resulting from comparing your circumstances against unrealistic personal dreams or how other blended families succeeded in different situations. Just stick with the reality of your own family circumstance. Begin by acknowledging those in the family who truly love God and each other. Then look for ways to praise each family member honestly—especially any who are more difficult to deal with. Encourage empathy. Try to understand each person's mind-set. Consider including noncustodial ex-spouses and extended family members. Plan out ways to memorialize family triumphs and good memories in scrapbooks and family photo albums or videos. Constantly encouraging family members to think positively will prompt them to *be* positive in their attitudes and actions.

Utilize available family assistance resources. Make a commitment to use Christian marital and family counseling on a *regular* basis—even if things seem to be going well—to maintain and preserve family harmony. Stay active in local churches and build relationships with other Christian families in similar situations. Consider joining local stepfamily support groups sponsored by local churches or the Stepfamily Association of America. Christian mediators provide a very valuable conflict resolution resource when problems arise with ex-spouses. Having others available to provide competent and timely advice to deal with problems and mediate family disputes provides powerful protection against division and family disintegration.

Make time for family fun! Each individual needs rest and relaxation from the pressures and stresses of blended family life. There are endless inexpensive ways for families to have fun and enjoy relaxing weekend and vacation outings together. Commit to having a "family night" of fun at least one day a week. Work hard to protect that time against the pressures of a busy schedule.

Allow room for change and growth, as God leads. As is true with making any life goals, build in flexibility for change over time. During Paul and Jo's fiftieth wedding anniversary celebration dinner, a friend asked Paul what seemed like an odd question: "Although your marriage to Jo has lasted fifty years now, how many wives have you had?" Paul knew instantly what he meant. After thinking for a moment, he replied, "Three or four. No, I would have to say five or six. Jo changed a great deal over these fifty years. The person I married was a sweet girl with blue eyes. What she has become is a very competent woman with many talents and interests, much like the woman described in Proverbs 31. And I have changed to keep up with her, while also trying to keep up with myself. Neither of us is the person we married!"

Church reformer Martin Luther didn't marry until he was forty. In doing so, he had very low expectations. Not long after he married, he wrote, "If I ever have to find myself a wife again, I will hew myself an obedient wife out of stone." Obviously, Luther wasn't one overcome with romance! Even so, through the years his relationship with his wife changed and matured. That seemingly sterile marriage blossomed into a beautiful tribute to biblical love. Toward the end of his life, he wrote, "I would not give my Katie for France and Venice together." She meant more to him than anything else in the world! Luther also passed this wise advice on to others: "Let the wife make the husband glad to come home, and let him make her sorry to see him leave."

So, as you make family goals, stick to them—but also allow room for review to change them as circumstances warrant. Remain in step with the natural life and growth in your family. Be sure to bend so your goals won't break!

BLENDED FAMILY TRAINING

Aside from setting family goals, the couple also needs to begin training all blended family members for what life will be like after the wedding. There are some practical measures individuals can undertake together to help ease the transition into blended family life, such as:

Discuss and agree upon roles, rules, and coparenting plans. Without roles and rules to help guide all family members, blended families would be like rudderless ships sailing without a captain at night through threatening shallow waters. Substantial planning is necessary to define the biblical roles of each family member, to develop household rules to maintain order and establish peace in the home, and to assign coparenting responsibilities.

• *Biblical family roles.* Husbands are to be the leaders and guides of the blended family, as they follow the example of Christ (Eph. 5:25). They are to love their wives as Christ loves the church, and not be harsh to them (Col. 3:19; Eph. 5:25–33). Fathers (including stepfathers) must not embitter or exasperate their children, and should avoid discouraging them (Col. 3:21). Instead, they should strive to bring them up in the training and instruction of the Lord (Eph. 6:4). Wives are to submit to their husbands graciously, as fitting to the Lord, and respect them (Col. 3:18; Eph. 5:22–24, 33). They don't seek to usurp their husbands' leadership role in matters not violative of Scripture. They *build up* their homes, rather than foolishly tear them down (Prov. 14:1). Husbands and wives together provide for their family (1 Tim. 5:8; Prov. 31). They keep watch over their children, always thinking and praying about their upbringing in the Lord and their best welfare. Children are to obey their parents (including stepparents) in everything, for this is right and pleases the Lord (Col. 3:20; Eph. 6:1–3).

The blended family, just like the church, is one body made of many parts. No one in the family can legitimately say to another, "I don't need you." Each family member needs the love, help, and cooperation of all others. God combines all members into a blended family so there will be no division in it, but each member should have equal concern for each other. If one family member suffers, all others suffer with him/her. If one member is honored, all family members rejoice with that person! You're forming a *single* blended family, and each member has a special role to fulfill as part of it.

• *Household rules.* One of the first priorities for the blended family is to make a list of all the household work. Who will pay bills, cook meals, grocery shop, do the laundry, take out the trash, clean house, etc.? Ask for volunteers for each job at a prewedding Family Conference (see chap. 8). Be sure to include the children in household work, as appropriate for their age. To help children keep track of chores, many families use a daily chart to monitor and praise completion. But in assigning initial family responsibilities, remember Josh McDowell's frequent warning, "*Rules* without *relationship* leads to rebellion." If you want to avoid rebellion in your home, make sure everyone receives proper praise and gratitude for their individual contributions.

• *Coparenting plan.* We address coparenting plans in chapter 9 as to children's issues, and in chapter 11 about coordinating parenting responsibilities with noncustodial ex-spouses. But it's important to have an initial parenting plan in place before remarriage. Ideally, it will have the blessing and cooperation of noncustodial ex-spouses as well. Your children deserve this planning on how to shepherd them through the bewildering process of blended family life. Be sure you and your mate have all the facts before working together on a parenting plan. Disclose to your partner *all* current parenting obligations so there will be no surprises or hurt feelings later on. One Christian wife I know didn't even know her husband had a daughter who was institutionalized until years into their remarriage. Imagine what a shock this was to their marriage! Unfortunately, with inadequate disclosure, the ones who suffer most are your children.

Focus on your children. You and your beloved have spent time getting to know each other and growing together as you prepare for remarriage. Your children may have missed this opportunity. Now as the wedding nears, each child notices that he/she must negotiate new family relationships. Not only is there a new stepparent to live with, but possibly stepsiblings as well as new grandparents outside the home. All these strangers are people the child might not have chosen to know, given a personal choice. The child has no opportunity to "court" these people or watch out for relationship "red flags" as his/her parent did in choosing a partner. If the parents overlooked something of concern to the child in these new instant-family ties, everyone must now work the issue out over time on the fly. That's very tough for a kid to do!

Stress the positive aspects of the new blended family to your children. Point out ways in which the remarriage will improve their lives. Plan out basic guidelines and ground rules for them in the new family. Set up weekly and weekend television and video privileges, division of chores, and allowances for each child. Jointly review these expectations. Write them out and post them in a prominent place so there's no misunderstanding later. Be careful not to overregulate the children in the beginning—just stick with the basics. To avoid jealousies among stepsiblings (and interspousal conflict), make sure these rules are consistent and fair based upon each child's age and maturity—though not necessarily identical for each child. Avoid making the potentially devastating mistake of not including *all* children in family plans. Prayerfully consider the needs of children who won't be living in your home, but only visiting from time to time. Make sure you have a copy of all medical records of each child spending any time in your home. Know their medical histories and any chronic health problems. Since stepparents have no inherent legal authority to authorize medical treatment for a stepchild, the biological parents should consider giving each stepparent a power of attorney or other legally recognized health authorization form granting this authority if the biological parents are unavailable during emergencies.

Above all, make your children a priority. Miami mortgage banker (and friend) Aris Sastre and his wife, Kelly, have a large family. They steadfastly support their children in a wide variety of endeavors, including taking them to sports tournaments all over the country. I asked Aris about the enormous time requirements of serving his children in this way. He replied, "Warren, I suppose I could be at the top of my profession and earning a lot more if this time were work-related. But Kelly and I decided together a long time ago that our kids would always come first. We're there for them. They know we love and support them. And I wouldn't have it any other way." No wonder the Sastre children have excelled in school and are now entering college with the goal of becoming doctors and other professionals! That same commitment needs to carry over into the ways we encourage, support, and *lead* our children through the family blending process.

Draw out a family tree. Unlike a first marriage beginning with just a husband and wife and their respective parents, many confusing logistical problems come with launching a remarriage/blended family. Children and stepchildren may be relative strangers to each other, wondering how they'll fit into the new family. Parents of the remarriage partners want to know who will become their grandchildren. Ex-spouses and their parents (grandparents to some or all the children in remarriage) have concerns about who will be living with their biological kin. They may fear possible custody and visitation interference. A whole bunch of folks become related at the wedding—folks who may not even know each other's names yet! There are parents, children, sisters and brothers, cousins, and multiple other extended family members. In reality, this is a *group* marriage. A remarriage/blended family isn't just a family tree—it's a family forest!

I'm reminded of the oft-quoted tongue-in-cheek essay written by an unknown author entitled "How a Man Became His Own Grandfather":

> I married a widow who had a daughter. My father visited our
> house frequently and fell in love with my stepdaughter and married
> her. Thus, my father became my son-in-law, and my stepdaughter
> became my mother, for she was my father's wife. My stepdaughter also
> had a son. He was, of course, my grandchild and my brother at the
> same time, because he was the son of my father. My wife was my
> grandmother, for she was my mother's mother. I was my wife's

husband and grandchild at the same time. Since the husband of a person's grandmother is his grandfather, I was my own grandfather!

Confused? Then you have some idea of how blended family relatives may feel!

It's helpful to draw a blended family tree on paper showing how everyone in the family, and extended family, relate to each other. Send copies to each person shown on the tree. This helps introduce people to each other and avoids unnecessary misunderstandings and confusion. For out-of-town extended family members, parents may want to videotape interviews by asking questions that inspire *stories*—not yes or no answers—to share with their children. Not only is it a great way to memorialize family history, but being able to watch family members share their lives makes them more real, friendly, and familiar to children. Also reverse the process—send videotapes of new blended family member interviews out to extended family members. The goal, of course, is encouraging all family members to know and love each other *before* the wedding, when they may be meeting each other for the first time.

Another good way to help everyone connect names and faces is by using photographs. Why not make it a fun game? Get two small pictures of each family and extended family member. Paste them on a small cardboard circle, with the person's name written just below his/her picture. Mix all the cardboard pieces up and place them face down on a table. Then play the "Match Game" by having each family member take a turn flipping over two cardboard pieces to match identical pictures. The one who makes the most matches wins a special dessert. You'll be surprised at how well this game works for all players. And by the time of the wedding, you and your mate can have fun watching your children proudly greet family guests by name!

Plan around existing and new family traditions. One potentially explosive conflict is understanding and appreciating existing traditions for each mate's family. Some families have large family reunions out of town on July 4, while others "always" go to the big fireworks celebration at the stadium or town square. Some families go boating and have a picnic lunch each Sunday afternoon after church while others come home and enjoy naps. Some open Christmas gifts on Christmas Eve after a church service while others "always" wait for the excitement of seeing what Santa brought on Christmas morning. The underlying potential conflict, of course, is when "our" microfamily way of "always" doing things a certain way conflicts with those of our mate's microfamily and "their" traditions. Potential family blowups are an even greater risk if neither microfamily even knows about the other's traditions. This might force surprise cancellation of long-standing plans! Why let these potential upsets come up by default? They'll only create power struggles and resentment later on.

Before remarriage occurs, it's much better for both family groups to share about their respective traditions and why they're so important. Talking these matters out allows everyone to review each tradition and question whether there's a better way of observing special events. What would happen if you did things differently?

Make a written list of each microfamily's traditions. Then have all family members brainstorm together about how to reconcile each person's current expectations about blended family life while also considering ideas for new family traditions. How can you resolve conflicts and create new possibilities? Here are some suggestions:

• *Use "increase the pie" options.* Using ultimatums and taking rigid "my way or the highway" positions increase conflict. Instead, as mediators often do in reaching settlements, increase the pie so everyone comes away with a bigger slice. You do this by adding options rather than subtracting them through default by allowing apparently contradictory options to cancel each other out. For Christmas, for example, why must everyone open gifts on Christmas Eve or Christmas morning? Why not both?

• *Allow for "opt-out" alternatives.* If most new family members want to continue a particular family tradition that creates a personal hardship or disappointment for others, be flexible. Allow for simultaneous alternatives. If some members like the idea of a picnic lunch and boating after church, they can enjoy that event together. If others prefer not to attend, they can stay home and nap if they wish (or younger children can stay with noncustodial parents, extended family, or friends for the afternoon).

• *Be sure to honor family traditions of ex-spouses.* Find every reasonable way possible to build bridges, not burn them, with ex-spouses (see chap. 11). One relatively inexpensive and considerate olive branch to offer them is to work around your ex-spouses' family traditions. If you have custody of children 330 out of 365 days a year, gracefully and cheerfully let your former spouse have special days with the kids, if possible. Try to bend so a good coparenting relationship won't break.

• *Don't ignore family tradition preferences of your children.* In the spirit of cooperation, however, don't ignore the needs of your children. For instance, some divorced parents logically think that Mom can have Sally for Thanksgiving, and then she can visit Dad for Christmas and New Year's (a longer period without school interference). Then next year, to be fair, they can reverse Sally's holiday visits with her parents. But what about Sally? She may have a preference about which holidays she spends with each parent. Therefore, see if you and your ex-spouse can agree on a longer-term arrangement that builds in more consistency as you prepare your prewedding coparenting plan. Of course, as children get older, their preferences should carry even greater weight in family decisions. For example, a teenager may want to take a trip with friends to go camping over the Thanksgiving holiday. Just be flexible.

• *Gracefully retire impractical family traditions.* Some family traditions outlive their usefulness. Create some new alternatives.

• *Plan for uniquely new blended family traditions.* One unique way to begin a shared blended family history is giving each family member a ring on the wedding day, as Cheryl and I did with Chase. Others give each member a gift, such as a silver cup personally engraved with the names of all family members and the date of the wedding, or other item to mark the occasion. Still others plant a tree to symbolize that as the tree grows and changes over the years, so will the family. In our family, we celebrate our wedding anniversary together—a wonderful memory relived and enjoyed! Why not start a family journal or scrapbook? Have each member write down thoughts and feelings about the upcoming wedding and his/her goals and expectations for the family. Then make it an annual family night event to update it. Begin searching for new family events and special occasions that will be the blended family's own—even *before* the wedding.

Review and evaluate family boundary issues. Before the wedding is the time to focus on specific boundaries at play in each microfamily group *before* living together in the same home creates encroachment friction and conflict. The key is *communication* among family members. Are existing family boundary patterns compatible with each other? If not, what compromises and adjustments may be necessary? Don't let these surprise you after the wedding!

Sara and her young boys have a very relaxed lifestyle. As a widowed single mom, she loves it when her little ones burst through her bedroom door and jump into bed with her to watch Saturday morning cartoons. Sometimes her little munchkins "cook Mommy a special breakfast" of chocolate milk and oreos. They share each other's toothbrushes and eat each other's meals. Sara's divorced husband-to-be, Doug, has a twelve-year-old daughter who's increasingly protective of her privacy as she matures. Doug and his daughter have very orderly lives, giving each other lots of room to live in their apartment. And they definitely *don't* like anyone sharing their toothbrushes! What will happen when these microfamily groups enjoy their first Saturday morning together as Doug and Sara decide to "sleep in"?

It's important that all blended family members understand and agree on some basic boundary matters *before* the wedding:

• *Respect each other's privacy.* Locked or closed bedroom or bathroom doors mean "Don't enter without first knocking and asking permission to enter" unless there's a legitimate emergency involving blood or broken bones, or the family member(s) affected say otherwise. (Some family members may want to keep a general "open door" policy, with only temporary lockouts to assure privacy for intimate moments.) Each family member will have privacy to bathe, undress, do homework, or talk on the telephone at proper times without unreasonable intrusion from others. Each person will receive unopened personal mail each day for private reading. Personal diaries remain private, telephone calls unmonitored, and rooms unsearched, unless parents have reasonable cause to believe conduct harmful to any family member, or a violation of the law, exists.

• *Respect each other's property.* Each person's personal property will be his/her own to keep or share as that family member determines best. No one will use other's personal property without first asking permission. After use, it'll be returned promptly in the same condition, or after repair or replacement due to any "accidents." No clothes, toys, or other personal property will be given or thrown away without discussing the matter first with the rightful owner and receiving his/her consent. If it becomes necessary to clean out a closet or get rid of outgrown clothes, the rightful owner will decide how to do it (except for very young children). No one's clothes sail off to Mexican missionaries without the owner knowing and agreeing to it first!

• *Respect each other's person.* Don't allow any hitting, spitting, or unwanted touching of any family members. Even if others tickle someone playfully, all tickling ceases whenever the person says stop. Limit unkind words or insulting comments among family members.

• *Personal boundaries must be consistent with overall family unity.* Each mature family member has freedom to establish personal boundaries meaningful to that person—even if others see no reason or need for the same—if consistent with overall family harmony. For example, if a child wants to spend video-game time alone, that will be honored. Similarly, that family member must agree not to interrupt game time of other children if they also want privacy. Blended family boundaries are a good thing! (See chap. 6.) They remind each family member of reasonable expectations, promote mutual respect, and maintain family order. Boundaries also help train children to be sensitive and loving Christians, as well as responsible citizens.

Make time for family worship. It's so true that the "family that prays together, stays together." How can conflict and division reign for long in any home if parents and children humble themselves before God, seeking his guidance in every situation and asking for forgiveness for wrongs done? In this age of fractured families and demanding schedules, it's vital that a vibrant and living faith undergird everything we do. Live Christianity *consistently* in the home, with Christ at the center of our existence as a blended family. It's vital for raising up our children in the faith. How is this done?

• *Read from God's Word.* There are many ways to do this. Some families take turns reading a passage of Scripture, or even an entire chapter, each day. Consider using topical or devotional studies, which really help family members understand and apply Scripture in a practical way. Cheryl and I prefer using a devotional guide with daily lessons geared for children so Chase always feels that he is an equal participant. But make sure the Bible text is in simple language, even by using a children's Bible if your youngest ones need it. This is an excellent time to memorize short verses of encouragement and meaning to the family!

• *Encourage discussion and practical applications.* Parents should keep family discussion moving in a positive direction by asking such open-ended questions as "Why did Moses make so many excuses when he stood before God in the burning bush?" "Why do you think Jesus brought Peter back into the boat after saving him from drowning in the lake?" Keep the discussion clear and concise while encouraging all family members to get involved. Use these family times creatively to help everyone see how the Bible really relates to every circumstance and need.

• *Pray together.* There are many things for blended family members to be thankful for so let God know how you feel! Be sure to ask each child if he/she has a particular prayer interest. This may lead to lots of prayers for gerbils, guinea pigs, and dogs, but that's okay. And remember, God likes to receive praise too! As part of prayer time, regularly confess personal ways we fall short of what pleases God. This vital part of family worship promotes healing of hurts and offended spirits while ensuring that family members walk in fellowship with Christ and each other (James 5:16; 1 John 1:5–10). Also remember to include personal requests and special intercession for other extended family members.

• *Keep a prayer journal.* Many families enjoy keeping a prayer list or notebook handy for each worship time. Tracking special needs and prayer requests focuses each family member on prayer and following up with the people involved. Regularly doing this encourages everyone to have a servant's heart and to truly be "other-centered" when it's easy to be selfish. Also record answers to prayer—a very positive family experience!

• *Let praise flow forth!* Family worship shouldn't be boring. Make it exciting by doing lots of different things, such as singing, acting out a Bible story, or making a craft to mirror a Bible lesson. Kids are really great at thinking of new ideas! Be flexible and yielded in allowing the Spirit to inspire the family (1 Thess. 5:19).

Ideally, family worship times should begin *before* the wedding. This allows everyone to feel comfortable in this setting early, with an easy transition after the wedding. You'll find this family worship time of special value—especially during the crucial postwedding adjustment period when so many other matters are in flux.

Resolve the name issues. We'll discuss the problems of how children address their parents in chapter 9, but there's a related issue for the remarriage couple as well. In recent decades, women have become increasingly sensitive about retaining their maiden names when they marry. This becomes more confusing when a remarriage.

When Cheryl first married, she took the name of her first husband. When they divorced, she changed her legal name to reacquire her maiden name, "Rybka." She used her maiden name to establish a very successful position in business before we met and married. She therefore believes it important to use three different names—Cheryl Kniskern, Cheryl Rybka-Kniskern (which, I'll admit, is a real tongue-twister!) or Cheryl Rybka, depending upon the circumstances. For example, in business she now uses the "Rybka-Kniskern" name to maintain the recognition she built up over many years. As part of Chase's school involvement, she uses "Cheryl Rybka." This is important because Cheryl also changed Chase's legal name to "Rybka" as part of the divorce from her first husband. We both believed it very important for Chase not to feel estranged when *none* of the parents in his life shared his last name.

Name differences between a remarried couple also may cause some confusion or hurt feelings for a few spouses. It also can create some uncomfortable, and perhaps unnecessary, "separateness" between mates. But there are some practical advantages to remaining flexible in this area as the couple prepares for remarriage. Think about it.

Maintain a good sense of humor! Good-natured humor and laughter certainly bring joy. But having a good laugh with your family is really about communication and intimacy, since the better you get to know someone, the more there is to laugh about! Laughter creates common ground out of different family experiences as you build relationships. It helps us cope with stress and the hassles of life. Sometimes it's great just to spend family time *primed* for laughter—looking and waiting for funny things to say. Once folks begin laughing, it isn't long before everyone joins in and begins playing off each other—almost like a food fight in the movies!

Sometimes well-timed humor can make a gentle but thought-provoking point. Lynn remembers one such event very well: "My husband and I, sitting next to each other on the bed, were having a disagreement in which neither of us would give an inch. Realizing I was getting nowhere in the argument, I said in frustration, 'You're impossible!' He turned to me and, with a smile, responded, 'No, I'm not. I'm *next* to impossible.'" Checkmate! They both shared a good laugh with each other on that one.

Begin early in keeping humor at the front of your relationships as you prepare for blended family life. Be sure to keep it going afterward too. Laughter is a gift that's always returned with interest!

There may be many other matters you need to plan for your blended family. But one very important goal is to try and eliminate as many unknown factors about your blended family as possible *before* the wedding. Then you can wisely *plan* and *prepare* to bring order and peace to your house while reducing the risk of potential conflicts and misunderstandings. Why wait until after the wedding to address these issues when so much else is going on?

So now you and your mate (and your kids) are ready to enter remarriage and blended family life. The wedding awaits.

THE WEDDING—THE ULTIMATE BLENDED FAMILY EVENT

What's remarriage all about? To civil governments, marriage is simply a contract—an agreement that a husband and wife make in the presence of witnesses. It's really not much different from buying a car or a house. From the church's perspective, Christians recognize the civil contractual element, but the spiritual dimension goes much deeper. Christians know that any marriage is a contract among *three* parties— the Lord, husband, and wife. For those entering remarriage with children from a prior marriage, there is even more—a pledge to love and care for each other, as well as each child in the blended family. And so the wedding is a confirmation of many precious commitments: compliance with civil law, church affirmation that God's at work in the husband/wife relationship, and the commitment of parents to care for their children.

A remarriage wedding, I believe, is the ultimate blending experience for a couple. Where else will they have so many different people together in one place during this uniquely special family time of commitment, vows, prayer, dedication, compassion, adoring love, and selflessness? The couple begins their new life together. The children are present and engaged in all that is going on. Grandparents and extended family members, perhaps from faraway places, come together to meet for the first time. And all this happens in a swirling excitement of a wedding! It's the first joyous project jointly undertaken by you, your mate, and your respective families. Few family projects are bigger than that!

Since the wedding is so important, let's look at some ways to help make it an extraordinary family blending event:

Make the engagement and wedding a family event. There are many wonderful and unique aspects of a remarriage wedding, but none quite so special as having your children there to enjoy it! Of course, it's natural that children feel somewhat awkward and out of place, especially if they see all the prewedding planning and actual ceremony focusing almost exclusively on Mom and Dad. They may experience other anxieties as well, such as realizing that the wedding means their divorced biological parents won't be getting back together as they'd hoped.

Cheryl and I wanted our relationship to include Chase in every way possible. We wanted to let him know, "You're a *very* important part of our new family!" This began from the time of our engagement. I proposed to Cheryl during a family outing to Clearwater Beach, Florida. We let Chase know of the good news the same day. We were all so happy that we did what any normal family-to-be would do—we filled up squirt guns and laughed as we doused each other! Shortly after Cheryl received her engagement ring, we took Chase out to a jewelry store to get fitted for a small gold ring of his very own. He was so excited about it. Each member of our family would receive a ring—including him! We rented a tuxedo for Chase to wear at our wedding so he would look just like his new stepfather *and* Cheryl's father (Chase's grandfather) as they walked down the aisle together.

Be sensitive to the children. It's easier to bring younger children, like Chase, into wedding preparations since they're usually eager to participate as a ring bearer or a flower girl. Older children may be more reluctant to be included. Let all of the children know they're welcome to join the ceremony to the extent they feel comfortable. Don't pressure them to do anything against their will. Invite children to get involved in planning the wedding. This encourages a positive attitude and minimizes feelings of being left out. But be sure to explain things along the way so they'll understand. Don't assume anything. I remember one little girl attending her first wedding whispering to her mother, "Why is the bride dressed in white?" "Because white is the color of happiness," her mother explained. "And today is the happiest day of her life." The child thought about this for a moment. "So why is the groom wearing black?"

Also be aware that some children won't decide what they want to do about the wedding until the last minute. Again, try to remain flexible and leave openings for them to slip in and participate with ease if they want to do so.

The "ex" factor. If you and your partner are like most couples, don't count on much cooperation from ex-spouses about the remarriage. The perceived threat presented by the new relationship may more than counterbalance your efforts to make an ex-spouse feel comfortable about your plans. Of course, if you're one of the fortunate few with an exceptionally good relationship with your ex-spouse, you'll enjoy much less stress and potential conflict. In most cases, it's best to make wedding arrangements around the children with minimum involvement by ex-spouses. Make sure you assume full responsibility for helping children dress appropriately, prearranging transportation to and from all wedding related events, and overseeing all other concerns.

Plan the wedding you want. Should a divorced or widowed woman who remarries wear a white gown?[2] Should she have the usual entourage of bridesmaids and attendants? Who'll participate in the wedding ceremony? How long will the wedding list be? Don't let other family members or friends push you into decisions against the best interests of your new family. Your wedding should be the way *you* want it to be, within the bounds of Christian marriage, church tradition, and the confines of good taste.

Your primary concern should be for the Lord, your mate, and your children in planning your wedding. Expectations of those outside your family-to-be are secondary.

Keep it simple. Why make a wedding a Hollywood production—especially for a remarriage, with all of its stresses and pressures? You can blow a gazillion dollars and spend a year of your life debating issues all the way down to whether to use an all-white or all-peach bridal bouquet, or you can plan your wedding in an hour, wear a sundress, carry daisies, and say "I do" on the beach at sunset. Either way, it can be spiritual, legal, and lovely! Remember, the risk of unforeseen problems increases almost geometrically as the number of people involved in your wedding grows!

Minister Jody Vickery of Norcross, Georgia, himself a wedding officiating veteran, shares this personal observation:

> The wedding, intended to be a commitment of the couple's love and affirmation by their families and the congregation, becomes one more symbol of status. Families spend enormous amounts of money and incur unnecessary debt to make a statement. I often tell couples to scale back their plans. In simplicity there is beauty. And room for the Spirit to work. Last year I conducted one of the most beautiful ceremonies I've ever seen. And one of the simplest. The bride's gown was simple, yet elegant. A groomsman led congregational singing. The groom's father led a prayer. The focus of the couple's lives was echoed in the tone of their ceremony. Their wedding was more worship service than fashion statement. The guests left commenting not about the elaborate decorations they had seen, but about the spiritual declarations they had witnessed.[3]

Whom to invite. There really is no right answer . . . with this important exception. Know *why* you're inviting particular guests and *how* they'll blend in! Will you acknowledge deceased or divorced parents of your children in any way? How about siblings of your children not present at the wedding? You and your mate should brainstorm about these possibilities with other family members to make sure you overlook no important matters of concern. Once you and your beloved decide a firm number to invite, stand by it together and you'll have a much easier time sticking to your goal.

Wedding bills. First-time brides receive the best resources their families can offer, with some parents gladly going into debt to provide the best wedding they can afford. In 2002, the average couple spends nineteen thousand dollars on a first marriage wedding.[4] But what happens the second time around? Like it or not, society doesn't give remarriages equal attention. Weddings aren't romantic week-long events featuring horse-drawn carriages, gourmet food, breathtaking scenes, string quartets, and doves released as you say, "I do." Gifts traditionally are of lesser value. Guests don't have the same eagerness to attend. Then there are those wedding bills! And they come when most couples suffer great financial stress from a prior divorce or other setbacks in life.

Unless parents or other family members help out with the expense, you and your partner should expect to absorb the full cost of the wedding and related events. Don't expect the father of the bride to pay for this wedding! This may mean sacrificing some of the expensive frills, but the ceremony still can be very special indeed.

• *Wedding planners.* Instead of having a wedding planner, use breaks at work to make calls to vendors, update your wedding calendar, or address a few invitations. But most experts believe that hiring a wedding consultant is money well spent if you're planning a larger wedding. They can save you time and stress at the most critical moments, and perhaps also reduce costs by securing discounts on services and food. Planners also can serve a mediation function, as when Broward County, Florida, wedding planner Karen Emery had to make peace between a divorced couple—the father and mother of the bride—who never could stand each other. She stepped in quickly to soothe ruffled feathers when the father snarled to the photographer trying to arrange a family group shot, "I am *not* standing next to *her!*"

• *Ministers/pastors.* Having your church minister perform the wedding may save you some expense, but remember that a worker is due his wages (1 Tim. 5:18). In fact, he may refuse payment for his services, but compensate him anyway for time away from his family while devoting himself to your wedding!

At our wedding, Cheryl and I actually had two pastors officiating—and not because we wanted to be doubly sure we were married! Our dear friend Dr. Kieth Mitchell (a church elder and minister, as well as our mentor and Christian marriage counselor) performed the wedding with Cheryl's brother, Michael Rybka, also a minister. Their individual contributions and perspectives blended so well! Their cooperation and encouragement truly blessed us on our special day!

But there's another important issue you might have to address. Some ministers choose not to perform remarriages simply because they find it difficult to know whether a couple is scripturally free to marry. Some church leaders also won't allow remarriages to take place on church property due to the same concerns. Therefore, make sure you build a relationship early with a pastor or minister satisfied that you and your beloved are indeed scripturally free to remarry. If your wedding location presents any problem for church leaders or members, simply be flexible in scheduling your ceremony elsewhere. Remember, God is everywhere—not just in church sanctuaries.

• *Wedding facilities.* Having the wedding at your church building, in a private home, or a local park should save on the expense of renting a facility. But be sure to ask the right questions: How many guests can the space accommodate? How long will a rental fee reserve the space? What are the overtime charges? Are there adequate kitchen facilities? What are the regulations on decoration, flowers, caterers, and photography, if any? Make sure you know all the details to avoid last-minute surprises.

• *Catering.* If your wedding is catered, consider having a morning wedding. Expenses for food, transportation, and hall rentals tend to be lower in the morning. Also avoid Saturdays, and June or September wedding dates, since these are the most popular (and expensive) wedding times. Be sure to ask prospective caterers some key questions: What's the estimated cost per person for a seated luncheon or dinner (or buffet), and what does it include? What is the staff-to-guest ratio? (For seated meals, you should have one service person per every eight to ten guests.) Do you have a set menu? Can you view the catering of another wedding party to check food display and service style? Can you taste foods on the menu you suggest? Questions like these root out any unreasonable expectations and make planning much easier.

• *Music.* How about music at your wedding and the reception to follow? Cheryl and I felt that live classical music was worth a little extra expense to make the occasion special. We hired a few students from the University of Miami College of Music. They played beautifully, and charged considerably less than other musicians. (But students are in short supply during the summer when school is out.) If you choose to have live music, be sure to ask about the musician's attire and work breaks. Consider hiring a small ensemble—three or four musicians—instead of a large band. Ask about overtime rates and cancellation terms, should you need to change or cancel the date. Negotiate minimum performance time. Avoid having live music at December weddings. It's holiday party time, so you'll pay premium prices for music. Also, if you book musicians for dates other than Saturdays, you can save as much as 35–40 percent.

• *Wedding dress.* Consider using a family heirloom dress or borrowing or renting one rather than buying a dress you'll only use once. (Cheryl borrowed her mother's beautiful cream formal dress and looked absolutely stunning!) Outlet stores often sell flawed, but easily repaired, gowns.

• *Flowers.* Flowers are a potential wedding budget buster. Bride and bridesmaids carry bouquets; groom and groomsmen wear boutonnieres. Parents on both sides receive flowers, and perhaps your children as well! There's an altarpiece for a church ceremony and a centerpiece for the head table at the reception. Some people buy (or even rent) silk flowers to save money. But there are other ways to save, such as mixing roses with red carnations, and especially avoiding weddings close to holidays when flowers are in the greatest demand and most expensive—Valentine's Day, Easter, Mother's Day, and Christmas. Instead of flowers, why not rent lovely and elegant candelabra twined with ivy as reception table centerpieces?

• *Economizing measures.* Consider folks in your congregation who would love to sing and play music at your special event. Fellow church members also can bring special home-cooked dishes for guests. Perhaps some attendees can bring beautiful garden flowers for the ceremony. Someone else might want to videotape the ceremony as a wedding gift. Can't afford a photographer? Try handing out disposable cameras. Decide what you want to splurge on—the wedding or the honeymoon, but not both. If you want to cut back the wedding a bit, dare to say no to tradition—no garter, no videotape, no veil, no band, no RSVP cards, and no bridal party beyond a best man and a matron of honor. Use some new wineskins—it's *your* day!

Get the extended family involved. At any wedding, especially a remarriage, expect gathering family members to feel uncomfortable meeting one another for the first time. (This is where the family-tree drawing we mentioned earlier comes in handy, if you previously delivered it to each guest!) Some couples at larger weddings offer attendees the option to wear name tags to help everyone get to know each other—an excellent suggestion to encourage "blending"!

Cheryl and I took the rather bold step of foregoing a photographer at our wedding. Instead, we bought disposable cameras for each guest. We asked them to have fun taking pictures of whatever they wanted. This was a wonderful, relatively inexpensive icebreaker—they had a great time! Our bonus was a wide variety of photos to choose from for our wedding album, with candid shots no professional photographer could have captured! The photos meant so much to us because beloved family members selected what caught their eye. This was much better than the standard posed shots from a dispassionate photographer.

Before and during the wedding, keep experienced extended family couples handy. Ask for their advice. They're wonderfully helpful in pointing out the little things that make a big difference, and they feel honored that you asked!

Keep the wedding Christ-centered. The ceremony and celebration should be Christ-centered and reinforce all the love and commitment issues we've discussed.

At our wedding, Cheryl touched my heart by sharing the words of Ruth, which captures the beautiful essence of commitment in a relationship:

". . . Where you go I will go, and where you stay, I will stay. Your
people will be my people and your God my God. Where you die, I will
die, and there I will be buried. May the LORD deal with me, be it ever
so severely, if anything but death separates you and me."
(Ruth 1:16b–17)

This passage isn't really a wedding or marriage verse, but it speaks volumes about the type of commitment marriage partners should make to each other! Remarried couples so desperately need the reassurance and encouragement of this type of commitment. With remarriages, convey the commitment that "I do, and I will" be everything I can be to help this blended family succeed with the Lord's help. What better way to express this promise than at a joyous wedding ceremony with family and friends present?

Include the children in the wedding. It's common for children involved in remarriages to stand near the couple. The couple's vows to each other frequently include promises to the children about their welfare and happiness. This is in keeping with the true meaning of "wedlock," which derives from the Anglo-Saxon word *wedlac*—*wed* means "pledge," while *lac* suggests "giving." Therefore, a wedding is a time of "pledge giving." The main purpose of a Christian wedding is to make vows.

Psalm 15:4 says that God honors the person "who keeps his oath even when it hurts." Why not include the children in this solemn commitment to one's spouse, as part of a family obligation? What better time to express promises to the children before God and assembled family witnesses in the spiritual, loving, and joyous atmosphere of a wedding? Weddings serve as excellent, concrete life-changing events that help each family member realize he/she is now part of a new family, bound together with voiced promises and commitments wrapped up in biblical love. The ceremony makes the new family real to everyone concerned.

Now, for a moment, let me take you to our wedding. After Cheryl and I expressed our vows to each other, with Chase standing beside us, I turned to our sweet little boy and got down on one knee to smile and look directly into his eyes. "Chase," I shared with him, "Mommy and I want you to know that we're all getting married today. We want you to be here with us and to share this beautiful wedding with everyone because you're a special part of our new family.

"You know, Chase, when Jesus was preaching to people, he was very busy. Some people listening to him wanted their children to be near him too. The disciples told the parents, 'Keep the children away.' But Jesus said, 'No, no. I *want* the little children to come to me.' Then Jesus reached out to the children, and touched them, and hugged them—just like I'm hugging you right now. That's the kind of relationship I really want us to enjoy together. I want to be a father figure to you so we can trust each other, and love each other, and be together for the rest of our lives.

"Did you know that you're a very special little boy, Chase? It's true! God loves you as his child. You also have grandfathers who love you, but now you are going to have another grandfather to love you. And you have a father, and now you are also going to have another father who will watch over you. So you're a very blessed little boy!

"Mommy and I have made some promises to each other today, called vows. But now we want to make a promise and vow to you. The Bible says fathers should tell their children about God's faithfulness. And that's what I vow to do with you. As we grow up together, I want to share with you about God's faithfulness.

"In Ephesians 6:4, the Bible says, 'Fathers, do not exasperate your children, but bring them up in the training and instruction of the Lord.' Do you know what 'exasperate' means?" Chase sheepishly shook his head to say no. "Well," I continued, "it's like when you shake your hands in the air and say, '*Augh!* I can't take it anymore!' The Bible tells us that parents are not to make their children frustrated and angry for no good reason. Chase, I want to make a promise to you that I will do my best to be a good father to you and not exasperate you as you, Mommy, and I live together.

"In Colossians 3:20, the Bible says, 'Children, obey your parents in everything, for this pleases the Lord.' So it's important that you obey Mommy and me, for this pleases the Lord. And we will take care of you. This is very important.

"And lastly, in Colossians 3:21, the Bible tells us, 'Fathers, do not embitter your children, or they will become discouraged.' So I will make a commitment to you, Chase. I'll always try to do what I believe the Lord wants me to do, but I'll do my best not to embitter you, because I don't want you to become discouraged. I want you to grow up and become a fine Christian man, as your Mommy and I really desire and pray for you. And I know you will. So I am committing that to you today.

"I promise to encourage you, and love you, and help you know how much the Lord loves all of us. Mommy and I will listen to you and make sure we're taking care of your needs so you'll be a happy and loving boy. We're so proud of you! It makes Mommy and me so very joyful in our hearts that you're here with us."

With that, I gently grasped his little hand and slipped his ring onto his middle finger (since his ring finger was too small). "Chase, this ring is a symbol of the promises and vows we're making here today. Mommy and I have our rings. This is your own very special ring to remind you of this day. Keep it and wear it as your link to our family." Then I leaned over to hug and kiss him as he gazed intently at the small gold ring sparkling on his finger.

Including Chase in our ceremony, rather than having him feel excluded or treated as an outsider, pleased us so much. We believe making vows to each other—including the children—is in keeping with what Jesus would want us to do as we try to be responsible parents.

But our wedding story with Chase didn't end there. With young children being what they are, there was a humorous postscript to Chase's participation in this joyous family event. After the ceremony, Cheryl and I noticed that Chase wasn't wearing his ring. When we asked him about it, he remarked rather matter-of-factly, "Well, we're married, right? So I threw the ring away. I thought that's what you do after a wedding!" This got a chuckle out of both of us before we explained how wedding folks do indeed keep their rings forever. (Fortunately, a sharp-eyed attendant found the ring on the floor and returned it to us for safekeeping.)

Children actually can be a source of *comfort* to the couple being wed. Miami banking lawyer William Jacobs, whose bride (Linda) was entering her second marriage, recalls his wedding day feelings this way: "Before our wedding, I bonded with Linda's children as much as I did with Linda. When I saw her coming up some steps from outside the church to walk down the aisle toward me, I remember feeling a little bit jittery about it all. But then I saw the heads of her children coming into view as they walked up behind her. Suddenly I knew that everything was going to be all right—we were all in this *together!*"

Rejoice! A wise person once observed, "Life isn't measured by the breath we take, but by the moments that take our breath away." Keep your sense of humor. Don't let obstacles kill your joy! The bottom line is that if you have the Lord, each other, your children, a preacher, and a marriage license, nothing else is really necessary to make your day very special. Make your remarriage a breathless moment in your life!

The honeymoon. Honeymoons are for couples who need a quiet place alone to decompress and focus on each other after a wedding. Remarriage weddings embrace children, extended families from multiple sources, friends and neighbors, and even entire communities. A public wedding confirms the sentiment of most everyone in attendance: "You're not alone. Your marriage isn't just important to you—it's important to all of us." By contrast, the honeymoon declares, "This is the time for *us.*"

Including children in the wedding is a wonderful way of beginning the family blending process. But let's be realistic—including the children in the honeymoon isn't! You and your new mate need this special time to yourselves without immediate family responsibilities. Thinking you have only a few hours alone before picking up children from a baby-sitter just doesn't meet most couples' needs. See if family or close friends can watch your children for at least several days. Sometimes, however, younger children won't understand why they're left behind, and may feel rejected. To soothe these youngsters, consider taking *two* honeymoons—one with your spouse alone, and another short separate family vacation with your kids.

As you successfully (and joyfully!) conclude your wedding and honeymoon experience, you must now face the daily realities of blended family life. Among the most important considerations (which really require decisions well before the wedding) are: "Where shall we live," "Where shall we worship," and "What about our careers?"

WHERE SHALL WE LIVE?

Agreeing on a place to live is one of the most important, and difficult, financial and emotional decisions that a couple will face together. No longer is it just a husband and wife planning for themselves; it is a major relocation involving two separate micro-family units. This decision involves moving out of one or both of the couple's separate housing environments into a new situation. It will affect church attendance, work commutes, school attendance, visitation of ex-spouses (and perhaps also custody), and interaction with extended family members—to name a few!

If both partners own their own homes, will they sell their houses and move into a new home together? Will one mate move into the other's home after the wedding? If so, will there be a "ghost" of a deceased or divorced spouse living there too in pictures, leftover clothes, or other personal items? Will the children become territorial with "strangers" moving into their home? Will they have to change schools? Will moving children farther away from a noncustodial parent make him/her bitter enough to seek a custody change? Will you furnish the new home with an eclectic collection of items from each partner's home, or new furniture? If the new family is larger than the housing space, how will children react by having to share bedrooms? So many questions arise that it's difficult to keep track of them all!

Many marriage counselors and experts recommend that couples move into a totally new home to begin family life. Some suggest this is more important to a wife and mother who may want the comfort of decorating and arranging the home as she feels best, without the trappings and preferences of prior residents. This gives the entire family a new environment in which to grow, with living arrangements beginning on an equal footing.

When we first met, Cheryl lived in Akron, while I was a lifelong Miami resident. I had an established law practice in South Florida, built up over twenty-five years. Cheryl held a new job position in Ohio, but received an opportunity to work in Florida with another company. Now she faced a dilemma. Should she marry me and move to Florida, or just skip it all and remain in Ohio? If she decided on a Florida move, would there be any conditions in doing so?

After considering all her options, Cheryl agreed to move to Florida—but *not* to the Miami area. Knowing I must work within reasonable range of my client base, she checked out many areas of South Florida. After a while, she stumbled upon Weston, a lovely new family-oriented community west of Fort Lauderdale. She loved it!

Living in Weston would mean selling my house in South Miami and relocating. It would require a long commute to my law office, then located in Coral Gables. But I viewed these changes as positive events. I would have loved it if Cheryl and Chase had chosen to move into my home in South Miami, but they really would have been moving into my life, rather than us making a new life of our own in that place. *All* of us would be moving to a totally new environment, making many of the same sacrifices in doing so. So the notion of equality (and "new wine"!) certainly applies here.

Moving may be heartbreaking for some, however. For widowed spouses, the thought of leaving one's beloved home for a new life elsewhere may seem like losing part of one's personhood. The touching way the following widower describes his home as he makes the final mortgage payment to his lender may capture the feelings of many:

Ladies and Gentlemen:

Please celebrate with me the fact that the final two mortgage payments . . . are enclosed in this envelope. It's been a long and varied 29 years since my young family moved into this house. Now the kids are raised and gone, my wife has died, and I'm left with a house full of sweet and wonderful memories.

But don't feel sad for me or my family. Instead, celebrate the fact that this house has been a significant part of the life of a family that has loved it and in return, seems to have been loved by this house. In this house, my wife and I weathered hurricanes; survived family crises of many varieties; more birthday parties than I want to count; and we have seen three lovely children reach maturity and live. This house has been a refuge and a haven for all of us to return to as we tried to meet the challenges of this crazy world in which we live. What comfort these four walls have given us, and what lovely memories we all have. And while we have never felt that this house wasn't ours, it's now very nice to know that the American Dream can be attained and the home is ours. What is sad, however, is that, in this day and age, so few families will ever again have the privilege of growing up and growing old in a house like this one.

I have no idea who, or even if, someone will read this letter. But if you do, smile for us and be glad that in doing your job, you helped make this one family happy and warm in their home.[5]

This man truly *feels* a house isn't only a financial investment—it's part of you. Each wall lavishly displays the fingerprints of your life. The floors captured every step you and your loved ones took, witnessed by chips and creaks. The tears you shed still rest on the windowsill. You can almost hear the joyous voices of family and friends still filling the air. But you also know that so many wonderful memories can almost overwhelm you as you enter certain rooms. Fancy dishes stacked high and away in the back of cabinets won't find their way onto family tables anymore. The house is just too big for one person. Also, how would your new mate feel about sharing all these wonderful memories with someone else? Sadly, many widowed persons resign themselves to beginning a new family story in another home. But for those who face this awesome life passage with those who remarry them, it's important to *feel* what they feel as they gently lay down a major part of their lives and move on with their futures.

Relocation concerns. Unlike first marriages where couples have virtually unrestricted freedom to move and live wherever they want, this definitely *isn't* the case in many blended family situations. The primary factor, of course, are the children involved. Any move away from familiar surroundings affects visitation rights of ex-spouses, school attendance, and friends, just to name a few! It's possible any child relocation may require court approval and consent of ex-spouses as well. Be wise about this vital concern, since some courts grant custody changes whenever a custodial parent relocates (see chap. 11).

WHERE SHALL WE WORSHIP?

Presumably, finding a mutually acceptable church when Christians remarry shouldn't be a problem. Not so! Conflict is inevitable if spouses are older and intimately involved in different church fellowships, have denominational bias, or cherish serious doctrinal viewpoints. Asking a mate to leave any religious heritages behind often brings an innate feeling of betrayal of God and fellow Christians that may run too *deep* for that person to bear!

Many couples entering remarriage believe they can "split the difference" by finding a new church fellowship offering a compromise between the groups individual spouses enjoyed previously. But a Creighton University study reveals that marrying someone from a different denomination makes it *more* likely that an individual will drift away from the church, and that the remarriage will end in divorce. Those marrying within the same denomination have a divorce rate of 14 percent, compared to 20 percent for interdenominational couples. But here's a surprising twist—if the bride and groom come from different denominations and later on join the same church, their divorce rate is only 6 percent![6]

Must there be a separation of church and mate? For those comfortable with it, the growing spirit of ecumenicalism and tolerance among different religious groups helps members adjust and work together in an increasingly diverse society. However, most couples want church options stressing biblical worship and practices that *both* partners can share in good conscience without compromise.

Cheryl pleasantly surprised me at our wedding when she committed to attend my church. But things did change for us. I had been with the same conservative church fellowship in Miami for more than twenty years, so making a long commute from our home wasn't a problem for me. But Cheryl felt differently. She deeply needed a church fellowship closer to our home, where Chase could be more involved with kids his age.

Cheryl and I agreed that she would find a Christ-centered church near our home that would be spiritually nourishing for her and Chase. Since this meant our family would be worshiping in different places, we worked out an accommodation to meet that need. We agreed that I would join Cheryl and Chase in worshiping at the Broward County church on every other Sunday, while I would worship with my Miami church family on the other weekends. For midweek services, our schedules were such that I could attend church in Miami after taking care of my appointments in the area during the afternoon. (Cheryl and Chase would attend the midweek services in Broward County.) This plan works for us although, admittedly, our preference would be to attend the same church all the time. Perhaps we shall in the future.

Couples, mature enough to have their spiritual needs met as believers, really would do well to focus on their children's spiritual welfare. What are their needs? Where will the kids grow best spiritually? Are there a lot of extra activities for children throughout the week? Obviously, continuity in one church fellowship is a concern, although it may not be determinative. Shifting from church fellowships can create anxiety in children and hinder development of important spiritual relationships. But making children's needs a priority may help the parents' decision.

How can a Christian couple resolve conflicts like these in a faithful, peaceful, and loving manner? Experts offer the following suggestions:[7]

Count the cost. Go into any remarriage with eyes open, being aware of "red flags" that faith differences will be a potential source of conflict. Are you and your beloved ready to work through your differences and collaborate on suitable accommodations and solutions? Realize you'll sacrifice some freedom—such as sharing spiritual intimacy in the same church fellowship with your spouse. In times of crisis, such as the death of a loved one or surviving a hurricane, how you react and adjust to these surprises from a spiritual viewpoint may be different from your mate. This often leads to a lot of discomfort and additional marital conflict.

Take your time. When you see that faith differences will be an issue in your remarriage, don't rush the relationship! Interdenominational remarriages require careful thought, fervent prayer, and wise premarital counseling. Many couples benefit from mentoring by other couples who successfully navigated this potential minefield, folks who can help focus the issues and provide spiritual guidance about possible conflicts ahead. Another excellent way to bridge the gap is by attending weekend encounter groups and classes providing greater insight and education into each spouse's church fellowship. Then you can make informed decisions.

Don't convert. Each person needs to "own" his/her own faith. If you agree to change denominations due to family pressures or a need to be a martyr and make the "big sacrifice," you'll probably end up hating yourself for doing it! Hold true to your spiritual convictions. If they're well-grounded in God's Word, don't ditch them!

Mutually decide the religion question for your children. Trying to split time between two church fellowships is simply too difficult for most children to handle. But don't ask them to rate each church and choose what they prefer. Author Joshua Peck notes, "You wouldn't say, 'Let the kids look at honesty and dishonesty and see which lifestyle they prefer when they grow up.'" Parents should choose the church environment *they* believe best for their kids without asking the children to choose between "Mommy's church" and "Daddy's church." Getting them consistently involved in worship and other church activities can come *after* making that initial decision. Research confirms that adults who went to church regularly as children are three times as likely to be attending church in adulthood as are their peers who avoided church during child-hood.[8] For this reason, the best interests of the children may be the deciding factor for the entire family, as long as there are no serious scriptural concerns.

Cultivate a spiritual "likemindedness" wherever possible. If attending the same church fellowship isn't reasonably possible for you (as with Cheryl and me), it's critical that the family make the home a spiritual refuge of likemindedness, resisting division. The apostle Paul's appeal to the Corinthian church could easily go to blended families in our situation as well: "I appeal to you, brothers, in the name of our Lord Jesus Christ, that all of you agree with one another so that there may be no divisions among you and that you may be perfectly united in mind and thought" (1 Cor. 1:10). Does this mean we strive for unity so personal differences don't divide us? Yes. Does it mean we must share the *same* mind and opinions about a church issue? No. Christ isn't divided, so that's where we begin. Focus on our common faith in Jesus in the home. Make family devotions and prayer special times. Emphasize everything from God's Word about which there's no difference of opinion. Be as flexible as possible without compromising biblical principles.

Interdenominational couples won't walk an easy road together in remarriage. They'll face struggles other remarried couples won't face, which (unfortunately) increases the risk of failure. But nothing's impossible with God working through a humble and yielded couple committing themselves to *listen* carefully and *respect* each other's opinions and beliefs.

WHAT ABOUT OUR CAREERS?

In most cases, single parents considering remarriage will be actively employed in order to survive financially. Relocating after the wedding could put jobs in serious jeopardy. How will this affect the blended family?

Should one spouse quit work to devote more time to the family? Can the family afford this income loss? Should a spouse change jobs? What about possible loss of seniority, penalties on pension and retirement benefits, or jeopardy of favorable health insurance benefits tied with the former job? If the family relocates while either or both spouses keep existing jobs, how will commutes affect family time? We can't ignore these issues if we're to remain good stewards of what God entrusts us with.

For a widowed or divorced single mother to quit her job upon remarriage may prove difficult. Giving it up could be an enormous sacrifice, possibly affecting her identity and self-esteem. But two-career families require numerous compromises, rearranged priorities, and major attitude adjustments. What if the wife keeps working after remarriage but receives a job promotion requiring relocation to another city or state? Who will wait at home for repairmen? Who responds to family emergencies? Whose career goals receive priority if there's a conflict? All these questions affect a remarried couple's family and job decisions.

We'll discuss some financial aspects of these issues in chapter 10, but here are a few suggestions to help you arrive at a mutually acceptable working arrangement:

Pray! Since God is the one who provides us with work and the ability to create wealth (Deut. 8:18), cast your indecision and anxieties upon him, knowing he cares for you and your family (1 Pet. 5:7). Ask, seek, and knock, waiting for him to open some doors for you (Matt. 7:7–11).

Agree on career goals. Evaluate the advantages and disadvantages of each spouse's job and the impact it has on the family as to income, time for commuting and work, flexibility to respond to children's needs and emergencies, personal job satisfaction, and insurance and retirement benefits. Review these matters in short-run and long-term contexts. What situation would be spiritually and economically best for the couple and blended family in general?

Make children a priority. The key word here is "sacrifice." You and your spouse may have to sacrifice to put your children's needs first. You may have to delay career goals or let them go. Material possessions may have to take a hit. Sacrifice isn't convenient, and may even be costly as one parent pulls out of a rewarding situation. But the ultimate question for the parents in a blended family before the Lord is, "What's best for my children and their future?" One possible compromise would be to have the stay-at-home spouse work part-time during the hours children are in school. (Fortunately, Cheryl continued her career by working part-time in our home office—an ideal solution for us.) Just make sure you meet your children's needs with the Lord's help.

Prepare a family work plan. If both spouses must work, determine your current blended family goals and needs, and how each spouse's job helps meet those goals and needs. A family work plan should include a list of priorities accounting for how to balance family, church, and work responsibilities. Give careful thought to addressing unexpected changes. This plan should have specific procedures for handling family emergencies and designating the person(s) responsible for responding. The plan also should delegate family responsibilities fairly among family members so they overburden no one. Who will take on family chores such as grocery shopping, meal planning and preparation, setting the table, washing dishes, and laundry? Who will take care of the yard and maintain the family vehicles?

In making a family work plan, keep four important points in mind: (1) allocate family chores so *all* family members get involved, (2) help all members learn to multitask by doing several chores or errands at once (such as doing laundry while also washing the dishes, or stopping by the grocery store on the way home from work), (3) spread household work out over a reasonable timeframe—especially weekends, and (4) don't feel guilty about hiring professional services if you can afford them.

Housing, family worship, and work responsibilities—three *major* areas for blended family planning. Put the skills discussed in chapter 6 into action as you work together toward mutually acceptable solutions best suited for your family.

"As the Twig Is Bent, So Grows the Tree"

That old adage is so true! The issues reviewed in this chapter follow a continuing theme in this book—prepare, prepare, prepare! The better you anticipate challenges and problems common to all remarriages and blended families and prepare for them, the more you increase your chances of success. How you handle family challenges early in your blended family life will set the tone for family unity. How will your family grow and change as everyone gradually and lovingly lays aside all the microfamily ties with the goal of truly being *unified*?

In the next chapter we'll review some specific ways to help your family run more smoothly in the blending process while growing in wisdom and loving more deeply!

A Message from Cheryl

There are so very many changes in a blended family . . . incalculable! Though adults have the venue to express and assert our needs and preferences, our children often take a backseat role in these decisions. Yet their stress and real (or perceived) fear of change is the greatest. Children thrive on constancy—a familiar meal, the same bedtime, consistent roles, friends, and yes, their own room. But now everything in their lives is open to change due to decisions *they* did not make. And this often comes after major turmoil from the death or divorce of a parent a few years earlier.

This is why I think the needs of children are perhaps the most critical in planning these changes. How can I keep a common name with my children? Can we avoid a change of schools? Can we keep the family pet? Can they have *some* family honeymoon time? Do they love their church? They need to see they still have the same importance in our lives after remarriage.

When Chase and I first moved to Florida in preparation for marriage, we invited Carole, my ex-mother-in-law, to live with us for a few months. Call me crazy, but we *love* Carole. She was a stabilizing influence for Chase in a sea of change! Carole also attended our wedding (but not her son) and took Chase on a "honeymoon" to visit family in Chicago to give us some time alone. She was the most important help to Chase at his time of change, and she remains a blessing to us still.

Our wedding was so simple and lovely. When you've previously been married for a decade (as I was), you realize how unimportant the trappings are. All I cared about was a spiritual environment to express our vows before those we truly loved. It was no big production, but it was meaningful and significant to each of the very few who shared it with us.

But I keep coming back to the children. When your children need your time and attention, don't lose them because you must address 150 wedding invitations to people you haven't seen in ten years. Your children are your most valued guests, and the only ones who will live with you and your spouse each day. Focus your wedding with that goal in mind.

Questions for Personal Reflection

1. Am I truly *unified* with my partner in planning for our remarriage and preparing for blended family life? In what specific areas could we experience more unity?

2. How will my remarriage affect my mate, my children, my ex-spouse, former in-laws, and me? Are there any special needs or concerns? What preparations have I made with my partner for the first two years of blended family life?

3. What goals for our life together do I need to discuss with my mate and family members? Are my goals realistic? Am I willing to be flexible and open-hearted about changing my goals as time and family needs warrant it?

4. Have I spent enough time with my mate and the children discussing family relationships, traditions, daily living arrangements, and family worship time so everyone knows what to expect? Are there any conflicts in these areas needing further discussion and compromise?

5. Are *all* of the children's needs really a priority for me and my mate? How can we make sure we aren't overlooking anyone or anything?

Chapter 8

BLENDED FAMILY LIFE AND THE BLENDED FAMILY <u>COVENANT</u>
Setting Up Your Household with Wisdom and Grace

What can you expect to happen after you remarry and begin blended family life? How can you and your mate rely upon the Lord and each other in maintaining balance, intimacy, and romance with so many matters in motion at once?

In sailing there is a term called "lift" which is both technical and poetic at once. It describes the moment of acceleration in a sailboat— the moment when the sails harden against the wind forcing the keel sideways against the water, and the boat begins to slide forward, faster and faster, until you suddenly feel . . . airborne. How something moving so slowly—about the pace of a moderate jog—can impart such exhilaration in this moment is probably unanswerable.[1]

While sailing is the topic of this warm passage, it struck me how much this description applies to successful remarriage and blended family life as well. Everyone piles into the blended family sailboat with all their gear. You feel the vessel creak a little bit and maybe wobble from side to side slightly as it settles a little bit lower in the water under all the weight.

Once everyone is aboard for the maiden cruise, they exchange "bon voyage" greetings with loved ones on the dock. Then they toss off the lines, and the boat slowly lumbers out of the harbor under the power of a small outboard motor. It takes a long time to clear the harbor, causing some impatience for the passengers who have hopeful expectations of the imminent voyage.

Once the boat hits open water, the family sets about the task of "turning to"— unfurling and raising the sails. There's a lot of pulling and grunting as each person yanks cables and lines and cleats them, but finally each sail is in place.

At first the flagging sails flap a little in the breeze. While the sheets are trimmed, the boat pauses somewhat, but then *Whap!* A big gust of wind fills the white fabric and stretches it to the limit. As the wind hits the taut sails, it *shoves* the boat into a forward glide. How can this heavy vessel move so gracefully with hardly a whisper but the sound of rushing water and racing wind? But it *is* moving . . . and you can feel it!

Then, as Chamberlain expresses it, you experience that magic moment—*lift!* You feel the rolls of the waves as the boat seems to fly over them. The sailboat, wind, and water work together now so the boat does what it's truly designed to do—skate over the sea in blissful harmony with God's creation. Then you know the wonderful joy of sailing!

But there's more to sailing than just aimlessly gliding over the waves. After achieving lift, it's up to the captain and crew to trim and set the sails just right to keep the boat moving on course. Those in the boat determine their direction; the wind just gives them power to move according to their choices.

Remarriage and blended family life begins with the goal of getting all your family members involved in moving your family boat out to sea. You want to "catch the wind" for smooth sailing and have your family experience the exhilaration of motion . . . and especially *lift*. Will your boat make it to this point? Exactly what does it take to get there? The power to move your boat is always available, but how can you catch the wind in your family's sails? It all depends upon getting your boat out of the harbor after the wedding and putting those sails up in the open sea of life. To do this, follow the proper procedures and rely upon God for the rest.

Your success in a blended family doesn't depend so much on whether you have an easier or more difficult time than others of us who have remarried. The Lord has given you the power and the experience to make your relationships work. What will you and your partner do with these resources? Will you commit the rest of your lives to doing whatever it takes to rely upon God? Will you chart your course toward Jesus, the bright Morning Star, through calm or stormy waters? Have you learned from the mistakes of past relationships? Do you have a better idea now of what God desires in your marriage? As poet Publilius Syrus once observed, "He is foolish to blame the sea who is shipwrecked twice." And so it all comes down to the decisions you and your family make—now and for the future.

To help you chart your course, let's take a look ahead and see what to expect as you sail into blended family life. Godspeed and bon voyage!

THE VOYAGE: THE STAGES OF BLENDED FAMILY LIFE

After decades of experience with family therapists and researchers, the Stepfamily Association of America (SAA) discovered that many blended families go through different phases as part of the blending process, which they call the "Stepfamily Life Cycle."[2] (The goal, of course, is to integrate microfamilies of each spouse into a blended family unified by a strong cooperative couple.) This life cycle has seven general phases spread over three different stages of development in a healthy blended family as follows:

Early Stage—Getting Started. This is the "getting to know you" stage of blended family existence, beginning right after the wedding/honeymoon.

• *The Idealistic Fantasy Phase.* For many remarried couples, a postwedding "honeymoon high" reigns. They begin their relationship with high expectations of healing each other's wounds from prior relationships and replacing what children lost from missing parents. "I will be the father her children never knew." "I love my husband, so of course I'll love his children just as much." "My kids will be thrilled to have new brothers and sisters their same age." Really? Many of these hopes and expectations are simply unrealistic. Children may want their real parents back and still hold on to that fantasy during this first phase.

• *The Emerging Reality Phase.* Fantasies begin to rub up against reality. Family members who always neatly hang up their outfits at the end of each day now find themselves living with those who drape every available chair and sofa with clothing of all kinds. Those who like leisurely dinners find themselves at kitchen tables with empty places as children (and perhaps a parent) are on the go to stores, at sports events, or working late at the office. Intimate times between husband and wife get interrupted more and more often. Family plans get sabotaged when an ex-spouse suddenly changes the visitation schedule. It seems like life's unraveling.

When children see changes and inconsistencies as part of these emerging realities, they may retreat into their comfortable microfamily relationship with a biological parent that was in place prior to the wedding. This may make a stepparent jealous or feel rejected, possibly leading to some withdrawal and distancing. Friction, confusion, and anxiety may increase between stepparent and stepchildren. Blended family members begin thinking, "Something's not right here, but I can't seem to put my finger on exactly what it is." Some think, "Maybe I'm the problem," while others begin mildly blaming fellow family members. To put it bluntly, the higher you climb in your idealism in the fantasy phase, the harder you may fall in this emerging realities phase. But this is normal for most blended families.

• *The Discovery/Disillusionment Phase.* Over the first few months together, blended families begin noting patterns and preferences of other family members. A formerly fuzzy picture gradually starts coming into focus as family members realize some fantasies are never going to be fulfilled. Now family members say to themselves, "Before, I didn't know what was going on, but I felt something wasn't right. Now I know what the problem is, and I don't like it!" A natural contradiction arises: the urge of biological parents to insulate their children from too much change and disruption while also yearning for deeper intimacy with a new partner, which requires new family rules and temporarily excluding children from "couple time." This is no easy balancing act!

During this challenging phase, many couples fret and worry that their remarriage may be shipwrecked. Either or both spouses reach out to others outside the family, sharing their discouragement and frustration. They ask, "Is my marriage and family situation normal? Should we worry about how things are right now? Do other blended families have these types of problems?" They want and need comfort and reassurance during this critical but very uncertain and unsettling phase. Christians especially pray more anguished prayers during this phase: "Help us, Lord. This is too much for us to handle!" Feeling the urge to pray and seek the Lord's help is a *good* result of this phase—we are facing the pain and learning to reach out for God in our distress.[3]

Middle Stage—Reorganizing the Family. At the beginning of this middle stage, blended family members (and particularly stepparents) are much more aware of their roles and responsibilities, as well as what they like (and don't like) about how the new family operates. Now disappointments and discouragement inspire family members to work more diligently in adjusting and blending. This middle stage is the time for more open family discussion of differences and mutual problem solving.

• *The Family Planning Phase.* Family members see things that need to change in order to restore peace and efficiency to the family. Family "change agents" emerge with pleas for "everyone to work together" in making some positive adjustments. This relieves some family members; problems come to the surface and get addressed. The family recognizes that roles and responsibilities may have to shift and adjust as part of workable solutions. Conflict resolution skills (chap. 6) come to the forefront as each family member seeks peace and reconciliation with others.[4]

• *The Family Reorganization Phase.* After thinking, praying, and planning together, the blended family experiments with different solutions. Instead of family members fighting each other, they now work together more often to fix what is lacking or weak. They're on the same side, figuring out ways to balance complex needs and interests of each family member. Sometimes a solution will require inventing or doing something entirely new, or "pulling together"—like a well-seasoned crew on a racing yacht! During this phase, a couple usually experiences greater unity of mind and purpose. Their relationship strengthens as they become more aware of personal sensitivities. Common ground is growing here!

In this phase also, biological parents begin releasing control over their children and slowly back away enough for stepparents and stepchildren to play more games together or work through problems by themselves. There's less need for biological parents to "run interference" for their children. (This even happens with teenage or adult children struggling with problems—even if the children no longer live at home.) The stepparent begins assuming more responsibility for correction and discipline of all the children.

Later Stage—Solidifying the Family. SAA describes the family at the end of the middle stage as having new, mature relational boundaries. This transforms the group into a combined blended family run by the couple working together as a *team*. This is the stage where, at long last, the blended family members begin to experience the early moments of that joyous experience of "lift" mentioned earlier in this chapter.

• *The Deepening Family Intimacy Phase.* Parents and children, regardless of what microfamily they were in before remarriage, are really getting to know and appreciate each other in new ways. They feel comfortable having heart-to-heart talks with each other. Conflicts that defied resolution in the past now get resolved in mutually satisfactory ways. Family members truly begin to understand and respect each other's differences with more of a team focus rather than everyone protecting their own interests. The family begins to rely on each individual's strengths to move the family forward.

• *The Family Unity Phase.* Husband and wife now feel joined in a bond of oneness that no one else quite understands, but all can sense when they're with the couple. They move closer to the Christian ideal of "likemindedness," experiencing the one-heart-one-mind life Paul describes in 1 Corinthians 1:10. They experience mutual respect, mutual love, and mutual acceptance. Remaining differences only highlight each spouse's uniqueness and captivating qualities that cause the couple to rejoice. They're truly partners in every sense of the word. The home environment's more familiar—less like a hidden minefield and more like a garden with familiar pathways running among beautiful flowers lovingly watered and groomed each day. The family has developed workable rules and guidelines, and enjoys refreshing new traditions. Family members trust each other more. They now know what to expect from one another. In every way, SAA describes this mature blended family as one having built "bonds without blood." I like that!

Isn't this what a "Christian blended family" is too? Lynne, a remarried military wife and stepmother of several children, said it well: "We've found that being far from 'blood family' as we learned to live together and moved with the military, our family pulled together even better as we mixed with our larger 'blended family' of singles, widows, and kids at church. This helped us realize how much unity in our Christian beliefs is even more important than blood bonds. Family by *choice*—not by chance— have even greater possibilities for better unity!"

How do these blended family stages and phases work? SAA has found that "fast" families can make it through all stages and phases in about four years from the wedding. "Average" families take about seven years to complete everything. The key difference is whether a family gets "stuck" in the particularly difficult and challenging early stage—a common occurrence in many blended families. Fast families take about a year in this early stage, while average families take three to four years. SAA has discovered that "stuck" families, who remain in the early stage for more than five years, often face disintegration and, in worst cases, divorce. Once a family moves on from the early stage, however, a majority of blended families take two to three years to move through the middle stage, with another year to complete the later stage.[5]

Processes like this, just like the grieving process, are normal aspects of blended family life and learning to adjust and live with others. Any change brings the *end* of one life phase and the *beginning* of another. The old passes away and the new comes. It's not something you ever fully prepare for, since there'll be some surprises and unexpected twists and turns along the way. The most important preparation you can make, as we emphasize throughout this book, is your mutual commitment to the Lord, to each other, and to your children. More than anything else, this commitment will help you sail on through some occasional dark waters into brighter days and calmer seas.

ROUGH WATERS: SIX WARNING SIGNS THAT YOUR BLENDED FAMILY NEEDS HELP

In chapter 4 we discussed "stop signs" in finding a suitable remarriage partner. Here are a few warning signs that may indicate that your blended family could be "stuck" in a particular stage or phase of development. These "red flags" signal that you and your spouse need counseling and professional help as soon as possible:

• *Spiritual apathy and neglect.* Are your family worship times becoming dull or nonexistent? Are your children, who embraced the Lord gladly before remarriage, now bored with spiritual matters while diving deeper into questionable worldly pursuits? Does God seem distant from your life? Growing spiritual apathy and neglect like this is slowly but surely pushing you and your family away from the Lord.

• *Poor communication.* Do you and your mate frequently avoid talking about controversial matters to spare arguments? Does your mind wander when your mate discusses important personal issues? Are you and your mate pursuing different activities at all hours of the day, day after day (such as one spending huge blocks of time on the computer while the other talks away for hours on the telephone)? Are you stuck in conversation ruts? Do you talk about family problems more with extended family members and friends than with your spouse? If you find yourself answering yes to such questions, there's a severe communication breakdown in your family.

• *Growing incompatibility.* Do you find yourselves spending less time together as your marriage continues? When you're together, are the periods of silence getting longer because you have less and less to say to each other? Are you nitpicking and nagging each other more? Are your sexual relations always the last thing on your "to do" list, while becoming less frequent and enjoyable as time goes on? If you experienced divorce in your former marriage, you may have a sinking feeling of "Here I go again!"

• *Excessive investment of your life in your children.* Do you or your mate regularly align yourselves with your biological children (premarriage microfamilies) and against each other? Do you and your mate strongly disagree about discipline of your children? Do either of you ignore each other's needs while devoting yourselves almost exclusively to your children's needs? Would you say that your children are the major, and perhaps only, factor holding your marriage together right now? If so, then you may be overinvesting your life in your children at the expense of your marriage.

• *Money conflicts.* Do you and your mate frequently argue over money matters? Do either of you secretly tuck away money to feel secure? Do you regularly argue over how to spend money? Do you find material things becoming more important than family members, church obligations, extended family relationships, and friends? Do you hide bills from each other? Do you regularly use money and gifts to appease and placate each other for inappropriate or offensive behavior? If you find yourself agreeing with these questions, *beware!* First marriages usually get underway with lots of love and little money. Too many remarriages reverse these resources—there may be more money than love.

• *Extended family boundary encroachments.* Do you or your mate get jealous or angry when the other must spend a reasonable amount of time working out scheduling and other coparenting matters with an ex-spouse? Does one partner try to limit or restrict the other's contact with his/her family? Do you invite extended family members into your home for excessively long visits or at inappropriate times? Do you or your mate regularly align with your extended family members or ex-spouses and against each other? Of course, many remarried couples have the usual boundary encroachment issues arising as children move between households. But loosely defined (or overly restrictive) boundaries involving former spouses, in-laws, and other extended family members can create major problems. Perhaps your partner is hanging onto feelings for a former mate. Maybe he/she needs affirmation that an earlier divorce wasn't a mistake. Perhaps you're not being as firm as you should about your ex-spouse telephoning or visiting at unexpected times. Boundaries become comfortable only after they're enforced consistently. Enforcement confirms there's a true emotional separation of adults with past marriage ties. Without this enforcement, excessive encroachments into your family's life are a warning sign! Your remarriage could be in jeopardy.

So what can you do? If you find yourself in troubled waters facing any of these warning signs, the Lord calls you to win your mate and family back, perhaps in the same way you and your mate nurtured each other while you were courting. Talk about all those wonderful qualities that led you to fall in love with each other. Think positively during troublesome times. Spend quality time together. Make your mate feel special! *Listen* attentively to your partner and your family. Reassure your family of your care and concern for each of them. Examine your own heart before God.

Recognize signs of incompatibility and begin working to reconcile your differences *early,* before the gap widens in your relationship. Let a competent Christian marriage counselor take a good look inside your family life to see how you can sail your boat in the right direction again (see chap. 4).

Think and pray about the specific needs in your family, and act promptly to meet those needs. Have a forgiving heart, and strive to be a family *peacemaker.* Carry the necessary faith in your mind and heart, to believe that things will get better. Pray diligently about your problems. Release the issues that defy resolution to the Lord for him to work out. In the meantime, be generous with praise and appreciation to your spouse and blended family—even if you receive little or nothing in return during the early years of your lives together. Keep the homefires burning by reaching out for each other daily!

Most importantly, pray for the Lord's help. Reach out for him. He is the *life* of your family, there to help guide you. Without his direction, you and your blended family may sail into dangerous shallow, rocky waters!

A FRESH START—SETTING UP THE BLENDED FAMILY HOUSEHOLD

Psalm 133:1 reminds us:"How good and pleasant it is when brothers live together in unity!" Unity definitely is the key to making blended families work. But how is this achieved? What issues and family challenges may sabotage this family unity?

Have you ever wondered how engineers build a complicated bridge across a huge gorge? Years ago they did it by flying a kite across the gap and allowing it to fall on the other side. Then they would tie a small cable to the end of the kite string and pull that across. This was followed by tying heavier and heavier cables to the ends of the other lines until gradually enough cables spanned that gorge that they were able to begin the work of building the bridge. It was a slow, careful process.

Here are some specific "gap-bridging" events in a typical blended family situation:

Reaffirm basic living rights. Each family member wants to feel loved and valued, and receive attention for personal needs, interests, and desires. One good gap-bridging measure is to acknowledge some basic rights of each family member. The goal here is to act like Jesus to one another!

• *The right to love, and be loved, unconditionally.* Does Jesus love us unconditionally? Does he ask us to love each other that same way? Yes (John 13:34)!

• *The right to be heard.* Does God hear our prayers? Yes (Prov. 15:29)! Each family member should have the freedom to make family requests by speaking openly and candidly, without fear of harassment or retaliation—unless he/she acts in an unreasonably offensive manner. (Of course, there need to be guidelines and boundaries about how to express feelings without whining, complaining, backstabbing, or tattle-tailing.)

• *The right to receive proper respect and courtesy.* Did Jesus ever act rudely, or was he unkind to anyone? No! Similarly, family members of all ages need to give each other proper recognition of their status in the family and basic human respect and courtesy. Modeling respect and civility to children is critically important between spouses. Would Jesus *say* it this way? Would Jesus act this way? Another good barometer is: Would I say these things, or act this way, if Jesus was sitting at the family dinner table?

• *The right to have some privacy.* Unless there is a good legal or parental reason to investigate, each blended family member should enjoy enough privacy to attend to basic human needs, prayer and Bible study, collecting one's thoughts, and just being alone at times. Privacy is vital to family members—especially with all the *commotion* found in most blended family situations. After all, Jesus left his disciples to be alone at times too!

• *The right to have personal beliefs.* The Lord didn't give us all the same fingerprints—or opinions! Each person is unique. Each family member deserves the right to hold personal convictions as long as he/she doesn't violate God's Word or unreasonably interfere with the daily life and growth of the family.

When family members truly honor and protect basic rights like these in the blended family home, it disarms them and eases an otherwise tense environment of personal competition and self-protection. Everyone can relax and be genuine with one another without fear of rejection, shame, or abandonment.

First-year blending. The first year in the early stage of your remarriage/blended family situation should focus on the *basics* of learning how to live with each other—nothing more. Look for ways to fulfill your commitment to each other and find alternatives to help *peace* reign in your home. Practice the basic communication and conflict-resolution skills discussed in chapter 6. Have regular family conferences (discussed in this chapter) to help communication and reduce conflict. Keep a spiritual focus in the family by regularly attending church services and having family devotionals and private worship in your home.

What can you expect during the first year of blended family life? Here are a few possibilities:

• *The shock of daily life.* When you and your mate courted, you probably had your children spend a lot of time with each other. Everyone got along well, for the most part, right? Well, expect some major differences between that premarriage togetherness and blended family life! Before the wedding, everyone had a good time together, but they all said good-bye at the end of the day and went to separate homes. It was easy to overlook minor annoyances when they were out of sight after the person went home. But now those aggravations are in the blended family home constantly. Here's where *flexibility* and *compromise* come into play, with wise oversight from you and your mate. Don't overlook any major annoyances that can be corrected. Encourage everyone to be patient, learn to change, and adapt to new circumstances. Most of the aggravations and differences do work themselves out over time if everyone's patient. You may need to have weekly, or even *daily*, family conferences for the first couple of months to sort through all the problems.

Remember that you and your spouse need quality "alone time" each day to regroup, while encouraging and refreshing each other. You also need personal time alone to fill up your soul through communion with God. You certainly cannot give to your mate and family if your internal reservoir is empty! This may require you and your partner to work hard in scheduling these times around the daily activities and bedtimes of your children. At least during the critical first year, you may need to pull back on some extracurricular activities, such as volunteer and church committee work.

• *Biological parent role adjustments.* If you are the biological parent of a child brought into the blended family home, you may experience some significant personal conflicts during the first year. You may feel pulled in too many directions. Your new spouse wants one thing. Your children want something else. Meanwhile, your ex-spouse demands more control over how you're parenting the children, while your extended family complains about not seeing you and your kids enough. Why not use family ties to your advantage? You share leadership with your mate in the new blended family. You know how to deal with your ex-spouse and extended family members. You therefore have a lot of influence in each group! Use your position to avoid being "caught in the middle" of any conflicts among these groups. After praying about your situation and seeking advice from your mate, carefully measure out how you can serve others after making your partner and children first priority. Strike a proper balance among these relationships and stick to it.

Examine your heart as your biological children warm up to your partner. How does this affect you? Do you find yourself feeling a sense of loss by watching your children bond with a stepparent? If so, you'll experience internal conflict between desiring your children to accept your partner while not feeling fully ready to entrust your sweet treasures with your mate. You may feel tempted to stand in the way of these fragile friendships at times. But don't do it! Allow your children to move toward your spouse, even actively *encouraging* them to do so. This will bring much good fruit in your family over the long term. A related problem arises if you have children living outside your blended family home who come to visit occasionally. You may want to favor them with special treatment during their brief stay. But think how this preference affects the children in your home, as well as your partner. Maintain some equilibrium in your relationships so no one feels favored or neglected.

• *Stepparent role adjustments.* To promote peace and harmony during the first year, focus on the relationships between stepparents and stepchildren. Research indicates that many blended families fail despite marital satisfaction between husbands and wives. Why? No positive stepparent/stepchild relationships developed. What keeps these relationships from growing? Conflicts over house rules, discipline, questions regarding parental authority, and family traditions. Stepparenting isn't easy! After all, biological parents have months and years to learn parenting of a newborn child. When a stepparent remarries, the "baby" he or she must coparent right away may be a fifteen-year-old teenager!

Stepparents thrust into immediate parenthood for the first time really need a "crash course" in parenting. Fortunately, resources are available. Why don't you and your new mate read some parenting books together or attend a couple of parenting seminars? Seek the advice of family counselors, church pastors, or other veteran stepparents with experience. Learn to observe your new stepchildren carefully. See what they want and need. Try to look through their eyes and feel what they feel. Sometimes the best way to know how to parent is using common sense as the children talk and act—they give lots of clues.

Bridging the gap for stepparents may mean biological parents sensitively taking the lead during the early years of remarriage. Stepparents need time to build the necessary skills, confidence, and affection to coparent their stepchildren in a godly and responsible manner. Children also need this vital time to build up the trust and respect for their stepparent! Stepparents need *lots* of empathy and compassion during the critical first few years of blended family life. Providing for your partner in this way will strengthen your remarriage and increase intimacy between you.

• *Child role adjustments.* After the wedding, boys in one microfamily may have to adjust to being around girls in another microfamily, or an only child may have new brothers and sisters to live with. "Pecking order" positions held by children in each microfamily could turn upside down as kids merge into the new family. Meanwhile, children helplessly watch the role of biological parent change as that parent comanages the blended family with the new stepparent. Kids may be jealous of their biological parents, while also fearing loss of significance among all the new blended family members.

As children struggle with their role adjustments in the new family (which is a good thing for them to do on their own as much as possible), parents should have understanding and compassion for the burdens their kids bear. Encourage them to be flexible and to welcome new change. Let them know that you may not be able to fix all the chaos and conflicts to their satisfaction, but you'll be with them every step of the way as everyone adapts and adjusts to each other. Also, be careful not to compare kids to each other. Instead, look for differences in each child to praise and appreciate. Above all, avoid gossiping about other blended family kids with your biological children. Nothing burns bridges and widens gaps between family members faster than the "us versus them" fires of disunity that gossip ignites!

• *Avoid repeating past mistakes.* One thing for everyone in the blended family to avoid—especially during the sensitive first-year adjustment period—is the mistakes of the past. Most family members will be on the lookout for old negative patterns from a prior failed marriage—the open fighting between parents, the put-downs and rejections, and the demanding lifestyles that spelled disaster. Do your best to leave the dysfunctions and difficulties of the past behind—nail them to the cross! Instead, constantly stress the unique, positive, and encouraging qualities and habits of your new blended family. If you see old patterns returning, act quickly to reverse course. Get counseling if necessary.

Remind everyone daily to be patient, flexible, and willing to change. There's really no stronger message for your blended family to hear during the early years of living together than that! Since my divorce from my first spouse, the wonderfully practical wisdom-in-a-nutshell of Reinhold Niebuhr's famous Serenity Prayer continually amazes me: "God grant me the serenity to accept the things I cannot change, courage to change the things I can, and wisdom to know the difference."

Many factors in setting up a blended family are beyond your control: new step-siblings thrust together, ex-spouses and inlaws who want time with your children, and many other complications of combining multiple microfamilies into one unified family. It truly can be overwhelming at times! So, for those things you cannot control or change, have the attitude of releasing them and letting them go. Let go and let the *Lord* take care of them (see chap. 1). Bend so you will not break on these immovable obstacles. There are many matters you *can* change: where you live, where you work, where you worship, and how you love and forgive others, to name a few!

The trickiest part, perhaps, is having the "wisdom to know the difference." This requires great maturity and experience, tempered by empathy, a godly and loving attitude, sensitive communication, and spiritual insight. Maybe you can legally keep your child away from his/her biological parent under certain circumstances. Or you may have the right and power to force a child to stay in your home, even if he/she wants to move out and live with the noncustodial parent. But, in the long run, will taking these positions help or hinder your child? Are they in your child's best interest?

In the introduction to part 2 of this book, we compared remarriage and blended family life to building your house either on the rock of Jesus Christ or on the shifting sand of worldly philosophies. These new life experiences also are like building the Golden Gate Bridge with a solid foundation, but also with a flexible cable system to keep that huge span moving with the winds and waves swirling around it over the years. These extremely important concepts merit emphasis once again here—root your family in the Lord, but be willing to be as flexible as possible so you can withstand the pushes and pulls of blended family life. If you have a rock-solid foundation in your family without the necessary flexibility, sooner or later you may find a crisis that could blow your house over. Alternatively, if you have a flimsy foundation of sand, but pride yourself on flexibility, you risk getting washed out! You must have both—flexibility *and* foundation—to survive as a blended family.

Be a wise parent to your kids. Create the best home environment for your children so your kids can make their own adjustments to the blended family as they're ready to do so. Here are a few suggestions:

• *Make the blended family home "child-friendly."* Treat children of similar age in similar ways. Avoid making special arrangements for occasions when noncustodial children visit your home. Keep life in your home as normal and regular as possible. Strive to be fair with all children living or staying in the blended family home without preferential treatment. Have the same general expectations of behavior for all children.[6]

Be sure to find space for each child in the home so no one becomes jealous. Make sure each child receives *daily* love and attention with a few minutes to talk with you privately. Think creatively about ways to help make a child's transition between homes easier by using familiar toys, fun places for transfer, and favorite events like going to a fast-food place with the family or getting an ice cream treat. In making your home "child-friendly," however, be careful not to go too far to the other extreme. Each child has the right and responsibility to develop his/her own relationships with other family members. Don't run interference for individual children, or this preferential treatment will create more conflict with the other kids. Refuse to take part in any kid competitions for your affections. Avoid forcing any children to share their activities and friends with each other if they are dead set against it. Just draw a circle around your entire blended family and let all the children know they're on the *inside* of that circle!

• *Preserve daily routines of children.* Give children living in the blended family full-time roles, responsibilities, privileges, and personal space and time. Don't change these daily routines whenever brothers, sisters, or stepsiblings visit. If you cannot avoid some changes, be sure to get input from all the children affected.

• *Help children visiting your home feel like residents.* Avoid treating visiting children like mere guests in your home. Instead, welcome them as temporary *residents* so they won't feel like outsiders. Include visiting children in household chores, all family events occurring while they're in your home, and even family conferences. But avoid pressuring these children to conform too quickly to your expectations—be patient! Most children are quite adept at catching up to the family pace when they're around long enough. Encourage them to make new friends in the neighborhood or, if it makes them feel more comfortable, even bring an existing friend along for the visit. Maintain good communication with the custodial parent during the visit.

UNPACKING BLENDED FAMILY SUITCASES

In remarriage, much more so than first marriages, each spouse probably has a lifetime collection of personal possessions, furniture, family photograph albums, and other items to bring into the blended family. Quite frequently, these items carry strong emotional ties for the owner, representing continuity in life. Memories attached to certain items make them familiar and comfortable, tangible evidence of stability through one's past. To a new mate, however, these items may pose a minor irritant or an outright threat.

When you remarry, you no doubt want to have a fresh start with your new mate. Is this a worthy goal? Yes! Will it happen? Probably not. Why? Because, try as you might, unpacking your suitcase in your new life, you'll probably find some things from your past that you don't want to leave behind, often with good reasons. But your mate and family may not understand or appreciate your reasons, which can create a gap between you and your new family.

What are we talking about here? Here are a couple of typical examples:

Gifts and treasures. Ken treasures a beautiful diamond necklace he had given his now deceased wife, Elizabeth, on their twenty-fifth wedding anniversary—just two years before she died of cancer. Since he had two grown sons, he kept the necklace in a safe deposit box. Now he's remarrying Claire, and he can think of nothing better than to have her wear this lovely jewelry on formal evenings out. He even has portraits of Elizabeth, glowing with a wonderful smile, proudly wearing this necklace too. (Ken even saved a few of Elizabeth's formal gowns that, as it happens, are just Claire's size!) Of course, the entire idea is repugnant to Claire, who's happy enough wearing the personal jewelry she fought hard to keep as part of her bitter divorce from Harry. Situations like these arise in many blended families.

Many years before I met Cheryl, a very dear friend gave me a silver cross necklace. It was quite unusual, with the inside of the cross cut out in the form of Christ. As you looked at it, the cutout portion suggested that Christ was once here, but now he is risen! I loved the cross, but the unusual nature of it meant even more to me. I've never seen anything quite like it before or since, and I enjoyed wearing it under my shirt.

So what's the problem? Well, this beautiful gift came from a former college love interest. She had a small inscription made on the back of the cross reading, "Love always, Judi." Well, about a year after I married Cheryl, I leaned over to kiss her and this cross fell out of my shirt to dangle in her face. "Oh," she said, noticing some writing on the back of the cross for the first time, "what's this?" She gently grabbed the cross and turned it sideways to get a full view. "Hmm. 'Love always . . .' And what does it say after that? '*Judi.*' Honey, I never knew this cross you've been wearing came from an old girlfriend." "But sweetheart," I quickly countered, knowing I was doomed, "Judi's a lifelong friend of mine! Besides, she's been married for years. The inscription was just her expression of the good feelings between us." "Well," Cheryl responded calmly, "I really don't think that's something you should be wearing now. I just don't feel comfortable with it—especially now that it has dangled in my face." While disappointed, I certainly could understand Cheryl's reaction. So, reluctantly, I put that cross away in a jewelry box and never wore it again.

By contrast, I let my first wife take all our china, silverware, and many other items she loved from our home. She left me some kitchen utensils (although I really never did know how to cook), including some Tupperware with her name inscribed on top in large, permanent, black ink letters. After Cheryl and I married and moved into our new home, I brought these kitchen items with me, thinking she might find them useful. As we were unpacking boxes, Cheryl spied the plastic containers and remarked, "Hmmm. Tupperware. And with your ex-wife's name on it too." I waited anxiously to see what she would do. "I think I'll keep it. Tupperware is *great!*" (File this one away in the "difference between men and women—go figure" folder!)

So what can you do about gifts and treasures from your past? First, determine whether the items are worth keeping. If you can let them go, do so quietly by privately selling the items or giving them away to family, friends, or charity. If they're just too personal to part with for the time being, bring the matter up to your mate sensitively and ask if it would be a problem keeping a few items around the house. If not, the problem's solved. If so, just tuck the items away in a box and stick them out of sight in the attic or garage until you find a better solution.[7] But learn from my mistake— definitely *don't* wear them around your neck so they bop your mate in the face!

My good friend Nancy Palmer, an outstanding Christian family lawyer and mediator who remarried into a blended family with stepchildren and adopted kids, experienced an interesting twist on this dilemma of personal treasures. She explains it in her excellent blended family book *The Family Puzzle: Putting the Pieces Together*:

> Shortly before my first husband left, he gave me a beautiful amethyst and diamond ring, and a matching amethyst bracelet. . . . Even though the amethyst is one of my favorite stones, that jewelry lacked luster to me. The timing ruined it. I rarely wore it. When Bill and I had been married a couple of years, our church was having a building drive, and I donated the ring and bracelet to the church.
>
> The following Christmas, I reached into my Christmas stocking and took out the gifts one at a time, oohing and aahing over each one. When I reached deep into the bottom of the stocking, I was absolutely shocked at what I found. It was the amethyst bracelet and ring. [My second husband] Bill had found out where they were being sold, and he had bought them back. He said, "Now you can enjoy them because they're from me."[8]

Isn't that a wonderful story of unselfishness? But it also highlights how you can turn situations around with your mate just by letting love rule! (By the way, Cheryl says, "I know what you're thinking, Warren. Forget it! If you donate your cross to a charity auction, I *won't* be buying it back for you!" Oh well . . . it was a thought.)

Family photographs and videos. Now we come to the most personal of property—pictures that capture part of our family history. Obviously, these items aren't easily left behind or tossed away. What to do?

The most obvious problem to avoid is making your new home a shrine to your former mate if you're widowed. Imagine the emotion if your mate glances over to your nightstand, only to see your dearly departed mate's photo looking wistfully over at the two of you during a romantic moment! The large portrait that used to hang over the fireplace in the old home won't work much better in the new living room either.[9]

Photographs and videos are important pieces of our past. They chronicle our lives. But they shouldn't create a stumbling block for the new blended family. Keep the personal photos and videos in your own space in the home—out of sight from others, preferably. If no one in the family objects, you might have a place in the home to keep a picture or two without too much trouble.

Plan ahead for incidents like these as you unpack your life in your new family. It is much better to lay aside all items from a prior marriage, since any attempt to recreate the past is loaded with risk of many problems in your new marriage. It's painful to admit, but they're old wineskins. At first, it may be practical and convenient for you and your mate to be patient with each other as blended family life begins. But if either of you is uncomfortable with relics from the past, the time must come to store away the controversial items, if not selling or giving them to others. Part of tasting the new wine of remarriage may mean purchasing new items of special significance to you and your mate alone.

MAKE TIME TO BLEND

If you're a Baby Boomer, you may remember the old Ed Sullivan television variety show. One frequent guest was a famous juggler/plate spinner, who balanced ten spinning plates at the same time on top of flexible cuestick poles. He constantly rushed back and forth, spinning new plates, while also frantically racing around to keep all of the existing plates rotating before they wobbled and fell off the various poles. It was quite a feat!

Launching a remarriage and blended family is plate spinning in real time. A woman who used to be a housewife in her first marriage may now have to juggle managing a new family, taking care of household chores, and working outside the home to make ends meet. A childless husband, used to coming home to a quiet and restful home each evening, now must cope with a wife and kids who each need special attention. Inevitably, spouses have a common complaint: "There's just not enough time in the day to do everything!"

Blended family life's a lot like living in Grand Central Station. Like most families, we get up and plan exactly what we'll do that day. But by the end of that same day, what we did may not look like anything we planned! Blended family life isn't made up of plans, but of unending interruptions! Many remarried couples feel Jesus was addressing them personally when he said, "Therefore do not worry about tomorrow, for tomorrow will worry about itself. Each day has enough trouble of its own" (Matt. 6:34). How true!

Having an overall game plan is essential for sailing your blended family through life, but not without building in significant flexibility for the day-to-day flow. Sure, use time-management techniques to organize your schedules, but be ready to scrap it all in an instant if your mate or another family member needs you. This communicates "nothing in my life is more important than you" and goes a long way toward building vital family trust and unity.

Here are a couple of suggestions to help you deal with the crunch of conflicting time demands:

Turn off the television and computer. Easy to say, but difficult to do in most households!

A few years ago, zoo officials in St. Petersburg, Russia, had a plan. They wanted to introduce their orangutans to the joys of family life by having them watch television together. The scheme backfired. The male orangutan soon became so engrossed in watching shows that his mate became very jealous and upset. Finally the exaspeated zoo director announced they were reducing the hours of television in an attempt to "salvage the relationship"![10] This is good advice for blended family couples as well!

If anything requires sacrifice, let it be the television rather than relationships in your family! This is especially true if it separates and isolates remarriage partners and other family members. If there is a special show to watch that others in the family have no interest in watching, at least tape the show and watch it during some personal free time when your family is away or busy doing other things.

Another relationship buster is the computer. Surfing the Internet can become such an acute problem that one spouse ends up going to bed alone most nights. What marriage partner wouldn't tire of playing second fiddle to a nineteen-inch box?

If television or computers interfere with the growth of your blended family, give them up! These pursuits aren't even worthy of exchanging a day of your blended family life. Then use your time to bridge the gaps in your family.

Turn on family creativity. Don't have enough time? Hold a family conference and look for creative ways everyone can work together to eliminate several chores at once. Does your family want to spend time together, but that dirty garage won't wait another week before boxes fall on the family car? Set aside Saturday morning for a special family breakfast, then have the entire family fix the problem! Are kids going to different evening sports events with no time for a family dinner? Take everyone out to eat and give the cook a night off! Everyone needs clothes and supplies for work or school? Load up the family and spend an evening shopping in a discount warehouse for everyone's needs. Pool your family talents and look for ways to save time. You'll be amazed at how many good suggestions your crew can generate!

Don't Rock the Boat: Keeping the Family Peace

"So It's Not Home Sweet Home—*adjust!*" So says the sign hanging in the kitchen of one remarried couple's home. Conflicts arise more often when family members are rigid and uncooperative with each other. The best way to avoid conflict? Adjust. In fact, the *more quickly* conflict arises in your family, the *sooner* you'll adjust to each other.

If you have a challenging blended family with lots of relationship fires to put out, you and your mate must resolve your own conflicts quickly and lovingly so you can devote your time helping your children adjust to new roles and responsibilities. (Unfortunately, some couples have so many personal issues, this isn't easy to do!) Children find ingenious ways to put each other down or create "accidents" to keep their siblings on edge. They'll fight over what television show to watch, whose turn it is to clean out the guinea pig's cage, who left the mess on the kitchen table, and who gets the last fudge bar in the refrigerator. In short, children need parental discipleship in conflict resolution (see chap. 6).

The best vehicle by far for promoting biblical conflict resolution in the blended family home is having a regular family conference, which we'll discuss in this chapter. Established procedures for working out family problems outweighs trying to resolve conflicts haphazardly on the fly. Take the initiative! Give the family conference your family's full effort for at least the first year of your life together. See if it doesn't significantly reduce your conflicts.

Develop family tact, timing, and sensitivity. Baseball veteran Cleon Jones, formerly of the New York Mets, once asked an umpire if he could get thrown out of a game for thinking. When the ump replied, "No," Jones said, "Well, then, I think you're doing a lousy job!"[11] Sounds like an exchange many blended family siblings might have in the home, doesn't it? Some define tact as the art of speaking your mind in such a way that you're long gone by the time they figure out what you meant. Training the family in tact, timing, and sensitivity includes everyone—even the youngest ones in the home. As politician Adlai Stevenson once noted: "No matter how limited your vocabulary, it's big enough to let you say something you'll later regret."

So how do you encourage family members to use tact and sensitivity? A major first step toward encouraging positive and uplifting communication in your home is helping everyone in your family feel secure and loved. Insecurity absolutely destroys good feelings and unity. During the short tenure of their remarriage, actress Pamela Anderson Lee reportedly kept a copy of her divorce petition taped on the refrigerator door to keep husband, rocker Tommy Lee, in line.[12] This not-so-subtle message didn't work. They later divorced. Surprised?

Family conferences help everyone understand issues and problems from different viewpoints. Empathy and understanding provide a solid foundation for sensitive and loving communication. Without these prerequisites in place, it's extremely difficult to avoid being offensive and inconsiderate of each other.

Insensitivity, tactlessness, and bad timing frequently reveal selfishness. You need to discover everyone's "hot buttons" and know that the *way* something is said can be just as controversial as *what* is said. Know to avoid certain unnecessarily inflammatory topics or discussions at certain times—such as when a spouse is paying the bills and not in the best of moods! There are some obvious "don't bother me now" signs family members shouldn't ignore.

Sure, everyone will make mistakes and be inconsiderate from time to time. Among the many "dumb questions I have asked Cheryl" are these: "Will you promise not to get mad if I ask you something?" "Uh, could you repeat that, sweetheart?" (which is a dead giveaway that I wasn't listening and didn't have a clue what she was talking about!), and my personal all-time favorite, "Are you asleep, honey?" But I *am* growing wiser by learning how *not* to say the same stupidly insensitive things over the years!

And of course the best blended family "heart tenderizer" is for each member to encourage and nourish each other in growing fruit of the Holy Spirit: "But the fruit of the Spirit is love, joy, peace, patience, kindness, goodness, faithfulness, gentleness and self-control" (Gal. 5:22–23a). When this is happening, tact, sensitivity, and timing are much easier to maintain!

The issues and problems you and your mate might face in your blended family could, I'm sure, fill a library of books. But hopefully you're picking up the general themes and principles that will serve you well over the years.

Now I'd like to offer another tool to help you and your family trim your sails with some stability and organization so you'll still enjoy smooth sailing when inevitable misunderstandings and uncertainties bring rough waters your way.

THE BLENDED FAMILY COVENANT—A BLUEPRINT FOR MANAGING BLENDED FAMILIES

The following is a brief summary of the *sample* "Blended Family Covenant" appearing in appendix B. You may want to refer to it as you read this section.

Concept of the Blended Family Covenant. Entering into remarriage without initial guidelines and goals is like trying to build a house without blueprints and a building code. It can be a futile and potentially fatal process! However, there are so many challenges and circumstances to face in a blended family that it's futile trying to anticipate and address all the specific issues in advance. To help bridge the gap in organizing your family, I would like to offer a general plan I call the "Blended Family Covenant." If your family will discuss and use these general, biblically based principles, you'll find yourselves well equipped to overcome almost any obstacle(s) in your way!

The primary purpose of the Blended Family Covenant is to remind everyone *in writing* of some self-evident truths and to encourage consistent living so as to reduce misunderstandings, unrealistic expectations, and conflict. By writing down some general ground rules and basic principles for blended family living, you and your family will find useful avenues for promoting unity, harmony, and peace in your home. If this idea enslaves you or your family, try something else. But this tool should provide a good benchmark by which you can measure your family's success.

Having a written agreement of this sort isn't intended to be legalistic. It merely reminds all family members to be consistently loving and encouraging to each other, while reducing confusion and distress. After all, *inconsistencies* in blended family living create the most conflict. The covenant provides a framework for family communication and a mutual agreement to work through inevitable conflict in a positive and conciliatory manner. In many ways, this covenant is similar to what the Israelites did before the Lord in Nehemiah's day (Neh. 9:38). Not intended to be engraved on stone tablets for your family, it should be a *dynamic* guide, subject to revision as necessary, growing and changing as your family adjusts and grows.

The covenant incorporates many of the familiar virtues and principles already discussed: (1) God loves each family member. (2) Each member has unique significance and is worthy of respect. (3) God calls each member to love everyone else in the family as he loves us. (4) Each person has God-given freedom and basic rights, which the family will honor and protect. (5) Each child is entitled to receive responsible and positive Christian parenting. (6) Each person has a right to be heard in family communication and conflict resolution procedures. (7) Each person has a right to know what's expected of him or her through house rules, respecting healthy family boundaries, and consequences of irresponsible conduct.

Let's review several of the most general provisions of a typical Blended Family Covenant:

Description of family roles. Use the Blended Family Covenant to highlight each family member's biblical role. This is a good opportunity also to address the authority of stepparents with stepchildren as a preemptive measure against the "you're not my mommy, so I don't have to listen to you" issues that will come up eventually.

House rules. Include some of the more permanent rules of conduct for your family—sharing rooms and toys in the home, fighting with siblings, unreasonable or excessive interference with other family members—in your covenant so everyone knows what to expect of everyone else. Of course, you can establish and revise short-term rules—bedtimes, curfews, use of the family car—from time to time as the need arises. Use a family conference to agree upon how to implement these short-term rules. House rules also might include allocation of chores to each family member, with a clear expectation of what needs to be done and when.

Family conferences. Good communication among all family members is crucial to success, making regular family meetings, or "family conferences," important.

• *What are family conferences?* They are special times (at least once a week for the first few months of blended family life, and once a month thereafter) when all family members gather without distraction to talk to each other, resolve conflicts, brainstorm about options and alternatives to make the family run more smoothly, and plan for the future. Any family member can request a special family conference at any reasonable time, but each month there is at least one regularly scheduled meeting.

• *What purposes do family conferences serve?* Family conferences encourage *teamwork*, promote communication among all family members, and reduce conflict. This is especially true during the first-year "getting to know you" early stage of blended family life. Creating opportunities for family members to see, communicate, and interact with each other really helps promote bonding and family unity. Individual participation like this significantly reduces misunderstandings and unwarranted assumptions. Family conferences also serve as a teaching tool, helping family members better define their roles and responsibilities. They also reinforce order and discipline in the home as God intends. Family conferences are an excellent time to learn about grievances, reconcile relationships, and coordinate expectations of family members.

• *How are family conferences run?* Ideally, all family members participate in a meeting for no more than an hour. Conferences occur on neutral ground in the home, such as the living room or family room. For consistency, they all begin at the same place and time. Be flexible about the agenda. To encourage participation, different family members run each meeting—but always with the oversight of parents when a mature child has a turn. Meetings should stay positive and solution-oriented, with guidelines on handling and deciding items on the meeting agenda. If a family member is unable to attend, those present may want to limit the scope of that particular family conference in deference to the absentee. However, exercise caution if one side of the blended family wants to participate in a conference while other family members do not. Proceeding alone risks dividing the family. Family conferences shouldn't serve as a stage for parental lectures, since the goal is for all family members to speak and listen to one another. At the end of each family conference, each family member should have a sense of ownership in the decisions that were made during the meeting.

Family conflict resolution and discipline. When it becomes necessary to resolve family conflicts and exercise discipline, it's important each family member is aware of how, when, where, and why these disciplinary procedures will occur and the person responsible for making things happen. As part of this family commitment to corrective discipline, you might agree on some general standards, such as the following:

• Discipline will be corrective measures applied with love and godly principles.
• Discipline will be uniformly applied to all children in the home (and visiting children).
• Discipline will respect age-appropriate boundaries of all children in the home (and visiting children).
• Discipline will balance encouragement, love, rewards, and correction.

Family time. Your Family Covenant may include a commitment to spend time together on a regular weekly basis, including vacation(s) for parents only, and other trips for the entire family. This written commitment allows everyone to know what to expect and plan so there'll be no surprises or hurt feelings. If there are new, universally comfortable family traditions, add these to your Family Covenant as well.

Child custody and visitation. If there are firm legal agreements in place for visitation/custody of children, your Family Covenant could include the specific plans for making sure everything runs smoothly with ex-spouses and other extended family members. How will everyone share space in the family home? When and what privileges (television, video or computer games, movies, etc.) will each child enjoy? Writing down general expectations really reduces misunderstandings and conflict.

Family finances. You might include a general description of how your family prepares annual budgets and spending priorities in your Family Covenant. Allow your children to have some meaningful input in this process.

Use the sample Blended Family Covenant in appendix B as a guide to prepare your own covenant tailored to your family's specific needs. Be sure each family member has a copy for future reference.

In this chapter, we've reviewed the general stages and phases of blended family life, as well as some warning signs alerting us to seek additional help for our family members. We discussed some of the many common problems many blended families face, and we learn that use of family conferences and a Blended Family Covenant can help bridge some relationship gaps. But to experience the "lift" in your remarriage that we mentioned at the beginning, you and your mate need to make sure three vital forces are working in your relationship—balance, intimacy, and romance!

ACTIVELY PURSUE BALANCE, INTIMACY, AND ROMANCE IN YOUR REMARRIAGE

Of all the marriage relationship issues any couple faces, three in particular merit special attention—especially in a remarriage. What are they? Balance, intimacy, and romance. You cannot have intimacy and romance in your marriage unless there is a certain equilibrium between you and your mate—a basic *balance* between your God-given gifts, needs, interests, desires, and personalities. You also cannot have true intimacy without some romance mixed in. Nor can you enjoy the richness of romance without intimacy. All these qualities build on each other.

The Importance of Balance in Remarriage

As two whole and complete individuals unite as "one flesh" in becoming husband and wife, they fulfill and balance each other in a "cooperative oneness" that's complete unto itself. Adam was a complete man. Eve was a complete woman. But they couldn't separately procreate, for example, without the one-flesh union of their bodies. So, in their union with each other they enjoyed a beautifully different form of completeness in the way God intended, that they couldn't experience independently. Marriage today is no different.

Building and preserving this cooperative oneness requires compromise and balance. The prophet Amos asked, "Do two walk together unless they have agreed to do so?" (Amos 3:3). Obviously not. Yet two people initially can agree to walk together, but later find they're so different that they wish they hadn't! *This can happen to Christians in a marriage (or remarriage).* Without balance between husband and wife, the marriage begins to wobble. This wobble affects everyone in the blended family. If they don't act promptly to correct this wobble with the Lord's help, remarriage partners risk becoming more out of step with each other and, eventually, unequally yoked in their relationship.

This keen secular observation about the need for balance in marriage, made in an old *McCall's* magazine article by Anthony Brandt, caught my attention:

> We live in no bed of roses. Our marriage, with stepchildren and money problems and all the other difficulties that typically accompany second marriages, is full of tension. But I've learned that I never again want to be with a woman who's not as strong as I am. I've also learned that I need a wife, that being married is part of my identity. . . . The great, slow dance that is marriage remains the best way for the vast majority of us to balance our masculinity with its opposite, to give point to our sense of responsibility and, finally, to bear the sometimes overwhelming burdens of this life.[13]

Even though we've had more than our share of difficulties in our remarriage, together Cheryl and I have a better balance between us than we ever enjoyed in our first marriages. We deeply regret it didn't happen with our former mates, but we cannot change the past. Instead, we rejoice that we're of one heart and mind in fulfilling the intent of Proverbs 27:17—as iron sharpens iron, we are sharpening each other in our remarriage and in life. Having a basic balance between us allows the courage we bring to the remarriage the love we give to each other, our coping skills, our shared love for Jesus, and our mutual commitment to make our marriage work to blossom forth and grow. Without this basic balance, we most certainly would become stuck and stifled in our relationship!

Regretfully, those who may have been well suited for each other upon remarriage can become unequally yoked over the years if they're not careful to continually adjust to, and balance, each other. Here are a few examples:

• *Power imbalances.* Sometimes, especially when chaos reigns in a blended family, one spouse or the other rises up to take too much control. Rather than continuing to negotiate who does what, one mate steps over the line and begins exercising too much authority. This may be an overbearing husband who demands that his wife "do her wifely duty and submit," or it could be the wife who tells her husband, "I'm tired of always doing things your way—now it's my turn!" (These attitudes reveal selfishness or rebellion too!) Power imbalances frequently arise when either or both mates are insecure about themselves or their marriage, or one mate is excessively passive, yielding, and dependent upon the other. This insecurity and impassivity may have carried over from childhood and family of origin or from mistreatment in a prior marriage, or both.

• *Functional imbalances.* Marriages with functional imbalances arise when spouses have extreme views of each other and how to manage the household. Many functional imbalances in blended families arise from dysfunctional nonbiblical role reversals between husband and wife. It also happens when children manipulate and control the household as parents fail, neglect, or refuse to fulfill their God-given parenting responsibilities. Codependent relationships, where one spouse is excessively enmeshed with the other, also create functional imbalances in remarriage. Marital roles become mixed up and confused. It is a very dysfunctional lifestyle that adversely affects the entire family.

• *Emotional imbalances.* Some spouses invest too much emotion and energy into forcing a relationship to work, while others unduly reserve their feelings and become emotionally distant. Some marriage partners will give and give while receiving virtually nothing back from their mates. They'll pursue their mates and appease them to avoid any conflicts in the hope of "getting the spark back into our marriage." Unfortunately, many of these pursuers have low self-esteem. They feel the need to please their spouses to feel whole and complete themselves. This isn't loving conduct—it comes from a dysfunctional and deficient lifestyle. There's very little intimacy in a marriage like this since an emotional imbalance exists.

• *Family conflict imbalances.* This occurs when one or both spouses stress the positive so much that they cannot bring themselves to deal with any negative issues at all. You may hear a wife tell her family, "Now let's not talk about anything controversial while we're all together—just happy stuff!" But this isn't reality. It's a retreat to the first idealistic fantasy phase of blended family life.

How can you deal with relationship imbalances? The short answer is *equalization*—like a seesaw tipping one way or the other, the spouses at both ends need to work together, push up on their respective ends, and shift their weight to achieve some balance.

The first step in achieving equalization for these relationship imbalances begins by defining what a healthy balance actually involves. Why not mirror with our spouses what Jesus tells us to do in loving God? "Love the Lord your God with all your *heart* and with all your *soul* and with all your *mind* and with all your *strength*" (Mark 12:30, emphasis added). Is your heart fully committed to God and to your mate as well? From an emotional standpoint, are you able to share what you desire, hope for, fear, believe in, and love? Can you open up your life enough to be totally honest and transparent so your mate can truly understand you?

How are you doing spiritually? Are you and your spouse able to pray together about your lives? Are you helping each other to become more Christlike? Are you regularly searching Scripture to understand God's perspective on your marriage and family life? Are you in touch with others' souls?

What about your mental outlook on the marriage and blended family? Do you know what each person in your family truly needs right now? What do they like? What don't they like? Is everyone growing spiritually, and intellectually expanding their minds? Are you and your family stimulating each other's creativity in finding new ways to love each other and grow closer together?

What about the physical aspects of your life? Are you content with your appearance? Do you appreciate the body God has given you, or are you held captive by an eating disorder or low self-esteem? Are you and your mate enjoying a healthy and uplifting sexual relationship? Do you regularly walk and talk together? Do you and your family do enough fun things together?

Successful remarriage partners know what they want and need to achieve and maintain a healthy balance with each other. Emotionally, spiritually, mentally, physically, and socially they strive for fulfillment and balance among all these vital life areas in their marriage and family, as they do in their individual relationships with God.

The next step in achieving equalization is for both spouses to yield and submit to God, and to each other, by honoring their biblical roles. Imbalances commonly occur when a couple takes their focus away from the Lord and begins keying on each other. Have you ever wondered how spinning Olympic ice skaters keep their balance? They set their focus on something fixed and stable while they're twirling around. Similarly, we must fix our eyes on Jesus, the author and finisher of our faith, to restore balance to our lives and marriages (see Heb. 12:1–3).

Achieving balance in your remarriage is a prerequisite for enjoying the intimate oneness God desires for all married couples.

Developing Intimacy in Remarriage

In A. A. Milne's famous story *The House at Pooh Corner*, Piglet sidles up to Pooh. "Pooh!" he whispers. "Yes, Piglet?" Pooh replies. "Nothing," said Piglet, gently taking Pooh's paw, "I just wanted to be sure of you." (For those who don't like the image of Pooh bear when talking about adult intimacy, my apologies. But don't miss the point here—intimacy is the comfort of knowing that your beloved is always there for you in ways that words cannot express at times.)

Intimacy comes from sharing common interests, companionship, trust, loyalty, commitment, love, raising children together, and enjoying a warm sexual union as God intended. Both partners feel free to say what they need to say to each other in ways that the other will understand. Intimacy grows from basic *trust* and a feeling that your mate, despite character flaws and shortcomings, is on your side. You can entrust your deepest feelings and fears to your mate, knowing they'll be lovingly and carefully handled. True intimacy roots itself in emotional security and safety that remains constant, even as loving feelings and romance vary from time to time. It is candid and serious communication on the deepest levels possible with your partner. It is sharing a powerful physical attraction to each other. But it's also sitting quietly with your beloved, feeling content and comforted merely by his/her presence. Intimacy is the trust that *nothing need be said*. You can tell when you have this genuine quality of intimacy. You'll know when your heart truly becomes knit together with your mate. How? You'll be *sure* of each other. And that's when you'll experience that wonderful sense of "lift" we mentioned at the beginning of this chapter.

But let's be honest. It's not easy feeling deep intimacy in a remarriage and blended family situation. Why? Because taking care of a family can really *drain* you at times. It's extremely difficult to be giving, loving, and intimate with your spouse when you feel overworked, overstressed, and totally frazzled! Then it's easy to become rather mechanical about relationship maintenance and fall into a dull, boring routine. Coasting in remarriage spares the extra work of creativity and developing a servant heart necessary to bond remarriage partners for the long term. But what happens? The marriage gets stuck, and intimacy becomes a distant memory.

So how do you develop intimacy in remarriage? Here are a few suggestions:

• *Build on a spiritual foundation.* We only know true intimacy by knowing him who created it—our loving and intimate Creator. We love and experience intimacy with each other because God first loved us and showed us what intimacy is all about (1 John 4:19). How often are you and your mate going to God to learn how to love each other more deeply and intimately? Are you passionate for his love? "As the deer pants for streams of water, so my soul pants for you, O God. My soul thirsts for God, the living God. Where can I go and meet with God?" (Ps. 42:1–2). Is that how you and your mate feel about the Lord? Spiritual intimacy springs from remarriages firmly grounded on the rock of Jesus Christ and the basic principles of the Christian faith. It comes from praying with, and for, each other—probably the strongest link the couple can share with the Lord and one another. It comes from feeding and caring for each other spiritually and keeping a collective focus on Christ. Then as the couple grows nearer to God, they naturally grow in love for, and intimacy with, each other.

Archbishop Temples once defined intimate worship with God this way: "Worship is the submission of all my nature to God. It is the quickening of conscience by his holiness, the nourishment of mind by his truth, the purifying of imagination by his beauty, the opening of the heart to his love, and the submission of my will to his purpose. All this gathered up in adoration is the greatest expression of which we are capable." Truly, if we're experiencing that kind of deep intimacy with our Lord, it's much easier to share a mirrored intimacy with our mates.

• *Intimacy requires hard work.* Take stock of your marriage. Do you share an emotional closeness with your mate? Has the "business" of keeping your blended family running smoothly gradually crowded out the tenderness the two of you once shared so naturally? Have you and your partner taken each other for granted and failed to appreciate and praise each other? Do you find yourself yearning for the early passion and excitement? If you see these things happening in your marriage, is it really a surprise that intimacy is slipping away?

How do you build emotional intimacy? Discover what's lacking in your relationship—what specific patterns in your life quench intimacy? Admit it's missing from your relationship. Pray that God will open your heart, and that of your spouse as well, so you can truly connect emotionally. Talk about it with your mate. Confess specific ways your actions contributed to the problem. Without blaming or condemning your spouse, repent and describe what changes you're willing to make. Ask for your mate's prayers, encouragement, and support. Spend as much quality time with each other as you can. Build up and encourage, praise, and appreciate each other.

• *Intimacy comes from having cherishing hearts.* Intimacy grows through communicating and truly believing that your mate is your treasure. You show this by the way you live. You let your mate know, "You're special to me and our family. I'm so proud of you. I believe in you. I'm so glad we married each other." Cherishing one another is one of those "love languages" that every person needs. You cannot enjoy true intimacy without it.

• *Intimacy flows from forgiving and accepting hearts.* Your mate needs to know you love him/her *unconditionally.* When your spouse offends you, be quick to forgive. Remember, most remarriage partners don't act out of malice; they aren't out to get their mates. Many offenses simply are temporary lapses and insensitive thoughtlessness. When your mate offends you, it's much easier to have an attitude of empathy and forgiveness by first putting yourself in his/her place. Ask yourself, "What was going on in his life at that particular moment?" Maybe he had too many things on his mind and simply forgot. Your partner needs your acceptance as a person, without having to change or be perfect before receiving your approval. Trying to see matters from your mate's perspective helps you have a forgiving heart also. Keep in mind that Jesus forgives us first so we can forgive others.

• *Intimacy celebrates the sexual union God created for married couples.* God created sex to mirror and reveal passionately intimate aspects of himself. In his infinite love and desire to please us, God created the sexual relationship for husbands and wives to enjoy to the fullest extent two human beings can do so. It's a joyous event! Sexual union is the ultimate intimacy builder, so it's difficult to imagine marital intimacy without a good sexual relationship. Sexual intimacy comes from having *balance* in your remarriage. If you and your mate are truly suitable for each other, your conversations and daily lives are intellectually, emotionally, and spiritually stimulating. This weaving together of your lives directly relates to your physical relationship as well, and makes you and your mate feel very comfortable, affectionate, and playful. Having a total, exclusive commitment to each other undergirds all your feelings of contentment, joy, and deep satisfaction.

One of the greatest joys of remarriage is learning from our immature mistakes and unrealistic expectations of youth and prior marriages. We have the capacity for a mature, deeper understanding and appreciation of our mates. Now we're better able to be *givers*, rather than takers. It's all so very natural—a new life beginning with a powerful head start! No wonder many documented studies of conjugal relationships confirm that husbands and wives enjoy sexual relations more often in remarriages, despite their age or the duration of their relationship!

But realistically, good sexual relations may not happen in all remarriages. Partners must now adjust to new spouses with established, and perhaps different, sexual habits. How does a husband help his wife when she's burdened with sexual problems arising as a result of criticism or neglect from her first husband? How does a wife help her husband whose first wife used sex as a manipulative tool to reward or punish him? Some men find their sexual drive increases in remarriage after they effectively recover from the stress and frustration of divorce. However, many males carry into their second marriages a variety of sexual inhibitions lingering from their former spouses. And there are so many other remarriage factors—instant families, lack of privacy, financial pressures, fear of another marriage failure, and odds against success of remarriage—that sexual dysfunction is a problem for more than a few remarried couples. Even so, remarriage is an opportunity to break old patterns, with freedom to try new ways of communicating and expressing love to one's spouse. If the couple truly can develop a sexual intimacy that is uniquely theirs, they'll find the Lord blessing and growing their relationship in ways they could never dream possible.

We've talked a lot in this book about the importance of you and your mate working together as a *team*. Intimacy is what makes this teamwork possible. This doesn't come naturally or automatically. You must cultivate it and nurture it like a priceless rosebush. Yes, it's all hard work—but *necessary* work. Your marriage may not survive any crisis for long without intimacy.

Balance. Intimacy. These are "glue words" in a remarriage. They thrive in a couple's love and commitment to each other. But there's that important third element—romance—that puts the icing on the cake!

The Power of Romance in Remarriage

When Lily and her husband, Tim, were courting, they loved and served each other in many creative and special ways. They went on impromptu picnics, sent flowers to each other for no reason, and left little love notes for each other in unexpected places. Their hearts leaped whenever they called each other just to say hello. But then . . . they got married. Kids from different families squabbled with each other. Mortgage payments rolled in. Housework and the laundry load quadrupled. Even when some routines smoothed out the chaos, a besetting familiarity washed out the romance. Now, a couple of years into their remarriage, when faced with the choice of sharing a passionate moment or watching television, they are casting their votes more and more for watching late night television.

Complaints about inattentive, unromantic, and less loving mates are common to all marriages. Quite often, it's the wives feeling neglected. They miss the little things—the unexpected compliments, or occasional bouquet of flowers—that let them know their husbands truly do care about them. But husbands yearn for greater closeness and romance too! Oh, we may not show it too much—we're prone to take our wives' adulation for granted. But when it's gone, we really miss it and want it back!

Romance thrives on surprises and adventures. Because humans tend to get bored very easily, routines and familiarity are the natural enemies of romance. This is why it's so important to break out of stifling patterns in a remarriage and take the initiative to do new things as part of receiving the new wine of remarriage.

Cheryl and I earnestly desire that this book not only be instructive and encouraging to you but very personal as well. In this spirit, permit us to share one very personal experience with you as an example among many of how to fire up the intimacy and romance in your remarriage.

It began when Cheryl, her three married sisters, and two sisters-in-law presented the men in the family with a challenge—create a romantic date for your spouse for under twenty dollars. The winner receives a prize. What a wonderful idea! My mind immediately kicked into gear on how to do it.

Here's how it all came about: One Saturday afternoon, while Cheryl ran some errands, I arranged for Chase's grandmother (Carole) to baby-sit him upstairs for the evening. A limit of only twenty dollars certainly restricted the options for a magnificent feast! This required some resourcefulness—a Boston Market newspaper discount coupon for two complete turkey dinners, some scented candles, a specially marked bottle of sparkling cider, some bubble-bath crystals, and a few packages of Post-It notes would just about bust the budget!

When Cheryl came home, I was waiting for her, dressed up in my suit. (This, in itself, was a nice surprise, since she knows how I hate wearing a coat and tie!) After encouraging her to leave her packages for later, I hugged and kissed her while leading her into our bedroom. When she opened the door, she found all the shades drawn and lit candles all over the room. At the foot of our bed was a card table with a white tablecloth and more candles and two glasses of bubbly cider, all graced by our turkey dinners, lightly simmering on china framed with silverware. This brought a giggling "Oh!" from my lovely wife.

As she enjoyed her meal and beverage, by candlelight I read Song of Solomon to her. More "Ohs!" from Cheryl!

Then she noticed that all around the room, on the bed, dresser, doorframes— *everywhere*—were yellow Post-It notes. Each had a message: "You bring in the mail each day, and take out the garbage every Wednesday night." "You dress me *up* when I want to dress down." "You jog and exercise, and watch what you eat to keep yourself looking beautiful." "You take my clothes to the cleaners and get out the chocolate stains." "You make the house look *wonderful!*" "You're the first one in the kitchen each morning to fix breakfast for our family." "You read what I write and tell me how to make it better." "You're an *excellent,* and *very savvy*, businesswoman!" "You take care of me when I'm sick." "You *special order* low-fat mint chocolate chip ice cream. *Yummy!*" There were about two complete packs of Notes everywhere, leading down the hallway to the bathroom. Cheryl read each one until the trail led her to the bathtub where more scented candles awaited, giving a warm glow.

"What now?" she asked. "Well, sweetheart, now comes a very special part of our romantic evening," I said with a wink. "Allow me to draw you a nice warm bubble bath so you can relax!" While kissing her warmly on her neck and shoulders, I slowly disrobed her and washed her gently in the suds. "Oh!" she squealed again with delight!

After drying her off with a large warm towel, I carried her to our bed. We made love in the flickering glow of our candlelit room before enjoying some more sparkling cider as we held each other close and listened to soft music on the stereo.

Although we had some very strong competition from some other family couples, we won the prize for the most romantic date. But who cares about winning the contest—the journey getting there was the real reward!

So how can you pursue romance in your remarriage? Here are some suggestions:

• *Be sensitive to what your beloved needs.* Focus on the Family founder and author Dr. James Dobson describes the importance of romance to women this way:

It is a wise and dedicated husband who desires to understand his wife's psychological needs and then sets out to meet them. Briefly stated, love is linked to self-esteem in women. For a man, romantic experiences with his wife are warm, enjoyable, and memorable—but not necessary. For a woman, they are her lifeblood. Her confidence, her sexual response, and her zest for living are often directly related to those tender moments when she feels deeply loved and appreciated by her man. That is why flowers and candy are more meaningful to her than to him. This is why she is continually trying to pull him out of the television set or the newspaper, and not vice versa. This is why the anniversary is critically important to her, and why she *never* forgets it. . . . This need for romantic love is not some quirk or peculiarity of his wife, as some may think. This is the way women are made.[14]

While men may not be as romantic as women, it's a rare person who doesn't appreciate it—regardless of gender!

• *Make a daily connection with each other.* If you and your mate are like most remarried couples with a blended family, your busy lives will work against connecting with each other. And if you're not talking and spending some quality time with each other, it sure is awkward to reach for your mate suddenly as he/she is falling asleep. That emotional connection has to be there during the day. It may be a quick phone call or even a voice-mail message to say, "You're on my mind, sweetheart," or "I wish I could be with you right now." Or it may mean getting up early to help your wife out with some of the laundry, or gassing up your husband's car. Believe it—those acts of appreciation and service will mean more to your mate than a dozen roses, or a ticket to his favorite football game!

• *Help each other out romantically.* What's a wife's frequent complaint about the romantic resourcefulness of her husband? "He just doesn't have a clue!" How about the husbands? "She won't tell me what she likes!" Her response? "If I have to tell you, it's just no fun!" But look at the big picture here. Without some meaningful communication between remarriage partners, what's likely to happen? Each mate floundering around trying to figure out what pleases the other in a haphazard, hit-or-miss, free-for-all in most cases. Take the initiative. *Tell* your mate what you need. Share how you feel. If you want "more romance," give some suggestions. Why not take some time for you and your mate to write down ten different romantic things you would like to happen, and then swap lists. Then, when you need inspiration, just pull out the list and try one!

Look for creative ways to enjoy romance with your remarriage partner! Nothing will keep the home fires burning brighter or help both of you to experience "lift" in your relationship than using these uniquely special and intimate ways of saying, "I love you with all my heart. I want you to be sure of me."

CAN YOUR REMARRIAGE SURVIVE "'TIL DEATH DO YOU PART"?

Given the few "sticky issues" discussed in this chapter, among many others remarried couples will face during their lives together, is it possible for the relationship to survive until "death do us part"? Absolutely! But it requires a healthy dose of realism, and accepting that marital stress is inevitable even in the best remarriages. There will be periods of crisis and change. Personality differences. Money problems. Family relocations. Career detours. Serious illnesses. Blended family issues. If you can imagine a conflict, remarriages are a prime candidate for it to occur. That's why divorce statistics for remarriages are so much higher than for first marriages. Even so, all things are possible with God (Mark 10:27)! If both partners lovingly commit to make their relationship a success, working diligently to submit to one another out of reverence for Christ, any remarriage will work with God's help.

A Message from Cheryl

Unfortunately, moving through the phases of blended family life is necessary. I work in the life insurance business. In our industry, *no one* succeeds the first year. They live in utter poverty as they struggle along. Those who make it through (and few do), often succeed beyond their wildest expectations.

The same is true in many remarriages. It will take years to "blend." Each of us feels "perfectly suited," smarter, and better prepared. Brace yourself: It'll be more difficult than you think. Like those insurance agents, you will struggle.

Now I would like to address a core fear. Each of us who is divorced would like to believe . . . if only I had married "the right person." So now, we chose better. (I certainly did.) However, there'll still be a time of disillusionment in each marriage. (Just ask Warren!) For some, it'll be a passing phase. For others, it may never pass.

So what is your commitment? What does God expect? The Lord doesn't expect this remarriage will be your happiness. He expects you to honor your vow, one way or the other. Are you marrying for happiness or for ministry? If you seek joy, what will you do when it eludes you?

A dear family friend writes beautiful poetry. She captured the reality of this issue in her poem entitled "Happy to Be Holy" (which she graciously permitted me to share with you):

> Full of expectations, happiness at hand,
> Happily ever after, I had found a man.
>
> Happiness and laughter were soon replaced by tears,
> Hopes and dreams fade away, with the passing of the years.
>
> Others seem so happy, life is just unfair,
> Clothed in my self-pity, I sank into despair.

When I hit the bottom, I began to pray,
"Lord, remove my heartache, send happiness my way."

That prayer he did not answer, yet faith began to grow,
God became my refuge, as this truth he did bestow;

"My grace, it is sufficient, I have a higher goal,
Greater than your happiness, the refining of your soul."

Casting off self-pity, now clothed with empathy,
Those who once seemed happy, now share their pain with me.

Joy relieves my heartache, yet my dream is still not dead,
But my goal is not my happiness, but holiness instead.

Be sure this is your beloved's vow as well as your own. Your blended family may not be able to endure another divorce.

Finally, as you go through what probably will be the most difficult times of your remarriage (during the first few years, often surrounded by children and conflict), be sure to take a break. Schedule both family fun times and romantic times alone. We all need a little incentive to hang in there and see the light at the end of our tunnel, the carrot at the end of our stick.

QUESTIONS FOR PERSONAL REFLECTION

1. What stage or phase of blended family life might create the most difficulties for my family, and why?
2. Which warning signs of a troubled remarriage should I be most alert against, and why?
3. What issues and challenges are my blended family most likely to face during the first year? How have I prepared for these matters?
4. How can we use family conferences in our blended family on a regular basis? What do we need to do to set them up properly?
5. How can my partner and I gain greater balance in our personal and family life? How can we develop a deeper intimacy with each other? How can we be more romantic with one another?
6. How well are we incorporating a Christian lifestyle into our blended family? Have we used godly principles in formulating our roles, our responsibilities, and our discipline? How are we looking to Christ for our contentment so we can give ourselves freely and honestly to each other?

Chapter 9

CHILDREN
How to Include Them on the Journey

Children. God's most precious gift after life itself. Their presence from the wedding of a remarried couple is what puts the "blend" in blended families.

Every once in a while, an event truly changes your life, making you think, "Whoa! I've got to change my entire perspective!" While we were courting, one afternoon outing with Cheryl and Chase shifted my paradigm as a divorced, childless man.

While Cheryl and Chase (then about four years old) were visiting me in Florida, I surprised Cheryl with an afternoon at the spa. "Sweetheart, enjoy yourself today. I'll take care of Chase. Don't worry about a thing!"

I dropped Cheryl off and took Chase to his favorite place—McDonald's. We ordered our food and sat down to have a prayer before our meal, when Chase interrupted, "Mr. Warren, I've got to go to the bathroom." Uh-oh! I wasn't prepared for this. I foolishly reasoned that Cheryl's earlier restroom stop with Chase would hold him until we rejoined her. Big mistake! But I put on a brave front and confidently asked, "Chase, can you hold it until after we finish lunch?" "Nope," he responded quickly. "Well, is it number one . . . or number two," I asked more apprehensively. "It's number two, and I need to go *real* bad!!" I asked a nearby customer to please watch our untouched meals, and led Chase by the hand for our very first adventure into the jaws of the foreboding men's room. Naturally, I didn't have a clue what to do once we got there.

"OK, Chase," I said less confidently, "Here we are. Go to it." "Well, Mommy always pulls my pants down and puts me on the toilet," he told me with an expectant look. "Okay . . .", I said reluctantly, "let's do that."

While Chase was in the stall, it took every fiber of my being to stand nervously at the other end of the restroom wondering what would happen next. I silently prayed, "Please Lord, if it's possible, let this cup that I'm about to partake pass from me!"

Then it happened. "Mr. Warren, I'm all finished now," Chase announced proudly. "Uh, okay, well just pull up your pants and come on out." (I was praying more fervently now.) "Well," Chase politely educated me, "Mommy always wipes me."

I thought . . . "My *life* is *over!*" But I mustered up enough courage to serve this beautiful little boy and meet his needs. How? By reminding myself, "Warren, you have a child in your life now. This is only a small glimpse into what remarriage will be like. This is *good* for you! Get used to it!"

As Chase and I returned to our cold meals, I knew I was a changed man. We tackled our first potty trip . . . and survived! In fact, while relishing this major life achievement, I thought, "You know, it really wasn't too bad!" As he chowed down on his Happy Meal and graciously forgot the sheer panic he had seen in my eyes during our stall encounter, Chase's rather matter-of-fact attitude encouraged me.

Such is the initiation of many childless single men and women who desire remarriage but receive the blessings of children as part of the bargain! This incident reminded me of a most encouraging Scripture: "Sons are a heritage from the LORD, children a reward from him. Like arrows in the hands of a warrior are sons born in one's youth. Blessed is the man whose quiver is full of them. They will never be put to shame when they contend with their enemies in the gate" (Ps. 127:3–5).

Children are a reward from the Lord; his precious gifts, entrusted to us for a short time. They fulfill us as human beings and remind us of joys and triumphs in life we'd miss if we didn't have those little eyes to help us discover things on life's journey. Does it really matter if youngsters are our biological children or not? They rely upon the adults to whom the Lord delivers them for care and direction. And we parents and stepparents shouldn't take this profound stewardship responsibility lightly!

With this blessing from the Lord comes the responsibility to teach our children and help them learn about God:

> Fix these words of mine in your hearts and minds; tie them as symbols on your hands and bind them on your foreheads. Teach them to your children, talking about them when you sit at home and when you walk along the road, when you lie down and when you get up. Write them on the doorframes of your houses and on your gates, so that your days and the days of your children may be many in the land. (Deut. 11:18–21a)

This privilege is our God-given opportunity to change history for his glory. As David expressed so well in Psalm 78, our children are our lifeline to the future:

> O my people, hear my teaching; listen to the words of my mouth. I will open my mouth in parables, I will utter hidden things, things from of old—what we have heard and known, what our fathers have told us. We will not hide them from their children; we will tell the next generation the praiseworthy deeds of the LORD, his power, and the wonders he has done. He decreed statutes for Jacob and established the law in Israel, which he commanded our forefathers to teach their children, so the next generation would know them, even the children yet to be born, and they in turn would tell their children. Then they would put their trust in God and would not forget his deeds but would keep his commands. (Ps. 78:1–7)

When we think about how important our children are to the Lord, and to us, it's heartbreaking that they must endure the most tragic consequences of death or divorce of parents. Yet we must try to understand how children think, feel, and cope with parents moving in and out of their young lives to help them grow in a new blended family situation. But this understanding begins with some self-examination. Childless widowed or divorced persons must ask themselves:

HAS GOD CALLED ME TO PARENT IN A BLENDED FAMILY?

In this book, we've assumed either or both remarriage partners bring children into a blended family. But a childless partner may have some reservations about remarrying a custodial parent and entering into a blended family because they aren't ready, willing, or able to accept additional responsibilities of parenting another's children. If you fit into this latter group, we urge you to reconsider your decision to remarry. If you cannot *fully commit* to parenting stepchildren, stop! Remarriage into a blended family could be a disastrous mistake for you and everyone else in the family.

Parenting is an awesome responsibility—a high calling. Has the Lord equipped you to fulfill his ministry to the next generation? Feeling inadequate to the task is *normal!* Few believe they have it all together as a parent (especially of a teen!). Feeling nervous and ill-equipped as a parent is one of God's ways to get you on your knees! But parenting a child definitely is a full-time job. Becoming an instant parent certainly isn't for everyone. Paul Reiser, costar of the *Mad about You* comedy series and author of the book *Couplehood,* echoes a thought many anxious childless stepparents-to-be might feel: "Ideally they should give you a couple of 'practice kids' before you have any for real. Sort of like bowling a few frames for free before you start keeping score."[1] There's no such luxury for instant parents. Perhaps you chose to remain childless in a prior marriage, a choice open to you and your former spouse. But with a remarriage into a blended family situation, no childless choices remain. Does this bother you?

Although children truly are a blessing, not every adult receives them as such. A child can be a heavy burden, with a decision to become a parent requiring many sacrifices. Don't think you can merely maintain the relationships with children until they grow up. Parenting takes much more work than that! Are you willing to count the cost and pay the price? Stepparents-to-be must *decide* to love and accept stepchildren as part of coming into a blended family.

Remarriage probably means you'll become a stepfather or stepmother to some wounded kids, grieving for a deceased or divorced parent they consider irreplaceable. Some children may never fully recover from the painful loss they feel at the core of their being. Can you live with, and love, these children even if they cannot (or will not) return your love?

Despite the liabilities, stepchildren are wonderful treasures needing a stepparent's love and acceptance. They extend little hands your way (usually covered in jam) and want you to admire and immortalize their scribbled "Picassos" on the refrigerator door. They desperately need you to be a hero by retrieving their balls from the garage roof, taking the training wheels off a bike, or removing a broken off pencil tip from their gums after they chewed on the wrong end. They ask you to shield and protect them by carefully bandaging a boo-boo only with the Scooby-Doo Band-Aids, being on call throughout the night to scare away monsters, or binding up their broken hearts when their fishing rods snap in two while going out the garage door. Can you listen patiently to a teen's occasional reverie of impossible dreams and foolish fantasies, sandwiched between many monosyllabic conversations? This means loving these youngsters without counting the cost. In exchange, they give you glimpses of God and a chance to be immortal in their eyes. Little ones will race to greet you at the door, bringing a smile to your face no matter how your day was at work or how well the stock market performed. Is this your heart's desire and passion?

If with clear conscience before the Lord you can resolve your doubts, receiving stepchildren as part of a remarriage package; and if, with sincere joy and sacrificial, biblical love you're ready to assume a stepparenting role, then Cheryl and I want to welcome you into the blended family club of remarried Americans! But before receiving initiation rights and responsibilities of blended family life, let's try to come alongside and *understand* these children coming from a prior marriage broken by death or divorce. What are these kids struggling with? What do they fear? What can parents do to help kids move from broken families into new blended families?

A Blended Family Child's Three Greatest Fears

One of Dr. Sigmund Freud's most compelling summaries is his consolidation of the many sources of anxiety to the anticipated threat of four major, universal, personal catastrophes: (1) loss of a loved one; (2) loss of the *love* of a loved one; (3) loss of physical or social integrity; and (4) loss of self-esteem.[2] One can easily see that children experience most, if not all, of these personal disasters with the death or divorce of parents, followed by adjusting to a new blended family of relative strangers.

Fear no. 1: Abandonment—My "real" parents have left me behind. Dr. Samuel Roll, professor of psychology and psychiatry at the University of New Mexico, summarizes abandonment issues this way: "Divorce . . . stimulates a child's fear that one or both parents will be lost forever. When asked about their three greatest fears, children frequently mention the loss of a parent: 'I'm afraid that my mom or dad might die,' or 'I worry that I will never see my dad again,' or 'I think that my mom might forget about me.'"[3]

This is a "where I've come from in life" fear. It's a basic survival issue for children. A child believes parents love each other and brought him/her into the world to love through childhood. If divorced parents stop loving each other, will they stop loving the child as well? Can the child trust Mommy and Daddy anymore? Children feel rejected and abandoned as they see parents become depressed or angry, absorbed in litigation, or working longer hours to make ends meet. Or a child may ask, "Why did Daddy have to die and leave me so suddenly? What will I do without him?" An absent parent, for whatever the reason, often confirms fears of rejection and abandonment. A child may become clingy and difficult to leave at school or with a baby-sitter. Even bedtime can bring nightmares. Children believe parents will leave them alone and unloved forever. The darkness of their bedrooms echoes what they feel inside. Older children, searching for their own identities, may not show outward signs of these fears, but they also remain vulnerable to similar feelings.

These feelings run *deep* with some children. Try to imagine how you, as a Christian, might feel if God died or withdrew from you. Think about it! Most of us would feel utter despair—that life wouldn't be worth living anymore. We would feel so vulnerable and afraid without his protection. Now consider how parents are in a godlike role for their young children. Everything you'd feel if God weren't alive and present may be what your children feel as a result of death or divorce of a parent.

How can you (and your remarriage partner) reassure your children while dispelling fears of abandonment after loss of a biological parent?

• *Keep in touch.* Listen, and allow ventilation of feelings. Be willing to spend quality time talking about a child's concerns. Encourage open discussions. Avoid immediate, critical, or judgmental reactions to whatever the child says. Patiently consider the child's statements and gently respond appropriately. Use relaxed body language that says, "I am going to hear you out for as long as you need to express yourself because I care for you." Offer facts and reassurances confirming that other loved ones will always try to be there for the child. Allow the child to cry as needed.

• *Remind your child that the Lord is near.* "Can a mother forget the baby at her breast and have no compassion on the child she has borne? Though she may forget, I will not forget you! See, I have engraved you on the palms of my hands" (Isa. 49:15–16a). God assures those who love him, "Never will I leave you; never will I forsake you" (Heb. 13:5b). Jesus' promise to his disciples extends to all Christians for all time: "And surely I am with you always, to the very end of the age" (Matt. 28:20). The Lord's near to us—there's no reason to be anxious about anything when we can present our requests to God with prayer and petition and thanksgiving in our hearts (Phil. 4:5–6). Pray with your child and read Bible stories together, illustrating how God keeps his promises and faithfully helps those in need.

• *Avoid criticism of an absent parent.* Criticism only reinforces abandonment feelings and self-blame, creating further confusion and anxiety for children.

• *If possible, encourage regular visitation with the noncustodial parent.* Professor Roll emphasizes the need for children to have predictable contact with both divorced parents: "Our general goal is deceptively easy to state: We must make the child feel, in the words of Isaiah, that the loved one is never far away and that the child is recorded in some indelible way on the parent. The child who feels emotionally related to the parent left behind and who has a sense of holding that parent close to his or her core will be at reduced risk."[4] Toward that end, each parent should try to keep normal schedules, rather than making each visit a special event.[5] Make sure your child knows the visitation schedule of a noncustodial parent. Give him/her reasonable input on when and where to meet. If possible, keep the telephone number of the noncustodial parent available. Encourage calls so the child knows the relationship remains intact.

Fear no. 2: Alienation/isolation—No one loves me now. Many children have an egocentric view of their world. They believe everything around them exists for their benefit. But with breakdown of a family through death or divorce of a parent, coupled with perceived isolation from others in the new blended family, it's easy to understand how kids may experience some alienation and self-blame. A child may even think God took a parent away in death because the child was disobedient. The child interprets the parent's absence as punishment for wrongdoing. This leads to further self-punishment, guilt, self-pity, and alienation from God. If the child lives with one divorced parent, he/she perceives this as personal rejection by the other parent. As family pecking orders get restructured among stepsiblings during the new family blending process, the child may feel detached and unimportant.

This is a "where I am right now" fear. "Not only have my real parents forgotten about me, but they've thrown me into a family of strangers where no one even likes me." Your child may be jealous of others who have both biological parents at home in an intact, traditional family. Your child may believe, "I'm the only one who feels this way about my life." What can you do?

• *Remind your child, "You're loved and appreciated!"* Come alongside your child and let him/her know how special and loved he/she is before God and among all blended family members. Consider having a family devotional where everyone can say to one another, "I appreciate you because . . ." Make sure no child is overlooked for praise and privileges. Look for family activities, such as board games or picnics, where each member has equal participation and enjoyment. Gently draw your child out of isolationist tendencies by being sure to include him/her in all family activities.

• *Encourage relatives and friends to recreate a circle of security for your child.* After death or divorce of a parent (and also upon entering a blended family), your child needs to see familiar faces. Regular contact with the usual friendly visitors in the home or at church provides a sense of continuity. This helps fill the gap left by a missing parent and provides rest from the strange new blended family environment.

• *Encourage your child to talk privately with others.* Church members, schoolteachers, friends, and especially new blended family members sharing similar adjustments would be good candidates. Children will learn that peers have families in transition, too, and they aren't alone.

• *Encourage your child to depend upon God.* If your child feels unloved by everyone, emphasize God's eternal love and that he's with your child always. Your child needs to know that if God is *for* him/her, who can stand against that team? Explain Romans 8:31–39 to your child in understandable terms.

• *Study biblical references about using love to deal with fear of rejection.* Psalm 23 is an excellent choice that you might encourage your child to memorize. Also explore the wonderful relationship between love and fear by explaining some of the concepts of 1 John 4:7–21 in terms your child can understand and apply in daily life.

Fear no. 3: Insecurity about the future—Too many changes are happening in my life. Simple fear of the unknown can spiral out of control when the most personal aspects of a child's life—home, parents, and livelihood—remain in constant change. It can be terrifying. The child knows parents (biological and stepparents) keep some marriage matters private, but he/she fears parental secrets will bring more terrible news. Children dread painful surprises that compound worries and anxieties. Worry breeds insecurity that surfaces in endless questions about the future, where parents will be, what will happen in the new blended family, and who will take care of everyone.

This is a "where I'm going" fear, as a child who already feels the upheaval and burden of losing a parent now sees family matters in constant change. Resolving this general fear of the future is very important *before* helping a child adjust to blended family life. Without adequate time and preparation, a challenging new blended family situation may worsen children's anxiety and insecurity rather than alleviate them.

• *Teach children to accept life's uncertainties.* Help them understand that everyone is powerless to control many of life's events, like the weather for example. But with God's help, anyone can be flexible and cope with whatever happens. The Lord asks us to trust him, be positive, and learn to adjust. Think of personal examples when good changes resulted from bad situations (Rom. 8:28). Teach children that nothing in this world—not even a marriage—can be anyone's sole source of security. That's why trusting God is so important.

• *Help your child cope and adjust with loss and change.* It isn't what people want or like, but it's not a matter of shame for the child. Cite examples of other children who fared well after losing a parent and then joining a new blended family. Talk about God's ultimate good plans to prosper those who love him and to give them hope for the future (Jer. 29:11). Do a Bible study on the life of Joseph. Focus on the many advantages of a new start in a blended family!

• *Give your child reassuring information.* Try not to allow your child's lack of information to propel negative thoughts out of proportion to actual circumstances. Reassure and comfort your child with positive facts and examples of upcoming events whenever reasonably possible. Explain to your child where everyone will be and what will happen to help the child guard against frightening surprises.

• *Search for positives.* Acknowledge negatives arising from loss of a parent and moving into a new blended family, but look for positive results as well. Instead of dwelling on the loss of a divorced parent, stress the advantages of having biological parents in two places, or living in two houses—including one with a *new* stepparent. Create a sense of adventure and excitement about new life in a blended family.

• *Prepare your child for changes.* If a move is necessary, visit the new location several times beforehand. Let your child adjust during a transition period. If the child must attend a new school, arrange to visit during school hours and meet the teacher.[6]

• *Encourage stability and consistency.* Help your children make a scrapbook of their lives, using photographs, birth certificates, special mementos, awards, drawings, and a narrative focusing on happy times and achievements. This reminds them that many good aspects of their lives will continue as in the past.[7]

With the many fears and anxieties children experience after the loss of a parent, coupled with the uncertainties of blended family life, it's vital that all parents (biological and stepparents) work diligently in coming alongside these youngsters, comforting and reassuring them every step of the way. These are natural fears, since a child loses a familiar family structure—something vital and precious to healthy development and maturity—and receives a new family appearing very strange and different. As a familiar family structure disintegrates, your child may feel like he/she is falling apart, too, worrying that the chaos and panic will last forever. Consistent love and attention to your children's needs will help them cope and mature through life's difficulties.

PREPARING YOUR CHILDREN FOR REMARRIAGE AND BLENDED FAMILY LIFE

When the time comes to talk to your children about a pending remarriage and blended family life, here are some practical matters to consider:

Speak privately with each child first. This requires diplomacy, love, and understanding. Speak honestly with the child about the death or divorce of the other biological parent. Avoid any negative put-downs of the absent divorced ex-spouse, but don't cover any obvious faults already known by the child.[8] Instead, foster a compassionate concern in the child for both biological parents. A mother may sensitively tell a child, "Mommy and Daddy have gone through a very difficult time with our divorce, but we both still love you and want you to love us too. Since Daddy doesn't live with us anymore, we all need to work together so Mommy and Daddy always will be a part of your life. But Mommy has prayed and believes it'd be best for us to move on into a new family life with Mr. _____. This will never change how you love Daddy, but it'll be a good thing for us. How do you feel about that?" Obviously you can tailor the conversation in different ways for older kids and teenagers, but be sure to cover the most important issues for you and your family.

Have your partner join you in discussing the remarriage. After your private talk, joint discussion reassures children that their greatest fear—abandonment—won't happen. It reinforces continuity of the parenting relationship as part of the remarriage. If the child sees his/her custodial biological parent and the remarriage partner talking calmly together, the child can view both adults as caring and loving parental figures. If both adults make clear that they believe it best to remarry, unity helps the child accept the former marriage is over. This united front also helps keep the child from pitting one parent against the other, and also ends the fantasy that Mommy and Daddy will get back together. Naturally, it's best for both remarriage partners to agree on a truthful, joint statement, tailored to their children's understanding, for everyone coming into the blended family. This common understanding beforehand is important to comfort, not frighten, the children and reduce the chance of giving any inconsistent messages while talking to each child. All along the way, continue emphasizing the many positive aspects of remarriage and blended family life!

Make plans clear. The *attitude* of each parent will convey more than any words to the child. Children search for reaffirmation from each parent. Don't overanalyze an upcoming remarriage. Keep it simple. Confirm the truth in a comforting way: "Mom and Dad both love you very much. We always will. But we have separate lives now.

You'll still see each of us as much as you want. Mom will still be your mommy, and Dad will be your daddy. That won't change. The good news is that, in addition to Mom and Dad being with you in different places, you'll have another new stepparent to love and care for you—a blessing many kids don't have!"

Give each child enough time to express feelings. It's tempting to move from meeting to meeting with each child since the discussions may be emotionally challenging and difficult. But resist the urge to do so. This isn't a time to be impatient with a child's expression of feelings. Encourage each one to let everything out—questions, angry words, fears, and anything else that's troubling. Pray with each child about all these matters! Each child should feel free to express reasonable concerns. Some children share inner feelings best by drawing pictures. Others respond to role playing, where they can ask "What if . . ." questions to either or both remarriage partners. Imposing *our* timing on our children can keep them bottled up and reap disastrous results later.

Reaffirm your child's place in the blended family. Many children coming into a blended family with new brothers and sisters feel very insecure. They wonder whether there'll be enough love for them. Children need to experience some stability when they feel vulnerable. They need to feel connected to the familiar and comfortable things in their lives. Since a young child may be unable to experience a personal and mature relationship fully with God yet, this means making sure that there is frequent and meaningful contact with *both* divorced parents, or other members from the deceased parent's family, *and* the new stepparent.

HOW REMARRIAGE AND BLENDED FAMILY LIFE AFFECTS CHILDREN

We've already discussed many specific ways in which remarriage affects children in this book, but you would do well to focus on these general concerns:

Custodial children/ex-spouse relationships. Remarriage is a highly emotional issue with ex-spouses, even if your relationship has been cordial and cooperative for a long time. Prepare yourself and your children—that may change! As parents' animosities rise, emotions overflow onto the children. Ex-spouses and children of divorce share one common fear—more relationship losses as a "stranger" (stepparent) enters the picture. A noncustodial parent may feel vulnerable and powerless, thinking the custodial parent gains an unfair advantage. Legal battles follow over custody, visitation, child support, and other restrictions directly impacting the children. This is why *information, cooperation, thoughtful sensitivity,* and *prayerful action* are keys to keeping the lid on a volatile situation. Keep your ex-spouse informed as to events *before* they happen. (Of course, be sure to get legal advice *first* if your ex-spouse is an abusive parent or presents a dangerous threat to your child. Circumstances like this may require a different course of action.) Reaffirm your commitment to cooperate and preserve his/her relationship with your children. Use mediation as needed if you and your ex-spouse run into personal difficulties working through these feelings (see chap. 11.)

Grief/loyalty issues. We try to make the best decisions for ourselves and our children—sometimes without fully understanding a child's viewpoint and desires. This is especially true in coping with grief. When we deal with our grief, we think our children progress at the same pace, which often isn't the case. The child may need much more time and help with the grieving process (chap. 2). With a remarriage, the child's grief compounds through loyalty conflicts—will the missing biological parent be replaced or forgotten if the child accepts a new stepparent? Many children are unprepared for this emotional onslaught, resulting in adjustment difficulties in the blended family, resistance to the stepparent, and perhaps the child's depression.

The best approach? Patience and understanding! You could help your child work through grief issues perfectly, but children still have problems dealing with one issue: many children of divorce desperately want Mommy and Daddy back together (as portrayed in the movie *The Parent Trap*). Help your children face their pain. Be honest and direct about the major issue of restoring the old family: "It's not going to happen. We're moving into a new family now. We love each other, and we're going to stay together." The Lord will heal your children in his time and at their own pace.

Parental guilt issues. Biological parents may feel extremely guilty about their divorce, with both subconsciously wanting to compensate their child for the family breakdown. A noncustodial father may become a "Disney Dad" by buying expensive gifts and making visitations lavish events. A custodial mother may let the child watch television, play video games, and eat junk food more than she would otherwise—all because of parental guilt. Stepparents also may shower the child with gifts and attention to gain favor over the noncustodial parent. But what happens? Parents really are spoiling the child. Children *love* all the extra attention, quickly learning how to play parents against each other to receive more privileges. Result? Overindulged, selfish kids brought into a blended family situation, where extraordinary privileges don't last long. You can predict the reaction! Refuse to let children use you or your remarriage partner. Hold the line and form a united front in all areas.

Blended family anxieties. After losing a biological parent through death or divorce, children will naturally cling to the remaining parent. With a remarriage, they may feel abandoned or resentful as their custodial parents appear to pay more attention to new mates and stepsiblings. Children also may feel the need for more isolation and self-protectiveness as stepsiblings intrude into personal belongings and private space. Obedience to a new, strange stepparent exercising authority where a missing, biological parent used to be a guiding force as well as new rules and unfamiliar household routines can create considerable stress and confusion. Children may long for "how things used to be" before the loss of a parent changed their lives so dramatically. But they also may fear breakup of the new family, complete with trauma and more loss!

This is why friendship dating and prewedding preparation work (chaps. 4–7) are so important in ministering to conflicted children. Take control of this potentially explosive situation. Use family conferences and prayer to encourage evenly paced, sensitive assimilation and cooperation among *all* blended family members.

Stepparent conflicts. Kathleen Fox, a mother of two and stepmother to three others, and author of *Making the Best of Second Best: A Guide to Positive Stepparenting,* provides this candid evaluation of some maternal stepparent relationships:

It's unlikely [that you] . . . will be growing to love your stepchildren exactly the way you love your children. As parents, we have bonds with our children that were first created with their conception. Threads were added to those bonds each time we held them, rejoiced over them, fought with them. We see in their features and characteristics our own, and those of our parents. They are the continuation of our bloodline, the passing down of our heritage. Even during times of conflict, even if we are sometimes different or uncaring as parents, those bonds remain.

When stepchildren come into our lives, of course we don't have the same bonds. How could we? We weren't there when they were born, when they learned to walk, when they spent time in the hospital with pneumonia. We don't know them in the same way we know our own children. And they don't know us. Bonds need to be created between us slowly, over time, as we live together and learn about each other and fight and share.[9]

Some stepparents feel they walk on eggshells in the blended family home to have relationships with their stepchildren. They feel inadequate assuming parenting roles for someone else's children. It's even more challenging if stepchildren are insecure and distrustful of their stepparents. Other conflicts arise if a stepchild's biological parent interferes with a stepparent's relationship with the stepchild. If a stepparent assumes a strong disciplinary role alongside the biological parents too early, it could cause a backlash of resentment from parents and stepchildren. Alternatively, if a stepparent becomes a "good guy" and doormat, stepchildren will lose respect. A stepparent walks a tightrope in trying to parent a stepchild while carefully not replacing biological parents. Each blended family child will be watching all parents carefully for any favoritism among siblings. A stepparent must find an appropriate balance between parenting stepchildren along with his/her biological children.

Take it *slow* —don't try to be SuperStepparent! Be realistic. You may be unable to love all your children and stepchildren equally, much as you desire it. You aren't always going to be absolutely fair in how you treat the children. For sure, you won't always have time and energy for everyone, though you'd like to! So *relax.* Let the children get used to you. Work your way around gently and lovingly. As your unique blended family patterns arise, you'll learn what to do next to meet your family's needs.

Sibling conflicts. As Kathleen Fox asks, "How would you feel if your husband came home one day with another woman—someone you've both known for some time—and said, 'Hi, honey, this is your new sister-wife. She's going to share our bedroom. I told her she could wear your new dress to work tomorrow. Oh, and by the way, please make a copy of your car keys because she'll need to use your car half the time. I'm sure you're going to love each other.' Would you welcome this interloper with enthusiastic warmth? Fat chance. So why should we expect our kids to welcome new stepbrothers and stepsisters?"[10]

When children of microfamilies blend, someone will feel like a loser. A child feeling displaced or disadvantaged may tell his biological parent, "Things were much better before you got remarried! Why can't we have things like they were before?" There will be rivalry, jealousies, and even outright hostility among the blended family siblings.

Most problems arise when parents ask some children in the blended family to make greater adjustments or sacrifices than others, or when there's competition for limited family resources, privileges, toys, or parental attention. To lessen sibling rivalry, emphasize Christian life principles of *empathy, communication, sharing and being other-centered,* and *flexibility* to meet the necessary changes. Give kids private, personal space in the home with clear, consistent boundaries they'll understand and honor. Make it easy for stepsiblings to do things everyone enjoys together. (Don't push too hard—let them think it's their idea. Make suggestions and open up possibilities for them to pursue.) Also apply household rules fairly and evenly, making each child feel accepted. Eliminate anything creating a root of jealousy or bitterness, or causing sibling conflicts. *Don't compare kids or label them—positively or negatively!* This only promotes competition and insecurity. Instead, emphasize how the Lord created each child differently and uniquely, and rejoice in their individual achievements. "Everyone, Caroline got a B on her big math test. Let's all go out and celebrate!" "Ben, you look great in that new suit. Let's get a picture!" Let each child know that he/she is equally precious to both remarriage partners. Above all, reaffirm "We're all in this family together," and deal promptly and decisively with any divisiveness.

The good news is you *don't* have to referee every child fight! Let kids try to resolve their conflicts among themselves first. Each child needs to learn how to be personally assertive and live in a blended family without getting stepped on or having constant parent protection. When intervention becomes necessary, remain neutral and listen to both sides as an impartial mediator. If the kids are upset and yelling at each other, give a time-out in separate rooms to help them cool down. Then help the children create options for conflict resolution together, to learn how to handle similar situations.

Realistically, most stepsiblings *won't* feel close during the early years of blended family life because while they share in common the remarriage of their parents, that's just not enough to promote intimacy. Bonding takes time. But they'll learn to love each other as they negotiate conflicts, adjust, and compromise. Eventually, they'll accept and appreciate one another as they share rooms, toys, pets, and other personal aspects of their lives. The key to bridging the gap is to keep the siblings talking and praying with each other—individually, at family gatherings, and in family conferences.

Child sexual conflicts. An only child coming into a blended family faces daily living with brother(s) and sister(s), or two sisters suddenly may find their mother's remarriage partner bringing his two boys into the family home. Teenagers of different sexes, only coming to grips with their own sexuality, may find themselves attracted to their stepsiblings or alternatively push them away to deal with those feelings. Some may feel sexual attraction to a stepparent. Children may see stepparents becoming affectionate with biological parents in ways never seen during the prior marriage, creating jealousy or confusion. And unfortunately, stepparents can experience attraction to their stepchildren. Result? More potential misunderstandings and conflicts unless remarriage partners *actively manage* their household, stressing Christian values of modesty and avoiding temptation, boundaries, and good communication. These situations all demand separation and guidance on how to deal with each other— especially matters of sexual differences.

Let's sort the issues. First, it's good for all children in the blended family to see a tender and loving relationship between remarriage partners. It may be difficult for children to accept initially, but they'll adjust more quickly if you and your mate do everything possible to help your child feel loved and secure.

Living spaces should have sexually appropriate boundaries, supported by house rules against any sexually provocative behavior—especially among teenagers. Everyone should wear robes or casual clothes, not undergarments around the house— especially in and out of bathrooms. Always have kids (other than infants) shower or bathe privately behind closed (and locked) doors. Each blended family member needs to be on guard, and resist, any obvious sexual advances. Cuddling, hugging, and even limited roughhousing may be OK from time to time, but not if it carries any sexual overtones. If you or your mate find it difficult to maintain loving and caring, but nonsexual, relationships among your children, seek counseling help without delay.

Dealing with child manipulation: You'd be a rare parent if you didn't hear these words come from your children at least once: "I don't like this arrangement. Change it, or I'm going to go live with Dad!" What a heartbreaking dilemma for a parent still feeling vulnerable in custody disputes with an ex-spouse! But you and your remarriage partner must remain strong and *united* against this threat, not giving way to this manipulation. Often, the threat's an empty one anyway.

Obviously, the child's threat grabs for power, but without understanding how destructive this tactic can be to the entire blended family. Therefore it's important to *educate* the child, lovingly (with tough love, if necessary) and sensitively, while hanging tough against any manipulation. The child must know from you and your mate in a calm, but firm manner: (a) children aren't in charge—we are; (b) no one makes unilateral decisions affecting our family—especially serious ones like this; and (c) there are limits to how far we can go with this matter—limits we fully intend to enforce if necessary. *Don't* allow your family to cater to this child or appease him/her by easing discipline or compromising family values and household rules. Continue to do the right thing for your family in general and your child in particular.

All parents need total *unity* in dealing with this situation. Ideally, remarriage partners have a cooperative relationship with the ex-spouse and have his/her full support as well. Nothing will have a more positive impact on stopping this manipulation than having the noncustodial parent tell the child, "No, it's not a good time for you to come live with me. You need to work out your problems in your own home." Talk about the problem with the noncustodial parent, and ask for him/her to back up your decision. Stress that joining this united front is in the child's best interest. If the ex-spouse doesn't cooperate, you and your mate must deal prayerfully with the circumstances alone, as the Lord guides you.

If the child's a teenager, you might want to use some tough love. Call the child's bluff: "If you really believe moving in with your father is what you need to do, we won't stop you. Remember, this isn't our desire or decision, but yours. We love you very much, but we cannot compromise our family values and principles to cave into manipulation. If you believe this is God's plan for your life, you can go whenever you want. If you need help moving out, just ask." Often, this is a wake-up call to the child that you mean business and the manipulation failed.

Above all, maintain your dependence on God's guidance, integrity, and self-respect. Other family members, watching how you handle situations, will see Christian values at work in your life and role model.

PREPARING A WORKABLE COPARENTING PLAN FOR YOUR CHILDREN

During the latter half of the twentieth century, as divorce rates increased, many courts and legislatures believed divorced spouses should separate, limiting further contact with each other and (as to noncustodial spouses) their children. But research by noted child expert Dr. Judith Wallerstein and others confirms that the impact of divorce is much more significant than originally thought. Many judges now affirm important public policy favoring continuation of children's contact with *both* biological parents. (Commendably, courts and legislatures also are realizing they *aren't* the best candidates to determine how best to parent your children!)

Research confirms that divorced parents are more considerate of their children's best interests when determining parental arrangements if they know how courts decide issues affecting their children and if they can provide meaningful input and make personal decisions about their children's welfare. So more states are looking for written parenting plans from parents, showing thoughtful and responsible provision for their children. A coparenting plan generally outlines how biological parents (and stepparents) will share parenting responsibilities and time with their children.

Coparenting plans make good sense. They help all parents—biological and stepparents—*cooperate* in coparenting their children with certainty and fewer surprises (the greatest source of conflict among ex-spouses). A coparenting plan reduces a child's loyalty conflicts between parents, enhances flexibility, and allows for addition of stepparents in parenting decisions. Most importantly, having both parents (*and* stepparents) coparenting sends a very positive message of unity and security to children.

Coparenting plan goals. Your coparenting plan should have at least three primary goals: (1) *unity* in coparenting a child so he/she receives a clear, consistent message from all parental figures; (2) *leading* each child by modeling a good example rather than forcing them to do things (which usually only results in driving children away);

and (3) backing up your words with *consistent,* loving action. Let your children know that you keep your promises and do what you say. Also use tough love, allowing a child to feel the pinch of the logical consequences of his/her *own* decisions.

Elements of a workable coparenting plan. It should include: (1) a role description of each biological parent (and stepparent); (2) an outline of parental decision making and responsibility (including discipline of children); (3) procedures for sharing of information and access to children; (4) methods for resolving conflicts and discipline; (5) educational, social, and religious involvement; (6) daily scheduling; (7) vacation, birthday, and holiday planning; (8) visitation by, and integration of, noncustodial parents and extended family members; (9) family relocation contingencies; and (10) financial planning.

1. *Parental roles.* You, your ex-spouse, and your respective remarriage partners have a God-given assignment to love and raise your children with the nurture and admonition of the Lord. This means modeling Christ in your attitudes and actions, and putting your children's interests above your own (Phil. 4). Ideally, parents will support and encourage each other—not because they like each other but because it's in their children's best interest. You may not want your ex-spouse to have much contact with your child, but he/she will always be the biological parent. Your child needs that contact to develop into a mature, secure adult. So work with your ex-spouse for your child's benefit. Your remarriage partner also may struggle with role adjustments, discipline, and loving your child, but he/she can accept this role in your child's life. Why? Because your partner loves you and wants what's best for your child. The bottom line for sorting out parental roles is this: What's in the child's best interest before God? Parental *cooperation,* rather than conflict, is what kids need most. All biological parents and stepparents should acknowledge this goal in writing.

2. *Parental decision making and responsibility.* Work out a mutually acceptable arrangement where the custodial parent decides the routine daily matters, such as meals, dress, playtime activities, bedtimes, etc., while keeping the noncustodial parent well informed. Discuss major decisions, like switching schools, surgery, or remarriage, in advance, and if possible, decide them jointly. Parents should agree to use private mediation to resolve major conflicts if they arise, *before* taking any legal action. It's important for each parent to pray that God will grant the necessary insight, patience, and wisdom to do whatever's best for the child. We need yielded and humble hearts, allowing him to make us more Christlike and loving toward our children (and ex-spouses!). This is a vital prerequisite to making any decisions affecting your child. We then have the responsibility to share the wisdom of God with our children and point them in the right direction in life (Eph. 6:4; Prov. 22:6). As part of fulfilling this task, we have the additional responsibility to teach and encourage our children to do what *Jesus* would do in different situations, rather than making selfish decisions. In turn, our children have the God-given responsibility to obey us, as their parents, according to God's standards. Parental responsibility requires being in tune with our children and investing quality *time,* joining in each child's life pursuits at home, school, sports activities, vacations, and family recreational events.

Above all, wrap decisions about children in prayer. Pray that all will understand your children's needs and interests. Ask God to guide your thoughts, words, and actions. Pray to be a good example of Christian living, worthy of imitation. Pray for unity of mind and spirit with stepparents and ex-spouses. Pray your children will think and reflect on their need for God in their lives and turn to him for guidance and strength when facing trials, trouble, or fear. Ask the author of love, grace, and mercy to grant your children humble, compassionate, and forgiving hearts and teachable spirits.

3. *Access and sharing of information.* Most noncustodial parents experience some jealousy and resentment toward ex-spouses and their remarriage partners simply because of child custody. Therefore, it's very important to include the noncustodial parent in the child's life, keeping him/her informed of doctor opinions; dental checkup results; when, how, and why your child was sick; and notify him/her well in advance of planned special events at school or sports activities (see chap. 11). Though you, as a custodial parent, will be taking care of the daily transportation, shopping, consulting, and nursing of your child, give the noncustodial parent frequent opportunities to get involved in any way he/she may be able or inclined.

4. *Conflict resolution.* Before you can resolve conflicts about parenting your children with your ex-spouse and remarriage partner, it's important you face your own anger, hurt, and resentment from the divorce so you can focus fully on parental cooperation. Try to keep personal feelings and attitudes toward your ex-spouse from interfering with issues. Pray! If you and your ex-spouse cannot agree on critical matters involving your children, use biblical conflict resolution measures (chap. 6). Use a mediator—perhaps a stepparent (if he/she has the trust and confidence of both biological parents), a church pastor or elder, or a Christian counselor. Only use court action as a *last* resort (see chap. 11).

Discipline. With all the complexities of postdivorce living, it's easy for parents to forget that their children *need* discipline. Instead, both may try to spoil children: (1) to gain favoritism over the competing parent; and (2) because neither wants to risk losing a child's love. (This is why stepparents can be quite helpful in intervening and giving children what they need—more objective discipline!) But children need age-appropriate boundaries and correction to have stability in their lives. Discipline builds character and teaches children to respect authority, exercise self-control, be considerate of others, and revere God by obeying him. Boundaries let children know what's expected of them. Discipline and boundaries prepare children for the future. Without discipline, our children can feel abandoned by both God and their parents and fall into the trap of destructive self-centeredness and pride.

There also must be a healthy, spiritual *balance* in discipline. Equalize rewards and punishment, undergirding both with consistent, loving encouragement. The Lord entrusts parents with his authority to correct and discipline children. This God-given responsibility includes the necessary disciplinary authority to influence and guide each child properly. Since stepparents share parenting responsibilities, they also have disciplinary *authority* from the Lord, notwithstanding a child's protest, "You're not my father, so I don't have to obey you."

To keep the peace with your ex-spouse, you both may prefer to keep your respective remarriage partners out of disciplining your children for a while. There are some noted experts who recommend this practice during the early years of a remarriage, allowing a stepparent to build a relationship and gain the love, trust, and confidence of a stepchild. But other parenting experts argue against excluding stepparents from discipline. For example, family psychologist and nationally known parenting columnist Dr. John Rosemond (himself a stepchild raised in two blended families) believes children need to understand that once remarriage vows are taken, the stepparent receives full parental responsibilities. Any arguments to the contrary, he asserts, merely protect the ego of an "absent" biological parent and unnecessarily avoid upsetting stepchildren. The real question, Rosemond argues, is whether a remarried couple is going to form a family or become "a single parent with a live-in parenting assistant." He counsels remarried couples this way:

> One of the reasons the failure rate for second marriages, when children are involved, is greater than that of first marriages is the failure of the mother to give her second husband full disciplinary privileges. You cannot be truly married and be a true family until you do. . . . So relax. Be married first and a mom second. By taking the leash off your husband, you take a burden off yourself. The most effective discipline is delivered from within the context of a functional marriage, not from one parent working alone.[11]

Regardless of what you and all other parenting partners of your children believe about this issue, try to cooperate and agree on whatever approach is best for your children and everyone involved.

5. *Educational, social, and religious involvement.* Religious and educational decisions for your children carry some risk of legal complications.[12] One parent wants his/her child to attend secular schools while the other insists on a private religious school or home-schooling. Some argue that home-schooling a child is contrary to the child's best interests. Unfortunately, providing children with a Christian education is no longer risk-free in court. For example, a Montgomery, Pennsylvania, trial court changed custody because the judge disapproved of the father's fundamentalist Christian beliefs and his children's enrollment in Trinity Christian Academy (notwithstanding the Academy's accreditation by the American Association of Christian Schools). The trial judge reasoned:

> On the surface this seems like an ideal adaptation under the circumstances, but it is the degree to which the father has pursued "life in the Lord" that has deprived the children of social and educational opportunities and has presented them with a singleminded approach to life that is very restricted in view and allows for no spontaneity, artistic expression, or individual development of rationale or logic or even just pursuit of ordinary curiosity. These children are being raised

in a sterile world with very rigid precepts, with no allowance for difference of opinion, and no greater breadth than the doctrinaire limits of
the religious beliefs.[13]

It's good to know that the Pennsylvania appellate court disagreed with the trial
judge, finding the "evidence does not disclose that the children's education was deficient in any way." But cases like this serve as a wake-up call to Christians. Use care in
making religious and educational decisions for your children—especially if the other
biological parent raises an objection. Agreeing on these matters in advance as part of
a written coparenting plan helps guard against misunderstandings and conflict later.

6. *Daily scheduling.* While custodial parents have primary responsibility for daily
decisions, it's appropriate for all parents to agree upon the child's typical week schedule. Be sure children aren't overburdened with activities or responsibilities and have
enough free time for flexible visits by the noncustodial parent.

7. *Vacation, birthday, and holiday planning.* Flexibility and compromise are key
factors (see chap. 7).

8. *Visitation with noncustodial parents and extended family members.* Courts are
cutting back grandparent and extended family visitation rights if biological parents
object to their involvement (see chap. 11). But why make this an issue? Unless there
are compelling reasons not to do so, maintain open relationships with all relatives of
your child. Each has something valuable to share that will enhance your child's life.

9. *Family relocation contingencies.* We discuss relocation issues in more detail in
chapter 11. This is a controversial matter with no easy answers for parents or courts!
Again, the key is flexibility and compromise. But a coparenting plan is an excellent
vehicle to brainstorm about contingencies and to plan options and alternatives in
advance—*before* the emotional heat of the moment clouds everyone's judgment.

10. *Financial planning.* A coparenting plan must include a *balanced* budget to
support each child. It should reflect the needs of each child and all other family
members (see chaps. 10 and 11). All parents should shoulder the responsibility of providing for their children, regardless of their financial circumstances. (Although stepparents have no *legal* obligation to subsidize court-ordered child support payments,
they assume support responsibilities before God upon remarriage.) Children
shouldn't suffer economic deprivation, especially while coping with the aftermath of
divorce and blending into a new family. Nor should they have their emotional and
economic well-being threatened by parents arguing about finances.

This child support commitment usually continues until the child legally becomes
an adult.[14] In making child support awards, courts usually consider the *net* income of
both biological parents (as determined separately from any remarriage partner's
income). Some states add both parents' net income together for a combined net
income. Then the court determines each parent's percentage share of child support by
dividing each parent's net income by the combined net income to arrive at a percentage. The court then multiplies the minimum amount of support needed for each child
by each parent's percentage to arrive at a monthly amount. (See *When the Vow Breaks*
for more details.) If you're the parent paying child support, meet your obligations

gladly. You're doing what's right before God. Your children will know that you care about them and will be less likely to harbor ill feelings against you. If you're the parent receiving support, be sure to use the money to benefit the child entitled to it, and let the paying parent know exactly how the money is used.

Coparenting plans are excellent tools for helping divorced spouses and their remarriage partners raise children coming from broken homes into blended family situations. But we still need to ask the question . . .

How Do Stepparents Fit into the Blended Family Puzzle?

When you remarry, you fully expect your remarriage partner will be exactly that—*your partner,* a role including most, if not all, decisions affecting any or all children in your family. The Lord grants scripturally remarried couples with this authority and responsibility. *But civil law doesn't view stepparents as fully empowered parents.*

Until the 1960s and the rapid rise in divorce rates, stepfamilies arose primarily following the death of a parent. The widowed survivor would remarry. The remarriage partner would adopt his/her stepchildren, thereby becoming a full-fledged parent. Such *isn't* the case for a remarriage partner wed to a divorced spouse. The key difference? The continuing presence of a child's biological, noncustodial parent. The stepparent takes a legal seat lower than biological parents, having legal status comparable to a child's grandparent or extended family member.

Courts and legislatures are extremely reluctant to grant rights involving children to third parties as long as both biological parents are fit and involved in their children's lives. The U.S. Supreme Court firmly recognized this basic constitutional principle in the 1923 landmark case *Meyer v. Nebraska,*[15] confirming each American's right "to marry, establish a home and bring up children" as a "liberty" guaranteed by the Fourteenth Amendment to the U.S. Constitution. Therefore, traditionally, a child's biological mother and father (assuming fitness) have the right to care and custody of their child. This holds true even in instances when others (such as a stepparent) have exercised some control over the child with the consent of either, or both, parents.

Legal concerns affecting stepparents and stepchildren. Because the law doesn't fully empower stepparents on a par equal to biological parents, stepparents don't have the *legal* status or authority necessary to fully parent their stepchildren. (Remember, this is civil law—not necessarily how God views the situation!) Beyond legal requirements for marriage, most state laws don't provide any uniform or clear definitions of a stepparent's rights or obligations. In fact, many state laws uniformly *terminate* a stepparent's relationship with his/her stepchild immediately upon death of, or divorce from, the biological parent. In instances of divorce, this means that obligations to support the stepchild, if there were any at all, immediately end as well. The stepparent also has no rights to visitation or custody of the stepchild, notwithstanding that the stepparent may have lived with and parented the stepchild for most of his/her natural life.[16] Who suffers most from these legal restraints? The stepchild.

Practical problems affecting stepparents. Since stepparents have limited legal authority over stepchildren, many logistical problems arise. For example, if your child needs emergency medical treatment, your remarriage partner may not have the legal authority to consent to this treatment in your absence (and that of the noncustodial biological parent as well). Also, your remarriage partner may have no legal way to prevent a court-ordered custody change to your ex-spouse upon your death, regardless of this stepparent's bond with your child and mutual desire to continue living together. You can give your remarriage partner a durable family power of attorney to act on your behalf and consent to matters involving your child in *your* place. But there's not much else a stepparent can do for your child in circumstances where only a legal parent can act. Keep this important matter in mind as you plan and decide your blended family's future with your remarriage partner.

Adoption alternative. One way for a stepparent to gain full, permanent parental rights is through adoption (discussed below), but that occurs only with consent of *both* biological parents. If a biological parent doesn't consent, there are very limited legal ways to have his/her parental rights terminated so an adoption can proceed. These include being an "unfit" parent because of abandoning the child; neglecting or abusing the child; being convicted of a felony making the parent unfit; being incapable of supporting the child because of developmental disability, mental illness, or mental disability (as portrayed in the 2002 movie *i am sam*); or disability due to alcohol, drug abuse, or moral depravity. But this is a very difficult legal procedure and most likely will be traumatic for the stepchild.

SHOULD YOUR REMARRIAGE PARTNER ADOPT YOUR CHILD?

Adoption means assuming legal, economic, emotional, physical, and spiritual parental responsibility for a child belonging to another biological parent. Although accurate data is difficult to obtain, perhaps 50 percent or more of the approximate 150,000 adoptive families formed each year are by stepparents or relatives parenting children who aren't their biological offspring.

Adoption of children after remarriage carries with it some spiritual implications for Christians. Pharaoh's daughter adopted Moses (Exod. 2:1–10). Although it certainly was a bittersweet event for his biological parents, we now know that God used this event as part of his marvelous plan for delivering Israel from Egyptian captivity. When her parents died, Mordecai adopted young Esther (Esther 2:7). As Christians, *we* also are adopted as God's sons and daughters through Jesus Christ (Eph. 1:5). We aren't slaves, but ones who received the Spirit of sonship (adoption), through whom we cry, "Abba, Father" (Rom. 8:15). By redeeming us from the Law of Moses, he graciously gives us full rights as sons and daughters—his heirs (Gal. 4:3–7)! So the whole concept of adoption has special meaning for Christian stepparents desiring to formalize their relationships with their stepchildren.

Unfortunately, some remarriage partners feel the selfish temptation to sever a noncustodial biological parent's ties to a child in a rather underhanded way through adoption so they can form a blended family without baggage from the past. Here's how it happens: Father and mother divorce. Mother and daughter live together, and may move several times. Father's visitation with daughter is sporadic. Father's child support payments may be inconsistent. Mother doesn't receive full support, becomes frustrated, and begins making visitation by father difficult. Mother remarries husband no. 2. Mother asks father to permit husband no. 2 to adopt daughter. As an incentive, mother tells father that he won't have to pay any more child support if he consents to daughter's adoption. Father reluctantly agrees since child support is a burden and visitation wars are a regular hassle. This is a "back door" legal way to receive a biological parent's consent to a stepparent adoption, but in essence, the biological parent is being bought off. Is this morally right before God? Is this truly in the child's best interest? Many don't think so!

Legal developments in family adoptions. A majority of states still recognize a legal presumption known as the "Parental Rights Doctrine" (also known as the "natural parent" preference) in dealing with child custody disputes between a child's biological parents and other individuals who have loved and cared for the child. This doctrine presumes that a fit biological parent, rather than a nonbiological parent (such as a stepparent), is best able to raise a child.[17]

The Parental Rights Doctrine is centuries old, from Roman times when the law viewed children as "property" of their fathers. The biological parents, simply because of a genetic link, had a superior right to determine what's best for their offspring over claims by anyone else. The doctrine worked well to protect families from fragmentation resulting from governmental intrusion and arbitrary removal of children.

Some courts apply the Parental Rights Doctrine in favor of fit biological parents having a true family relationship with their child under these basic circumstances: (1) a biological relationship between parent and child; (2) an intact marriage relationship; and (3) an active, emotional, and psychological involvement in the daily activities of raising the child. But since some of these elements don't apply in post-divorce situations, judges are questioning whether this doctrine should apply.

In recent years, child-care experts also have questioned the heavy-handed nature of the Parental Rights Doctrine—especially if a biological parent has little or no involvement in a child's life. In fact, the child may have bonded to a stepparent or other parental figure caring for the child on a daily basis. Many legal experts refer to this caregiver individual as a "psychological parent."[18]

Obviously the Parental Rights Doctrine becomes a major problem in instances where the biological parent has played no significant role in the child's physical and emotional development over time. During that same period, the child has viewed a "psychological parent" as a "real" parent. If a biological parent wants custody of the child, it could mean destruction of an interactive, loving family that truly meets the child's needs. The doctrine, when legalistically applied, really devalues the mutual love and respect developed between a child and a psychological parent, and demotes that person to nothing more than a "makeshift stand-in" despite the individual's active parenting of the child. Here the law's bias toward a biological parent's blood ties, as opposed to the loving and nurturing relationship between a child and a psychological parent, doesn't work very well. Often it leads to harsh, tragic results, dramatically affecting a child's welfare.

Now, however, most states require a valid consent from *both* biological parents for adoption by a stepparent or "psychological parent," unless the biological parent declining to consent is judicially declared to be "unfit" or that parent's consent has been dispensed with for a recognized legal reason under a valid state law.[19] While the Parental Rights Doctrine remains the predominant legal precedent affecting custodial decisions and adoptions of children, however, it's clearly eroding. More courts are considering what circumstances might justify a legal determination that a biological parent is unfit, thereby clearing the way for a psychological parent to adopt *without* consent of the biological parent, based upon the following factors:

- the length of time a child has been with the prospective adoptive parents.
- the strength of the attachment between the child and the prospective adoptive parents.
- the relative stability of the child's future with the biological parent and with the prospective adoptive parents.
- the sincerity of the biological parent's desire to parent the child.
- the age of the child when care is assumed by the adoptive parents.
- the emotional effect of the adoption on the child.
- abandonment by the biological parent, either before or after the child's birth.
- failure to support or visit the child.

The bottom line in adoption is that children cannot put their lives (and hearts) on hold while adults bicker about who'll be the better parent. Any adoption decision needs to be finalized promptly, to avoid hurting the child emotionally. If a non-custodial biological parent won't consent to adoption by a stepparent, it's wise not to press the issue any further.

THE NAME GAME

One typical scenario arises when an ex-wife tries to change a child's surname to the mother's maiden name. Courts acknowledge that changing a child's name so he/she no longer bears the name of the child's father is a serious matter undertaken only when it's in the child's best interest.[20] One parent's desire, or customary practices in renaming children, generally aren't legally sufficient reasons for change.

Many child psychologists believe it important for all children in a family to have the same last name. They're concerned that a child with a different name may feel guilty, or perceive the difference as a handicap. So they recommend changing a child's name to match the same family surname. But other experts believe a name change causes estrangement from the child's natural father and takes away the child's freedom to use two different names in two different households, depending upon custodial living arrangements and visitation.

In 1995 the nation watched in horror at just one such parental conflict over a name change for a three-year-old child in Pennsylvania. Karen Deremer decided to call her son Scott, "Scott Deremer" rather than "Scott Gubernat" with the surname of his father, Alan Gubernat. They battled the issue out in court. The trial court stated: "[A] father's desire to have . . . someone carry on his name is proper. It's a right that a father has." So Scott Thomas Deremer became Scott Thomas Gubernat . . . until May 11, 1995, when a unanimous New Jersey Supreme Court held that the name selected by the custodial mother is presumed to be in the child's best interest and will be upheld, in absence of evidence to the contrary. In so ruling, the court found that the "historical justifications that once supported a tradition . . . for children to bear paternal surnames have been overtaken by society's recognition of full legal equality for women." The court also added: "The love of the parent, and not the name of the parent, is the cohesive (sic) that binds parent and child."[21] Result? Scott's name went back to "Deremer," as his mother intended.

Scott's father seemed to accept this decision. Since he supported his son and had visitation rights, it seemed to be no problem when the father picked up his son for a family gathering on the following Sunday (Mother's Day) after the court's decision. But this time things were different. Distraught, Alan Gubernat took his son up to a second-floor bedroom in the father's home and surrounded him with toys carefully inscribed with "Scotty Gubernat 1995." He then shot the boy and himself. In the aftermath, Gubernat's lawyer reflected on the tragedy, saying, "I think the Supreme Court decision was one element, the straw that broke the camel's back. . . . I think [Gubernat] felt the relationship with the child was slipping away from him, and he had nowhere to turn." The attorney also noted that Gubernat disliked personal depictions as a "male chauvinist" for wanting his son to have his name. In fact, Gubernat had offered to compromise with his son's mother, willing to give the boy a hyphenated name, but the mother allegedly refused.[22]

Changing a child's name can bring powerfully tragic reactions from parents. This is why it's vital that biological parents communicate and remain flexible with each other when walking over such emotional ground. Legally, when a state has statutory procedures for changing names, it's prudent to follow these procedures rather than unilaterally changing a child's surname.[23] Again, private mediation could be a valuable resource for exploring options and compromises to resolve conflicts—especially since litigation only fuels the fire of bitterness and resentment.

Legal considerations. To determine whether name changes are in a child's best interest, courts review the following factors:
- the effect of the change on the preservation and development of the child's relationship with each parent.
- the identification of the child as part of a family unit.
- the length of time a child has used a surname.
- the child's preference, if he/she is of sufficient maturity to express a meaningful preference.

- whether the child's surname is different from that of the child's primary residential parent.
- the embarrassment, discomfort, or inconvenience that may result when a child bears a surname different from that of the primary residential parent.
- parental failure to maintain contact with, and support of, the child.
- any other factor relevant to the child's interest.[24]

Child identity issues. Generally, very young children aren't really aware of identity issues. If so, changing the child's name is less traumatic. One factor in keeping a child's given birthname arises when everyone in the child's life knows him/her by that surname.

Timing. It's less traumatic to change a child's name before beginning grade school, when the child's name becomes known and used by peers and other adults.

Use hyphenated or affectionate names. Culture's important here. For example, it's customary for Hispanic parents to use compound or hyphenated names. This may be a way to keep everyone happy. Rather than get into potential conflicts over names, or whether a child should call his/her stepparent "Mom" or "Dad," why not use an entirely different approach? Since Chase was very young when Cheryl and I married, we became "the Doggy Family," primarily because Chase's favorite toy was a little stuffed dog. I became "Daddy Doggy," Cheryl "Mommy Doggy," and Chase (you guessed it) "Baby Doggy." We loved this endearing little game, especially since it helped us address each other in disarming ways that didn't upset Chase's father.

Keep matters simple. Listen for your children's preferences in how they feel most comfortable addressing parental figures. Be flexible and accept their preferred names in the blended family home, as long as they show proper respect for everyone concerned. Stepparents shouldn't be ashamed of having their stepchildren introduce them as children choose.

WHAT ABOUT HAVING MORE CHILDREN?

Many parents entering into remarriage, particularly those with older children, may not want to have any more children. A childless partner, however, may desperately want to have children of his/her own. For many women in this position, they can empathize with Rachel's plea to Jacob—"Give me children or I'll die" (Gen. 30:1)! This can create a classic catch-22 dilemma for the childless remarriage partner—does he/she put pressure on a mate to have more children and risk resentment and bitterness in one's beloved? Would it be better to forego having children and remain personally unfulfilled in experiencing childbirth? This isn't an easy problem to solve!

Cheryl and I faced this challenge early. Cheryl prayed for years to have a child. Chase's birth, occurring just before her divorce, answered her prayers. After the divorce Cheryl devoted her full attention to parenting Chase. Being a single mother, she released the thought of having more children. Meanwhile, I came into our remarriage with the hope of having children with Cheryl—especially to bless Chase with a brother or sister he dearly wanted. Cheryl was reluctant at first, but willing to let the Lord lead. We received our answer from him. We weren't able to conceive a child naturally. Disappointed, we tried invitro fertilization and actually received two embryos, but they lived only a few days. Since we prayed and tried every available resource to have biological children without success, we accepted the Lord's will for us. With glad hearts, we now rejoice in giving Chase our full attention (as does he!).

Your story may be different. A child born into a blended family is such a wonderful event! This little one is the first common genetic and historical link to *everyone* in the family, being the biological child of the remarried couple and a half-brother or half-sister to all of the couple's other children. The child may be living proof to his/her siblings that the parents are committed to staying together and parenting the entire family. But a birth may not be welcome to everyone. Jealous siblings may see the baby as a competitor for parental attention. Overjoyed parents may feed this jealousy upon seeing their physical characteristics reproduced in this child and feeling the sense of fulfillment he/she represents. The best remedy? Make sure *all* children receive enough time, attention, praise, and love, reinforcing the message, "We're becoming even more *united* as a blended family. Praise God!"

TRAINING A BLENDED FAMILY CHILD TO GROW AND GO

After death or divorce of a spouse, we must parent our children without the daily teamwork we once shared. Upon remarriage, our new mates may not fill all the holes left by the absent spouse/parent. What's the best approach to help our kids grow through the emotional roller-coaster ride we've experienced?

"Train a child in the way he should go, and when he is old he will not turn from it" (Prov. 22:6). This is much more than memorizing Scripture and perfect attendance at Sunday school. It means loving discipline. It's patiently taking enough time to *know* a child, individually and intimately. It means pruning a child's tender leaves at every opportunity, helping him/her work through pitfalls in life. Notice the verse says we're to train up the child in the way *he* (or she) should go—not necessarily where we, as parents, decide we want the child to go. God has made each child unique and complex. He's made a way for this child to go in his/her own search for a personal relationship with himself. This may not follow our path. It may not be the way of our ex-spouse or our parents. Other children who turned out well may march to a different drummer. We are to seek *our* child's way—the way best for him/her.

Cheryl, Chase, and I frequently vacation in Juno Beach, Florida, right on the beach fronting the Atlantic Ocean. It's such a beautiful patch of God's earth, with crystal clear waters in wonderful hues of turquoise. It's no wonder that this stretch of sand has been a favorite nesting place for many sea turtles, despite encroaching developments along the shore. We love to watch the enormous "momma turtles" lumber slowly out of the water late at night. These turtles exercise tremendous strength in paddling uphill through the sand before digging out a hole to lay their eggs and return, exhausted, to the sea. But this event's a double blessing! A few months later, the eggs hatch, and the sand over the nest bubbles and boils as dozens of little turtles fight their way to the surface. Then they instinctively begin their long march to the sea and new life. Seeing these little critters sashay down the beach with their tiny flippers working so hard makes anyone want to step in and help them out by carrying them to the water. But that's the *worst* thing to do! Why? Because God created these creatures to struggle through the sand *before* hitting the water so they would build up enough strength to live in the sea. Without this vital new life exercise, the baby turtles have a much lower chance of survival. And so it's true with our own children as well! Without letting our children struggle through some of life's problems, they may lack the preparation necessary to meet life's challenges.

Our children are running the race of life. They'll fall down and get beat up at times. They'll lose races. They'll stumble on life's hurdles. But we parents serve our children best by nurturing and encouraging them to finish *their* race, difficult though it may be! What's our most important parenting role? "He who fears the LORD has a secure fortress, and for his children it will be a refuge" (Prov. 14:26). Our children need to see God in our lives. Parents who continually model praise and thanksgiving to our loving God in an active prayer life make their mark in a child's eyes. Children need to see each parent's life confidently pointed into the future with clear purpose and direction. Then they'll crave the sweet fruit that only the Spirit can offer—love, joy, peace, patience, kindness, goodness, faithfulness, gentleness, and self-control (Gal. 5:22–23). Putting these principles into practice is the best legacy we can leave to our children as part of any remarriage.

A Message from Cheryl

Perhaps no role in life calls for more unselfish sacrifice than that of stepparent. The natural parental role requires *daily* unselfish giving to your children, but it's easier to do because they're *your* children. Although a stepparent accepts this same responsibility in remarriage, I believe it's more challenging because he/she doesn't have the same natural inclination at times. A stepparent's efforts may be hindered somewhat as he/she encounters the effects of long-term parenting mistakes of others.

Children also need to know the truth about their parents, but in age-appropriate doses. I believe it's important to shelter them from as much hurt and conflict as possible until they're ready to handle it.

I clearly remember the evening I was bathing little Chase a few years after my divorce, when our conversation went just so: "Mommy, why can't I have a brother?" "Well, Chase," I replied, "Mommy isn't married. You can't have a baby when you aren't married." He paused and thought for a moment. "But Mommy," he countered with a big smile, "you had *me!*" "Oh, but Mommy was married when I had you!" "You were?" he asked with a perplexed look, "Who were you married to?" "Chase, don't you know?" Thinking for a moment more, he asked, "Aunt Juli?" Now I sensed Chase was ready to learn a little more about his history. "No, dear," I explained, "I was married for eight years to your daddy." He didn't stop there. "But why didn't you stay married, Mommy?" (Ah, the defining question! But what does *he* need to know now?) "Well, Chase, you know sometimes people make bad decisions? Well, your daddy made some very bad decisions and we couldn't stay married. Later, he asked me to forgive him, and I did."

This conversation stayed with Chase. When Warren and I were making our plans to remarry, we found Chase terrified of another divorce. We felt it would increase his concerns if he knew Warren also had been divorced years earlier. Yet, he did need to know the truth at the appropriate time. As years passed, and Chase became more secure, the Lord presented the perfect opportunity to turn a great hurt into a great lesson of faith.

When he was eight years old, Chase and I were discussing how God works in our lives. Our conversation went something like this: "Chase, I have a story to tell you. There was a man who loved his wife very much. He wanted to stay married forever, and *very* much wanted children. One day his wife told him, 'I don't want to be married anymore.' He was very sad, and tried for two years to change her mind. But she left him alone. He was in his old house with no wife, no children, and no family. He was so sad. He cried, and prayed that God would send him a family. Well, years later he met a nice woman in another city whom he began to love. And guess what, Chase . . . she had a beautiful little boy! The man loved the little boy so much. He was the child he never had but always wanted. The boy brought great joy to the man. And the three of them got married and lived happily ever after. The man then had a wife *and* a beautiful son. The son also had a daddy at home, and his mother had a good husband." Chase listened carefully, and asked, "Is that a true story, Mom?" "Yes it is, Chase," I reassured him, "and you know this man too!" "Wow! That's such a happy ending!" he replied, "But who's the man, Mom?" Well . . . you know the rest.

Our greatest grief can become a lesson of God's goodness and security. Let him work in your life and the lives of your blended family members as well!

QUESTIONS FOR PERSONAL REFLECTION

1. Has each of my children adequately coped with grief over a deceased or divorced parent? How about the children of my remarriage partner?

2. Is there anything my mate and I are doing that could adversely affect the current child custody orders of our children? *(Be sure to check with your attorney about these important matters* before *you take any action!)*

3. Have I prepared a coparenting plan with my ex-spouse? What revisions do we need to make to include my remarriage partner in parenting my children?

4. Specifically, how have my remarriage partner and I prepared our children for blended family life? What difficulties have we encountered? How have we resolved these problems?

5. Do we desire to have more children as part of our remarriage? What plans have we made in this regard? What impact will this have on our existing children?

6. How have we kept our children focused and growing in their individual relationships with the Lord? How could we work together better in encouraging their spiritual growth?

Chapter 10

REMARRIAGE FINANCES
Planning for a Family Merger,
Not a Hostile Takeover

*Money. Its power is exceeded only by its controversy. What should
our attitude be toward money? How do we account for "yours,
mine, and ours" in remarriage?*

Surveys and polls confirm it. Money—more than sex, children, or in-laws—is the
most common source of conflict among America's married couples.[1] Divorcees cite
financial disputes in 50 percent of the divorces in America. You may think these statistics come from financially strapped couples. Not so!

Most marital money issues arise in three areas: (a) accountability for expenses,
(b) honesty in handling a financial situation, and (c) different expectations in managing money.[2] The *compelling* problem underlying each of these hot issue areas?
Corrupted *attitudes* toward money and how to use it—we simply *love* money too
much!

Money is a tool, and a symbol, in society. It means different things to different
people, but to many it can be a metaphor for power and control. Men generally measure worth by income. Consequently, husbands may feel they're entitled to make the
financial decisions. As the old Yiddish proverb says, "Those with the pay have the say!"
But that's not God's way!

You and your beloved *will* have very different money attitudes and viewpoints,
many of which aren't readily apparent. Family backgrounds, culture, peers, and emotional concerns all contribute to one's monetary belief system. Parental fiscal habits
particularly influence a child's monetary policy, which he/she carries into adulthood
and marriage. Many single parents struggle valiantly to survive after death or divorce
of a spouse. (Studies show, in the year following a divorce, a woman's income plum-
mets by 25 to 45 percent.) So, after successfully digging themselves out of this monetary Grand Canyon, *they never again want to lose financial security.* Result? Many
formerly married women may come into remarriage inclined toward defensiveness

and suspicion—unable to trust a new husband fully with family finances. Each person's life experience uniquely affects their financial mind-set for years to come.

Even "money personalities" clash and create conflicts. Some years ago, University of Minnesota financial psychologist Ken Doyle outlined four classic personality types: (1) the *analytic person*, for whom money means control; (2) the *expressive person*, for whom money means esteem; (3) the *driven person*, for whom money means competence; and (4) the *amiable person*, for whom money means affection. Try putting an analytic person with a mate who's expressive and watch the sparks fly! As Doyle explains it, "It's the case of an accountant married to an entertainer. The accountant says, 'Don't you have any concept of earning and saving?' and the entertainer says, 'Loosen up! You're driving me crazy!'"[3]

Gender differences play a significant role as well. Typically, men tend to be rather noncommunicative about finances. They confidently make independent money decisions and revel in the power and prestige it brings. Women generally desire sharing and exploring money decisions with others as part of emotional bonding with their partners and advisors. Men are more likely to read financial journals, believe they have adequate financial resources, and prefer selecting their own investments. Women are more likely to believe getting rich isn't a realistic investment goal, consider stock investments too risky, and seek help with their finances.

Soon after remarriage, it isn't unusual to see spouses polarize, as each mate becomes increasingly uncomfortable or critical of the other's spending (or nonspending) mind-set. They fail to appreciate and understand their different backgrounds and financial personalities. Instead of exploring ways to *combine* their individual strengths, they harp on their perceived weaknesses. Rather than sharing and assessing their respective talents and needs, they clam up.

If you want to avoid problems with your beloved, it's critical that you and your partner evaluate how family backgrounds, money personalities, gender differences, and other personal factors influence each other *before* remarriage. *You and your partner must talk out these money issues.* Ask each other pointed questions: How was money treated in your childhood home? How did that affect you? What's your approach to using credit? What debts do you currently owe? To some spouses growing up in poverty, money can be a constant source of survival anxiety and fear. For those from a wealthier background, it's very natural to have a relaxed attitude about spending. The key for future financial success or conflict in remarriage is each partner's *attitude* about money.

FINANCIAL HARMONY BEGINS WITH THE RIGHT SPIRITUAL ATTITUDE

Consider the apostle Paul's warning in 1 Timothy 6:10: "For the love of money is a root of all kinds of evil. Some people, eager for money, have wandered from the faith and pierced themselves with many griefs." It's *not* money that's the problem, but our *love* of it. It's making accumulation of money an end in itself, rather than using it as a tool to provide for our families and those less fortunate.

What's our attitude problem with money? We want it because we think having lots of money will satisfy all of our needs and desires. We believe it'll fulfill our desire for power, significance, and self-gratification. But it never does. Why? Because real satisfaction only comes from being right with God. As Paul warns us: "But you, man of God, flee from all this, and pursue righteousness, godliness, faith, love, endurance and gentleness" (1 Tim. 6:11). Life-fulfilling satisfaction comes from enjoying the fruits of God's blessings that money cannot buy—love, joy, peace, patience, kindness, goodness, gentleness, and self-control (Gal. 5:22–23). It comes from seeking *God's* kingdom *first,* rather than running after the things of this world (Matt. 6:25–34).

Wealth and possessions distort our priorities in life. In 1997 the *London Mirror* described Queen Elizabeth II and some royal family members this way: "The Queen's eyes were glassy and she appeared to struggle with her emotions. . . . The Princess Royal [Anne] dabbed her eyes with a handkerchief, and the Prince of Wales [Charles] shook his head. It was the most remarkable display of feelings in her 45-year reign," said the paper, quoting a palace official as saying, "[The Queen] has never shown such emotion in public before."[4] You might assume that the royal family was reminiscing about the late Princess Diana. Not so! The tears welled up and emotion brewed over the retirement of the royal yacht, *Britannia.* The often-quoted proverb still rings true: "Possessions weigh me down in life, I never feel quite free. I don't know if I own my things . . . or if my things own me!"

Money attitudes also impact our family lives. *Spy Magazine* once published a very politically incorrect child's guide to the economic status of one's family this way: "If your father comes home from work at 4:30, you're lower middle class. If your father comes home at 5:30, you're middle class. If your father comes home at 6:30, you're upper middle class. If your father never comes home at all, you're rich. If your father never leaves home, you're poor."[5] Sadly, this humorous analysis isn't too far from the truth!

Why is it such a problem to want more money? Because, as Jesus says: "No one can serve two masters. Either he will hate the one and love the other, or he will be devoted to the one and despise the other. You cannot serve both God and money" (Matt. 6:24). Our hearts and minds can become so divided that we're ineffective and unproductive, forgetting what life's all about. Furthermore, it's foolish to spend our lives collecting money and possessions. Why? Because it tears us away from loving the Lord and our families. We *worry* about it constantly! As Jesus points out in Matthew 6:19, our possessions will wear out, rust out, or be taken out by thieves. The time, effort, and worry about what we own immobilize us and make us hostages to circumstances.

What should our attitude be toward money? A right attitude comes from trusting and believing that God will give us what we need (not necessarily what we *want*) if we put him first in our lives (Matt. 6:33). It also comes from knowing our roles and responsibilities. As stewards or trustees receiving wealth and possessions as God's *blessings,* we have personal responsibility to use these resources for *his* glory (not ours). What should our attitude be? Loving *people* and using *things,* rather than the other way around. Remarriage partners need to strive for *oneness* in financial matters by thinking of how to lovingly and responsibly provide for each blended family member's needs. We need to use God's Word not only as a plumb line to build our financial house as God intends but also as a spiritual scalpel to cut through any impure thoughts and attitudes of our hearts. If you or your beloved desire self-protection more than self-denial, then spare yourselves great anguish—*don't* remarry! A sacrificial *unity* in Christ and with each other is what makes for successful remarriages. Without it, you risk becoming another grim statistic.

INVENTORYING OUR BLESSINGS AND RESPONSIBILITIES

Who blesses us with *all* we have? Of course, it's the Lord. Not only that, but God gives us the *ability* to produce wealth (Deut. 8:18). Since it all really belongs to God and we're only *stewards* of his bounty, we need to ask ourselves what, if any, boundaries belong among these blessings as we enter remarriage and blended family life. Do we favor our biological family members? Should we ignore our deceased mates' inheritance wishes for our children when we remarry? Should we make a new start by putting *everything* into the pot with our new remarriage partners and families?

What about our premarriage responsibilities and obligations to others? There may be family members to care for—children of prior marriages, ex-spouses, or invalid parents. There may be financial commitments—alimony payments and child support. There may be other beneficiaries having a stake in our retirement plans and business interests. Should remarriage partners share all these premarital obligations as well? There are *many* issues to sort out.

It's relatively easy for most remarried couples to agree that money earned from their joint labors for the family after remarriage should be "our money" and debts they jointly incur be "our debts." But what about our personal assets and liabilities *before* we remarry? Addressing issues like these brings us back to an important concept introduced in chapter 5.

THE QUESTION OF FINANCIAL SEPARATENESS

Separateness is a very "sticky issue" in remarriage. One great temptation facing those who remarry is building self-protective walls around their premarital microfamilies. In essence, though "remarried," partners may try to live independently from their spouses in too many ways. In fact, it's quite easy to do. If you're a marriage veteran who has survived by steadfastly maintaining self-control and determining your own destiny, it may even be second nature! This type of selfish separateness is destructive and divisive in a remarriage.

But there's a *constructive* separateness arising from responsibly using healthy family boundaries. She takes the joint checkbook, but forgets to enter checks she writes. He has the credit card when she needs it. Solution? Keep separate checking accounts and credit cards to avoid misunderstandings and conflict.

The issue of separateness becomes most apparent in how couples handle their premarital assets. Let's review a few aspects of this puzzle.

Vickie, a widow with four children, received a sizable life insurance settlement from her deceased husband, earmarked for their children's college education. She later married Roger, a divorcee with two kids of his own. Soon thereafter, Roger's business fell on hard times. Creditors asked for missing loan payments. Would Roger lose the business or find a way to salvage it? He chose the latter, asking Vickie to "loan" him the life insurance/college fund proceeds. This created a gut-wrenching conflict for Vickie. She wanted to be supportive of her husband, but how could she justify risking the only solid means of support left to her children by their deceased father? Not knowing what to do, she reluctantly turned the money over to Roger. Within a year, creditors wiped out these funds and Roger lost the business. Now Vickie's children have nothing left.

Vickie and Roger might have avoided this double tragedy had they more carefully evaluated Roger's business prospects going into the remarriage. They also could have agreed in advance, perhaps through a separate private trust for the children, to hold these insurance proceeds in a "don't touch under any circumstances" account before the emotions of economic hardship led them to do otherwise. (We'll discuss use of private trusts and premarital agreements later in this chapter.)

What are some of the underlying factors at play here?

The psychology of separateness. Couples entering first marriages usually begin on a fairly equal financial footing. Not so with remarrieds, many of whom have received multiple financial blessings from long careers, divorce settlements, or inheritances. More often than not, there's a financial imbalance between the spouses. This imbalance can affect each spouse's self-concept. From a worldly perspective, a spouse with few assets may fear this imbalance could keep him/her imprisoned by financial limitations that may not affect the wealthier spouse. This isn't to say such feelings are healthy or proper for Christians, but it's reality for many individuals!

Unreasonable separateness causes the "ours" aspect of the relationship to fall away into "this is yours" and "this is mine." He owns the house the blended family moves into. No matter what else is said, it'll always be "his house" to his wife. Or a wife may come into the remarriage with an inheritance and a sizable investment portfolio that he doesn't own. If he doesn't have some access and shared control over this asset, it'll always be "her investment portfolio" no matter how many times she dips into it to help pay for marital expenses. This can lead to great frustration and resentment.

Outwardly the spouse with the monetary assets may be genuinely perplexed. "But Sweetheart, both of us directly benefit from all that we own, jointly or separately. Everything I have is for both of us, and our family, to use and enjoy." (If these words have a familiar ring to them, you're right! The father in the parable of the prodigal son used a similar plea in persuading his older son to rejoice over the return of his younger brother [Luke 15:31].) The wealthier spouse might be convinced that his/her personal management style is prudent and generous. However, that isn't always how the money flows day to day. If assets remain in one spouse's name alone, there's no shared control. These actions speak louder than any words, and the asset-laden mate may not even be aware of how deep this problem goes!

Legal considerations of separateness. As those who have experienced divorce know all too well, if a couple cannot resolve financial issues in a divorce settlement, countless attorneys and judges stand by to give them an education in division they'll never forget! If they weren't aware of how to handle their assets before divorce, they'll learn the high cost of their mistakes after it's too late to remedy them.

If you intend to preserve assets for the future, you must understand how the courts view what's "yours, mine, and ours." Don't bury your head in the sand about these matters! After all, government and laws of the land are ordained by God (Rom. 13:1). Christians need to be wise as serpents and innocent as doves about these issues (Matt. 10:16). Before you remarry, obtain legal advice of how property distribution laws in your state work upon your demise or if you or your remarriage partner ever become disabled or divorced.

Property ownership. Like any trustee, it's important for Christians to inventory their blessings before, during, and after remarriage. This also means knowing how the law allocates ownership of those assets and liabilities. Generally, everything gets put into either of two pots: *joint assets* and *personal assets.*

Joint assets include:

- assets acquired, and liabilities incurred, *during* remarriage by either spouse individually, or jointly by both of them;
- increases in value of any personal assets (described below) resulting from the efforts of either spouse during remarriage, or from use of marital funds or assets, or both;
- gifts between husband and wife during remarriage;
- benefits and funds gained in retirement, pension, profit-sharing, annuity, deferred compensation, and insurance plans during remarriage; and
- all real property (such as a personal residence) held by the spouses as joint property for the remarriage, whether bought prior to, or during, the remarriage.

By contrast, *personal assets* include:

- assets acquired, and liabilities incurred, by husband or wife *prior to* remarriage (such as personal credit card debt), or exchanged for new assets and liabilities (such as debt-consolidation agreements or personal home equity loans);
- assets acquired *separately* during remarriage by husband or wife by gift or inheritance (other than between the husband and wife themselves) and any other assets bought in exchange for such assets;
- all income earned from personal assets during remarriage (such as interest on a trust fund inheritance), *unless* the income is treated, used, or relied upon by the spouses as a *joint asset;* and
- assets and liabilities specifically *excluded* from joint assets by agreement of the spouses (such as by a trust or premarital agreement), and *included* among personal assets of one spouse.

Courts use these factors (or others like them) to put all joint assets into one pot. A remarried couple may assume they own this pot of joint marital property on a 50-50 basis (although before distributions occur, courts frequently adjust this 50-50 split).[6] Personal assets generally belong to the spouse owning those assets.

If it's your intention to maintain the personal asset nature of any property you own during a remarriage, it's legally important that you keep those assets separate *without commingling them with any joint assets.* Otherwise all these assets (such as an inheritance from a deceased husband) you thought forever belonged to you and your biological children could get tossed into the joint assets pot for division with your spouse and his/her children should the issue ever arise.

How do you deal with separateness? Quite often, one inevitable result of financial separateness is a widening emotional distance between husband and wife. It's truly amazing how often money issues become so intricately entangled with vital intimacy issues among remarried couples. As one spouse withholds assets, that person also is, in many ways, withholding himself or herself. Your mate may fear being cast aside and "poor again." This fear particularly haunts many formerly single mothers. The couple separates emotionally as anger and resentment build. Sexual feelings shut down, leaving the couple dry and empty. A marriage meltdown begins.

Why let this happen to your remarriage? Here are a few suggestions to keep separateness from overwhelming you and your family:

• *Talk out your feelings and needs first.* Instead of letting separateness creep into your finances and encroach on your remarriage, talk out your feelings and concerns with your partner. What are your fears? Are you able to let go of whatever past events scarred you financially? Are you afraid of being abandoned or manipulated by the financial imbalance in your relationship? Express those fears and concerns directly. If one spouse bringing assets into the remarriage wants those assets to go to his/her biological children and any new children born in the remarriage, how can the remarriage partners meet this need without the other spouse (and his/her biological children) feeling rejected? Couples need to put issues like these on the table for discussion rather than defaulting to pragmatic decisions.

Candid and thorough communication promotes harmony and helps a remarried couple plan around the pitfalls and traps ahead. Most importantly, pray about these matters and seek the Lord's guidance. (Financial issues are so sticky, I recommend praying together, and separately, before and after "the talks" to invite God into this area of life covered with so many hidden emotional landmines.) Talking alone with your spouse without the Lord goes nowhere. Also try to isolate where the power differentials are in your relationship. Give each other sufficient time to express feelings about those imbalances. Look for ways to help *equalize* matters. If the discussion becomes too heated, take a break to think and pray, setting a time and date to come back and pick up the process once again. In the meantime, read Philippians 2 several times to get a better handle on God's perspective! Deal with these matters before remarriage!

• *Mutually decide on a plan of action.* This takes hard work, creativity, and negotiation to establish balance with equally shared power and control between you and your remarriage partner wherever possible. Continually ask for the Lord's help in achieving unity and peace. Begin by focusing on all financial areas where joint control and responsibility *won't* pose any significant problem. Ask for the Lord's direction, then make a written list of what you will jointly own and earn together in the remarriage (all joint assets) to build up a sense of sharing power equally. One or both spouses may need a separate checking account to track personal assets, but why not use a joint checking account to receive and spend joint marital funds? The same would be true of credit cards. This encourages and promotes cooperation and trust. You also may decide to have mutual spending limits and "check with each other" agreements before making major purchases, setting up a savings plan, and agreeing on investment strategies for joint funds. The key is to emphasize joint cooperation in any action plan.

• *Wisely integrate assets.* It's foolish and reckless for a remarried couple to say, "Oh, so what? Let's just dump everything together and forget about all these issues!" That merely buries the feelings and needs, which require focus and attention. And it leads to a whole host of other problems as well! The mature and responsible approach is for the remarried couple to ask themselves, "How can we use all the assets under our joint and separate control in the way God wants us to take care of our family, promoting trust, commitment, and unity between us?" In all events, bring all heart attitudes and fears up before the Lord. It's critical that a couple fully trusts each other first, or lingering doubt will remain, prompting the asset-laden spouse to maintain control over the other spouse. It usually takes years (not months) of working hard to build up trust in the remarriage, although the groundwork should be in place by the seventh or eighth year of the relationship, according to remarriage experts.

• *Don't let your assets become a liability.* Have the mind-set of wanting to serve and reassure your spouse whenever possible. Is it really better to hang on to a position of control at the expense of wounding your mate? Filter each of your decisions through prayer and a gracious, loving, and sacrificial spirit as much as possible. Your primary concern and commitment must be to the one you marry! Avoid letting any separateness in finances tempt you to into selfishness and exploiting your remarriage partner.

• *Don't let separateness build upon itself.* The real danger of separateness is that it can act like a cancer in your remarriage. If you have joint and separate financial interests and this situation engenders anger and frustration for either or both spouses, what's the result? Withdrawal of feelings and limited personal involvement. What happens then? More separation in other areas. Little by little, the couple becomes like two single individuals linked only by a marriage certificate, rather than interactive and loving remarriage partners. It may be prudent and wise to have some separateness in finances—certainly in the beginning years of a remarriage. But hold the line on just how far the separateness goes. Be alert for drifting feelings and withdrawal. If you see this happening in your remarriage, it's time for immediate marital counseling and reaching out for each other!

We'll come back to how separateness affects consideration of private trusts and premarital agreements later in this chapter. But let's back up a bit to where most couples considering remarriage begin—the "getting to know you" and financial planning stage of entering into a lifelong partnership. Then we'll see how unique and different remarriage issues often change our goals and plans.

Getting Started: Planning Your Financial Future

As a remarriage candidate, focus on how you and your spouse can best merge your financial lives together: How about monthly overhead? Have you discussed tithing to the Lord and how much to save as a couple? When do you want to buy a house, and how much should you spend? Are you going to have more children? How about retirement savings? Whether your financial situation is simple or complex, it's very important to discuss these matters well in advance of the wedding. The penalty for failing to do so can be very severe.

Watch out for any "red flags" as you discuss matters together. If your partner feels family finances are exclusively his/her domain or if there's any deception about finances, then remarriage may not be appropriate. Ignoring warning signs and unresolved differences while plunging ahead into a remarriage is a recipe for disaster. You risk heading into divorce.

If you and your beloved do share some common perspectives, how can you fine-tune matters to build a smooth entry into remarriage? Here are a few suggestions:

Know your partner's financial habits (as well as your own) before remarriage. The New England proverb is true: "If you want to know what a man is really like, take notice how he acts when he *loses* money." What is your beloved's attitude about money? Is he a saver or a spender? Does she live within her means by spending less than her income? Does he responsibly balance today's *desires* against future *needs* by making small sacrifices now as part of building up savings for future spending? Try to view financial matters through the eyes of your beloved. What do you see? Don't assume things—appearances can be deceiving! This brings to mind the story of the young wife who found her husband gazing intently at their baby's crib with a mixture of emotions. She slipped her arms around him. "A penny for your thoughts," she said, her eyes glistening. "For the life of me," he replied, "I can't see how anybody can make a crib like this for $84.97." Make sure you know and understand your beloved's perspective and values!

Know the facts. Before remarriage, both partners should reveal to each other their annual income, assets, and debts; legal obligations for ex-spouse and child support; expected future inheritances, pensions, and retirement accounts; and insurance policies (and beneficiaries of each). Honest and complete premarital disclosure is critical so there are no surprises after the wedding. For example, one spouse may have several delinquent credit card accounts. These should be disclosed. One good way to foster trust and cooperation in this area may be for both spouses to order a copy of their own credit reports (you cannot order someone else's report without their permission) and then review them together. Don't think you know everything about your credit report—*you* may be surprised! In any event, you certainly don't want a credit problem coming up for the first time when you and your spouse apply for a home loan!

Financial values and goals. Remember that important first step? Pray first! Then talk about your vision of life together. Brainstorm with your partner about how to provide for your new family. Discuss where you want to live. Share expectations about your daily lives. Put all financial issues on the table for discussion. Then review each issue—one by one—focusing on your shared Christian values. Decide what's most important to both of you, given that there may be some differences of opinion.

Use the "five values, five years" plan. Write down the five highest priorities *both* of you share for the first five years of remarriage. Spirituality? Freedom? Family? Security? How do these values interface with each other? Then write down a brief explanation stating why those values are important. Do you feel God's approval and direction? Include the desires of each child coming into the blended family. Pledge to review these shared values on each anniversary of your remarriage so you won't lose perspective on how you began life together. Remember, these values are your *highest* priorities.

Next, focus on specific goals geared to each of your five priority values. Before remarriage, each partner has personal goals for career, budget management, and savings and investment philosophies. After the wedding, a couple should have *team* goals. Do you both agree about how to use your individual and joint incomes and expenses? How about dealing with debt? Should retirement savings be a priority, even over saving for a child's college education, to ensure you won't financially burden your children? Candidly discussing financial topics like these reveals individual and shared team goals *and* how to maintain some personal goals within your new team goals. Work toward *unity* of agreement as God leads you both.

Prepare a budget. Gloria Steinem was right about one thing: "Rich people plan for three generations. Poor people plan for Saturday night." It isn't enough thinking and praying about shared values and goals unless you use them to prepare an annual budget of income and expenses, focusing on how to seek the Lord's help in making those goals a reality.

For each goal, you and your partner may want to use a cost/benefit analysis. Is the cost of achieving a particular goal worth the benefit received? Can you reduce the cost while increasing the benefit? Be creative in making necessary budget cutbacks while reducing the expense of inconsequential things. It's a rare couple indeed who has more money than they know how to spend. The Lord blesses those who manage limited resources well with more responsibilities later on (Matt. 25:14–30).

Having a budget is very important, but being sure to *balance* your budget is critical! As Senator Phil Gramm once noted in talking about our national budget, "Balancing the budget is like going to heaven. Everybody wants to do it. They just don't want to do what you have to do to make the trip." If you find your annual expenses exceeding your annual income, it's not difficult to see that your budget may not be workable or wise. An unbalanced budget is a "red flag" that you must find ways to increase your income or decrease your expenses by scaling down your lifestyle. Calvin Coolidge said it well: "There's no dignity quite so impressive, and no independence quite so important, as living within your means."

Charitable giving plans. Remarried couples need to review and discuss personal charitable giving goals and preferred charities. One spouse religiously gives 10 percent of his or her *gross* income to charities—nothing more, and nothing less—while the other spouse prefers only giving from *net* income, but at a 20 percent rate. One spouse gives primarily to a home church while the other partner loves spreading donations around to many charities and parachurch organizations—some of which may be objectionable to the other mate. If there's enough disparity in giving guidelines, increasing conflict awaits unless the couple compromises and agrees on a *joint* charitable giving plan.

No matter what charitable giving plan you and your partner decide upon, be sure to give generously to the Lord's work. It's he who gives the increase (Mal. 3:6–12)! As Jesus tells us, "Give, and it will be given to you. A good measure, pressed down, shaken together and running over, will be poured into your lap. For with the measure you use, it will be measured to you" (Luke 6:38). Remember, it's not so much what we give to the Lord but *what we have left* that's the measure of sacrifice. Give God what's right . . . *not* what's left.

Discuss how to make financial decisions. Keep it a team effort. Always make significant financial decisions *together.* This means talking matters through and brainstorming about options and alternatives. When a financial problem persists, who will you turn to for wise and prudent advice? How will you work through deadlocks and disagreements? *How* to make specific financial decisions isn't as important as mutually agreeing on a general philosophy of handling money.

Who will be the family bookkeeper? Most remarried couples find it works best when one partner handles all the bill-paying chores so nothing's overlooked. Perhaps it's my legal background or detailed mind-set, but paying bills and tracking our income and expenses are ways I love to serve our family. I make sure we pay our bills on time and our checkbooks balance. Cheryl's a wonderful cook (all I "cook" are peanut butter sandwiches!). She enjoys having complete discretion over buying groceries, deciding the family menus, and surprising us with wonderful meals. But we monitor bills and write checks using different styles. She makes quick work of this task in her personal accounts using an occasional running balance in her checkbook, which works well for her but could be a problem for our family finances. So we divide up our chores according to our strengths, keeping in mind how we can best achieve our family team goals.

Agree on number and use of checkbooks. Some couples simplify household bookkeeping by using one joint checkbook instead of having separate accounts. In fact, some believe this unites a couple, as an extension of the intimate nature of their one-flesh relationship. Others find common checkbooks create problems, especially when one partner has the checkbook at times when the other needs it. There's greater risk for bill payments, account reconciliations, and other matters being overlooked.

Other couples—especially remarried partners—prefer having separate checking and credit card accounts. Many also believe it's important that each spouse preserve a personal financial identity for privacy reasons (*not* secrecy). But separate accounts also tend to create and preserve separateness between remarriage partners—a hurdle the couple may want to minimize over time, not enhance. Also, separate accounts may not be wise for spouses who don't manage money well, or tend to overspend, since this can create a family financial crisis before the couple has enough time to prevent it.

One possible compromise is by having both joint *and* separate accounts. The joint checking account receives all marital income. Checks for all major monthly family bills (mortgage, utilities, etc.) come out of this account. A couple then makes disbursements from that joint account to each partner's separate account(s) for personal spending money and household purchasing responsibilities (groceries, clothing, etc.). Of course, you may want to handle payment of your blended family's bills in a different manner. That's okay. Just be sure you and your partner agree with each other on your household setup and act as a team. If one method doesn't work, simply try something else.

Discuss general spending procedures/limits. What about spending limits in using joint income? How much is each partner free to spend without the prior approval of the other partner? Some couples agree to secure *mutual* approval before spending more than fifty or a hundred dollars of joint funds, except during emergencies. Other couples prepare a detailed budget and make monthly disbursements to a particular spouse for each line item in the budget, with preauthorization to spend up to, but not exceed, the budgeted allocation. For some, agreeing upon specific spending rules may seem legalistic and require too much busywork. They may prefer more general spending guidelines. Whichever option(s) you and your spouse choose, the goal is to have both partners know what the spending rules are *in advance* and to mutually agree to honor them as a team. This builds trust!

Budget for housing expense. Buying a residence is one of the biggest investments most couples make in their lifetime. Given this major expense, all costs of acquiring and maintaining the residence need careful evaluation and planning. Would it be better to rent rather than buy? What type of mortgage will you need? Can you afford the monthly payments? How much housing can you really afford after remarriage? Two ratios mortgage lenders commonly use in reviewing home loan applications are: (1) the housing expense ratio, and (2) the debt payment ratio. The housing expense ratio compares your *total monthly housing expenses* (mortgage payment, plus real estate taxes and insurance) to your gross monthly income before deducting income taxes. Lenders believe your housing expense shouldn't exceed 28 percent of your family's gross income. The debt payment ratio compares your *total monthly payments on all debts* (including a home mortgage) to your gross monthly income before deducting income taxes. Accordingly, that percentage should not exceed 36 percent of your family's gross income. Of course, these are only guidelines to help determine whether your dream home is within reach. But the housing issues definitely need to be discussed between remarriage partners—preferably before the wedding.

Most married couples face many of the foregoing issues, but remarriages are different. That's why we also need to review some unique aspects of financial planning for blended families.

SPECIAL BLENDED FAMILY FINANCIAL ISSUES

Remarriage is a complex mix of many personalities and financial issues. The couple needs to manage money coming in from different purses, and often going out to several different households. Into the mix are preexisting good (and bad) credit ratings, spending habits, and debt obligations of each spouse *and* ex-spouse, to name a few! Also, don't overlook child-support payments, retirement plans, and college funds of children *and stepchildren,* in addition to added cost for food, day care, entertainment, and so many other daily expenses that test any blended family's strength. It can be a monetary minefield! Here are a few important considerations:

Remarriage estate planning. How will you pass along assets to your current spouse, children from your current and former marriages, and perhaps even your ex-spouse? The only way to know is by completing some estate planning. Sure, estate planning's a topic we'd rather not think about because it reminds us of our mortality. Why plan for the death of either or both remarriage partners even before remarriage? But then you hear the horror stories.

A newly married young friend and client of mine had his first child on the way some years ago. I urged him to secure some estate planning and adequate life insurance, but he resisted. As he walked in downtown Miami one day, a man in a stolen car whipped around a corner and sheared off a stop sign, which became a projectile striking my friend in the head. He died after being on life support for twenty-four hours. The medical expenses depleted his paltry twenty-five-thousand-dollar life insurance policy. His young widow not only had to cope with this terrible loss, but desperately tried scraping together enough contributions from family and friends to pay for his funeral. Before giving birth to their child, she had to sell the family home and move in with her parents to survive financially. How tragic!

Ana summed up the problem well as she recalled her husband's sudden death from a heart attack at age thirty-seven: "No one wants to talk about how a survivor will sort out the details of a sudden death. I know I didn't. When my husband died, he had no will and was underinsured. We both knew these were two areas we would *eventually* resolve, but we never did. Neither of us ever expected the other to die so young. If only I had prepared. If only I had followed the advice of our lawyer and our accountant."

The unfortunate fact is that three out of four Americans die without a will. Financial planners estimate that about half of all Americans also are underinsured or not insured at all. This lack of preparation can be devastatingly costly at a time of emotional upheaval—especially with the additional complexities of a blended family! Christians in these circumstances must search their hearts, "Am I adequately providing for my family, as the Lord requires?" (1 Tim. 5:8).

Estate planning establishes long-term goals for preserving and managing assets and wealth in the event of death. We plan for the most efficient and productive way to establish financial security, reduce taxes, and preserve what the Lord has blessed us with for those loved ones who survive us. We achieve our goals through gifts, wills, trusts, insurance policies, and many other methods. This critical planning work isn't only for wealthy individuals—everyone has a responsibility to exercise sound financial planning for the maximum benefit of the blended family.

• *Wills.* Too many couples entering remarriage haven't even looked at their existing wills from a prior marriage. Imagine their surprise upon discovering their former spouses remain named as sole beneficiaries of their estates! (Fortunately, in most states a divorce invalidates one's will for this reason.) A will is one basic element of estate planning. This document provides assurance that upon your death your property will go to those you designate. If a person dies without a will (which the law refers to as dying "intestate"), a probate court will distribute that person's assets according to state law. And if the state decides how to distribute your property, odds are good that it won't be the way you would have liked!

Your will covers not only property distribution but also allows you to select a trusted person or bank to act in your place as an "executor" or "personal representative" after your death to decide matters consistent with your wishes. Even more importantly, your will states who should have custody of your minor children. It's true that if the other biological parent is alive and legally fit, that parent usually gains custody—despite active daily parenting by your spouse/stepparent (see chap. 9). Even so, it's important to include specific child custody instructions in your will. Why? Because your ex-spouse may die before you do, or he/she may fail, neglect, or refuse to assume custody of your child even if the law allows it.

• *Probate.* It's necessary to probate a will at death. That means that when you die, your executor must take your will to the local county courthouse for a court-supervised procedure to establish what you own and to determine who receives it as you directed. The probate process also oversees payment of taxes, claims, and expenses of your estate. After completing all these procedures, the probate court distributes what remains of your assets to your beneficiaries. But probate can be a costly and time-consuming process. And having only a will is a one-way ticket to probate court. So depending on the state involved, many remarried couples plan their financial affairs to avoid probate, if possible.

• *Living trusts.* One way to avoid probate is to have a living trust. You transfer your estate assets to a trust while you're alive. Nothing changes, except the trustee of your trust (usually yourself) holds title to those assets. Your life continues as it did before, with you having complete control over all the assets in your living trust. When you die, a successor trustee you select takes over your trust and can immediately distribute your assets after paying applicable estate taxes, rather than wait for completion of a long probate process. [A word of caution here: Make sure your successor trustee is competent and trustworthy. Probate courts investigate and qualify personal representatives under wills, but your appointment of a successor trustee requires no such court verification in most cases.]

Living trusts also can help with child custody concerns. Given the likelihood that your child's other biological parent may gain custody upon your death, you may not feel comfortable placing any of your child's inheritance into your ex-spouse's hands.

What can you do? Why not set up a trust for your child and name a trusted person to serve as trustee, thereby ensuring your estate assets do indeed go to your child? Without a trust, any money left to your child winds up in a court-directed guardian-ship proceeding—another very costly and time-consuming process! Then a judge you've never met will decide how to spend your money on your child. No thanks! In addition, without a trust, guardianships in many states end when the child becomes a legal adult—still very young in years and maturity. What might your child do if he/she receives a large sum of money at college age? Can you spell "Porsche"? For these and other reasons, it may be wise to establish a trust for your child that not only protects the assets from your ex-spouse but also protects your child against his/her own imma-ture inclinations for awhile.

• *Durable family powers of attorney.* Each remarriage partner also needs to give a durable family power of attorney to a trusted agent (usually one's spouse or another trusted family member) providing legal authority to handle one's legal affairs if he/she is unable to do so. Make sure your attorney-in-fact also has signing privileges on crit-ical checking accounts and access to safe deposit boxes to keep the family afloat dur-ing emergencies!

• *Estate and gift taxes.* The estate tax is a tax on the act of transferring property at your death—not a tax on the right of your beneficiaries to receive their inheritances. Your estate pays the tax. Therefore, the tax your estate pays reduces the value of your property going to your beneficiaries. The good news is that some or all your assets may be excluded from estate tax liability. In 2001 the exclusion amount was $675,000, meaning that if your estate was worth $675,000 or less, it may not be taxed at all on the federal level. (States also may have inheritance taxes, so be sure to check with your estate-planning advisor about this additional expense.) Beginning in 2002, the exclu-sion amount gradually increases until it tops off at $3.5 million in 2009. You may think you're not wealthy enough to exceed these thresholds, but after adding the value of retirement plans, equity in your home, and especially life insurance proceeds, your estate value rises very quickly!

Estate planning involves taking advantage of tax laws. The Tax Reform Act of 1976 combined gift and estate taxes into a single tax applicable to gifts made during our lives or to estate inheritance transfers made to others upon one's death. The mas-sive Economic Growth and Tax Relief Reconciliation Act of 2001 also made many changes that reduce applicable estate taxes over a period of years (as noted above). The tax laws keep changing, so proper estate planning and compliance with changing laws reduce taxes paid to the IRS. Your benefactors will then enjoy more of what you pass on to them. Be sure to see a competent tax or legal advisor about these important matters!

• *Estate planning for blended families.* Typical "simple wills" won't work in most situations involving a remarried couple. Why? Because most "standard wills" assume that both spouses have married only once, all children were born during that mar-riage, and everything the couple owns are joint assets. These wills further assume each spouse's primary desire at death is to provide for the surviving spouse. But remarriages are different, especially when children exist from a prior marriage. Sometimes a remarried spouse wants jewelry or antiques to remain "in the family," meaning with biological children. If a parent isn't specific and clear about who receives this valuable property, it may go to a stepparent and eventually the step-parent's biological children. Carefully address these matters in all estate planning documents.

One way to direct inheritances to one's biological children is for each parent to set up a separate trust for his/her own children and to transfer premarital personal assets into the trust before remarriage. Each parent then names his/her own biological children as the beneficiaries of that parent's trust. In most states, this preserves children's inheritances of premarital assets from their biological parents. In the meantime, each parent can enjoy the benefits of his/her respective trust as specified in their individual trust agreements. With all estate-planning considerations, be sure to use competent legal and financial advisors who are very familiar with your particular circumstances.

Administration of retirement plans. Be sure to check into *all* differences in retirement plans *before* you remarry! Who are the beneficiaries of your plans, insurance policies, and investment accounts? Upon remarriage, you may want to add your new spouse as a beneficiary on particular assets, such as an insurance policy, as part of your estate plan. If you have a 401(k) retirement plan, watch out—your new spouse may have an *automatic* claim on those assets, even if someone else is listed as a beneficiary, unless your spouse waives any claim. Each spouse also should carefully compare and coordinate retirement plans to get the most out of each plan. For instance, if both spouses contribute the same amount to their individual plans each year, but one spouse's plan has a dollar-for-dollar match for contributions while the other plan doesn't, the couple may want to increase contributions to the matching benefit plan while reducing contributions to the other plan.

Retirement and social security benefits. In completing your divorce, you may have received a Qualified Domestic Relations Order (QDRO), which awarded you a portion of your ex-spouse's retirement benefits. Under existing survivor benefit rules, the law considers your ex-spouse's *current* spouse at the time your former spouse retires (or upon his/her death prior to retirement) as your ex-spouse's "surviving spouse." So if your ex-spouse remarries, this could affect *your* benefits unless you're clearly named as the "surviving spouse" in the QDRO. Check with the attorney obtaining your QDRO for specific advice and options.

Also be aware that under current rules your ex-spouse could receive one-half of *your* social security benefits if: (a) you and your ex-spouse were married for ten years before you divorced; (b) your ex-spouse hasn't remarried; (c) your ex-spouse is sixty-two years or older; and (d) your ex-spouse isn't entitled to his/her own social security benefits that equal or exceed one-half of your benefits. Be sure to plan for contingencies like these in providing for your new spouse and blended family.

Coordination of insurance. The most critical insurance for a remarried couple to review first is health insurance. What health insurance does each spouse carry? What coverages are included? What are the applicable deductible amount(s)? Which policies allow you to select your own doctors? How much coverage will each child receive under each plan? Does any health insurance of ex-spouses cover the children?

• *Health insurance.* Generally, the least-expensive health care options are continuing coverage of your biological children under your ex-spouse's group plan or switching them to your own group plan. For example, the Employee Retirement Income Security Act of 1974 (ERISA)[7] (and as amended) provides that children may keep health care coverage when their parents divorce. You also may be able to obtain a qualified medical child support order (QMCSO, or "Kiddie QDRO") requiring employer-provided health systems to continue providing such medical insurance. In addition, COBRA coverage pursuant to the Consolidated Omnibus Budget Reconciliation Act of 1985 (COBRA)[8] guarantees continuous coverage under an ex-spouse's group plan for a limited period after divorce (usually eighteen to thirty-six months). Check with your current health insurance carrier to learn more about your options in extending and/or converting coverage maintained by your ex-spouse.

If you plan on having more children with your remarriage partner, you may want to consider other health plan options, such as switching to a health maintenance or a preferred provider organization that covers all well-baby care. (You may need to add a new child to the plan within thirty days of birth, or risk losing coverage until the next open enrollment period.) If a basic health insurance plan is unavailable or too expensive, don't go uninsured and put your entire family at financial risk! At least check available major medical insurance policies with high deductibles to protect your family against any disastrous health problems. You and your partner need to agree on which options offer the best coverages for greatest value. Health insurance should be in place and ready to use by everyone in the blended family from the wedding date forward.

• *Life insurance.* Make sure each spouse has enough coverage to provide the surviving spouse and family with the ability to enjoy the same lifestyle after death of the insured. Life insurance also allows a spouse of modest means to generate an inheritance for his/her children. For example, the surviving spouse might inherit the decedent's interest in the marital home and all joint accounts while the children receive the life insurance proceeds in trust for college expenses. Be sure to review your divorce settlement. It may specify that your biological children are beneficiaries of your ex-spouse's life insurance. Also keep in mind that insurance companies won't pay proceeds directly to a minor. To avoid management by a guardian, consider using a trust for that child's benefit, with the chosen trustee named as policy beneficiary so the trustee can invest and use insurance proceeds for your child's benefit.

How much life insurance do you need? Discuss your family situation with a qualified and knowledgeable insurance agent. The amount of insurance also depends on how many children you have and how old they are. Estimate your family's expenses if either remarriage partner died, then subtract the joint assets available for the blended family. Insure the resulting financial gap with life insurance. Many financial planners recommend that parents of two children carry policies equal to seven to ten times the combined annual family income. Remarriage partners also may consider purchasing a "widow's shock absorber"—a separate life insurance policy on each spouse's life in the amount of a year's gross salary. This ensures the surviving spouse can grieve and take care of the blended family's needs without the severe financial pressure of meeting daily expenses for at least a year.

• *Disability insurance.* Realistically, there's a much greater risk that you'll become disabled in the next few years than be deceased. Even so, too many people are uninsured or underinsured for disability. You may have coverage at work or otherwise be eligible for social security disability benefits, but that coverage isn't unlimited. Make sure you know how much each pays and how long payments continue. Then purchase a disability insurance policy to fill the gap.

Title to personal and joint assets. How will you and your remarriage partner own assets—jointly, separately, or both? Obviously these decisions directly affect tax planning, so it's critical you consult a tax advisor before taking any action. Perhaps either or both of you sold a personal residence before remarriage with the intent of purchasing a new home together. How will you account for the funds from your respective house sales? How will you allocate the expense of your new home? Whose name(s) will be on the title to the new residence? If a spouse and his/her children insist on staying in the same residence they lived in before remarriage, what happens if that spouse refuses to add the new remarriage partner's name to the title? You can bet the new spouse will feel like an outsider!

Subject to estate planning and tax considerations, you could title each remarriage partner's assets in the way the couple wants them to be treated upon any disability, death, or divorce. Assets the couple purchase with joint funds after remarriage could be titled in both spouses' names, for example. If you want to keep premarital personal assets separate, keep the title to these assets in the individual owner/spouse's name. This makes it easier for your executors and others to determine your intent.

Support sent to ex-spouses and noncustodial children. Frequently *spouse* support payments coming *in* from ex-spouses to either or both remarriage partners lapse by force of law or other reasons upon remarriage. Meanwhile, support obligations going *out* to former unremarried spouses and children may continue—a classic catch-22 financial bind. Less income is coming into the new blended family account while other expenses remain constant! Sometimes a remarried husband's jealous ex-wife brings him back to court to *increase* her spouse support payments. Result? The remarried couple may have to absorb additional legal fees as well as any support increases awarded by the court. This can depress the couple's living standard as a blended family. Perhaps a remarried, noncustodial husband gives his ex-wife, secretly or otherwise, even *more* money than his support obligation requires because of a deep sense of guilt over the divorce, or fear of not being able to see his children. This also penalizes his current wife and family.

These situations bring up many tough questions for any remarried couple. Should a remarried husband's salary pay for all blended family expenses, *including* the additional expense of his biological noncustodial children? What if his wife isn't working, but she has separately owned property generating an income—should she help support her husband's noncustodial children from this income? How about contributing toward her husband's spouse support payments to his ex-wife? Should the couple use blended family income to put a remarried wife's son through college—especially if her custodial ex-husband refuses to pay for it? These questions aren't easy to answer. Yet discussing them early in the couple's relationship helps avoid many misunderstandings, conflicts, and heartache!

It may be very difficult to write monthly checks to an ex-spouse for spouse and/or child support. But keep your focus on your overriding priority and goal: Provide for your children as if you had not divorced. Keep in mind Paul's admonition in 1 Timothy 5:8: "If anyone does not provide for his relatives, and especially for his immediate family, he has denied the faith and is worse than an unbeliever." Don't let an ex-spouse's greediness, lack of cooperation, or other annoying conduct distract you. Also, be generous and willing to adjust the amount periodically if your child has unusual expenses, such as special sporting events or medical needs.

Support and retirement benefits received from ex-spouses. Remarriage may end a divorced spouse's support benefits from an ex-spouse. Make sure you know how to replace this income if it's lost. Also, if a divorced spouse lives in a former marital residence, remarriage may create an obligation to sell the house and split up the proceeds with the ex-spouse. Possibilities like these need full evaluation from a financial and tax standpoint.

Unlike spouse support, remarriage may *not* directly affect child support responsibilities. Those obligations of a noncustodial spouse usually continue after remarriage of the custodial parent. However, life's harsh reality is that many custodial parents don't receive the full amount due from ex-spouses. This is even more true when less fortunate ex-spouses see their former mates remarry a financially secure partner. They don't want to pay as much because they feel the newly remarried couple can afford it. Wrinkles like these need to be factored in to any blended family budget rather than just assuming you'll continue to receive all child support payments.

The good news is you now have more legal tools to enforce child support obligations against your ex-spouse than ever before. It's important that he/she share financial responsibility for the expenses of your biological children. If you cannot win your ex-spouse's cooperation voluntarily, you owe it to your children, your remarriage partner, and yourself to use these laws to enforce compliance. This isn't being mean or vindictive. It's the essence of using responsible "tough love." At the same time, be willing to be fair and flexible. Absorb your fair share of providing for your biological children. If you receive more income in relation to your former spouse, consider using that income and demanding less from your ex-mate. Prayerfully seek ways to have *peaceful* relationships with all concerned, as long as this doesn't lead to any appeasement postures (which usually backfire and make matters worse). Above all, never hold your child back from seeing his/her biological parent solely because a child support payment is late or missing. This vindictive action deeply wounds your child more than anyone else (see chaps. 9 and 11).

Holdover joint debts with ex-spouses. Divorce courts usually split debts of a former marriage in the same manner as assets, but most lenders and the Internal Revenue Service often hold *both* ex-spouses personally liable for the *entire* debt. So if your ex-spouse doesn't pay his/her fair share of jointly incurred debts from your former marriage, you could be forced to pay it all—no matter what your divorce decree says! Before remarrying, it's prudent to verify what joint debts with your ex-spouse remain outstanding, if any, so you can arrange to have them paid if possible. You don't want these obligations coming back to haunt you and your new spouse! On some debts, such as a mortgage on the former marital home, you may be able to have the lender agree to look only to the one having sole title to the residence—especially if the value of the home is significantly greater than the remaining balance on the loan.

Financial impact of family relocation on ex-spouses. If the remarriage involves relocating the children of the former marriage to a new area, this obviously restricts the ex-spouse's access to his/her children and increases the amount of expense everyone must absorb for such costs as airline tickets, long-distance telephone calls, out-of-town meals, and similar charges. You must be sure to budget for these expenses (see chap. 11).

College expense of children and stepchildren. Many child support obligations end when the child becomes a legal adult. This support usually doesn't continue for college expenses. However, many parents continue helping their biological children through college and even beyond. Discuss future plans like these in detail prior to, or early in, the remarriage. Budget for the expense accordingly. Also be aware that the federal government and many colleges determine financial-aid eligibility based on income and assets of the custodial parents *and* stepparents. Make sure you factor in any additional tuition expense if aid isn't available.

PUTTING YOUR REMARRIAGE FINANCIAL PLAN INTO ACTION

Experts offer the following general guidance for handling marital finances:

Make joint financial decisions. This is true even if one spouse earns all the family income. Remember, you and your spouse are a financial *team*.

Schedule regular talks about finances. Be sure you have enough time to review and discuss all the issues—preferably on a weekly basis. Plan your talks at specific times when there's no additional pressure. View it as an intimate way to get to know each other better. Listen to each other's opinions regarding money without being judgmental. Each spouse should prepare an agenda in advance of this meeting, listing topics of concern. Make sure each partner receives equal time. And, above all, don't forget to *pray* first!

Keep accurate and complete records. Why do disreputable businesses operate primarily on a cash-only basis? The same reason you shouldn't—the money's untraceable. Computer programs such as Quicken and Microsoft Money easily help track a family's annual income and expenses. They provide very helpful and informative reports, and even graphs, to keep a remarried couple fully informed as to their financial plan. But you don't need a computer to track your family finances. Some couples simply use a loose-leaf binder. In one column they record all income, with the date and amount of each bill for the next three months logged in the next column. In minutes they know exactly where the family money's going.

Disclosure. Share information. Make sure each spouse knows the blended family's current financial status. A woman who doesn't know about her husband's finances and becomes a widow may find out—too late—that her husband's pension plan or life insurance is inadequate to support her and her children, or that he ran up debts for which she may now be responsible. But just as it's important for the bookkeeper spouse to input the data and provide reports to his/her mate, it's just as important that the receiving spouse *read* the reports to keep up with what's going on. I know of one husband who provided his wife with regular family financial reports, offering to review and discuss the details at her convenience. She refused, saying, "I don't want to know about this stuff. You take care of it." But when the couple later divorced, one of the first complaints made by the wife's attorney was that the husband didn't keep his wife informed about finances!

Decide whether to pool assets. You and your remarriage partner must make a joint decision whether you want to blend incomes, pool your assets, or keep some assets separate. "In some marriages, both partners have their own pools of money, because they realize they're two separate individuals with two brains," notes Diane Sollee, director of the Coalition for Marriage, Family, and Couples Education, an information clearinghouse in Washington, D.C.[9] For other couples, however, having independent finances may prove to be a big problem, undermining intimacy and the "cooperative oneness" necessary to make blended families work. Having completely separate finances could be a "red flag" for deeper problems down the line. Prayerfully discuss these issues with your mate, deciding what's in your family's best interest. Give high regard to how your decisions affect your children.

Carefully monitor blended family debts. Since either spouse could become liable for his or her remarriage mate's personal debts, each spouse should be aware of how much indebtedness exists—especially since joint and personal liabilities can adversely affect *both* partners' credit ratings. From 1989 to 1998, the average American family's net worth jumped 20 percent. That's the good news. The bad news is debt also increased. In 1990 the average household credit-card balance was $2,985, but by 2000 the average balance had more than doubled to $8,123. And while 401(k) contributions increased dramatically during the nineties, Americans didn't save cash. Savings plummeted from 10.9 percent of disposable income in 1982 to *negative* 0.1 percent in 2000.

According to Debtor's Anonymous, there are three different aspects of debt problems: (1) *compulsive spending,* meaning an inability to control spending; (2) *unsecured debting,* such as using credit cards to build up a mounting debt load; and (3) *underearning,* or spending more than you earn or ever have a chance to earn. By far, one of the greatest problems facing most married couples is credit card debt. In a 1977 survey, 27 percent of people said credit cards were "bad" for consumers. By 2000 that number jumped to 51 percent, with 41 percent agreeing that everyone would be better off if credit cards didn't exist.[10] Even so, cardholders are charging faster than ever as their credit cards feed frivolous shopping and nurture a "luxury fever" that sinks too many families into bankruptcy. Savings are falling while spending and tardy mortgages are rising.

According to the National Foundation for Credit Counseling, here's how to bail out: (1) shelve your credit cards for a while and curb spending, since you cannot reduce your debt by constantly adding to it; (2) total the debts you have and the respective interest rates you're paying; (3) develop a repayment plan, paying off the credit cards with the highest interest rates first, and always paying at least the minimum amount to avoid late fees; and (4) raise extra money by cutting expenses, holding garage sales, taking a part-time job, etc. Once out of debt, stay debt-free by never charging anything you cannot pay off in ninety days. And, although it does carry the advantages of interest being tax-deductible with a lower rate than credit cards, resist the urge to refinance and increase your home mortgage. Why? You just don't get out of debt by borrowing more. Debt consolidation in a home mortgage is like putting "Band-Aids on bullet wounds." If these steps don't solve the problem, get professional help and credit counseling.

Maintain an emergency fund. If possible, it's prudent to set aside a "rainy day" emergency fund of after-tax income equal to three to six months of household expenses in easily tapped, interest-bearing savings accounts or money-market funds. But the real amount may be more or less, depending on how much you make and spend, as well as the particular needs of your blended family. These funds help pay for life's unexpected events (illness, job loss), while covering regular living expenses.

Each spouse should have discretionary funds. Each spouse needs some "fun money" to spend without feeling that every expenditure needs to be accounted for, or "begging" for money from each other.

Understand tax returns. Ask questions—don't worry about sounding ignorant. Don't clam up simply because you feel it isn't romantic to deal with these issues. Ignorance about tax matters can be very costly! Upon remarriage, you and your spouse need to make sure the married names used on your tax returns match those registered with the Social Security Administration. Any mismatch between a new remarried name on the tax return and a social security number under a spouse's former married name could unexpectedly increase a tax bill and reduce the size of any refund.[11] Remember also that a remarried couple must provide social security numbers for each dependent child claimed on the tax return.[12]

Never sign contracts you don't understand. Whether it's a contract to buy or sell a house, purchasing a maintenance contract on home appliances, or even your own estate-planning documents, make *certain* you know what you're signing. If you're unsure about anything, ask questions first—not later. Seek legal counsel.

But there's still another "sticky issue" that many couples considering remarriage after death or divorce of a spouse cannot ignore—the inevitable subject of . . .

Private Trusts and Premarital Agreements

Note: The following section about private trusts and premarital agreements is, perhaps, one of the most controversial sections in this entire book. However, as a Christian lawyer, I believe it's important that you and your remarriage partner fully inform yourselves as to all your options and alternatives. Then you'll be better able to plan for your future and make the best decisions for your blended family, as God leads you. In presenting this material, neither Cheryl nor I take any position on the advisability of using such private agreements. It's my intent simply to present the issues, examine the pros and cons, and leave the final decision to you and your mate about how to proceed. In all events, never use a private trust or premarital agreement without first receiving spiritual and marital counseling, as well as advice from a competent family lawyer!

Newlyweds gingerly tiptoe around the subject. Usually it takes a family crisis or divorce to become brutally honest. What am I talking about? It's the practical question nearly everyone dreads: "What happens to our family and assets if one of us dies, becomes disabled, or even if our remarriage fails?" It's an inevitable spinoff of the separateness issue discussed earlier in this chapter.

In 1970, prior to enactment of "no fault" divorce laws, the vast majority of wedded individuals married for the first time. But now the numbers are almost equally split between first marriages and spouses entering a remarriage, according to the Census Bureau. And a growing majority of remarried couples are using private trusts and/or premarital agreements. Perhaps that's why the best-selling book in Amazon.com's marriage category during 1999 was *How to Write Your Own Premarital Agreement.*

Using a private trust and/or a premarital agreement is an *option* for consideration by remarriage partners—especially if one or both spouses has children from a previous marriage, owns a personal residence, has retirement benefits accrued over many years, or has substantial savings and investments through family inheritances or otherwise. Never mind that Donald Trump believes any wealthy individual who marries without a premarital agreement should be institutionalized.[13] Forget those who justify themselves, saying there's a time when romance must yield a little bit to a dose of realism. *You must make your own decision about this matter, especially in light of God's Word and the material appearing at the beginning of this chapter concerning the importance of having biblical attitudes on wealth and possessions.*

What are premarital agreements? A premarital agreement outlines property division, spouse support, and other important matters in the event anything happens to either spouse or the marriage. Premarital agreements are a fairly recent development among married couples. Until recently, courts generally wouldn't recognize contracts between husband and wife, based in part on society's interest in protecting the family and the belief that it's difficult to have fair and balanced negotiations about marital rights. But courts slowly began changing this legal position, realizing that marital agreements could benefit some married couples if death ended a marriage. Eventually this change led to using these agreements for other marital situations as well.

Then in 1983 the National Conference of Commissioners on Uniform State Laws noted the increasing frequency of multiple marriages and the growing popularity of premarital agreements. After addressing the concerns of many lawyers about the uncertainty and lack of uniformity in enforcement of premarital agreements, the commissioners adopted the Uniform Premarital Agreement Act (UPAA).[14] Adopted in a majority of states as of 2002, this Act provides that married couples may contract for virtually everything in a premarital agreement, except child support and custody matters, as long as the agreement is, in the words of the Act, "not in violation of public policy."

What are private trusts? Trusts are legal agreements that divide ownership of assets from management of those assets. Beneficiaries hold legal title to trust assets, but trustee(s) use and manage those assets for the benefit of these owners during the trust term. There are revocable trusts, where the person setting up the trust reserves the power to amend or revoke the trust; or irrevocable trusts, where this power has been surrendered.

Private trusts serve important practical purposes. For example, in the earlier case of Roger and Vickie and use of the life insurance proceeds belonging to Vickie's children, Vickie (or her deceased husband) might have made these funds "untouchable" by putting this money into an irrevocable private trust for the sole benefit of their children, with a bank or other trusted person serving as trustee. The children then would be the rightful owners of these funds, but the trustee would have control over how to invest and spend those proceeds until the time came for fulfillment of the trust's purpose—paying for each child's college education. A private trust of this sort might have taken some of the pressure off Vickie in resisting Roger's demand that they dip into these funds to save his business. It would have been easier for Vickie to say, "But Sweetheart, we both knew in advance that neither of us would ever use this money for anything else but the children. It's in trust for them—we can't touch it."

What purposes do private trusts and premarital agreements serve?

• *Ownership and use of premarital assets.* If a couple chooses to "throw everything into one pot" (an unusual step for many blended families), a premarital agreement may describe any retained ownership privileges and responsibilities in writing so there's no future misunderstanding. If some personal assets are to be set aside for specific persons or purposes, then a private trust could be helpful. What about each spouse's individual retirement plan—will each partner's plan remain his/her own asset? How will the couple make additional contributions—from joint or personal funds? The couple can specify this in a private agreement. If a couple purchases a residential investment property in their joint names, but each spouse contributes unequal amounts of premarital funds to buy the home, they could agree to share in any appreciation of their investment in the same proportion as they contributed to the purchase price. For example, if the husband contributed 60 percent of the purchase price while the wife put in 40 percent, on any resale of the home they could split the appreciation in the same percentages. Or they could agree to just reimburse themselves for their contributions and then split the appreciation 50/50 after that. All these planning measures are appropriate in premarital agreements.

• *Payment of premarital debts.* Both spouses could agree that each partner remains responsible for his/her own debts incurred prior to remarriage, as is typical in many premarital agreements. Or one spouse may commit to helping his/her mate pay off premarital debts in specified ways under certain conditions. There are many options available, as long as both spouses are fair and considerate of each other.

• *Provisions for biological children.* Just as a private trust might have helped Vickie and Roger's situation, many older couples want to protect and provide for their biological children, and perhaps even grandchildren, from a prior marriage. They may not want anyone else to receive assets or monies earmarked for those children. Premarital agreements can list and categorize these personal assets, designating which children will receive them upon any disability, death, or divorce of a parent/grandparent. Alternatively, private trusts can keep these assets separate for the exclusive benefit of the children.

• *Protection of family businesses.* With the greatest intergenerational transfer of wealth in history to occur in the United States over the next decade—an estimated $10 trillion to be passed from parents to baby boomer children—much of this wealth is tied up in family business stock. Private business trusts and premarital agreements help keep family businesses from becoming the spoils in any marital disputes. Premarital agreements even include confidentiality clauses, barring spouses from revealing family or corporate secrets.

Advantages of private agreements.

• *Guards against future misunderstandings.* Guidelines and restrictions in private agreements resolve issues in advance—before emotions run high after a death, disability, or divorce occurs. A couple decides potentially controversial matters at the beginning of a remarriage, when each partner is lovingly cooperative. From a legal and economic standpoint, partners begin with a partnership agreement. A remarriage partnership may be no different. Each "partner" brings unequal assets and commitments into the relationship. How will they share their respective privileges and responsibilities? Unwarranted assumptions can lead to major conflict!

• *Allows couples to tailor their lives to their family circumstances.* Private trusts and premarital agreements provide you and your spouse with a wide range of options to consider in deciding how best to plan for the future. For example, one spouse wanted to provide for his elderly parents and children from a first marriage upon his death. His premarital agreement provided for leaving his estate to his parents and children, but also required him to secure and maintain a suitable insurance policy for his second wife. The possibilities are almost endless.

• *Reduces interference from lawyers and courts.* Without private agreements, you concede authority to dispassionate judges and warring lawyers who decide your affairs during a vulnerable family time (disability, death, or divorce) with little input from you and your remarriage partner! You may want to retain some control over your life by voluntarily expressing your desires in advance, rather than having some judge tell you and your family that you must do something against your will.

Disadvantages of private agreements.

• *Brings an element of doubt into the remarriage.* This single factor is a critical disadvantage! To a couple in love, the entire issue can communicate "I don't trust you." The underlying message is that you're planning for a remarriage that may not last "until death do we part." Divorces can happen, even to committed, remarried Christians, but it's quite a different matter to prepare for that eventuality with such an agreement. It can have the emotional effect of saying, "I'm hedging my bets on this marriage," a potentially cancerous message and attitude! This perceived mistrust also can become a self-fulfilling prophesy. If a spouse perceives mistrust, he/she may act accordingly. To spouses who are business-oriented, an agreement may be good. Although not pleasant to think about, planning is prudent—like making a will or buying life insurance. But there's no doubt that from an emotional standpoint these agreements can be devastating—even to the most mature and secure person!

• *Brings lawyers and legal concerns between a couple in love.* I recall a cartoon showing a wedding couple facing a minister who was reading from a script prepared by a lawyer standing nearby: "And now Mr. T. A. Hester of Fulton, Hestor & Parker will read a brief synopsis of the prenuptial agreement."[15] Who wants that? Yet legal matters like trusts and premarital agreements can be extremely complex, so lawyers must become part of the process. Even so, few couples want to tangle with the hassle and expense of financial self-protection issues and lawyers when weddings and relationships are on everyone's mind!

• *Invites unreasonable family pressure.* Some parents even insist their sons and daughters use private trusts and premarital agreements, or they lose any stock in the family enterprise—often called "scotchguarding a business." Sometimes parental pressure becomes overwhelming. Billionaire financier Ronald O. Perelman, chairperson of Revlon Inc., in a much-publicized feud, boycotted his son's wedding ostensibly because the son refused to secure a premarital agreement from his bride.[16]

The psychology of private agreements. Regardless of the legal arguments made for using private agreements, you must balance everything against the major psychological toll these agreements may impose on the heart, mind, and soul of each spouse. The perceived lack of trust, and other negative emotional messages coming with it, really cut to the heart! What about the common goal to *establish* trust? If each partner has lawyers and counselors involved in preparing such agreements, where's the Lord in this process? *Whose* assets are under consideration here—ours or the Lord's? Nagging questions like these, coupled with any adverse effects of such agreements, can carry forward for years, cropping up in many other relationship areas. That's why it's so important to pray about this controversial subject *before* taking any action.

The real force behind such private agreements is *fear*—one partner may fear the remarriage might bring an immediate claim on premarital property if and when a divorce occurs, while the other may fear losing an entitlement that he/she believes is earned merely by entering into remarriage. If one spouse feels the need for a premarital agreement, he/she has something of value needing protection—something the other spouse doesn't own. So a premarital agreement could *freeze* an imbalance in property and power in favor of the spouse receiving the agreement. Realistically, there's little chance the remarriage will escape hurt feelings in these circumstances. And hurt feelings frequently lead to some *very* adverse consequences!

Legal considerations. Obviously, attorneys and tax advisors need to tailor premarital agreements to a couple's situation, but here are a few important legal matters to consider:

• *Adequate notice without pressure.* Some very short-sighted souls actually have tried to deliver a premarital agreement to their prospective spouses on the way to the wedding. Not only is this idiotic, cruel, and manipulative, from a legal standpoint it's doubtful that a court would enforce it. Each partner needs enough time to read and evaluate provisions of an agreement, using counsel of independent attorneys and tax advisors without pressure. Entering into the agreement also must be voluntary—not under duress. Ideally, this should be done shortly after the couple's engagement—well in advance of planning any wedding—to allow time to count the cost of whether proceeding with the remarriage is appropriate.[17]

• *Full disclosure.* In discussing how to provide for children from a prior marriage, as well as ownership and use of premarital assets, each partner must list all premarital assets and liabilities. This may mean designating what each spouse contributes to the remarriage, as well as those personal assets kept separate. Premarital agreements are creatures of precise detail—there are no shortcuts!

• *Consistent actions.* One major legal trap undermining the legal effect of premarital agreements is allowing day-to-day living practices to run counter to the written provisions of the agreement. One primary problem arises when spouses have agreed on what is "yours, mine, and ours" and have set up separate personal assets and debts, but then they begin commingling marital and premarital accounts and assets. This makes it difficult, if not impossible, for any court to determine what belongs to whom later.

• *Questionable provisions.* There are some matters you may not be able to address adequately in a premarital agreement. For example, many states won't allow you to decide child custody issues in advance of any divorce, which may not occur. (The best interests of each child will almost always prevail in determining appropriate custodial care at the time of any divorce.) You also may not waive any legally applicable child support obligations. And while parties to a premarital agreement may agree on where they'll live, how they'll jointly or individually pursue career opportunities, and children's upbringing, they may not prescribe a child's religious upbringing after any divorce. This would require a court to encroach upon the basic right of individuals to question or change their religious convictions, as protected by the Free Exercise and Establishment Clauses to the U.S. Constitution. Religious freedom is inalienable—no one can bargain it away.[18]

• *Judicial review.* Parties to a premarital agreement may contract away numerous rights and benefits or *add* responsibilities beyond the minimum limits the law requires, but the entire agreement remains subject to judicial review as to *fairness* and enforceability. In doing so, a judge will make sure neither spouse automatically passes from misfortune to prosperity or from prosperity to misfortune. As one judge phrased it, "The basic criterion is fairness between the parties, which will be evaluated in light of the facts touching [one spouse's] property and the question of whether the provisions made for [the other spouse] will enable [that spouse] to live after dissolution of the marriage in a manner reasonably consonant with [that spouse's] way of life before the dissolution."[19]

Even if a premarital agreement is clear, unambiguous, and otherwise legally valid, a court may still not enforce it if a party to the agreement proves that fraud, duress, deceit, coercion, or overreaching occurred by the other party. That's why it's so important to promote equality and balance in premarital agreements, with each spouse having the benefit of using independent legal counsel, and marital counseling as well if necessary. (Again, it's vital for you and your partner to carefully [and prayerfully] review this entire process in light of God's Word, and use a private agreement *only* if it doesn't destroy your spirit of unity. If these prerequisites fail, *don't* go any further!)

Resolving conflicts and differences in using private agreements. When the issue of private trusts and premarital agreements comes up, many partners find themselves caught on the horns of a dilemma. Do they walk away from the remarriage before it begins and sacrifice a promising future together, or reluctantly agree to such private agreements "just to get it over with" (which certainly breeds frustration, anger, and resentment)? Donald Trump's ex-wife, Marla Maples, expressed her feelings about this conflict just prior to completion of their divorce in 1997. She admitted not wanting to take the time to even read her premarital agreement, which then husband-to-be Trump asked her to sign two days before her 1993 wedding. "I refused to read it because I felt it was sealing our fate," she told the *New York Daily News*. "I'm sure I would not have signed it. I probably would not have gotten married either."[20]

Is there any way to bridge the gap here? Fortunately, there's room for some negotiation, creativity, and compromise, provided each spouse steps back to consider each other's feelings and needs:

• *Focus on underlying feelings and concerns.* To resolve this deadlock and counter any fear, both partners need to reassure each other of their love for one another, with an overriding commitment to protect and provide for each other during the remarriage—regardless of issues addressed in private agreements. Fully discuss the underlying reason(s) for needing a private agreement, such as providing for biological children from a prior marriage.

• *Sunset provisions.* Why not include a provision that allows the spouses to renegotiate a premarital agreement and adjust its scope to meet changing circumstances? Many agreements allow for such renegotiations at intervals of five or ten years. Another possibility would be using an agreement for a limited time during the remarriage, with the stipulation that it dissolve after the couple has time-tested the remarriage for a specified number of years. By then they will have learned to trust each other more fully, while also building up enough joint assets for their mutual benefit. Sunset provisions like these help keep spouses from feeling locked into an agreement that may not work out the way they initially intended.

• *Joint asset pools.* Similar to a "sunset provision," a remarriage couple may begin the relationship with premarital assets owned separately. The couple also agrees to make annual contributions into a new joint asset pool. Year by year, the joint asset pool grows as each spouse's separate asset holdings diminish. Over time, this has the effect of equalizing what each spouse owns, resulting in a feeling of shared power and control.

• *Expense subsidies.* Although personal assets may be a spouse's separate property, the couple might agree that if budgeted family income doesn't balance with expenses in any particular year, the spouse with personal assets will use some of those assets and funds to provide a subsidy for the family. Then both spouses and the family can feel good that their budget will balance each year—a blessing many blended families don't have!

• *Other ownership options.* Simply keep personal assets separately titled in the name of the spouse owning them, and then be sure not to comingle any income with any joint marital funds. Try using private trusts rather than premarital agreements. One reason is obvious—premarital agreements contemplate divorce consequences, while private trusts generally don't, in most cases.

The bottom line on private agreements. Private agreements should benefit *both* parties in some way—not be a declaration of war. This is an opportunity to candidly discuss critical issues and prevent serious misunderstandings in the future. For Christians struggling with this issue, perhaps a good Bible study on having a biblical perspective on wealth and materialism should precede any discussions. Each person might want to read the parable of the rich fool in Luke 12:13–21 or Jesus' admonitions in Luke 16:10–13. If a Christian couple can, from their hearts, be at peace with themselves and the Lord about this matter, then it may be appropriate for them to proceed. However, if the potential upset and hard feelings threaten the remarriage, be wise and forget it! In any event, it's important that you and your remarriage partner choose wisely in this matter.

Now let's shift forward into the remarriage and consider one final matter—teaching financial responsibility to children in a blended family.

MODELING GOOD FINANCIAL CONDUCT FOR BLENDED FAMILY CHILDREN

Finances are a major factor in many blended family decisions. Certainly it is no less so in dealing with children. Financial management can provide positive reinforcement, encouraging a child to mature and grow in assuming responsibilities and developing proper, godly values. Or it can become a destructive tool, such as when a stepparent uses money to buy the compliance or affection of a stepchild. Will blended family children become accustomed to gifts and few hardships in life, or learn the true value of material things through hard work, patient saving, and rewards for excellence? Parents who wrap their children in a protective bubble with no financial struggles unwittingly deprive them of learning the basic skills of life management that enable them to cope with an unforgiving world.

We have the God-given responsibility to disciple and parent all children in our blended families into becoming responsible Christian adults. If our kids grow up with the "gimmes," becoming selfish and materialistic, this won't escape the Lord's notice! So how can you faithfully help your children prepare for life and financial responsibility? Here are some suggestions:

Lead by example. We need to *show,* not just tell, our kids how to be compassionate, generous, and spiritual stewards of God's blessings so they'll develop godly attitudes and become responsible good citizens as well as smart consumers. We need to make opportunities to talk with them about some of the financial decisions we make, and walk them through a few options and alternatives. As we do so, our children learn self-discipline and how to make sound decisions for themselves. Since their strongest temptations may come from worldly commercials and advertisements, we also need to help them decode sales approaches and the subtle messages they present. Most importantly, we need to teach and stress biblical principles of gracious and loving financial management—using the many insightful parables and lessons from God's Word—while cultivating a charitable spirit.

Let experience be a guide. Kids who have a voice in how they save and spend their money learn wisdom and prudence quicker than those who don't. Experience is a great teacher! For young children, this may mean giving them an allowance and encouraging them to put money in the plate at church, or letting them pay for a store item and receiving the change. For older children and teenagers, it may be allowing them to decide about expensive clothes by struggling with the question, "Is this something I truly need or just want, and how important is it?" or letting them handle returns and complaints about defective purchases they make.

Don't miss those golden opportunities to help your children learn about financial responsibility. Cheryl's brother, Larry Rybka, is a great example. One Christmas holiday, Larry was driving his seven-year-old daughter, Laura, to the mall to shop for presents. "Sweetheart, what are you going to buy Mommy?" Larry asked as he gazed at his daughter in the rearview mirror. "Well, I'm going to buy her a necklace, some perfume, some shoes, a pocketbook and a . . ." the list went on and on! "Well, honey," Larry gently interjected, "how are you going to pay for all those nice things?" "Easy," Laura chirped, "I thought I would do the *picking,* and you could do the *paying!*" Larry smiled to himself before pointing out, "Well, if I bought your gifts for Mommy, I really would be the one giving the gifts—not you." After hearing this, Laura was very quiet for a time while staring out the car window. Finally she said, "You know, Daddy, I've been doing some more thinking about this. I believe Mommy would like it much better if I made her something for Christmas—a clay statue of me!" Oh well. Laura did learn about personal giving nonetheless!

Don't bail our your children if they've spent all their allowance and want or need something else. Let them learn by facing the logical consequences of their own decisions! Let your children learn that resources have limits in fulfilling needs versus desires. This helps a parent avoid getting hooked into a child's inevitable, "Mom, can you buy me . . ." whims on shopping trips. Now the response becomes, "Well, do you have the money to buy it? If not, maybe you'd like to save your allowance until you can."

Allowances. Should you give each child a regular allowance? If so, how much? What, if anything, should a child do to earn it? Will doing chores be a prerequisite to receiving an allowance, or will each child receive payment for completing specific chores? In lieu of an allowance, will each child receive spending money for specific items, such as clothes or entertainment? What if a teenager has a regular job and already earns enough spending money? The blended family needs to review these issues together at a family conference to avoid sibling wars in the household.

Why are allowances important? Because each child needs to learn how to manage money. How can they do it without having any funds themselves? Allowances also are basic tools for helping our kids learn about family values, setting priorities in life, and using our resources wisely to glorify God and serve others. It's best not to tie allowances to chores such as making the bed, taking out the garbage, folding the laundry, setting the table, or caring for a family pet. Why? Because doing chores is part of being a blended family and helping one another. If parents pay kids for chores, it can change a kid's perspective. Instead of altruistically thinking about being a helpful family member, children may begin thinking selfishly about what's in it for them. Each family member has a personal stake and responsibility in helping family life run without receiving payment to do it.

In a letter to *USAA Magazine* some years ago, Dana Panter of Conroe, Texas, outlined her sound philosophy about allowances for her kids:

> In our family, I pay allowances once a month as a means of teaching children how to manage money. The money is divided into five categories: tithing, gifts, clothes, savings, and spending. The children do have weekly chores which are considered a part of being a member of our family. There are consequences (privileges taken away, etc.) if chores are not done. I believe it is wrong to tie allowance to chores in that children then tend to expect money for *everything* they do and don't learn a sense of "duty" in life.[21]

Gifts from ex-spouses and grandparents. It will happen sometime—your ex-spouse will lavish expensive gift(s) on your biological child while your stepchildren look on enviously. Or your parents will take your biological child on a fabulous trip but overlook their step-grandchildren in your household on their birthdays. You may feel guilty, and your spouse resentful, at the disparity adversely affecting his/her biological children. Meanwhile, intense rivalry may grow among children in the blended family. Though difficult problems, these situations do help kids learn that people don't have equal advantages in life. Sure, you can ask extended family members to be sensitive and empathetic to how *all* children in your family react to selective gifts. You might even limit how a child uses a gift that other children in your family don't receive. But these circumstances help discipline and mature kids for how the real world can be at times.

Emphasize fairness. It will be very difficult, if not impossible, to treat all children in the blended family equally in all situations. Why? Because they have so many different needs, which are in an almost constant state of change. One child may have severe medical problems and need much more time and attention. Another child may be a gifted athlete and need more financial support for sports gear and league fees. Another child may feel "caught in the middle" in the blended family, just needing some bucking up and more encouragement than others. Even in the most balanced blended families, the time, money, and attention each child receives may be unequal. But it's important each child sees the remarried couple striving to be *fair* in meeting legitimate family needs without bias or prejudice. If the kids see fairness, it'll keep them from exercising their natural tendency to keep score of what each child receives.

Encourage giving from grateful hearts. This is the most important financial lesson to instill in children living in a blended family. Talk to them about the importance of giving generously to the church and helping those in need. Help them to become "other-centered" as part of their love for God love for their parents and siblings. There are no greater commandments than fulfilling these goals in life—for your children . . . or yourself (Matt. 22:34–40).

A Message from Cheryl

As an older and independent woman, I found finances in a second marriage to be very complicated. I work in the area of financial planning. My experience is that most remarried couples have great conflict here—and for good reason!

To begin with, we're older, more independent, and set in our ways. Second, we've been through some type of unsettling by death or divorce of a spouse. The experience can't help but make us more cautious and acutely aware of the emotional and financial risks we take in remarriage.

Third, great conflicts of interest exist, particularly with children from a prior marriage. Most first marriages set things up to provide for spouses first and then children. But if there's only one natural parent providing for the children, their needs rightly may come before those of a new spouse.

I'm very opposed to a relationship that looks like a partnership agreement. You pay for half of the electricity, and I'll pay for half of the groceries. If you don't trust your spouse more than that, certainly don't risk your children to him as a stepparent! The children are a greater risk than money. But if you have money accumulated for the benefit of your children, perhaps through a death benefit or divorce settlement, it may be foolish not to set that money aside from a remarriage. This may be done effectively by separate titles or a trust agreement if a premarital agreement is distasteful or if assets aren't a great amount.

As far as daily expenditures are concerned, Warren and I quickly found we needed separate checking accounts. I needed freedom to make some daily financial decisions. I was used to writing checks, choosing a blender, or paying a mortgage. I had a budget. I didn't want to account to someone for my daily purchases—not because it's wrong but because I'd become much more autonomous as a mature single parent. So we have a budget and we abide by it. But I also have daily autonomy about how I spend some categories of our budget. We deposit some of our monthly budget money into my account, out of which I pay for things I oversee (clothing, groceries, gifts, etc.). I kept a credit card of my own, and these bills come to me. So if I spend too much on a dress (which happens often), I can make it up somewhere else. Warren doesn't worry. He doesn't see the bill (which keeps me out of trouble); he just sees the dress and baked beans for dinner!

Even our giving is different. Warren tithes to the church. I have a habit of scattering charitable gifts all over . . . school, a parachurch ministry, a single mother in need, or a religious politician. So, I have some of our tithe money to give away at whim, while Warren has some of our money budgeted to give faithfully to the church. Both of us have joy in giving as we are led without resenting each other's preferences.

It took us a while to figure all this out, but since then it has worked very well for us because it takes into account our unique personalities. The most important thing is to recognize that you have two mature adults here, and things aren't going to work the same, or as simply, as they did for your parents, who were married for forty years, or as it did (or didn't) work with your former spouse. Be creative. Talk a *lot*. Get good advice.

Don't ever feel that financial planning is unspiritual. Quite the opposite—the Bible's filled with advice on being cautious with money. I hope you come to your compromises easier and quicker than we did.

QUESTIONS FOR PERSONAL REFLECTION

1. What's my attitude toward money? What's the attitude of my remarriage partner? Are we compatible in our attitudes?
2. To what extent will my remarriage partner and I keep our premarital assets and liabilities separate? Does this separateness bother me? Does it bother my mate?
3. What are my values and goals for remarriage? What are the values and goals of my partner? In what ways do they differ? How are they the same?
4. What specific estate planning and other financial matters are a concern to me in remarriage? What concerns does my partner have? How have we addressed those concerns?
5. What specific financial challenges can we foresee in supporting a blended family? How will our ex-spouses and others affect our financial plans? How can we best disciple our children in financial matters?

Chapter 11

THE TANGLED WEB AFTER DIVORCE
Dealing with Ex-Spouses and Ex-Inlaws

One of the most challenging tasks of remarriage is trying to keep peace in the blended family—especially with ex-spouses. Are there ways to make these relationships loving and helpful to remarriage partners and their blended family members?

During our early courting days, Cheryl and Chase (then a toddler) flew from Ohio for a brief visit to South Florida. Her ex-husband, Michael, and I waited side by side at the airport gate to greet them. (We had met several times before this day, with good progress on building a cordial relationship.)

Chase, eager to run after a long flight, leaped ahead of Cheryl as they made their way from the plane. Spying Michael and me standing together, Chase raced toward us with squeals of delight . . . only to wrap his little arms around my legs and look up at me adoringly. Meanwhile, his father stood patiently beside me . . . alone.

Although it was a matter beyond my control, I still felt terrible about it. I can only imagine how Michael felt after making a long drive just to see his little boy. Gently peeling his little arms away from my legs, I got down on my knees to look Chase in his eyes. I hugged him tightly, while greeting him warmly. Then I quickly added, "Chase, I'm so glad you're here and that you're happy to see me. But your father came here to greet you also. Why don't you give him a big hug and let him know how much you love him?" He turned his head to smile at his father, and reached out for him.

Little Chase hardly knew how his actions impacted Michael and me. To his credit, Michael never made any issue of this event. Instead, he courageously took it all in stride as if nothing had happened. But putting myself in his shoes, I think this incident would have wounded me deeply. I would have felt jealous and hurt as I thought, "Who is this fellow anyway? He's just a guy my ex-wife is dating—not even family! And here's my *only* son, hugging him like *he's* the father!" Empathy for Michael flooded my soul. I've never forgotten it.

Sometimes the most innocent events can bring deep emotional wounds to noncustodial ex-spouses. Michael's mature and sensitive reaction was exceptional. Too

311

many ex-spouses react negatively to potential remarriage partners coming into the lives of ex-mates and biological children. It's important to understand why this happens before we can try to resolve the problems.

UNDERSTANDING THE MIND-SET OF EX-SPOUSES/NONCUSTODIAL PARENTS

A noncustodial ex-spouse/parent is excluded from home and children following a divorce. Outwardly, many of these parents may appear calm and self-controlled, but there's a lot more going on in their hearts. After dealing with attorneys, judges, and the family court system that may discount their parenting qualifications, they lose custody of their children. This causes them to seethe with anger and resentment toward their ex-mates while experiencing deep inner guilt and helplessness.

Noncustodial parents may feel guilt about the divorce causing their children pain, even if they didn't initiate the split. Feelings of inadequacy also arise from seeing the children too infrequently. (Some custodial parents also can't resist pouring a little fuel on this fire by accusing noncustodial parents of letting his/her children down by not being there for them.)

Many noncustodial parents feel utter helplessness as they watch their children grow and change without their input or direction. Remarriage causes these "outside" parents to look in on a blended family as being intact, almost like a traditional family. This makes many noncustodial parents feel unnecessary and useless. No surprise the pressure becomes so intense for some noncustodial parents that they choose to withdraw, perhaps even move away, cutting off further contact with their children. But who are the ultimate losers? The children.

Of course, a noncustodial parent's hostility about divorce and remarriage frequently transfers to anyone filling a stepparent role with his/her children. Who wouldn't feel hurt, displaced, and discounted watching from a distance as the kids bond daily with a stepparent they call Daddy or Mommy?

What about the emotional impact of ex-spouses watching former mates remarrying new partners, with all the resulting negative competition and comparisons? What former wife wouldn't feel wounded by her ex-husband remarrying a much younger woman? Factor in depression over losing a mate, stewing in low self-esteem, and it's easy to anticipate this emotional pot bubbling over. Marta gives us some insight into this feeling:

> My ex-husband, Garrett, is remarrying next month. I'm not handling it well. Garrett's bride is twenty years his junior—not to mention tall, blond, thin, looking like a supermodel. He recently bought a large, expensive house, and his fiancée is decorating it lavishly. My ex-husband's able to do a lot for our ten-year-old son financially. My son and I are very close, but it's hard to compete with Dad's hot tub, fancy car, and luxury vacations. I'm worried that when our son gets a little older, he'll want to live with his father because of the

luxurious surroundings and all the things his father can afford to give him. I feel very insecure about this situation.

Of course, Marta's allowing materialism and superficial competition to overshadow the truly meaningful values in life—that of loving her son and raising him to love God while guarding against empty worldly pursuits. Even so, many can identify with Marta's insecurities.

Remarriage brings other concerns for a noncustodial ex-spouse. A father worries: "Will this mean *less* time with my children because they need to spend more time with their new stepsiblings?" "Won't this remarriage and blended family life among strangers confuse my child?" "What will happen if my ex-wife and her new husband move to another state and I can't see my children every other weekend?" A desperate mother asks, "What if my daughter loves her new stepmother more than me?" These are all reasonable concerns.

Like it or not, custodial parents and their partners absolutely must remain empathetic to the intense emotionally and psychologically gut-wrenching feelings running through a noncustodial parent's mind and heart. Why? For the sake of the children. Because it's the right thing to do before the Lord. And for peace to prevail. But how can you make this happen with the Lord's help? Here are a few suggestions:

Pray for your ex-spouse. Even if you view your ex-mate as your enemy, Jesus says:

But I tell you who hear me: Love your enemies, do good to those who hate you, bless those who curse you, pray for those who mistreat you. If someone strikes you on one cheek, turn to him the other also. If someone takes your cloak, do not stop him from taking your tunic. Give to everyone who asks you, and if anyone takes what belongs to you, do not demand it back. Do to others as you would have them do to you. (Luke 6:27–31)

If an ex-spouse insults or hurts you in some way, what should you do? The Bible tells us more:

Bless those who persecute you; bless and do not curse. Rejoice with those who rejoice; mourn with those who mourn. Live in harmony with one another. Do not be proud, but be willing to associate with people of low position. Do not be conceited.

Do not repay anyone evil for evil. Be careful to do what is right in the eyes of everybody. If it is possible, as far as it depends on you, live at peace with everyone. Do not take revenge, my friends, but leave room for God's wrath, for it is written: "It is mine to avenge; I will repay," says the Lord. On the contrary: "If your enemy is hungry; feed him; if he is thirsty, give him something to drink. In doing this, you will heap burning coals on his head."

Do not be overcome by evil, but overcome evil with good. (Rom. 12:14–21)

Strive to identify with their interests and struggles in an even-handed search for common ground. Look for opportunities to make peace with your ex-spouse, if for no other reason than to provide level paths for your children to walk on peacefully.

This means cultivating some empathy for your ex-spouse. We know we're to *love* our neighbors. Don't ex-spouses qualify? We're to talk with them face-to-face. Communicate with them. Put ourselves in their place to understand them, more than force them to understand us. Love is more powerful than retaliation. And then, while loving our enemies, we're to resist evil conduct by not compromising the truth. "Turn from evil and do good; seek peace and pursue it" (Ps. 34:14). This means pursuing peace *actively*, like a hunting dog searches out game. It does *not* mean that a person doing evil things escapes judgment for injustice. As this passage clearly says, the Lord avenges unrepented sins. But the Lord deals with this person directly (Ps. 34:16; Prov. 24:19–20). We're to leave vengeance to the Lord. The Lord asks us to exercise grace, mercy, forgiveness, and love in doing to others as we would have them do to us (Luke 6:31).

But how do we resolve conflicts with our ex-spouses—especially when they become our enemies and hate us? It doesn't mean picking up the weapons of this world—guns, government, or going to court—to assert our rights. A Christian's tools for conflict resolution are truth, righteousness, peace, faith, salvation, and the Word of God (Eph. 6:13–17). Sometimes this means not resisting an evil person. It may mean turning the other cheek. It may mean going the second mile. Jesus tells us the best way to resolve conflicts with our enemies is to love them, pray for them, and give to them as God does. Winning a former spouse over into a spirit of cooperation through kindness is one of the most exhilarating experiences in life!

These are powerful principles—in theory for sure, but even more so in practice! Unfortunately, you and I know we cannot resolve every conflict with our ex-spouses, even by using these spiritual tools. Some conflicts defy resolution despite our best efforts. Even so, we cannot manipulate or control others to seek resolution and reconciliation. This is why we must embrace Romans 12:18 by striving to live at peace with our adversaries, as much as it depends upon us, and then turn the conflict over to God. But if opposing parties make the effort to go and meet with each other, face-to-face; if they allow wise and competent mediators to help resolve their dispute and restore the relationship without going to law against one another, it will work. Mediation also helps bring the peace that surpasses all understanding (Phil. 4:7).

Have a forgiving heart. Both spouses have a stake in the failure of a marriage. Have you confessed to your ex-spouse your part in whatever led to your divorce? Even if you weren't completely wrong, you can still tell your former marriage partner with a sincere heart, "I'm truly sorry for my part in how our marriage failed and how this hurt you. I don't want to cause you more pain. Please forgive me so we can work together on parenting our children as the Lord wants us to do." Graciousness like this will have its effect! You'll find it bringing down barriers and obstacles with your ex-spouse. Most importantly, it will make a real difference to your children.

As we've said, forgiveness is an unnatural act—it isn't our natural tendency to forgive others and release bitterness and resentment. In fact, we have to *learn* it from the Lord. Yet it's vitally necessary for us to move on in life. But there's more to forgiveness than that. We also must forgive our ex-spouses for what they did to offend us and our children—not primarily for their benefit, but for ours. This action cleanses our hearts of bitterness and resentment that poisons our lives and makes us depressed. Consider this statement from Kathy, a divorcee in New Mexico:

> In 2001 my son's father and I divorced. I harbored a lot of resent-
> ment toward him because he didn't contribute anything to our house-
> hold, nor did he help care for our baby. During our marriage, my
> savings ran out while he refused to look for a job. After our divorce,
> I spent a lot of time and energy being angry with my ex-husband for
> the way he behaved. I went back to college to get a better job, but my
> heart wasn't in it and my grades showed it. This severely depressed me.
> Then I read a real gem in an Ann Landers column: "Resentment is let-
> ting someone you despise live rent-free in your head." I read that sen-
> tence twenty times over and repeated to myself over and over whenever
> I felt hurt and angry at my ex-spouse. It no longer mattered to me that
> my ex-spouse never asked to see our son or never paid child support.
> I decided it was *his* problem. He would be the loser in the end.

Outdo your ex-spouse in flexibility and cooperation. If you have certain legal rights granted in a custody/visitation order, consult your attorney about more flexible visi-tation privileges. Nothing is keeping you from being more generous than the law requires. Be compassionate and empathetic about your ex-spouse's situation. Although you and your remarriage partner may feel vulnerable to manipulation and control, or like doormats for your ex-spouse, over time you'll see the wisdom of this gracious attitude as it disarms your child's parent and serves the best interests of all your kids. Be generous in adjusting visitation and holiday plans. Remember, if you're the custodial parent and have the children full-time, you're in the better position to cut your ex-spouse some slack and end potential conflicts and resentment in the process. Most noncustodial parents won't overlook or forget your kindnesses.

Respect your ex-spouse's privacy. Admit it—aren't you curious about what's hap-pening in your ex-spouse's life, especially since you send your child into that home for visits? Many divorced parents want to know how their ex-spouses spend their time and money, what their remarriages are like, and who they count as friends. Naturally, it's tempting to pump your kids for information. *Resist this urge!* Respect your ex-spouse's boundary of privacy. Doing so will encourage him/her to respect yours. This is a very important trade-off when you and your remarriage partner have enough troubles of your own in blended family life.

Assume the best of your ex-spouse. Inevitably there will be disagreements, no mat-ter how hard you and your ex-spouse try to work with each other. But don't play into Satan's hands by jumping on problems without having all the facts *first.* Give your ex-spouse the benefit of any doubt. Assume the best, rather than the worst, until you confirm an offense. Then discuss the matter *directly* with your ex-spouse. Also, resist the temptation to second-guess your ex-spouse's parenting decisions when your child is away on visitation. Yes, reveal your concerns and appeal for cooperation, but don't bad-mouth your former partner to your children or your current mate. Negative criticism tends to have a life of its own, and creates more problems.

Work out a fair and mutually beneficial coparenting plan. Discuss the need for consistency in house rules and discipline for your children. Just as a united front is necessary with your remarriage partner, it's even more important with a child's biological parents. Consistency requires advance communication, coordination, and cooperation without overruling each other's short-sighted decisions. Plan a workable visitation calendar allowing for flexibility in rescheduling. Especially plan for holidays to make sure you fully account for children's needs and expectations in a loving and considerate manner. Mutually pledge not to surprise each other with last minute changes that would disrupt either parent's household, unless a legitimate emergency arises. If you and your ex-spouse must negotiate any sensitive matters, do so in a neutral location, like a park or an office conference room without any children around.

Cooperate with your ex-spouse on visitation environment matters. Quite often, when children visit the noncustodial parent, that parent may not support your rules or boundaries for your children. Perhaps their values and faith are different, or nonexistent. They may have a live-in lover, drink heavily, or have a more "expansive" vocabulary. For many, this is the most difficult task to face. You must hand over your precious treasure to an ex-spouse you may not trust. There's no easy resolution in this trial, unless abuse occurs. But it's also true that reducing conflict with an ex-spouse makes the visit less stressful overall for your children (as hard as that might be).

We really have no control or authority over noncustodial parents. However, this challenge does present us with an excellent opportunity to take a moral stand with our children at an early age. Cheryl and I encouraged then seven-year-old Chase to tell his father he's allowed to watch only G-rated movies, and that he would leave the room if necessary should any other movies come on. This could be a useful lesson as he grows older and must stand up to peer pressure. It's not an ideal situation, but once we accept the reality, we can do our best to help our children build character.

Keep in touch with your child's feelings about visitation. One eight-year-old asked her mother, "Why don't you visit Daddy with me? You married him. I don't think it's fair. You should have to visit him too!" We need to help children like this youngster understand that both parents love them and want to spend time with them. It may not be easy for them to accept at the time, but later they'll see the wisdom of what you're doing.

Encourage remarriage partners to develop a good working relationship. After Laura and Peter remarried, Peter's grown daughter (of whom Laura became very fond) had family gatherings where Laura saw Peter's ex-wife, Peggy, more than she cared to. But Peggy, not feeling the same way about Laura, graciously sent an anniversary card to Laura and Peter, which included an invitation to Laura to meet for a lunch date. Laura reacted negatively to this gesture. She had no interest in "getting chummy" with Peggy. But Laura missed an excellent opportunity. Many remarriage partners see the value of staying on friendly terms with their spouses' ex-mates simply because it keeps a stable, peaceful environment for the children and eases conflict.

Getting to know one another's remarriage partners relieves many fears and doubts, but also just makes good sense! No parent would place children in another person's care without first checking that person out. Also, if divorced spouses have a strained relationship, either or both of their respective remarriage partners can help mediate personal conflicts. (Of course, it's better to let former spouses work out parenting and visitation matters between themselves. But when they hit a snag, who's better informed and available to help their mates work through sticky issues than remarriage partners?)

Obviously, introducing remarriage partners requires tact, sensitivity, and empathy among everyone concerned. Toward that goal, it's especially important that your remarriage partner remain humble and respectful of a noncustodial parent and his/her new spouse. First meetings can set the tone—good or bad—for future interaction. If you or your remarriage partner are defensive or demeaning to your ex-spouse and his/her mate, the success of your relationship can suffer for a long time. A "Cathy" cartoon illustrates this point. As Cathy attends the wedding of a former boyfriend (Alex), his bride runs up to Cathy with a big smile and open arms: "You're Cathy! Alex told me so much about you!" gushes the bride. "Alex talked about me?" Cathy asks with a look of some apprehension. "Are you kidding?" the bride chirps, "I helped him *recover* from you!! It was awesome!! We shared! We wept! We bonded over you! We owe our whole marriage to you! You were the focal point of our couple's therapy!!" Cathy blushes and thinks, "Fifteen minutes of fame is fourteen minutes too many."[1]

Some natural insecurities also may arise with some remarriage partners. Tom, the father of a fourteen-year-old daughter, and his ex-wife worked hard to maintain a cordial relationship after their divorce, for their child's sake. Now Tom, since remarried, has another problem:

> I recently married a woman who's terribly insecure. She thinks
> I shouldn't have any contact with my ex-wife unless it directly affects
> my daughter's health. I find this extremely restrictive, since there are
> school functions and athletic activities that my ex-wife and I want to
> attend. Each year, my ex-wife and I celebrate our daughter's birthday.
> This year, my daughter invited my new wife to come along. But my
> wife is physically ill over the prospect of being there, and insists I have
> no business going. She says my presence would encourage my daughter
> to think her parents will get back together. I have spoken to my daugh-
> ter about this, as has my ex-wife. Believe me, the teenager has no illu-
> sions about this annual get-together. Also, I have no intention of
> returning to my ex-wife, regardless of my daughter's wishes.

Tom indeed has a problem—not with his ex-wife but with his insecure remarriage partner! If Tom's wife feels uncomfortable attending the party, she's free to skip it. But how tragic that she feels she must interfere and upset a good coparenting relationship that Tom and his ex-wife created!

Fortunately, there are good stories to share. It's not uncommon for remarriage relationships to blend exceptionally well. An adult stepchild involved in one such family coalition shares this report:

My parents were married for twenty-five years before they divorced thirteen years ago. Their parting was amicable, and they both married other people within a few years. Since then, every holiday includes both sets of parents and stepparents. My mother and stepmother are good friends. Sometimes we take family vacations together. My children have benefitted from having extra grandparents, and there's no confusion or ambivalence. Our situation isn't typical, but there's never been any ex-spouse bashing or competition for the children's affection. Our family circle has expanded in size and love. I don't think I've ever thanked them adequately for turning what could have been a devastating event into one that's a joy. They've been exceptional role models.

I'm so proud to be part of such a loving, extended family!

Unusual? Yes. Impossible? Definitely not! Relationships like these prove that love is stronger than bitterness, resentment, and hatred. The aftermath of divorce need not continue destroying lives.

Try to eliminate uncertainties. Few people like unpleasant surprises—especially involving one's children. Make it your goal to be open and honest with your ex-spouse about matters affecting your kids—time, money, and other parenting responsibilities. Act the same with your children, considering their age and maturity.

Keep focused on the future. You can't change the past. Let it go, with all its baggage. Today's a new day. Start fresh and work with your ex-spouse from where you are right now, building a *new* coparenting relationship for your children.

Mediate your differences. Litigation frequently means that everyone loses—certainly in time and expense. Once you run on the litigation track, it's difficult to get off. Litigation exposes the worst in people bent on retaliation. If you can resolve nothing else with your spouse, try to agree on this: "We will use mutually trusted third parties to help us work through our conflicts." You and your ex-spouse won't regret it!

"EX-COMMUNICATION": KEEPING YOUR EX-SPOUSE INFORMED ABOUT YOUR CHILDREN

Divorced parents retain a lifelong connection through their kids. To assure a peaceful, healthy setting for your children's benefit, you and your ex-spouse must find ways to get along. The key to achieving success is communicating effectively and making sound mutual decisions in Christian humility and wisdom (Phil. 2:4).

Keep discussions focused on your children. Stick to an agenda of issues. Speak calmly and evenly in all situations, doing your best to keep a peaceful dialogue. Set parameters for your conversations, dealing only with your children's issues of most concern to your ex-spouse. Your blended family's business is, and should remain, private. This guards against any jealousies or insecurities your remarriage partner might have about contact with your former spouse.

Make specific requests. Being specific in scheduling visitation or fulfilling mutual coparenting responsibilities helps avoid many potential misunderstandings and conflicts. Pray and prepare for discussions with your ex-spouse in advance. Write your requests in clear, concise language. Run them by your remarriage partner. If the request requires multiple decisions, or contains too many details to discuss by telephone, write a letter and deliver or mail it with a reasonable timeframe for response.

Encourage direct communication between parents and children. Schedule reasonable times for the noncustodial parent to contact your children regularly by phone. These conversations facilitate important bonding for your children's benefit. Without a schedule, expect calls during the dinner hour or at the kids' bedtime! This is why many parents arrange early Sunday evening calls as a good way to begin a new week. Then, if Mom and Dad need to discuss coparenting matters, they also have time to talk after the kids have gone to bed. Avoid the temptation to "listen in" on your child's telephone conversations with a parent or to monitor their times together. This creates hard feelings, and could drive your ex-spouse and children into secrecy.

Maintain a parenting notebook. Some divorced parents, unable to communicate about their children due to emotional upset, make use of a parenting notebook, which travels back and forth with the child on visits. The notebook contains helpful information about changes at home, special achievements and upcoming events, as well as important medical information, school schedules, and vital telephone numbers for emergencies. Parents can attach folders of photographs and drawings as an added bonus. The only two ground rules are: (1) All entries should be positive and encouraging (in case your child reads it), and (2) for privacy reasons, there's no discussion about life in each other's homes, beyond the child's involvement.

Notification of specific school, sports, and social events. Without too much inconvenience and trouble, try to send the noncustodial parent copies of letters and notices about school, athletics, and other activities well in advance of the events. If this is too burdensome, point the noncustodial parent in the right direction to plug into the information pipeline. Direct notification relieves the custodial parent of blame if the noncustodial parent misses an event for lack of notice.

Fortunately, many schools acknowledge noncustodial parents' rights to participate as school parents (unless they're specifically denied by a court), although remembering to provide duplicates of everything can be problematic. One school principal offers these practical suggestions to help overcome this obstacle:

One way to help noncustodial parents stay informed about report cards and school events is for them to submit ten legal-sized self-addressed, stamped envelopes, which can be used by the school office to forward notices, copies of report cards, newsletters, etc. The parent can number each envelope one through ten, so when he or she receives envelope no. 8, the parent will know it's time to supply the school with more envelopes. Parents also can provide a few larger envelopes with extra postage for bigger mailings. They also should provide E-mail addresses to the teachers, as well as to the school office. Sometimes individual teachers send notices home in the child's backpack, so the office has no copies. Asking the child to supply both parents with this

information is unreliable. Some teachers, if asked, are willing to com-
pile a weekly packet for pickup by the noncustodial parent. I also recommend that both parents attend parent-teacher conferences together.
With so many divorced spouses, it becomes a burden on teachers to
schedule separate conferences for each parent.[2]
Be sure to add the noncustodial parent's name to all school emergency contact lists.

Be honest about behavior problems. Many custodial parents fear loss of custody if
they disclose a child's behavioral difficulties to a noncustodial parent. Usually, this is
an unwarranted concern. In fact, ex-spouses may be struggling with the same parenting problem! Why not relax and discuss the matter calmly and rationally together?
Join forces to deal with the matter directly, rather than avoid each other.

REAPING THE GOOD FRUIT OF COOPERATIVE COPARENTING

When former spouses can work through personal issues and truly cooperate with each
other, they can wipe out years of heartache, pain, and expense. It *is* possible!

This warm letter sent to Ann Landers by a Virginia divorcee touched my heart:

I would like to surprise my former husband with this tribute,
which I hope you will run on Father's Day. . . . My children's father has
always been a strong, positive influence in their lives. He not only
made his child-support payments on time, he also participated enthu-
siastically in our children's activities. He coached our son's Little
League team and bought season tickets to the symphony for our
daughter when she was learning to play the violin.

My ex and I separated when the children were very young, but the
kids have spent at least two nights a week with their dad ever since we
parted. We both juggled full-time jobs, but he was always available to
help take care of them when they were sick or had doctor's appointments. . . . We discussed the children frequently and he was always generous with his time. I made sure the children saw their father often,
and encouraged them to allow him to participate in every facet of their
lives. Too many ex-wives use their children's schedules as an excuse to
keep them away from their fathers. They may gain some personal satisfaction from this maneuver, but they sabotage one of the most important relationships their children will ever have.

I did my best to be gracious, and my ex returned the favor. He
never said one bad word about me. In fact, he tried to build me up
every way possible. Although I knew the kids liked him better, he
always told me, "That's not true. They love you just as much."

Divorce does not have to be divisive and painful if you put your
children's welfare first. We agreed that a good relationship with *both*
parents was vital, and did everything we could to make that possible.
We all turned out to be winners, because my ex-husband met me more

than halfway. I would like to thank him for that, and wish him a richly deserved Happy Father's Day.[3]

Isn't that a wonderful tribute to *both* of these divorced parents? What a noble example they are for former marriage partners!

Empathy, cooperation, and loving others as God loves us—these qualities help break through conflicts and bitterness with ex-spouses. But now let's review a couple of very sticky issues between divorced parents: nonpayment of child support and relocation of the custodial parent and children.

WHAT IF YOUR EX-SPOUSE DOESN'T PAY CHILD SUPPORT?

We hear and read about children living in substandard housing, inadequately clothed, with no insurance, while noncustodial parents live in relative luxury, paying little or no child support. Your situation may not be as drastic, but missing child support payments still present a problem for many blended families. Your children need and deserve this support!

Experts estimate that about 51 million Americans have child support obligations—either owing it or receiving it. About 85 percent of custodial parents are mothers. Meanwhile, U.S. Census Bureau figures for 1996 indicate that only 39 percent of all custodial parents in the U.S. received the full amount of court-ordered support. An almost equal proportion—37 percent—received *no* support at all from noncustodial parents. Another quarter only received partial payments.

Steven J. Silver, an Arizona assistant attorney general and head of that state's Enhanced Enforcement Unit, has prosecuted hard-core child support violators for years. "What is really appalling and painful to watch is the damage people do to their children," he notes. "It's going to affect these kids throughout their lives in their own ability to have trusting relationships, and it's going to affect their own parenting skills."[4]

Some noncustodial parents with court-ordered child support obligations mistakenly believe this obligation ends if or when a custodial parent makes more money or remarries a wealthier person, reducing the need for financial assistance. Not true! The legal obligation remains on *both* biological parents to support their children. Other noncustodial parents think they're excused from paying support to their biological children if they remarry and have stepchildren to support. Also not true! Parents still must support their biological children despite any added responsibilities for supporting stepchildren. Children, unlike baseball cards, cannot be traded with other parents!

The problem of "deadbeat parents." What about the truly hard-core cases—"deadbeat parents" who fail, neglect, or refuse to obey a court order directing payment of child support? This includes parents who can afford to pay child support, but don't do so; those who are voluntarily unemployed (or underemployed); and still others whom lawyers humorously refer to as suffering from R.A.I.D.S. (Recently Acquired Income Deficiency Syndrome). A true deadbeat parent makes *no* child support payments, rather than reduced payments. Florida Judge O. H. Eaton Jr. elaborates:

True deadbeats have no money or assets. They live off the income of others, usually day-by-day, or they rely upon the generosity of friends for assistance through the hard times. Deadbeats believe they have nothing to lose. They have no job. They have no status. They have no property. They perceive themselves to be creatures deserving of sympathy due to their pathetic state which was caused by the custodial parent who now is to blame for the whole thing. The usual civil remedies such as income deduction orders and writs of execution or sequestration do not produce needed monetary support. To add to the frustration, the custodial parent is usually destitute, or nearly so, and cannot afford counsel. Sometimes the court files in these cases are voluminous because the deadbeat [represents himself in court] and is making a career out of dragging the custodial parent to court over trivial matters, thus jeopardizing employment and putting the custodial parent even more at the mercy of the deadbeat. . . . It is not rational to refuse to pay child support. It is not rational for an ablebodied person to refuse to earn a living in order to avoid paying child support. Deadbeat parents justify their irrational behavior as a way to get back at the custodial parent, or to get the custodial parent back.[5]

Many deadbeat parents do have the necessary funds for support, but refuse to pay because they're angry with their ex-spouses. They ignore the fact that child support is a vital contribution to the physical and emotional well-being of their children, and they selfishly put their own needs first. If a divorce decree requires an embittered noncustodial parent to carry insurance for his/her children, that parent may try to withhold information on the policy, use sloppy handling of claims to "get even," or allow the policy to lapse. But the children losing critical coverage suffer the most!

Unmet child support obligations create great frustration and volatile emotions for everyone concerned—even judges. After dealing with deadbeat parents in court for many years, Judge Eaton believes attorneys and courts should get tough by using indirect *criminal* contempt proceedings to force these parents into meeting their legal support obligations—pay up or go to jail! He believes having a deadbeat parent arrested, booked, and fingerprinted, followed by prosecution before a jury (many of whom themselves regularly pay child support) is eye-opening for a deadbeat parent. (If a custodial parent is destitute, Judge Eaton notes that invoking the criminal process usually is without cost to the custodial parent, since taxpayers pick up the tab.)

New child support enforcement laws. Since defaults on child support obligations reached epidemic levels in the latter half of the twentieth century, Congress took action by enacting the following:

• The Personal Responsibility and Work Opportunity Reconciliation Act of 1996 (PRWORA) ended welfare as we knew it for the past sixty years.[6] It also included some significant child support enforcement amendments, including establishing new federal and state registries for support orders. It enhanced interstate enforcement by requiring all states to enact the Uniform Interstate Family Support Act (UIFSA) (which is complementary to the Full Faith and Credit for Child Support Orders Act [FFCCSOA][7]) by January 1, 1998, to keep federal funding for child support programs. (By April 1998, this was done.) The Act also expanded use of the Federal Parent Locator Service, and required states to enact tougher enforcement measures, such as authorizing the placing of liens on occupational and professional licenses.

• The Debt Collection Improvement Act of 1996 denies federal loans to parents owing child support, and intercepts federal payments to parents to pay debts.[8]

• In 1995 the Child Support Recovery Act (CSRA)[9] created a federal offense for those willfully failing to pay legal child support obligations for a child who lives in another state. The Deadbeat Parents Punishment Act of 1998[10] strengthened the CSRA, and also makes nonpayment of child support a federal felony, punishable by fines and up to two years in prison and mandatory restitution. Defendants can be convicted—even upon showing they couldn't pay the full amount ordered—if they also failed to pay the portion they could afford![11]

Congress's intent is to centralize collection and distribution of support funds in each state, provide for automatic wage-withholding orders for each child support order, streamline enforcement of orders across state lines, and use technology to track parents trying to hide their assets from child support enforcement agencies. Even so, collection of child support remains a serious problem in America.

These laws are *tough!* Congress wants all states to get serious about making deadbeat parents pay child support so children no longer have to suffer the consequences of their failure to do so. Federal prosecutors also are becoming more aggressive in criminally prosecuting those who repeatedly flout state court child support orders. In August 2002, they arrested 102 deadbeat parents in 29 states who together owe more than $5 million in unpaid child support.[12]

Both biological parents, custodial and noncustodial, have a spiritual, legal, and moral obligation to take care of their children. Deadbeat parents still try to find legal loopholes to "beat the system." But those loopholes are rapidly closing. And certainly there are *no* loopholes in parenthood obligations before God!

What's really broken here? It isn't child support defaults and legal obligations—it's *parenthood*. David Blankenhorn, author of *Fatherless America*, offers this insight: "Our current deadbeat dad strategy fails even to acknowledge our society's crisis of family fragmentation and declining child well-being. For what is broken in our society is not the proper police procedures to compel small child-support payments from reluctant men. What's broken is fatherhood."[13] Secular sources agree. A few months after Blankenhorn made these comments, New York Bar Association Matrimonial Law Committee member Sy Reisman made this observation:

> There is nothing simple about divorce, and the seething anger that
> surrounds the imposition of [support] cannot be diverted even with
> the legal arsenal Washington is considering. If we are really serious
> about tackling the multibillion-dollar problem of deadbeat parents, we
> need to look at how visitation and custodial rights are handled by the
> courts. The strongest weapon we have for solving the deadbeat parents

problem is to ensure they have ample access to their children and a significant role in their upbringing.[14]

So *why* do many noncustodial parents (with fathers comprising about 85 percent
of that group) fail to pay full support? Quite often, it's because they *feel cut out of their
children's lives!*[15] It's not morally right to do this, and support obligations should be
met regardless of feelings, but we still need to *understand* how noncustodial parents
view their circumstances so we can work out an appropriate solution. And it's a fact
that when noncustodial parents don't feel disenfranchised from their children, they do
pay more support.[16]

You really have two alternatives to deal with an ex-spouse who's behind on child
support—the "hammer" of criminal prosecution that the world offers, or the *loving
hand* that Christ says we should use (with "tough love," if necessary). Here are a few
more practical suggestions to help you deal with your situation God's way:

Make your children a priority. This is the best approach in dealing with child support issues with hostile or cooperative ex-spouses. Most ex-spouses can work through
problems if *mutual* concern for their children remains foremost. Support funds benefit children, and are not for parents' personal expenses. Quite often when parents
bicker over child support, they've lost sight of their children's needs.

Many family mediators can help parents keep the focus on their children. One
begins initial sessions by asking ex-spouses for pictures of their children, which he lays
on the table, saying, "Folks, these are the most important persons we need to think
about here. They did nothing wrong, yet they suffer more from the consequences of
your divorce than anyone else."

Be generous with visitation. Be as cooperative as possible in permitting frequent
visits by the noncustodial parent—perhaps even more than your custody order allows.
Keeping a noncustodial parent active and involved in the child's life avoids many
problems. If you or your remarriage partner has serious concerns about the lifestyle
of a noncustodial parent, why not suggest *inclusive* visits where your blended family
invites the other parent to visit with the child in a semi-supervised way while everyone enjoys a family picnic or a sports event? There are ways to make visitation work
in relieving everyone's concerns.

Account for child support expenditures. Most custodial parents use support money
wisely. Certainly it's their legal prerogative to decide how to use these funds in their
children's best interest. Even so, many noncustodial parents doubt whether custodial
parents truly spend support funds on the children, rather than on personal expenses.
Allay these concerns by being upfront and honest. Periodically provide your ex-spouse
with an accounting for how you spent the support money. Even better would be to tell
your ex-spouse, "Sam, Mark needs some clothes for school. Rather than pay the full
amount of child support this month, why don't you deduct $150 and take him shop-
ping so he can see you buying the clothes for him directly? I'll be glad to provide you
with a list of what he needs." The custodial parent now controls a portion of the support money and gets to be the hero. The child also sees an active and involved parent
fulfilling support obligations in a personal way.

Don't be petty about your children. Custodial parent Chip remarried Judi, bringing his seven-year-old son, Tim, into their new blended family. The family agreed that everything they give Tim stays at their house. They send Tim on visits to his mother, Martha, with only a few old playclothes. Judi and Chip didn't tell Martha about this rule because they once bought a new outfit for Tim, which Martha accidentally ruined by putting too much bleach in the washer. Martha replaced the outfit, but if she finds out about the "rule," she may become irritated at Judi and Chip. Do material possessions take precedence over relationships? Is it a loving, godly act to risk involving the child in an interfamily dispute? How does this "secret rule" promote peace? Judi and Chip would do well to rise above the bleach incident and forgive Martha, since everyone will gain more in the long run. The bottom line on child support: Always keep the big picture in mind, and don't let trivial matters jeopardize relationships.

Try private mediation. Even the best parents run into conflicts regarding support obligations. Use biblical conflict resolution measures (chap. 6) to work through problems if you're unable to do so directly with your ex-spouse. You'll be amazed at how much less expensive, and more rewarding, mediation can be if everyone actively participates with the desire to cooperate!

Here's an example: Before Keith and Sue remarried, Sue's former spouse, Mark, wasn't paying support for his daughter despite having a good job. Since Sue was financially secure, she didn't complain—she was just pleased to have peace with Mark. But was Sue thinking more about her daughter's well-being, or just wanting to save herself the trouble of trying to enforce the long-standing support default? Money wasn't the only problem. Wasn't it important for Mark to take a personal stake by supporting his daughter? Both parents were dropping the ball, with Sue appeasing Mark's negligence—all at their daughter's expense. Keith urged Sue to reconsider the situation. She reluctantly concurred that Mark should make current payments, even if she preferred to let past due payments accrue for now. No one wanted a court battle, but something needed to be done.

Solution? They used private mediation, considered various options and alternatives, and agreed on the following plan: Use available legal procedures to have Mark's employer deduct support payments directly from his paycheck and send them to the court registry, for forwarding on to Sue. This spares Mark the monthly anguish of writing a check to his ex-wife, while ensuring payments arrived in Sue's hands on time. (After beginning this procedure, payments haven't been a problem.)

After Sue and Keith remarried, another problem arose. The Lord blessed them with a very comfortable lifestyle. While Mark certainly wasn't poor, he lived more modestly. Mark resented sending support to Sue when she and Keith already provided Mark's daughter with a better lifestyle than he was able to afford. To appease Mark, Sue quietly began refunding some support money to Mark. Again, they were backpedaling into an appeasement/negligence posture with each other.

This called for a creative win-win solution. The mediator told Sue, "I understand why Mark feels some resentment paying money to you while you and Keith enjoy a comfortable lifestyle. However, it isn't morally or legally right for Mark to ignore his responsibilities and obligations to your daughter. I'm also aware that Keith, as your daughter's stepfather, wants to show he loves her too through supporting her. So why don't you and Keith assume 100 percent of your daughter's daily living expenses, and put every dollar of Mark's support into a trust fund for your daughter's college expenses? That way, Mark can truthfully tell his daughter he's paying for her college education and feel good about paying support. Mark's contribution helps you and Keith save for your daughter's education as well. Win-win." Everyone loved the idea! When creative solutions work, *everyone* feels good about it!

Despite financial issues, and regardless of each parent's emotions, the focus of child support always should be your *child's* best interest. If conflict and confusion arise over child support payments, parents probably have muddied the waters by self-interest. Understandably, it will be difficult, perhaps impossible, for the parent paying support to enjoy sending money to an ex-spouse. An unforgiving spirit feeds this pain. But whether an ex-spouse owes you support or vice versa, make the payments owed as if paying it to the Lord for your children's benefit.

Use legal remedies only as a last resort. Custodial parents owed child support now have a powerful arsenal of legal remedies to enforce payment from delinquent ex-spouses. But, to escape bitterness and resentment toward you, your children, your remarriage partner, and your blended family, avoid threats. Use available legal resources only if private negotiation and mediation fail. Be sure to consult with a good family law attorney before taking any action. (Also keep in mind 1 Corinthians 6:1–8, if your ex-spouse is a Christian. In that instance, God's Word counsels us to absorb the loss rather than litigate with fellow believers.)

Moral of the story regarding child support defaults of an ex-spouse? Work out a cooperative coparenting plan with your ex-spouse to make sure he/she has significant interaction with your children. Give the noncustodial parent lots of good reasons to care and get involved! This should provide motivation to provide the necessary support without complications.

WHAT IF YOUR FAMILY RELOCATES AFTER REMARRIAGE?

Emily received sole custody of her children as part of her divorce from Beck. A working single mother in Miami, she was transferred four years later to Atlanta. When Beck arrived on a visitation appointment ten days before the scheduled move, Emily handed him a letter advising him of her new job and address. She informed him that he could have the children during part of the summer, and could visit them in Atlanta anytime. Beck was furious, and filed a petition with the court granting their divorce, demanding immediate custody of the children.

Janis, the mother of two boys, lived in Nashville near her country singer ex-husband, Carl, for many years after their divorce. Now she's remarrying a minister from a large Southern Baptist church in Texas. Janis and the boys will move with the minister into a church-owned house. Carl, more resistant to religion since the divorce, is doubly angry about this move "halfway across the country" and how Janis is "brainwashing my sons with Christianity." He hires an attorney to block Janis's move or change custody, with references to a "cultlike church." So begins another angry, self-centered court battle with children in the breach. How the Lord must weep as he watches hurting people struggle for control while mutilating each other and those they love in the process!

Across America, many laws encourage frequent, positive interaction by *both* parents in the rearing and development of their children, reinforcing views of numerous child experts and studies that children generally benefit from such continuing relationships. But our highly mobile American society demands frequent relocation for any number of reasons. During 1996–97, 16 percent (42.1 million) of Americans moved, with 19 percent of that number moving between counties, and 15 percent across state lines. Of these, 1.6 million female single heads of household relocated, while 480,000 male single heads of household moved.[17] Each year approximately one American in five changes residences, with the average adult moving about 10.5 times in a lifetime. Most moves are employer-initiated job transfers. Certainly each American has the constitutional right to travel. As noted researcher Dr. Judith Wallerstein advised a California court, "To require divorcing parents to spend their lives in the same geographical vicinity is unrealistic."[18] But this raises the question: Should children move with their custodial parents to preserve stability at the expense of the noncustodial parent?

This single problem—relocation—perplexes and plagues parents, psychologists, lawyers, courts, and legislatures more than any other family controversy. Ex-spouses face excruciatingly difficult life choices dealing with postdivorce matters—decisions impacting them and their children far into the future. Normal, healthy, and desirable life changes occur for ex-spouses as they build separate lives, change jobs, pursue new careers, remarry, have new children, and relocate. But relocation stands as a major turning point for postdivorce family members. Divorce does enough to disrupt each parent's involvement and access to their children, but relocation can shut down interaction for long periods. Despite previous good communication and cooperative coparenting between former mates, *major* resistance often springs from relocation decisions. An amicable relationship can turn sour—perhaps forever. It invites anger, defensiveness, stonewalling, and revenge if not handled sensitively and lovingly. Few issues are more complex, controversial, and heart-wrenching than relocation. No wonder this is a major battleground between ex-spouses!

Relocation generally leads to one of three alternatives: (1) allowing relocation by the custodial parent (which means less access by the noncustodial parent); (2) not allowing the relocation (leaving the child in the custody of a frustrated parent who cannot move); or (3) changing custody, thereby freeing the former custodial parent to move—but without his/her child. There are no easy choices here!

When a competent custodial parent wants to relocate with a child for good reasons, what about the noncustodial parent's interest to keep involved in the child's life? And how about the child's close connections and relationships in the existing community? Will severing ties harm him/her? If there's any chance of postdivorce litigation, relocation of a custodial parent will be the lightning rod receiving multiple strikes from a disappointed, frustrated, and angry noncustodial parent unless mercy, grace, compassion, and compromise prevail!

Legal problems with relocation decisions. Unlike most legal issues where courts render decisions based upon *past* behavior of people, child custody/relocation cases force courts into predicting *future* behavior of parents, and how they might handle relocation. They also must foresee how children will react and adjust to changes.

In considering relocation cases, courts and child experts try to measure potential harm to a child arising from the move, compared to what might occur if the child remained in the same community, with a custody change—an almost impossible task! In doing so, courts balance child and parent factors in a cost/benefit analysis, which leads to inevitable guesswork. If a court determines that relocation of a child one hour away from the current home isn't harmful, would a move of two hours be enough to deny relocation? In 1999 a Colorado court determined that a mother who moved from New York with a young child was undermining the relationship with the child's father, which harmed the child. But removing the child from the mother's custody would create even more harm than that which the mother caused. The court had to choose between all the harm done to find the *least* detrimental solution for the child—a horrible dilemma![19]

And what happens to children during all this legal wrangling? Renewed conflict between parents in courthouses piles on children's emotions and severely threatens their sense of security. The court system terrifies many young children—particularly proceedings involving child evaluations. They suffer through even temporary separation from the custodial parents and other legal disruptions of daily family life. After experiencing major life trauma in seeing their parents separate and divorce, a black-robed stranger sitting behind a big desk in a large, cold courtroom now tells them which parent they *must* live with, as the other parent becomes geographically distant! How can anyone avoid lasting psychological damage to children in these sad circumstances? As Dr. Judith Wallerstein notes, in the child's mind this conflict confirms "a view of the world as an armed camp in which the child can trust no one."[20]

Is this what God wants? No! How can we put practical Christian principles and godly attitudes to work in keeping this from happening to those we love?

Relocation factors. After handling many complex relocation cases, legal experts have helped fine-tune the issues we also need to focus on as Christian parents.

Two primary questions must be considered: (1) Is relocation in the best interest of the *child* (not the parents)? (2) Would relocation be harmful to the child? This tandem consideration obviously isn't made without difficulty. While relocation may not be in a child's best interest, would it be sufficiently harmful to justify not relocating? Also, how does one quantify harm? At a minimum, any child will experience some emotional distress and adjustment problems in any significant relocation.

The American Academy of Matrimonial Lawyers prepared a model relocation act with standards to guide those grappling with these decisions, offering the following factors to consider:

- the nature, quality, extent of involvement, and duration of the child's relationship with the person proposing to relocate, and with the nonrelocating person, siblings, and other significant persons in the child's life;
- the age, developmental stage, needs of the child, and likely impact of relocation on the child's physical, educational and emotional development, taking into consideration any special needs of the child;
- the feasibility of preserving the relationship between the nonrelocating person and the child through suitable visitation arrangements, considering the logistics and financial circumstances of the parties;
- the child's preference, considering the age and maturity of the child;
- whether the person seeking relocation has an established pattern of conduct of promoting or thwarting the nonrelocating person's relationship with the child;
- whether the relocation will enhance the general quality of life for both the custodial party seeking relocation and the child, including but not limited to financial, emotional benefit, or educational opportunities;
- the reasons each person seeks or opposes the relocation; and
- any other factor affecting the best interest of the child.

The first three factors are the most contentious issues between parents fighting over relocation, particularly when many argue that frequent and continuing contact between *both* parents and minor children is a priority. Nevertheless, these factors provide us with an excellent checklist to evaluate and pray about how any relocation will affect our children and *both* parents.

How do courts and legislatures balance all these factors? As of this writing, the majority agree with child psychologists and other experts: A child's relationship with his/her primary residential parent and caretaker—the custodial parent—is the most important factor affecting the child's welfare when the child's parents don't live together. So courts generally keep the custodial household intact and permit relocation if there are no compelling reasons against doing so, notwithstanding diminished contact with the noncustodial parent. They believe forcing a custodial parent to forego relocation in a desperate effort to retain custody puts that parent in the unenviable position of making a "Solomonic choice," which unreasonably tests parental ties.[21] The only instance courts in most states may deny relocation, or order a custody transfer, is when the noncustodial parent establishes: (1) the relocation will prejudice the child's welfare, and (2) changing custody will bring less harm to the child than permitting relocation with the custodial parent/primary caretaker.

But how will *you* and your ex-spouse balance these factors? Try to be objective and yielded to the Lord as you consider each one. If you can do so without extreme upset, review each one with your remarriage partner and your ex-spouse. Seek the advice of Christian counselors and church elders. Strive to define the issues affecting *your* move, and begin developing options and alternatives to reduce conflict.

Listen to your children. Children need to *know* that both parents love them—even when they're separated. So it's vitally important that parents have sensitivity and awareness about each child's adjustment to relocation—physically, emotionally, and spiritually—since they're also grieving over separation, loss, and abandonment issues from the divorce. Think and pray carefully about their feelings and preferences. But be careful! Children are notorious people-pleasers—especially with parents. They often seek to favor and support the more unstable or needy parent—even at their own developmental expense. Although younger children are easily manipulated, older children can be self-serving, and heavily influenced by which parent will be the more lenient. Children's preferences don't always reflect true feelings or the true relationship with each parent. Nor do their views show accurate recollection of experiences with both parents, or even their own best interests. Therefore, *understanding* the reasons behind a child's preferences is crucial. But if a child is of sufficient age (usually, seven or older), with capacity to reason and form an intelligent preference about custody, most courts won't ignore this input. Neither should parents.

Compromise and cooperate whenever possible. Parents who truly love their children will be cooperative, compromising, and sacrificial in working through all relocation problems. No doubt a child's postdivorce adjustment moves forward best when *both* parents support a coparenting relationship. In relocation, *adjusting* that coparenting plan to reinforce the relationships helps reduce conflict, reduce loss and expense, and greatly helps preserve the peace. Cooperation confirms that both parents are striving to be peacemakers without acting rashly, while sharing the goal of sacrificially considering the child's needs first.

So how can you work peacefully with the noncustodial parent in making a relocation decision? First, don't surprise your ex-spouse with a decision to relocate. Except when domestic violence is a threat, custodial parents should provide noncustodial parents with reasonable prior (not less than sixty days) *written* notice of any proposed relocation, which should include a *proposal* for a revised visitation schedule if the move makes the current schedule unworkable. Your ex-spouse will appreciate your advance disclosure and willingness to compromise early.

Review the relocation factors with your former mate. Remember, keep your focus on your *children*. What problems need to be addressed? List each one so you can pray about them and seek further advice. Brainstorm together on options and alternatives to make any relocation less burdensome for everyone concerned. If your ex-spouse is willing to cooperate on a relocation, but has concerns about the travel expense to see your children, perhaps you can provide some help by using support funds to subsidize visitation trips. You also may agree to visit your current city each year to increase contact between your ex-spouse and children. Maybe you can agree to meet at a fun, neutral location, such as a Disney World trip. Lots of avenues are open to you if you and your ex-spouse can discuss them calmly and sensitively.

Physical distance need not be a barrier. Noncustodial parents and relocated children can still have meaningful contact—even on a daily basis. If you're the custodial parent, take the initiative! Telephone calls, letters, and especially instant E-mail and video greetings through the Internet help bring separated family members together in ways that were impossible a decade ago. Help your ex-spouse and children use regular telephone chat times or E-mail sessions. Cooperate with reading of bedtime stories by telephone or by sending tapes you can play for your children. Have your child send the other parent special drawings, essays, and poems. Encourage parent and child to exchange photographs and videos of life events. Your ex-spouse will appreciate your cooperation in promoting the relationship, while your child has the security of knowing *both* parents' love. Personal visits then become another element of the relationship, rather than an isolated special event.

Work out travel plans. Arrange for the noncustodial parent to visit your child, sparing travel problems for your child. The visiting parent can see the child (and the child's peers) in their home and school environments. But it will be necessary for the child to visit his/her noncustodial parent as well. This is important, since it gives parent and child the sense of living together for a time, as opposed to merely visiting each other, and also provides interaction with stepparents and stepsiblings. Try to agree upon a fair sharing of travel expense, and a liberal extended visitation schedule during the summer months and holidays.

Get counseling help. Counseling is necessary for both parents, their respective remarriage partners, and especially the children to reduce the adverse effects of any relocation. Don't try to do this on your own unless you and your ex-spouse have a very cordial and cooperative coparenting arrangement!

Use mediation. If you and your ex-spouse cannot agree on how best to handle a family relocation matter, don't rush into court! Mediation can help you work out mutually acceptable solutions tailored to your circumstances. Allowing *parents* (not judges) to determine what's best for their children, with the assistance of an unbiased, competent mediator, reduces conflict and ultimately brings more satisfaction. It's certainly what the Lord would want. Mediation provides more opportunities for both parents to work out creative, individualized visitation schedules while counterbalancing any adverse effects on the noncustodial parent's relationship with the children. Adversarial court litigation over relocation issues would only be a last resort.

Like many other consequences of separation and divorce, there are no easy answers. The New York Court of Appeals provided this thought-provoking observation on the extremely difficult challenges facing legislatures and courts in relocation cases:

> Like Humpty Dumpty, a family, once broken by divorce, cannot be put back together in precisely the same way. The relationship between the parents and the children is necessarily different after a divorce. . . . Accordingly, it may be unrealistic in some cases to try to preserve the noncustodial parent's accustomed close involvement in the children's everyday life at the expense of the custodial parent's efforts to start a new life or to form a new family unit.[22]

But where courts and legislatures throw in the towel, Christians can keep moving in a positive direction by working out loving and mutually acceptable relocation solutions with the Lord's guidance!

COPING WITH BITTER, VINDICTIVE, AND CONTROLLING EX-SPOUSES

Hostile noncustodial parents/ex-spouses are loose cannons who've taken a bitter pill of resentment into their hearts. They believe rejection they feel from their children or former marriage partners justifies backlash and revenge. Because they're unable to forgive you or accept their losses, you must prepare yourself for extreme behaviors that disrupt and actively interfere with your life, and the lives of those you love.

In her book *To Love Again: Remarriage for the Christian,* author Helen Kooiman Hosier shared one good example of how bitter and resentful ex-spouses can poison the foundation of good relationships:

> I know of one woman who flew to another state to visit her ex's favorite aunt. There she unloaded all her stored-up venom, convincing the elderly lady that her nephew had wronged her terribly. The aunt, now up in years and not as capable as she once had been of sorting things out, believed this vicious woman, wrote her nephew telling him she never wanted to hear from him again, and that she was ashamed of him. She berated him for stepping out of God's will, for going against the teachings of the Bible, and for deserting his wife. The tragedy of this story is that because the man had never received much love from his mother, this aunt had been as a surrogate mother to him, and when he received the letter from her he was heartbroken. He wrote several letters in reply; he called her on the phone, but she hung up. Finally she wrote him back stating she never wanted to hear from him again. The relationship was severed, never to be restored.[23]

Alex's ex-wife, Jeannie, also made his life unbearable. As part of their custody agreement, Alex settled for much less visitation than he wanted with his ten-year-old daughter, believing it best for her if he and his ex-wife limited contact. He loves his daughter very much, and sees her regularly—without a hint of criticism about her mother. Whenever he takes his daughter on an annual vacation with his new wife and family, he always tells Jeannie where they're going and for how long. Jeannie always has his cell-phone number for emergencies, and Alex makes sure his daughter regularly checks in with her mother. But this never seems to satisfy Jeannie. Although Alex has never done anything to warrant her concerns, Jeannie wants the names, addresses, and phone numbers of every hotel and destination on his family trip (even though some arrangements haven't yet been made), as well as every friend Alex may visit, whether he actually sees them or not. Alex resents having to subject his daughter, his family, and friends to what he perceives as obsessive and controlling behavior.

Parental Alienation Syndrome. Even worse are the instances where parents feel the need to destroy the bond between their children and the other parent. Experts confirm what most parents know already—children need the love of *both* parents in order to mature and develop to their full potential in life. Divorces often destroy family relationships for generations to come—why make it even worse for the innocent children? And yet some do just that.

One classic example of how this destruction occurs arose in the case of Richard and Laurel Schutz. After six years of marriage, they divorced in November 1978. The former Mrs. Schutz received sole custody of their two young daughters, while Mr. Schutz had visitation rights. In the following years, the mother moved the children from state to state without notifying Mr. Schutz before each move. When Mr. Schutz found his children, they "hated, despised, and feared" him.

Mr. Schutz went to court for help. The judge determined "the cause of the blind, brainwashed, bigoted belligerence of the children toward the father grew from the soil nurtured, watered, and tilled by the mother." The court believed "the mother breached every duty she owed as the custodial parent to the noncustodial parent of instilling love, respect, and feeling in the children for their father. . . . She slowly dripped poison into the minds of these children, maybe even beyond the power of this Court to find the antidote." Consequently, the judge ordered the mother "to do everything in her power to create in the minds of [the children] a loving, caring feeling toward the father . . . [and] to convince the children that it is the mother's desire that they see their father and love their father."

The mother wasn't content with this decision, however. She appealed the ruling to the Supreme Court of Florida, arguing that her First Amendment rights guaranteeing free speech protected her from any legal obligation to undo the harm to the children. The court agreed that she had freedom of speech. But the father of her children, and the state of Florida, had a stronger interest in encouraging a good relationship between father and child. If it were otherwise, the court reasoned, any such encouragement would do no good if the mother could undo it. No one required the mother to express opinions she didn't hold (a practice disallowed by the First Amendment). She was, however, required to take those measures necessary to restore and promote frequent and positive interaction (such as visitation, telephone calls, letters) between father and children, and to refrain from doing or saying anything likely to defeat that end.[24]

Sadly, the real victims in the Schutz case were the children. Despite the best efforts of the judicial system, will they ever appreciate their father fully after the damage done? Sowing seeds of resentment and bitterness in young, impressionable minds of children against a parent reaps a whirlwind (cf. Hos. 8:7; Gal. 6:7–8).

The Schutz case highlights a major problem among ex-spouses—bitterness and revenge overflowing from adverse effects of divorce. Psychologists and courts call it "Parental Alienation Syndrome." It is conscious (and subconscious) brainwashing, causing a child's alienation from the other parent. As one parent deliberately and systematically teaches a child to defame the other parent, a child becomes obsessed with shunning or hating the other parent without embarrassment or guilt. The child views the "loved" parent as all good and the "hated" parent as all bad, resulting in long-lasting animosity without any compelling reasons for such hatred.

Parental alienation also can be self-inflicted. Rebecca, a single mother with custody of her children wrote this revealing note to her ex-spouse (who has since remarried):

I know the children haven't spoken to you for several months.
They're old enough now to call and visit you on their own if they wish.
I have asked them to call you today because I think it's important they
stay in touch with you. I didn't do it for your sake. I did it for theirs.

You've been telling people I "turned the children against you."
I didn't have to do that. You did it all by yourself. You criticized and
yelled at them during court-ordered visitations. When you refused to
pay child support, I had to get your wages garnished—twice. Then you
lied about your income, putting some of your money in your new
wife's name. You should be ashamed. You profess to love your children,
but you don't want to support or care for them.

You might want to know how your children are doing, but you
never bother to call. You haven't sent them a birthday card, graduation
card, or holiday gift in years. These aren't stupid kids. They know you
just bought a big house with a swimming pool. When you refused to
help pay their college tuition, they figured out where that money went.

Get to know these three great kids while they're still willing. It's
becoming harder every day to get them to make the effort to call you.
One of these days, it'll be too late.

How do you deal with challenging and powerful situations like these?

Take prompt, decisive action. One cannot ignore parental alienation, since it
destroys any chance for a child to have a healthy perception of the defamed parent and
severely affects custody, visitation, and other contact between both parents and the
child. Early diagnosis and prevention are *essential* to an aggrieved parent in avoiding
permanent damage. Prevention may require an immediate change in custody (if the
abusing parent is the custodial parent), or limiting or temporarily ending visitation
rights of a noncustodial parent. In court, ask the judge to withhold visitation unless,
and until, an abusive ex-spouse receives competent psychological evaluation. Also
secure immediate intensive counseling of the child (since it will be problematic having a child live with a hated parent). To reverse alienation, the child may need to spend
more time with the bashed parent so he/she can experience that parent's love and
attention. In violent situations, quickly alert the local police, and secure a protective
court order, if necessary.

Combatting parental alienation also requires *fervent* prayer to the Lord, and making active use of all available counselors, mediators, child experts, and the courts if
necessary, *without delay.* This is *child abuse!* The damage to a child's psyche can
become entrenched and irreversible if it takes root! (Also make certain *you* don't fall
into the trap of bad-mouthing or bashing your ex-spouse, and brainwashing your
child, or you may find the courts ruling against *you!*)

Protect your children. Children want to remain loyal to both biological parents, so
they get trapped between two battling parents who want them to take sides. *Don't put
them in the middle!* When parents manipulate children, they selfishly use them like
chess pieces for personal gain. This isn't love! To the extent you can reasonably do so,

make an appeal directly to your ex-spouse. Stress the many benefits of mutual cooperation, emphasizing any past constructive and positive outcomes. Then demonstrate
how your ex-spouse's negative behavior adversely affects your children (child nightmares, depression, etc.). Review the consequences of any continued negative behavior
(restricted visitation, custody change, etc.). Pray continually that the Lord will work
on your ex-spouse's heart!

Avoid unproductive arguments. The Bible tells us plainly,

> Don't have anything to do with foolish and stupid arguments,
> because you know they produce quarrels. And the Lord's servant must
> not quarrel; instead he must be kind to everyone, able to teach, not
> resentful. Those who oppose him he must *gently* instruct, in the hope
> that God will grant them repentance leading them to a knowledge
> of the truth, and that they will come to their senses and escape
> from the trap of the devil, who has taken them captive to do his will.
> (2 Tim. 2:23–26, emphasis added)

If you (and your remarriage partner) can reason with your ex-spouse, do so—but pick
your battles carefully, sticking to the most important issues and letting trivial matters
slide. Above all, keep doing what you believe is loving and best for everyone—especially your children.

Don't repay evil for evil. Treat ex-spouses with good manners and respect even if
they don't reciprocate. Never seek revenge for inconsiderate or evil actions—this will
only make matters worse for you and your blended family. Instead, leave room for the
Lord to handle the situation as he determines best. Also take heed of the old truism:
"Keep your words soft and sweet. You never know which ones you may have to eat."

Don't respond to unreasonable demands. Just let them slide. If a response cannot
wait, let it come with mediators present; don't try to do this alone.

Don't become overly emotional with an ex-spouse. Remain calm and matter-of-fact
in your tone and conversation. Try to come alongside your ex-spouse in a psychological way to understand the cause of any problem. Search for a way to shift your
ex-spouse's focus off you (or your remarriage partner) and onto the problem, so you
work together finding a solution. But, above all, don't ratchet up the emotions if your
ex-mate is uncommunicative. Give him/her time to calm down. If any conversation's
out of control, simply tell your ex-spouse you cannot help find solutions when he/she
is so upset. Promise to talk about it at another specific date and time.

Communicate in writing if necessary. This has multiple advantages, allowing you
to draft and redraft your thoughts until your letter has proper tone and substance.
You'll have a chance to review the content with your remarriage partner or another
advisor before delivering it to your ex-spouse. A letter puts this important matter
directly into your ex-spouse's hands so he/she can review it multiple times with less
risk of misunderstanding.

Use mediation. Apply biblical conflict resolution measures to your situation; enlist
the aid of a neutral third party to serve as mediator and messenger for exchanging
sensitive information. A good mediator will cut to the chase by asking pointed,

eye-opening questions, such as, "Which is more important, your children or your hate for each other? You do have a choice. But if you choose to hang onto your hate, realize that you may sacrifice your children in the process."

Trust that your children will see the difference. David's divorce from his ex-wife, Rhonda, was bitter. During one meeting shortly before the divorce, Rhonda's rage became so excessive that she attacked David with a screwdriver as he tried to call the police for help. Then she grabbed the telephone and beat him with it. David happily remarried a few years later. Unfortunately, Rhonda, the custodial parent, remained bent on revenge. David must maintain contact with Rhonda or never see his two children, but Rhonda continues to make life extremely difficult for him. On one occasion she screamed, "Why don't you just disappear, like most divorced fathers?" David quietly and consistently kept weekly visitations with his children, taking them to church each week and arranging birthday parties and sleepovers with their friends. He paid child support promptly without complaint. Years later, his then-grown children told their father, "Dad, we love Mom, but we know she has a problem with her emotions and anger. Thanks for being there for us when we needed you the most." *Your children see and understand more than you may know!*

Many different issues may arise with ex-spouses, but if you and your remarriage partner will put some of the principles discussed above into practice, you'll find there are few circumstances beyond your reasonable control with the Lord's guidance.

But now let's take a look at the bigger picture—what you and your remarriage partner may face with extended family members.

THE IN-LAWS (AND OUT-LAWS) OF DIVORCED SPOUSES

Most stepparents know their blended families include not only their mates, their mates' children, as well as immediate family, but also a rather amorphous group of extended family members of ex-spouses as well. These extended family members don't cease to exist after divorce, and add to the complexity remarriage partners face in experiencing multiple marriages. Extended family seems to grow exponentially!

I recall another cartoon about that same wedding of Cathy's ex-boyfriend, Alex, mentioned earlier. The strip shows Cathy milling among various guests at the refreshment table. "I'm the ex-husband of the second wife of the bride's uncle on her stepmother's side," says one man. "I'm the sister-in-law of the daughter from the groom's grandfather's first marriage," adds a woman standing beside him. "I'm the bride's half-sister's best friend's ex-wife's cousin," chimes in another woman behind her. Still another man introduces himself as "the ex-boyfriend of the ex-fiancée of the groom." Cathy's reaction? "Nothing like a wedding to make you feel part of the family."[25] Some of us who remarried into large extended families can relate to this confusion!

It's really surprising how many couples plan for remarriage and combining their children into one blended family without fully considering how their children not only have noncustodial parents but grandparents, aunts, uncles, nephews, nieces, and half-siblings biologically linked through those noncustodial parents too! And most of these extended family members aren't content to share brief visitation time with a noncustodial parent—they want the children to come visit them as well. Don't overlook these important relationships!

Many remarried couples also fail to adequately guard against conflicts and intrusions with their in-laws. Some in-laws can be real troublemakers, disturbing family peace. In fact, in-law problems destroy many marriages, and rank among the top four reasons for marital unhappiness, along with money, sex, and kids. When in-laws become family interlopers, they're called "out-laws." Many blended families overreact by barring out-laws, who remain on the outside—never welcomed by family members. As estrangement results, however, children lose more relationships with these blood-related family members—another tragedy after divorce.

Remarried couples do need to deal decisively with out-laws. John, stepfather to twelve-year-old stepson Timmy through remarriage, shared this experience:

My wife's ex-husband, Timmy's father (Ray), has spent most of his adult life in jail. Ray was paroled a year ago, but made no effort to see Timmy. Unfortunately, Ray's mother (Grandma Rose) had other ideas. For weeks, Grandma Rose urged us to make sure Timmy sees his father. She always made sure to say it in front of Timmy. We decided to give it a try, but it was a disaster! When we took Timmy to visit him, Ray's language was terrible, and he regaled the boy with stories about what a big shot he was in prison. He's covered with obscene tattoos, and told the boy he should have some done. The visits really affected Timmy's behavior, so we decided to curtail visits until Ray could take some parenting classes. Since then, we haven't heard from Ray. Grandma Rose, however, won't leave this alone. She tells Timmy how much his father loves him and wants to see him. Now, Timmy is nagging us to let him go live with Ray. I have asked Grandma Rose to stop stirring the pot, but she doesn't listen. Meanwhile, Timmy's behavior becomes troublesome whenever Grandma Rose is around, and Ray has shown absolutely no interest in cleaning up his act.

Cara and her first husband divorced, leaving her with three children. Her ex-husband's great aunt (Phoebe), a wealthy woman, formed a close relationship with Cara and her children during the marriage. Secretly, Aunt Phoebe set up trust funds for Cara's three kids, but only after making Cara promise she wouldn't tell her then husband. As Cara explains it:

Not long after my husband and I divorced after ten years of an unhappy marriage, we established joint custody of our children, and they share equal time with us. Several months after the divorce, I received a check in the mail from Aunt Phoebe, along with a letter saying how fond she was of me and to please accept her gift. This money was a complete surprise to me, and a pleasant one. Being recently divorced, I had many expenses and needed a place to live. That was three years ago, and I have since remarried. But Aunt Phoebe now wants me to return the money. She said I didn't deserve it because I allowed my ex-husband to share joint custody of the children. She thinks they should be living full-time with me and shouldn't see their father at all. She said I could keep the money if I arranged to have sole custody and have my children live with me and their new stepfather.

Unfortunately, stories like these aren't uncommon. Manipulation and control can come from most any source—and there are *many* such sources from prior relationships affecting the lives of blended family members! Remarriage partners striving diligently to help their families get a good start certainly don't need these bad influences!

But let's look at the other side of the equation for a moment. How do these extended family members feel? Often they may feel a deep sense of insecurity and loss when a divorced parent of children they love decides to remarry. Of course, the situation becomes even more complicated when the remarriage partner has children from one or more prior marriages. For example, grandparents of children on the non-custodial ex-spouse's side must adjust to a custodial parent getting remarried to a stranger, possibly reducing contact with their grandchildren. But these grandparents also may have step-grandchildren in this new blended family—some strange new fruit on their now "instant family" tree over which they have little or no control! It's understandable why extended family members, under this pressure, may not always act in sensitive and loving ways.

Don't be overly skeptical of all these extended family relationships. It's quite common for a warm relationship to exist between a remarriage partner and his/her ex-in-laws. Some individuals even have long-standing work relationships in family businesses that don't cease with divorce. Remarriages shouldn't destroy these existing ties.

Parents of an ex-spouse are as important to their grandchildren as a custodial parent's own parents. In fact, they can have a wonderfully special influence on a blended family. Jake and Jennifer, a remarried couple with three children, are a military family. When Jake was sent to Iraq for a year, no one lived near Jennifer and the kids except her ex-spouse's parents, Lee and June. These grandparents did their very best to fill the hole left in Jennifer's family. Lee served as a surrogate father for the children, always available to retrieve them from school or drive them to ballet lessons or baseball practice. He helped Jennifer with house and car repairs while she was at work. Grandma June greeted the kids each day after school busying herself baking cookies, vacuuming the house, and watering the plants. These grandparents also encouraged Jennifer, cash-strapped as she was, to talk long-distance to Jake at the forward military base—at their expense. They took pictures of Jennifer and the kids, and then sent them along to Jake in frequent letters to him. There are many folks who would *love* having former in-laws this special!

Cheryl and I feel so blessed to have Chase's grandmother on his father's side, Carole, stay with us for extended periods. Carole and Chase absolutely adore each other. Carole helps us in so many ways by coaching Chase with his homework, cleaning out our guinea pig cage, and even sliding down water shoots with him at Disney

World's water park. The bonus for Cheryl and me is to sneak away for a date night of our own while Carole and Chase eat popcorn and play games on Saturday night. Most importantly, Carole loves the Lord. We know Chase needs her wise, spiritual influence in his life, as Timothy needed from his grandmother, Lois (2 Tim. 1:5)!

Regrettably, not everyone sees the great value of many loving and helpful grandparents and extended family members. Following divorce, some parents cut off all ties with *anyone* related to their ex-spouses—including grandparents. This prompted the American Association of Retired Persons (AARP) to sponsor passage of grandparent visitation laws in all fifty states between 1966 and 1986. The battle cry among these seniors was, "We have the right to see our grandchildren!" While differing in details, most of these laws authorize visitation orders for grandparents if a judge thinks it's in the best interest of the grandchildren. But the battle didn't end there.

In June 2000 the U.S. Supreme Court ruled in *Troxel v. Granville*[26] that a Washington state statute allowing grandparents (and others) to petition for visitation at any time was too broad and interfered with a parent's Fourteenth Amendment due-process interest in parenting a child without undue state interference (unless there is harm to the child involved). Thereafter, supreme courts of other states began striking down various grandparent visitation laws, considering them "unconstitutionally applied," or violating a parent's right to privacy. A notable exception was a 2001 Louisiana case involving Jeffrey Alan Harris, a widower with custody of an infant daughter. Harris argued that Louisiana's law, giving grandparents reasonable visitation if a spouse dies or is imprisoned, interfered with his parenting. In that case, however, the U.S. Supreme Court let stand an earlier Louisiana court decision upholding the visitation law. The Louisiana court judge told Harris and the grandparents: "You're going to need some help raising a little girl, so that would be a very good resource for you. . . . Try to get past this litigation and get on with your lives."[27] Well said!

So how do you deal with these extended family members while trying to make a blended family work with a remarriage partner?

Encourage children to maintain ties with extended family members. Julia, a stepchild many times over, expresses her feelings well on this point:

> Both my parents have been married three times. I've had a series of revolving-door siblings, aunts, uncles, and grandparents. Every time someone remarries, I'm expected to welcome the new relatives with open arms. Whenever someone divorces, I'm expected to disown my stepsiblings and act as if they never existed. It's painful to ignore people who treated you as a close relative for years. I decided early on that just because my parents couldn't get their lives straight didn't mean mine should be torn to pieces. I have excellent relationships with my ex-stepsiblings, ex-stepgrandparents, and other family members. Children shouldn't be expected to turn their feelings on and off whenever an adult relationship sours. No one can tell me whom to love.

For the sake of your children, do your best to keep positive relationships with grandparents and other extended family members, allowing for easy access to the children. Make every effort to *cooperate,* rather than alienate them from their grandchildren.

Be gracious, loving, and forgiving. Contact with extended family members is unavoidable, so make the best of it. In fact, it's a *good* thing in most cases. Grace, diplomacy, and lots of patience help soothe any irritations, and keep relationships running smoothly. If you're uncivil and hostile, you reap what you sow. If your remarriage partner has a good relationship with his former in-laws and other extended family members, be flexible and understanding. It's unreasonable to expect your mate to end these relationships upon remarriage, after building them up over many years. (Your remarriage alone may create some distance between your spouse and his/her extended family, which may serve as a reasonable buffer for your family anyway.)

Stepparents can be a powerful force for change in these relationships—particularly when it's difficult for a remarriage partner to cope with all the emotions involved. Loretta is a good example:

When I first met my husband's former in-laws, they were warm
and friendly. Shortly after our wedding, however, they became cold and
downright insulting. I never did anything to provoke such hostility,
and it was difficult to endure. At one point, my husband said, "That's
it! We're never going to see those people again." I knew my husband
wanted all these people to get along with his children, though, so I
refused to give up. I swallowed hard and let them know I was available
when they had problems seeing my husband's kids. I invited them to
our home for dinner. I made a big deal over any nice thing they did for
my stepchildren. It took almost ten years, but at last, I'm considered
part of the family. My stepchildren adore their grandparents, as well as
their cousins, aunts, and uncles of their mother. We truly are a happy
extended family group now. The best reward? My husband knows his
children are enjoying time spent with all their relatives.

Enforce your blended family boundaries. You may not have out-laws quite as intrusive as Israel's King Saul, when he tried to hunt down his son-in-law, David, with murderous intent—although it may seem that way at times! But in-laws or out-laws can cross over the line of responsibility and respect by dropping in for surprise visits, meddling in your family's personal affairs, or just making a remarried couple feel smothered or controlled. Guard against harmful intrusions by enforcing clear family boundaries (see chap. 6). Whenever you feel an encroachment arises, make sure: (1) a problem exists and isn't merely a misunderstanding; (2) you and your remarriage partner correct any contributions you made to the problem (Matt. 7:1–5); (3) you and your partner confront those causing the problem directly, gently, and lovingly (Matt. 18:15; Eph. 4:13) with a *united* front; and (4) those confronted understand and acknowledge what boundaries must be imposed and *why* these limits are necessary. Healthy boundaries are good solutions for *all* family members, who feel chafed by intrusiveness, favoritism, or other encroachments and conflicts. They provide everyone with some much needed breathing room.

Prepare a coalition plan with extended family members. By asking remarried couples what they need, extended family members can help relationships run smoother (rather than making unwarranted assumptions). Also, not giving advice unless asked and *listening* and *watching* from a distance can help extended family members develop some empathy and understanding about what a blended family is dealing with. Remarried couples need *lots* of praise and encouragement too! Now that's what extended family members *should* do, but many of them don't. Why? They may not know how. So we remarried couples must help disciple them.

It begins with a family coalition plan among all adults involved in a child's life (similar to a coparenting plan with an ex-spouse). The remarried couple and extended family members agree on ground rules for communicating and visiting with children in a loving and orderly fashion, so everyone feels comfortable and welcome. Extended family members acknowledge the remarriage couple is in charge, having primary responsibility for nurturing and protecting the blended family group. The plan acknowledges that the security and growth of the blended family always remain a priority—the interests of extended family members come second. Beyond that, however, the plan emphasizes *teamwork* among all concerned, wrapped up in mutual praise and encouragement, prayer, forgiveness, and lots of unconditional love. Family coalition plans also set aside time on a regular basis to share feedback with extended family members, and work on ways to improve the relationships. This valuable feedback allows everyone to update and revise their coalition plan to meet current needs.

Encourage extended family members to play to their strengths. Extended family members can offer blessings the remarriage couple cannot always provide for their children. Use them! Grandparents can share their family history with grandchildren to give them a better sense of who they are. Making copies of cherished family photographs for the grandchildren and sharing stories about other interesting people in the family tree can strengthen and bond relationships. A five-year-old just learning to ride a bike might love to hear about grandpa's first bike, while a teenager might enjoy learning how this grandparent saved up for a car, or how the grand couple met and married. Extended family members also can establish many meaningful connections with children by promising to pass along a precious family heirloom or special item of personal significance, such as a jewelry case or a favorite fishing rod. Why not take advantage of it? Take the initiative. Turn potentially troublesome out-laws into allies by promoting good friendships and healthy interaction between those in your blended family and extended family members!

As we near the end of this chapter (and this book), we've reviewed many issues and problems remarriage partners and blended families face. In these remaining pages, let me call you to a higher standard of Christian living that will serve you well in blended family life, and life in general, as God wills for all of us.

THE TRUE MARK OF A CHRISTIAN: LOVING AND GIVING TO THE UNLOVABLE

Are you ready now for the ultimate test of your faith? Consider these words of Jesus:
"You have heard it was said, 'Eye for eye, and tooth for tooth.' But
I tell you, Do not resist an evil person. If someone strikes you on the
right cheek, turn to him the other also. And if someone wants to sue
you and take your tunic, let him have your cloak as well. If someone
forces you to go one mile, go with him two miles. Give to the one who
asks you, and do not turn away from the one who wants to borrow
from you." (Matt. 5:38–42)[28]

More than a few individuals believe that if preachers really preached what Jesus taught, people would run them off! Perhaps those holding this view had this passage in mind. Too often we may have "softened" the words of Jesus with the familiar refrain, "Now he says this, but what he really means is . . ." This passage is a prime example tempting us to ask, "Does Jesus really mean what he says here? Is he talking literally? Can I accept this?"

This isn't a natural way to live. It's the antithesis of how we normally respond to problems. It's an unnatural act. Biblical forgiveness (chap. 2) also is an unnatural act. It's not how we would respond without God's guidance about those who wrong us.

In so many ways Jesus works contrary to our thinking and desires in life. He says, "Blessed are the poor in spirit" (Matt. 5:3a). He must be wrong. We know the successful, aggressive, and resourceful people who gather an enormous fortune are the ones blessed in the world, right? "Blessed are the meek" (Matt. 5:5a). Surely you're kidding, Jesus! The meek are the doormats who get walked over and spit upon. They're the wimps and weaklings who make stomachs turn. But Jesus does know better than we do. This is no mistake. His teachings may conflict with our perspective of the world. And this conflict leads us to a choice. Will we live as Jesus challenges us to live, or will we go our own way? If we live the life Jesus calls us to, it won't be natural for us. It'll be an uncomfortable fit for a while. It won't be easy. But over time, we feel ourselves adjusting and stretching, just like breaking in a pair of new shoes. Finally the fit feels good. Ultimately we'll be *different* people, with God's help. Then we'll truly be the salt of the earth, and light of the world.

Jesus tells us, "Do not resist an evil person." But James says, "Resist the devil, and he will flee from you" (James 4:7b). The apostle Peter notes: "Your enemy the devil prowls around like a roaring lion looking for someone to devour. Resist him, standing firm in the faith, because you know that your brothers throughout the world are undergoing the same kind of sufferings" (1 Pet. 5:8b–9). We also know that Christians resist each other, as Paul did in opposing Peter publicly for his hypocrisy in dealing with the Jews and Gentiles (Gal. 2). How can we reconcile these verses? By understanding the *nature* of the resistance.

First, the Old Testament principle of "eye for eye, and tooth for tooth" (Exod. 21:22–25; Lev. 24:17–22; Deut. 19:15–21) commands that punishment *by the authorities of God* (not persons in *private* disputes) fit the crime committed. It's a principle guiding legal action by the governing authorities for certain *criminal* activities—not private transactions between individuals. Nowhere in the New Testament does God give us the right to take vengeance upon others with whom we privately disagree. To the contrary, vengeance is the Lord's exclusive privilege (Deut. 32:35; Rom. 12:19). If it were otherwise, as some have said, we would be a world of eyeless, toothless people!

Second, Jesus' words don't deprive us of self-defense or self-preservation if others threaten us (or our children) with bodily harm. We have the right to run. We can ward off blows against us without retaliation. But Jesus addresses the *attitude* behind resisting an evil person with several illustrations.

If a person strikes you on the *right* cheek, it probably means a right-handed person slapped you with the *back* of his hand—an insulting blow. How should you handle the insult? Our natural reaction is to slap those who slap us, to retaliate and pay back harm for harm. (You'll recall that Judge Eaton wholeheartedly endorses this approach in dealing with deadbeat parents.) But Jesus encourages us to turn the other cheek to this person. Don't retaliate.

Turning the other cheek isn't symbolic or figurative. This is the way Jesus lived:

> I offered my back to those who beat me,
> my cheeks to those who pulled out my beard;
> I did not hide my face
> from mocking and spitting.
> Because the Sovereign LORD helps me,
> I will not be disgraced.
> Therefore have I set my face like flint,
> and I know I will not be put to shame.
> He who vindicates me is near.
> Who then will bring charges against me?
> Let us face each other!
> Who is my accuser?
> Let him confront me! (Isa. 50:6–8)

When they brought Jesus into the courts of evil men, how did he react? The Gospels record he gave no response. He remained silent in the face of his accusers who condemned him to death, spat upon him, beat, and mocked him (John 18; 19; Isa. 53). When the authorities came to arrest him, he didn't resist. At his trial, he didn't resist. When they took him to be crucified, he still didn't resist. He set us an example:

> But how it is to your credit if you receive a beating for doing wrong
> and endure it? But if you suffer for doing good and you endure it, this
> is commendable before God. To this you were called, because Christ
> suffered for you, leaving you an example, that you should follow in his
> steps. "He committed no sin, and no deceit was found in his mouth."
> When they hurled their insults at him, he did not retaliate; when he
> suffered, he made no threats. Instead, he entrusted himself to him who
> judges justly. (1 Pet. 2:20–23)

Jesus then gives another illustration. If a man takes you to court and sues you for your tunic or coat,[29] give him your cloak as well. Brothers and sisters in Christ, made so by God, have no right to be in court against each other, as we clearly know from 1 Corinthians 6:1–8. But remember that, in Matthew 5, Jesus is talking to a multitude of people—not just believers. He says that if *anyone* sues you, it's best to settle quickly. Why? Because if you battle it out with a skunk, you're going to end up smelling like one! More than that, settle on unfavorable terms if necessary. If someone wants your tunic, give him the shirt off your back as well to settle. Fighting matters out in court is a losing proposition. For Christians, it's a spiritual defeat—a much greater loss indeed! Do everything you can to suffer wrong, before you do wrong (1 Cor. 6:7).[30]

There's great practical wisdom in heeding this advice of Jesus. Pursuing our perceived "rights" at the expense of others, either by filing legal actions or by aggressively resisting actions by others against us, tends to steamroll and create more conflict. How? Christian Legal Society attorney Thomas Strahan describes it this way:

> Many Christians are as quick to start a lawsuit as anyone else and want to assert every legal right available to them if they get into some difficulty. However, if we are acting on the basis of some particular right, our action is actually based primarily on our own self-interest. Assertion of a "right" will often tend to cause alienation and division between individuals and groups. This division will first manifest itself between those contending for the "right" and those who believe that this claimed right will be gained at their own expense or diminish their position in some manner. A chain reaction is often triggered because other persons observing the struggle, but who were not initially involved, become worried that they are not getting enough for themselves and then they, too, begin clamoring for some "right" of their own to protect and enhance their position. It thus often ends up that people operate on fear or suspicion, resentment, envy, jealousy, or mistrust instead of faith, hope, and love. Jesus tells us not to stand on our legal rights, but to take the further step of willingly giving the wrongdoer more than that which was taken from us.[31]

Think about it. In most instances, is peace ever promoted by filing lawsuits? Isn't it more likely that it promotes hatred (Prov. 10:12), pride (Prov. 13:10), quarrels and strife (Prov. 26:21), anger and division (Prov. 29:22), and an unhealthy interest in controversies and arguments that are the source of constant friction (1 Tim. 6:3–5)? Does one who pursues a lawsuit really want peace, or do they seek a personal vindictive "justice" by wanting the other party to suffer?

One man not holding these truths in his heart once demanded of Jesus, "Teacher, tell my brother to divide the inheritance with me."[32] Asserting his "rights" consumed this man. He wanted a judge to see matters his way. He was thinking selfishly, putting property above his relationship with his brother. Jesus quickly replied, "Man, who appointed me a judge or an arbiter between you? . . . Watch out! Be on your guard against all kinds of greed; a man's life does not consist in the abundance of his possessions" (Luke 12:13–15). One wonders what Jesus' response to this man might have been if he had asked, "Teacher, how can I *love* my brother without letting our disputes separate us from each other?"

Jesus continues with one more illustration. If a man compels you to go one mile with him, go with him two miles. The Persians and Romans had the right to stop anyone and command that person to carry baggage for one mile. This was very insulting to the Jews, already struggling with domination under Roman rule during the time of Jesus. The Jews wouldn't go one inch farther than one mile when pressed into this servitude. The natural way was to carry the load one mile and dump it on the mark.

Jesus says to go two miles (actually, four miles—two miles down the road, and two miles back to the starting point). But mileage isn't on Jesus' mind as much as the *attitude* of dealing with distasteful inequities and insults. He's almost saying that, short of a longer walk together for "two miles," one cannot become acquainted with an oppressor and learn to love that person individually and unconditionally to win him/her over to repentance.

It's natural for us to say relationships are a 50-50 proposition. But Jesus would say that true *commitment* to a relationship is *0-100*—you may end up putting everything into a relationship and receiving nothing back! This doesn't mean being a wimp; it's *strength under control*. Going the second mile keeps remarriages and blended families together. It keeps churches together. It keeps relationships together. And it'll help keep matters civil with your ex-spouse and extended family too! Will you go the second mile in resolving problems presented by divorce, remarriage, and blended families— even if you have to go with no one but Jesus by your side?

I'd like to close this chapter with an outstanding example of how these principles are put into action with grace and love in a modern Good Samaritan story involving a remarried couple, Gail and Tom (as told by Helen Kooiman Hosier). Years earlier, Tom's ex-wife took their two daughters and left him for another man. But see how this loving couple worked through any bitterness they might have had:

> Shortly after their remarriage, Tom's first wife learned she had terminal cancer. Her new husband, who didn't want to be saddled with a woman who was going to die of cancer, walked off—taking the television, the car, and leaving her and her daughters high and dry. Destitute, she appealed to Tom. Gail and Tom had her and her daughters moved from another state back to the community where they lived. Because she was unable to work, they provided for her every need. She actually lived longer than the doctors estimated she could survive. This was, understandably, a terrible financial drain on Gail and Tom. Gail never complained, and pitched in, using much of the money she'd been left by her deceased husband to help out. In the end, they lost their home.
>
> I think the thing that stands out the most in my own thinking is what Gail did for this dying woman, her husband's first wife. She visited

her in the hospital and assured her she'd never try to take this woman's place with her daughters, but that she would care for them and give them a mother's love. Because the dying woman had lost all her hair, she was wearing wigs, and Gail took it upon herself to clean and set the wigs, helping this woman to maintain her appearance as best she could right until the moment she died. She also insisted that Tom be with his first wife and the daughters as much as possible, and that he be there at her bedside when she died.[33]

Having a loving and gracious spirit like this is what life is all about! How about you and your remarriage partner?

A Message from Cheryl

No relationship stirs one's emotions more than that with an ex-spouse.

Often Warren and I consult each other on difficult business relationships. When our emotions run high, we help each other refocus with one question: "What's our ultimate goal here?" This is the question that can define your relationship with your ex-spouse.

Beginning immediately after a divorce with children involved, and assuming that reconciliation with an ex-spouse isn't practical or possible, I see two healthy, primary goals in an ongoing relationship with a former mate: (1) to continually encourage him/her and be a living testimony and witness pointing that former marriage partner toward the Lord; and (2) to foster a close and mutually beneficial relationship with the children. End of story. It's no longer appropriate to be a counselor, or to direct an ex-spouse's life (or vice versa).

Assume for a moment your ex-spouse is your child's teacher, calling to discuss your child. What would you do if the teacher began asking how much money you spent on a new dress, or commented on your parents, or criticized your husband. Naturally you would set boundaries and state, "I'm sorry, those are inappropriate remarks. Let's go back to the topic of Joan's schoolwork."

Equally important is understanding *your* position in your ex-spouse's life. You're limited to the enhancement of his/her relationship with your children. You're no longer your former marriage partner's confidant or spouse. Your job isn't to improve your ex-spouse or to teach, correct, or criticize—just be a cooperative parent for the best interest of your children.

Some of us cannot seem to detach from an ex-spouse. If you're recently divorced, that's understandable. But if it's been a year or more, chances are there's another reason personal ties beyond the children remain. Perhaps you haven't forgiven your former mate. Maybe you haven't let go of the relationship and moved on. (Both of these factors usually relate to each other in a number of ways.) If you cannot work on coparenting your children in an appropriately detached and healthy manner, pray and work through the major issues of forgiveness and letting go (see part 1).

A wise man once said, "Many of our problems are not nearly as big as we make them out to be." Remember, no one can truly ruin your life unless you allow them to do so.

Herein lies the difference between believers in Jesus and the world. God expects us to be different. It's absolutely possible to be divorced and remarried, *and* to be a godly and forgiving Christian through it all.

QUESTIONS FOR PERSONAL REFLECTION

1. Put yourself in your ex-spouse's shoes. How would you view your coparenting relationship? What would be bothering you most about the divorce? The remarriage? What would you need or want the most, and why? How would you act to obtain what you want or need?

2. Is there any way I can make my former mate's responsibilities to me and our children more of a joy rather than a burden? What incentives can I give my ex-spouse to make child support payments in a timely manner for our children's benefit?

3. Am I planning to relocate my family? How can I discuss this matter sensitively and empathetically with my ex-spouse? How can I make the transition easier for my children and their other parent?

4. Are any extended family members creating difficulties for me, my remarriage partner, or our children right now? What would be the best approach to dealing with these specific problems?

5. In relationships within and outside my blended family, am I willing to go the second mile? Am I willing to unconditionally love and give without expecting anything in return, as Christ did for me?

CONCLUSION

What are the key concepts vital to any remarriage within the context of where we've come from, where we are right now, and where we want to go in life? Healing and recovery from past relationships. Building a rock-solid foundation on Jesus Christ, rather than the sand of the world. Flexibility in adjusting to change. Finding a suitable partner. Experiencing biblical love. Counseling and preparation for remarriage. Striving for *unity* with a remarriage partner in everything. Loving communication. Healthy family boundaries. Biblical conflict resolution. Compassion for blended family children. Cooperative coparenting with ex-spouses and extended family members. Blended families are living testimonies of the two greatest commandments: loving God, and loving others as ourselves (Matt. 22:35–40)!

Right now, this book may leave you asking yourself, "How can I keep all these plates spinning at once?" Without the Lord, it's very difficult—if not impossible. But remember, all things are possible with God (Matt. 19:26)! Our best advice to those entering remarriage is this: Move *slowly*, move *wisely*, and *always* follow the Lord's lead. Why? "Unless the LORD builds the house, its builders labor in vain. Unless the LORD watches over the city, the watchmen stand guard in vain" (Ps. 127:1). Don't feel inadequate to the task facing you when the Lord is with you. Worldly wisdom from family experts may sound practical and true, but the Lord won't steer you wrong. After all, he used amateurs to build the ark, while "professionals" built the *Titanic*. Just give God your best and let him take care of the rest. You'll never regret accepting his judgment on any questions.

You don't have to know it all. That's not the problem. Many people know what to do, but few of them *do* what they *know!* To paraphrase Claude Pepper: remarriage, as with life, is like riding a bicycle—you don't fall off unless you stop pedaling. Start with the little things you do know, and work your way through to a few more changes each week.

Cheryl and I aren't experts in remarriage and blended families. We're struggling and learning as we go forward, just as you are! As Howard Hendricks wryly noted, "Nothing kills a man's testimony more than an eyewitness." But we trust our lessons learned from hardship will enable you to profit from our experience.

In closing, we challenge those joining us in the ranks of the remarried: Love as if you've never been hurt. Accept responsibility for mistakes. Remove the shackles of yesterday's failures. Communicate honestly and lovingly. Create win-win solutions in resolving conflict. Be consistent. View uncertainties as opportunities approached in faith. Pursue a mission greater than yourself as you serve your family. Give God the glory!

Appendix A

FACTS AND STATISTICS ABOUT <u>FAMILY RELATIONSHIPS</u>

Anyone who conducts an argument by appealing to authority [and statistics] is not using his intelligence; he is just using his memory.—Leonardo da Vinci

There are two kinds of statistics, the kind you look up, and the kind you make up.—Rex Stout, author

[*Author's note:* Beginning in 2000, the U.S. Census Bureau no longer included a box for citizens to indicate whether they're married, single, divorced, or widowed on forms received by most Americans. Also, the National Center for Health Statistics cut back their work in gathering complete national divorce statistics in the nineties.]

General trends:

- The overall U.S. divorce rate had a brief spurt after World War II, followed by a decline in the 1950s. The divorce rate rose again in the sixties, and even more quickly in the seventies, before leveling off in the eighties and declining slightly.
- Measuring the divorce rate today is difficult, and perhaps impossible, to determine—especially since statistical data is limited.
- In a report released in June 1999 and produced by the National Marriage Project at Rutgers University, the overview stated: "Key social indicators suggest a substantial weakening of the institution of marriage. Americans have become less likely to marry. When they do marry, their marriages are less happy. And married couples face a high likelihood of divorce. Over the past four decades, marriage has declined as the first living together experience for

couples and as a status of parenthood. Unmarried cohabitation and unwed births have grown enormously, and so has the percentage of children who grow up in fragile families. . . . As an adult stage in life course, marriage is shrinking. Americans are living longer, marrying later, exiting marriage more quickly, and choosing to live together before marriage, after marriage, in between marriages, and as an alternative to marriage. A small but growing percentage of American adults will never marry. As a consequence, marriage is surrounded by longer periods of partnered or unpartnered singlehood over the course of a lifetime."[1]

Marriage and family—general:

- Married couples with children represented only 26 percent of households in 2000.[2]
- According to the National Center for Health Statistics, the percentage of Americans getting married is at an all-time low. Meanwhile, the number of divorces has increased almost 200 percent between 1960 and 1990. In 1960 there were 73.5 marriages for every 1,000 unmarried women and 9.2 divorces for every 1,000 married women. By 1987, there were only 55.7 marriages, but the number of divorces had risen to 21 per 1,000 married women.[3]

Divorce—general:

- The often quoted statistic that 50 percent of all U.S. marriages end in divorce is inaccurate. This statistic arose when someone at the Census Bureau noticed there had been 2.4 million marriages and 1.2 million divorces in 1990. Comparing those two figures without taking into account the 54 million marriages already in existence gave birth to this quotable, but highly inaccurate, statistic.[4]
- Approximately 45 percent of new marriages will end in divorce.[5]
- Approximately 40 percent of all married adults in the nineties have already been divorced.[6]
- Approximately 43 percent of first marriages end in either divorce or separation within fifteen years. One in three first marriages dissolve within ten years. One in five first marriages terminate within five years.[7]
- Divorce rates rose in 44 of 50 states after adoption of no-fault divorce legislation.[8]
- In 1998 approximately 10 percent of adults (19.4 million) were "currently divorced," according to the U.S. Census Bureau.
- According to Barna Research Online in August 2001, born-again Christians are just as likely to get divorced as are adults who are not born again.

Children of divorced parents:

- The number of children whose parents divorced grew by 700 percent from 1900 to 1972.[9]

- About 25 percent of Americans aged eighteen to forty-four are the adult children of divorced parents. Approximately 67 percent of children grow up with divorces and remarriages of one or both parents. Only a fraction bonded with all members of the blended families. More than one million children a year have experienced parental divorce since 1970.[10]

Widowed persons:

- Approximately 45 percent of women sixty-five years and older were widowed. Of the elderly widows, seven in ten lived alone.[11]

Single parenting:

- The number of children living with both parents declined from 85 percent in 1970 to 68 percent in 1996. Between 1970 and 1996, the proportion of children under eighteen years of age living with one parent grew from 12 percent to 28 percent (20 million), according to a 1998 U.S. Census Bureau Report.
- According to the U.S. Census Bureau, during the ten-year period ending in 2000, households headed by single mothers increased by more than 25 percent, while those led by single fathers grew by almost 62 percent.
- According to the U.S. Census Bureau, the percentage of children in single-parent families has risen from 9 percent in 1960 to 28 percent in 1998.
- Based upon current trends up through 2001, it is predicted that half of the children living today will spend at least part of their childhood in single-parent homes.[12]

Remarriage—general:

- In 1993, approximately 80 percent of all divorced persons remarried. About 83 percent of all divorced men, and 75 percent of all divorced women, remarried. Approximately 50 percent of those whose first marriages ended in divorce remarried within three years. Approximately 80 percent of divorced men, and 70 percent of divorced women, remarried within five years.[13]
- In 1998, the median age for remarriage of widowed men was 63.1 years, and 54 for widowed women.[14]
- Approximately 46 of every 100 marriages in 1998 were remarriages for one or both partners. Of those, 24 were remarriages for both persons.[15]
- According to noted researcher Judith Wallerstein, in 2000 approximately 60 percent of remarriages will end in divorce.[16]
- According to the National Center for Health Statistics in 1995, remarriages ending in divorce lasted an average of 7.4 years for men and 7.1 years for women. The average age of men divorcing from their second marriage was 42 years; for women it was age 39. For those divorced three or more times, the average age of men was 46.5; for women it was 42 years.
- One-half of all women who experienced divorce in first marriages and remarried, did so within two and one-half years after their divorce.[17]

- Approximately 39 percent of all remarriages dissolve within ten years. But age makes a difference. If a woman remarries under twenty-five, the likelihood of separation or divorce is 47 percent. If she is twenty-five or older, the likelihood falls to 34 percent.[18]

Stepfamilies—general:

- According to the U.S. Census Bureau, the number of stepfamilies increased 36 percent from 1980 to 1990, to 5.3 million. About 21 percent of all married couples with dependent children now include at least one stepparent. In 1990, 7.3 million children were in stepfamilies.[19]
- In 1990 20.8 percent of all two-parent families had stepchildren, up from 16.1 percent in 1980.[20]
- In 1990, one of three Americans was either a stepparent, stepchild, stepsibling or other stepfamily member. Approximately thirteen hundred new stepfamilies were formed every day in the 1990s.[21]

Appendix B

SAMPLE BLENDED FAMILY COVENANT

Christianity has its roots in the words of Jesus Christ, memorialized for us in the Bible, the living Word of God. America was founded on the Declaration of Independence and the U.S. Constitution, the dynamic documents of our freedom as American citizens. All these precious covenants guide and direct us in maintaining order and peace in our lives. So it's very appropriate and prudent for a complex blended family to have a covenant to help each member understand and appreciate that the whole family body works together best as each member does his or her part.

[*NOTE:* This Family Covenant is only a *sample.* Use it as a guide to create your own covenant. This sample is prepared for blended family parents addressing their children.]

PREAMBLE

The purpose of our Blended Family Covenant primarily is to acknowledge some truths our family holds as being "self-evident" and to encourage consistent living in order to minimize misunderstandings, unrealistic expectations, and conflict. It isn't intended to enslave anyone in our family, but merely be a tool and benchmark by which we live together in *unity* and *cooperation.*

As members of the same blended family, we mutually acknowledge the most important biblical principle in building up our relationships: "Unless the LORD builds the house, they labor in vain who build it" (Ps. 127:1). Therefore, in everything we do we mutually need and desire that our Lord be a part of our plans. Otherwise we'll be planning in vain. Since we fully expect to succeed in our family life together, we'll live our lives firmly grounded on what the Lord tells us in Scripture.

Our Family Covenant reminds us of some important biblical virtues and truths: each family member is loved by God, with unique significance, and is worthy of respect; each family member is called to love everyone else in our blended family; each person has God-given freedom and basic rights to be honored and protected; each child is entitled to receive responsible and positive parenting; each person has a right to be heard in family communication and conflict-resolution procedures; and each person has a right to know what's expected of him or her through house rules, healthy family boundaries, and fair warning of adverse consequences for irresponsible or unloving conduct.

Having a written agreement of this sort helps each of us remember to be *consistently* loving and encouraging to one another. This acknowledgment is similar to what the Israelites did before the Lord in Nehemiah's day (Neh. 9:38). We know inconsistencies in blended family living create the most conflict. We don't want this to happen within our family. Not intended to be engraved on stone tablets for our family, we expect to use our Family Covenant as a *dynamic* guide, which can be revised as necessary—growing and changing as our family adjusts and grows.

As family members, it's our mutual hope and prayer that having this covenant will promote family unity, harmony, and peace in our home. Striving for individual happiness isn't enough—we need to develop a *team* mentality in a loving, committed, trusting, interdependent, spirit of "we-ness." In working out our relationships and family management according to this covenant, we mutually commit to focus on promoting *stability* within our family, with *security* and *mutual respect.*

LOVE COMMITMENT #1
EACH FAMILY MEMBER IS LOVED INDIVIDUALLY

God loves each one of us, regardless of how we feel about each other. Our individual and collective goal as a family is to make the most of every opportunity to help each other grow in grace and our faith in God. We commit ourselves to making sure that we do everything in our power to help all family members be saved for eternity.

1. *All parents love all children:* Children, your biological parents and stepparents all love you. We, your parents, commit ourselves to look out for your best interests, as the Lord guides us. Children are a vital part of our families. We're glad each child has an opportunity to spend quality time with each parent (biological and stepparent). No matter what our differences are, all parents are agreed that we want what's best for you.

2. *All children love all parents:* Each child will have every opportunity to love all parents and stepparents without feeling guilty, pressured, or rejected. We, your parents, want you to love God with all your heart, mind, soul, and strength, and to love us as well.

3. *We commit to love regardless of expectations:* We mutually commit to loving each other for each other's greater good. We won't keep a record of rights and wrongs. We won't love on a ledger sheet, keeping track of each other's good and bad deeds. We will love *unconditionally.*

LOVE COMMITMENT #2
EACH FAMILY MEMBER HAS BASIC RIGHTS

Each of us has the right to nurture and love each other, and our extended family members, without criticism or harassment. We have the right to be treated courteously and with respect. We have the right to attend and participate in special activities involving other family members. Each of us has the right to privacy unless it's something potentially destructive or dangerous to each other or the family in general.

Love Commitment #3
Each Family Member Has a Right to Expect Positive and Responsible Parenting

Children, we commit ourselves as your parents to strive for unity in all matters—especially in our parenting responsibilities. We won't air our personal differences in front of you. We commit ourselves to not speaking negatively about each other in front of you or asking you to hear about any difficulties we have between us. We commit to practicing what we preach and modeling good behavior for our family. We'll be responsible for handling the finances for our family. With the Lord's guidance and blessing, we assume full responsibility for understanding the true needs of each family member and for providing adequate shelter, food, clothing, and protection of our family. We commit ourselves to resolving any personal disputes promptly and lovingly, if reasonably possible. We further commit ourselves to seeking godly advice and counsel from competent spiritual advisors whenever we're unable to agree on issues or are uncertain about how to pursue matters. We'll keep ourselves refreshed by attending at least one Christian marriage event or conference a year.

1. *Parenting plan:* We commit ourselves to preparing and following a written parenting plan based upon godly principles that focuses on serving the best interests of everyone concerned in our family. Each child will have every opportunity to develop an independent and meaningful relationship with each parent—biological and stepparent. Each child will be loved, disciplined, and protected by each parent. No child will be asked to choose between parents. In every way, we commit ourselves to letting each child *be* a child without having to make adult decisions or take on adult responsibilities.

2. *Interaction with noncustodial parents:* We commit ourselves to acting lovingly and spiritually with your noncustodial parents and coparenting you in a manner that is in your best interest. We'll respect and appreciate the personal differences of all parents without unreasonably judging them. We won't ask any child to be a messenger between parents. We commit to not using any child as a bargaining chip in any negotiations between parents.

3. *Living within our means:* In keeping the family finances, we commit ourselves to making sure that we live within our means as the Lord has blessed us. Each child will be given the best economic support we can reasonably provide with God's help.

4. *Focus on the future—not the past:* We commit to doing everything reasonably possible to help each family member grow and mature into being Christlike men and women. While we'll learn from the mistakes of the past, our focus will be on making our future together everything God wants for our family.

5. *We commit to being peacemakers:* Like Jesus, we pledge to be peacemakers, rather than peacebreakers, with each other. We'll follow the biblical principles for conflict resolution as set forth by Jesus in Matthew 18:15–17 in a prompt and timely manner. If there are any conflicts we cannot resolve ourselves, we commit to asking trusted and competent church leaders, counselors, or friends to help mediate our discussions

in an effort to reconcile any brokenness in our relationships. Above all, we mutually commit ourselves to having loving, accepting, and forgiving hearts so no root of bitterness and resentment creates a barrier between any of us.

Love Commitment #4
Each Family Member Has a Right to Be Heard

While we, your parents, are responsible before God for final decisions affecting our family, we want—and *need*—input from each of you, our children. To make sure each of us thoughtfully and prayerfully considers the personal cares and concerns and unique perspectives of each family member, we commit ourselves to holding regular family conferences, at least on a monthly basis, to discuss these important matters. Family conferences will provide us with a safe place to exchange ideas, discuss suggestions as to how to make our lives better, resolve complaints, and generally discuss issues confronting us as a family.

Everyone will have an opportunity to share—no one will be overlooked. We commit ourselves to allowing each family member to freely express his/her concerns without criticism or ridicule. We also want these family conferences to be *solution-oriented,* meaning that we don't want to just discuss problems—we also want to put our heads together to find creative solutions to those problems in which every family member "wins," if reasonably possible.

1. *Scheduling of family conferences:* Our regular family conference will be held on the first Sunday night of each month after our family dinner together. However, any family member may call a special family conference at any time if there's a good reason for it. It's important that each family member attend all meetings.

2. *Agenda for family conferences:* Mom or Dad will prepare a written agenda for each family conference and hand it out to each family member at least a day or two before the conference occurs. This will allow each family member sufficient time to think and pray about the issues to be discussed. If you'd like to have a topic discussed, put your *positive comments* and *suggestions* in the "Family Matters *Joy* Jar" in the kitchen and ask to have them placed on the agenda. If you have a *complaint,* put it in the "Family Matters *Grievances* Jar," also in the kitchen, which will become an automatic agenda item. Sign your name if you wish, or you can type it on the computer and make it an anonymous submittal if you wish.

3. *Performing family conferences:* Mom or Dad will head our family conferences, although we may ask one of you children to take over this responsibility from time to time. Regardless of who chairs the conference, everyone will have an opportunity to speak on every issue for a reasonable period of time. Everyone is encouraged to be completely honest. All family members commit ourselves not to interrupt, raise our voices, or show disrespect or lack of courtesy to one another.

4. *We'll be solution-oriented and communicative:* We further commit ourselves to be creative and innovative in bringing suggestions and solutions for family problems to our conferences. The chairperson will be responsible for preparing written minutes of our conferences, distributed to each family member as soon as reasonably possible after each conference. If any family member believes the minutes for any conference don't accurately reflect our discussions, that person may ask for a special family

conference to correct any misunderstanding. To make sure we do understand each other, and in case we forget anything important, we may agree to tape-record our family conferences for our own benefit.

5. *Making decisions at family conferences:* All decisions will be made on a majority basis, but Mom or Dad each have the right to veto a decision whenever it is reasonably necessary in the interest of our family unity and harmony.

6. *Adjourning family conferences:* We ask each family member to do his/her part in ending each family conference with at least two positive and encouraging comments about the family in general, and at least one sincere compliment about another family member. This family time should be an event where everyone leaves with a sense of accomplishment and good feelings.

7. *Family communication in general:* We want to learn how best to communicate with each other and understand how each of us thinks and feels about life. Toward that goal, we would like each family member to commit to *actively* listening to each other by putting down whatever is in his/her hands, looking at each other eye-to-eye, and maintaining eye contact during conversations, giving full attention. We agree to focus on what's being said without interruption or distraction from our surroundings (such as the telephone ringing). We'll assume the *best* of each other—without jumping to conclusions—until we have facts to the contrary. If a family member wishes to discuss a matter and it's not a good time to talk, the other family member commits to rescheduling another time to do it. If the topic is controversial, and if time allows for it, we won't say no right away, but keep our minds open and hold our emotions in check with each other. If we don't understand each other, we'll ask for clarification. To make sure we understand what's being shared, we'll restate the matter in our own words and ask for feedback from the speaker before making any other response. We commit to devoting our full effort to learning the *facts* and trying to understand *why* and *how* things happened before reacting.

LOVE COMMITMENT #5
EACH FAMILY MEMBER HAS A RIGHT TO KNOW WHAT PERSONAL CONDUCT IS EXPECTED OF EACH OTHER

We desire, and need, order, peace, and unity in our family. Toward that goal, each family member needs to know how to act and live for the greater good of our entire family. By living together, we'll discover matters about ourselves and our lives together that will need guidance and direction to avoid misunderstandings and unreasonable conflict. We'll also need to write some guidelines so we won't forget what we've agreed upon.

1. *House guidelines:* After we discuss house guidelines and adopt them at a family conference, Mom and Dad will prepare a list of these family guidelines and provide a copy for each family member to review and remember. An additional copy of our list will be placed on our refrigerator for easy reference. We'll also rank each house guideline in order of priority and importance. Each family member commits to modeling godly behavior and wholehearted compliance with these house guidelines.

2. *Enforcement of house guidelines:* We commit to allowing each family member to face the logical consequences of his/her own decisions with a minimum of

interference, to allow the Lord to work in each person's life. We'll use responsible "tough love" principles as necessary without appeasing sinful behavior. Compliance and noncompliance with a house guideline will have a consequence. Compliance brings praise from other family members and a specific blessing. Noncompliance brings a specific consequence, leading to *consistent* discipline fitting the infraction. This discipline will be enforced for a specific time period, with the purpose of encouraging responsibility, self-control, and the need for obedience in the offender. As a family, we'll decide together what these blessings or consequences are *in advance* at our family conferences. Mom and Dad will be the enforcers of all house guidelines.

3. *Discipline principles:* As part of our family commitment to discipline, we agree that:

- discipline will be corrective measures applied with love and godly principles;
- discipline will be uniformly applied to all children in the home (as well as visiting children);
- discipline will respect age-appropriate boundaries of all children in the home (as well as visiting children); and
- discipline will balance encouragement, love, rewards, and correction.

LOVE COMMITMENT #6
EACH FAMILY MEMBER HAS A RIGHT TO SHARE MATTERS IN CONFIDENCE

We commit ourselves not to betray each other's confidences unless it's a matter that violates God's Word, is unlawful, or is potentially destructive or dangerous to any family member or the family in general. Before sharing any matter in confidence, we'll ask the person desiring protection of the confidence if he/she will permit disclosure. We'll respect each other's decisions in those circumstances.

LOVE COMMITMENT #7
EACH CHILD HAS A RIGHT TO LEARN FINANCIAL MANAGEMENT

We commit to being good models in showing our children how to be compassionate, generous, and responsible citizens in using the material blessings the Lord gives us. We'll talk with our children about some of the financial decisions we make so you'll learn some of these details toward the goal of self-discipline, sharing in a charitable spirit, and exercising sound decision making.

1. *Children shall have opportunities to learn personal financial lessons:* We believe our children should have a voice in how our family saves and spends our money. We want you to be informed and prudent stewards of the Lord's blessings. We will provide financial guidance for our family, but we know you also need firsthand experience in deciding how to handle your own money. Toward that goal, we'll let you manage your allowance money and spend it as you determine, unless decisions violate God's Word or the law, or it's potentially destructive or dangerous to any family member or the family in general.

2. *Children shall receive allowances:* Each child shall receive a monthly allowance based upon age, as Mom and Dad shall determine after annual discussions of this

matter at our family conferences. Mom and Dad will provide the basic things in life such as food, shelter, education, medical care, and basic clothing. Children will then use allowances to purchase anything beyond these basic necessities. We'll regularly discuss with you the importance of giving generously to the church and helping those in need. We want to help our children become "other-centered" as part of your love for God and love for their parents and siblings. We all recognize there are no greater commandments than fulfilling these goals in life as family members (Matt. 22:34–40).

LOVE COMMITMENT #8
SPECIFIC FAMILY MATTERS

Our family also makes the following specific commitments to each other:

1._____

_____.

2._____

_____.

3._____

_____.

Agreed to and signed at our family conference on _____, 20___.

Dad:

_____

Mom:

_____

Children:

_____

_____

_____

Appendix C

RESOURCE LIST OF GROUPS AND ORGANIZATIONS

This list of resources provides contact information about groups and organizations you can call or write to help you cope with difficult family matters. Consult your local directory for organizations or groups in your area.[1]

BLENDED FAMILY PARENTING, CHILD SUPPORT, AND OTHER CHILDREN'S ISSUES (SEE ALSO MARRIAGE/FAMILY)

Association for Children for Enforcement of Support (ACES)
2260 Upton Avenue
Toledo, OH 43606
(800) 738-ACES (2237)
Internet: www.childsupport-aces.org
(Provides information and assistance in collecting support. Largest child support self-help group in U.S., with 45,000 members and 400 chapters in 48 states. Has 57 percent success rate finding absent parents.)

Child Support
(800) 622-KIDS

Confident Kids (founded 1990)
330 Stanton Street
Arroyo Grande, CA 93420
(805) 473-7945
Fax: (805) 473-7948
Internet: www.confidentkids.com
(Bible-based support group outreach to help children cope with life circumstances.)

Fathers for Equal Rights, Inc.
(founded 1973)
P.O. Box 50052
One Main Place Station
Dallas, TX 75250-0052
(214) 953-2233

Internet: www.fathers4kids.org
(Strong advocate organization for equal parenting responsibility and strengthening father-child relationship.)

Federal Office of Child Support Enforcement
Administration for Children & Families
370 L'Enfant Promenade, SW
Washington, DC 20447
(202) 401-5439
Internet: www.acf.dhhs.gov
(ACF is a federal agency funding state and local organizations to provide family assistance [welfare], child support, child care, and other programs relating to children and families. National information clearinghouse.)

For Kids Sake, Inc. (founded 1974)
P.O. Box 313
Lake Elsinore, CA 92530-0313
(909) 600-0158
Fax: (909) 600-1380
Internet: www.forkidssakesocal.org
(Christian-based program towards early recognition, intervention, and prevention of child abuse and molestation through education.)

Lost Children's Network
(877) 898-5678
Internet: www.lostchildren.org
(Nonprofit volunteer organization, founded to search nationwide for missing children via television programs broadcast throughout the country.)

National Center for Missing and Exploited Children (founded 1984)
Charles B. Wang International
Children's Building
699 Prince Street
Alexandria, VA 22314-3175
(800) THE-LOST (843-5678), or
(703) 235-3900
Fax: (703) 274-2200
Internet: www.missingkids.com
(Cofounded by John Walsh of
"America's Most Wanted" television
show. Serves as clearinghouse of information on missing and exploited
children. Provides technical assistance
to citizens and law enforcement agencies, and training programs.)

National Child Abuse Hotline
(800) 4-A-CHILD (422-4453)

National Child Pornography Tipline
(800) 843-5678
Internet: www.cybertipline.com
(Tipline run by National Center for
Missing and Exploited Children in conjunction with U.S. Postal Inspection
Service, U.S. Customs Service, and FBI.
Handles calls
from individuals reporting sexual
exploitation of children through
pornography.)

National Runaway Switchboard
(800) 621-4000
Internet: www.nrscrisisline.org

National Child Support Enforcement Association
444 North Capitol Street, NW,
Suite 414
Washington, DC 20001-1512
(202) 624-8180
Fax: (202) 624-8828
Internet: www.ncsea.org
(Organization representing a workforce
of more than 60,000 in the child support community.)

National Youth Crisis Hotline
(800) HIT-HOME (448-4663)
(Provides national referral service as to
crisis intervention for runaways and parents of runaways, rape and abuse victims, drug and alcohol addictions, etc.)

Parents Without Partners
(founded 1957)
1650 South Dixie Highway, Suite 510
Boca Raton, FL 33432
(561) 391-8833
Fax: (561) 395-8557
Internet:
www.parentswithoutpartner.org
(Largest international organization
devoted to interests of single parents and
children. Has 50,000+ members—55
percent female, 45 percent male—in 400
chapters. Provides information on support enforcement as well as support
groups for separated, divorced, and widowed parents.)

Stepfamily Association of America, Inc.
650 J Street, Suite 205
Lincoln, NE 68508
(800) 735-0329
Fax: (402) 477-8317
Internet: www.saafamilies.org
(National organization dedicated to
providing support and guidance to
stepfamilies.)

Stepfamily Foundation
(founded 1975)
333 West End Avenue
New York, NY 10023
(212) 877-3244
Fax: (212) 362-7030
Internet: www.stepfamily.org

Tough Love International
(founded 1980)
P.O. Box 1069
Doylestown, PA 18901
(215) 348-7090
Fax: (215) 348-9874

Internet: www.toughlove.org
(For help when dealing with out-
of-control behavior of a family
member.)

COUNSELING/ PSYCHOTHERAPY

Adult Children of Alcoholics World Service Organization, Inc.
P.O. Box 3216
Torrence, CA 90510
(310) 534-1815
Internet: www.adultchildren.org
(Provides 12-step program for individ-
uals growing up in alcoholic or other-
wise dysfunctional homes.)

Alcoholics Anonymous
(founded 1935)
Grand Central Station
P.O. Box 459
New York, NY 10163
(212) 870-3400
Internet: www.alcoholics-
anonymous.org
(Provides well-known 12-step program
for recovering alcoholics, with more
than 2 million members.)

American Association of Christian Counselors
P.O. Box 739
Forest, VA 24551
(800) 526-8673 or (434) 525-9470
Fax: (434) 525-9480
Internet: www.aacc.net
(Provides listings of 50,000 profes-
sional, pastoral, and lay counselors
whose counseling services are based on
Christian principles.)

American Association for Marriage and Family Therapy (founded 1942)
112 South Alfred Street
Alexandria, VA 22314-3061
(703) 838-9808
Fax: (703) 838-9805
Internet: www.aamft.org

(Represents more than 23,000
marriage/family therapists
internationally.)

American Psychiatric Association
1400 K Street N.W.
Washington, DC 20005
(888) 357-7924
Fax: (202) 682-6850
Internet: www.psych.org
(Represents more than 38,000 psychiatric physicians internationally. Your
local APA can refer you to psychiatrists
in your area.)

Christian Counseling and Education Foundation
1803 East Willow Grove Avenue
Glenside, PA 19038
(215) 884-7676
Fax: (215) 884-9435
Internet: www.ccef.org
(Christian counseling organization)

National Board for Certified Counselors, Inc. (founded 1982)
P.O. Box 651051
Charlotte, NC 28265-1051
(336) 547-0607
Fax: (336) 547-0017
Internet: www.nbcc.org
(Monitors a national certification sys-
tem with more than 31,000 certified
counselors internationally.)

National Christian Counselors Association (founded 1983)
3650 17th Street
Sarasota, FL 34235
(877) 887-2870
Fax: (941) 951-6676
Internet: www.ncca-usa.com
(Association of minisers, professional
Christian counselors, testing specialists,
medical doctors, and teachers
who believe that counseling is self-centered and useless unless it is founded
upon, and directed by, the Word of
God.)

Overcomers Outreach
P.O. Box 2208
Oakhurst, CA 93644
(800) 310-3001
Internet: www.overcomers-outreach.org
(Nondenominational ministry providing national support group network for individuals and families within evangelical Christian churches providing a two-way bridge between biblical principles and the 12-step program of Alcoholics Anonymous.)

RAPHA
(founded 1986)
3021 Gateway Drive, Suite 290
Irvine, TX 75063
(800) 383-HOPE (383-4673)
Fax: (972) 258-0449
Internet: www.raphacare.com
(Provides Christ-centered in-patient psychiatric treatment and professional counseling for Christians suffering from emotional problems or substance abuse. "RAPHA" comes from the Hebrew name for God, literally meaning "Our God who heals you.")

CREDIT/FINANCIAL MATTERS
Major national credit bureaus:

Trans-Union Credit Information
P.O. Box 2000
Chester, PA 19022
(800) 888-4213
Internet: www.transunion.com

Equifax Disclosure
P.O. Box 740241
Atlanta, Georgia 30374-0241
(800) 685-1111
Internet: www.equifax.com

Experian National Consumer Assistance Center
P.O. Box 2002
Allen, TX 75013
(888) 397-3742

Internet: www.experian.com
(Most people have credit files at one or more of the foregoing three major credit bureaus. A copy of your file can be obtained by contacting them.)
Other credit and financial management resources:

Christian Financial Concepts
P.O. Box 2377
Gainesville, GA 30503-2377
(800) 772-1976 or (404) 534-1000
Internet: www.cfcministry.org
(This organization is under the oversight of Larry Burkett, one of the most highly regarded financial counselors in the country using Christian principles.)

CreditGUARD of America
5301 North Federal Highway, Suite 230
Boca Raton, FL 33487
(800) 500-6489
Internet: www.creditguard.org
(Nonprofit debt management and credit counseling organization.)

Debtors Anonymous (founded 1968)
P.O. Box 920888
Needham, MA 02492-0009
(781) 453-2743
Fax: (781) 453-2745
Internet: www.debtorsanonymous.org
(Provides international assistance and support groups to those wanting to stop incurring unsecured debt.)

Internal Revenue Service Hotline
(800) 829-1040

National Foundation for Consumer Credit (founded 1951)
801 Roeder Road, Suite 900
Silver Spring, MD 20910
(800) 388-2227 or (301) 589-5600
Fax: (301) 495-5623
Internet: www.nfcc.org

(National network of more than 1,300 agencies providing assistance to those dealing with stressful financial situations. Ask for the "Do-It-Yourself Credit Repair and Improvement Guide.")

Social Security Administration— Department of Health and Human Services
Office of Public Inquiries
Windsor Park Building
6401 Security Boulevard
Baltimore, MD 21235
(800) 772-1213
TTY: (800) 325-0778
Internet: www.ssa.gov
(Ask for the booklets "Understanding Social Security" and "Survivors," both printed in January 1991.)

DATING RESOURCES
eharmony (founded 1998)
300 North Lake Avenue, Suite 1111
Pasadena, CA 91101
Internet: www.eharmony.com
(Provides Christian matching system based upon numerous compatibility factors, supported by 30 years of research. Founded by relationship expert Dr. Neil Clark Warren to help people find a suitable marriage partner and build successful, long-lasting relationships with a Christian emphasis.)

Match.com (founded 1995)
P.O. Box 3870
McAllen, TX 78502
Internet: www.match.com
(Secular online dating service with profiles of more than 3 million members. Christians should use caution!)

DIVORCE AND SPOUSAL DEATH SUPPORT AND RECOVERY
Church Initiative
(DivorceCare/GriefShare Ministries)
(founded 1993)
P.O. Box 1739

Wake Forest, NC 27588
(919) 562-2112
Fax: (919) 562-2114
Internet: www.churchinitiative.org
(Founded by *Steve & Cheryl Grissom.* [See *Foreword* to this book.] International Bible-based ministry provides outstanding video series and other Christian resources for divorcees and widowed persons, and their children.)

Fresh Start Seminars/Life Counseling Services
P.O. Box 968
Duluth, GA 30096
(888) 373-7478 or (770) 495-7440
Fax: (770) 495-1287
Internet: www.freshstartseminars.org
(Christian ministry to separated and divorced individuals, with local seminars/support groups across U.S.)

DOMESTIC VIOLENCE AND EMOTIONAL ABUSE
National Domestic Violence Hotline
(800) 799-SAFE (799-7233)
TDD: (800) 787-3224

Parents Anonymous, Inc.
(founded 1970)
675 West Foothill Boulevard, Suite 220
Claremont, CA 91711
(909) 621-6184
Fax: (909) 625-6304
Internet: www.parentsanonymous.org
(For parents who are, or fear they may become, out of control in disciplining their children.)

LEGAL RESOURCES
American Bar Association Family Law Section
750 North Lake Shore Drive
Chicago, IL 60611
(312) 988-5584
Internet: www.abanet.org

American Academy of Matrimonial Lawyers (founded 1962)
150 North Michigan, Suite 240
Chicago, IL 60601
(312) 263-6477
Fax: (312) 263-7682
Internet: www.aaml.org
(Association of 1,500 members in U.S.)

Christian Legal Society
(founded 1961)
4208 Evergreen Lane, Suite 222
Annandale, VA 22003-3264
(703) 642-1070
Fax: (703) 642-1075
Internet: www.clsnet.org
(Largest national nondenominational Christian organization of attorneys, judges, law professors, and law students. Advocates biblical conflict reslution and voluntary/low-fee legal assistance for the needy. Provides local referrals.)

MARRIAGE AND FAMILY
Association of Couples for Marriage Enrichment (founded 1973)
P.O. Box 10596
Winston-Salem, NC 27108
(800) 634-8325 or (336) 724-1526
Fax: (336) 721-4746
Internet: www.bettermarriages.org
(International organization promoting better marriages by providing enrich-ment opportunities that strengthen couple relationships and enhance per-sonal growth, mutual fulfillment, and family wellness with a Christian focus.)

FamilyLife Today
(founded 1978)
P.O. Box 23840
Little Rock, AR 72221-3840
(800) FL-TODAY (358-6329)
Internet: www.familylife.com
(Organization overseen by noted mar-riage experts Dennis and Barbara Rainey. Offers numerous Christian marriage seminars and resources [including Homebuilders Series on

Remarriage], with volunteer network of more than 10,000 couples.)
Focus on the Family
Colorado Springs, CO 80995
(800) 232-6459
TDD: (877) 877-8227
Fax: (719) 531-3424
Internet: www.family.org
(Organization founded by noted author and psychologist Dr. James C. Dobson. Dedicated to strengthening the Christian home. Produces several national radio programs and magazines as well as family-oriented books, films, videos, and audio cassettes from a Christian perspective.)

Marriage Builders, Inc.
12568 Ethan Avenue North
White Bear Lake, MN 55110
(651) 762-8570
Internet: www.marriagebuilders.com
(Ministry overseen by noted marriage expert Dr. Willard F. Harley Jr. Helps couples overcome marital conflicts and restore love.)

MEDIATION
Academy of Family Mediators
5 Militia Drive
Lexington, MA 02421
(781) 674-2663
Fax: (781) 674-2690
Internet: www.mediatorsadr.net
(Contact source for family mediators.)

American Arbitration Association
335 Madison Avenue, Floor 10
New York, NY 10017-4605
(800) 778-7879 or (212) 716-5800
Fax: (212) 716-5905
Internet: www.adr.org
(Largest international alternative dis-pute resolution organization.)

Association for Conflict Resolution
1527 New Hampshire Avenue, NW
Washington, DC 20036

(202) 667-9700
Fax: (202) 265-1968
Internet: www.mediators.org or
www.acresolution.org
(Represents and serves diverse international audience of more than 7,000
mediators and others involved in conflict resolution and collaborative decision making. Offers referral service.)

**Association of Family and
Conciliation Courts** (founded 1963)
6515 Grand Teton Plaza, Suite 210
Madison, WI 53719-1048
(608) 664-3750
Fax: (608) 664-3751
Internet: www.afccnet.org
(International and interdisciplinary
association of family, court, and community professionals dedicated to
the constructive resolution of family
disputes.)

Peacemaker Ministries
(founded 1982)
1537 Avenue D, Suite 352
Billings, MT 59102
(406) 256-1583
Internet: www.hispeace.org
(Ken Sande, author of *The
Peacemaker*, heads up this outstanding
international, ministry of Christian
mediation which trains mediators and
provides mediation, services as well as
other excellent mediation resource
materials. Affiliated with the Christian
Legal Society.)

NOTES

Introduction

1. Dan Piraro, "Bizarro," *Miami Herald,* 2 December 1999, 12EB. Bizarro © 1999 Piraro. Dist. by Universal Press Syndicate. All rights reserved.

Chapter 1

1. "A Great Emptiness," *Newsweek,* 7 November 1983, 120.

2. Ibid., 124.

3. According to the U.S. Census Bureau, November 1998, men comprised only 49.8 percent of the population in the 30–39 age group. This percentage then declines to 49.4 percent among those aged 40–49, 48.4 percent in the 50–59 group, 46.5 percent for those 60–69, 42.8 percent in the 70–79 group, 35.4 percent for those 80–89, and 25.1 percent in the 90–99 group (*Newsweek,* 15 February 1999, 6).

4. Ana Veciana-Suarez, "A Pain Hard to Bear, a Question with No Answers . . . and a Vow," *Miami Herald,* 22 January 1995, 5J; 29 January 1998, 2A.

5. David Gelman, ETAC, "A Great Emptiness," *Newsweek,* 7 November 1983, 124.

6. Jason Cole, "Wannstedt Builds Team to Be Weather-Proof," *Miami Herald,* 29 November 2000, 6D.

7. Ann Landers, *Miami Herald,* 18 January 2002, 64G.

8. If divorce or death of a spouse is difficult for you, look into Fresh Start Ministries or the DivorceCare/GriefShare ministry of Church Initiative (see appendix C). Single parents also may want to check into Parents without Partners. The Fresh Start and DivorceCare ministries offer seminars emphasizing personal interaction in a comfortable and nonconfrontational setting among attendees who have gone through a separation or divorce. From personal experience, I can tell you that these seminars provide excellent help in moving toward a healthy acceptance of your own situation.

9. *The Week,* 5 April 2002, 8.

Chapter 2

1. President Franklin D. Roosevelt, first inaugural address to the nation, March 4, 1933.

2. In 1970 Dr. Elizabeth Kubler-Ross received national attention for her book *On Death and Dying.* She pioneered the idea that terminally ill persons go through well-defined states of grief—denial, anger, bargaining, and depression—before accepting impending death. While Dr. Kubler-Ross confined her research to the terminally ill, wide acceptance of her ideas led to more recognition that survivors of other crises also go through stages of grief.

3. George Scriven and C. C. Converse, "What a Friend We Have in Jesus." Public domain.

4. The apostle Peter's speech in Acts 2:14–41 to the crowds in Jerusalem who had crucified Christ is an excellent example of how God helped the Israelites feel objective guilt that motivated them to repentance and salvation.

5. According to the National Depressive & Manic-Depressive Association, warning signs of depression are: (1) extreme loneliness; (2) sleeplessness or sleeping excessively; (3) withdrawal from others; (4) neglect of appearance; (5) compulsive overeating, or drastic diets and weight loss; (6) frequent or unexplainable crying spells; (7) feeling hopeless, believing "I'll never get over this,"; (8) loss of interest in a job, family, friends, and hobbies that once brought joy, and getting little or no pleasure out of anything in life; (9) overreacting with excessive irritability over trivial matters; (10) loss of energy, with difficulty in thinking and concentration, memory loss, and inability to make decisions; (11) low self-esteem and self-blame; and

(12) if depression is severe, recurrent thoughts of death or suicide. If you are experiencing some, or many, of the symptoms of depression, it is time to seek competent professional counseling without delay!

6. "Study Shows Sharp Rise in Depression Treatment," *Miami Herald,* 9 January 2002, 12A.

7. William Shakespeare, "Much Ado about Nothing," Act III, Scene 2.

8. This doesn't necessarily mean getting remarried to an ex-spouse, although no one who remains single after divorce should reject this possibility. There may be circumstances where remarriage to an ex-spouse may be unwise, inappropriate, or even unbiblical. (See chap. 3.) What it *does* mean, however, is that we can restore *peace* to the relationship and not let past sins jeopardize current interaction with our ex-spouses.

9. Larry Crabb, *Inside Out* (Colorado Springs, Colo.: NavPress, 1988), 32.

10. For an in-depth biblical study on many practical ways to depend upon God after loss of a spouse, please refer to chapter 8 in *When the Vow Breaks* (Nashville, Tenn.: Broadman & Holman, 1993), 115.

Chapter 3

1. God created man and woman as equal counterparts in their nature, not different beings, but different expressions of the same human creation. From the beginning, Eve was created as a "helper" or "help meet" (Hebrew, *neged,* meaning a "part opposite; specifically a counterpart, or mate") in the sense of being spiritually, physically, emotionally, and intellectually complementary with Adam. Sharing the same nature didn't negate the differing *roles* of headship and submission that the Lord established between Adam and Eve, and which remain applicable to husbands and wives today. Some believe Eve first assumed a submissive role in her relationship with Adam as a result of God's judgment in Genesis 3:16. In other words, they believe headship and submission arose from punishment in the Garden. But it is more likely that God established the roles of authority, headship, and submission *prior* to this discipline.

2. It is possible for an unmarried man and woman to be of "one flesh" in an illicit sexual sense only. But marriage, in God's eyes, arises as he joins *those desiring marriage*—the "leavers" and "cleavers"—into "one flesh." There is nothing else on earth that quite matches this special union.

3. The husband gave his wife a "get" (coming from the Hebrew word for "document"). Only men could issue this document. No similar right existed for women under Jewish law, although a wife could ask a Jewish court to compel her husband to give her a "get" under certain circumstances (e.g., husband was impotent or had a loathsome disease). A "get" was a twelve-line document written by a scribe in Hebrew and Aramaic describing a written release from marriage. The certificate of divorce had to meet all the expressed or implied requirements of Jewish law and be properly signed by the husband, dated, and witnessed to be valid. It specifically recited that the woman was now free to marry any man. Another man who married the divorced woman with a valid certificate of divorce did not have to worry about the first husband claiming any rights under the first marriage. The executed certificate was effective with delivery to the woman by putting it in her hand. All of this is described in Jewish law and traditions, *not* in the Bible.

4. Hebrew, "tame," or "to become unclean." Leviticus 18:20 and Numbers 5:13–14 use the same term to refer to adultery. In context, this defilement may exist only in the wife in relation to her first husband, but not with other men.

5. Leviticus 18:7–8; Genesis 2:23–24. Those holding this view argue on the basis of kinship. In other words, since the wife has become "one flesh" with her second husband, she thereby made the first and second husbands brothers. If the wife remarried the first husband, it would be similar to a man marrying his sister. This may be a rather far-fetched explanation however.

6. This argument assumes that the wife may have received a divorce settlement *(ketubah)* from the second husband and become a "rich divorcee." As such, the first husband would profit from her fortune while hypocritically overlooking his original objections to her during the first marriage. However, logically this would mean that the Lord was more concerned that the first husband not be unjustly enriched in a material sense rather than allow reconciliation of the original marriage.

7. As debates and religious politics absorbed the Pharisees' attention, what was Jesus concerned about? He was preaching humility and servanthood as true greatness. Notice what Jesus discussed in Matthew 18 through 20. His teaching on divorce is nestled between expressions of his love for children. He draws these little ones to himself and praises their innocence and trust as living testimonies of what pleases God (Matt. 18:2–7, 10–14; 19:13–15). He also emphasizes the importance of resolving interpersonal conflicts in relationships through unlimited forgiveness. The Pharisees focused on debate and points of law.

8. The Greek root word is *suzugnuo*, used only in Matthew 19:6 and in Mark 10:9. It means to "fasten to one yoke, or to yoke together" as two oxen are yoked together to pull a plow.

9. The root word for "not separate" (Greek *chorizo*, meaning "to separate, divide, part, or to put asunder") also appears in Romans 8:35 and 39. Nothing can *separate* us from the love of God in Christ Jesus. In 1 Corinthians 7:10, 11, and 15, Paul uses this term to instruct Christians not to separate from their mates. It clearly expresses that breaking a marriage bond is not pleasing to God. Husbands and wives can physically sever their relationship with each other (unscripturally, if no marital unfaithfulness *[porneia]* occurs) and change their marital status to "unmarried" by leaving a marriage with no intention to return. This is considered a divorce. However, they are not free to remarry as long as no porneia exists and both mates remain alive (Matt. 19:9; 1 Cor. 7:10–11).

10. However, there may be circumstances where it is *necessary* to separate, as when there is unreasonable duress through verbal, physical, or mental abuse that endangers the lives of a spouse and children. There's no specific Scripture that commands or authorizes separation under these circumstances, but implicitly God's Word protects and preserves human life wherever reasonably possible. Consequently, most believers wouldn't counsel any battered spouse to put his/her life at risk by not separating from a confirmed abuser.

11. The word *divorce* in verse 7 refers to the same term in Deuteronomy 24:1 and 3. The Hebrew term is *kerithuth*, from the root word *karath*, meaning "to cut off." This term also appears in Isaiah 50:1 and in Jeremiah 3:8 where God says he has given faithless Israel a certificate of divorce. In Greek, the root word is *apostasion*, meaning "divorce or repudiation of marriage." The term "send her away" in verse 7 refers to the Hebrew word *shalach*, meaning "to send away," as Abraham did with Hagar in Deuteronomy 21:14. The corresponding term in Greek is *apoluo*, meaning "to loose from, sever by loosening, undo, repudiate, dismiss from your house." A few Bible scholars have tried to distinguish between *kerithuth* and *shalach* by defining the latter as a cruel and harsh expulsion without a divorce, which may allow for another marriage. But most scholars believe that both terms refer to the same action—that of divorcing one's spouse with the intent of ending the marriage.

12. Although neither the Pharisees nor Jesus specifically cite this passage, it is the only germane portion of the Law of Moses. This specific passage also was the subject of vigorous debate between the Shammai and Hillel schools at that time.

13. Greek *epitrepo*, meaning "to permit, allow, as a concession" used also in Mark 5:13 and Hebrews 6:3.

14. Greek *skleerokardia*, meaning "a characteristic of one whose heart is hard, harsh, stiff," similar to how Israel refused to listen to God in Ezekiel 3:7. The term is used in only two other instances in the New Testament—Mark 10:5, in a parallel passage on divorce, and in Mark 16:14, where Jesus rebuked his disciples for their stubborn refusal to believe those who had seen him after he had risen. An excellent New Testament description of hard-heartedness is in Ephesians 4:17–18.

15. We may ask, "Aren't the hearts of men and women still hard today? Why doesn't Jesus permit divorce as Moses did?" Perhaps it is because *we* can have a personal relationship with a risen Savior during our lifetimes. God has given us the power to live the Christian life in a way not available during Moses' time. Before Christ fulfilled the Law of Moses (Gal. 3:15–29), God graciously made concessions to those under the law due to man's failure to live a righteous life. His people desperately needed grace and forgiveness because of missing the mark and falling short of God's standard. Jesus paid our penalty on the cross. Jesus confirms that divorce under Moses was an *abnormal* stopgap measure.

16. What is the Law of Moses? It is rooted in the covenant God first made with Israel through the Ten Commandments (Exod. 20:1–17; Deut. 5:1–22). But God decreed, centuries before Christ, that he would make a "new covenant" with all those who believe in Jesus. Christ, as mediator of this new covenant, fulfilled the purpose of the first covenant given through Moses. Unlike the Ten Commandments written on stone tablets, the living God spiritually writes this new covenant on our hearts as we come to him (Jer. 31:31–34; 32:40; Heb. 8:1–13).

17. For example, in the Sermon on the Mount (Matt. 5), notice how many times Jesus says, "You have heard it said . . ." He refers to the Law of Moses on murder, adultery, divorce, oaths, retribution, and dealing with enemies. In each instance he follows this up by saying, "But I tell you . . ." Then he focuses on the root causes of these sins in the *heart*.

18. Greek *hos an*, meaning "whoever or whosoever."

19. If true, Jesus tacked an addendum onto the Law of Moses that applied for a very short time (certainly less than three years until his death on the cross). What if this were true of John 3:16 and similar

verses? Could Jesus have told the world *anything* about the new covenant of grace before his death on the cross without it passing away with the law?

20. This may be one reason why the New Testament, rather than the Old Testament, includes the Gospels, even though many of the events in the Gospels occurred while the Law of Moses was still in full force and effect.

21. Greek *apoluo,* or "to loose from, sever by loosening, undo, repudiate, dismiss from your house." This term is used sixty-nine times in the New Testament, including Matthew 1:19, where Joseph considered putting away Mary due to her pregnancy. It should be said that, just as the Bible specifies no ceremony for marriage, it's true that no divorce procedures are prescribed either. It's a matter of private decision between husband and wife. Even so, a couple's decision to divorce, or compliance with a human civil court procedure for divorce, are irrelevant to God if his requirements are not met. Unless marital unfaithfulness *(porneia)* occurs in a marriage, a civil divorce doesn't end the relationship even if a court says it does.

22. Greek *gameo,* meaning "to lead in marriage; to take a wife; to get married." We find this word throughout the New Testament, including Mark 6:17 and 1 Corinthians 7:9, 10, 28, 33, 34, 36, 39 discussed later in this chapter.

23. For example, assuming that verse 9 has universal application to all humankind, different people interpret this verse as: (1) not permitting divorce at all (Mark 10:11–12); (2) permitting divorce only after marital unfaithfulness has occurred, but *not* remarriage under any circumstance as long as both spouses live; (3) permitting divorce for "something indecent" *and* remarriage as Hillel interpreted Deut. 24:1 (meaning divorce for almost any reason and freedom to marry others); (4) permitting divorce for both spouses, but with remarriage to another partner *only* open to the spouse not guilty of marital unfaithfulness; or (5) permitting divorce *and* remarriage for *both* spouses after either or both spouses commit marital unfaithfulness (which can occur before or after divorce, or when one spouse marries another person).

24. In Verse 9 Jesus is directly speaking of divorce in general. The unique problems of marriages between Christians and non-Christians arising after his resurrection may not be directly addressed here by Jesus. In 1 Corinthians 7, Paul may provide a special exception permitting divorce for *Christians* in such "mixed faith marriages."

25. Some argue that marriage is a covenant, and divorce breaks a covenant to remain married and faithful for life. Support for this view focuses on Israel's turning away from God in spiritual adultery (i.e., idolatry, Jer. 3:1–14). But *porneia* goes beyond nonsexual covenant-breaking or even figurative adultery. The term includes all forms of *sexual* infidelity. (The NIV translation—"marital unfaithfulness"—is somewhat misleading.) In addition, it is possible to *violate* a covenantal relationship while not *dissolving* it. (For example, Saul *violated* the covenant of Israel with the Gibeonites by putting some to death (2 Sam. 21:1–9), but he did not *terminate* the covenant, which continued for many more centuries.) In a marriage, a husband may *violate* a covenant to love his wife as himself (Eph. 5:28) in many ways not involving any sexual infidelity, but *breaking* this covenant doesn't authorize dissolution of the marriage. By making this exception in verse 9, Jesus implies that *sexual infidelity* is what breaks the "one flesh" relationship and can destroy the marriage relationship through divorce—not mere "covenant-breaking."

26. Thayer, Arndt, and Gingrich, to name a few.

27. *Porneia* is broadly defined to include adultery. All adultery is *porneia,* but not all *porneia* is adultery. *Porneia* covers a wider range of sexual sins that includes, but is not limited to, adultery. *Porneia* is what violates God's plan for marriage.

28. Some may wonder about the whole concept of infidelity and how it really begins. Is it exchanging secrets with someone else about matters that your spouse doesn't even know? Is it having lunch with someone you're attracted to without your mate knowing about it? In terms of sexual infidelity, does this mean intercourse or some other sexual activity short of it? Isn't an emotional involvement with someone outside the marriage just as devastating to a marriage as a sexual situation? This in turn tempts people to wonder, "How far can I go and still be considered faithful to my spouse?" I believe, however, that if these thoughts are running through one's mind, the *desire* to commit *porneia* may be growing. It won't be long before some *opportunity* arises to commit the *porneia* Jesus describes in Matthew 19:9. Also, it highlights the idea that one's *heart* isn't right before God!

29. God endured Israel's spiritual adultery for hundreds of years before divorcing her. (He also took her back after divorce.)

30. Matthew 18:15–18 may not apply here. The "two or three witnesses" in that passage are present to verify the *response* of one being challenged for past sin—not witnesses of the sin itself.

31. *Leonard v. Leonard,* 259 So.2d 529, 530 (Fla. 3d DCA 1972).

32. God's graciousness should cover any errors in that belief. In any event, if the errant spouse has already divorced his/her mate unscripturally and remarried, adultery has occurred. But remember, the key isn't to focus on justification for divorce. (God *permits* it but does not *require* it!) Instead, we must turn our hearts toward forgiveness and reconciliation to *preserve* a marriage as God has willed. Even if sexual infidelity has occurred, it is reasonable to believe that God would still approve of reconciliation between spouses (in the same spirit that God reconciled with Israel—even after divorce—and Hosea took back Gomer). If that fails, it's time to move on.

33. It's a sin to murder someone else. But once the murder has occurred and the victim is dead, the murder doesn't continue. One doesn't keep on murdering a dead person. Some argue the same thing occurs with *porneia* in breaking a marriage bond.

34. This assumes that the spouse committing adultery by remarriage to another person is, in doing so, terminating the first marriage, thereby rendering the remarriage no longer adulterous. But there are some serious problems with this view. For example, if God is seen to approve of a man and woman in an initially adulterous (but immediately thereafter legitimate) remarriage, is he somehow participating in their adulterous act? Does this view also allow an adulterer to legitimize an unscriptural divorce from a faithful spouse by remarriage to a lover? Does this view actually *encourage* people to commit adultery while pursuing remarriage?

35. Actually, the sentence structure in Matthew 19:9 is quite similar to Mark 2:12 about the healing of the paralytic at Bethesda. The paralytic got up (past tense, one-time event), picked up his mat (past tense, one-time event) and walked (*continuous* action, *not* one-time event, as in "keep on walking").

36 *Cf.* Mark 6:18; 1 Corinthians 5:1–5. However, if *porneia* occurs through consummation of the adulterous remarriage, doesn't this make the formerly unscriptural divorce in the first marriage (i.e., without *porneia*) now effectively a *scriptural* divorce? If so, how can adultery continue if the first marriage is now terminated scripturally?

37. What happens if the divorcer has already remarried? How does the unfaithful divorcee repent and receive forgiveness now? *Porneia* led to a divorce of the unfaithful divorcee. But is this an unpardonable sin? Few would deny that repentance and godly sorrow for the wrong done brings full forgiveness. If the marital unfaithfulness has stopped, then one can resolve not to repeat it. But if the divorcer has scripturally ended the marriage and remarried someone else, the marriage is over. Repentance through reconciliation (similar to the prodigal son) of the marriage partners is now impossible. Therefore repentance and forgiveness should be complete. Can this formerly unfaithful divorcee remarry despite committing *porneia* and breaking up a marriage, or does this person face mandatory celibacy for life?

38. This implicitly assumes that the divorcer's spouse is still alive since death also terminates a marriage (Rom. 7:2–3).

39. This brings us back to the question of whether a person can return to a spouse from a prior marriage if this remains an abomination to God as described in Deuteronomy 24:1–4.

40. Matthew adds, "for any and every reason" (Matt. 19:2).

41. The word "causes" in Greek is *poyeo,* meaning "to be the author of; to cause; to make ready; to prepare."

42. This is in accord with Romans 7:2–3 and 1 Corinthians 7:10–11, which we will review later on in this chapter.

43. 1 Corinthians 7:8. It's possible that he married at one time as a voting member of the Sanhedrin, the Jewish Supreme Court and the highest religious tribunal in Jerusalem. (Members of the Sanhedrin were married.) If so, we don't know what happened to his wife.

44. See, for example, 1 Corinthians 7:40.

45. Such as devoting oneself to prayer (1 Pet. 3:7).

46. But in context with 1 Corinthians 7:10–11, the unmarried (formerly married) Christians referred to here include only those *scripturally eligible* to remarry.

47. Greek *chorizo,* meaning "to separate, divide, put asunder; depart, go away." This is the same word used by Jesus in Matthew 19:6 and by Paul in 1 Corinthians 7:15 in referring to unbelievers. Husbands and wives physically can sever their relationship and become "unmarried" by terminating normal marital

relations and leaving the marriage with no intent to return. This is a divorce. But it does *not* necessarily break the marriage bond. Since God established marriage by joining husband and wife, he must tell us in Scripture when it is *scripturally broken*. A *scriptural* divorce changes one's *marital status* before God, with freedom to remarry thereafter.

48. Proof Paul refers to divorce here is his description of the separated wife as "unmarried" in 1 Corinthians 7:11, meaning no longer married. The warning not to separate is *strong*, using the same word used to assure us that nothing separates us from the love of Christ (Rom. 8:35, 39).

49. Greek *katallasso*, meaning "to reconcile; return into harmony and favor." It is used in the same spirit of forgiveness and love that God reconciles man to himself through Jesus Christ (2 Cor. 5:18–20).

50. See also 1 Corinthians 7:39; Romans 7:3. Although Paul doesn't mention the "marital unfaithfulness" exception of Jesus, this doesn't nullify its validity. He is most likely addressing Christian spouses divorced for reasons *other than* marital unfaithfulness *(porneia)*. In any event, verses 10–11 are consistent with Matthew 19:9. Unless the marriage is scripturally broken, forgiveness and *reconciliation* are God's will.

51. Greek *apistos*, or "unfaithful; unbelievers;" also used in 2 Corinthians 6:14–15.

52. The word used for "divorce" in these verses is *aphieemi*, meaning "to send away; to order to go away or leave." It is not the word used by Jesus in Matthew 19:9, but conveys a similar meaning of leaving a marriage with no intent to return.

53. Again, the obvious implication is that Paul addresses Christians only, not all people as Jesus did in Matthew 19:9.

54. Although Paul doesn't specifically address the unbeliever's situation *after* he/she leaves a marriage, the teachings Jesus gave to all the world on marriage and divorce in Matthew 19:9 fully apply to the unbeliever.

55. Greek *douloo*, meaning "to make a slave of; reduce to bondage," as one becomes a slave of God (Rom. 6:18, 22).

56. This is important in comparing the teachings of Jesus and Paul. In Matthew 19:9, Jesus tells us that validly married spouses who divorce may not remarry without committing adultery as long as both spouses live and no *porneia* occurs. Remarriage to others after an unscriptural divorce is improper. Why? Because the couple is still *married* in God's sight. Paul echoes this command in 1 Corinthians 7:10–11—the couple must remain separate or reconcile. But in 1 Corinthians 7:15, Paul addresses a *believer* separated from (divorced by) an unbeliever. In context with verses 12–16, Paul says the believer is "not bound" to the unbeliever. By implication, Paul's inspired judgment is that the believer's marital status before God is no longer "married," but "unmarried" and free of the marriage bond. Consequently, since Paul didn't give the believer the same command in verse 15 that he did to another believer in verse 11, it is *possible* the believer is no longer "bound" to the marriage or "married" before God. Therefore, they may be free to remarry without committing adultery. (Remember, adultery arises when a validly *married* spouse remarries.)

57. Some believe it is possible for a Christian to become totally apostate by actively and voluntarily turning away from God—so much so that he/she literally becomes an unbeliever within the meaning of 1 Corinthians 7:15 (*cf.* Heb. 6:4–6; 10:26–29; 2 Pet. 2:20–22). Others believe the eternal security of believers makes "falling away from the faith" into unbelief impossible (*cf.* Jn. 10:28–29). Regardless of which viewpoint you hold, if the divorcing spouse is a Christian acting disobediently, it appears to me somewhat of a stretch to equate a Christian in sin under Matthew 18:18, who is to be treated by his/her church "*like* an unbeliever," with a *literal* unbeliever in 1 Corinthians 7:15 in order to make this particular passage apply to divorce between professing Christian spouses.

58. Greek *deo*, meaning "to bind; put under obligation to another."

59. Greek *koimaomai*, meaning "to be still, calm, quiet; dead."

60. Greek *apothneesko*, meaning "to die; pass away."

61. Greek *elutheros*, meaning "free, exempt, unrestrained, not bound by an obligation." Jesus used the term in John 8:36 in promising that he sets people free.

62. Greek *katargeo*, meaning "to be separated from; discharged from; loosed from; to terminate all intercourse with."

63. The key Greek root words are: [1] *monan*, meaning "only; alone," (also used in Eph. 1:21 and James 2:24, which says we aren't saved through faith *alone*, but by an obedient faith); and [2] *kurios*, referring to God. Unfortunately, the NIV takes some editorial license by translating this phrase "but he must belong to the Lord," which could affect a proper interpretation.

64. In keeping with 2 Corinthians 6:14–18 about not being yoked together with unbelievers.

65. A related question is, why wasn't the same restriction put on formerly married or virgin Christians? Once again, this issue isn't clear from Scripture. It is *highly advisable* that a Christian (scripturally divorced, widowed, or never married) only marry another Christian. Then he/she can share the precious privilege of a common faith in Jesus Christ with a mate. Each Christian must make a personal decision about this issue as God speaks through Scripture.

66. We get confused by the civil process of divorce. If a state court tells us we are divorced, we may believe this somehow legitimizes a divorce. Not so with God! The only divorce God recognizes is one that is *scripturally* permitted. If no such divorce occurs, the marriage continues—even if separation between spouses, or a civil divorce, has occurred. The couple's status in God's eyes remains "married." And, if the marriage relationship isn't properly ended before God, remarriage to someone else can result in adultery.

67. This freedom doesn't arise from innocence or guilt of the spouses involved, but by their *unmarried status* before God. Some have analogized it this way: Imagine a husband and wife bound together in handcuffs. If the handcuff is removed from one spouse, the other is no longer bound either. Each is free to move in a different direction. But this creates a serious moral issue for many. If remarriage is available to *both* spouses after one spouse commits *porneia* to break up their marriage, what are the consequences of this sin? The "guilty party" should repent of sin and seek forgiveness from God (and the former spouse). But by being free to remarry simply by virtue of no longer being married, is this moral and just? After all, the exception in Matthew 19:9 literally applies only to the one who *divorces* a spouse for "marital unfaithfulness." The "guilty spouse" is the one *divorced* for misconduct. Therefore, should the "guilty party" have any right to remarry? These are difficult questions! But remember, God holds all unrepentant sinners accountable at judgment. It is not our role to punish these people, but leave vengeance to the Lord.

68. May a spouse guilty of *porneia* and break-up of a marriage remarry? Some of the arguments *against* allowing remarriage are: (1) it gives the guilty spouse an incentive to commit *porneia* in order to get out of an unwanted marriage; (2) the guilty spouse receives the same freedom to remarry as the innocent spouse, without punishment for the sin of breaking the marriage; (3) it allows a guilty spouse to maintain an adulterous remarriage; and (4) the guilty spouse is allowed to remarry when other parties to an *unscriptural* divorce (without *porneia*) may *not* remarry (e.g., the "innocent spouse" in Matthew 5:32b, and a Christian couple referred to in 1 Cor. 7:10–11). On the other hand, the Christian faith focuses on mercy, not sacrifice, and grace to motivate everyone to repentance. What is the consequence of the guilty spouse's adultery? What does repentance require? Is the answer to both questions that the guilty spouse forfeits an opportunity to remarry? The ultimate answer requires that we carefully review this person's situation. *Porneia* breaks the marriage bond. The guilty spouse's marital status before God is that he/she is no longer a "married" person. Can any adultery continue if the marriage is broken? Furthermore, if the guilty spouse has remarried, does repentance (and restitution) require breaking up the remarriage? Won't this cause more problems? What about the inequity arising with others who also commit *porneia* but *don't* scripturally forfeit the right of marriage? For example, *unmarried* persons committing *porneia* with a married person aren't specifically prohibited from marriage (or remarriage) in Scripture. Neither are widowed persons who previously committed adultery, or adulterous spouses who murder their mates (or drive them to suicide). Should there be a distinction between these situations? Perhaps not if the key factor is whether a valid *marriage* still exists in God's view. And that's precisely the point—if the guilty spouse is no longer "married," why would he/she be treated any differently than those mentioned in the foregoing examples who also sinned? Many of the issues in the story of David's adultery with Bathsheba and subsequent murder of her husband Uriah appearing in 2 Samuel 11 are germane to our consideration of this difficult question. Remember God's graciousness in that situation!

69. A related question is how does one repent of an unscriptural *divorce*? If the spouses *continue* in a divorced state, is this pardoned by God? Some argue that divorce is like murder—it happened, but no one can bring the victim back to life. Furthermore, 1 Corinthians 7:11 says that an unscripturally divorced spouse has a choice—to remain unmarried or to reconcile. Therefore, God recognizes a state of separation or divorce (without remarriage) to another person. Others would say, however, that one shows repentance from causing a divorce by having a *willingness* to reconcile with one's spouse.

70. Questions of incest exist in Mark 6:17–18 and 1 Corinthians 5:1–5 that makes those relationships *inherently* wrong. Unlike adultery (which may or may not be a continuing state of sin and is dependent upon whether a prior marriage still exists), incest doesn't change over time. Relatives married to each other

never cease to be relatives, but adulterers married to each other may cease to be adulterers if the prior marriage(s) dissolve. The same logic applies to marriages involving homosexuality or polygamy—also being sinful relationships that are *inherently* wrong regardless of remarriage issues. Paul says in 1 Corinthians 7:27–28 that a *husband* freed from a *wife* may marry again without sin. He *doesn't* say that two men may marry without sin. Both adultery in a remarriage and homosexuality are sins involving illicit sexual intercourse. But the difference, of course, is that two men married to each other violates God's basic design for marriage. That will never change even if the homosexuals repent while married.

71. A common analogy used to illustrate this is of a British citizen coming to the United States. He or she is not an American citizen. This person hasn't sworn allegiance to this country. But American law applies to this person's conduct as much as it does to native citizens. If the British citizen murders someone in this country, he/she violates American law though still subject to British law by citizenship. Similarly, God's law applies to all creation—the entire world. If anyone violates God's law, that person will be subject to whatever God provides, though he/she may not yet be a citizen in God's kingdom.

72. In 1 Corinthians 7:20, Paul tells Christians to remain in the situations they were in at conversion. But this refers to *cultural,* not sinful, situations. Paul surely didn't counsel new converts to remain in sinful situations or he would not have, for example, commanded the church in Corinth to expel the man referred to in 1 Corinthians 5.

73. Repentance by an abusive spouse needs careful consideration. It may require a real willingness and commitment to admit the problem and agree to participate in long-term counseling and rehabilitation. One of the challenges making this consideration very difficult is the tendency of many abusers to make massive, sweeping apologies after a rampage. They "lament" their actions later on, but this is not real repentance. Usually the abuser apologizes profusely for losing control, but still blames his/her victim for "causing" the abusive action to occur. In many cases, extremely complex psychological factors trigger abuse. Unfortunately, the cure rate for men in abuse rehabilitation programs is notoriously small. Why? Because the abusers remain in denial that *they* are the problem. *Extreme caution* is necessary! Repentance involves a *change of heart*—not just an empty apology without confirming action.

74. Also cited is 1 Corinthians 7:2 where Paul acknowledges the prevalence of immorality and calls for each man to have his own wife, and vice versa. But in context, 1 Corinthians 7:9 must be read in conjunction with 1 Corinthians 7:11 and Matthew 19:9, or Paul contradicts himself in the span of just two verses. First Corinthians 7:9 must address unmarried (formerly married) persons who are *scripturally free* to remarry—those to whom verse 11 that follows is not applicable. Also, in the Greek, 1 Corinthians 7:2 addresses *married* persons. It literally says that each spouse should have sexual relations with his/her mate. It addresses the problem of married persons withholding conjugal rights from each other, not a natural right to have a mate.

75. I desire, and need, to remain open to reason and correction. You may have an insight from the Lord that I don't possess. I would welcome an opportunity for you to share that with me if you wish. The Bible encourages us to reason *correctly* (Acts 17:11; 1 Thess. 5:21; 1 Pet. 3:15). Understanding God's truth in a deeper way is something I desire with all my heart.

Chapter 4

1. "Oh Happy Day," *Miami Herald,* 1 December 1981, 3C; 17 January 2001, 4A.

2. Tim Grissom, *Books in Brief,* reviewing Joshua Harris, *I Kissed Dating Goodbye* (Sisters, Oreg.: Multnomah, 1997). *Current Thoughts and Trends,* September 1997, 31.

3. Ibid.

4. "Cathy," Cathy Guisewite. *Miami Herald,* 16 May 1995, 6B. © 1995, Reprinted with permission of Universal Press Syndicate. All rights reserved.

5. "Cathy," Cathy Guisewite. *Miami Herald,* 12 June 1985, D6. ©1985, Reprinted with permission of Universal Press Syndicate. All rights reserved.

6. *RD, Face to Face,* "Getting Better All the Time," *Readers Digest,* November 2001, 84.

7. As quoted in *Investors Business Daily,* 15 February 2002, A3.

8. NBC *Today Show,* 6 March 2002, as part of interview with NBC *Today Show* consultant Dr. Gail Saltz.

9. *WorldCLICKS/WINNING! Magazine,* 6 February 2002.

10. "Cathy," Cathy Guisewite. *Miami Herald*, 3 February 2000, 6D. © 2000, Reprinted with permission of Universal Press Syndicate. All rights reserved.

11. Dr. Neil Warren, "Finding the Love of Your Life: How Not to Choose the Wrong Mate," *Focus on the Family Magazine*, November 1992, 2.

12. As quoted in *Clarity*, October/November 1999, 72.

13. "Bizarro," Dan Piraro. *Miami Herald*, 11 January 2002, 59G. © 2002, Reprinted with permission of Universal Press Syndicate. All rights reserved.

14. "Cathy," Cathy Guisewite. *Miami Herald*, 26 September 2000, 6D. © 2000, Reprinted with permission of Universal Press Syndicate.

15. As quoted in *Marriage Partnership*, Fall 2001, 11.

16. *Readers Digest*, November 2001, 80.

17. *Marriage Partnership*, Fall 2001, 11.

18. "Bizarro," Dan Piraro. *Miami Herald*, 28 September 2001, 55G. © 2001, Reprinted with permission of Universal Press Syndicate. All rights reserved.

19. As quoted in *Investors Business Daily*, 7 September 2001, 4.

20. As quoted in *Investors Business Daily*, 26 February 2002, A2.

21. As quoted in *Investors Business Daily*, 14 November 2001, 4.

22. Interview with *Prime Time Live*, 31 March 1994.

23. Psychologist David H. Olson developed PREPARE in 1979 for use by couples considering marriage. (A similar program, ENRICH, helps married couples.) PREPARE helps you: (a) get your marriage off to a good start; (b) build upon the strengths you have as a couple; (c) more clearly identify areas of your relationship that may be problematic or in need of enrichment; and (d) better communicate your feelings and ideas with each other about a variety of important topics. The foundation of the PREPARE program is a scientifically developed questionnaire that you and your partner take individually. It focuses on thirteen important areas: communication (feeling that you are understood and able to share feelings), religious orientation (agreement on religious values and beliefs), family and friends (having a good relationship with parents, in-laws, and friends), leisure activities (having shared interests while enjoying time together *and* apart), conflict resolution (being able to discuss and resolve differences), financial management (having realistic budget experience and agreement on financial matters), realistic expectations (about demands and difficulties), personality issues (liking a partner's personality and habits), children and parenting (with agreement on the number of children and child-rearing responsibilities), sexual relationship (feeling comfortable discussing sexual issues), egalitarian roles (agreeing on how to share decision-making and responsibilities), family adaptability, and family cohesion. Each partner then rates, on a scale from 1 (agree strongly) to 5 (disagree strongly), personal reactions to statements such as: "It is very easy for me to express all my true feelings with my partner" and "My partner and I are adequately prepared for the realities of marriage." Based on each person's responses, the organization prepares a personalized "PREPARE Computerized Report" identifying strength and growth areas as a couple.

24. McManus developed the "community marriage policy." Churches set up minimum standards for a couple about to wed. This plan includes extensive premarital counseling, a detailed "premarital inventory" of a couple's strengths and weaknesses, classes on morality and making marriages work, and working with a volunteer mentoring couple from a local church. McManus discovered that divorce rates in communities following these premarital standards are dramatically below the national average.

25. Dr. Harley authored the classic marriage book *His Needs, Her Needs*. Couples attending these seminars learn how love is created and destroyed, how you can identify and meet a couple's most important emotional needs, how to protect each partner from the other's destructive predispositions, and how fair negotiation can help a couple fall in love and stay in love. After the weekend, the couple immediately begins Harley's twelve-week course: "His Needs, Her Needs: Habits for a Lifetime of Passion," supported by six hours of audiotape. During this twelve-week course, Harley sends weekly assignments by E-mail to assist in developing the couple's love for each other and to monitor their progress at regular intervals. Harley also offers an eight-week course, "Love Busters: Overcoming Habits That Destroy Passion," based on his other well-known book *Love Busters*. This course features four hours of audiotape instruction, weekly E-mail assignments, and follow-up.

26. FamilyLife also offers the HomeBuilders Couples Series, a small-group Bible study program for couples on a wide variety of topics. The series consists of interactive six-to-seven-week small-group studies

designed to help couples open up to each other in fun, nonthreatening interactions. Participants build stronger Christ-centered relationships themselves and with other couples. In 2001 this series added a study entitled "Making Your Remarriage Last," designed especially for couples considering or entering into remarriage.

27. In an attempt to reduce the divorce rate by making it tougher to wed in haste, in 1980 the Archdiocese of Miami began requiring South Florida Roman Catholics who plan to marry in the Catholic Church to notify their parish priests *at least four months in advance*. Priests then assess the couples through use of a 143-question premarital inventory designed to gauge attitudes in areas ranging from religion and philosophy to children, in-laws, and sex. Vicki Salloum, "Catholics Tighten Rules on Marriage," *Miami Herald,* 29 May 1980, 1A, 12A.

28. *Focus on the Family Magazine,* February 1999, 2.

Chapter 5

1. Herald Editors, "Accountability," *Miami Herald,* 10 September 1997, 12A.

2. Doug and Naomi Mosely, *Making Your Second Marriage a First-Class Success* (Rocklin, Calif.: Prima Publishing, 1998), 27.

3. "Cathy," Cathy Guisewite, *Miami Herald,* 4 February 1993, 8D. © 1993, Reprinted with permission of Universal Press Syndicate. All rights reserved.

4. Herald Editors, "An Unanswered Prayer," *Miami Herald,* 4 April 1992, A2.

5. *Emerging Trends,* April 1999, 812.

6. In the Greek, the root word for "submit," *tasso,* means "to appoint, rank, order or arrange." In the Greek translation of the Old Testament it's used of appointments in the army (1 Sam. 22:7) and of God's ordering of nature (Jer. 5:22). Similarly, in the New Testament it's used of soldiers (Luke 7:8) and particularly God's ordering of things (Acts 22:10; Rom. 13:1). Combining *tasso* with *hupo* (meaning "under"), we have the verb *hupotasso* (the word used in Eph. 5:21–24), which means "bring into submission" or "to put yourself under" or "to arrange under"). By contrast, *antitasso* means to rebel against order. It (submit) isn't the same as *obey* (*peitharcheo*). Actually, to submit encompasses more than obeying the will of another—it means *voluntarily* doing the will of another. It's not coerced, nor does it hinge on inferiority or superiority of personhood.

7. Dr. Juliana Slattery, *Finding the Hero in Your Husband* (Boca Raton, Fla.: Health Communications, Inc., 2001), 51.

Chapter 6

1. Although love is unconditional, relationships do have some conditional elements. For example, if a spouse *or* children experience domestic violence or abuse, that's an unacceptable situation—a condition prompting them to leave the abuser. Even so, *love* can remain unconditional.

2. Edward and Sharon Douglas, *The Blended Family: Achieving Peace and Harmony in the Christian Home* (Franklin, Tenn.: Providence House Publishers, 2000), 17. Used with permission.

3. As quoted in "Thoughts on the Business of Life," *Forbes,* 8 January 2001, 276.

4. Kenneth Heiting, "Ineffective Communication—The Fine Art of Disagreeing," *Marriage and Family Living,* vol. 61, no. 1, January 1979, 16.

5. Parents can feel the same way too! Trying to maintain a relationship with a noncustodial child may seem too painful for the parent. He/she needs acceptance by the child but experiences overwhelming fear of rejection, so the parent may cut off the child emotionally. This psychological boundary rooted in self-protection makes it easier for the parent to feel better by forgetting the child.

6. Henry Cloud and John Townsend, *Boundaries in Marriage* (Grand Rapids: Zondervan Publishing House, 1999), 17.

7. Some believe tough love contradicts unconditional love. They argue that unconditional love *doesn't* set up limits on another person's conduct. They view such limits as conditions in an effort to control the love object. They believe that unconditional love requires one to love others no matter what they *do* and without trying to change them. Not so! There's a difference between *unconditional love* for a *person* and *unconditional acceptance* of what they *do*. The former is biblical and loving, but the latter isn't biblical at all. Unconditional love *doesn't* mean "anything goes." God loves the whole world—Christians and pagans alike—but he accepts into heaven only those choosing to believe in Christ (John 3:16). The Bible has numerous examples of loving the sinner but hating the sin. Unconditional love for people and using tough

love to set limits on acceptable conduct aren't contradictory at all, but are very consistent with helping people see their need for personal repentance.

8. When specifically noted, Peacemaker® Ministries graciously granted permission for me to use material drawn from their copyrighted resources in this section on conflict resolution. For more information about this excellent ministry, visit their Web site at *www.HisPeace.org,* or contact Peacemaker Ministries at 1537 Avenue D, Suite 352, Billings, Montana 59102; 406-256-1583.

9. As quoted in "Thoughts on the Business of Life," *Forbes,* 8 January 2001, 276.

10. Les and Leslie Parrott, "Do We Fight Too Much?" *Marriage Partnership,* Spring 2002, 22.

11. Greek *diallasso,* meaning "*exchanging* hostility, hatred, prejudice, aggression, or rejection for good-will, comfort, friendship, joy, love, and *unity.*"

12. This may be why Jesus emphasized how important it is to approach the offender and "show him his fault."

13. Helen Kooiman Hosier, *To Love Again: Remarriage for the Christian* (Nashville: Abingdon Press, 1985), 175. Used by permission.

Chapter 7

1. Edward and Sharon Douglas, *The Blended Family: Achieving Peace and Harmony in the Christian Home* (Franklin, Tenn.: Providence House Publishers, 2000), 36–37. Used with permission.

2. Some folks discourage brides from wearing white in remarriage. For what reason? The traditional white wedding dress was first popularized by Anne of Brittany, who wore one in marrying Louis XII of France in 1499. Before that time, a woman just wore her best dress. In fact, brides and grooms in biblical times wore blue bands around their wedding attire, since blue—not white—symbolized purity. (This is where the idea of the bride wearing "something blue" comes from.)

3. Jody Vickery, "How I Stopped Dreading Weddings: Bringing Grace and Peace to Tension-Filled Extravaganzas," *Leadership,* Spring 2000, 110.

4. *Miami Herald,* 17 February 2002, 5BI. According to "Bride's 2000 State of the Union Report," the average wedding has 186 guests. Receptions average $7,246; rings—$4,042; photos/videography—$1,263; bridal gown—$790; flowers—$775; music—$745; invitations—$374; mother-of-the-bride's dress—$198; other expense (veil, limo, fees, etc.)—$3,441. As quoted in *Readers Digest,* September 2001, 178.

5. As quoted by Nancy Barnette in "A Letter from a Borrower," *Fund Concept,* vol. 27, January 1995, 14.

6. *Pastor's Weekly Briefing,* 30 July 1999, 2.

7. Holly Miller, "Separation of church and mate?" *Clarity,* January 2000, vol. 2, no. 3, 26–30.

8. "Adults Who Attended Church as Children Show Lifelong Effects," *Barna Update* (Barna Research), November 5, 2001.

Chapter 8

1. Tony Chamberlain, *Boston Globe,* 20 July 1979, C2.

2. This life cycle is outlined in "Stepfamilies Stepping Ahead: An Eight-Step Program for Successful Family Living," a compendium prepared by members of the Stepfamily Association of America (Lincoln, Neb.: Stepfamilies Press, 1989), 31–48.

3. As Cheryl and I went through this phase of our remarriage, we knew what we needed to do—get professional marriage counseling. We hit some of the usual roadblocks and detours that most married couples face, but we needed input from an unbiased source to help us work through some of our problems. I cannot tell you how disarming it was for us to have this counselor smile warmly as he listened carefully and helped us work through conflicts—and especially to hear him say, "You two really are so good for each other!" We thought we were self-destructing at times!

4. In this phase, Cheryl and I really started putting our heads together, trying to create workable options and alternatives. For example, this is when we decided that I would move my office to Weston and end the daily commute to South Coral Gables. I could buy back my life and have more family time. Cheryl adjusted to a new church fellowship closer to our home. We planned more family nights and date nights, while being very protective of them against scheduling conflicts. We also used this phase to plan for Chase to change schools, with the goal of giving him a better Christian education. The roots of our new life together grew deeper.

5. You might assume each stage and phase of blended family life progresses in logical order, with each phase ending one day, followed by the next beginning the day after. You also might assume that everyone in your family will be in the same stage/phase at the same time. Of course, neither assumption is true. Reality is that all these stages and phases move in circular motion and repeat themselves at times. Your individual family members also will go back and forth between stages and phases at different times, depending upon each individual's feelings, circumstances, and desires. However, overall these stages and phases represent a long-term logical progression of blended family life. After a decade or two, you should be able to look back on these first years and see how all the pieces fell into place.

6. Pledging to treat your children fairly and objectively obviously isn't going to be easy. For example, if your eight-year-old son isn't permitted to ride his bicycle down the street, but your mate's eight-year-old daughter can, some compromise is necessary to keep the family peace. If one child likes being a "bathroom tenant," what will happen as the other new kids in the family wait in line? Obviously the customs of the past must give way to the new courtesies and guidelines of the present.

7. One solution is to box up your nonvaluable memorabilia and treasures you want to save. Mark the boxes and date them. If you don't need the items, or haven't even looked at them in two years—throw them out. But this advice does *not* come from personal experience, since I'm a habitual packrat!

8. Nancy S. and William D. Palmer, with Kay Marshall Strom, *The Family Puzzle: Putting the Pieces Together* (Colorado Springs: Pinion Press, 1996), 181–82.

9. You may even have the reverse situation occur with your loved ones. What if they want you to *keep* photographs you really want to get rid of? Cheryl's mother loves a beautiful portrait of Cheryl in her wedding gown, taken at her first wedding. Since the groom isn't in the picture, no problem . . . right? Well, Cheryl doesn't want to see it, nor does she want her mother to display it anywhere. Respectfully, her mother complies . . . at least whenever Cheryl visits her parents. We later found out that her mother rehangs the picture on the wall in her home immediately after every one of Cheryl's visits!

10. Editorial Staff, *World Magazine,* 16 January 1999, 13.

11. Editorial Staff, *Miami Herald,* 1 April 1993, 3D.

12. Editorial Staff, *Miami Herald,* 21 May 1997, 3D.

13. Anthony Brandt, "What Divorced Men Are Looking For," *McCall's,* May 1984, 16.

14. Dr. James Dobson, "Vive la Difference," *Focus on the Family Magazine,* February 1993, 6.

Chapter 9

1. As quoted in "People in the News," *Miami Herald,* 30 September 1994, 2A.

2. Sigmund Freud, "Inhibitions, Symptoms and Anxiety," *The Standard Edition,* vol. 20, (London: Hogarth Press, 1926), 87–174.

3. Samuel Roll, "How a Child Views the Move: The Psychology of Attachment, Separation, and Loss," *Family Advocate,* American Bar Association, vol. 20, no. 2, fall 1997, 28.

4. Ibid., 30.

5. Some psychologists recommend keeping pictures or a videotape of a child's happy times with the noncustodial parent handy to share with the child whenever lonely times come between visits.

6. Before moving, work with the child in looking over his/her current bedroom with an eye toward finding ways to improve it in the new place. Make it a game. In planning for setting up the child's new room, cut up a brown paper bag and use it as a floor plan to stick on cutouts of the bed and other furniture. Involve the child in decision-making by asking, "Where will your bed go?" "Where will you do your homework?" and "Where will your stuffed animals live?" As the child participates in the planning, positive expectations develop about the move. Take advantage of free children's moving kits that many moving companies offer, with pages to color, stories, stickers, puzzles, and games. Anticipate some postmove adjustments, but assure your child that you'll discuss these matters as they come up. If possible, pack the child's room last as part of the move, and make it the first for unpacking in the new location. Keep the child's favorite toy or keepsake unpacked so it can always be kept close at hand for comfort.

7. There are many ways to illustrate the continuity of life to children. In *Group Magazine* (September 1989), Cindy Parolini and Rick Lawrence suggested buying a healthy plant, such as a philodendron, and cutting off a sprig just beyond the joint. By pointing out the fact that the sprig can still grow even though broken off from the plant, prove it by planting the sprig in new potting soil and nursing it into a healthy plant. Helpful Scriptures to share as part of this exercise are Psalm 34:17–18, 51:16–17; and Isaiah 61:1–3.

8. Why not disparage the absent ex-spouse? Simply because the child has developed his/her self-concept from *both* parents. In running down the ex-spouse, the child may view it as a personal attack. This will only backfire on the parent making the comments. More importantly, it's not a Christian way to behave.

9. Kathleen Fox, *Making the Best of Second Best: A Guide to Positive Stepparenting* (Rapid City, SD: Foxcraft, Inc., 1998), 77–78.

10. Ibid., 73.

11. John Rosemond, "The Dilemma of Children, Discipline, and Second Marriages," *Miami Herald,* 1 September 2001, 7E.

12. Courts generally maintain an attitude of strict impartiality between religions. They use restraint in disqualifying or changing custody, or limiting biological parents from taking their children to a particular church. This conforms to the constitutional separation of church and state. (Even so, this "wall of separation" has been crumbling over recent years.) An exception arises where clear and affirmative evidence confirms that religious practices are illegal, immoral, or present a substantial threat of imminent harm to the child. *Munoz v. Munoz,* 489 P.2d 1133, 1135 (Wash. 1971); *Osteraas v. Osteraas*; 859 P.2d 948 (Idaho 1993). See also *Compton v. Gilmore,* 560 P.2d 861 (Idaho 1977). Now the "exception" should be even more cause for concern by custodial Christian parents!

13. *Stolarick v. Novak,* 584 A.2d 1034 (Pa. Super. Ct. 1991).

14. At age eighteen or twenty-one, depending upon the state. However, this may differ if the child is mentally retarded or impaired or otherwise dependent upon the parent paying child support.

15. For an overview of U.S. Supreme Court cases first recognizing, and subsequently reaffirming principles of, family autonomy and its underlying values, see e.g., *Meyer v. Nebraska,* 262 U.S. 390, 399–400 (1923); *Pierce v. Society of Sisters,* 268 U.S. 510, 534–35 (1925); *Wisconsin v. Yoder,* 406 U.S. 205, 232–33 (1972); *Santosky v. Kramer,* 455 U.S. 745, 753–54 (1982); *Smith v. Organization of Foster Families,* 431 U.S. 816, 843–44 (1977); *Cleveland Board of Education v. LaFleur,* 414 U.S. 632, 639–40; *Stanley v. Illinois,* 405 U.S. 645, 651 (1972).

16. The only exception to this is the common law doctrine known as *in loco parentis* (literally meaning "in place of a parent"), whereby a stepparent *temporarily* can acquire the status of a parent in relation to a stepchild for certain limited duties and obligations. *Miller v. United States,* 123 F.2d 715, 717 (8th Cir. 1941). This legal doctrine asserts that a stepparent isn't legally obligated to support a stepchild, but if a stepparent receives the stepchild into his/her home and supports the child, most parental rights and obligations adhere. Many state courts are very reluctant to apply this doctrine, however.

17. This "Parental Rights Doctrine" makes it easier for a fit biological parent to raise his/her own children. The courts usually won't overrule this presumption unless there's proof the biological parent is unfit or the parent isn't serving the child's best interest. Nonbiological parents (such as a stepparent) have a tougher burden. They must prove to the court they're fit to parent the stepchild. The court must review this evidence and rule in their favor for an adoption to occur.

18. A "psychological parent" means a fit adult who: (a) has actually acted as or assumed the responsibilities of a parent, (b) has formed a parent-child relationship with the child, (c) has continuing daily interaction and companionship with the child, (d) meets the child's daily physical needs, (e) has fulfilled the child's psychological needs for a parent, and (f) is viewed by the child as his/her parent.

19. For example, a father's conviction for murdering a child's mother properly had his parental rights terminated in an adoption proceeding. *In re Adoption of A.P.,* 982 P.2d 985 (Kan. Ct. App. 1999), *review denied.* A father's consent to adoption by a stepfather was not required in an Indiana case where the father had not provided child support and had limited contact with the child for a number of years. *Irvin v. Hood,* 712 N.E.2d 1012 (Ind. Ct. App. 1999); see also, *G.T. v. Adoption of A.E.T.,* 725 So. 2d 404 (Fla. DCA 1999) (where former husband abandoned child born to marriage, his consent was not needed for adoption).

20. *Lazow v. Lazow,* 147 So.2d 12 (Fla. 3d DCA 1962).

21. Editorial Staff, *Miami Herald,* 13 May 1995, 6A.

22. Editorial Staff, *Miami Herald,* 16 May 1995, 6A.

23. See, e.g., *Acevedo v. Burley,* 994 P.2d 389 (Alaska 1999).

24. See, e.g., *In re Willhite,* 706 N.E. 778 (Ohio 1999).

Chapter 10

1. Sherry Suib Cohen, "Don't Let Money Wreck Your Marriage," *Parade Magazine,* 12 March 1995, 24, citing a survey of 2000 men and women completed by Roper Starch Worldwide.

2. Ginger Biss, "Till Debt Do Us Part," *Virtue,* March-April 1998, vol. 20, no. 4, 30–33.

3. Ken Doyle, "What's Your Financial Personality Type?" *Kiplinger's Personal Finance Magazine,* July 1991, 65.

4. London Mirror as quoted in "People in the News," *Miami Herald,* 7 September 1997, 2A.

5. As quoted in "People in the News," *Miami Herald,* 25 October 1992, 2A.

6. For example, if one spouse is in more financial need than the other, the court may award more property toward the support of the needy spouse. Child custody issues also can affect property distributions, such as awarding the homestead to the parent having primary custody. If one spouse has clearly worked harder in making a joint marital asset more valuable, that also affects the distribution percentages.

7. 29 U.S.C. §§1001–1461 (1993).

8. Public Law 99–272, 7 April 1986, 100 Stat. 82.

9. As quoted by Janine S. Pouliot, "Don't Let Money Troubles Ruin Your Marriage," *Parade Magazine,* 16 April 2000, 25.

10. Daniel McGinn Et al, "Maxed Out," *Newsweek,* 27 August 2001, 36–37.

11. It's easy to inform the Social Security Administration of name changes by filing Form SS–5 at any local agency office. It usually takes about two weeks to have the change verified.

12. If the couple has any adopted children without numbers, the parents can apply for an adoption taxpayer identification number, or ATIN (used in place of a social security number on the tax return), by filing Form W–7A with the Internal Revenue Service.

13. Editorial Staff, "Prenuptial Agreements Can Be Essential for the Wealthy," *Tampa Tribune,* 20 August 1997, 7.

14. 9B Uniform Laws Annotated (Master Edition) 369 (1987). The full text of this act can be found on the Internet at http://www.law.upenn.edu/bll/ulc/fnact99/1980s/upaa83.htm.

15. *Florida Bar News,* 15 October 1998, 9.

16. Anita Sharpe, "Prenuptial Pacts Shield Businesses from an Heir's Ex," *Wall Street Journal,* 19 June 1996.

17. The longer the time—at least thirty days—the better. Most attorneys want about seventy-five days prewedding lead time to begin drafting a proper premarital agreement.

18. *Zummo v. Zummo,* 394 Pa. Super. 30, 574 A.2d 1130 (1990).

19. *Del Vecchio v. Del Vecchio,* 143 So.2nd 17 at 20 (Fla. 1962).

20. As quoted in "People in the News," *Miami Herald,* 22 October 1997, 2A.

21. Dana Panter, "From Parents' Perspectives," *USAA Magazine,* August-September 1996, 14.

Chapter 11

1. "Cathy," Cathy Guisewite, *Miami Herald,* 25 September 2001, 4E. © 2001, Reprinted with permission of Universal Press Syndicate. All rights reserved.

2. Lynda Tripp, principal, Lynnwood, Washington, as quoted in Ann Landers' column, *Miami Herald,* 11 May 2002, 7E.

3. As quoted by Ann Landers, "An Ex-Wife Thanks the Father of Her Kids," *Miami Herald,* 18 June 2000, 2KB.

4. As quoted by Margaret Graham Tebo, "When Dad Won't Pay," *ABA Journal,* September 2000, 60.

5. Florida Eighteenth Judicial Circuit Judge O. H. Eaton Jr., "Frustrated by a Deadbeat Parent? Try Invoking the Dog Law," *Florida Bar Journal,* March 2000, 64.

6. Pub. L. 104–193, 110 Stat. 2105 (1996).

7. 28 U.S.C.A. §1738B.

8. Pub. L. 104–134, 110 Stat. 1321–358 (1996).

9. 18 U.S.C.A. §228 (1995).

10. Pub. L. No. 105–187, 112 Stat. 618 (June 24, 1998).

11. *United States v. Mattice,* 186 F.3d 219 (2d Cir. 1999); *United States v. Ballek,* 170 F.3d 871 (9th Cir. 1999); *United States v. Mathes,* 151 F.3d 251 (5th Cir. 1999).

12. Editorial Staff, *Miami Herald,* 19 August 2002, 10A.

13. David Blankenhorn, interviewed in *Insight Magazine,* 27 March 1995. In his excellent book *Bringing up Boys,* Dr. James Dobson, Focus on the Family president, also makes a powerful case for how important it is for fathers to be proactive with their sons for their mutual best interest.

14. Rich Bard, "Deadbeat Parents," *Miami Herald,* 28 May 1995, 3C.

15. Certainly this isn't the only reason parents fail to pay support. Even writing a monthly check to an ex-spouse may cause extremely negative feelings. But automatic wage deductions can relieve noncustodial parents of this emotional task. Because the noncustodial parent doesn't see the money going out, he/she may be better able to adjust to living without it. But loss of contact with one's children is a *pervasive* problem.

16. The U.S. Census Bureau confirms that fathers who have joint custody or regular visitation with their children pay child support about 70 percent of the time, while those with little or no visitation pay only about 35 percent of the time.

17. Current Population Reports: Population Characteristics, P20–510, U.S. Department of Commerce, July 1998.

18. Judith S. Wallerstein, *Amicus Curiae Brief of Dr. Judith S. Wallerstein, Ph.D,* filed in Cause No. S046116, *In re Marriage of Burgess,* Supreme Court of California, December 7, 1995, 21–22.

19. *Steving v. Brown,* 980 P.2d 540 (Colo. Ct. App. 1999).

20. Judith S. Wallerstein and Tony J. Tanke, "To Move or Not to Move: Psychological and Legal Considerations in the Relocation of Children Following Divorce," *Family Law Quarterly,* vol. 30, no.2 (Spring 1996), 311.

21. Wallerstein, *In re Marriage of Burgess,* 913 P.2d 473 (Cal. 1996).

22. *Tropea v. Tropea,* 665 N.E.2d 145 (N.Y. 1996).

23. Helen Kooiman Hosier, *To Love Again: Remarriage for the Christian,* (Nashville: Abingdon Press, 1985), 149–50. Used by permission.

24. *Schutz v. Schutz,* 581 So.2d 1290 (Fla. 1991).

25. "Cathy," Cathy Guisewite, *Miami Herald,* 29 September 2001, 6E. © 2001, Reprinted with permission of Universal Press Syndicate. All rights reserved.

26. *Troxel v. Granville,* 530 U.S. 27 (2000), in which the Court, in a 6–3 decision, struck down a Washington state judge's order that required a reluctant mother to turn over her daughters once a month for weekend visits with the parents of her deceased boyfriend. No one suggested that the mother, Tommie Granville, was unfit or had harmed the girls in any way. And the grandparents, Jenifer and Gary Troxel, hadn't raised the girls or served as caregivers. Nonetheless, when these grandparents sued for forced visitation, the judge ruled it would be "in the best interest of the children to spend quality time" with them. Disagreeing, Justice Sandra Day O'Connor said the U.S. Constitution "does not permit a State to infringe on the fundamental rights of parents to make child-rearing decisions simply because a better decision could be made." The Court's decision stopped short of declaring all grandparent visitation laws unconstitutional, but the case does alert judges to tilt the scales in favor of a biological parent's wishes.

27. "Grandparent Rights Won't Go to Court," *Miami Herald,* 14 November 2001, 16A.

28. I remain indebted to Ancil Jenkins, former minister of the Sunset Church of Christ in Miami, Florida, for opening my eyes to much of the meaning behind this passage.

29. A tunic is an outer garment similar to a poncho with a hole in the middle for one's head. It kept one protected during the day, and warm at night. It was so precious that the Law of Moses didn't allow one's tunic to be offered as security for a loan unless the one receiving it gave it back at the end of each day so the person could sleep with it (Exod. 22:25–27).

30. This illustration focuses on elevating *spiritual* issues above *property* disputes and avoiding further damage to the one being wronged. It doesn't necessarily mean that a Christian should always give to anyone who sues, or wants to sue, any or all of his/her property. And it certainly doesn't mean turning over custody of one's child to an abusive ex-spouse, since the child's life and protection are the custodial parent's God-given responsibility!

31. Thomas Strahan, "Should a Christian Assert His Legal Rights?" *The Word and the Law: A Biblical Studies Guide,* vol. 1 (Oak Park, Ill.: Christian Legal Society, 1977), 64.

32. The Law of Moses provided that the firstborn son received two-thirds of the inheritance and the younger son one-third (Deut. 21:15–17). It's likely the one complaining here is a younger son who wants more than his share of the inheritance.

33. Hosier, *To Love Again,* 163.

Appendix A

1. David Popenoe and Barbara Defoe Whitehead, "The State of Our Unions: The Social Health of Marriage in America," the National Marriage Project, Rutgers University, 1999, 2. To access the report via the Internet, please see http://marriage.rutgers.edu.

2. Judith Wallerstein, "The Unexpected Legacy of Divorce: A 25-Year Landmark Study," quoted in Karen S. Peterson, "Happily Ever After: Children of Divorce Grow into Bleak Legacy," *USA Today,* 5 September 2000.

3. *Current Thoughts and Trends,* November 1994, 13.

4. "Divorce," *Leadership,* Summer 1996, 69.

5. Wallerstein, as quoted in Peterson, "Happily Ever After."

6. Ibid.

7. Karen S. Peterson (quoting Center for Disease Control and Prevention, based upon a 1995 Federal study of 10,847 women aged 15–44), "43% of First Marriages End in 15 Years—Study Finds Age Linked to Success," *USA Today,* 25 May 2001.

8. Karen S. Peterson (quoting University of Oklahoma researcher Joe Rodgers), "Saying No to the Notion of No-Fault Divorce," *USA Today,* 25 January 1996.

9. Kingsley Davis, "The American Family in Relation to Demographic Change," in Charles R. Westoff and Robert Parke, eds., *Demographic and Social Aspects of Population Growth,* vol. 1, Commission on Population Growth and the American Future, Government Printing Office, 1972.

10. Wallerstein, as quoted in Peterson, "Happily Ever After."

11. U.S. Census Bureau Report, "Marital Status and Living Arrangements: March 1998."

12. "Breakdown on Family Breakdown," *Washington Times,* 25 March 2001, B2.

13. James B. Meyer, "Beyond a Reasonable Doubt: Positive Psychology in Marital Agreements," *Florida Bar Journal,* February 1994, 71.

14. Dick Randall, "Remarrying Can Bolster Self-Esteem," *Miami Herald,* 1 June 1999, 3C, citing National Center for Health Statistics information.

15. Carl Brecheen, "Helping Stepfamilies," *Christian Chronicle,* February 1999, 12 (and sources cited therein).

16. Wallerstein, as quoted in Peterson "Happily Ever After." See also National Center for Health Statistics, "National Vital Statistics Report: Births, Marriages, Divorces and Deaths, Provisional Data for 1998," vol. 47, no. 21.4, PHS 99–1120.

17. Margaret L. Usdansky (quoting from Census Bureau Report, "Marriage, Divorce and Remarriage in the 1990s"), "1990s' Wedding Bell Blues–New Report Echoes Trend of the '70s," *USA Today,* 9 December 1992.

18. Peterson, "43% of First Marriages."

19. Karen S. Peterson, "Out of Step—Some Worse off When Parent Marries Again," *USA Today,* 14 January 1996.

20. Usdansky, "1990's Wedding Bell Blues."

21. Brecheen, "Helping Stepfamilies," 12.

Appendix C

1. This list doesn't include every organization dealing with remarriage and blended family issues. Inclusion on this list doesn't constitute endorsement by the author or publisher of this book. Neither the author nor publisher exercises any control over the work performed, or materials provided, by any organization on this list or any fees charged.

TOPICAL INDEX